Postcolonial Servitude

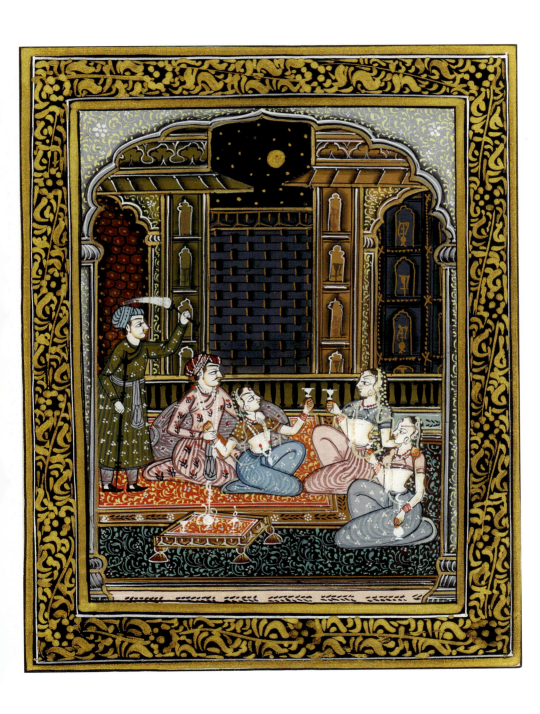

Postcolonial Servitude

Domestic Servants in Global South Asian English Literature

AMBREEN HAI

OXFORD
UNIVERSITY PRESS

Oxford University Press is a department of the University of Oxford. It furthers the University's objective of excellence in research, scholarship, and education by publishing worldwide. Oxford is a registered trade mark of Oxford University Press in the UK and certain other countries.

Published in the United States of America by Oxford University Press
198 Madison Avenue, New York, NY 10016, United States of America.

© Oxford University Press 2024

All rights reserved. No part of this publication may be reproduced, stored in a retrieval system, or transmitted, in any form or by any means, without the prior permission in writing of Oxford University Press, or as expressly permitted by law, by license, or under terms agreed with the appropriate reproduction rights organization. Inquiries concerning reproduction outside the scope of the above should be sent to the Rights Department, Oxford University Press, at the address above.

You must not circulate this work in any other form
and you must impose this same condition on any acquirer.

Library of Congress Control Number: 2023056795

ISBN 978–0–19–769800–6

DOI: 10.1093/oso/9780197698006.001.0001

Printed by Integrated Books International, United States of America

Contents

Preface vii
Acknowledgments xiii
A Note on the Cover xv

Introduction 1

PART ONE

1. Constituting (from) the Background: The South Asian Literary Servant in the Margins, or, Early South Asian English Fiction from Below 49

2. The Servant('s) Turn, in the Middle Ground: Rushdie and Transnational Writers After Rushdie 96

PART TWO

3. Foregrounding the Servant: What's New About Daniyal Mueenuddin's Interlinked Short Stories 141

4. From Periphery to Center: The Male Servant as Narrator and Protagonist in Romesh Gunesekera's *Reef* 174

5. In the Driver's Seat?: Aravind Adiga's *The White Tiger* 207

6. Sharing Space: Alternating Female Servant-Employer Narratives in Thrity Umrigar's *The Space Between Us* 252

7. Legacies of Servitude, Global and Local: Kiran Desai's *The Inheritance of Loss* 284

Conclusion 322

Notes 333
Works Cited 373
Index 381

Preface

Over the years that I have been working on this book, when people, often non-academics, asked me what I was writing about, and I would say, "Servants in literature, from South Asia—India, Pakistan, Sri Lanka, Bangladesh," I have had a range of reactions, from puzzlement, surprise, and confusion, to a certain awkwardness or embarrassment. Sometimes I got looks that I found hard to read. "Domestic servants," I would elaborate, "cooks, cleaners, maids, chauffeurs, watchmen." I did not use euphemisms like "the help," or "domestic workers."

"They write about it themselves?" was a common query.

"No," I would reply, "Most servants in South Asia are servants because they cannot read or write. I study fiction. . . . Award-winning fiction," I would add defensively, "I'm looking at how writers of fiction who are themselves of upper or middle-class backgrounds imagine, describe, or call attention to the condition of servants in their societies."

"Like *Downton Abbey*?"

"No, not quite," I would struggle to explain.

Two moments in particular stand out in my memory. One, soon after I began work on this project, and mentioned it to a dear American friend and college professor, she told me of a visiting Fulbright scholar at her institution, an Indian woman who (she reported), could not understand how American women maintained their careers without servants. Life was so much harder for the middle classes in the United States than in India, this Indian scholar would exclaim, especially for women! "American self-sufficiency and democracy" seem to have "substantially reduced the privileges of even modestly middle-class people," she observed, who have no help, no servants to drive, cook, or clean. Years later, when I had progressed further with the book, I was talking to a new acquaintance who was struck by my topic. She said she had just had a conversation with an Indian woman doctor who said she had given up working as a doctor upon arrival in the United States because life here was so difficult without servants. It took too much time, energy, attention, she said, to do the housework, groceries, cooking, family laundry.

What is common to both these stories, passed on to me by kind listeners, is that both involve the perception, and insistent assertion, by professional middle-class Indian women, that life is more difficult in the United States than in India because of the *absence* of servants. (Since I received both stories secondhand, and have not met these particular individuals, I regret I cannot give them more texture. I wonder if they would have said the same thing in the same way to me, since I am also South Asian. They might have assumed I would automatically understand.) What is also significant is that they both evidently felt strongly enough about it to emphasize the comparison to their audience of white American middle-class women. I want to pull out from these stories three elements. The first is the taken-for-granted assumption among South Asians that servants are necessary to, in fact constitutive of, modern middle-class life. Instead of focusing on the (putative) absence of servants in America, what if we were to turn the lens back on South Asians and ask instead: Why is it so necessary to have individuals in the home at one's beck and call? How would our sense of ourselves, our identities, and our relationships with others (spouses, children, family members, and not least of all our "helpers") change if we (the we who can hire domestic workers) paid more attention to the fact and assumed necessity of having such omnipresent help, if we did our personal work ourselves, or redistributed responsibility for it, or questioned how we regard those on whom we often do not acknowledge our dependence? The second is the assumption that housework and household management is or must be women's responsibility, itself gendered labor. It is important that it was Indian *women* who talked of the need for servants, not men. The third (and this is my suspicion) is the perceived need by those Indian middle-class women to imply that life in India is qualitatively better (for them) than in America. I hear a certain postcolonial class pride and defensiveness in their claims, the need to assert that they were not dying to immigrate to the United States. Why would they want to suffer such loss of privilege?

More recently, I was having lunch with a colleague who asked me if I would include in this book something about my own experiences with servants in Pakistan. My first response was to say no, I would not, for I did not want to predispose a certain kind of sanctimonious self-righteous American reader to see me as "privileged" and therefore automatically disqualify or discredit what I had to say before they even read it. But upon second thought, recognizing my own defensiveness (and legitimate wariness), it seems to me wiser to explain, as I did to my colleague, that unlike North America, where servants are limited to the very elite, in South Asia even the lowest middle classes have servants, even if it is someone who comes in for a few hours daily to clean. In the 1970s and 1980s when I was growing up in Pakistan, urban middle-class families like mine usually had a live-in cook and ayah, and sometimes also a full-time driver, part-time gardener, watchman, and certainly a daily cleaner (a "jemadarni" or sweepress who came from the slums and did not live in the servants' quarters attached to middle-class houses). You do not have to be rich to have servants. The saying about Calcutta, that everyone either has a servant or is one, remains true broadly across South Asia.

This book is not an autobiography. Nor is it sociology. Though rooted in close personal observation and understanding of lived realities, it is very much an act of literary analysis, imbricated in cultural analysis, that examines how a new generation of transnational South Asian writers has begun to take a new look at a pervasive cultural institution—domestic servitude—that most South Asians take so much for granted that it is almost unremarked upon, among us. It is there in all the literature, and yet as literary scholars, especially postcolonialists, we have not given it much attention. In between the extremes to which we have paid attention, from the Dalit to the social elite, domestic servants are positioned between extreme indigence and privilege. Servants constitute a curious blind spot, caught in the interstices of domestic middle-class life, ever present yet unnoticed, or noticed only when absent. In the introduction that follows, I will explain more. In this preface, I begin with these stories to provide context for this project, to suggest where it comes from, to draw out some reasons for why we need to pay attention to South Asian attitudes to and practices of servitude.

Many years ago, I published an article about a Pakistani Partition novel, Bapsi Sidhwa's *Cracking India*, that focused on the novel's use of the figure of a servant woman, the Ayah. Perhaps that is when I started thinking about servants. Since that essay was published a long time ago, it is not part of this book. Soon after my first book was published, an Indian friend told me I had to read this amazing new Pakistani American writer, Daniyal Mueenuddin, whose first book, a collection of stories, had just appeared. I did, and found myself compelled to write an essay that grew longer and longer, as I tried to explain how I thought what Mueenuddin was doing was excitingly new. Perhaps that was another moment that started me thinking more broadly about servants in South Asian literature, to expand to how other writers did and did not write about servants, and tipped me into realizing that this had to be my next book.

As literary critics, we often plunge right away into impersonal, often quite intimidatingly cerebral theoretical frameworks and analyses. Before proceeding to the analyses that follow, and that I hope are written so as not to appear arcane and uninviting to read, I want my readers to know of some of my own recollections that I think animate my analytical work. As I think back now to my middle-class childhood in Karachi, here are some memories of servants and servitude that keep returning to me, that had an impact, even if I was unconscious of it at the time.

When I was about eleven, I remember listening to a servant woman confiding in my mother about her eleven-year-old daughter whose marriage had just been arranged by her Pathan father, up north. The issue was not that the girl was not willing, but that even her mother was not willing. Men arranged these things and the mother was not even consulted. What I heard, remember, and understand more fully, now that I have teenage daughters, is the mother's agony. I remember her resignation, as she expressed it to my mother. But the fact that she expressed it suggests also a level of protest, made to another woman, a refusal to accept it, perhaps a tacit call for help, woman to woman, mother to mother. Perhaps she thought my mother, or my mother via my father, could make a difference. The girl had just begun menstruating, said her mother, as had I. Perhaps that, and the fact that I was the same age, and had just learned about sex, made me pay attention to this conversation. It was not a private conversation, for both my mother and the servant woman knew I was in the room. Maybe there were other such conversations that I had not heard or understood.

My mother nodded, and sympathized, but though she evidently thought it was wrong, she did not and could not do anything to stop it. My parents never interfered in servants' private lives—I wonder now what would have happened if they had tried. As middle-class immigrants to Pakistan from North India, maybe they felt vulnerable among people who claimed a different kind of belonging to the land, the imagined larger whole that was the new nation, and were unwilling to rock the boat or arouse resentment. I can imagine that a different kind of employer, a woman who was also of the land, a Punjabi perhaps, or Pathan, might have used her privilege to talk to the woman's husband, to persuade him to wait. Not that she would have been necessarily effective. A year later, her mother reported, the girl, now twelve, had had a baby—stillborn. I remember her mother's voice when she told my mother. I do not know what happened to that girl. I remember how she used to come to our house with her mother, shyly holding back, hiding behind her mother, bearing that air of knowledge that she was inferior, lesser, hesitant to put herself forward. Of the many, many, many stories I heard growing up, this one particularly stands out in my mind—emblematizing the utter helplessness of women in that extreme patriarchal framework—the girl, her mother, and even my mother, unable to intervene. The men who orchestrated these women's lives, poor illiterate migrants from the rugged northern mountains to the large, teeming metropolis, Karachi, exerted their manliness precisely by reasserting their ties to their homelands, sending back their young daughters, reverting to intransigent tribal codes of honor when they themselves lived deeply precarious, impecunious lives, with little hope of a future in the city, with no education or chance of more remuneration than a pittance from construction work or domestic service.

Another memory haunts this book, from when I was maybe nine. We had a cook, a gentle, courteous, quiet man. He was so good at his job, and so trusted by my parents, that when some of their friends were looking for a cook, they asked him to find a cook for them like himself, to refer one of his friends, which he did. Soon there was a robbery at my parents' friends' house: valuable jewelry was taken; it seemed an inside job. The police were called in, and unsurprisingly, their cook promptly disappeared, perhaps because suspicion fell inevitably on him. (It turned out later that the employers were getting divorced, and the husband had set up the robbery to do away with his wife's valuables—whether to steal or be vindictive, was unclear.) But our cook was taken in by the police for "questioning," perhaps to help them find his acquaintance, the vanished cook, since he was the only one with any clue to the man's whereabouts. Our cook came back to our house after some time, not without the intervention of my father, who kept visiting him at the police station, doubtless not only because he was concerned but also because my mother complained about having no help in the kitchen. I remember the heart-thumping sense of shock that I felt, even as a child, when I saw him. He looked thinner, somehow broken, his face wrinkled, as if he had aged in that short period. He gave us a wan smile. "He was beaten," I heard my father tell my mother quietly. We children were not supposed to hear that. Our cook seemed angrier somehow, as if his body emanated a restrained resentment. I don't know what happened between him and my parents, but something changed. The good-humored atmosphere was gone. After a short while he left, possibly by mutual agreement, or possibly he was let go. Maybe he resented my parents for having not stood by him, for not getting him out sooner, for allowing him to be implicated. And they sensed it, and did not feel they could trust him entirely any more. We never saw him again.

Both these memories speak to a sense of employers having failed to fulfill an unspoken obligation, of failing their servants, while all were caught in a peculiar ethos of servant-employer distance and dependence, expectation and rejection, involvement and abstention. This book is not an act of compensation—it cannot be—but it is undergirded by such memories of injustice and oppression that I witnessed, if only partially, as a child. They also speak to themes we will see often in the fiction explored in this book: gendered injustice, solidarity between women or its failure, male servants suspected of theft and subjected to police brutality, the breakdown of trust between employers and servants.

There are many more stories I could tell, of women servants subjected to physical violence by their husbands, turning to my mother for support, or asking my mother to keep their earnings to prevent their husbands from spending them on drink or drugs. I'll restrain myself to one more. Once, after a male cook had left, my father went down to the servant's room to check something. He came back looking a bit shocked and mystified. He had found something scrawled on the wall in Urdu. "*Zillat ki zindagi.*" It meant, "a life of humiliation and degradation." By the 1980s in Pakistan, it was not completely unusual for some servants to know how to read and write. A handful had completed a few grades of primary school. Maybe this servant had left, or been more resentful, precisely because he was more educated. But why did he write that on the wall, my father wondered. My father's demeanor suggested that he could not understand what the servant may have meant. Why was it so humiliating to be a servant? Wasn't he treated well? Wasn't he fortunate to have a job, and free food and shelter along with it, to say nothing of free running water and electricity, unlike any of the villages or urban slums that might otherwise have been his site of residence? My mother agreed. Even then, as a teenager, I knew my parents were missing something. Who did that vanished servant write it for, I wonder now. Was it for himself, as a form of expression of feelings he could not suppress? Or was it a message to his employers? Or was it a warning to other servants, telling them that my mother was worse to work for than most employers? I don't know the answer, of course, but that was a rare moment that we heard in a servant's words what he may have wanted us to know about how he felt about his servitude. Was my mother worse than other employers? She would get irritated with servants' mistakes; she was not always respectful or kind. Male cooks took it worse than female ones. It was gendered, of course—it threatened their masculinity to take orders from a woman. But how did my mother compare to other employers? I don't know because I never saw how others really treated their servants in the privacy of their homes. When I visited friends, their mothers seemed courteous to their servants, but was that normal or just a show for visitors?

We still know very little about these often multiply subordinated beings who exist on the fringes of the consciousnesses of their employers, people of different ethnicities, geographical origins, ages, genders, on whom upper classes depend not just for everyday comforts but also for their very sense of identity. We know little of the real feelings, the mix of trust and mistrust, dependence and independence, the resentment and gratitude, the attachments and distances, the complex dynamics that underlie the everyday existence of and interactions between employers and servants. In this book, I argue that a new wave of South Asian writers has begun to pay this complex a new kind of attention, calling upon readers to rethink those entrenched, habituated forms of practice, attitude, and feeling, in the hope, not only to tell servants' stories, to find new ways of telling stories, but also to change minds, to inspire new ways of seeing, and ultimately, perhaps, to effect social change.

Acknowledgments

Early versions of portions of the Introduction and Chapter 3 were previously published in my essay "Postcolonial Servitude: Interiority and System in Daniyal Mueenuddin's *In Other Rooms, Other Wonders*" in *Ariel* 45.3 (July 2014): 33–74. An early version of Chapter 6 was published as part of "Motherhood and Domestic Servitude in Transnational Women's Fiction: Thrity Umrigar's *The Space Between Us* and Mona Simpson's *My Hollywood*" in *Contemporary Literature* 57.4 (Winter 2016): 500–540. A few pages from my article "'No One in the House Knew Her Name': Servant Problems in R. K. Narayan's Short Stories" in *South Asian Review* 39.3–4 (2019): 335–353 reappear in my Introduction. I am grateful to Johns Hopkins University Press, the University of Wisconsin Press, and Taylor and Francis for their permission to reprint this material.

I owe thanks to Smith College for its generous sabbatical policy, which has provided me time over many sabbaticals and financial resources to pursue the research and writing for this book. Thanks also to my colleagues in the English Department for their support and encouragement over the years, and for their collegial engagement when I presented this work in its earliest stages. Thanks also to the many audiences that have offered feedback and advice on portions of this project at various international conferences over the years, including the Modern Language Association, Postcolonial Studies Association, South Asian Literary Association, and the University of Madison–Wisconsin's Annual Conference on South Asia.

I am also extremely grateful to the anonymous reviewers at Oxford University Press for their helpful comments, which have helped strengthen this book. My thanks also to Hannah Doyle, my editor at Oxford University Press, for her kindness, enthusiasm, and help in bringing this book to publication.

And finally, to my family, to whom no thanks can be adequate: my husband Kevin, my daughters Anya and Amara, and my sister Mehreen, for believing in me and in this project and for sustaining me through the years.

A Note on The Cover (Frontispiece)

Many years ago, in the late 1990s, when I was visiting my parents in Karachi, I went with my mother to Zainab Market, a slightly kitschy little shopping area that caters mostly to foreign tourists. At one little stall, almost unnoticeably tucked away amid the others that sold batik fabrics, hand-woven rugs, marble ornaments, carved walnut wood furniture, leather jackets, cheap handbags, seashell trinkets, and other such goods, I found some faux Mughal-style miniatures. They were all court scenes, cheap imitations, hand-painted on fine cloth, about 8 x 10 inches, with frayed edges. I liked their unpretentiousness, their ersatzness. They made no claims to be authentic or priceless. They were not replicas of actual paintings, as far as I knew, just approximations, imagined scenes cast in that recognizable, familiar, stylized idiom. I bought four: a Mughal emperor presiding over his courtiers, dispensing justice; another Mughal spearing tigers, surrounded by his admiring men; another relaxing over goblets of wine with a group of women; and one of Mughal princesses by themselves, dancing in a circle around a blue god, with no men around. I had them framed when I returned to Northampton, Massachusetts, where I live. The framing cost about ten times more than the art itself. They hang in our dining room. Folk art, from my erstwhile home.

There is no artist's name on any of them, so I asked the man I was buying them from who had painted them. It was an innocuous question; I was just curious to know more. My mother sighed and shifted uneasily next to me, letting me know wordlessly that I was transgressing bounds of class and gender decorum: middle-class women like us were not supposed to have unnecessary conversations with lower-class men; we were supposed to demand, bargain, buy, and leave. I ignored her. He was polite, courteous, happy to oblige. He told me they were the work of local artists from his community, Hindus who had lived for generations, since before Partition, in Karachi. I am not religious, but I knew that he understood that I belonged to a Muslim family. Knowing about the difficulties that minorities, especially Hindus, face in Pakistan, I struggled to word my solicitude with tact, to phrase carefully my inquiry about their well-being. "What happens when there is a communal riot, or conflict with India?" I tried to ask. How had they fared when tensions between India and Pakistan had recently escalated? Had there been threats or violence? I was surprised by what I learned. "The police look after our community," he assured me. "They arrive pre-emptively to provide protection." I hope what he said was true.

The image on the cover and frontispiece of this book is of one of these paintings, which I am happy to own. I like the fact that they were made by Hindus who continue to live in Pakistan, precarious though their lives must be. I also like that in both style and content, the paintings call upon a strangely hybrid past, of Mughal rulers, migrants to South Asia from West and Central Asia, who settled and merged with those they governed, and that the paintings themselves enact an unembarrassed syncretism, placing blue Hindu gods amid Mughal princesses, Muslim emperors who cheerfully share alcohol with women who calmly bare their midriffs and raise glasses of wine.

But it was not until I was almost halfway through writing this book, as I was wondering about an image for the cover, that it suddenly struck me that I had it right there, hanging on my wall. This image presents a Mughal king or noble, enjoying wine with three women, all seated at ease. One leans against him, the others may be friends, relatives, poets, intellectuals, or courtesans. In the background, on the edge to the left, slightly cut off by the frame, stands a man who is a servitor. He is not sharing in the festivity. With one hand, he holds above the king's head what appears to be a feathery fan or a lamp—the brush work is ambiguous. With his other hand he holds, and slightly leans on, what may be a spear. He is clearly a servant, not an equal, so much in the background that he is not even fully in the picture. And yet he completes it. He is there to signal the status and power of the others and to enable their leisure. He stands, while they sit. He works, while they relax. He is incomplete, while they are complete. He threatens violence to potential intruders or enemies, risking harm, inviting injury to himself, so they can be safe. He protects, while they are protected. And yet, in all the eight years or so that I had studied South Asian literature about servants in the background emerging into the foreground, I had not paid attention to him on my wall. Until now. To see this painting, I literally had to open the door behind which it was hidden, and close the door to another room, my office.

This book zooms in to look more closely at such servant figures in the margins—the margins of history, society, art, literature. Literally and figuratively, socially and formally, the servant in this painting is marginal. He is rendered multiply marginal: by socioeconomic frameworks, by the artist, and by the onlooker who has learned not to see him. To be more precise, this book attempts to close in on literature that zooms in to look closer at such figures and that centers on them. What does it take to see the margins? How does it change what and how we see? What happens when the figure usually in the margins is placed in the center? How does it change the art? How would that disrupt our (usual, official, or officious) modes of reading, knowing, understanding? What doors do we have to open, or close? To bring the servant into prominence is to disrupt something. For the servant to bring herself or himself into prominence is to disrupt something.

It is possible of course, that this scene of companionability and revelry, enabled by the servant, is itself about to be disrupted by the servant. For perhaps he raises that unidentifiable object in his left hand to strike the king. Perhaps it is a weapon. Perhaps the artist has caught this moment just before it is ruptured. I know that that is a perverse reading, probably not at all what the artist intended. Perhaps such a reading itself is driven by fear—fear of the servant, of the militant Muslim, of the other, fear driven by those who really are themselves to be feared. We can, however, read both with and against the grain of a text. We must. We can consider and weigh the possibilities that may seem outlandish, that break decorum, for the answers may teach us something we didn't know. We can ask what lurking resentments, emotions, desires, hopes, ambitions, lie hidden perhaps, beneath the mask of servitude that the servant wears, that he must perforce wear. What hidden suggestions lie waiting beneath the surface of the painting, beyond its apparent intentions, conventions, recognizable frameworks? What if we were to go beyond, to ask, if not perverse, then difficult, troubling questions of what we think we know?

It is also worth noting that the faces of the two men in this painting, master and servant, are exactly the same. They mirror each other. What similarities do they evoke? What connections, despite difference? What relationships, literal or figurative? And, as it happens, so are the faces of the women. All five faces are identical. Family resemblance? The artist's laziness or ineptitude? Maybe. Or a joke. A surreptitious act of leveling. A way of showing the connections between us. Whatever it is, it puts in question assumed differences of class and gender. We will see such mirrorings again and again in contemporary servitude fiction, where the servant serves as a double, or a projection, or where the servant desires affectively both to be the master and to emulate the master. And like the ambiguities adumbrated in this painting, in this literature as well, the servant can both protect and threaten, support and betray, care and resent.

The evocative scene of precolonial servitude in this painting continues to tease us, puzzle us, challenge us to keep asking, if not answering, questions, and to keep looking. It is painted by a contemporary Pakistani artist who retains the powerful forms of something much older and revered, who, though himself working class, replicates the conventions that keep the servant in the background, cut off from telling his own story. I focus on writers, not themselves servants or working class, who move the servant into the foreground, who reject or rework those conventions. With this image as an opening prompt, I ask my readers to turn with me to look more closely at postcolonial servitude in contemporary literature which asks, and to ask of it, similar and yet more probing questions.

Introduction

In her short story "For Whom Things Do Not Change" (1970), Ghanaian writer Ama Ata Aidoo presents a haunting encounter between Kobina, a progressive young doctor in newly independent Ghana, and Zirigu, an aging "Ex-Serviceman" who has worked as a houseboy and gardener for his colonial masters, served in many British colonies in World War II, and is now cook and keeper of a Government Rest House (23).[1] At one point, Zirigu asks Kobina this key question:

> When a black man is with his wife who cooks and chores for him, he is a man. When he is with white folk for whom he cooks and chores, he is a woman. Dear Lord, what then is a black man who cooks and chores for black men? (17)

As the story's title suggests, national independence, with its promise of freedom from colonial servitude, has not changed things much for Zirigu, who continues in his humble position of domestic servitude, disillusioned by the realization that even after decolonization, while around him some men prosper, his "own people" will not grant him even the benefits of "electricity and a water closet" in his servants' quarters (28). The ultimate question this dilemma tale poses occurs in its simple last sentence, when Zirigu resignedly asks, "My young Master, what does Independence mean?" (29). For a nation created to be free of colonial servitude, what indeed does that freedom or postcoloniality mean if its most vulnerable citizens are re-inserted into the same structures of disenfranchisement and servitude, with black instead of white men on top? For whom—and how—do things change and not change?

Disillusionment after independence and critique of oppressive and corrupt neocolonial regimes are not new to postcolonial literature.[2] But Aidoo's story calls our attention more specifically to the condition of *domestic* servitude in the context of postcoloniality, and to its classed, gendered, and racialized effects.[3] Kobina's well-meaning but naïve egalitarian efforts—to have Zirigu sit with him, eat with him, and address him by first name instead of "Master"—fail because no single encounter can displace deeply entrenched habits, behavior, and expectations inscribed upon the psyche, nor can one individual change a social and economic system that remains firmly entrenched and supported by most of whom it privileges. Moreover, as Zirigu's words suggest, his sense of his identity, particularly his manhood—his gender and sexuality—is also shaped by the specificities of his work. Although cooking within one's own home is understood as feminine and hence effeminizing work for a black man, Zirigu learned to make an exception, to cook "the white man's chop" for his English masters as a way of making a living within the racial/colonial system (17). His fragile sense of gender and ethnic/racial identity has been shored up by his wife Setu, who shops and cooks their family's regional food "of the land," saving him from cooking what they themselves eat, because within their system, only women must cook and serve their food (17). When Zirigu has to cook and serve (the white man's) food to another black man, this fragile hierarchy is partially disrupted. His question, "what then is a black man who cooks and chores for black men?," suggests its own unpleasant answer, for not only (to his understanding) is such a black man betrayed by his own people, but he is also unmanned, forced into a servile, effeminized, and perhaps (homo)sexualized relationship via his labor. This can be second only to the humiliation he suffered earlier, he indicates, of washing the "underclothes of a white woman" younger than himself (23). When Kobena tries to rectify things by asking Zirigu to cook the native "food of the land" and not "white man's chop" for him—to serve his new black postcolonial master—he unintentionally worsens even that fragile state of affairs by pushing Zirigu into the position of "woman" he has struggled so long to avoid.

Aidoo's short story is unusual not only because it elaborates on the intersecting complexities of classed and gendered postcolonial servitude, but also because it makes a servant character central, giving him voice and interiority in a dialogue that is designed not just to educate the upper-class character but to pose broader dilemmas for its readers to ponder (and eventually solve).[4] In much contemporary global or postcolonial literature and film, domestic servants, when they appear, still tend to be marginal or subsidiary, not central protagonists. But nonetheless, such texts call upon the figure of the servant to perform key functions. Indian-Canadian filmmaker Deepa Mehta's 1996 film *Fire*, for instance, depends heavily on a male servant figure for its plot development and its exploration of sanctioned and unsanctioned sexual desire. Famous for its controversial depiction of a lesbian relationship between two Hindu middle-class sisters-in-law, the film has garnered much attention, but few have noted the significance of Mundu, the family servant who lives in the house, spies on the women when they make love, reports them to the master of the house, and hence serves as the pivotal instrument of exposure and precipitant of narrative crisis.[5] However, in contrast to Aidoo's *foregrounding* of the servant figure Zirigu, which poses the question of servitude as central to postcoloniality and modernity, Mehta's film keeps Mundu in the *background*, as more typically a barely noticed minor character, rendering him marginal even when necessary to its main narrative and concerns.

Mundu is introduced early in the film, when the younger brother Jatin brings his new bride Sita to his joint-family home to live with his aged mother (Biji), older brother Ashok, and sister-in-law Radha. A liminal and comical figure, Mundu is both (literally) part of the welcoming family circle, and outside because subordinate to it: he squats on the floor while they stand or sit on chairs; he is part of the household but not "family" by blood or marriage. Mundu is responsible for looking after the disabled Biji and is kept in his place by Jatin through routine insult. "Shut up," Jatin tells him roughly (00:7:25), or "You'll end up in the lunatic asylum" (00:7:50). Paralleling Jatin's treatment of Mundu in its portrayal of the servant, the film uses recognizable servant stereotypes to associate him with untrustworthiness, betrayal, illicit sexuality, and the lower body: Mundu forces Biji, who has suffered a stroke and can neither speak nor walk, to watch porn films with him while he supposedly takes care of her; he pees against a historic building, which suggests that he makes and is dirt; he harbors a secret crush on Radha, the oldest daughter-in-law of the household, posing a sexual threat to the purity of the patriarchal household; and he acts as a sexual voyeur, a peeping Tom who spies on the two female protagonists while they engage in sex, and then betrays them. The film thus sets up, but does not explore, a contrast between Mundu's problematic (hetero)sexual transgressions and the women's (more sympathetically portrayed) queer desires, though clearly, Mundu's ethical violations disallow any equivalence between their different ways of flouting normative sexuality and domesticity.

As the servant insider/outsider in the household, Mundu has a paradoxical power because he knows and can expose intimate secrets.[6] (In dominant narratives produced by members of upper classes, as I elaborate below, a good servant is often defined by his or her loyalty to the employer's family, as one who does not tell secrets, or who finally tells them when most beneficial for the family.) Despite his lower-class status, Mundu exerts masculine power over the women of the household—he acts as arbiter and enforcer of gender roles and sexual decorum, and as the eyes of the master for purposes of surveillance of the women—and considers his primary allegiance to Ashok, not to Radha. And paradoxically, as a servant, he is vulnerable precisely because of this power. Ashok, as the patriarch, fearing disgrace in a culture that burdens women with the obligation to maintain family honor, and unwilling to share seeing with the servant what he himself fears to see, throws Mundu out and threatens him with the police to ensure his silence. He rejects Mundu's loyalty when it threatens him. The film thus presents many characteristic features of the condition of servitude: for the family, the servant is always expendable in crisis, ejected from the family despite their repeated self-serving rhetoric that he is family. (Ironically, as Bruce Robbins reminds us, the word "family" is derived from the Latin *famulus*, for servant or slave, linking all who form a household, living under one roof; 111.

Modern users of the word "family" forget this root meaning when they assure servants that they are part of the "family," only to demonstrate in action that they are not.) As if in fuller recognition of this ambiguous belonging, Mundu's reaction is complexly dual, including both knowing anger ("Bastard, doesn't want me to see his shame," he reflects bitterly) and fearful self-abasement ("Sahib, don't throw me out, this is my home," he begs Ashok). In the last scene in which we see him, the film evokes a rare affect of pathos for Mundu, as the camera remains for some moments on his face, his head bowed, crushed by the boomerang effect on himself of what he has engineered, in his miscalculation of what would constitute loyalty to this fractured family.

Unlike Aidoo's story, *Fire* both depicts and itself reinforces the marginalization of the servant figure, even as it requires Mundu to perform necessary functions within its representational economy. Mundu's final words suggest the servant's *abjection*, as Julia Kristeva brilliantly defines the concept, as the part of the self that must be rejected, disowned, disavowed, in order to constitute the self as separate from that within the self that is considered undesirable, dirty, or impure (Kristeva, 1–6). Ashok's rejection of Mundu functions psychoanalytically as a displacement of that within the family that must be externalized and denied; he rejects Mundu for knowing, and hence embodying, the horrifying secret of his family. Yet, despite the moment of pathos, Mundu, as a self-serving upholder of heteropatriarchy, is also presented by the film as getting his just deserts for betraying the two central female protagonists. The film is not interested in pursuing his story for its own sake, or in exploring the similarities in his position of powerlessness and domesticity compared to the women's, or in contrasting his form of violation of sexual norms and theirs.[7]

I begin by juxtaposing these two examples of representations of domestic servants in postcolonial fiction and film because the comparison, which makes visible both their differences and congruencies, poses some of the key questions central to this book. What kind of work—cultural, political, aesthetic, thematic—does the figure of the servant do in each text? What does it mean for a postcolonial writer (or filmmaker) to notice or not to notice, to call attention to or to redeploy dominant social ways of positioning, demeaning, exploiting, or using domestic servants in elite or middle-class South Asian homes? What contradictions accrue when cultural production that seeks to be daringly progressive in some respects (as a proponent of gender equality or same-sex sexuality) does not extend its egalitarian politics to a particular kind of subalternity, to the domestic servants it requires to perform other functions, and falls into regrettably classist, lazy modes of representation? How do writers who seek to intervene in and change both actual socio-cultural practices and mindsets, as well as discourses and modes of representation, invent new literary forms, or adopt modes of representation that engage the problems of postcolonial servitude in compelling, progressive, productive ways? How do they address the particularities, in specific contexts and histories, of the intersections of servitude, which is primarily determined by class, with other vectors of identity such as gender, sexuality, ethnicity, religion, nationality, or age, given that servitude in South Asia carries deep stigma and shame and is often understood as an unchangeable marker of identity? How are we to read and assess representations by relatively more privileged writers and cultural producers of relatively less privileged others?

This book explores how a diverse range of twentieth- and twenty-first-century global, transnational, award-winning writers with origins in India, Pakistan, Sri Lanka, and Bangladesh engage with the complexities of postcolonial domestic servitude as a problem not only for the nation but also for the novel. I focus on what I identify as an emergent wave of global Anglophone South Asian fiction that centers, explores, and elucidates the problems of contemporary servitude and strives to develop more self-aware, ethical, and egalitarian formal techniques and strategies of representation to do so. I chart how, pushing back against much early to late twentieth-century South Asian English writing, in which the figure of the domestic servant traditionally remains in the *background*, a peripheral but nonetheless ubiquitous, constitutive figure for usually elite-focused narratives, this new body of writing instead *foregrounds* and humanizes that lower-class figure, the other of the other, both as protagonist and as a nexus of a range of concerns. I suggest that this fiction, however, does more than represent: it makes an argument. Implicitly, it argues against what is, and argues for what might be. Offering critique and imagining alternatives, it does cultural and political work: it seeks to intervene in existing discourses and practices, and to change normalized ways of seeing or not seeing.

The internationally acclaimed writers to whose work I devote most of my attention—Daniyal Mueenuddin, Romesh Gunesekera, Aravind Adiga, Thrity Umrigar, and Kiran Desai—all devise different ways to shift the margin to the center of their narratives, to refocus instead on bringing out the interiority, subjectivity, and perspectives of a segment of humanity usually represented from the outside and cast as subsidiary; they call attention both to servants in particular and to the problems of servitude in general. Indeed, as we will see, they all emphasize views from below, often in contrast to views from above, to showcase what subordinated, non-dominant perspectives can see that dominant ones miss; and they experiment with or adapt formal and generic literary conventions to achieve their goals. Collectively, their work constitutes what I identify as a dynamic new literary genre and movement: postcolonial servitude fiction written in English. Servitude fiction (or more accurately, *anti*-servitude fiction), I argue, does not merely call attention to the plight of the mistreated "domestic"; it seeks to defamiliarize, to intervene, and it crafts new narrative forms to offer alternative ways of seeing and imagining the world. This global, transnational fiction,

I suggest, does something new as it makes servitude both its central subject and a key optic for understanding and rethinking the relation between the home and the nation, the domestic and the national, the private and the political, upper and lower classes, the workings of power and the intersection of the high and the low. The term "domestic," after all, as Rosemary Marangoly George reminds us, is a keyword that includes the complex interconnections between "the private home and all its accoutrements" and "hired household help," between "the 'national' as opposed to the foreign" and "the 'tame' as opposed to the 'natural' or wild'" (88).

Cutting across national boundaries, domestic servitude, to be distinguished from slavery, indenture, or other forms of menial labor, has a long history in South Asia as a distinctive cultural formation and as a complex, pervasive, and exploitative system. I am interested in the ways that servitude constitutes a complex of relations that include and exceed issues of labor, social injustice, gender and sexuality, and economic and political precarity. Servitude is predicated upon enormous disparities of class, power, and privilege, and yet, because it uniquely takes place in the intimate spaces of the (employer's) home, which is the servant's workplace, it remains unregulated and unobserved, an occasion for abuse as well as mutual dependence, and complicated concomitant attachments and antagonisms, resentments and obligations, trust and distrust, symbiosis and fear. It is a site of intimacy, a contact zone for the interface between classes, an occasion for the greatest physical and emotional proximity for those located socially and economically at great distance.

As sociologist Raka Ray and historical anthropologist Seemin Qayum have shown in their groundbreaking book *Cultures of Servitude* (2009), domestic servitude has a distinct culture in South Asia that has morphed greatly from feudal to modern capitalist to postcolonial societal arrangements, and that yet remains a highly prevalent norm not only for the upper classes, but also for the middle to lower middle classes.[8] Unlike the West, which has seen a disappearance and recent reappearance of domestic service work, in South Asia servitude has had an uninterrupted though changing trajectory.[9] Attendant upon servitude in South Asia are expectations of servility, self-abasement, ingratiation, subordination, indignity (for the servant), and command, distance, detachment, dignity (for the employer). Servitude in South Asia carries humiliation, and dehumanizing and demeaning behaviors for servants, and for the employer, unsurprisingly, not only release from domestic work, but also a boost to their social status and prestige. Indeed, as an "institution that lies at the bedrock of Indian [and South Asian] domestic middle- and upper-class existence," servitude enables "the constitution of the classes on both sides of the employer-servant relationship" (Ray and Qayum, 2). Via servitude, Ray and Qayum argue, employers produce themselves as "the class destined to lead [the nation] to modernity, and servants as a distinct class, premodern and dependent" (2). Servitude is premised upon lack of opportunity or viable alternatives, in turn based upon illiteracy or lack of basic formal education. A common strand in postcolonial servitude fiction is thus the effort to find alternatives and ways out of servitude, and hence an emphasis on access to education and upward social mobility, within the changing conditions of modern postcolonial nations.

Despite the persistent recurrence of servants in modern South Asian literatures, such that it is hard to find South Asian literature that does not mention servants, servitude is often invisible to or overlooked by postcolonial literary scholars perhaps because it is assumed to be straightforward and unworthy of notice, or because it falls short of conditions of extreme subalternity such as untouchability, or because it is situated in the hidden spaces of the home. And yet it is widely, implicitly understood in South Asia in terms of stigmatization, disempowerment, and abjection. Addressing what it identifies as a blind spot in contemporary postcolonial literary studies, this book understands servitude not as a taken-for-granted, simple phenomenon, but as fraught and multivalent, as a contact zone for disparate classes, constituted by profound and paradoxical inter-class intimacies and interdependencies, power relations, asymmetries, and affective interpersonal relations, as at once a source of stigma and shame, and a site of identity formation, constituted and intersected by such vectors of identity as gender, sexuality, ethnicity, religion, and age. This is the first full-length study to focus on the presence, indeed the persistent recurrence, of domestic servants in Anglophone postcolonial or South Asian literature and to pay close attention to their political, thematic, and formal significance. *Postcolonial Servitude* reframes central questions in postcolonial literary studies and also offers fresh readings of South Asian Anglophone writers ranging from early to contemporary, well known to less known, from Rajo Rao, Mulk Raj Anand, and Anita Desai to Salman Rushdie, Mohsin Hamid, Shyam Selvadurai, and Monica Ali. It identifies a cultural shift in the twenty-first century postcolonial novel, a new attentiveness, altruism, and self-implication in addressing an ethical concern for the other on whom the self depends.

In reading these texts, my approach emphasizes the *how* as well as the *what*, paying close attention to form as key to addressing content. I am concerned not just with the issue of making the invisible visible, but also with how writers attempt this with particular narrative techniques and strategies. To understand how these writers invent new ways to achieve new goals, I examine how they use different genres, such as interlinked short stories that provide diverse and contrasting perspectives; how they may depart from social realism to adapt satire or humor into a new idiom; how they may break from novelistic conventions such as the Bildungsroman or the marriage plot to redesign and restructure new kinds of plots, how they devise new modes of telling, deploying the unreliable autobiographical servant narrator, or the more reliable limited third-person omniscient narrator, or alternating multiple narrators and protagonists, in order to explore the connections and disconnections between servants and their employers.

Postcolonial domestic servitude becomes, I suggest, a site of particular attention for these writers because it constitutes a nexus of many concerns: the complex affective dynamics and gendered micropolitics among individuals placed in situations of close proximity, intimacy, and asymmetric dependence across multiple and vast power differentials; the intersectionality of class with gender, sexuality, age, ethnicity, religion, caste; the constitution and performance of servant and employer identities; the effects of subordination, stigmatization, and abjection on servant psyches; the self-perception of individuals subjected to servitude over generations; servants' often covert modes of resistance, negotiation, or exertion of agency; the generational legacies and familial costs of servitude; the ethical obligations and responsibilities of those more privileged toward those who serve daily in their own homes; and the political responsibilities of the state toward some of its most vulnerable citizens. These writers are thus broadly also interested in the relation between the domestic and the national (what happens in the privacy of the employer's home, which is also the servant's workplace, and what is a concern of the state). The precarity and pervasiveness of servitude in South Asia also becomes a litmus test for the promised freedoms of democratic nationalism, a signifier of the failures and disillusionments of the anti-colonial liberation movements that led to political independence but not to basic rights for many postcolonial citizens.[10]

Because domestic servitude in South Asia remains unregulated, legally unprotected, and part of the uncounted "informal sector," no one knows exactly how many domestic workers exist in each country. There is no doubt, however, that servitude in postcolonial South Asia, with a long history from before colonial times, persists, often in new forms, and that it is highly gendered. In India (with a population of 1.4 billion in 2021), estimates of current domestic workers range from 4.2 million to 50 million, the majority of whom are women (75% or more) and many are underage children.[11] The International Labor Organization (ILO) in India states:

> Domestic work refers to housework such as sweeping, cleaning utensils, washing clothes, cooking, caring of children and such other work which is carried out for an employer for remuneration. Domestic work provides an important livelihood source for illiterate women or those with very little education. Official statistics place the numbers employed in India as 4.75 million, (of which 3 million are women) but this is considered a severe underestimation and the true number to be more between 20 million to 80 million workers. However, numbers alone do not describe the importance of their work, or the

hardships they face. Many of these workers do not even receive the minimum wage (in States where it exists), work extremely long hours and often do not get one day's rest.[12]

Sociologist Sonal Sharma notes that whereas up to the 1970s the Indian domestic worker was predominantly male, by the 1980s that demographic had flipped to predominantly female (536). In Pakistan (with a population of 231 million in 2021), the ILO cites the most recent estimate of domestic workers as 8.5 million, "mostly women and children," though this number may be severely undercounted (Asrar, 2021). According to one source, "every fourth household in [Pakistan] hires a domestic worker, and the majority of these workers is females (especially children)."[13] In Bangladesh (population 169 million in 2021), the estimated number of domestic workers is 10.5 million,[14] and in Sri Lanka (population 22 million in 2021) it is 80,000, of which 60,000 are women.[15] These astonishing figures bespeak the sheer pervasiveness of domestic servitude in contemporary South Asia and suggest its roots in poverty, illiteracy, gender inequality, and a widely accepted, normalized culture of servitude.

In *Cultures of Servitude*, Ray and Qayum argue that in India "the institution [of domestic servitude is] . . . central to understanding self and society," and is "intimately tied to the self-conscious evolution of a 'modern' Indian elite" (2). This argument applies as well to other South Asian nations with shared cultural traditions, such as Pakistan, Bangladesh, and Sri Lanka. In this book, I examine how Anglophone South Asian literature, itself an institution that narrates the nation to itself and to others, both helps constitute that elite and has lately begun self-critically to question that constitution and its dependence on servitude. The servitude fiction writers I identify address various dimensions of servitude; the socio-economic, political, and historic conditions that lead to servitude; the ways that servitude functions as an in-between condition that provides refuge from extreme destitution, homelessness, starvation, and the occasion for intimate forms of coercion and exploitation; and the compounded effects of the lack of governmental regulation, oversight, or protection. It also demands a rethinking of servitude itself and of the constitution of servant identities as the premodern or simple other of the elite. Without necessarily recommending that servitude be abolished altogether, they offer critiques of the ways it is constituted in their societies and the radiating effects of such an unquestioned domestic and cultural arrangement. They suggest imagined alternatives and attempt alternative forms of representation as they urge their readers toward new ways of seeing and rethinking habituated modes of acculturation to servant-employer relations.

These writers of what I call servitude fiction are thus not only concerned with issues such as class divides, social inequalities, gender discrimination, or exploitation and abuses of power, though these are all part of the mix. They are also concerned with something more subtle, complex, and fine-grained, something that is both interpersonal and political at micro and macro levels, something that literature is uniquely positioned to explore and grapple with: individual inner lives, relationships, interactions, self-understandings, perceptions, and misperceptions, as impacted by institutions of servitude. Literature can explore interiority, psychology, multiple perspectives, and the complexity of human interrelations even as it places all these in the context of a larger social context or complex.

It is precisely because domestic servants occupy the space of the employer's home, in which they must be trusted with the employer's most intimate secrets, precious possessions, and vulnerable family members (young children, aging elders) that they are invested at once with fear and anxiety, with animus as well as connection. And because servants have the (imagined) power to withhold their labor, or to enact covert resistance by messing up the work on which their employers depend, servants are often viewed (by employers) as having undue power. Salim, the Indian African narrator of V. S. Naipaul's *A Bend in the River* (1979), describes his family's Arab African servants as "limpets" living in the "smaller houses" his wealthy family provides for them in the compound of their home (18). With overt contempt, he casts these families of servants as irrational beings who manipulate their employers into caving to their demands: "I could imagine the scene. I could imagine the screaming and the stamping and the sulking. That was how the servants got their way in our house; they could be worse than children" (30). In Jessica Hagedorn's American Book Award–winning postcolonial novel *Dogeaters* (1990), a German visitor to the Philippines expresses his unease at having servants present in the luxurious home provided to him: "That's the problem with these colonial situations of yours. . . . Servants. They end up knowing your secrets, they always end up knowing too much. It's a kind of insidious power" (145).[16] Servitude fiction pushes back against such perspectives.

Servitude fiction might instead suggest how the (often misplaced) fear on the part of employers is matched by (justified) fear on the part of servants. Indeed, it explores the complex effects of servitude on the psyche and emotionality of a servant. Paradoxically, it is often because servants, despite their extremely precarious positions, have some power/knowledge to hurt or expose their employers, that they must continually ingratiate and work to win and retain that trust. Given that their livelihoods are dependent on employers' whims, approval, or displeasure, servants cannot be truly open or frank before employers, they must develop a dual demeanor and mask their words and actions to maintain the frail security of their conditions of work. For employers as a class, servants can become a site of unreadability, inscrutable strangers in their own homes, who must be at once depended on and, at some level, feared. For servants, on the other hand, knowing and understanding the employer carries high stakes. How well then can one know oneself, when constituted by servitude? One writer suggests that servitude produces such complexities of interaction, so deeply structured by power inequalities, that it occludes the possibilities not only of mutual knowledge, but also of self-knowledge, for both employers and servants.

At a key moment in Aravind Adiga's Booker-prize winning novel, *The White Tiger*, Balram, the narrator-protagonist, reflects that he does not even fully know or understand his own feelings as a servant:

> I put my hand out and wiped the vomit from his lips, and cooed soothing words to him. It squeezed my heart to see him suffer like this—but where my genuine concern for him ended and where my self-interest began, I could not tell: no servant can ever tell what the motives of his heart are.
>
> Do we loathe our masters behind a façade of love—or do we love them behind a façade of loathing?
>
> We are made mysteries to ourselves by the Rooster Coop we are locked in. (*White Tiger*, 160)

I will say more in Chapter 5 about the "Rooster Coop," Adiga's key metaphor for the deep grip of ideology, for the structures of fear that entrap poor people in servitude, convince them of the futility of resistance, and terrorize them with the real threat of violent retaliation upon their families. What I want to note here about this passage, though, is the intense emotional ambivalence that Balram, as a servant, expresses about a master who has both grossly exploited him and who yet also, in a state of drunken self-indulgence, depends on him like a helpless child. In this extraordinary moment of self-dissection, while self-knowing about his concomitant resentment and attachment, Balram unmasks another aspect of servitude, making clear the impossibility of knowing, even for the servant himself, how to separate self-interest from altruistic fellow feeling. Indeed, as he peels back layer upon layer of his own consciousness, the question Balram raises is whether altruism is extricable from, or is even possible without, self-interest in a relationship founded upon extreme inequalities of power. It points also to the habitual mask of servitude that servants must wear to remain unreadable to their employers, and to the invisible emotional labor that they must regularly perform, in addition to the physical labor that is their obvious task, to the extent that they may become unreadable to themselves.[17]

Postcolonial domestic servitude has been overlooked in critical scholarship, I think, for at least two reasons. First, among South Asian and postcolonial scholars, most of whom hail from middle- to upper-class backgrounds, it is so routine and normalized as a condition of domestic and social life, that it remains unquestioned and unseen. Those who attend to precarity and disempowerment have tended to focus on the most extreme kinds of subalternity: untouchability, urban and rural poverty and migration, political disenfranchisement, dispossessed or starving peasantry, war-ridden populations, and so on. But servitude has escaped scholarly attention in South Asian literary and cultural criticism, perhaps because servant-employer power dynamics inhere in the more hidden, intimate, ostensibly private space of the employer's home (which is paradoxically the workplace of the servant). In her recent book, *Maid in India*, the Indian journalist Tripti Lahiri comments on this blindness among employers to regular mistreatment and injustices to servants:

> The gulf between what we say we believe in, as members of [India's] elite, and how we actually live is so immense that it doesn't even merit being called hypocrisy. Hypocrisy requires at least some awareness of the great distance between one's actions and one's claims. And nowhere else is this distance so visible—and yet we seem blind to it—as when we are at home. (25)

Second, for Western, non–South Asian scholars, servitude remains invisible perhaps because those who have not lived in South Asia do not realize how pervasive it is, or how deeply ingrained in everyday life as a condition of existence.[18] Such scholars tend to focus on issues of race/colonialism, gender, sexuality, class, and caste, but not on servants. When class is foregrounded, again, extreme cases occupy attention and servitude falls out of the picture.[19] Westerners also tend to think of servants as a privilege of the extremely wealthy, as it is now in the West. In South Asia, however, middle and lower middle classes can almost be defined by their constant dependence on servants.[20]

As I will show in subsequent chapters, the work of early to contemporary South Asian writers, from R. K. Narayan to Mulk Raj Anand, from Salman Rushdie to Arundhati Roy to Kamila Shamsie, seems predicated on references to domestic servants. Even when they are little more than occasional, even subliminal presences, servants mark the emergence, continuation, and distinctiveness of a colonial and postcolonial upper and middle class. And this is true not only of Indian writers, but also of Pakistani, Sri Lankan, Bangladeshi, Afghan, Irani, and Nepali ones. In a telling moment, for instance, Pakistani American writer Daniyal Mueenuddin, in his short story "Lily," describes the protagonist's parents, living on a tiny retirement pension in Islamabad, as having only two servants: "They had almost no money—worrying about electricity and gas, about the car breaking down, [they] kept only a cook and a bearer" (172). In other words, despite having come down in the world, this elderly couple employs at least two full-time house servants. Moreover, only the live-in, full-time servants are mentioned, as markers of the family's descent in the world; the part-time help also additionally relied upon—the daily cleaner who comes from the sweeper colony, the gardener who lives in the slums—goes without saying. Likewise, Nepali writer Samrat Upadhyay's short-story collections *Arresting God in Kathmandu* and *The Royal Ghosts* portray numerous middle- or lower-middle class characters and families in late twentieth-century Kathmandu, often struggling to maintain their class status in a changing world, all of whom have at least one or more household servant, and who distinguish themselves sharply from the ubiquitous servant class.[21] Afghan writer Khaled Hosseini's bestselling first novel *The Kite Runner*, set in 1970s Afghanistan, turns upon the well-to-do male narrator-protagonist's childhood relationship with Hasan, the servant boy who lives in his house, and who turns out eventually to be his illegitimate half-brother. Iranian memoir writers like Marjane Satrapi and Firoozeh Dumas, who hail from the pre-Revolution middle class, describe servants as an inextricable part of the life in Iran they left behind.[22] And in Arundhati Roy's *The God of Small Things*, the first novel by an Indian woman to win the Booker Prize, Kochu Maria, the "vinegar-hearted, short-tempered midget cook," is the last servant left in the rundown family home, a suitable companion and lower-class counterpart to the aging evil aunt Baby Kochamma (16). Much attention has been paid to Roy's approach to the problems of caste in postcolonial South India, but servitude in this novel is overlooked, though embodied and stereotyped in this figure of malice and prejudice, whose relatively privileged status in the household enables her to treat viciously the vulnerable others she fears and resents: the untouchable Velutha, the children, and their divorcée mother.

From James Joyce to Ngũgĩ wa Thiong'o, Kiran Desai and Mohsin Hamid, postcolonial writers have long used the idea of the servant or servitude figuratively, as a metaphor to represent the positionality of the colonized subject, subordinated by imperialist power or political tyranny. Early in Joyce's *Ulysses*, for example, Stephen looks at himself in a mirror "cleft by a crooked crack," and reflects bitterly, "It is a symbol of Irish art. The cracked lookingglass of a servant" (6). Soon after, he elaborates, suggesting through repetition the powerful hold of the word: "I am a servant of two masters, . . . an English and an Italian [England and the Catholic Church]" (17). In *A Grain of Wheat*, his major novel about the Kenyan struggle for independence, Ngugi wa Thiongo presents the white colonialist racist imaginary as dependent on the discourse of servitude. Thompson, a British colonialist administrator, decides to resign his post and leave Kenya on the eve of independence because he sees the colonized as his servants rising out of their proper place: "why should [white] people wait and go through the indignity of being ejected from their seats by their houseboys?" (55). To express his outrage, this man who sees himself as "Prospero" explicitly uses the term "houseboy" (for male domestic servant) to refer to Kenyan freedom fighters, as if imagining that his black servants, both literal and figurative, would displace their white masters (54). Even postcolonial subjects imagine themselves in terms of servitude when addressing new forms of national or global disempowerment. In Kiran Desai's *The Inheritance of Loss*, the separatist Nepalis of India who want their own nation voice their resentment of second-class citizen status in a postcolonial state: "We are kept at the level of servants" (174).[23] Changez, the Pakistani protagonist-narrator in Mohsin Hamid's *The Reluctant Fundamentalist*, realizes that even as a Princeton graduate and highly paid financial analyst in New York city, he has unwittingly behaved like a brainwashed captive, serving the interests of twenty-first century American imperialism: "I was a modern-day janissary, a servant of the American empire at a time when it was invading a country with kinship to mine and was perhaps even colluding to ensure that my own country faced the threat of war" (153).

But what is the forgotten actuality, the literal ground for this metaphor, the hidden ubiquitous basis that is so regularly seen that it becomes unseen, that provides the vehicle for this tenor? In this book, I focus not on figurative servants or servitude, but on the literal, material conditions and representations of subordinated individuals who work in the homes of a formerly colonized elite, and who are, despite the end of colonization, still deprived of the equality and agency promised to them by nationalism and the struggle for independence. Understanding the subtleties and extraordinary degradation of servitude in South Asia incidentally also helps us understand what postcolonial writers mean when they use the term metaphorically. In his famous essay, "Outside the Whale," for instance, Rushdie proposes a more assertive political stance for writers and uses the corrosive metaphor of servitude to castigate George Orwell for proposing quietism:

> [Orwell's] view [in "Inside the Whale"] excludes comedy, satire, deflation; because of course the writer need not always be the servant of some beetle-browed ideology. He [sic] can also be its critic, its antagonist, its scourge. (*Imaginary Homelands*, 98)

When we can understand what Rushdie is talking about, what a servant in South Asia literally has to be and to endure—the self-effacement, the self-abasement—then such remarks gain more power and meaning. Rushdie's use of metaphor becomes clearer when grounded in the very gritty reality that he knows up close.

Because servitude is predicated upon proximity and relationality across severe social divides, and because it creates an interdependence often unacknowledged by employers, it necessitates subtle negotiations on both sides, coding and decoding across vast differences and power divides. Servitude fiction is interested in unraveling the subtle forms of resistance, negotiation, and acquiescence, the paradoxical intimacies among unequal persons who are perforce placed in close contact; it is interested in exploring the complex inner lives of, and microdynamics between, people at once closely connected yet separated by enormous differences of power and social status. While social science can study and analyze broader patterns, fiction can tease out the subtleties of such relationships and interactions, set in concretely realized situations within narratives that historicize and chronicle individual lives and relationships, that provide a before and after. Fiction can show not tell, it can explore interiority and psychology as well as socio-economic and political contexts, indeed it can reveal how they interfuse. And, as we will see, though links between empathy and action remain contested, through narrative techniques such as first-person narration or free indirect discourse, narrative fiction is able to evoke empathy, care, and concern, to elicit both understanding and affective responses, if not (occasional) identification. I argue in this book that servitude fiction explores these questions by shifting emphasis to servants' perspectives, often setting up comparisons to those of their employers, that it highlights or gives weight to the inner lives, consciousnesses, interiority, and personhood of servants as literary characters, and that it attempts to devise new, more respectful and tactful modes of representation, as it seeks to rehumanize those who have been dehumanized, to challenge dominant discourses and understandings of domesticity, servitude, and subjection. Ultimately, it makes both ethical/political and formal/aesthetic interventions, as it urges readers toward a re-seeing of servitude as in institution, and a rethinking of the relation between servitude and postcoloniality, it also crafts literary strategies or reworks given conventions that befit its goals.

In canonical British and European literature, domestic servants have long served as minor, necessary but functional figures, enabling the plot, revealing crucial information at crucial moments, providing comic relief, and so on. They are not usually central protagonists with deep subjectivities to be explored. This is hardly a surprise, given that literary and literate storytellers historically emerged from middle to upper social ranks and primarily addressed the ruling classes, not the ruled. *The Servant's Hand*, Bruce Robbins' pioneering study of servants in European literature, begins by noting both "the exclusion of the people from literary representation" (ix) and the more surprising literary "effects" of the "power" of their invisible presence in the form of servants (ix, xi). Many academic literary studies have since explored different dimensions of servants in Renaissance, eighteenth- and nineteenth-century British, and early twentieth-century American literatures.[24] In Europe and America, the era of domestic servants was supposed to have ended with the end of World War II, and the socio-economic political changes it brought; though as many social scientists, particularly feminist scholars, have begun to note, global servitude has made a comeback with globalization and the feminization of care-work, as women from the Global South migrate to the North to provide childcare and housekeeping services to enable relatively affluent women to have careers and release from domestic responsibilities.

Literary scholars, however, seem not to have noticed that just as domestic servants disappear from post-1945 Western literatures, they re-appear in modern non-Western or postcolonial literatures, especially in South Asian fiction.[25] Indeed, it is hard to find Anglophone South Asian fiction that does not include some reference to servants. Modern South Asian English literature depends on servants in some form, not least, as postcolonial writing, in order to highlight the distinctions between different ranks of the colonized—to highlight either the existence of a long-entitled ruling class, or the emergence of an educated upcoming middle class that is defined by its household servants. Servitude in South Asia, as we will see, has a long and different history than in Europe, and depends on different cultural formations. It constitutes not only a "structure of feeling," in Raymond Williams' words, but a structure of *being*, central to all the societies in the region. And yet there is so far no book-length study of servants or servitude in postcolonial, or South Asian, literatures.

Postcolonial literary critics, though much interested in the general idea of the subaltern, have not really paid attention to the specificities or questions that servitude raises, to the prevalence of servants in their (our) elite and middle-class homes (in reality and in fiction), servants on whom the upper classes depend and build their own identities.[26] Nor have they attended to what I will argue is the recurrent, *constitutive* presence of servants in even earlier South Asian literature, or examined what kinds of functions (political, ideological, aesthetic) the servant figure performs in this literature.

Defining Servitude More Closely

Unlike American literature and film, where employers are white but servants are often people of color, descendants of slaves, or recent immigrants, in African, Caribbean, or South Asian postcolonial literatures, servants are frequently of the same putative race as their employers, often even the same ethnicity and religion, also citizens of a new democratic nation. Yet the postcolonial servant is marked by extreme disadvantages of class and education, locked in cultures of servitude that seem to necessitate the enactment of self-abasement, humility, and extreme deference to an elite class of employers. In South Asia in particular, what almost defines domestic servants is their illiteracy or meager, interrupted formal education, their inability or low ability to read or write, which thereby limits their options and constrains them to work as low-paid, supposedly unskilled labor hidden in other peoples' homes. When in Neel Mukherjee's 2017 novel, *A State of Freedom*, a rare servant girl knows how to read, she conceals it from her peers, who challenge her when they find out: "How come you're coming with us to work as a servant if you can read?" (222).

Raka Ray and Seemin Qayum define a culture of servitude as:

> one in which social relations of domination/subordination, dependency, and inequality are normalized and permeate both the domestic and public spheres. . . . By "normalized" we mean, first, that these social relations are legitimized ideologically such that domination, dependency, and inequality are not only tolerated but accepted; second, that they are reproduced through everyday social interaction and practice. . . . In a culture of servitude, servitude is normalized so that it is virtually impossible to imagine life without it, and practices, and thoughts and feelings about practices, are patterned on it. (Ray and Qayum, 3–4)

Embedded deeply in "structures of feeling" (5), domestic servitude in India, they remind us, has "long unbroken histories" (2), having morphed from feudal to modern systems and imaginaries (2). It is an unregulated "institution" that encompasses a "nexus of relations," hegemonies, and economic and social arrangements (4–5) that constitutes class identities, subjectivities, self-identities, and perceptions "on both sides of the employer servant relationship" (2). While servitude has clearly evolved and adapted to social changes, some key structural features remain constant and unique to South Asian norms of servitude, such as the dehumanization and expected obsequiousness and self-effacement of servants, the routine abusiveness of employers, and the degrading practices that enforce distance and distinction.

Servitude thus becomes a legible constituent of identity, marked upon a human being's body and bearing, recognizable to others, and internalized deeply as constituting one's being and place in the world. The middle-class narrator of one of Mueenuddin's short stories, for instance, recognizes an old feudal servant by his gait and clothing, by picking up the cues readable within a shared cultural sign system:

> The next evening, . . . I found an old man standing by the portico with the timeless patience of peasants and old servants, as if he had been standing there all day. . . . By his language and manner I knew him to be a serving man of the old type, of the type that believes implicitly in his master's right to be served. (106)

The narrator knows that the servant knows that he must wait, humbly, outside, in intemperate weather, to present his supplication, that the old man has absorbed deep within himself an acceptance of his inequality and degradation as the status quo. What is unusual, however, is Mueenuddin's attentive evocation of the servant's internalized acquiescence to this system, the compassionate reading from the outside of the psyche within.

It is no surprise that the figure of the domestic servant should be present in, even essential to, twentieth- and twenty-first-century fiction from India, Pakistan, Sri Lanka, Bangladesh, Nepal, Afghanistan, and Iran, given the socioeconomic structures of inequality, rural to urban migration, reliance upon domestic labor instead of electrical appliances, and hence ubiquitous presence of servants in lower-, middle-, and upper-class homes in these countries (much as was the case in Britain until World War II). In an era of postcolonial modernity and globalization, industrialization and agricultural change, such systems of domestic service are arguably on the rise, as more and more urban households employ as menial "unskilled" "help" (cooks, bearers, nursemaids, cleaners, kitchen-workers, chauffeurs, gardeners, watchmen), individuals who have few other employment options in households that do not have widespread access to laundry machines, dishwashers, or even vacuum cleaners, and where such work must be done by manual labor.[27] In literatures emergent from nations newly freed from European colonization, and founded upon hopes of creating modern democratic and egalitarian societies, both the invisibility *and* visibility of servants thus take on new meanings as middle-class postcolonial writers either fail to notice, or call attention to, the continuing disenfranchisement of servants (*the other of the other*, the serving people of a formerly colonized bourgeoisie) present in their midst.

To be clear, by "domestic servitude" I refer to a complex of relations distinguished from both slavery and indentured labor.[28] In much of South Asia, a domestic servant is (nominally) paid for his or her labor, and though constrained by severe lack of choices and informal networks of emotion, obligation, or tradition, and is able voluntarily to enter or leave the service of an employer without notice and without any binding legal or written contract. That said, she or he is nonetheless also among the most vulnerable in society, unprotected from abuse or injustice, and powerless to prevent sudden termination of employment and loss of shelter or lodging at the whim of the employer. I want to focus on domestic servants not as generalized representatives of subaltern or impoverished classes (which might include agricultural workers, factory workers, shopkeepers, Dalits, beggars), but more specifically as individuals who work and often live in the homes of employers who can afford to retain and pay them, and whose interactions with their employers thus present the intimate interface between unequal classes, the paradoxes of close contact and distance between individuals from very different social strata.

Domestic servitude in South Asia is understood to be a deeply stigmatized position, as a permanent not temporary constituent of identity, often passed down through the generations, that produces expectations of loyalty, deference, even self-abasement from servants, and varying degrees of obligation from employers.[29] It is distinct from other forms of work or "classic capital/labor relationships" that are constituted by the "market," as Ray and Qayum argue, because it "inhabits the private, intimate space of the home" (192).[30] The employer's home or "domestic life" is a workplace even for the live-in servant. The home becomes a site of intimacy where the private and public, leisure and work, contractual and affective relations intersect, producing in many cultures of servitude what Ray and Qayum call a "rhetoric of love" and "family," a "complex discourse" that both conceals exploitation and makes it "bearable" on both sides (93).

It is also important then to distinguish domestic servitude, especially in South Asia, from other more visible forms of labor that exist outside the home, such as factory work. In a telling moment in Salman Rushdie's *Midnight's Children*, when Saleem's family migrates to Pakistan, Saleem as narrator comments on how his father, Ahmed Sinai, started a new business manufacturing towels, and "began treating his workers as peremptorily as once, in Bombay, he had mistreated servants, and sought to inculcate, in master weavers and assistant packers alike, the eternal verities of the master-servant relationship" (397). But the factory workers resist:

> As a result, his workforce walked out on him in droves, explaining, for instance, "I am not your latrine-cleaner, sahib; I am qualified Grade One weaver," and in general refusing to show proper gratitude for his beneficence in having employed them.... he let them go and hired a bunch of ill-favored slackers who pilfered ... but were willing to bow and scrape whenever required to do so. (397–398)

Rushdie's purpose here is to critique the classist, high-handed arrogance of a bourgeois elite businessman like Ahmed Sinai. Yet in order to do so, he shows how all, including factory workers, assume the normality of the abuse and degradation of household servants. Far from envisioning solidarity with other kinds of workers, the factory workers insist on their higher status as artisans even in a capitalist system, as separate from menial servants. Because they have more visibility and power, they resist such being treated as servants. When Ahmed Sinai tries to replace them with more servile, less qualified workers, his business flops. This is not to say that servants cannot resist abuse—they can, and they do, as we will see—but often their resistance takes covert or delayed form, or involves complex negotiation. Or, more often, servants may be forced to submit or resort to the hidden revenge of the helpless: spitting into food, inflicting small forms of damage, pilfering small objects.[31] Rushdie's passage also implies that servants cannot walk out as easily as factory workers can, and are understood as more expendable. The normalized mistreatment of domestic servants here serves as a low benchmark against which, in a changing postcolonial market, the relative dignity, self-respect, and capacity of skilled factory workers to protest is measured.[32]

In this book, I use the term "servant" (instead of recent euphemisms like "the help" or "helper") for several reasons. First, the English word "servant" is the term used broadly throughout South Asia, and is the closest cultural equivalent to words like "naukar" (Hindi/Urdu for servant). It is also the term used in all the fiction discussed in this book. As an England-returned Bengali narrator in Neel Mukherjee's *A State of Freedom* (2017) ruefully recognizes, his preference for the term "domestic help" is out of sync with reality: "My mother's generation still called them servants. My politically correct tag had not a jot of correlation to their status: their position in the Indian social hierarchy or economy had never changed" (35–36). Second, "servant" aptly conveys, instead of washing out, the sense of stigma and power to ascribe identity to those to whom the term is applied. It carries the structure of feeling, the culture of servitude that constitutes the matrix of relations and being that servitude fiction seeks to address and redress. "Domestic worker" is an important, very recent term that has begun to be used in the United States as a way to restructure the nexus of servant-employer relations, to claim more dignity and respect for individuals paid to work in other peoples' homes, but it bespeaks a different kind of (imagined or actual) relationship, while the term "servant" conveys the nature of the (ongoing) problem that is the focus of this study and of servitude fiction. I worry about minimizing, or worse, erasing, the historical and contemporary realities of servitude addressed by servitude fiction if I were to use another term. Third, it would also be anachronistic to use a term like "domestic worker" in discussions of earlier literature, and even of contemporary literature that itself emphasizes, even as it questions, the servantness of servitude. As I elaborate in my conclusion, "domestic worker" is rightly the terminology used by organizations now increasingly mobilizing and arguing for social and legal reforms for systems of servitude in various South Asian countries. In contexts of reform, I would urge the use of the term "domestic worker."

It has become a commonplace in politically oriented literary studies to identify and valorize various forms of resistance on the part of subordinated subjects. However, social scientists who study servitude remind us that to employ the binaries of domination and subordination or "romanticized" notions of "subaltern resistance" can be simplistic; Kathleen Adams and Sara Dickey propose instead an approach that understands "hegemonies and their multiple hierarchies as constantly negotiated," seeing "multiple vulnerabilities and dependencies, axes of opposition, and contestations of representations on all sides" (7). By reading closely the *micropolitics* of servant-employer interactions we can plumb their complexities and avoid seeing them in terms of either cooptation or resistance and instead understand them as a process of necessary and continued negotiation, as enactment of (limited) agency. I thus propose a shift away from the lens of *resistance* to that of *negotiation*, a recognition of the multiple ways that those subject to power negotiate their ways around and through these power dynamics, and creatively construct their own ways of exerting power. At the same time, I would say, *pace* Foucault, in our drive to validate resistance, we also need to remember and recognize that not all those subjected to power or oppression are able or willing to resist, that many do in fact submit, and are nonetheless no less (or even more) deserving of attention.

Rather than presupposing servitude to be an already understood, easily dismissed, simple condition, I read it as complex and expansive; as inclusive of affective interpersonal relations, paradoxical intimacies, and dependencies; as deeply fraught by intersecting axes of power, embedded in various intersecting hierarchies; and as therefore demanding of attentive, nuanced reading and historicizing. Focusing on servitude is not just a way to think about class differences or cross-class relations but to examine a social formation defined by a unique proximity and intimacy between individuals of very different classes or social ranks. Domestic servitude also offers (internal to postcolonial societies) what in the context of colonial cross-cultural encounters Mary Louise Pratt has termed a "contact zone"—a site of simultaneous intimacy, distance, and mutual adaptation. Instead of treating colonizer and colonized as sealed and separate entities, Pratt's focus on contact foregrounds "the interactive, improvisational dimensions of colonial encounters," emphasizing "how subjects are constituted in and by their relations to each other," via "copresence" and "interaction, interlocking understandings and practices, often within radically asymmetrical relations of power" (7). I borrow this notion of the contact zone to examine internal or intra-cultural dynamics within modern postcolonial societies—employer-servant relations in contemporary transnational postcolonial fiction—where similar asymmetries of power operate for individuals of radically different socio-economic and educational backgrounds, though often of the same nationality, similarly locked into close proximity.

Focusing on servitude is also very much a way to think about the inflections and effects of gender as it intersects with class and other vectors of identity and what meanings they accrue in particular contexts. Hence, the subjectivities, experiences, and the dynamics between servants and employers are necessarily shaped by the gender of both employer and servant. In the two examples I began with, in Aidoo's story and Mehta's film, the servants are male, one old, one young. But, as South Asian literature demonstrates, servitude is obviously very different for women, who are usually hired for different (gendered) tasks than men, and are subject to different expectations and experiences. In South Asia, women exclusively serve as ayahs or nannies to provide childcare, or as maids who attend upon higher-class women, while men exclusively serve as drivers or chauffeurs, gardeners, bearers (who fetch and carry), watchmen, or guards. The overlap areas are cooking and cleaning, undertaken by both men and women, though men are usually paid more for the same jobs. Thus, obvious hierarchies exist among servants: drivers are paid more, for instance, because their work is perceived as based on more specialized training. In Adiga's *The White Tiger*, Balram, the servant-narrator-protagonist, exemplifies the downtrodden peasant underclasses, brutalized by bloodsucking feudal landlords, and deprived of economic or social opportunity by the gross corruptions of the postcolonial state. But when, thanks to his unusual enterprise, Balram becomes a highly paid chauffeur for his feudal landlord's son in New Delhi, it is also clear that despite his multiple disadvantages, Balram benefits from the privileges of his gender in being able to move alone to the city, and to obtain both the training and the job, which comes with a (filthy but free) room in the servants' quarters. If he had a sister or a wife, she could only be hired as an ayah (nanny), maid, or cleaning woman; no woman would be hired to serve as a driver. By contrast, Bhima, the aging female protagonist of Umrigar's *The Space Between Us*, can only eke out a subsistence from part-time menial work doing much lower-paid cooking, cleaning, and housework while paying for her lodgings in a filthy slum with no amenities.

Women servants are also more vulnerable to sexual exploitation from male employers as well as male servants in the households where they work. As we will see, women writers (Hosain, Umrigar, Sidhwa) highlight this issue of sexual predation, though some male writers (Mueenuddin) certainly do too. Servant-employer interactions are necessarily shaped by the gender of both. Relationships between female servants and female employers permit greater familiarity and intimacy and produce greater attachment and animosity than those between (male or female) employers and male servants.[33] Male servants are usually not permitted within the intimate spaces of the home accessible to female servants (especially bedrooms), in part to protect elite women from lower-class men. Female servants, however, must enter spaces—bedrooms, bathrooms, kitchens—in which they may be alone with predatory male employers. Hence younger female servants become, inevitably, more vulnerable to sexual predation by male employers or male servants. The circumstance of upper-class women having authority over male servants also produces a chiasmic or crossover effect of gender versus class power, if men resent and resist being ordered about by women.

I would emphasize therefore that my approach is that of *intersectional feminism*, which understands gender as not stand-alone but as simultaneously intersecting or interlocking with other vectors of identity such as class, race, nationality, and dis/ability. These, as contemporary feminist theory has taught us, are not additive but mutually constitutive, or *interactive*—in other words, each shapes the other. What I attempt is an analytical approach that recognizes this holistic phenomenon, rather than singling out one category in isolation. As Ray and Qayum note, "class . . . more than caste or gender frames the potentiality of becoming a servant or being born a servant" (2). Recognizing class as a primary determinant of servitude, the chapters of this book are also structured around the gendering of servitude, and are interested in teasing out the nuances of gender as it intersects with servitude and other factors. Chapters 1 to 3 are all framed in terms of the gender of servants, as well as their race/ethnicity, age, and so on. Chapters 4 and 5 focus on and compare male servants and their first-person narratives, and the challenges to masculinity and homoerotic tensions between male employers and male servants. Chapters 6 and 7 focus on the dynamics between employers and servants (either between women, or between a young woman of the employer class and an old man who is the household servant), and the intergenerational legacies of servitude, all of which I foreground as heavily shaped by gender.

Literary History and the Method of Close Reading

To set up a contrastive benchmark, a literary tradition and context against which to measure the departures or interventions of servitude fiction writers, I begin, in Part One (Chapters 1 and 2), by examining how some earlier and recent Anglophone South Asian writers have written about servants as a side-note to other concerns. I show how early pioneers like Raja Rao and R. K. Narayan to Salman Rushdie, call upon servants primarily to enable the emergence of upper-class (male) subjects, and how early women writers, like Attia Hosain, Zeenuth Futehally, Kamala Markandaya, and Nayantara Sahgal, are more attentive to the complex gendered dynamics between upper-class women and servants within the domestic realm. I also discuss how, after Rushdie, a younger generation of well-known contemporary transnational South Asian writers like Shyam Selvadurai, Monica Ali, and Mohsin Hamid rely upon servitude for key purposes while not making it central to their fiction. In Part Two (Chapters 3 to 7), I analyze the work of more recent, millennial writers, male and female, citizens of many nations—Pakistani American Daniyal Mueenuddin, Sri Lankan British Romesh Gunesekera, Indian Australian Aravind Adiga, Indian Americans Thrity Umrigar and Kiran Desai—who center on the servant to produce a new wave of what I call servitude fiction.

Because my argument depends on examining the micropolitics and subtle nuances of minute interactions, in unraveling the intricacies of form and language, my method is grounded in a politically and theoretically informed close reading. I propose, and practice, a mode of attentive literary analysis that is not opposed to and that enhances or enables culturally and politically oriented approaches with a deep attentiveness to the unexpected and unique, to textual details and layers of meaning, to such things as tone, irony, narrative voice—and that can engage in the unraveling of multiple, coexistent, and sometimes contradictory meanings. I pay attention to what Derek Attridge has called "the specificity and singularity of texts" and eschew pressing a text into the service of a pre-made frame or grid (13). Close reading and theory, or close reading and postcolonial or feminist critical approaches, have come to be seen as opposed, perhaps because formalism, in the form of New Criticism, was practiced and subsequently viewed as apolitical and ahistorical. However, as many critics have argued, this seeming incompatibility is a belated accident of a historical contingency and not an inevitability. In his recent book, *Literary Criticism: A Concise Political History*, Joseph North argues that for I. A. Richards, the founder of practical criticism in the 1930s, close reading was originally designed as a way to train readers and citizens to cultivate critical and political sensibilities. The later (mis)adaptation of Richards' methods by Southern white male New Critics in the United States emptied it out (14–15). Indeed, I would contend, reading politically well depends on reading closely, with nuance. As Terry Eagleton, the Marxist scholar and exemplar of political and theoretical literary criticism, argues in his recent manifesto, *How to Read Literature*, paying attention to the literariness of a text is to attend to both "how" it means as well as "what it means," to practice a "particularly vigilant kind of reading, one which is alert to tone, mood, pace, genre, syntax, grammar, texture, rhythm, narrative structure, punctuation, ambiguity—in fact to everything that comes under the heading of 'form'" (2). Unlike much work in postcolonial literary criticism, this book pays attention to form as well as theme or content; indeed, my method of reading regards them as inextricable.

And finally, my interest, to be clear, is not in literature as *mimesis*, in the mere depiction of servants, or the extent to which fiction may or may not capture reality. Nor is it limited to how literature seeks to intervene in that reality. Rather, I am interested in *both* the political and the literary, in the cultural work of the representation, and the formal/aesthetic implications of the literary figure of the servant in the contemporary postcolonial fiction. I draw upon Bruce Robbins' key distinction between *actual* and *literary* servants. Literary servants both mirror actual servants and, within the text, engage in both diegetic and non-diegetic work. The literary servant doubles as a functionary who performs two kinds of work: domestic service within the imaginary world of the text (cooking, cleaning, etc.), and literary or narrative service within the dynamics of the text (revealing a key secret, interrogating elite normative ethos, exploring forms of gendered cross-class interaction, etc.).

In *Pride and Prejudice*, for example, Mrs. Reynolds, Darcy's housekeeper, serves both the mimetic purpose, within the world of the text, of supervising other servants and showing visitors around the house, and the non-mimetic, literary one of enabling Elizabeth to see Darcy in a new, more favorable light. But literary servants can at best only approximate the realities of actual servants; they more importantly serve other purposes in a text. As Robbins explains, "the literary servant does not represent real servants, or at most does so only tangentially" (11–12); instead, "the field of objects that [he] call[s] 'servants' refers less to an occupational group, defined, outside of slavery, as non-kin paid to perform menial labor in the house, than to the conjunction of that group with a certain body of aesthetic functions" (41). I am interested in formal as well as social and ideological questions, in exploring how the presence of the servant, or the shift to making the servant central, affects the meanings of a text, and how the focus on servitude and underrepresentation changes the very form or structure of each novel. How do writers, given their own class positions, take on the task of representing servitude? When the margin becomes the center, how does it unsettle narrative conventions that are so established that they remain unquestioned? In order to read, analyze, and assess servitude fiction as something new, I have endeavored to build an interdisciplinary theoretical and conceptual framework as I elaborate below.[34]

Domestic Blind Spots and Transnational South Asian Writers

Servitude fiction addresses what I would call a critical and cultural blind spot in public and private discourses in South Asia. It exposes an oddity, an anomaly: domestic servitude is on the one hand a pervasive, widely accepted institution in South Asia; yet, on the other hand, it seems to go unnoticed, evoking little protest or contestation, even among progressives who oppose more flagrant forms of social injustice based on caste, gender, ethnicity, religion, and so on. To take a recent example that hit international headlines: in December 2013, Devyani Khobragade, India's deputy consul general in New York was arrested by American authorities and "subjected to strip and cavity searches and treated [she claimed] like a 'common criminal'" with no "dignity" because she was charged with visa fraud, or, more specifically, falsifying a visa application for her maid.[35] According to CNN, Khobragade obtained a work permit for "her nanny Sangeeta Richards" by promising to pay her $9.75/hour but in fact paid her $3.31/hour, far below the minimum wage.[36] After Richards fled Khobragade's home and went to the police, American authorities were led to investigate Khobragade's misstatement about the lower-class Indian woman she had brought to the United States to care for her children.

In India, the reaction was widespread fury, outrage, and vocal protests over the Americans' scandalous failure to treat with respect a female Indian diplomat, a woman of evident high rank and a representative of the state. But, interestingly, no parallel concern was expressed about the diplomat's treatment of her female Indian domestic worker.[37] While American newspapers highlighted fraud, exploitation, and abuse of privilege by Khobragade, by contrast, Indian newspapers described Sangeeta Richards as "the absconding maid" who was "overpaid" not underpaid; Richards was even accused (by Khobragade's relatives and the Indian government) of attempted extortion, blackmail, and dereliction of duty.[38] While certainly it should be questioned why any person (regardless of their position, class, race, or nationality) should be subjected to a strip-search, I want to call attention here to the servant, not the diplomat on whose behalf Indian outrage eclipsed empathy or compassion for her servant, and to the normalization of the subjugation of servants that created such a blind spot among Indians to a powerful employer's exploitation of her powerless maid, to the extent that the maid was attacked for enacting resistance to the conditions she lived under.

Indian External Affairs Minister Salman Khurshid addressed the Indian Parliament, which was united in support of Khobragade: "It is no longer about an individual. It is about our sense of self as a nation and our place in the world."[39] To my mind this remark poses many questions: if the mistreatment of a woman diplomat is a matter of concern for the *nation*, then why is the mistreatment of a servant woman not equally a national issue? Why must the "dignity" of a prominent elite professional be so vociferously defended while the subjection to routine indignity of a poor voiceless woman is not only ignored but the servant is actually blamed and denigrated in the Indian press while the diplomat claims immunity?[40] What cultural norms enable such attitudes and inhibit others? What produces such extraordinary invisibility? Sumit Ganguly, professor of political science and Indian cultures and civilizations at Indiana University, commented: "Something we [Indians] don't want to talk about or think about is how we treat domestic workers. For God's sake, we treat them like chattel... This is a national shame we have not confronted."[41] What does it take to confront, if not the shame, then the cultural habitus of servitude? The fiction I study in this book attempts to prompt answers to this question.

In South Asian public discourse, it is only when there is a rupture in the norm, when a servant protests or refuses to go along with expectations of acquiescence, that the issue of servitude bursts into view. In another recent servant-related incident in India that made international news, servant resistance to employer abuse evoked surprise and called into view what otherwise remains unquestioned and routine. In July 2017, a *New York Times* article titled "Maid's Dispute in India Erupts into Class War" described how a violent riot broke out between maids and their "madams," or the maids' families and their employers in Noida, a gated community outside New Delhi, as a culmination of longstanding disputes. In strikingly discrepant reports, the employer accused her maid of stealing money, whereas the maid and her family accused the employer of withholding two months wages, and then assaulting her and locking her up overnight in their apartment, not allowing her to return home to the shantytown where she lives. What was rare about this event was the united and public resistance of the poor, the angry protests of her community on behalf of the maid. The *Times* noted that while "conflicts between domestic workers and their employers are a regular feature of Indian crime logs," such a full-scale expression of resentment of the rich by the poor, or confrontation between socially marginalized, precarious domestic workers and affluent, socially powerful employers, is new, given servants' and employers' mutual dependence in a "symbiotic" social system built on inequality, disempowerment, stigmatization, and the threat of police violence.[42]

Again, in India, this resistance was met with outrage; the servants were cast as uppity. *The Washington Post* commented, "For centuries, India's elite have employed servants, but economic liberalization and the rise of the middle class has meant that the number of cooks, maids and drivers has grown exponentially in recent decades . . . Hundreds of thousands have migrated from villages to India's five major urban centers to tend to the needs of the elite."[43] The *Post* quoted from Tripti Lahiri's *Maid in India* (2017), which describes the routine abuse of servants by employers, lack of legal or social protections, culture of habituated inequality, and performance of deference and subordination: "We eat first, they eat later . . . we live in front, they live in the back, we sit on chairs and they sit on the floor, we drink from glasses and ceramic plates and they from ones made of steel and set aside for them, we call them by their names, they address us by titles."[44] Strikingly, both examples highlight the problem of a pervasive cultural tendency, evinced in South Asian public discourse, *not* to see the problem of abuse and exploitation of domestic servants by employers. Both prompt the question why contempt for and mistreatment of domestic workers are so normalized that they are invisible, and why those who enact resistance are further blamed and attacked for so doing. The writers I discuss in this book seek both to address this blind spot, to defamiliarize via the act of imaginative representation, and to contemplate possibilities for efficacious resistance and change.

If it is set in South Asia, and focuses on exclusively South Asian contexts, in what sense can this fiction be considered transnational or global? As English-language fiction, this literature is transnational and global in multiple senses: it is addressed to multiple audiences, both within and beyond the nations that may be the reference points for its narrative situations; it is written by writers with multiple national allegiances, with more than one citizenship and residential location; it often concerns characters whose experiences and subjectivities are shaped by the forces of globalization and migration; it may explicitly or implicitly address or respond to transnational forces, issues, and questions of globalization, or explore transnational experiences and identity formations. The novels I discuss may be *differently* transnational from one another (i.e., transnational in different senses), but they are all transnational in the broader sense defined by Paul Jay: "English literature in the age of globalization is increasingly transnational, whether written by cosmopolitan writers like Salman Rushdie, . . . or by a host of lesser-known writers working in their home countries or in diasporic communities around the world" because the "globalization of English" is "a simple fact of contemporary history" (25). Rather than see these novels as limited to their specific national contexts or readership, we might understand them as global English fiction, as always already transnational or "born-translated" (to use Rebecca Walkowitz's term), thanks to contemporary circuits of publication and readership, not just produced in one national context and read in another, but addressed to multiple audiences around the world.[45] They are at once both local and global. They address the complex of domestic servitude in this transnational context, inviting readers globally (if we recognize that readership is itself a condition of relative socioeconomic privilege) to think about their implication in circuits of care that depend on workers whose work undergirds their (our) everyday comforts.

The double vision, or privileged insider-outsider perspective of writers who belong in more than one place, and who often move back and forth between nations, may enable, I suggest, a re-seeing afresh of what is so taken for granted that it becomes unseen, an awakened critical capacity to see and question what one might have otherwise become habituated not to see. Thrity Umrigar has said, for example, that returning to India while living in the United States provided her with "the critical distance . . . to be able to write about India" and critique its system of servitude in her novel *The Space Between Us* ("Looking Back," M10). Likewise, in speaking of his interlinked short story collection, *In Other Rooms*, Pakistani American Daniyal Mueenuddin has described himself as "internally displaced" but consequently enriched by that double belonging.[46] Both suggest that their insider-outsider status enables them to see what perhaps insiders locked into the system cannot see. All these writers seem enabled by their "flexible citizenship," as Aihwa Ong has named it, the simultaneous allegiances and affective connections to multiple nations or homelands, by the concomitant defamiliarization of habitation elsewhere and return, and the commitment to and desire to intervene in the discourses and practices of the postcolonial nations they write about, and that they regard in some sense as home.

All these writers also belong to a post-Rushdie, younger generation, who were educated and came of age in a turn-of-the millennium era. One might dub them "midnight's grandchildren." Writing half a century or more after political independence, they may be more ready to concentrate on servitude, as perhaps a less flagrant, less visible form of social inequality, injustice, and abuse of power because it takes place *in the home*, in the daily ordinariness of everyday lives, and seems less an issue of political or national concern, than earlier writers like Anand and Markandaya who focused more (respectively) on the problems of the caste system (in *Untouchable*, 1935), or the destitution of landless peasants by feudalism and colonial capitalism (in *Nectar in a Sieve*, 1954). This new generation of transnational writers is more attuned to recognizing servitude as social injustice, and, more attentive, after the critiques mounted by postcolonial, feminist, and critical race scholars, to the thorny problems of representation across "social difference" or (in Donna Haraway's term) "significant otherness" (Black, 3).

Ray and Qayum quote a Kolkata truism: "everyone has a servant who is not himself or herself a servant" (169). The truism applies equally to other South Asian countries, to Nepal, Pakistan, Sri Lanka, and Bangladesh, among others. I focus in this book on Anglophone South Asian writers on servitude because, regardless of national, linguistic, ethnic, or religious boundaries, and divergent histories, they share in the understanding of a culture of servitude that connects them and that somewhat distinguishes what they are addressing from servitude in other parts of the world. When I began thinking about this project, my ambition was to work comparatively with postcolonial and transnational literatures from across the Anglophone corpus, including, for example, Nigerian, Zimbabwean, and Jamaican texts.[47] I soon realized, however, that the project would benefit from a closer focus on South Asian writers, allowing for more regional specificity and exploration of shared histories in South Asia, even across national divides and other differences. Traces of that original ambition remain in the comparative references I make to West Asian, African, and Caribbean writers, though I focus on the writers named above.

This project is also unusual for the comparative framework it extends across national divides within South Asia. Recent scholarship on South Asian Anglophone literature tends to observe national boundaries: Arvind Mehrotra's magisterial *History of Indian Literature in English*, Priyamvada Gopal's *The Indian English Novel*, Pranav Jani's *Decentering Rushdie*, or Priya Kumar's *Limiting Secularism* are important recent examples that focus for good reasons on the Indian Anglophone literary tradition and its development. With its collection of essays, the recent *Routledge Companion to Pakistani Anglophone Writing* likewise attempts to chart the contours of a Pakistani Anglophone literary tradition; Goonetilleke's *Sri Lankan English Literature and the Sri Lankan People 1917–2003* maps a Sri Lankan Anglophone tradition.[48] It is more rare for South Asian literary scholars to attempt to make cross-national comparisons or connections, to cross the divides that they insist are arbitrary and historically contingent.[49] *Postcolonial Servitude* explores the connections between and pervasiveness of a phenomenon or social structure that links both *societies* in India, Pakistan, Sri Lanka, Bangladesh (and Nepal, Afghanistan, and Iran, as the range of references to writers addressed shows) and the twentieth- to twenty-first-century transnational, often culturally hybrid *writers* who emerge from these societies and seek to explore the implications of those social norms of servitude in their fiction. Since Anglophone South Asian literature has become a global phenomenon, circulating in an international market, especially post-Rushdie, writers from different countries read one another, and certainly do not work in isolation. Even if the South Asian writers discussed in this book do not necessarily know of one another (I am not arguing for old-fashioned influence or a movement so much as for intertextuality) they work within the gambit or matrix of shared transnational writing, and can, I believe, be read productively together.

Indeed, I would argue both that the contemporary transnational writers studied here are doing something new in the context of South Asian literature in English, insisting on changes in habituated or acculturated ways of seeing and representing, *and* that they belong in a broader global wave of fiction that is attempting something similar. This global servitude fiction, which includes such texts as Kazuo Ishiguro's *The Remains of the Day* (1989), Monique Truong's *The Book of Salt* (2003), Chimamanda Ngozi Adichie's *Half of a Yellow Sun* (2006), Mona Simpson's *My Hollywood* (2010), Jo Baker's *Longbourn* (2013), Zadie Smith's *The Embassy of Cambodia* (2013), Imbolo Mbue's *Behold the Dreamers* (2016), and even Kathryn Stockett's controversial *The Help* (2009), has begun, in different forms and wide variety of contexts, to re-think the invisibility of servants and servitude, and to address servant interiority, agency, and vulnerability as a form of social and cultural intervention. I identify servitude fiction as distinguished by at least three traits: it centers the servant, it emphasizes the interiority of the servant, and it critiques servitude as a system.

In contemporary literary and cultural studies, race, gender, sexuality, class, and nationality have increasingly come to be taken for granted as significant and mutually constitutive, historically contingent, categories of analysis. However, we (especially in postcolonial literary studies) have not paid sufficient attention to domestic servitude as a similarly significant social, economic, or cultural form of identity construction and formation or dimension or marker of identity and constituent of human interaction. While social scientists (notably anthropologists and sociologists) have amassed a wealth of invaluable work that explores servitude in its manifold aspects and contexts, there needs to be much more work done by literary scholars on how contemporary postcolonial and/or global transnational literature engages with these questions.

Literary Servants, or Servants in Literature of the British Empire

In canonical white-authored British drama and fiction from the Renaissance to the nineteenth century, a lasting legacy and foundational tradition that various Anglophone postcolonial writers both adopt and repudiate, servitude is rarely a central concern, and domestic servants rarely appear as central protagonists. As marginal figures, they are present, as Robbins argues, not as representatives of an *actual* underclass, but to serve a variety of aesthetic or *narrative* functions in texts that are primarily concerned with their social superiors: as signifiers of their employers' socio-economic status; as comic relief; as messengers, go-betweens, or enablers of the plot; as reliable witnesses who provide crucial information and family history for the protagonists; as unequal parallels to the master('s) narrative; to provide local color or setting; and a tool to critique the dominant classes.[50]

In the rare instances when servants appear as narrators, like Nelly Dean in *Wuthering Heights*, or Gabriel Betteredge in *The Moonstone*, they tend to serve from the sidelines primarily to tell their employers' stories, not their own. In even rarer cases, when servants are both narrators and protagonists, as in *Pamela* or *Caleb Williams*, they emerge as exceptional (unlike other servants) and as ideological mouthpieces for authorial didacticism. In these exceptional cases, it is worth recalling that the narrator-protagonist turns out to be in fact middle class, educated, and above those charged with doing menial labor, such as cleaning, cooking, or childcare. Pamela, as revealed at the end of the novel, is not from the laboring class; her parents are educated but suffered misfortune (Richardson, 455). She frequently distinguishes herself from the "common servants" (458). Caleb Williams occupies an intermediary position as the educated secretary of a gentleman, and is not a menial servant. Exceptions tend to prove the rule: with the exception of a rare naturalist novel like *Esther Waters*, British fiction does not focus on servants as major characters or protagonists.[51]

It may appear to some that the widespread genre of nineteenth-century British governess novels undermines my claim, but I would emphasize that it is a category mistake to confuse governesses with menial domestic servants, who historically occupied a different social class altogether. The ranks of domestic servants included household workers, from maids to butlers, with agricultural or working-class origins, who are hired to undertake manual, physical demanding labor, but not governesses (like the Brontë sisters' Jane Eyre and Agnes Grey or Jane Austen's Jane Fairfax in *Emma*) whose education and middle-class affiliations (or gentility) placed them in an intermediate but significantly different social position. It is important to distinguish between the liminality of the governess figure in nineteenth-century British (and American) fiction and society, forced to earn her keep, but via *intellectual* labor, and the unambiguous lower status of the maidservant who has to do arduous physical and menial "dirty work" like emptying chamber-pots, or the footman whose trained body must comport itself to stand still interminably or fetch and carry. Despite their poverty, these young governesses are always linked at least to the middle class, evinced by their familial connections, eventual marriages, inheritance (as in the case of Jane Eyre), and most importantly, their education.

It is no accident then that *Jane Eyre* begins with Jane reading, and an illuminating dispute between young Jane and a servant woman, regarding who is the other's superior.

> "What shocking conduct, Miss Eyre, to strike a young gentleman, your benefactress's son! Your young master."
> "Master! How is he my master? Am I a servant?"
> "No; you are less than a servant, for you do nothing for your keep."
> (Brontë, *Jane Eyre*, 9)

Ironically, it is an unnamed lady's maid who rebukes the penniless young orphan Jane for fighting tyranny (in the form of Jane's bullying older male cousin), though both Jane and the lady's maid are subordinated by the interlocking systems of gender and class oppression. In this proto-feminist English classic, Jane offers an early instance of resistance; her fighting violence with violence is presented by Brontë as both naïve and heroic, linked to Roman slaves protesting injustice. But Jane also fights the maid: unlike the maid, Jane asserts, she is not subject to a "master," the over-entitled John Reed. Jane thus also asserts her superiority to the maid by casting her selfhood as distinct from servitude, challenging the language and ideological subordination of the maid. While Jane repudiates the identity of servant, which she understands as one who must serve a master, the maid claims an alternative superiority: for the maid, to be an orphan is worse (and "less") than to be a servant, because Jane is a dependent, the putative recipient of unearned charity, whereas the servant earns her keep through her labor. Jane will fight this challenge too as when she grows older, she will learn (and yearn) to earn her own keep, to work for her independence, but she will never be a servant. She defines her identity from the beginning as precisely not-servant.

And the novel insists on confirming Jane's superiority to the nameless servant-woman. In a telling scene, right before she leaves Lowood school for Thornfield, Jane is visited by Bessie (the Reeds' servant) who declares her a "lady" for having learned to play the piano, speak French, and paint, skills that place Jane clearly in a class well beyond that of servants like Bessie herself (78). When Jane arrives at Thornfield, her class status above servants is affirmed by Mrs. Fairfax, the housekeeper, herself distantly related to Mr. Rochester, and who, despite, or because of, her own in-between position as employee, makes clear the need to maintain distance from servants:

> I am so glad you are come; it will be quite pleasant living here now with a companion. . . . one feels dreary quite alone, in the best quarters. I say alone—Leah is a nice girl to be sure, and John and his wife are very decent people; but then you see they are only servants, and one can't converse with them on terms of equality: one must keep them at due distance, for fear of losing one's authority. (*Jane Eyre*, 82)

If in domestic British fiction, servants served to highlight class divides, to assert the distinct positionality of the middle and upper, aristocratic classes, in overtly colonial British fiction servant figures recurrently appear as racialized and subordinated others, deployed, unsurprisingly, for further ideological purposes: to emphasize and normalize both class and racial divides, and to provide an implicit justification for colonialism and imperialism. In the work of popular nineteenth-century imperial writers like Rudyard Kipling, Flora Annie Steel, Robert Louis Stevenson, and H. Rider Haggard, "native" servants appear as caregivers, providers of domestic needs to colonial officials and administrators, or helpers in adventure and discovery for these white men without white women, out on the colonial enterprise. These non-white servants are usually depicted as lesser beings to be managed by the white narrator with indulgence, humor, nostalgia, or contempt, undeserving of more.

The ex-colonial administrator H. Rider Haggard's highly iconic and popular adventure novel *King Solomon's Mines* (1885), for instance, features three white Englishmen in southern Africa, seeking both mythical treasure and a lost brother. They end up finding both, but not without the aid of five African men as guides and helpers required from the start: "a driver, a leader, and three servants" (45). Predictably, like expendable redshirts, two of the servants die early on in the adventure. One, "Khiva, the Zulu boy," the stereotypically loyal good servant, voluntarily sacrifices his life to save "his master" from a marauding wild elephant (62). (With unselfconscious irony, it is the white man he saves who is named "Good.") He "died like a man," proclaims the narrator, confessing to a "lump in his throat" (62). The second, "the Hottentot Ventvögel," also brave but not as hardy, cannot handle the extreme cold as the white men can, and quietly succumbs to death by freezing in a cave where they are all huddled together (96). The literary-ideological purpose of these racially designated servant men, then, is to establish both the challenges these white colonialists face and the greater manly toughness they demonstrate.

The third servant, however, proves an interesting exception. Umbopa, introduced as "tall, handsome-looking man, . . . very light-colored for a Zulu," later turns out to be Ignosi, a Zulu prince in disguise who has been cheated by an evil usurper of his rightful kingdom (46). His difference from regular, presumably "natural," servants is hence marked from the start. But even he is described with racist condescension as "a cheerful savage" though "dignified," of whom the white men "all got very fond" (51). And he acts like their servant at least until they reach their destination, cutting off the "best meat" from an antelope and carrying it for them, using his lesser technology while the white men have guns (104). The white men help restore Umbopa to his rightful place, for which he repays them with fervent loyalty, diamonds (the treasure they have taken from his land), and a declaration of brotherhood (251), as they recognize him as "every inch a warrior king" (of the Zulus) (211). Thus while Haggard distinguishes Umbopa from the other servants because he is a king, ideologically, Umbopa serves a deeper imperial purpose, for the novel establishes that even such a magnificent king among Africans owes his kingship to the white men, recognizes their rights to the resources of the land, and is ultimately no more than their servant, in a broader political and racial sense.

These modes of representation inherited from the imperial British literary tradition, inculcated through the elevation of British literature (above South Asian or even American literature) in colonial and postcolonial educational systems, provide a lasting and influential legacy, against which some contemporary writers push back, and that other postcolonial writers adopt, often unthinkingly, in their own writing. As we will see in Chapter 1, early twentieth-century Indian writers often adopt similar modes of representation (the good servant, devoted but foolish, or the bad servant, deceitful, unreliable, ignorant) though with importantly different goals (to elevate the emergent Indian middle class or elite), in their writing.

In the context of British India, the most well-known and influential colonial writer is Rudyard Kipling. Kipling's Indian writings teem with Indian servants. His 1937 autobiography, *Something of Myself*, begins with his earliest memories, framed by servants, in Bombay: a Roman Catholic ayah and Hindu bearer who introduced him to their respective places of worship, and taught him "stories and Indian nursery songs all unforgotten" (4). Kipling claims, through his putative closeness to these childhood servants, a primary Indianness and knowledge of "the vernacular idiom," though he makes clear always the superiority of all things English. The ayah instructs him to "speak English" to his English parents, and is described with condescending indulgence as having "a servant's curious mixture of deep affection and shallow device" (4). In Kipling's book, even the (good) servant is sincerely devoted yet disingenuous and not very smart. For Kipling, there is no question that his parents were the ones who gave him more advanced knowledge, or that "Home" was ultimately England, and not India, where he was born.

Kipling's groundbreaking fiction about the British in India likewise recurrently turns upon Indian servants who serve a variety of literarily subordinate and colonial ideological purposes. In "The Strange Ride of Morrowbie Jukes," a stunning 1885 story, itself perhaps an allegory of the white man in India, the eponymous English protagonist is rescued from a nightmare pit of horror, by his loyal and humble Indian "dog-boy," Dunnoo, the good servant, who followed the footprints of Jukes' pony to track down his vanished "Sahib" (24). Dunnoo reaches the edge of the pit, which he knows is inhabited by the living dead, and returns to get help from Jukes' (bad) servants, "who flatly refused to meddle with anyone, white or black, once fallen into the hideous Village of the Dead" (25). Enterprising and undeterred, this good servant returns alone with ropes and ponies to "haul" out his fallen master. The story ends without any further reference to what happens to Dunnoo, whether he receives any reward, uplift, or reciprocal rescue from the pit of servitude. The servant appears here only as a plot device at the end, yet he both reinforces the white man's precariousness in India and dependence on the native, and enables his return to the norm, where racial and social hierarchies of power again obtain, and where he is again master. Despite his terrifying sojourn in a place where it does not matter whether he is "black or white," Jukes returns to a world where good servants believe in those hierarchies. In a predictable binarism, the colonial stereotype of the good servant is matched by that of the bad one, the ones who refuse to help, who bow to another authority than that of the British Empire.

Unlike most other colonial writers, however, Kipling presents his Indian servants as caricatures with some complexity, with a mix of patronizing affection and derision while leaving no doubt of their lower status—racially, socially, or mentally. One kind of servant is docile, dependable, and loyal, but foolish; speaks in ornate, flowery language; and obsequiously accepts verbal abuse. In an 1891 story, "At the End of the Passage," for instance, when a colonial official finds another young colonial official dead from overwork, he notices the "look on the dark face" of the "personal servant," and asks what he thinks, leading to the following exchange:

> "Heaven-born, in my opinion, this that was my master has descended into the Dark Places, and there has been caught because he was not able to escape with sufficient speed.... Thus have I seen men of my race do with thorns when a spell was laid upon them..."
>
> "Chuma, you're a mud-head. Go out and prepare seals to be set on the Sahib's property."
>
> "God has made the Heaven-born. God has made me. Who are we, to inquire into the dispensations of God? I will bid the other servants hold aloof while you

are reckoning the tale of the Sahib's property. They are all thieves, and would steal."[52]

At least Kipling gives Chuma the servant a name and a voice. But this Indian servant's superstitious, circumlocutory voice is used to emphasize both the distance in his outlook from that of the rational British, and the acceptance by the servant of his own inferiority, emphasized by his purportedly self-identified "race." Kipling then also attributes to Chuma, as commonly held knowledge, the usual stereotypes about servants as "thieves," from whom Chuma is distinguished for his self-proclaimed honesty. Kipling is more complex and ambiguous than most imperial writers: the story also suggests that perhaps the peremptory white man is too hasty to reject Chuma's point of view, for Chuma may have an insight into the darkness of whatever caused his master's death, a mystery that the white writer can only hint at, but not deliver in his story.

But Kipling's servants, while often given voice and some complexity, are equally prone to lie and deceive, or worse, murder their masters. In an eerie 1891 ghost story, "The Return of Imray" (originally titled "The Recrudescence of Imray"), a colonial administrator narrates how one night he, together with Strickland (a recurring white character in Kipling's stories), discovered the murdered corpse of Imray, another young colonial official, hidden between the roof and ceiling cloth of his bungalow. Immediately suspicious of Imray's servants, who are now serving Strickland, who is now renting Imray's bungalow, the narrator and Strickland discuss how best to find the culprit:

"If I call in all the servants they will stand fast in a crowd and lie like Aryans. What do you suggest?"
"Call 'em in one by one," I said.
"They'll run away and give the news to all their fellows," said Strickland. "We must segregate 'em." (216)[53]

Dependent though they are on the labor of these servants in the intimate spaces of their homes, these white men band together against the presumed unity of all Indian servants in their shared solidarity with their dead comrade and their presumed knowledge of native deceit and racial otherness. However, before they can act on these plans, the culprit reveals himself, as Bahadur Khan, Strickland's (and formerly Imray's) "body-servant," described as "a great, green-turbaned, six-foot Mahomedan," who exposes himself by arriving and concocting an obvious and unnecessary lie (216).

While reinforcing white colonialist fears of the violent Muslim, as the putatively hyper-masculine, almost white-but-not-quite, light-skinned Pathan or Afghan from the northwest mountains, Kipling also gives this servant a voice and an important twist. Confessing to the murder, Bahadur Khan explains why he murdered his master:

> "Nay, Sahib, consider. Walking among us, his servants, he cast his eyes upon my child, who was four years old. Him he bewitched, and in ten days he died of the fever—my child!"
> "What said Imray Sahib?"
> "He said he was a handsome child, and patted him on the head; wherefore my child died. Wherefore I killed Imray Sahib in the twilight, when he had come back from the office, and was sleeping." (217)

With a similarly exoticized, overly courteous language, the Pathan servant explains his apparent treachery via his dangerously unscientific belief that Imray had admired, bewitched, and therefore killed his precious male child, with his "evil eye" (217). But Kipling also gives this servant a distinct sense of manly honor and pride. Instead of hanging, Bahadur Khan chooses to die then and there of snakebite:

> "I come of land-holding stock," [he explains] . . . "It were a disgrace to me to go to the public scaffold: therefore I take this way. Be it remembered that the Sahib's shirts are correctly enumerated, and that there is an extra piece of soap in his wash-basin." (218)

A conscientious servant to the last, caught up in the mundane trivialities of servitude, Bahadur Khan is presented as impossibly illogical, but still worthy of some measure of respect. The two white men, in the end, shake their heads over Imray's folly, his naiveté in failing to understand the "nature of the Oriental," for it is the white man's responsibility to know those who serve him (218). The story maintains the racial and social hierarchy, and the unreliability and unknowability of even long-term Indian servants, while also highlighting the vulnerability of the innocent white man newly arrived in India as he takes on the white man's burden. In Kipling's fiction, the Indian-born white man Strickland survives, by contrast, because he knows native ways, and can "go native" to learn their otherwise secret ways, in order to bring them to colonial justice. At the end of the story, the narrator "shudders" to think of the unreliability of his own servant (who has been with him for four years, as long as Bahadur Shah was with Imray), another intimately proximate "body-servant" who remains "impassive" about the rough justice he has just witnessed (219).

If a long tradition of British (and even American) literature places the servant in the background, as peripheral though necessary to its main concerns, what implications accrue when contemporary Anglophone writers place the servant at the center of the narrative, to position him or her as the central protagonist? Clearly, they are working against a long and powerful set of conventions that subordinate the servant. To undo that tradition is not only, then, a matter of changing content, but also of rethinking and reconstructing the very form of these inherited traditions. In his important book *The One and the Many*, Alex Woloch explores the "governing tension between the one and the many" (11), between the protagonist, the "central individual who dominates the story," and the minor characters, the "host of subordinate figures" in a narrative, as critical to narrative form (2). Woloch argues that literary characterization depends on this "distributional matrix," where "the discrete representation of any specific individual is intertwined with the narrative's continual apportioning of attention to different characters who jostle for limited space within the same fictive universe" (13). Noting how servants also serve as minor characters in nineteenth-century fiction, he makes an important distinction between "narrative subordination" and "social subordination," which, he notes, are often linked (25); the "narrative work" that servants do in the fiction is doubled by the work they perform within the fictive universe (27). Hence, writes Woloch, *"minor characters are the proletariat of the novel"* (27; original emphasis).

By contrast, I would contend, contemporary South Asian servitude fiction *upends* this double minoritization, and instead makes the servant character a major character or protagonist, exploring his or her interiority, and hence produces a disjunction between the (major) narrative role that the servant figure plays in the novel versus the (minor) social status and social subordination he or she continues to experience. In other words, the very form of late twentieth- and twenty-first-century servitude fiction disrupts the narrative legacies that tend to align the narrative and social significance of a character. Woloch distinguishes usefully between what he calls *"character-space* (that particular and charged encounter between an individual human personality and a determined space and position within the narrative as a whole)" and *"character-system* (the arrangement of multiple and differentiated character-spaces . . . into a unified narrative structure)" in order to think about both characterization and the importance of "distributed attention" within the realist novel (14). He hence explores the different ways of apportioning attention, the varied "character systems" of asymmetric nineteenth-century European fiction, "where *any* character can be a protagonist, but only one character is" (31), and where at the same time an "increasing political equality, and a maturing logic of human rights, develop amid acute economic and social stratification."[54]

However, the attempted inclusivity of nineteenth-century fiction, though it may stretch from the aristocracy to the bourgeoisie and even to some working-class figures, rarely extends (as I suggest above) to servants as major characters in their own right. In looking at South Asian Anglophone servitude fiction, I too am interested in the different ways that different novels re-apportion character-space and hence restructure the character-system, in the shift in narrative form from a central protagonist to alternate forms such as alternating perspectives that require equally shared narrative space, or multiple perspectives that re-order character-system in new ways. What is novel about these novels and short stories, however, is that in all, the narrative dominance of the protagonist, given the character-space that he or she occupies, is always starkly at odds with his or her social subordination, throwing the narrative itself, and its address to educated middle- or upper-class readers who cannot easily identify or align themselves with such protagonists, into radical disarray. Servitude fiction, then, sets itself the difficult challenge of addressing itself to readers who cannot be expected to identify or experience easy connection, empathy, or sympathy.[55] This fiction has to call in other ways upon to its readership, emotionally and cognitively, to attend.

Servants and the Problems of Literary Representation

Given that South Asian servitude fiction, at least at this historical point, is inevitably and necessarily written by members of an educated class, themselves privileged in many ways, who are not and have never been related to servants, and who belong not to the class of those serving but to that served, an important question arises: how suspicious should we as readers be of those who choose to represent servants, when they have no identification with or experience of servitude themselves? This frequently asked question takes various forms and opens a formidable can of worms. What right do well-to-do writers have to represent those who cannot (yet) represent themselves? In what ways are these seemingly altruistic writers being self-serving, or themselves exploiting, literally and symbolically, those they write about? What about the irony that in order to write their servitude fiction, many of these writers depend, literally, on the domestic labor of servants in their own homes? Even if sympathetic and well-meaning, how well can they understand, portray, or avoid the self-aggrandizing effects of portraying those disempowered and othered by their own class? Given what we know of a long tradition of those in power representing those with relatively much less power (colonizers-colonized, men-women, white-black, and so on), should we not be wary of writers who may enact, even unknowingly, similarly problematic modes of representation?

I think we need to be wary but not a priori dismissive of servitude fiction. Inevitably, literary representation raises thorny questions about the capacity or right to represent, the presumption of speaking for an "other," a subaltern who may not be heard even if he or she does speak.[56] These are important questions that need to be raised, but it would be unfortunate if they led us to dismiss out of hand, without closer examination, what a writer may have attempted or achieved, or what kind of conversations, among what audiences, the work seeks to engage. I would grant at once that the writers discussed in this book are upper- to middle-class writers, and that I carry no romantic illusion that we are looking at authentic voices or experiences as seen from the perspective of a real servant.[57] My interest is rather in the literary, cultural, and social work performed by such higher-class narratives that are addressed simultaneously to international as well as national readers of English, not to prejudge them as specious, but to ask more productive questions about what they seek to do and in what contexts, given the current realistic limitations on the production and dissemination of writing by members of servant classes in Third World nations.

In her important book, *Fiction Across Borders*, Shameem Black argues that while late twentieth-century postcolonial, feminist, and ethnic minority criticism has produced necessary exposés of orientalist, sexist, or racist forms of representation, and shown how the socially empowered writing-self mirrors itself in representations of less privileged others, this work has led to the critical fallacy that *every* representation of those in less privileged social locations is an act of imaginative invasion and does representational violence. This fallacy, she contends, has limited both what is considered legitimate for contemporary writers to write about and how critics may approach contemporary fiction. "Although the political problem of speaking for others stems from historical injustice and unequal social privilege, border crossing fiction need not always remain a passive casualty of such inequities of power" (Black, 61). Black proposes alternative modes of reading late twentieth-century and twenty-first-century fiction that is aware of such critiques and strives to address them, modes that allow us to "attribute positive ethical significance to telling stories about others" (19–20) and to "consider why some representations may be less prone toward representational violence than others" (31). While I find Black reductive in her description of postcolonial criticism as merely "charting representational failings" (66), I take seriously her exhortation to read efforts to imagine socially significant otherness with a more generous, alternative lens. For I agree that while "writing about alterity has often been described as dangerous, *not* writing about the lives of others may be equally troubling" (Black, 61). I read servitude fiction, the work of the writers I discuss in this book, as exemplifying such "border-crossing fiction."

Indeed, many of the writers who are the subject of this study themselves take up this question. In an interview, the Pakistani American writer Daniyal Mueenuddin reports being asked, "How can you presume to speak for characters like Saleema or Nawabdin when you have never been hungry for even a day in your life?" He replies: "But that's what fiction writers do—write about others' lives. I am not writing about Daniyal Mueenuddin's life" (*The New Yorker*, March 3, 2009).[58]

His response, which argues for a more capacious understanding of imaginative and empathetic reach, suggests how contemporary writers are often placed in a Catch-22 by narrow, identity-politics-minded criticism: accused of inauthenticity or presumption if they write about others, and of narcissism if they write only about themselves. The kneejerk self-righteousness that denounces any writer with relative privilege for presuming to represent (or create the voice or imagine the perspective of) a person with less privilege bespeaks a broader critical problem that stems, I believe, from prevalent misreadings of Spivak's important essay, "Can the Subaltern Speak?," that take the essay as indicting *any* or *every* attempt to represent the subaltern.[59] Spivak critiques European intellectuals (Foucault and Deleuze) and positivist social scientists (historians, anthropologists) who assume they can act as transparent transmitters of the consciousnesses of those lost in official records or dominant discourses. But at no point in her essay does Spivak attack the literary effort of imagining socially significant otherness.[60] In fact, she distinguishes between two senses of "representation" collapsed in the English term—the German *vertreten* (to speak for, as elected representatives are authorized to do) and *darstellen* (to re-present, as in art) (70), the difference between "proxy" and "portrait" (71). To attempt to portray via imaginative, empathetic literary means is then not the same as to "speak for" and claim historical truth. "The intellectual's solution is not to abstain from representation," Spivak states (80).

Yet only too often, writers like Mueenuddin are attacked just for attempting to write fiction about subaltern subjects. Clearly, we do need to be cautious about *many* forms of representation of socially significant otherness, as feminist philosopher Linda Alcoff notes in her important early essay, "The Problem of Speaking for Others." But, like Black later, Alcoff presents a vigorous argument for *some* kinds of speaking for. Alcoff focuses on how we may determine *when* it may be valid to speak for others (12), and how to lessen the dangers (24). For surely silence, as she points out crucially, is also an ethical problem, and not an alternative: "if I don't speak for those less privileged than myself, am I abandoning my political responsibility to speak out against oppression, a responsibility incurred by the very fact of my privilege?" (8). Her answer is clear: "Even a complete retreat from speech is not neutral since it allows the continued dominance of current discourses and acts by omission to reinforce their dominance" (20).

I would argue that transnational writers like Mueenuddin, neither subaltern nor metropolitan, situated in that third space of postcolonial class privilege, take on precisely this political responsibility. They are aware of the dangers, but also of the culpability of remaining silent. The stakes are high for such storytelling, which seeks to disrupt the continued dominance of ideologies of servitude that maintain and reinforce oppression within postcolonial Pakistan, India, or Sri Lanka, and to represent, in both senses, imagining and speaking for those who of necessity are not yet at least able to reach a national, let alone global, audience. Does their fiction avoid some of the dangers of representational violence, given their position vis-a-vis-those he represents? Readers will differ, but this book attempts to show that a nuanced reading must take into account the subtle techniques and representational choices of a writer instead of automatically dismissing his work based on his positionality alone.

Hence, I would add, it is crucial to avoid a fallacious equivalence between what Neil Lazarus terms an author's "social location" and "political or philosophical position" (6). The former does not determine the latter. This is not to say that social location has *no* effect whatsoever on a writer's politics or allegiances, since clearly it does have influence, even if unconsciously, by shaping the ideological frameworks that structure their world views. But it is to say that individual writers can and do struggle against, complicate, and often reject, the ideologies associated with their class positions, and that it is simplistic to assume a straightforward connection between class position and ideology. Such an assumption also fails to take into account the important lesson of *intersectional* thinking that opposes reductive identity politics. In "Mapping the Margins," her foundational essay on intersectionality, Kimberlé Crenshaw distinguishes between identity politics, which fixates on one aspect of an individual's identity while overlooking others, and intersectional thinking, which recognizes the mutually constitutive fact of multiple interlocking aspects of identity, such as race/ethnicity, gender, class, sexuality, and age. Black women, for example, experience their race and gender differently than black men do because race and gender are mutually constitutive. And, as we will see, upper-class women writers, who have to be more attuned to the psychodramas of domesticity than upper-class men do, pay far more attention to the gender constraints, violence, and sexual vulnerability experienced by women servants than do male writers or even men who are also servants.

The postcolonial critic Rob Nixon, in his path-breaking book, *Slow Violence*, likewise takes on the difficult question of "the literary right to represent," and the problem of the "inevitable distance" between Global South writers who have "ascended not just into the literate but into the publishing classes" and "the impoverished people about whom they write" (26). His answer is illuminating:

> In the scheme of things, this hardly seems to me the most suspect kind of distance. Relative to the invisibility that threatens the marginalized poor and the environments they depend on, the bridge-work such writer-activists undertake offers a most honorable counter to the distancing rhetoric of neoliberal "free market" resource development. (Nixon, 26)

Nixon also points out the dangers of flattening out all forms of privilege, of assuming a simple binary of privilege and non-privilege. He notes that in fact such public intellectuals (Ken Saro-Wiwa, Richard Rodriguez, and James Baldwin, among others) were often themselves among the first generation in their families to obtain university educations, and, combined with the complex intersections of gender, race, sexuality, or nationality or immigrant status, had "to negotiate the vexing terrain of unfamiliar—and unfamilial—privilege fraught with an anxious sense of collective responsibility" (26). The writers I discuss are not situated in as close proximity to the indigence or servitude they describe, but like the writers Nixon names, they also evince this strong sense of collective responsibility and undertake this necessary "bridge-work" as "go-betweens" or "intimate, highly motivated translators" (Nixon, 26–27).

Shameem Black argues that border-crossing writers reveal their self-awareness and locate themselves and their standpoint in their fiction, while Alcoff concludes: "anyone who speaks for others should only do so out of a concrete analysis of the particular power relations and discursive methods involved" (24). Early twenty-first-century servitude writers both position themselves clearly via extra-textual commentary (such as interviews), and analyze in their fiction precisely the systemic power relations and discursive politics involved in the nuanced interactions they present between servants and non-servants. Alcoff adds that for us (as readers) "to evaluate attempts to speak for others in particular instances, we need to analyze the probable or actual effects of the words on the discursive and material context. One cannot simply look at the location of the speaker or her credentials to speak, nor can one look merely at the propositional content of the speech; *one must look at where the speech goes and what it does there*" (26; emphasis added).

Servitude fiction is designed to speak to multiple audiences, both local and global, and to perform cultural work on at least two important levels. One, *within* the nation, it addresses itself to elite (educated middle- and upper-class) South Asian readers who routinely employ servants who remain invisible to them. Many testify to the eye-opening experience this entails. Here for example is a blog written by a young Pakistani woman from Lahore, now living in New York:

> Mueenuddin's stories left me puzzled, stunned ... Nawabdin, Saleema, Zainab, Rezak ... were alien to me, foreigners, their private lives detached from mine by an invisible wall. Of course I knew people *like* them—we kept servants at home, like any well-off Pakistani family, and most of them came from the villages surrounding Lahore. But I really knew nothing about them, ... I knew nothing beyond the rudiments, the apparent facts. ... would I ever know what they really thought about me, or any of us, what they said to each other in the confidence of the kitchen?[61]

Even if servitude fiction succeeds in making middle-class South Asian readers see the workers in their homes as not merely furniture, it has achieved something. More broadly, in addressing the nation (India, Pakistan, Sri Lanka), this fiction implicitly critiques that postcolonial nation for so utterly failing those among its most vulnerable citizens. It examines the complex consequences to vulnerable individuals located at different levels of a carefully analyzed feudal system passed down to an ineffectual postcolonial state as a colonial legacy. These writers' insider-outsider focus on the servant asks for a re-vision of the nation, de-familiarizing what is taken for granted, making visible what is unseen. Different writers uses different techniques, shifting perspectives from servants to employers and back, to invite readers to *see* differently. Fiction, as Dominic LaCapra notes, "may have transformative effects more through its style or mode of narration than in the concrete image or representation of any desirable alternative society or polity" (4).

And two, at the same time, this transnational servitude fiction also writes *beyond* the nation, addressing international readers, educating them about complexities of postcolonial societies, insisting on layers of power and dimensions unknown to or ignored by dominant global media. It forms an emergent wave of world literature that examines and calls attention to the subtleties and invisibility of servitude across nations. Mueenuddin's fiction, for example, is both rooted in the specificities of a postcolonial Pakistani context at the same time that it is part of an emergent trend in world literature. David Damrosch contends that "world literature is not . . . [a] canon of works but rather a mode of circulation and of reading" (5), and concludes: "World literature . . . is a double refraction, one that can be described through the figure of the ellipse, with the source and host cultures providing the two foci that generate the elliptical space within which a work lives as world literature, connected to both cultures, circumscribed by neither alone" (283). Both the national and the global, the originating and the receiving cultures, he suggests, are at once necessary and simultaneous foci for reading world literature. As global English fiction, this servitude fiction likewise is not just produced in one cultural or national context and read in another, but addresses both audiences, local and global; it is always already transnational, so that a focus on either one context would delimit an adequate reading. The servitude fiction discussed in this book is hence global, and not merely "regional."

This book is divided into two parts. First, in Part One, in Chapters 1 and 2, I outline some key contours in Anglophone South Asian literary history, identifying significant patterns in the modes that authors use to represent and call upon servitude in fiction from the 1930s to the present. These first two chapters provide a point of departure and foundational contrast against which to showcase the work of the servitude fiction writers I examine in the rest of the book. Chapter 1 charts how pioneering Indian male writers (the so-called forefathers R. K. Narayan, Raja Rao, Nirad Chaudhuri, Ahmed Ali) write instrumentally about servants primarily as a contrastive backdrop for the emergence of upper- or middle-class protagonists, and compares the significantly different attentiveness of mid-century pioneering women writers (Attia Hosain, Zeenuth Futehally, Kamala Markandaya, Nayantara Sahgal, Anita Desai) to the affective dynamics of servants and employers in the home. Chapter 2 examines how, starting with *Midnight's Children*, Rushdie gives servants and servitude a new, greater prominence in his fiction, and yet concomitantly deploys a distancing humor that puts down the very servants he brings into the middle ground. By comparison, I look at how, after Rushdie, some other well-known contemporary transnational writers (Shyam Selvadurai, Monica Ali, Mohsin Hamid) highlight servitude more critically in significant ways even though they do not make servitude central to their fiction.

In Part Two, I turn to what I argue is a new wave of contemporary or millennial servitude fiction from Pakistan, Sri Lanka, and India, which adopts three distinctive strategies. In Chapter 3, I explore how Daniyal Mueenuddin uses the interlinked short story form with a self-absenting and self-abnegating third-person upper-class narrator, to render with unprecedented sensitivity both servant interiority and the systemic matrix within which Pakistani feudal servitude is located. In Chapters 4 and 5 I compare how Romesh Gunesekera and Aravind Adiga invert the usual margin and center of much South Asian fiction. Both use a first-person male servant narrator to construct the voice of a subaltern who tells his own story and tracks his own complex trajectory toward independence and freedom from servitude. In Chapters 6 and 7 I compare two women writers, Thrity Umrigar and Kiran Desai, who choose in their novels *The Space Between Us* and *The Inheritance of Loss* to alternate servant and employer perspectives and hence to present, through comparative juxtaposition and a shift in the character system, the contrasts, connections, and disjunctions between servant and employer modes of seeing. In all these divergent forms, I argue, servant figures are no longer relegated to serving as subsidiaries to upper-class narratives, but are instead themselves the subject of the narratives, with unprecedented subjectivity, who demand that we rethink our preconceptions not only about servitude, but also about postcolonial fiction itself.

PART ONE

1
Constituting (from) the Background
The South Asian Literary Servant in the Margins, or, Early South Asian English Fiction from Below

In Rohinton Mistry's *Family Matters* (2002), a novel occupied with the dynamics and difficulties of a Parsi family in Bombay, the narrator pauses briefly to notice what often goes "unnoticed" both in the home and in South Asian English fiction:

> Her presence was slight, and went unnoticed. But when illness or indisposition kept her away, she was seen everywhere: in the dirty cups and saucers, upon the dusty furniture, in the sheets of unmade beds. (64)

The unnamed "she" here is the family's domestic servant whose labor is noticed only when it is absent, a female body on whom the household depends but who is "seen" only in the physical traces of work not done, a person defined negatively in terms of "unmade" beds and unclean cups (64). In fact, this female servant is not actually seen even in Mistry's novel, from which, upon being noted as unseen, she disappears. However, Mistry's percipient observation is unusual, not only because it calls attention to the invisibility of servants who are counted upon as ubiquitous, indispensable presences in South Asian upper- to lower-middle-class homes, but also because it poses a challenge for South Asian fiction and its readers, and prompts a range of questions: What would it mean to notice that servant when and wherever she *is* present in the text? How can we read domestic servants both with and against the grain of the texts in which they appear? How have South Asian writers paid attention to servants and servitude, for what audiences, and for what purposes? What kinds of paradigms or templates have they created that subsequent writers have to work with or against?[1]

In Salman Rushdie's *Midnight's Children* (1980), Saleem the narrator-protagonist likewise interrupts his narrative to notice briefly the servant Musa, who as a good, trusted servant, has learned to stay silent about family secrets and to keep himself "in the background" (87):

> Musa, the old bearer, kept his mouth shut. He kept himself in the background of our lives, always, except twice . . . once when he left us; once when he returned to destroy the world by accident. (87)

In fact, Saleem's egotistical storytelling also keeps the servant in the background, keeping the focus on himself and his family. And yet, Saleem insists, that servant *is* a necessary constituent of his story. As he keeps saying, "to know just the one of me, you'll have to swallow the lot as well": Saleem's gargantuan life-story depends on his family, friends, acquaintances, and numerous servants (4). In *Midnight's Children*, servants emerge from the background at crucial moments to transform, irrevocably, the course of events and hence of Saleem's narrative. Rushdie's self-reflexive, meta-narratival cues indicate that servants are quietly indispensable to his plot, themes, and figural structures. Compared both to Saleem, and to the South Asian writers who preceded him, Rushdie is more self-aware in his narration, highlighting the significance of the servant, and self-consciously calling attention to acts of backgrounding, moving the servant to the middle ground of his narratives.

The servitude fiction that is the focus of this book centers on various conditions of gendered postcolonial servitude, on hierarchies and relations among servants as well as between servants and employers, on the corrosive effects of habituated servitude on subjectivity and identity, on forms of resistance and negotiation in response to almost unlivable realities. In so doing, writers like Mueenuddin, Adiga, Umrigar, and others push back against, and rework, key paradigms of representation established by writers before them, and that may still be in play in the work of some of their contemporaries. To establish a measure of what these emergent writers are working against, and points of comparison for their aesthetic and political departures, in this chapter and the next I chart some dominant approaches to servitude that recur in the work of early to relatively recent South Asian English writers. I show how, in South Asian English fiction from the 1930s up to the 1990s, servants are almost never protagonists or subjects of the narrative; how instead, they primarily serve to constitute the background to elite narratives, and to constitute, in another sense, by contrast, elite identities *from* that background. Even when the servant figure serves to enable critique of that elite class, or of social injustices and inequalities, servitude is not central to the narrative or its main concerns. Paradoxically, the servant is both needed and placed in the background. By reconstructing a literary history of South Asian Anglophone fiction from the underside, as it were, I hope to offer an angle of vision that challenges those established paradigms and reveals some fresh, unexpected, and illuminating connections and disconnections between well-known and lesser-known texts.

In this chapter I examine how early to mid-twentieth-century Anglophone South Asian writers address servitude. I begin with four prominent, pioneering, influential male writers from the 1930s to 1940s (R. K. Narayan, Nirad Chaudhuri, Raja Rao, and Ahmed Ali), roughly coincident with the first wave of

Indian English writing that built an Anglophone literary tradition. I show how they use the servant-figure to provide the unobtrusive backdrop against which the upper- or middle-class colonized subject or community may emerge. Often seeking to establish for Western readers the existence of a "civilized" Indian bourgeoisie, or an earlier aristocratic class, and their forms of privilege, these writers call upon servants as minor, generic, shadowy presences in narratives that focus on employers as protagonists, sometimes concerned about, but usually unable to understand their culturally and psychologically remote servants.[2] I also discuss, as an important exception, Mulk Raj Anand, who uses servants either to offset the most disenfranchised at the far end of the social spectrum, or to critique the more powerful classes of Indians or British colonials. By comparison, five path-breaking women writers from the 1950s and 1960s (from the less-known Zeenuth Futehally to the more well-known Kamala Markandaya, Nayantara Sahgal, Attia Hosain, and Anita Desai) pay more attention to servants in the home, to the gendered dynamics between servants and employers. Compared to their male predecessors or contemporaries, these women writers rely on the presence of servants in their writing for somewhat different, though still secondary, purposes.[3]

With the exception of Attia Hosain's short stories, about which I will say more below, in *none* of these writers' work is a servant a central, primary, or even secondary figure—as protagonist, antagonist, or narrator. Yet in all their work the figure of the servant recurrently appears as necessary, semi-visible in the background, useful for a variety of reasons. I argue in this chapter that, whereas in the work of the early male writers, the literary servant primarily helps to identify, critique, or constitute the upper class or upcoming middle class, in that of the first women writers the servant fulfills more complex tasks, as the secret sharer whom women, responsible for the domestic realm, must supervise, observe, depend on, control, engage, or offer as contrast. Even in their occasional attention to servitude, women writers tend to be more sympathetic and complex, more nuanced in their understanding of the individuals and the micropolitics and power dynamics in the interactions between servants and employers. In what follows, I make no claim to be exhaustive, and aim to chart broad outlines through careful attention to textual details and asking of questions that have not been asked of these writers. I thus hope also to offer fresh insights and readings of this early body of literature.

Many years ago, what began as a joke became what is now known as the Bechdel test for gender representation and sexism in film. As an extremely minimal benchmark measure, and yet shockingly revealing "litmus test" of the reinforcement of gender norms and inequalities in popular visual media, one can simply ask if a film: (1) has at least two female characters (2) who talk to each other (3) about something other than a man.[4] Since various studies show that less than 30 percent of Hollywood films pass this test, or the idea of it, has become unexpectedly powerful.[5] (Other tests and modifications have been added: that the characters be named, or that the women's stories include a range of concerns and depth, or have a narrative arc that is not there merely to support a man's story.) As a thought experiment, if we were to borrow from Bechdel to devise a roughly equivalent test to assess what literary texts reveal about attitudes or attentiveness to servitude, we could ask if a narrative has: (1) at least one named servant character (2) who is a protagonist or is otherwise central to the narrative and (3) whose perspective or interiority is presented or, more ideally, occupies some narrative space. (One could of course ask for more, such as a range of concerns and depth of characterization.)

Why these three criteria? First, whether a character has a name matters, as a minimal indicator of individuality.[6] Second, casting servants as protagonists, giving them character space, shifts attention to the importance and agency of individuals usually overlooked because they are both humble and not humble enough, and therefore not seen as worthy of attention, and asks readers to concern themselves with their stories in themselves, and not in service to someone else's story. Third, acknowledging the interiority of any individual intensifies their claims to subjectivity and humanity; showing their perspective enables seeing the world from *their* eyes, both giving value to their standpoint and enabling readers to see how they see and what they may see differently. Servitude fiction, as we will see, fulfills all these three minimal conditions, and does much more.

I am not actually proposing a Bechdel test equivalent as a mode of analysis for this chapter or book. My point is simply that, astonishingly, *none* of the texts discussed in this chapter or the next would pass such a servitude test. Some, to varying degrees, may name the servant, as a minimal marker of individuality, but in none is a servant a protagonist, and all are narrated from an upper-class employers' perspective. None offer a sustained interest in a servant's interiority. Even Attia Hosain's exceptional short stories would pass the first two criteria, but not the third. In some cases, the servant's perspective is available through reported dialogue, but retold via an upper-class narrator. To be clear, I am not arguing that the writers are upper class and therefore cannot or should not attempt to represent the lower-class character. (As I have elaborated in the introduction, both would be highly problematic claims, limiting, even obviating, the possibilities of imaginative fiction.) Rather, my point is that these early writers do not *attempt* to imagine or render the subjectivity or inner consciousness of a lower-class person as a full human being, of interest in their own right, when they could. Only the millennial writers I discuss in Chapters 3 to 7 do, and fulfill all three criteria above, either via indirect narration (third-person limited or interior monologue—Mueenuddin, Umrigar, Kiran Desai, Neel

Mukherjee) or via first-person narration, either in an attempt to approximate the voice of the servant (Adiga), or to allow the servant to narrate his own story in standard English, without attempting the verisimilitude of the speaking voice (Gunesekera). In servitude fiction, in most cases, we are asked to imagine the character speaking in Hindi or other South Asian languages, even when the text, though it is written in English, does not attempt to approximate that non-English language. My goal in this first chapter is to provide an overview, to examine closely the predominant ways that 1930s–1970s South Asian writers call upon servants in their fiction and to identify and establish some significant patterns or modes of representation of servitude.[7]

For those unfamiliar with this time period, it is worth recalling some key historical contexts. In brief, the period (roughly 1930–1970) was obviously one of great political and social transformation and turbulence. The British had ruled India since the eighteenth century. The 1757 Battle of Plassey initially gave the British East India Company control of Bengal. By 1857, the year of the Indian "Mutiny" or First War of Independence, when Indian soldiers turned against British officers, the British Crown had taken control of large parts of India. In 1858, the British Crown disbanded the Company and took full control of India; Queen Victoria was crowned "Empress of India" in 1876. The Indian National Congress was founded in 1885, and the All-India Muslim League in 1906. By the 1930s, the Indian struggle for independence and self-rule was well under way. After the 1919 massacre of unarmed civilians at Jallianwalla Bagh in Amritsar, Gandhi launched the non-violent Non-Cooperation Movement in 1921. In 1930, Gandhi led the famous Salt March civil disobedience movement to protest British taxes on salt. The Indian Congress passed the Quit India resolution in 1942. With a much-weakened empire after World War II, Britain agreed to grant India independence in 1947 and to partition British India into what became the modern states of India and Pakistan. Partition, and the horrific violence that ensued, occurred in August 1947. (In 1971, after a genocidal civil war, East and West Pakistan separated, and East Pakistan became Bangladesh.) Ceylon, also a British colony, gained its independence in 1948. (The name was changed to Sri Lanka in 1972.)[8]

This was also a time of great social change and upheaval. In the early twentieth century, women's education was a subject of much debate, discussion, and reform, with highly differential practices and policies among different classes and ethno-religious groups. Because of pervasive gender discrimination among all groups, men were the first to be educated; the privileged were sent to England. (Even Attia Hosain, daughter of an aristocratic clan, educated in a prestigious English school and college in the city of Lucknow, was not allowed to attend the University of Cambridge, where her brother studied.) It took another generation, even among the upper classes, before women received schooling outside the home or higher education. Hence, the first Anglophone writers were all men. Writers in regional or Indian languages reflected similar asymmetries. In 1936, the All-India Progressive Writers Association held its founding conference, which included Urdu and Hindi women writers like Rashid Jahan and Ismat Chughtai. Upper- and middle-class women's participation in politics was a new thing, encouraged to varying degrees in the service of the struggle for national independence. Among the working classes from which domestic servants emerged, literacy and education were rare. Anyone with the means to receive a higher education could not and would not by definition be a servant.

When Servants Were Still Servants: Early Male Writers from the 1930s to 1940s

Early in R. K. Narayan's novel *The Bachelor of Arts* (1935), the young male protagonist returns home late from a busy day at college to "shout at the cook to hurry up" and bring his dinner (29). Working against colonial stereotypes of Indians, seeking to educate an English-speaking Western readership about a new Indian middle class, Narayan presents this homecoming scene to establish the status of the protagonist's South Indian Brahmin Hindu family. In a typical gender divide, the commanding patriarchal father waits for his son in the front of the house and monitors his son's British Indian undergraduate education and socialization into adulthood, while the mother waits on the back verandah, where, having fulfilled her domestic responsibilities, she has retired to perform *puja*, to think about "her husband, home, children, and relatives," under the tranquility of "coconut trees waving against a starlit sky" (29–30). She can enjoy her evening leisure, her husband can supervise their son, and the son can focus on his English studies because the family has a cook available to make the food and be ordered to serve it. The briefly appearing figure of the nameless servant thus serves in Narayan's novel as a signifier of this family's upper-caste and upwardly mobile class status, their combination of tradition and modernity. In the home, his diegetic work (within the world of the novel) is also to serve as a familial intermediary between mother and son. Deferentially but firmly, he informs Chandran that his mother expects him to have dinner, and responds to her subsequent inquiries when her son has hurriedly eaten and left the house. "Didn't he eat well?" she asks the cook, who replies with equal concern: "No. He took only rice and curd. He bolted it down" (30). Not strictly a member of the family himself, the domestic servant serves to help maintain the bourgeois household, inculcating the young in proper filial behavior, and enabling communication between young and old, men and women, interior and exterior spaces of the bourgeois home. The servant in Narayan's early fiction thus serves an important literary non-diegetic function: he becomes the necessary, indeed constitutive, backdrop against which the bourgeois colonized subject may emerge.[9]

Likewise, in Narayan's first novel, *Swami and Friends* (1935), a nameless cook again serves as a signifier of a family's status, but here the cook also enables light comedy to send up the absurd pretensions of bourgeois children and reveal the complex dynamics between servants and their employers' children. Swami, the child protagonist, visits the house of his new school-friend Rajam, the son of a Police Superintendent, who tries to impress his schoolfriends by trying to boss the cook who brings them a plate of snacks:

> Rajam felt that he must display his authority.
> "Remove [the plate] from the table, you—" he roared at the cook. The cook removed it and placed it on a chair.
> "You dirty ass, take it away, don't put it there."
> "Where am I to put it, Raju?" asked the cook.
> Rajam burst out: "You rascal, you scoundrel, you talk back to me?" . . .
> The cook obeyed, mumbling: "If you are rude, I am going to tell your mother."
> "Go and tell her, I don't care." (26)

With gentle humor, Narayan pokes fun at the fragile egos of young middle-class boys, who, precisely because they are relatively powerless and insecure, try to assert their class and gender status by exerting power over a servant. Rajam is clearly not accustomed to being served food in his room, and is enacting a performance for his two visitors. The servant, notably, does not overtly resist the abuse the child has evidently learned from watching adults, itself revealing of the lower status and mistreatment of servants. But this cook, even as he indulges the child's misbehavior, has the power of mild resistance, in that he can threaten to report the child to his mother, a greater figure of authority, and refuse to follow the child's orders. The comedy unfolds as Rajan's ineffectuality is exposed: upon being cursed, the cook "quietly" takes the plate away, telling Rajan to "come and eat in the kitchen" instead. This is both a "great disappointment" to the two boys watching the drama, and a "terrible moment" for Rajam: "To be outdone by his servant before his friends!" (26). Unable to control the cook, Rajam sheepishly tries to save face by retrieving the plate from the kitchen and explaining this to his friends as follows: "I had to bring this myself. I went in and gave the cook such a kick for his impertinence that he is lying unconscious in the kitchen" (27).

Rajam's hilarious fib highlights the middle-class child's needs, desires, and aspirations via the rare inclusion of a servant whose own story, needs, or desires remain unaddressed. The novel focuses, as the title indicates, on Swami and his friends. The servant appears on occasion in Narayan's text as a necessary underside to its action. Within the world of the novel, the cook does what he is supposed to: in part helping to discipline the unruly child by establishing limits, and, at the same time, functioning as a subordinate member of the household. For the narrative, the cook serves to establish the reality of social distinctions, the psychology of the upper-class protagonist, and the self-constitution of the elite via, or by contrast with, the servants in their homes. The process of elite self-constitution is thus revealed as precisely a process. Soon after, making this even clearer, Swami re-enacts what he has learned from Rajam. Concerned about his own comparatively less posh household, and about projecting his own bourgeois image when Rajam returns the visit, Swami instructs his own cook: "Look here, you can't come to my room in that dhoti. You will have to wear a clean, white dhoti and shirt" (36). Linking servitude with dirt, shabbiness, and poverty, Narayan presents Swami's nameless cook as not speaking, so we do not know to what extent he follows this child's demands. Part of the comedy of the narrative, of course, is that the children do not see themselves as comic, but the point of the servants' presence is that these children *have* servants to lord over and who care for them.

In a more serious vein, a similar use of a servant figure appears early in Nirad Chaudhuri's monumental 1951 memoir *Autobiography of An Unknown Indian*, as the adult narrator details his self-formation through accounts of his Bengali childhood and describes the heavy monsoon season: "Everything was wet to the marrow of the bone. Neither we nor our clothes were ever properly dry. . . . [By contrast,] our servants were always wet, and their brown skins were always shining" (9). In a move familiar from colonial discourse, Chaudhuri defines his self in terms of a socially subordinate other: the privileged higher-class Indian subject wears the clothing that represents civilization, in contrast with bare-skinned Indian servant bodies purportedly closer to nature, and the objects of the (narrator's) gaze. (The collective "we" refers here to the male "children" in Chaudhuri's family and does not include those clearly separated by the term "our servants"; 9.)[10] With striking unselfconsciousness, this "unknown" Indian, who thus makes himself known to his readers as the (colonized) subject of his own narrative, is eager to establish his *difference* from his servants, not to equalize all humans under the same elements, but to distance himself from his (yet more unknown) lower-class domestic workers. Chaudhuri seems to need these references to servants to establish both difference and yet *some* similarity with himself: the Indian servant's body provides a way to speak indirectly of his own. In this early South Asian memoir, the servant body can be read as a metonym or lesser double for the narrator's own: as if unable to mention his own brown skin, he calls upon the servant body to indicate elliptically his own un-English and non-white racial status, for he too is a brown-skinned Bengali (albeit a clothed one) similarly drenched by the rain.

Later in the same chapter, Chaudhuri's servants reappear briefly to serve a different purpose. The narrator reminisces about his boyhood innocence and horror of prostitutes, whose colony of "small huts" was located on the bank across the river, "enclosed . . . by a high screen" (29). This spatially and socially marginalized community is blocked from the young Chaudhuri's view, but he learns of it via his servants: "Although the servants, the shopkeepers, and other small fry seemed to take much interest in this part of the town, we hated the sight of the screen, and we hated still more the simpering women whom at times we saw sailing out from behind the barrier" (29). Establishing his own distance from the women and the male servants or "small fry" who are together linked with illicit or uncontrolled sexuality, poverty, and dirt, the middle-class boy (and adult narrator, who ironizes his youthful naïve self but does not distance himself from that youthful self-righteousness) emphasizes his own bourgeois disgust and internalization of social prohibition. But the domestic servant also suggests proximity to the narrating subject: it is through (dis)identification with the male servant that the boy learns indirectly of his own (future) sexuality; it is through the servant's mediation that he learns about these women; and it is via contrast with the servant's "interest" that he intimates his own, for we also learn that the boy "hated" the screen, perhaps not only because of what it hid, but because it hid what he wanted to see, almost as if he unconsciously envied the servant for having access to what was to him forbidden.

Such instrumental uses of the figure of the servant are not interested in servant individuality or interiority, or in exploring the condition of servitude in itself, but rather, by way of contrast and contiguity, serve to elevate and self-fashion the bourgeois (post)colonial subject, and to reinforce employer prejudices about servant unreliability and prurience. (By contrast, as we will see in Chapter 3, in "About a Burning Girl," a story that explores the warped perspective of such an employer, Daniyal Mueenuddin turns the self-absorption of a middle-class male narrator into the butt of comic satire, and eschews such instrumental uses of the servant figure.) My purpose here is not to engage in finger wagging or mere ideological critique at the expense of these pioneering early male South Asian English writers, but rather, to note the significance of what is and is not noticed by them, and what they do and do not ask their readers to notice, in order to identify commonalities and trends that help us see both what subsequent women writers do differently, and the novelty of what more recent writers have begun to do. Part of my point is precisely to recognize the myopia of much earlier South Asian writing to conditions of servitude that are nonetheless taken for granted. A goal of this chapter is to investigate the literary and political functions of the appearance of servants in these early texts, to see how servant figures are both relegated to the background and required to perform various literary tasks. Early to mid-twentieth-century male South Asian English writers often dwell briefly on figures of male servants—cooks, household helpers, valets—emphasizing their uncouthness, or noting their existence, as a way to indicate the relative wealth, power, or prestige of their elite Indian employers to a Western audience as well as a form of self-representation to readers within the nation. Doing important political and cultural work in this national and international literature, these references become part of a project of self-constitution of the elite.

This is not to imply, of course, that domestic servitude is new to South Asian societies, or unique to a Westernized elite subsequent to colonization. As Raka Ray and Qayum note, servitude in South Asia has a "long, unbroken" history and continues in changing forms into the postcolonial present (2). Raja Rao's groundbreaking first novel *Kanthapura* (1938) makes clear the taken-for-granted presence of servants even in the rural, traditional hierarchical Indian society it describes as it explores the impact of Gandhian ideas on this remote, southwestern region. While the problems of reforming untouchability and the caste system are primary to the novel's concerns as it dramatizes the difficulties of bringing about change in a society deeply entrenched in these hierarchical beliefs and practices, domestic servitude appears as something common and in-between the highlighted opposition of Brahmins versus "Pariahs" (the term used in the novel for Dalits).[11]

Kanthapura is narrated by an elderly Brahmin woman who is at first openly resistant to the social egalitarianism promoted by Moorthy, an educated young Brahmin man. To begin with, though the narrator describes daily routines of household work, religious practices, and agricultural and market activities, she does not mention servants as doing any of this work. However, the ubiquity of servants and her implicit assumptions about servitude surface on occasions when her narration needs a marker of the low, a measure of debasement. When Moorthy has been threatened with "excommunication" by the village Swami for "mixing with the Pariahs like a veritable Mohammedan" (36), and his mother is so upset with him that she cannot serve him food as is proper for a Brahmin male, the narrator reports: "Moorthy sits by the threshold and eats like a servant, in mouthfuls, slowly and without a word" (42). The narrator (who mostly uses the pronoun "we" as if her voice is a representative of the village, although she speaks only for the Brahmin segment of it) is clearly ironized by Rao, who makes visible her prejudices against two kinds of undesirable outsiders: "Pariahs" and Muslims. Particularly striking here is the narrator's likening Moorthy's fallen position in the home to that of a servant's: he eats at the "threshold," a border space, and he eats in an improper way, unseemly and inappropriate for a man born into his caste and position. What marks his fall is the comparison, not to the figure at the lowest end of the hierarchy, the putative "Pariah" (for despite his transgressive interactions and mingling with Pariahs, Moorthy cannot yet be equated with untouchables), but to the servant, as if the narrator can only bring herself to describe Moorthy's disgrace in terms of something intermediate, the lowly servant whose caste is higher than that of the "Pariahs," and who is therefore allowed to enter the home and kitchen and eat in it.

Later in the novel, as British injustices at a nearby coffee estate increase, Moorthy succeeds in persuading more villagers (Brahmins and Pariahs) to unite in forming a Congress group, and leads the villagers in anti-British non-violent actions that are met with violent retaliation by the police. In another rare but revealing reference to servants, Moorthy, now celebrated by the villagers as a hero, is asked for help by an elderly village woman who reports how the revenue collector (who works for the British) maltreats the villagers and coerces them to pay taxes: "Raghavayya . . . takes bribes and beats his wife and sends his servants to beat us. . . . [C]ome to our village, son, and free us from this childless monster" (134). The indignity of violence against village women, especially women of higher caste, is exacerbated by the fact that the oppressor sends "his servants" to inflict the physical violence, crossing lines of class, caste, and social rank, as well as of gender. It is significant that this employer of servants, Raghavayya, is a rich man, grown wealthy from his role as an agent of extortion for the British government, and that his ignominy is indicated by his use of his undue power and wealth when he sends *his* agents, servants, to inflict violence upon the aged and weak. The detail about his servants thus also furthers anticolonial critique; it indicates both the power and the abuse of power by Indians who collude with British colonialists. In this pre-Independence nationalist novel preoccupied with casteism and the difficulties of the anticolonial struggle, these rare passing references to servants reveal both pervasive cultural attitudes and literary uses of servitude for particular political ends.

Hence it is important to distinguish class from caste. Class may overlap with but does not necessarily coincide with caste: in texts that present Hindu households where employers are upper caste and upper class and servants lower on both scales, servants are not untouchables (Dalits), because people designated as untouchable would not have access to such proximate areas of work in household interiors as food preparation or childcare.[12] In Mulk Raj Anand's pioneering 1935 novel *Untouchable*, Bakha, the titular protagonist, is contrasted with servants whom he regards (accurately) as more privileged than himself, and whose position he has no hope of ever occupying. *Untouchable* remains a landmark in its exposition of the injustices of the caste system, as it explores the subjectivity of a young man who accidentally brushes against an upper-caste man and is reviled for polluting him. Yet despite his unusual sense of outrage at the series of injustices he experiences during just one day (in contrast with his father Lakha, who urges acquiescence), Bakha is shown to have so deeply internalized a sense of stigma and lowliness that he is overwhelmed by the extraordinary condescension of another upper caste-man, Charat Singh, who gives him a hockey stick and orders him to fetch coal from his kitchen and tell the cook to bring his tea, tasks normally never assigned to an untouchable. "The boy stood wonderstruck. That a Hindu should entrust him with the job of fetching glowing charcoal in the chilm which he was going to put on his hookah and smoke!" (106). Bakha is still being ordered about to fetch and carry and do menial tasks, but these are normally the tasks of a domestic servant, of higher caste than Bakha, to which Bakha, who sees himself as "an unclean menial," cannot aspire (107).[13]

Notably, the unnamed cook, engaged in the cleaner task of "peeling potatoes," assumes that Bakha, in spite of his appearance, cannot be an untouchable, otherwise his master would not send him to the kitchen, a place of food preparation, and hence particularly vulnerable to feared pollution (107). Servitude, when it appears in *Untouchable*, serves an unusual function: it becomes a marker of difference from something much worse, namely untouchability. (Needless to say, in this novel the servant figure—the cook—also functions at the same time as a signifier of the employer's status and power.) Anand's focus on untouchability, while indisputably primary and admirable, nonetheless forecloses attention to servitude, which is overlooked or cast as a lesser evil, both in this novel and in scholarly studies that continue into the present. It is surely time now for literary scholars to attend to servitude, in addition to other forms of social injustice, as a form of injustice that, while lesser, exists alongside the injustice of untouchability, and is likewise complicated by its intersections with gender, region, religion, age, and so on.

That said, it is important to recognize that Mulk Raj Anand's work *is* exceptional for its time. Unlike the examples from Narayan, Chaudhuri, and Rao discussed above, Anand, in his second novel *Coolie* (1936), does attempt to present the interiority and subjectivity of a servant, and calls attention to the routinized humiliations and injustices of domestic servitude in South Asia. *Coolie* details the painful experiences of a young orphaned boy, Munoo, a migrant from the hills who is dispatched by his relatives to work in the city. Like much of Anand's fiction, *Coolie* is interested not specifically in servitude but more generally in highlighting various social systems of inequality, oppression, and exploitation. *Coolie* elaborates the extreme and systemic mistreatment of the marginalized underclasses, and particularly the abuse and lack of protection for (male) children, and the effect on the psyche of living under such systems. (None of these texts address female servants.) Munoo's trials in this episodic, anti-picaresque novel begin and end with servitude: he first becomes a servant in a humble Indian bureaucrat's household, then, after he runs away, a factory worker, a coolie, a rickshaw puller, and finally (again) a servant before he dies of tuberculosis at the age of fifteen.[14]

Anand focalizes the narrative mostly through Munoo, presenting via choice details the village boy's bewilderment and curiosity about the novelties he encounters in a 1930s urban middle-class Indian household. Munoo is struck by his new mistress's *sari* draped in a way quite unlike that of "hill women" he knew (12), and by her Anglicized custom of serving tea in china cups with milk in a separate jug and teapot, respectively described from Munoo's baffled viewpoint as "utensils of polished 'white chalk,'" and "big pot with a beak like a pig's nose" (15). He cannot understand why he is not offered any food after his long journey "according to the custom that prevails in all Indian homes" (13). Central to Munoo's oppression as a servant is this ill-tempered mistress (whom Anand portrays with remarkable misogyny). She is the foul-mouthed domestic tyrant who orders Munoo about, gives him stale leftovers, suspects him of theft and lasciviousness, and berates, curses, or blames him for failing at the household tasks she does not train him to do. The text thus reveals the gendered dynamics of a female employer with a male servant, and the criss-crossing of gender and class inequalities. The mistress is more vicious to her servant than her husband is in part because she has less social power as a woman. But Anand seems unaware of these gender issues and focuses exclusively on class-based inequalities.

Anand is the first among South Asian Anglophone writers to explore the effects on the mind and soul of a boy abjected by servitude, and to attempt to delineate what he might think or feel. But Anand adds plot twists and patronizing commentary that undermine his well-intentioned portrayal. Despite Anand's leftist-socialist leanings, his depiction of Munoo tends toward self-contradiction, as it alternates between sympathetic treatment and condescension or reaffirmation of upper-class prejudices about lower-class servant men as uncontrollably hyper-sexual or violent. As an early attempt that sets out to critique the combined effects of both Indian social hierarchies and British colonialism on the oppressed underclasses, Anand's portrayal of Munoo as a servant is concomitantly indignant and condescending, sensitive and clumsy, even crude. The morning after Munoo arrives at his first employers' home, he pees outside the kitchen door, unable to contain himself after a night spent without basic facilities. Anand thus reproduces the association of the servant with dirt and disgust, even as he presents the bodily aspects of subjection and its psychological consequences: "Munoo felt humiliated. He did not know how to face people if they were all going to be told what he had done this morning. He realized finally his position in this world. He was going to be a slave, a servant who should do the work, all the odd jobs, someone to be abused, even beaten . . . He felt sad; lonely" (31). It is very rare for writers in South Asian Anglophone fiction of this period to give readers access to a servant's interiority, or to accentuate his realization of its ignominy.[15] But Anand's mode of representation remains awkward. The paragraph ends in bathos, with the short, simplistic final sentence. Anand's narrative choices add to the stylistic problems. Munoo is sexually aroused by his employers' prepubescent child, imagines her naked (54), and, carried away as he plays a game of monkey to please her, bites her cheek, and is violently beaten by her father as a result (57–59). Thus, even as he critiques Munoo's employer's prejudiced perceptions of Munoo as an uncouth rustic, Anand's own depiction of Munoo reconfirms some of those perceptions.

Emphasizing the damaging effects of systemic injustice, the narrator explains how Munoo has been socialized to accept inequality: "his ego [had been] conditioned by the laws and customs of the society in which he had been born, the society whose castes and classes and forms had been determined by the self-seeking of the few, of the powerful" (35). But, Anand adds, Munoo, lacking better models, "sought all the prizes of wealth, power and possession exactly as his superiors sought them"; he aspired blindly "in the confusion of froth" to imitate the narrow self-interested self-advancement of those around him, unable to recognize the "fatuity of his desire to be like his superiors" who were themselves subordinate to the British (35). Like Kipling's Kim in a similarly critical moment, Munoo questions his own identity and realizes that servitude constitutes him, that he is defined by his position as servant:

> "What am I—Munoo?" he asked himself as he lay wrapped in his blanket, early one morning. "I am Munoo, Babu Nathoo Ram's servant," the answer came to his mind.
> "Why am I here in this house?" a further question occurred to him. "Because my uncle brought me here to earn my living," his mind reflected vaguely, the waves in his brain struggling to flow....
> It did not occur to him to ask himself what he was apart from being a servant, and why he was a servant and Babu Nathoo Ram his master. His identity he took for granted, and the relationship between Babu Nathoo Ram, who wore black boots, and himself, Munoo, who went about barefoot, was to him like sunshine and sunset, inevitable, unquestionable. (34)

While asking his readers to understand and empathize with a subaltern individual not unlike one likely working in their own homes, Anand's narrator puts Munoo down, inserting his own heavy-handed commentary ("the waves in his brain struggling to flow"). Anand here stereotypes the servant boy as unintelligent and incapable of questioning the social degradation in which this social system entraps him at the same time that Anand attempts to show how that system disallows self-awareness or independence of mind and promotes this internalization of identity and habituation to a sense of inferiority.

Even for Anand, however, servitude is not in itself a central concern; it is there to serve other narrative goals. In *Coolie*, another function of the literary servant is to enable critique of British colonialism and its effects on the aspiring, upwardly mobile Indian middle class. In a central episode, Munoo's employer, Nathoo

Ram, seeking advancement within the system created by the British, invites his new English boss (named Mr. England) to tea at his home in an attempt to ingratiate himself and secure a higher salary and promotion. The tea party is, predictably, a disaster (in a nod perhaps to the failed tea parties in E. M. Forster's *A Passage to India*). The over-excited Munoo rushes in with teacups and drops the tray with a resounding crash, shattering "all the expensive china" together with the family's pretensions. The literary servant thus serves even in this novel as a comedic tool in an episode designed to satirize how the Indian middle-class act both literally and metaphorically as "servants" to the British:

> "Sir," said Nathoo Ram, his under-lip quivering with emotion. I had hoped you would partake of the simple hospitality that I, your humble servant, can extend to you.... Tea, oh! Munoo, bring the tea!" (44)

It is no small irony, Anand suggests, that Munoo, the servant of the "servant" of the British, is the one who undoes the "tea-party," because he is made so anxious by his master's over-anxious efforts to please.

Anand also uses Munoo's servitude at the end of the novel to critique (though in highly sexist terms) a character named Mrs. Mainwaring, a mixed-race divorcée who claims whiteness, and is so sexually promiscuous that she even tries to seduce Munoo, her new child-servant:

> Mrs. Mainwaring had found that India was a veritable paradise for the white woman. She had not spent her time trying to bleach her colour in England in vain.... For *India was the one place in the world where servants were still servants*, and one could laze through morning and sleep through the afternoon, happy in the assurance that the cook and the "boy" will look after breakfast, lunch, tea and dinner, ... where one could come in to dress and leave the discarded garments in a heap on the floor, to be collected and folded away by the servants, whose mending needle stitched up every rent unbidden, and who picked up the ladders in one's stockings with uncanny skill! (267, my emphasis)

Through a notable phrase that satirically identifies 1930s India (from the "white" woman's perspective) as "the one place in the world where servants were still servants," Anand makes clear that the system of British colonialism in India is built upon and aggravates the effects of an already exploitative precolonial system. He uses servitude to critique the pretensions of an intermediate power group, white and Eurasian women, who take advantage and benefit from this system of racialized colonialism at the expense of the most downtrodden in India.

Servitude in South Asia is not, of course, unique to Hindu households, cultures, or fiction. Regardless of religious affiliation, it is central in every South Asian household that claims respectability, and remains so over time. Ahmed Ali's important historical novel, *Twilight in Delhi* (1940), which charts the decline of an aristocratic Muslim family under British colonialism, addresses servitude in an Indian Muslim context and, unlike Narayan, Chaudhuri, or Anand, also includes female servitude. Set in the early twentieth century, *Twilight* presents in nostalgic detail the dying world of old Delhi Muslim culture that faced erasure after the 1857 "Mutiny" or Rebellion and subsequent fall of the Mughals. Although the novel focuses on a decadent patriarch, Mir Nahal, and interactions among diverse members of his large extended family, included among its plethora of characters are servants, some of whom are named and given individual narratives and histories. Like his male contemporaries, Ali casts servants as backdrop, barely there, as extremely minimal figures, in whose thoughts or feelings the narrative has little interest. But Ali's effort to give texture to the collective and to the way of life he commemorates leads him to weave in servitude as its significant component, and to illuminate some key gendered and sexual aspects of servitude.

Early in the novel we are introduced to Dilchain, the "maidservant" who is ordered out of her sleep by the lady of the house to serve food to the master when he returns home late at night (7). Dilchain, whose name literally means "the one who brings peace to the heart," is a flat minor character. She alone "underst[ands]" her incapacitated mistress's speech and provides care, while grumbling, "There is no peace for me, O God" (18–19). As a servant within this world, Dilchain is at everyone's beck and call, performing various household tasks: cooking, cleaning, fetching, carrying. As a literary servant, Dilchain functions non-diegetically to enable Ali to establish the relative power and comforts of the women in the zenana, the hierarchies and divisions of labor within the household, and to hint at more complex dynamics of gendered sexual exploitation. Unmarried Dilchain had illicit relations long ago with her master and, consequently, "a son who died" (45). Ali's presentation of this hushed-up family scandal, however, as remembered by Mir Nahal's now-adult children, does not call for sympathy for Dilchain or outrage at female servants' vulnerability to routine predation by male employers.[16] We are not told if Dilchain was willing or unwilling in this affair. Rather, Mir Nahal's children evoke this past between the female servant and their father as the reason for their mother's mental illness, and for their unhappy childhood. If read against the grain of the text, however, this startling detail complicates our understanding not only of Dilchain, but also of the relations among women in this joint family, who, though differently positioned, are differently disempowered by the patriarchal system and are forced to live together despite histories of betrayal and resentment, and where the aging mistress becomes increasingly "dependent" on the aging female servant with whom her husband had sex (253).

Ali's representation of servants, though it gestures toward more complexity than, say, Chaudhuri's, nonetheless reinforces similar gendered and classist stereotypes. Dilchain is also presented as unreliable and mischief-making, as a threat to familial privacy: she misuses her proximity to her employers and contributes to the conniving and dissension among women in the household when she eavesdrops on a conversation between Begum Nihal and her daughter and exposes their secret (71). That this behavior is supposedly typical of female servants is reinforced by the similar behavior of an unnamed sweeperwoman in another incident that leads to a rift in the family (273). With class and religio-ethnic prejudice, Ali describes Dilchain as ignorant and superstitious, "with the simple credulity peculiar to the people of India," attributed (via a detail that he reveals surprisingly late in the novel) to her having once been Hindu, even though "she had long ago been converted to Islam" (perhaps because she was of lower caste and found work in a Muslim household) (279).

Ahmed Ali deploys different negative stereotypes for male servants. Ghafoor, Mir Nahal's valet, who waits upon his master but is not allowed into the zenana (women's quarters), is presented as a sexual threat, as an over-sexed, hyper-masculine, dandyish, but grotesque imitation of his master: "He too was a gay bird. He was not only strong and virile, but possessed great charm. With his Tartaric ferocious eyes, his hairy chest, the oil trickling down over his brow, and his fine white long coats smelling of strong attar, he was a favorite with the prostitutes" (38–39). Ghafoor talks crudely of his voracious sexual appetite, which, Ali implies, so over-strains the young girl he marries that she dies of "ulcers in the womb" (209). Such representations of the male servant serve to highlight his distance from the more respectable aristocratic men he serves (even though they are equally promiscuous), or simply to contribute "color" to Ali's portrayal of old Delhi. In so doing, however, Ali plays into, and replicates, deeply pernicious, classist, and orientalist ideologies.

While servant characters serve to elucidate the complex textures of this once aristocratic family and culture, Ali's novel also uses servitude as a marker of the stigmatized and undesirable, against which are measured the heights or claims of old Muslim aristocracy and nobility. One of Mir Nahal's sons, Asghar, wishes to marry a young woman whose family is considered unsuitable by his parents because she had an ancestor who was a servant. The novel thus reveals Mirza Nihal's hypocrisy—he seduces a servant woman and gets her pregnant, but will not allow his son to marry into a family that has a distant link to servitude—and underscores servitude as that from which respectable families distance themselves. Begum Nihal makes this taint of ancestry explicit: "In Mirzaji's wife there is the blood of a maidservant. I am not going to bring her daughter as my daughter-in-law" because "the good-blooded never fail, but the low-blooded are faithless," she states (60). This rejection of alliance or connection with servants in Ali's novel serves to intensify the aristocratic pretensions of old Delhi Muslim families, who insist on their erstwhile status in 1911 precisely when it is severely diminished. Likewise, in a startling moment, the narrator comments on the shameful depths to which the British have reduced Indian royalty, where the female descendants of the last Mughal king, Bahadur Shah Zafar, have had to marry their own servants to survive: "In Delhi to this day there were innumerable princes and princesses alive, daughters and granddaughters of Bahadur Shah. Many cut grass for a living, others drove bullock carts to keep body and soul together. The princesses had married cooks and kahars, their own servants, or served as cooks and maids" (142). This account of the steep descent of princesses becomes a way (both for Ali and for his aristocratic characters) to highlight and denounce the deep ignominy of the British, who have thus destroyed the social system and prestige that prevailed before. In a novel proliferating with references to servants yet not concerned with or about them, Ahmed Ali illustrates how, like his contemporaries, as an early male Indian writer, he both needs servants in his fiction, and yet overlooks them as human beings or characters worthy of importance in their own right.

"One Must Live": Women Writers from the 1950s to 1970s

A rather different approach to the representation of servitude and servants appears in the work of South Asian Anglophone women writers from the 1950s to 1970s. Given that women have been traditionally assigned the responsibility of the home and the supervision of staff needed to run it, and that, as Ray and Qayum note, with the rise of a modernized, educated middle class in India, a "civilized" household was defined by a wife's ability to govern servants and manage a home (50), it is understandable that post-Independence, middle-class women writers pay more attention (than their male counterparts) to the internal spaces of the home, the politics of gender, and the micropolitics of employers' relationships with their servants. Many explore cross-class (same-sex) homosocial intimacy between women or the (cross-sex) paradox of women employers having authority over male servants within the arena of the home.[17] Interested in domesticity, their writing shows more awareness of its secret sharer, the figure of the *domestic*. Many of these pioneering women writers, from Zeenuth Futehally to Attia Hosain, Kamala Markandaya and Nayantara Sahgal, show greater attentiveness to and sympathy for servants, especially women servants, and their conditions and choices, compared to preceding or contemporaneous male writers. Though usually centering on (upper- or middle-class) female protagonists, these women writers address the nuanced and often conflicted, alternately affectionate and antagonistic, interactions between upper-class protagonists and their servants, interactions that often become integral to narratives of the female protagonists' identity formation, gendered acculturation, and initiation into sexuality. Nonetheless, with the important exception of Hosain, in none of these writers' work are servants cast as protagonists, nor are questions of servitude central. Even when servants are given prominence in their fiction, the emphasis remains on the upper-class protagonist(s), often a first-person narrator, whose education and coming-of-age they enable. And, as with the male writers discussed in the previous section, some of these women writers' representations of servants may be still imbued by bourgeois prejudices about servant unreliability, criminality, and sexuality, or framed by implicit distancing calls for pity, while the focus remains on the necessarily removed protagonist or narrator.

Zeenuth Futehally's 1951 novel *Zohra*, arguably the first novel published by an Indian Muslim woman in English, opens with the words of Unnie the "old nurse," reproving a younger maidservant, Gulab, for pushing Zohra, the eponymous aristocratic young protagonist, too high on a swing (1). While entirely focused on Zohra and her struggle not to sacrifice her desires (artistic, political, romantic) to the duties of her social position, providing access only to Zohra's interiority, the novel includes a broad-ranging portrayal of Zohra's pre-Partition world of Hyderabadi Muslim aristocrats and includes illuminating glimpses of their household servants and the servants' interactions with one another. Unnie has served as Zohra's mother's wet-nurse, and hence occupies a "very special position of trust and privilege in the household," as at once foster-mother and servant, loved and respected, though not of equal status (1). She now lives permanently with the family in the zenana, monitors the other servant women (earning their resentment), and watches lovingly and protectively over Zohra and her sister. She even presumes to advise and instruct Zohra's mother, Begum Zubaida, who indulges Unnie's "high-handed" interference in her supervision of servants and family, recognizing a deep form of belonging: "For where could one find another like her? Such devotion only came through lifelong service in the family" (16).

As a matriarchal upholder of custom and tradition within a patriarchal set-up, Unnie thus serves multiple functions within the novel. From the beginning, she establishes and polices, literally and figuratively, the gendered and classed boundaries of Zohra's 1930s world, discouraging Zohra's love of learning (2), denouncing the neighbor's son for peeking into their garden (3), guarding Zohra from prying eyes to maintain her purdah (6). "In our days, girls behaved like girls," she exclaims, "girls never entered the outer garden" (2). She voices strong disapproval of girls' education, marking the changes that have occurred among upper-class Muslim families in the early twentieth century, and expresses both her sense of entitlement as well as the distance in rank between herself and Zohra's family: "it is for such fears [that girls will exchange notes with boys] that we poor folk discourage our girls from learning to read and write" (6). As a somewhat stereotyped mouthpiece for convention, and representative of the societal constraints that surround Zohra, Unnie is also discredited by the narrator for her penchant for exaggeration and gossip: "Unnie, like all those given to exaggeration, deceived herself into believing she would have spoken the truth" (5).

Yet the figure of Unnie also enables Futehally to explore the complex sense of identity and structures of feeling entailed in such traditional frameworks of lifelong servitude. Most unusually for this time, we are given glimpses into Unnie's interiority. Unnie sees herself as belonging to the family she serves, proudly, fiercely loyal, and protective of their interests. In part also serving as a contrast to her kinder mistress, she criticizes the hangers-on whom the master generously invites for dinner, and is in turn criticized by the narrator for her paradoxical classism: "In this, Unnie revealed the snobbery of servants working in aristocratic households. Had all the guests been nawabs, no trouble would have been too great for her, but for impoverished people, she had only contempt" (18). Futehally thus suggests how servants participate in enforcing the social hierarchies that elevate their employers above others (and that thereby secondarily elevate them). Futehally also emphasizes the closeness, intimacy, and sense of reciprocity between mistress and maidservant, as Begum Zubaida herself sews clothes for Unnie's children and infant grandchildren, keeping up with each milestone in their lives. "Tomorrow is the naming ceremony of Unnie's granddaughter, and I must finish this. It seems only the other day that I was sewing her daughter's trousseau, and in the twinkling of an eye here is the child," this royal descendent tells her husband (10). This portrays a relation less unequal, quite different from the visibly forced distance and austerity between English aristocrats and their servants that structures nineteenth-century British or American fiction.

Indeed, as an Indian Muslim writer, Futehally implicitly critiques both British and Hindu customs of distinction between servants and masters, as she describes how, after a day of fasting in the month of Ramazan, in accordance with a disappearing Muslim tradition, all the zenana women break their fasts to feast together in Zohra's mother's dining room: "In the democratic fashion that a few Muslim homes still preserved, Unnie and the other women-servants and maids joined them in the repast" (33). That this is somewhat unusual even among Muslim families is noted in the novel itself, for later when Zohra moves in with her in-laws she notices that "none of the servants [women] were asked to sit with [her and her mother-in-law] at meals, even when both of them were alone without Bashir. Here a servant was treated as a servant, and not a member of the family, as was done in her mother's house" (64–65). The novel does not claim that social inequality was eliminated among all Muslim women of higher classes and their servants, but Futehally does point to variations in practice, to relatively less abjection, and to unexpected forms of intimacy, attachment, and relative egalitarianism within the indubitably unequal structures of a classed feudal system. Social stratification exists, but is very different from the rigid barriers of the Hindu caste system. In yet other households, the novel suggests, maids enjoyed that sense of belonging and investment in the family they served. When Zohra's sister gets married, her prospective in-laws arrive with maids who are equally eager to inspect the new bride, and whose curiosity is indulged: "The menfolk were received in the men's quarters by Nawab Safdar Yar Jung, while the ladies had travelled in closed cars and carriages with their maidservants who were also anxious to see their young master's future bride" (20). Even in a novel devoted to the trials of an upper-class female protagonist, Futehally gives surprising room to the interactions and desires of servants, particularly women. Futehally's portrayal of this world of servants thus provides an instructive contrast to Ahmed Ali's, in that Futehally provides far more texture and feeling, and avoids the highhanded stereotypes of Ali's depictions. She also makes use of literary servants, but with more sympathy and nuance, to portray a variegated, disappeared world of Indian Muslims, as part of a political strategy to assert the contested citizenship of Indian Muslims post-Partition.[18] What we do not see, however, is a critique of servitude per se, as a degrading and dehumanizing system.

In *Zohra*, Unnie, together with the other women servants in Zohra's parents' home, also serves to illustrate the complex dynamics among older and younger servant women, and the fluidity of boundaries of power in a Muslim zenana, even with its feudal traditions.[19] At Zohra's pre-wedding festivities, "maids mingled with mistresses freely joining in the fun," splashing colored water on each other, laughing, crowding around the bangle seller. Such enabling of pleasure and mingling among women, regardless of rank, was socially sanctioned, Futehally suggests, for Zohra's mother looks on "indulgently" as the maids "neglected their work" (42). However, when Unnie, the over-zealous champion of her employers' interests, predictably takes it upon herself to "reprimand" the younger maids, exerting her power, Futehally also includes their feisty responses: "The maids looked at one another, winked, and made wry faces behind [Unnie's] back.... Gulab, looking wretched, exclaimed, 'Does this mean-spirited woman really think she's doing all the work? Indeed she bosses enough for ten, or even twenty. Perhaps that's what she means by saying she does the work of ten!'" (42). Futehally thus presents an important mix of women's interactions: Zubaida's indulgence, Unnie's officiousness, and the maids' spirited though covert resistance (to the older servantwoman, not to their mistress). She gives them names, and histories: younger Gulab, for instance, is attractive but "disfigured" by childhood smallpox, and has an embattled dynamic with Unnie, whose surveillance and chastisement she frequently endures (17). She also provides a glimpse into male-female servant interactions: Gulab enjoys a flirtation with Mohammed, a male servant, as she runs errands and relays messages between the zenana and the men's quarters (16). Futehally thus both links servants with illicit indulgence in forbidden sexuality while making clear how the protection of purdah, which Zohra finds restrictive, is also a form of protection afforded only to upper-class women, and not to servant women like Gulab.

In a novel committed to critique of gendered oppression, particularly the purdah system, arranged marriage, and the curtailments placed on women's education, Unnie further serves as an indicator of the degree of protection nonetheless afforded to young upper-class women by their families. After Zohra's wedding night, of which we are told little, we learn that Unnie alone has been sent with Zohra to her in-laws' house:

> The following morning, after the bridegroom had left, Unnie eagerly entered Zohra's room. She had accompanied the bride, as an old and trusted servant. Her duty was to wait on Zohra who would be hesitant to order about the servants in the home of her new parents. She also had to keep Zohra's parents informed as to how the bride was faring in her new life. Unnie started to ask Zohra oblique questions, but the latter maintained a studied silence. (58)

This brief passage alone is remarkably revealing about gender and servitude in Indian Muslim custom. First, Unnie, as at once female servant, guardian, and representative of Zohra's family, is entrusted with the important task of providing care and comfort to a young bride in a new, possibly alien environment, especially after her first sexual experience, and reports back to her parents on the conditions of her new home. Yet Unnie is expected to move residence, without regard for her own comfort, with Zohra, to subordinate her own needs to those of the family she serves. (Unnie later returns to Zohra's mother, and we hear of her throughout the novel, accompanying Zohra's parents on pilgrimage to Mecca, expressing concern at various stages of Zohra's life. Unnie is a lifelong, feudal servant.) In Zohra's in-laws' house, however, Unnie is subjected to unaccustomed differential treatment: she is relegated to the servants' quarters, and not invited to eat with Zohra and her mother-in-law, "a slight that the old woman resented" (65). Second, Unnie's prurient curiosity and concern are resisted by Zohra, who builds a wall of silence to barricade herself and her new privacy in her marriage even from the maternal servant figure who has known her since birth. Third, the passage also suggests the tentative, liminal position of a new bride in her in-laws' home, where she does not yet have the authority to command their servants, also part of the new family, and must rely on the familiar (in every sense) servant from her parental home.

As the novel moves on to Zohra's marriage and emotional entanglement with her husband's brother, Hamid, we hear about various unnamed servants who populate her in-laws' household—the ayah who looks after her children, the chauffeur who drives them around, the maids and bearers who bring tea, the loyal servants who carry stories of Hamid's doings to his mother—who serve both as markers of their employers' affluence and to express the servants' sense of belonging within this family as well. In an interesting scene, Futehally suggests the complex gendered and classed dynamics between Zohra, now a young wife and mother, and Abdul, an old male servant. Abdul (whose name emblematically means servant, making clear that he is present in the novel explicitly and exclusively in the capacity of servant), expresses his concern that Hamid is overdoing his Gandhism by giving away his grand clothes and wearing homespun. Revealing how, as an observant servant, he has noted Zohra's influence over her brother-in-law, he tries to persuade her to dissuade Hamid. At first Zohra smiles and "listen[s] intently," indulging Abdul as if he were a male version of Unnie: "His long years of service with the family had given him the privilege of expressing his opinion of her brother-in-law whom he had looked after since his birth" (163). But as he moves too close, speaking "even more intimately," she becomes "uncomfortable as he bent over her, and she could not help drawing back a little" (164). Zohra remains dignified and reassuring, and Abdul respectful and solicitous, but this interaction also suggests how, even though Zohra is now out of purdah, the familiarity of the older male servant requires the reassertion of class and gender boundaries. Zohra, for all her kindness, feels the need to maintain them, preserving a necessary distance and personal space from the incursions of a male, lower-class, family retainer who is, ultimately, not family. Though the dominant strain of this novel is the story of Zohra, centrally concerned with gender restrictions and Indian Muslim nationalism, these moments constitute a significant minor strain, as Futehally also offers a nuanced exploration of the gendered and classed complexities of servitude in this pre-Partition context, to illuminate, post-Partition, the complexity of a minority community both forgotten and misunderstood.

Kamala Markandaya, one of the most well known of early Indian English women novelists, also evokes, in small moments, the complexity of servitude in fiction that is primarily about something else. Her classic first novel, *Nectar in a Sieve* (1954), focuses on the harrowing challenges faced by Rukmani, a landless Hindu peasant woman who reflects on her experiences of floods, famine, drought, repeated loss, abandonment, and the deaths of her children and husband—disasters exacerbated by systemic injustice under feudalism and the combined changes wrought by colonialism and modern capitalism. Both before and after Independence, Indian fiction that sought to raise awareness of subalternity was understandably concerned with extreme conditions of oppression and precarity, as faced by Dalits or agricultural workers living under stringent, exploitative conditions that barely allowed subsistence. However, in an instructive episode, Markandaya describes how Rukmani and her aging husband, having lost the rented land they have tilled all their lives, go to the city looking for help from a son who has become a servant. The novel thus offers a critical explanation for domestic servitude (from a servant's family's perspective), as the slightly better alternative that rural migrants choose when they seek relief in the city from feudal landlords, tenant farming, bloodsucking moneylenders, and the economic changes wrought by colonialism that only heighten their vulnerability.

For Rukmani, this fruitless trip becomes the occasion to mourn the loss of her son, Murugan, who has vanished. *His* story remains incomplete, for we never learn what his experiences were, why he left two successive servant positions, or whether he found something better. But Markandaya provides a powerful if brief glimpse of gendered differences in servitude via her portrayal of wives of male servants who live in the "servants' quarters" and themselves work as servants (159). Rukmani is disappointed not to find her son at his original place of employment, but she receives temporary welcome from the wife of a male servant who explains her generosity as the extension of a kind employer: "We are fed free," she tells Rukmani, "the doctor is very good to us and gives us rice and dhal. Today she sent extra for you" (160). Markandaya takes time to detail the rudimentary physical conditions in which servant families live, raise children, cook, and share toilets. The servants' quarters are spatially separate, "behind the house and some distance away," consisting of "three godowns standing in a row, square rooms with brick walls and stone floors, each with a separate low doorway. . . . Inside it was half-dark, for there was only one window high up on the wall and thin blue smoke was rising from a corner where a young woman was cooking" for her children (159). A "godown," derived from the Malay word for storehouse, is a contrived, cramped residential space assigned to those who serve the big house. Yet even this accommodation is understood as generosity and is jealously guarded by other servants, like the woman's husband, who is "none too pleased" at having to share his precious resources (158). The employers' houses, by contrast, are guarded by men who visibly emblazon their employers' wealth, "wearing the white tunics of servants," who assume Rukmani and Nathan are beggars, and whose task it is to keep out potential encroachers and supplicants (157).

Markandaya also suggests how a destitute young servant woman has to resort to sexual labor to survive, when conventional morality becomes an unaffordable luxury. And here we do see a glimmer of an early critique of servitude as a system, with a chain of gendered and sexual consequences for dependent others. In her search for Murugan, Rukmani is next sent to the Collector's house, where Murugan subsequently served, and where he left his wife and child two years earlier. Now living hand-to-mouth herself in a similar godown room with two children, their daughter-in-law Ammu is unwelcoming, resentful of her in-laws for their son's abandonment, suspicious of what they may expect of her. She too has become a servant, sweeping and cleaning for a pittance. The infant on her hip, she tells them, is not their grandchild. We are not told who is the child's father, or what Ammu had to do to feed her first child and keep the roof over their heads. " 'One must live,' she repeated, defiant, challenging, sensing reproach where none could be" (164). Rukmani sorrowfully agrees, reiterating her daughter-in-law's words: "for it is very true, one must live" (164). In response to Ammu's refusal to express shame or apology, and to her determined, resonant words, "one must live," Rukmani offers understanding, and guilt at her son's actions. Grieving the loss of family and the erosion of older systems of support and community, she offers help to this younger woman, imbued perhaps with the memory of her own daughter back in the village who turned to prostitution to feed a starving child. Rejected, Rukmani reflects, "There is no touching this girl . . . Misfortune has hardened her, which is just as well, she will take many a knock yet" (165). Through Rukmani's non-judgmental, compassionate and foreboding perspective, Markandaya's portrayal of this passing figure in the novel calls attention both to the need for generosity of understanding and to the grotesque struggle and sacrifices that a young servant woman must endure as a single mother in this harsh social and economic system. (As we will see in Chapter 3, in his short story "Saleema," Daniyal Mueenuddin explores more fully the interiority and choices of such a servant woman.)

Some Inner Fury (1955), Markandaya's second novel, focuses, in an interesting rewriting of E. M. Forster's *A Passage to India*, on the difficulties of romantic love between an affluent Hindu Brahmin woman, Mira, and a white Englishman, Richard, during a time of political turmoil and hostility in pre-Independence India. Although centered, in complete contrast to her first novel, on the doings of elite, affluent, Westernized characters, *Some Inner Fury* relies on frequent references to various types of servants who serve, again, to highlight the Hindu family's status and needs. Multiple nameless servants are strictly supervised by Mira's mother and cannot be "entrusted" with important tasks (41); "half a dozen servants" regularly accompany the family to their summer retreat in the hills (57) and are remembered by Mira the narrator-protagonist as a "phalanx of servants" or protective barrier between the family and the hoi polloi (143)—the male "chauffeur" who drives the family around (5, 15, 177), the male "bearers" who serve as butlers or footmen for various household tasks, and the male "gardener" and "watchman" who guard the boundaries of the "compound" to keep out village children seeking free food amidst preparations for a family wedding (42). Sometimes named and identified for their differentiated tasks and religio-ethnic diversity, these include Das, the "well-trained," "old and experienced servant" who alone can be trusted to accompany Mira when she travels by train (66–67);

Richard's bearer, a "tall impassive Northerner" (137); the "broad, squat, . . . slit-eyed" Gurkha chowkidar (from Nepal) hired to guard the ripening mangoes and frighten children with his "kukri" (weapon) (42); and Arikamma, the low-caste "indoor sweeper" who has to complete her work early in the morning before other servants can start theirs and is "bullied if she didn't" (100). Amid the novel's other concerns, Markandaya maintains an unusual attentiveness to the nuances of servitude in the colonized society she describes, even as she deploys servitude in this novel for unexpected and new purposes.

Early on, Mira the narrator describes how Richard, her brother's English friend who has just arrived from England and is staying with the family, dons "a dhoti and chappals scandalously borrowed from one of the servants" before the two young men go off to explore the town (6). "The Englishman has a lot to learn," remarks her father sardonically, "I do not think his countrymen will approve of his unconventionality" (6). Mira's parents' amused disapproval stems from their recognition that the scandal lies in Richard's transgression not only of British colonial racial norms, but also of Indian class and caste ones. Kit, Mira's brother, remains in his "finery"; such bodily intimacy as sharing servants' clothing is highly inappropriate among upper-class Indians and can only be enacted by a clueless new arrival (6). But sixteen-year-old Mira speaks up unexpectedly in Richard's defense, aligning her with him for the first time, and prefiguring their future affinity: "I think it is very sensible of him to dress for the climate—even if he had to borrow servants' clothes" (6). It is via this transgression relating to servants that the author hints at the interracial and sexual crossing of borders that Mira and Richard will later undertake.

Nonetheless, servants remain minimal and functional in these early novels by Markandaya as well; they are there to illuminate, by suggestion, something about those above or below them, the elite or the peasantry, not to focus on servitude per se. *Some Inner Fury* also offers a new attentiveness to subtle historic and social changes that affect upper-class women, highlighting how a distinct local tradition of servitude continues in this South Indian Hindu culture, while a shift to something new is happening alongside it. She notes how more Westernized households have begun to adapt, or imitate, the British Anglo-Indian culture of servitude, so that the two co-exist or the latter replaces the former, imposing a new responsibility upon Hindu women. It is at first awkward for Mira's mother to host Richard, because they are orthodox vegetarian Brahmans, as are their in-house servants. To accommodate colonial guests, Mira notes, their "house itself was equipped to cope with both Europeans and Indians: there were two dining rooms, two kitchens, even two sets of servants, the one lot knowing Indian cookery and service, the other, trained by European memsahibs, knowing how to deal with such abominations as meat and capable of waiting at table" (19). However, the servants trained to pander to Europeans are only prepared for occasional visitors, not for a house-guest. Richard's constant presence necessitates further accommodation. Later, when Kit, Mira's brother, becomes a civil administrator, his wife Premala has to learn a new kind of housekeeping. Their house, furnished by a European firm, has "nothing that was Indian about it," and Premala reports that though she has "good servants," a cook and butler trained by British women, who make her task easier, she remains in awe of them (71–72).

Markandaya's nuanced attentiveness extends to the abuse of servants within both these traditional and evolving systems of servitude, and also serves the important purpose of revealing something about employers as individual characters. When Premala, Kit's wife, decides to adopt an orphan child from a nearby village, Kit, autocratic, Westernized, but attuned to the necessities of maintaining his reputation among both Indians and his British superiors, objects: "people will think I've slept with the serving maid and this is my bastard and you're just being nice about it" (119). Kit is right; "there was talk," the narrator confirms (119). The detail, however, allows Markandaya to call her readers' attention to another point: that sexual exploitation of servant women was common but unacknowledged even among this "select and small" circle of Kit's Westernized friends; the problem is the apparent acknowledgment of it. In highlighting this hypocrisy, Markandaya also reveals that Kit, though unjustly suspected here, is in fact guilty of another kind of (verbal) abuse: it is normal(ized) for him, when his chauffeur fails to fix an apparently malfunctioning car and disappears to look for a mechanic, to exercise his class and male privilege by calling the chauffeur names: "I *knew* it wasn't the car's fault. . . . I *said* it must be that idiot driver. . . . Bloody incompetent ass" (68).

Unlike her first two novels, which focus respectively on the extremely indigent and affluent, in her third novel, *A Silence of Desire* (1960), Markandaya explores the troubles of a young middle-class clerk whose wife refuses the ovarian surgery she needs because of her fear of modern medicine, and places her faith instead in a Swami, a traditional medicine man, leading to erosion of the couple's relationship and of the family's precarious finances. Interested in the opposition between a Westernized mindset, with its faith in science and reason, and a belief system invested in faith healing, the novel is focalized almost entirely via the perspective of the husband, who remains unsure whether the alternatives promised to his wife are ultimately exploitative or psychologically therapeutic. However, in a minor strain, as an almost negligible but continuous presence in his household, and hence in his consciousness, Markandaya presents the figure of a servant girl who serves several important purposes in the novel. This female servant is first introduced as a marker of the lower-middle-class family's upward mobility, of the male protagonist's pride in having secured a modicum of financial comfort despite his social and economic position: "He was a senior clerk and they employed a servant girl, and it gave him real and considerable pleasure to think he could do as much for his wife" (9). Servitude is clearly crucial for a middle-class family as well to mark its relative status. Via this figure, Markandaya also establishes the different gender-based responsibilities in this urban, semi-traditional home: Dandekar, the husband, takes pleasure in being thus able to alleviate the menial household tasks that are understood as his wife's responsibility; Sarojni, the wife, is frequently seen "directing" the servant girl (39). Normality in the home is manifested when Sarojni is engaged in such supervision, fulfilling her role as housewife, or when she is able to talk to Dandekar about her day and complain about the girl: "for once I managed to get some work out of Janaki . . . but really we must get another maid" (33). As an important nuance, they can only afford to employ one servant "girl" to undertake multiple tasks from kitchen work to childcare, not numerous servants or even one male servant (9).

It may seem surprising that in this novel Markandaya, as a woman writer, does not provide a woman's perspective or explore relationships among women. However, I would argue that by focusing on the husband's perspective, Markandaya chooses instead to highlight his ineptitude and gendered and classed attitudes about domesticity and servitude. Happily oblivious of household management, Dandekar is befuddled one day when he returns home to find his wife inexplicably absent. Predictably, he "shout[s] for the maidservant, a wizened girl of fifteen" for information and is irritated by her giggling ignorance: "He recalled that she did not know how to tell the time. She was an utter fool. She did not know anything. He vented his rising ill-humor on her" (11–12). With tongue-in-cheek humor, Markandaya thus showcases Dandekar's contempt and failure of authority as the maid bursts into tears, as does the infant she is carrying, producing domestic chaos until, to his relief, his wife returns and "order" is "restored": "The maid was invisible, which was what Dandekar most desired she should be" (13).

Evidently, if a husband has to ask a maid where his wife is, there must be disorder in the household. As things go wrong, as Sarojni begins to neglect her household responsibilities, and tensions erupt because Dandekar suspects her of adultery, the maidservant becomes both a representative of social convention and a potential agent of surveillance. She exerts a silent, unwitting constraint on the couple's actions, interactions, and expressions of emotion. Her presence inhibits Dandekar even as he wonders if he can use her as a household spy. "Servants talk," says an officemate, as the men discuss whether an Indian wife could get away with infidelity (45). Dandekar debates whether he should stoop to "ask the maid" about his wife's doings: "But who on earth would gossip with that imbecile? he said to himself angrily" (50). When Sarojni sacks Janaki, he grows more suspicious; when she hires a new servant girl, he worries, as he tries to unlock his wife's trunk, about the "curious looks from the new hireling" (56).

After their first fight, as the couple try to conceal the tension from the new maid, "before whom they must posture and play-act," Dandekar resents the presence of the servant whom he also needs (86).

Markandaya draws on the figure of the servant girl for multiple purposes in this novel, but primarily to highlight the bourgeois male householder's distanced, disengaged relation to the very domesticity on which he depends, and the gendered abjection of the female servant as well as her indispensability to the post-Independence bourgeois Indian household. The servant girl is not even a minor character; one girl is interchangeable with and replaced by another who is no different, highlighting their functionality to both the household and the text. However, each servant girl becomes a marker of what Dandekar does not know and cannot do, and of some minimal growth in his consciousness. Markandaya draws attention, in fleeting moments, to the second girl's precarity. As his suffering increases, so does Dandekar's capacity for empathy, as he begins to pay attention to those around him. When he becomes ill, he realizes, "I don't even know her name" (93). With his wife is increasingly absent, neglecting him and their children, he returns from work and suddenly becomes aware of the girl working in his home: "Despite his abstraction he noticed the maid hovering anxiously. She started work in the mornings at seven, but there was no set time for her to leave; she went when she was told. Poor child, he thought, she must be longing to get home" (96).

Through these subtle but sustained, minor moments, Markandaya establishes concomitantly the material conditions under which a young servant girl works, the failure of both employers to recognize or care about how they use her, and the gendered difference between husband and wife, where the husband is more oblivious. The maid serves ultimately to expose the system in which they all live: what women know and do as housewives, compared to their husbands; what men fail to notice; what women employers take for granted; and hence what women servants have to endure. Later, when the maid is absent, as is his wife, and his child is hungry, Markandaya highlights Dandekar's cultivated helplessness: "He went uncertainly into the kitchen. In all his life he had never cooked a meal, never fried a chili or a potato. Men never did, unless they were cooks, and even cooks wouldn't cook in their own homes" (156). As a woman writer, Markandaya offers this pointed reminder, via the details of what Dandekar cannot do, of male dependence on layers of gendered labor—from the wife to the female servant—and the systemic devaluation of that labor in the home even in a system where some men are paid to cook in other men's homes. Implicitly, Markandaya also suggests a critique of the inattentiveness of her male Indian contemporaneous writers, whose work similarly both depends on and disregards this labor.

Among early Anglophone Indian women writers, Nayantara Sahgal, given her highly elite status and privileged connections to the Nehru family, might not seem a likely candidate as a writer attentive to connections between domestic servitude and gender constraints. Yet even Sahgal's early novels (from the 1960s)—though mostly focused on the problems of political leadership in post-Independence India or on the struggles of upper-class Hindu women trapped in unhappy marriages—draw upon servants as a regular frame of reference for elite Indian families, and express a strong, often critical, awareness of the burdens placed upon upper-class women of by servant supervision and of the abuse faced by servants themselves.

Set in 1950s India, *A Time to Be Happy* (1958), Sahgal's first novel, uses a male narrator who describes both his own pre-Independence anticolonial activism and his observations of the changes experienced by two generations of an elite Hindu family as they shift to post-Independence. However, compared to earlier male writers like Chaudhuri, who used servant figures mostly to signify a family's upper-class and caste status, or to signal the servant's links with sexuality and dirt, Sahgal does something very different. In Sahgal's fiction, the degree of entitlement and habituated comfort of various characters, indicated by the way they treat their servants, becomes a significant barometer of an individual's character, separate from his or her elite status. The narrator describes, for instance, his wealthy old friend Govind Narayan, a family patriarch, as blissfully unconcerned with the problems of a changing world, by comparing him to the legendary Nawab of a fallen city, who, upon hearing that he ought to escape before the British arrived to kill him, replied, "Indeed I ought, but the servants have already fled and there is no one to fetch me my slippers" (4). Through this humorously exaggerated comparison portrayal of the indolent Nawab, who cannot bestir himself even to save his own life, Sahgal implies the decadence of such a deeply ingrained attitude of elite male privilege and dependence upon servants even among mid-twentieth-century Indians. Govind becomes a representative of the old ways, in contrast to the changing social attitudes of the modern Indian man, represented by the Gandhian narrator.

By further contrast, Sahgal suggests, women of Govind's own family differ significantly in their approach to servants. Govind's widowed mother, despite her age, refuses to depend on servants: she was "the only member of the Shivpal family who did not summon a servant to do what she could do herself" (20). Govind's wife, tasked with the housewifely responsibilities of keeping servants and children under control, is praised for keeping them out of the way of her husband: "Lakshmi had responded to his devotion by providing him with a smoothly run household where the quarrelling voices of servants or the crying of children had seldom been heard. Her children and servants adored her" (73). Sahgal thus makes clear that this is a gendered expectation, placed upon women, who are judged by their ability to manage their households perfectly in order to gain social and familial approval.[20]

At the same time, Sahgal shows, all housewives in this context are not equally benign. The narrator describes his aunt, an imperious matriarch, as follows:

> With Rohan Masi, money was either saved or wasted. . . . Though extremely well off herself, she had never employed a personal maid. She had no use for the feminine vanities a maid would cater to. Her one luxury, if he could be called this, was her servant, Ramdin, an ill-starred individual whose sole purpose in life, it appeared, was to carry her pändän wherever she went. It was his job to replenish it regularly with fresh pän leaves wrapped in a damp cloth, finely chopped areka nut, cardamoms, and tobacco. He was invariably summoned by the irate cry of "*Arë kambakht*! Hast thou died in thy sleep?" As a youngster, I thought his name was *Arë kambakht*. (51)

Interestingly, this lady reveals a gendered scorn for the female servant (considered lower in status than a male counterpart), who, like an English lady's maid, might attend to "feminine vanities" of dress or adornment. Refusing such luxury, she demands, however, another kind of service of a male attendant, who must pander to a different luxury, the regular availability of pän. The word *kambakht* in Urdu/ Hindi literally means "less blessed," "unfortunate," or "wretched"; idiomatically the epithet translates as "Hey, idiot" or "Hey, misbegotten one". The fact that the narrator, as a child, actually thought that the servant's name was "*Arë kambakht*" thus offers a humorous but telling critique of the routine dehumanization and verbal abuse suffered by this male servant who was never blessed by the use of his actual name, and was in fact *rendered* wretched by the mistreatment he received from this high-class woman. Sahgal's gentle satire makes fun, not of the servant, but of the female employer who mistreats him.[21] Sahgal and Markandaya's work offers such occasional moments of critique of servitude as a system.

It is not until her fourth novel, however, that Sahgal offers, in a pivotal moment, a powerful structural assessment and critique of the position of upper-class women in relation to their servants, highlighting both similarities and differences. *The Day in Shadow* (1971) addresses the profoundly unjust divorce settlement that Simrit, a writer and an upper-class Hindu woman, is entrapped in by her ex-husband and the Indian legal system, and the development of her more positive relationship with Raj, a progressive Indian Christian politician who tries to help her release herself from her socialized acquiescence to the strangleholds of marriage, religion, and patriarchy. At a key moment in her unhappy marriage, Simrit breaks down at a dinner party hosted by her husband, after she becomes aware of a bearer, a male servant, as she presides elegantly at the head of the table:

> At the corner of her vision a dark shape hovered, not clearly visible in the mirror, neither quite stationery nor quite mobile, which she identified when

it came forward as the bearer. Forwards and backwards he moved, like a dark moth with a rhythm but no life of its own. A moth on a string pulled by the food on their plates. She turned in spite of herself to look full at him, to invest him if she could with personality, and at once he was at her elbow, waiting courteously for her command. What have I done for him, she thought aghast, that he should have to do this for me, days without number as long as he can work? (86)

At first the human being who is serving her is literally in the background, a "dark shape," an "it," not quite human, ungendered, as if undifferentiated from the furniture. When she becomes aware of him, he seems again "dark," both in a racialized, negative sense of being literally darker-skinned (associated with being lower-class and -caste), and figuratively as one on whom light (attention, blessing) does not fall. He is, in every sense, in the shadows, not the limelight. Like her, she realizes, he is an automaton, there to serve others, a "moth" without agency drawn to a flame, a puppet "on a string pulled" by the needs and demands of others.

It is significant that Simrit is looking at herself in the mirror when she becomes aware of this figure, on the literal peripheries of her vision. In fiction, occasions when a character looks at herself in a mirror are loaded with signification, often catalyzing crises of identity, of self-recognition and cognitive dissonance. The character sees not just herself, an image, in the Lacanian sense, but experiences the dissonance between the inner self as experienced from within and the self as seen from without by others, as carrying different (gendered, classed racialized) meanings ascribed to her by social contexts, and begins to see herself dually, as at once inner self and as something located in a world frequently at odds with that inner self.[22] Right before this moment, we are told, "she presided meticulously," dutifully, over that table, from where "she could see herself doing her unblemished hostessing in the mirror opposite with her queerly static face reflected in it" (86). What Simrit sees at first is herself, as she is seen, as if she almost cannot recognize herself, as if she is separated from the self she sees enacting the role of the perfect wife and hostess, as if there is a mismatch between her interiority and the reflection in the mirror. Yet the non-normativity of the "queerly static face" also suggests that her own inner dissonance and unhappiness are reflected in the face she sees in the mirror. It is a moment of awakening, of coming to self-awareness, of realization of the charade she has been enacting as a hostess and as a wife.

It is then that she becomes aware of the bearer. In this weirdly dual moment of doubling, he becomes both a reflection of herself, an other self, a queer double, a secret sharer, *with* whom she experiences affinity, and *for* whom, perhaps for the first time, she experiences a sudden empathy. It is Sahgal's stark insight here that even the upper-class woman becomes, in the traditional structure of a patriarchal Hindu marital framework, comparable to a domestic servant, there to serve the demands of her husband, paid in kind with a certain prestige and status, but likewise expected to deny her own selfhood and needs, to sacrifice her personhood. And, in the case of Simrit, she has to subordinate her ethical instincts in order to promote her husband's wants and desires. This is the structural similarity between domestic servant and female mistress to which Sahgal calls attention through this scene of doubling. It is important that Simrit resists that subordination as she turns to look deliberately at the bearer, to try to "invest him *if she could* with personality," to refuse to cast him any more as a nonentity, and ironic that her violation of social norms elicits from him only a misrecognition, a reaffirmation of his servanthood as he misreads her attention as a call for further service.

In this comparison, Sahgal is careful not to suggest an equivalence, only a similarity. For Simrit is still an upper-class woman with power over the bearer, who evokes in her now a terrible remorse, and awareness of structural exploitation, as she wonders, with both identification and disidentification, how she could have elicited from him such subordination. "What have I done for him, she thought aghast, that he should have to do this for me, days without number as long as he can work?" (86). In this climactic moment, she recognizes herself as both likewise oppressed (as wife), analogously acted upon by a system to which she has succumbed, to work till the end of her days on earth, *and* as oppressor (as employer), beneficiary of the system of servitude that places her in a position of command over him. The scene ends with Simrit in tears, literally unable to see, her outer vision destroyed as she is swamped by what she has just seen: "Her image in the mirror was all blurred by that time" (86). Her weeping subsequently shatters the charade she has been forced to enact, as well as the party, as she is retreats to her room, in a turn that leads to the end of her marriage. In this stunning and critical scene, it is important to note that the unnamed servant is not a primary or even secondary character; he has no agency or control over bringing the protagonist to her recognition. But he becomes the potent catalyst, the "dark" figure that precipitates that recognition and subsequent shift in her self-awareness and actions. He remains symbolically potent, enabling Sahgal to make a powerful series of points about class, gender oppression, marriage, and self-realization. Sahgal however does not enter into his consciousness or experience; he is not her focus, Simrit is.

Servants in this novel thus serve, in relation to the upper-class woman, as a measure of her, of her awareness of others and of the degree to which she herself becomes a "cog in the machine" in a "situation . . . with which it was impossible [for her] to live" (38). Simrit's unusually disenfranchised wifehood is highlighted by the way her husband, Som, shows his disrespect for her, mediated through their servants. Earlier, we are told, Som overrules her even within her domain of servant supervision, disallowing her control in the household, undermining her authority, and thus diminishing her position overall. She has not been allowed to make up her own mind about anything, from "marriage" to "children," she thinks, "not even about chair covers and curtains. Even there Som had had a veto. Not even about the servants. She had dismissed the cook twice for drunkenness and bad behavior and Som had kept him on" (38).

In Sahgal's early novels, women and wifehood are defined through the complex relations of upper-class women to their servants. In *This Time of Morning* (1965), her second novel, Sahgal actual coins a new term—the neologism "servantless"—to describe a new generation of post-Independence Indian diplomats' wives who have to live abroad without servants, as if these women lack a body part: "Their wives spoke a smattering of several languages and had had babies and learned to keep house, *servantless*, all over the world.... The diplomatic corps was a nationality of its own" (5, emphasis added). To be without servants, for upper-class Indian women, Sahgal implies, is to be practically unwomanned, to face new challenges not faced in their own country, to become perforce a new "nationality," so integral to the constitution of the middle to upper classes in South Asia is the possession and availability of servants.

However, despite all these nuances, and the centrality of servants to an understanding of domesticity, for none of these pioneering Indian woman writers of the 1950s and 1960s are servants of interest in their own right. At best, servants are present as necessary appendages, accessories to their main subject, pertinent to the exploration of upper-class women's subjectivities and gendered constraints in mid-twentieth-century India. At worst, for other mid-century women writers, as well as for male writers like Chaudhuri and Ahmed Ali, servants are often cast as an encumbrance for those they serve, subjected to stereotype and denigration, a means by which to measure the difference of the upper class from the lower, and upon whom are projected the anxieties and fears of a rising middle class. Nor do any of these writers offer any imagined way out of servitude. It is therefore a powerful departure when later South Asian writers like Mueenuddin, Adiga, and Umrigar focus on servants as central characters or protagonists, and explore servitude as a subject of interest in itself.

The Exceptions: Attia Hosain and Anita Desai

I want to conclude this chapter with a brief discussion of servitude in the work of two of the most well known of Indian women writers of this period, Anita Desai and Attia Hosain, both of whom reveal some anomalies or departures from the patterns that emerge among the writers discussed above. Compared to Futehally, Markandaya, and Sahgal, Desai's contemporaneous work reveals a surprising negativity toward domestic servants, even as it stresses their necessity to the bourgeois Indian home. What it shows, perhaps, is that even though women writers pay more attention to servants in their fiction, they do not all do so with equal sympathy or empathy. Attia Hosian, by contrast, gives servants more importance than do any of her peers, though with significant limitations.

Desai's first novel, *Cry, The Peacock* (1963), explores the gradual descent into mental illness of Maya, a young middle-class Hindu woman whose wealthy but emotionally distant husband is unable to understand or care for her. Surrounded by numerous nameless servants, of whom she is dimly aware, Maya repeatedly bemoans her "loneliness," as if the humans who serve her are incapable of relieving her desire for human company (14, 24, 28). The novel opens with Maya weeping hysterically over the rotting corpse of her pet dog, while the gardener refuses to bury the animal as she demands, shunting that task to the sweeper, lower in the chain, and "sen[ding] his wife to take [Maya] into the house and keep her there" (7). With this beginning, the novel establishes the constant presence of a retinue of servants, and their complex hierarchies and gendered divisions of labor, even as they all work to take care of Maya. Told alternately by Maya in the first person and by a third-person omniscient narrator who sometimes filters Maya's consciousness, the novel presents Maya as an idle, inactive member of the household, a passive recipient of work done by others. "The tea-tray had been brought to the table beside her, neatly decked with the grandmotherly silver tea-pot, the biscuit tin and the sliced lemon, and the curtains had been drawn as the sun had gone down" (8). The passive voice effectually absents the labor, not specifying how this housework is done, or by whom. The precision, the attention to detail, suggests the work that is completed to fastidious specification, yet the mistress remains oblivious to the doers of that work, not even acknowledging them in her sentence structure: "The verandah chairs had been taken out on the lawn for us, two large, comfortable cane chairs, rather battered, rather old, and we sat down, as we did each evening, to glasses of fresh lemonade" (16).

Desai thus presents the myopic self-absorption of a certain privileged class that takes for granted the service it demands of invisible others. She describes how upper-class characters see their servants—as noisy, dirty, unsightly, burdensome, best kept out of sight. With the typical desire to maintain class distinction, for instance, Maya's father forbids her older brother from playing "with the servants or their children," convinced that he is too good to them: "what was his money spent on if not on the feeding and rearing of the many servants and their impossible families who lived in the quarters behind the trees?" (116). Likewise, adult Maya recalls how "a row of papaya trees... hid the servants' quarters from view" but "did not shut out the sound of their voices, or of the small drum someone was thumping, or the chant of 'Radha-Krishna, Radha-Krishna'" (26). Such descriptions indicate the desirability of removing servants from view, linking them stereotypically with noise, and an alien, mindless religiosity. While these attitudes are ascribed to not very admirable upper-class characters, Desai's narrative does not challenge them or offer a corrective, to render them suspect or to signal such prejudice as unwarranted.

Indeed, Desai's own mode of representation and her plot construction participate in and reinforce these attitudes and negative stereotypes about servants. Maya's neuroses originate, or have been exacerbated, Desai suggests, by a visit Maya undertook as a young child with her ayah to an astrologer who predicted an early death "by unnatural causes" soon after her marriage (30). Maya's father consequently throws out the ayah, "the foolish woman" whom he blames for infecting his motherless child with her ignorant superstitions, and threatens both the servant woman and the "charlatan" astrologer with prison (36). But, the novel suggests, irrevocable harm has already been done by the servant woman; Maya can never recover from the dire prophecy she has heard. The novel ends with Maya making the deranged choice to fulfill the prophecy by killing her husband in order to save herself from the prophesied death. Problematically, Desai renders servants here as not only unpleasant but also dangerous. A vulnerable child's proximity to servants does long-lasting harm, to her, to her marriage, and eventually to the man she murders.

Anita Desai's representations of servants show some notable developments over the course of her work. Her prize-winning later novel *Fire on the Mountain* (1977) explores the reclusive psyche of an aging widow, Nanda Kaul, who has chosen to retreat from family obligations to live alone in the foothills of the Himalayas, in a solitary house perched on a barren ridge above a hill-station. Although the novel focuses on Nanda's desire for solitude and her mixed reactions to the unexpected arrival of her great-granddaughter, it gives unusual narrative space to her male servant, Ram Lal, on whose services she depends for her daily existence. Desai emphasizes how despite, or precisely because of, her isolation, Nanda depends heavily on the full-time live-in cook who does all the housework and serves single-handedly as bearer, guard, messenger, and, eventually, childcare provider for her great-grandchild. At the same time, Desai presents him, via Nanda Kaul's perspective as well as her own narration, with a surprising degree of antipathy, even casual disgust, as a stereotypically volatile, grumpy old man, callous to animals, and prone to tell tall tales to frighten and control children. (By contrast, as I will show in Chapter 7, Anita Desai's daughter Kiran Desai's Booker Prize–winning *The Inheritance of Loss*, set in a similar Himalayan hill-station, seems to revise her mother's novel, and instead alternates the perspectives of the cook and the unwelcome granddaughter of the equally reclusive, retired judge, rendering them both far more sympathetically.)

In *Fire on a Mountain*, we first meet Ram Lal as he puffs up a hill with a bag of groceries, wearing tennis shoes a size too big for him. He is described as a little ridiculous, taciturn, "stiff," and "dour," grunting at and not offering not "much company" to the old postman who must also make the steep climb (11). The narrative shifts then to Nanda Kaul's perspective, who is literally and figuratively looking down on both the "bent-backed" lower-class men as "they toiled up the steep path [to her], stones slipping from under their feet, in a way that wildly irritated Nanda Kaul . . ., for she always made a point of keeping her back straight as a rod" (11). This scornful sense of superiority is the first thing we hear about how Nanda feels about her servant. The moment becomes emblematic: Nanda irritated judgment, based on her view from up high, is oblivious to her own privilege (she can keep her back straight because she literally does not have to carry burdens for others). But Desai does not counter with the cook's view of his mistress. Soon after, Nanda's perspective is complemented by the narrator's own more negative description of Ram Lal as he scatters the chickens crowding around him: "he started flinging chopped vegetable heads at them, each one accompanied by a word of filthy abuse" (12). Thus, while Desai presents the cook with more attentive detail than do previous writers, she does so with a remarkable absence of sympathy or concern for his interiority or humanity; he is shown as seen from the outside, and linked with dirt and latent violence.

Undoubtedly, Desai presents Nanda Kaul as disdainful, elite, exhausted by a life spent as wife and mother, resentful of intrusion, full of distaste not only for servants, but for all human company. But the narrator's own mode of representation shows a relative alignment with her protagonist's attitude to servants. In a telling passage, Desai describes Nanda Kaul's memory of her past, when she ran a large household:

> There had been too many servants in the long long row of whitewashed huts behind the kitchen, so that the drains choked and overflowed, and the nights were loud with the sounds of festive drumming, of drunken singing and brawling, of bathing and washing and wailing children. (29)

Again, for Nanda, servants represent noise, excess, dirt, civic irresponsibility (the servant's families choke the drains with excrement and improper rubbish disposal), uncontrolled reproduction, and sexuality. To be fair, the Nanda's memory-list includes "too many guests coming and going," too "many rooms full of guests," "too many trays of tea" "meals," "dishes on the table," and "shortage of privacy" (29). But her disgust is most intense for the servants. When she remembers the "slovenly neurotic ayahs she had had to have because there was such a deal of washing and ironing to do and Mr. Kaul had wanted her always in silk," she resents the husband's demands that required her to perform upper-class wifehood, but it is the fellow women, the ayahs, whom she resents more, and whom she sees as "slovenly," as a burden imposed on *her* even when *they* retrieved her of the burdens of physical housework and childcare (18). Desai seems to endorse her character's attitudes when she casts the ayah as feeding Nanda Kaul's child "opium at night, under her fingernails," and reinforces the upper-class view of the unreliable and dirty servant who betrays the trust placed in her by doping her vulnerable charge to keep him quiet (34).

Desai does complicate Ram Lal, as she presents an unacknowledged mutuality between him and Nanda Kaul. When she receives her daughter's letter informing her that the child is being sent to her, "in distress and agitation," Nanda goes to the kitchen to tell Ram Lal, ostensibly to tell him to prepare, but in fact to seek some comfort and reassurance (31). Ram Lal knows her, he can sense her distress, the change in the atmosphere: "she spoke to him with a nervousness that alarmed him as a thunderstorm in the air might have alarmed him" (31). This is the closest we get to his perspective in this novel, one of the few times we get a glimpse of how he sees his mistress. Desai's language suggests both his percipience and Nanda's power: he needs to be able to read her, to calibrate the emotional changes that transform the conditions of the environment he inhabits. But Desai still casts him as unable to provide that requisite human support, even as he listens and nods, "trying to sound to reassuring, but failing" (31). He cannot rise to the level of providing comfort; a lifetime of servitude has rendered him incapable of responding to her distress, even as he recognizes it.

Desai shows perceptively, however, how he must negotiate the delicate micropolitics of server and served. He knows how to maintain Nanda Kaul's upper-class status. When she asks him what he will cook for the child, he enacts servitude, deferring to her, "his eyes downcast" (32). His sudden inspiration, "All children like potato chips!" prefigures the difference between them that will later become clearer: he understands and will connect with the child better than Nanda Kaul will. But, as if to undercut this suggestion of elevation, and repudiate the momentary link, Desai describes his "bloodshot eyes," suggestive perhaps of drugs, or other indulgence or indiscipline. As he keeps a "wary eye on the Memsahib" when she walks unsteadily back to the house (he needs to, for he would be answerable to her family if she should injure herself), and recognizes a certain affinity, "She is old, I am old. We are old, old," again Desai puts him down: when a hen pokes its head in to his kitchen, he "flung his filthy market-bag at in rage," indicating again his slovenliness, his sudden, unpredictable, uncontrolled shifts of mood, and his latent anger and brutality (33).

Indeed, soon after, when Raka, the great grand-daughter, peeps in on Ram Lal sleeping, Desai describes him as almost animalistic: "In the room next to the kitchen, still smaller but somewhat brightened by the myriad magazine and calendar pictures stuck to the smoky walls, Ram Lal lay on his string cot, his limbs flung out to its four corners, his cap on his nose, lifting and falling with the low growls and sudden snorts that came and went beneath it" (42). Even as the details indicate the impoverishment of a servant, the minimal furnishings, the lack of luxury, they also suggest his bad taste and association with mass culture, the garish pictures from pulp magazines, his noisy abandonment in sleep, rendering him almost porcine. Even when he is humanized (he connects with Raka, providing a companionship that Nanda Kaul envies him; 76–79), he is undercut, cast as the stereotypical servant (similar to colonial servants in Kipling's Indian fiction) who spreads superstition and fear, telling exaggerated stories of danger, warning of jackals and ghosts to restrain the child's solitary wandering (44).

In the last scenes in which he appears, Desai's depictions of Ram Lal emblematize both her ambivalence and awareness of the importance of servitude. Toward the end, Nanda Kaul is obligated to invite an old friend to tea. The chapter opens with this highly crafted description, as of a stage set for a play:

> Tea was laid on the veranda table. On circles and hollows of china, it lay perspiring under cloths weighed down with embroidery and with beads. The thwarted flies buzzed in dismay, nuzzled the fine cloth for a spot of jam, a flake of cake. (107)

Again, Desai absents the labor that makes this tea-table possible. Even the food is more animate, and the flies more notable, than the servant whose work and existence are indicated at best through the passive voice ("tea was laid"). Ram Lal is present, off-stage but adjacent to the scene, "squatting outside the kitchen door," "watching the path" that would bring the awaited guest (107). Like Nanda Kaul and Raka, who are also waiting—for their tea—he serves as a shadowy counterpart, in every sense, the underside to their story, making it possible.

When the guest finally arrives, he materializes, rushing on-stage to fulfill his duties:

> *In the background*, Ram Lal hovered, waving away flies, putting down tea pot and milk jug, whisking away beaded nets to reveal the fruit of his day's unusual labor. It was not every day they invited someone to tea. (115; my emphasis)

Strikingly, here the servant is actually noted as existing "in the background," as part of the tableau. He is there as part of a performance, to perform the labor that is required of him by his employers, which is both to serve and to impress the visitors. In this almost self-reflexive moment, the text highlights how in it the servant also performs literary labor for the construction of the bourgeois domestic scene. What he does for the ladies within the text is what he does for the text itself: he enables Desai to present and construct the (self-constituted) social elite. Desai's text makes clear that he does what he does for the benefit of the guests and the hosts, to establish for each who they are, so that they can enact their roles as upper class, as not dirtied by domestic labor. His labor on this occasion is "unusual" not because it is domestic labor—for he performs his usual tasks as servant every day—but because drama is added to it, for the edification of a guest, as he almost magically whisks away the nets to reveal the snacks he has prepared for their consumption, and magically whisks into place the set upon which they can enact their roles as civilized Westernized subjects, as ladies of leisure.

That they are all playing roles they have been taught becomes even clearer when the tea-party ends, and Ram Lal returns to clear the table he has set. The old ladies silence themselves when he appears, stopping the conversation they are having about the difficulties of social work. They have been trying to persuade lower-class men living nearby to stop child marriage:

> Now he busied himself, taking off the fly-specked nets, piling the crockery on a wooden tray, shaking out the folds of the aged tablecloth that cracked with stiffness, while the old ladies discussed the weather in his presence, as they had been taught to do. (130)

For all their dependence and need, the women know that a male servant represents the threat of lower-class male sexuality, and that they must maintain the illusion of distance and stiff formality that would ensure their safety and distinction from the servant whose proximity must be thus contained. Aware of the decline of the Anglicized Indian elite, they remember the more stringent practices of their pre-Independence childhoods, when their parents maintained this distance through the symbolic and real practices of distinction.[23] "Their servants wore white cotton gloves" (as if their physical touch would pollute) and uniforms, and "a skirted nanny" timed the ayah who took the baby for a walk in its perambulator (11). Anita Desai calls attention to the details of the effort, the labor involved (for employers as well as servants) in this maintenance of domesticity, which also requires the maintenance of requisite distance, the refusal and disavowal of intimacy. In its unexpected and gruesome conclusion, the novel reaffirms this notion of the lower-class male as threat, when a villager rapes and kills Nanda Kaul's friend as she walks home from the tea party.

By contrast, Attia Hosain takes a very different tack. It is ironic that in her 1988 introduction to the Virago re-issue of Hosain's 1953 short story collection *Phoenix Fled*, Anita Desai praises Hosain for her empathetic attention to servants, a kind of attention absent in Desai's own fiction:

> Her greatest strength lies in her ability to draw a rich, full portrait of her society—ignoring none of its many faults and cruelties, and capable of including not only men and women of immense power and privilege but, to an *equal* extent, the poor who labored as their servants. Perhaps the most attractive aspect

of her writing is the tenderness she shows for those who served her family, an empathy for a class not her own.²⁴

Hailing from a powerful and wealthy aristocratic *taluqdar* Indian Muslim family, educated in Lucknow's elite English schools, Attia Hosain moved after marriage to England, where she lived, after the 1947 Partition, for the rest of her life, and where, from a transnational diasporic perspective, she looked back at the past life on which she based her short stories (collected in *Phoenix Fled*, 1953) and her 1961 novel, *Sunlight on a Broken Column*.²⁵ Retrospectively evoking a lost feudal pre-Partition world, her fiction does indeed pay unusual attention to servants and servitude, though not, I would argue, to as "equal" an extent as Desai claims.

Six of the twelve stories in *Phoenix Fled* are centrally concerned with servitude, with servants as central protagonists. Together they present a range of figures, male and female, child and adult, young and old, Hindu and Muslim. Hosain is, I would argue, the first writer of South Asian English fiction to place servants at the center of her narratives, and to pay detailed attention to servant consciousness and to intra-servant as well as servant-employer relations.²⁶ Set within the domestic space and boundaries of various South Asian homes, her stories are the first to focus on relations of dependency and intimacy across class between *women*, both serving and served. Attia Hosain thus becomes a bridge figure for my argument in this book. She both fits and does not fit in this chapter. Though writing in the 1950s and 1960s, Hosain created a mode of writing about servitude that was well ahead of the work of her male and female contemporaries, and that connects her more surprisingly with the transnational writers (Rushdie and more recent transnational millennials) I discuss in Chapter 2.

With its textured understanding and analysis of classed and gendered relations of unequal power in contexts of intimacy and domesticity, and with its focus on servants as fictive subjects in their own right, Hosain's pioneering exploration of servitude makes a significant departure from and intervention in the modes of representation of servitude in contemporaneous Anglophone South Asian literature discussed so far in this chapter. Many scholars have paid attention to Hosain's novel, but her short stories remain relatively neglected. Reading Hosain's short stories and novel together reveals interconnections and continuities as well as important shifts over time as her evocations of servitude evolve from sympathetic though self-consciously partial representation in the stories to fuller political critique in the novel. I would argue that while the form of the short story enables Hosain to foreground the individual servant and servant subjectivity, the form of the (bourgeois) novel allows for a more historicized, continuous, and interwoven account of a greater social matrix and a greater diversity of servant characters in comparison and interaction with one another as well as with members of higher classes.²⁷

In her stories, Hosain breaks new ground and extends her imaginative and empathetic reach to those ordinarily overlooked even in twenty-first-century fiction. But her servant stories also reveal some inevitable limitations in their representations of servants and their subjectivities. None of the stories is told from the point of view of a servant or narrated from a servant's purported voice. The servant stories in *Phoenix Fled* center on servants as subjects, but remain locked within the subjectivity or point of view of upper-class narrators who seem to recognize their inevitable distance from their servants. Those that deploy first-person character narrators provide no access to the interiority of the servant characters that become not the subjects, but the objects of the story's interest. Instead, Hosain's stories draw attention, through modernist techniques, to the limitations and partiality of often fallible upper-class narrators. Those that use a third-person omniscient narrator offer intermittent access to the interiority of servant characters, but still remain limited to the distanced, occasionally distanced point of view of an upper class that finds its servants ultimately remote and unreadable. To elucidate, though I cannot elaborate more fully here, I offer below a brief example of each.

In a story titled "The Loss," Hosain uses a male upper-class first-person narrator, who describes how he is awakened one night by an old woman servant distraught because she has been robbed of her life savings. The story begins by suggesting the alienation and attachment that coexist for this employer regarding the old woman, "the ugliness of [whose] face suspended above [him]," and whose "misshapen quivering mouth" and "tortured eyes" at first terrify him when he is jolted out of sleep (117). But, he insists, as he recovers consciousness, that in this "face, familiar to my mind and heart, of the woman whose heavy breasts had nourished me, whose rough hands had tended me, there was no ugliness" (117). She was his wet nurse when he was an infant, and is now his dependent: he has provided her with a permanent home in his household. He calls her "Amma" (mother), his children call her "Granny"; she addresses him as her "child" and is "privileged to correct" him, to scold and lord it over new servants (125). Her distress at the loss of her steel money-box so upsets him that he pressures a friend in the police to spare no efforts to find the thief. "Her grief obsessed me," he says, as he "remembered the warm shelter of her love in all childhood sorrows" (119). Though he sees her as "a simple peasant woman" who failed to follow his advice that she entrust her valuables to a bank, he takes responsibility for her ignorance (120). "Her simplicity shamed me," he reports (120), explaining how as a young widow, she had been brought from his ancestral village to serve as his "foster-mother" while her own son, Chand, had been taken "from her breast and fed on cow's milk" (123). The story thus speaks to the complex bonds of guilt, obligation, and attachment, across differences of power, class, and gender, as it locates those bonds in lifelong histories of service, interaction, and cohabitation, and what Ray and Qayum call a "feudal imaginary" (8).

The story elucidates, however, less the interiority, psyche, thoughts, or feelings of the unnamed old servant woman, and more of the narrator, focusing on *his* discoveries and realizations, as he gradually comes to understand her better. At first, he is astonished that, despite his guaranteed lifetime provision for her, she cares so much about the loss of savings that she will not need for herself. Her priorities and desires are made clear, however, through reported dialogue. These savings were for her son's future, she insists: "Everything I have saved, every pice. All my jewellery, too, and gold I had put aside for Chand's wife when he marries" (120). But the focus remains on *his* astonishment as he discovers how much money she has saved, and its significance, "I saw her poverty and self-denial with intense clarity in the light of her lost savings" (122). When he reports her crying "Who am I? I am a beggar at the mercy of the lowest" (125), we glimpse her feelings, but the narrative reports his reflections: "I saw it now, clearly. It had not been enough, the abstraction of love and respect; it had not made poverty and hard work bearable. The power had been in the little box under the bed. The money and gold had brought her no visible comfort, but were an assurance of it. The rich foundation was gone, and her poor life crumbled" (125). This is a nuanced and important realization, important to relay to upper-class readers who may hence begin to understand those who serve them as more complexly human than they had perhaps assumed. But the emphasis of the story is on what the upper-class narrator learns about the servant, on his underestimation of her complexity.

The story turns, moreover, not on his discovery that the thief is actually Chand, the old woman's son, but on the employer-narrator's surprise upon discovering that to her, the loss of her life savings is worth less than the loss of honor that would ensue if it became known that her son was the culprit. "If my son were to steal from me I would that he were dead, and I with him," she declares (133). The title refers then not only to the "loss" of the money-box, but also to the loss of her son and her son's honor, both more precious to her. Throughout these stories, Hosain emphasizes servants' concern for their honor or reputation, which often surprises their employers, and which is understandable precisely because of the servants' precarity: their reputation matters to them because they materially have so little, because they are so deprived of dignity, and because, due to their physical access to the employer's household, they are the first to be suspected of theft and dishonesty and threatened with police violence. "The Loss" grants unusual complexity and agency to this old woman servant, in that the narrator respects her reasons and listens to her instruction to stop the investigation: "I felt thrust aside. My decision was made" (133). The story gives us strong glimpses of the servant woman's interiority. Not only does it affirm that she has one, but

Hosain also suggests the difficulty of knowing or understanding the woman's interiority from the point of view of the upper-class narrator, at the same time that Hosain emphasizes the importance of trying to understand it. But, despite the remarkable attentiveness and psychological complexity she awards in this story to the elderly woman servant, Hosain maintains the focus on the narrator who learns more about the unnamed woman he thinks he has known all his life. She does not offer readers more direct access into the subjectivity of the woman herself. In fact, Hosain does something in-between with the first-person narration. She creates a dual focus: both on the male narrator who tries to understand the ayah, and on the servant as not quite understood by him. And, with some self-contradiction, in making the servant woman's son the thief, Hosain also confirms the stereotype of the lower-class male's dishonesty and untrustworthiness.

In a gender crossover, in "The Street of the Moon," Hosain uses third-person omniscient narration to present the thoughts and feelings of a middle-aged male cook, in a voice that suggests the simultaneously sympathetic and yet somewhat condescending perspective of a female upper-class employer. The story begins: "Kalloo the cook had worked for the family for as long as he could remember. He had started as the cook's help, washing dishes, grinding the spices and running errands" (24). This narrative voice seems sympathetic, giving us an entry into Kalloo's consciousness, what he could remember, detailing his lifetime of labor from childhood onward, the restrictiveness of his life. It hints at the implicit racism or colorism to which Kalloo has been subject from childhood. Kalloo is a diminutive epithet, not a proper name, which means "the black" or "dark-skinned one," or perhaps the one who is blackened by working in the kitchen). But then it continues:

> When the old cook died of an overdose of opium Kalloo inherited both the job and his taste for opium. His inherent laziness fed by the enervating influence of the drug kept him working for his inadequate pay, because he lacked the energy and the courage to give notice and look for work elsewhere. Moreover, his emotions had grown roots through the years, and he was emotionally attached to the family. (24)

The story suggests the exploitativeness of the system that has positioned Kalloo as a servant—the low pay, the lack of training or opportunity to seek alternatives—and habituated him not to seek redress. But the wording ("his inherent laziness," he "lacked courage") also suggest that this is partly Kalloo's own fault, for he is too innately lazy and self-drugged to seek betterment. Like the cook before him, he takes opium—perhaps, this narrative voice implies, servants take drugs to numb themselves to the harshness and tedium of their lives, or alternatively, perhaps because that is who they are, that is what servants do.

Hosain's omniscient narrator's external perspective thus both evokes sympathy and contributes to the confirmation of upper-class biases against servants as a class, and against male servants in particular. This choice of technique reveals a certain ambivalence, as this narrative voice alternates between a sympathetic focus on Kalloo's thoughts and feelings, and a tendency to make distancing judgmental comments or putdowns that undercut the understanding that the sympathetic focus generates. Kalloo's opium habits lead him to sexual depravity, to seek out prostitutes at the eponymous "Street of the Moon." In order to curtail this behavior, an old woman servant arranges his marriage with the beautiful young daughter of another servant woman in the household, while commenting, "You men, you are all animals, even when your feet hang in the grave" (25). The story details, in the end, Kalloo's disillusionment as his young wife leaves him to become a prostitute. Hosain thus indirectly gestures at the girl's agency and desires, but does not explore her consciousness or the process by which she makes such a decision. The third-person narrator provides brief glimpses into both servants' interiority, complexifying them in new ways while also partially reaffirming negative stereotypes about servant sexuality and unreliability.

By contrast, Hosain's novel *Sunlight*, though told entirely from the point of view of Laila, its upper-class narrator-protagonist, includes detailed evocations of a diverse servants' lives, voices, and perspectives, and gives a new kind of sympathy and importance to Nandi, the servant girl who breaks the rules, talks back to power, and serves as both a double and model for the initially more timid Laila. In a powerful early scene, for example, Laila becomes witness both to the sexual exploitation of female servants, and to the possibilities of female resistance within a patriarchal system that entraps her as well. Within the feudal household, Nandi is publicly shamed and accused of sexual promiscuity because she has been seen talking to a servant boy. Laila's uncle Mohsin, delegated to enact the patriarch, tries to discredit Nandi's attempt at self-defense, "This slut of a girl is a liar, a wanton" (28). In response, Nandi turns the tables on him, breaking her silence to reveal that in fact he is a hypocrite, a sexual predator who has tried to molest her:

> Nandi looked up with fear-crazed eyes, looked around at that cruelly silent, staring ring of trappers and cried out: "A slut? A wanton? And who are you to say it who would have made me one had I let you?" (28)

As young girls, both and Nandi and Laila are punished: Nandi is sent away, and Laila made to apologize for trying to defend Nandi. But Hosain, with an intersectional understanding of gender and class, makes clear both her critique of the purdah system that thus enables violation and violence, and the importance of the courage and agency that Nandi exemplifies, precisely from her multiply disadvantaged position. As the novel develops, Nandi, though not the central protagonist, grows into a much stronger figure, rendered with depth and nuance, more complex than the servant women in Hosain's earlier short stories, and stronger even than Laila. Nandi educates Laila, and looks after her at a time of crisis when Laila's family members abandon her. More importantly, Nandi stands up repeatedly against injustice and oppression, not only for herself but for other women. In many ways she is more of a feminist than Laila. Nandi finally defies the system to carve out a life of her own, against the rules of her society.

To conclude: as we have seen in this chapter, without exception, both male and female Indian writers from the 1930s to 1970s seem impelled to call upon servants—as minor figures, or generic references, with none or very little character space—in their fiction. None, with the exception of Attia Hosain, attempt to evoke the servants' individuality or interiority to any extended degree or to make servants central to their work. While most are focused on the position and subjectivities of men and women of middle and upper classes, others, like Anand and Markandaya, focus on the lowest of the low in their societies—respectively, those of the lowest caste, or displaced peasants victimized by both feudalism and colonialist capitalism—to whom they give their fuller sympathy. Servants fall in between these extremes, and yet prove useful, even necessary, to highlight and define those both above and below them. In nearly all these writers' work, the servant figure remains instrumental, functional, there to establish the status or critique the indulgences of Indian bourgeois or elite classes, each defined by the number of their servants and the duration of their employment. For many of these writers, even the instrumentality of their servants is very limited. These servants are rarely even to be learned from, as is the case with some later writers like Bapsi Sidhwa and Khaled Hosseini.[28]

But important gender differences emerge in the ways early Indian writers use servants in their fiction. The early writings of male writers (Narayan, Chaudhuri, Rao, Anand, Ali) use servants and servitude to establish or occasionally critique the upper class or the effects of colonial rule.[29] Some reinforce stereotypes of dirt and sexual promiscuity associated with servants. Anand's work is unusual, but still remains self-contradictory and limited in its approach to class and servitude. These male writers also show very little interest in women servants and the complexities of gender dynamics. Women writers, by contrast, though by no means exempt from such prejudices, tend to be more nuanced, attentive, and sympathetic, particularly toward women servants. They explore relations between women, and emphasize the importance of servitude to domesticity and upper-class women. Many (Futehally, Sahgal, Markandaya, Hosain) draw upon occasion on servants in their narratives for more progressive ends. But as yet, except for Hosain's stories, their fiction is not focused on servitude per se nor invested in a critique of servitude as a system. In gathering these traces of servitude in these early writers, these vanishing marks or rare instances that nonetheless attest to the power of servants' presence, I have had to read against the grain of these texts. Each instance offers, however—from the unselfconscious sideways references, to the anxious self-distancing, to the occasional sympathy to the barely concealed repulsion—powerfully illuminating signs of each writer's priorities, politics, orientations, ideologies, concerns, and commitments, as well as overall patterns and a tradition of representation that subsequent writers both learn and depart from.

2
The Servant('s) Turn, in the Middle Ground
Rushdie and Transnational Writers After Rushdie

In Amitav Ghosh's 2004 novel, *The Hungry Tide*, Piya, the Indian American female protagonist, rejects Kanai, a successful Indian entrepreneur, as a potential love interest because of his "remote" servant-enabled lifestyle: "She tried to think of his life in New Delhi, and she imagined a house filled with employees—a cook, a driver, people to fetch and carry" (276). Here, as in the work of earlier Indian writers, servants still serve to define bourgeois Indian male identity, but now, from the perspective of the egalitarian, progressive, second-generation American environmentalist, Kanai's (assumed) accustomed dependence on servants renders him at once ethically suspect and romantically undesirable. Ghosh thus identifies a new critical sensibility in a millennial generation of diasporic Indian returnees represented by Piya, a shift in political orientation and ideology, a change in attitude with regard to servitude and things Indian. More recently, in Neel Mukherjee's 2017 novel, *A State of Freedom*, another Indian American returnee, controlling his irritation at his driver, reflects, "More than twenty years of life in the academic communities of the East Coast of the USA had defanged him of the easy Indian ability to bark at people considered as servants" (6). Mukherjee likewise presents a shift in consciousness in the returning diasporic South Asian, produced by immersion in a particular progressive sub-culture that enabled seeing—both the self and others—with new eyes, and a new unwillingness to participate in the old normalized, habituated routines of abusiveness toward domestic servants. Mukherjee's metaphoric language emphasizes the violent animality of that erstwhile mode of being that this narrator is aware still sits deep in him, of which he hopes to be "defanged," in order to desist from "barking" at those who serve him.

I explore in this chapter how, in contrast to the writers from the 1930s to 1970s discussed in the previous chapter, a new generation of transnational Anglophone South Asian writers from Salman Rushdie onward takes a more self-aware, critical stance against servitude, even when servitude is not a primary or central concern of their fiction. Energized themselves, like the two characters above, by a new double vision, the insider-outsider perspective of belonging

Postcolonial Servitude. Ambreen Hai, Oxford University Press. © Oxford University Press 2024.
DOI: 10.1093/oso/9780197698006.003.0003

and unbelonging enabled by departure and return, having lived elsewhere and learned to see otherwise, they call attention to and question normalized, routinized forms of domination and subordination across classes in the home.[1] In none of the fiction discussed in this chapter do servants or servitude occupy major status. But these transnational South Asian writers look at servitude from a fresh angle, and give it a new importance, both thematically and formally, in the ways that they structure servitude into their fiction. They move it out of the periphery, or the margins, closer to the center. Revealing, over time, a gradual ideological shift in South Asian fiction, they question, rather than accept, the status quo, and emblematize, through their fiction, the role of the progressive intellectual or educated upper-class subject who challenges, rather than acquiesces to, the system he or she benefits from.

Whereas the writers I discussed in Chapter 1 place servants in the *background*, and the writers of servitude fiction I focus on from Chapter 3 onward place servants in the *foreground*, I argue that the writers I discuss in this chapter place servants in the *middle ground*, and thus form a bridge between the earlier South Asian tradition discussed in Chapter 1 and the innovations of contemporary servitude fiction. I draw upon the language of the visual arts, which define "the three zones of recession in linear perspective," based on proximity to the viewer, as follows: the foreground is "the part of a composition that appears closest to the viewer"; the background the part that appears the "farthest"; and the middle ground "describes the part of a composition between the foreground and background."[2] Undoubtedly, this vocabulary pertains to the static conditions of painting or photography, whereas narrative is more dynamic and fluid, as characters move in and out of positions of importance. Nonetheless, this terminology can help us to recognize the overall degree of importance or space given to particular characters or issues in a narrative. As I show below, Salman Rushdie, Mohsin Hamid, Shyam Selvadurai, and Monica Ali all bring servants forward into the middle ground, with a new, defamiliarizing, critical attentiveness to servitude.

I begin with Salman Rushdie's pathbreaking, most influential early novels (1980s to 1990s), which offer, though subordinated to other concerns, both a critical view of South Asian norms of servitude, and a concomitantly sympathetic but somewhat self-contradictory, ridiculing mode of representation of servants that undercuts Rushdie's progressive moves. Rushdie's work becomes, I argue, a critical turning point in the shift toward the writers that are the focus of this book. I then look closely at three recent, younger writers as examples of millennial fiction (late 1990s to 2000s) that highlights and critiques South Asian servitude from a diasporic insider-outsider perspective, without Rushdie's self-contradictions: Sri Lankan Canadian Shyam Selvadurai's novel *Funny Boy* (1994), Pakistani American Mohsin Hamid's *Moth Smoke* (2000), and

Bangladeshi British Monica Ali's *Brick Lane* (2003). Though none of these three make servitude a central or prominent issue in their fiction, they bring servitude into the middle ground, in illuminatingly different ways. All are contemporaneous with the writers I focus on in this book, and all are similarly attuned to problems of mistreatment and discrimination, which they deploy for different ends. These writers constitute what I would call an intermediate step toward servitude fiction, offering both an advance in the outlook and narrative strategies of the writers discussed in Chapter 1, and a contrast to those discussed in the following chapters.

This is not to imply that all diasporic or millennial writers are necessarily or uniformly politically progressive, or even attentive to servitude. They are not. In fact, many in their fiction, like Kamila Shamsie in her early novels, may reveal a continuing inattentiveness to or acceptance of norms that they do not question.[3] Those whose fiction is set outside South Asia, in Britain or the United States, like Jhumpa Lahiri, barely mention servants at all (except as a feature of homes left behind), itself indicative of the inextricability of South Asian servitude from its particular locations. Servitude is not a preoccupation of diasporic writers who set their fiction outside South Asia.[4] But it is noteworthy that the writers who make servants and servitude a central focus of their work, and who will be the subject of subsequent chapters of this book, are diasporic or transnational returnees, whose work is set in South Asia.[5] All look back, or upon return, with a questioning eye, at an institution that is neither new to them, nor so normalized that they cannot see or challenge it. All seek to promote social justice, highlighting the microdynamics, micropolitics, and structures baked into the domestic spaces of the home, but are interfused with the broader forces that structure the nation and society at large. I begin, in this chapter, with Rushdie, and then turn to the transnational writers who, after Rushdie, pay attention to servitude, though without yet making servants or servitude central to their narratives or narrative concerns. In so doing, I hope to establish, by comparison, both the links and differences between these transnational writers and the writers who foreground servitude as their central concern, and whose novelty thereby becomes more manifest.

Caught in a Strange Middle Ground: Rushdie's Servants

South Asian English writing took a definitive turn with the publication of Salman Rushdie's *Midnight's Children* in 1980. With its broad historical and geographical sweep (stretching from 1914 to 1978, and from India to Pakistan and Bangladesh), and its interest in the challenges of newly decolonized nations, especially the proximity and contrasts between the rich and poor,

THE SERVANT('S) TURN, IN THE MIDDLE GROUND   99

Midnight's Children drew new attention to what Rushdie would later call "intimate strangers," the ubiquitous domestic servants on whom the upper classes depend (*East West*, 178). Its plot hinges on Mary Pereira, the hospital nurse turned ayah who, at the moment of Independence in 1947, switches two babies at birth (the narrator Saleem and his alter-ego Shiva). Mary, often referred to as one of his mothers, hence inaugurates Saleem's life as a middle-class child. She presides over his childhood and, at the end, provides him with both refuge and the key metaphor for his writing: history as pickling, preserving memories of forgotten truths for the "amnesiac nation" to consume (549). Saleem thus appropriates her domestic (and later commercial) labor as the ground for his nationalist labor of rebuilding a damaged nation by retelling history, including forgotten and suppressed truths. Saleem is also paired with Padma, his cook-mistress-audience-critic, who enables (or, when absent, disables) his writing: she "leaks" into him, changing the way he tells his story (38); she provides the "necessary counterweights," the "paradoxical earthiness" without which his narrative is reduced to the "one-dimensionality of a straight line" (177–178). Rushdie therefore repeats, with variations, two common literary servant tropes—the older woman servant as desexualized surrogate mother or nanny (for the employer's child), and the younger one as sexualized and available body (for the male employer)—though both are intermittently highlighted as significant propellants of Saleem's narrative. An old male family servant, Musa, has a key role as well—in his rivalry with the newcomer Mary, he catalyzes the major downward spiral in Saleem's life, occasioning Mary's revelation of her "crime" and of Saleem's true origins—and is likewise drawn with broad outlines, cast at once as somewhat pathetic and absurd (303).

Thus, even though Rushdie gives much more importance to servants than most writers who precede him, bringing servants into the middle ground, and granting them a new kind of space in his narratives, his comic, external narrative standpoint and often condescending mode of representation allows little interiority or fullness for the servant figure who is thereby flattened and othered. Throughout Rushdie's fiction, servants are still subsumed to the self-absorbed upper-class male narrator's story and patronized from his perspective.[6] Rushdie's first four major novels, set primarily in India or Pakistan, reveal a curious ambivalence about servitude. On the one hand, they call attention to the indignities suffered by servants and the consequent resistances induced by South Asian systems of servitude, and, in a fresh approach to servitude, increase the significance of the literary servant and character-space allotted to such figures. On the other hand, simultaneously, Rushdie also diminishes the servant through reductive caricature, comic putdown, inflation or deflation, stereotype, and exaggerated dialogue. A close reading of servants in his early novels, starting with *Midnight's Children*, reveals continuing self-contradictions in Rushdie's writing. While

Rushdie calls attention to servants and the oppressions of servitude, he also reduces, ridicules, and stereotypes servants; while he is attentive to the different conditions that servants endure because of their gender, he himself reinforces those gender stereotypes and power asymmetries in his mode of representation.

Servants, both named and unnamed, are everywhere in *Midnight's Children*, though few literary critics have addressed their significance. From the beginning, Rushdie casts these servants both as warranting attention, and as somewhat ridiculous. Early in the novel, when Aadam Aziz first arrives in the "opulent" house of Ghani the landowner, where he will meet his future wife, he notices that "the servants clearly took advantage" of the blind widower Ghani: dust lay everywhere and rooms revealed "a state of violent disorder" (17). Typically noticing servants through their absence, via work not done, Rushdie stereotypes them as shirking duty in the absence of a supervising mistress. Dr. Aziz next encounters the large, muscular women who serve as bodyguards to Ghani's nubile daughter: one, addressed by Ghani as "ayah," is "a woman with the biceps of a wrestler" whose "sari told him she was a servant; but she was not servile"; two more are "also built like professional wrestlers" (18–19). Unlike his male predecessors, Rushdie asks his readers to notice these figures usually relegated to the background, calling attention to their social position, signaled by their clothing, their unusually assertive manner, and forthright speech. At the same time, he makes fun of them and their supposedly masculine bodies, dubbing them "lady wrestlers" who threaten the masculinity of the young doctor (19), or "earplugged guardians" who intrude on the privacy of the newly affianced couple (25). Nameless and unimportant in themselves, they serve, having moved into the middle ground, to hold up the infamous perforated sheet, and provide the aura of protection and indulgence for the courtship of Saleem's grandparents. Undoubtedly, Rushdie's mode is not realist fiction, and his humor is not reserved only for these servant women; his comic style targets all the characters in this novel, making them all slightly exaggerated and absurd, impossible to take seriously. But the degree of vulnerability of each character, correspondent to their relative power and social location, affects the edginess and tenor of the humor, whether it can be read as top-down, or bottom-up, punching-up, or punching-down. When servants (or women) are mocked, it carries a different resonance than when Rushdie makes an elite politician the butt of his satire.

This humor at the expense of servants is contradictorily coupled with an egalitarian impulse, and complicated by Rushdie's provocative tendency to challenge the complacency of the educated implied reader, to poke fun at assumed snobbery. Early on, when Saleem, in one of his meta-comments, reveals that he works with condiments, he teases his imagined Indian reader, mimicking the inversions of spoken Indian English: "But now, 'A cook?' you gasp in horror, 'A khansama merely?' How is it possible? And, I grant, such mastery of the multiple gifts of cookery and language is rare indeed; yet I possess it" (38). Saleem is right: in South Asia, a household cook is unlikely to have the education to demonstrate the facility in English that Saleem does; Saleem has both the gifts "of cookery and language" because he straddles the class divide, having been raised as an upper-middle-class child in Bombay and then returned to the slums after the loss of his family and his experiences in the war of 1971. Rushdie here both challenges the assumption that a narrator-protagonist cannot be a cook or servant, and affirms that assumption—Saleem, his protagonist-narrator, is in fact not just a cook.

As the narrative of *Midnight's Children* moves through various generations of Saleem's family and their households and neighborhoods, it introduces a plethora of servants, exploring, through them, as do the women writers we have seen in the previous chapter, key elements of South Asian societies: gender and domesticity, interdependence and affective relations between and across classes, and servants' acquiescence and resistance. Naseem Ghani, now married to Aadam Aziz, takes pride in "supervising the cook," Daoud, over whom she reigns with territorial ferocity, keeping her husband out of the kitchen, both scolding and "confiding" in Daoud in a complex relationship (41, 42). Daoud later suffers extreme pain when, subject to her self-imposed regime of silence, he is confused by her wordless commands, and drops boiling gravy upon his foot "and frie[s] it like a five-toed egg" (63–64). The horror of this bodily injury to a servant is coupled by a humor that dispels and reduces. Rushdie's mode of representation creates, through absurd comparison, a sense of unreality, deflecting empathy from the cook, and directing attention to the power of the mistress.

As Saleem's narrative moves into the 1950s and the early days of India's post-Independence era, nameless generic servants are constantly mentioned as part of the texture of Saleem's upper-class family's life, and used to cue readers in to significant points. In Methwold's Estate, servants of the upcoming Bombay elite wear the discarded unwanted clothes of the departing British, so that the new post-Independence generation of children is tinged by that legacy, "cared for" by servants who still literally and figuratively carry on their bodies the burden of continuing (double) colonialism (149). Throughout, Rushdie twins the descriptions of privilege and luxury enjoyed by the Indian elite with the abject labor and deprivation endured by the lower classes, and particularly by the servants who live in close proximity and wait upon that upper class. Heavily pregnant Amina has to be physically carried by "two manservants" who must "form a chair with their hands to lift her" (116). Musa, the Sinai's old bearer, who moves with them from Delhi to Bombay, proudly boasts to "the other servants, in the kitchens of the red-tiled palaces, in the servants' quarters at the backs of Versailles and Escorial and San Souci" of the "whopper" ten-pound baby whose birth is imminent in his household, demonstrating his own sense of identity as derived from the family he serves (116).

Servants literally occupy the backs of the houses of the new urban elite, Rushdie points out, hidden from view, placed in a different physical geography. Again, Saleem calls attention to the functional, separate-use "servants' spiral iron staircase," quite different from the grand architecture enjoyed by employers (243). In a telling moment, when Amina Sinai's guilt-induced empathy enables her to become a confidante for her neighborhood circle, "one of those rare people who take the burdens of the world upon their backs, . . . [she] heard about servants being beaten and of officers being bribed," Rushdie suggests how the routine corruption of the elite includes abuse of their servants in the secrecy of their homes (187). The questionable character of Ahmed Sinai, Saleem's putative father, is indicated by the fact that he habitually "mistreated servants" (93, 387). When rich neighborhood children fight, surrounding "servants couldn't pull them apart," notes Saleem, conveying both the servants' ineffectuality, and the sense of responsibility that prompts them to intervene (270). And, in a strange (and unrealistic) demonstration of loyalty, Saleem writes, "when [his] mother left her second husband, all the other servants walked out too," suggesting, through his ambiguous syntax, that Amina, as upper-class wife, also effectually occupies the position of servant to her husband, analogous to that of the domestic servants who are both her subordinates and comrades in subordination and resistance (341).

Two named, highly individualized servants rise to prominence in *Midnight's Children*—Musa and Mary Pereira—to whom Rushdie self-consciously, repeatedly, meta-fictively calls attention as crucial to his plot. Saleem introduces Musa early, before his birth, and, in a proleptic, ominous sentence, warns how Musa will emerge from the background to transform the lives of Saleem and all his family:

> Musa, the old bearer, . . . kept himself in the background of our lives, always, except twice . . . once when he left us; once when he returned to destroy the world by accident. (87)

Repeatedly, Saleem warns, Musa, "for all his age and servility," is a ticking "time-bomb," waiting to explode (89, 121). As narrator, Saleem creates suspense, alerting his readers to anticipate Musa's importance, building up expectations to be fulfilled later, when old Musa's rivalry with the newly arrived Mary will lead to the revelation of her secret. And yet, as Saleem's words also suggest, "the world" thereby destroyed is really only *his* world, the tiny circle of his family, and of his place within it. Musa's importance in Saleem's narrative is therefore only subsidiary, relevant only to the extent that it will change (or re-adjust) Saleem's identity and the family that has raised him. Likewise, with Mary Pereira, while we know by the end of Book One, a quarter of the way into the novel, that she switched Saleem and Shiva as babies in 1947, we do not know when she will reveal her secret; throughout Book Two we are told of her growing guilt, also building a sense of anticipatory dread, forewarning readers about the impending catastrophe (for Saleem) to be caused by her.

Unlike the many unnamed generic servants in *Midnight's Children*, Mary and Musa serve in this novel not just to propel the plot, or to trigger a critical turn of events, but also to reveal the complex, gendered, psychological effects of servitude on individual subjectivities. Rushdie gives them both specific histories and asks readers to understand the socio-economic material realities and inequalities that drive their behavior. At the same time, however, he presents them through the flattening lens of the slightly ludicrous, using neither social realism nor magical realism, but a kind of heightened absurdism that renders them cartoonish rather than sympathetic, reduced even when he grants them motivation imbued by a sociological understanding.

Mary engineers the baby-switch because she wants to ingratiate herself with Joseph D'Costa, the violent communist for whom she suffers unrequited love, and to satisfy whose "virulent hatred of the rich" (121) she engages in "her own private revolutionary act, thinking, "he will certainly love me for this" (135). Rushdie grants Mary here neither psychological complexity nor motivational plausibility. Complaints of lack of realism may seem misplaced for a novel presented mostly in the mode of magical realism, but even so, I would contend, it is worth unraveling the class and gender implications of such portrayals, and recognizing that Rushdie diminishes Mary, making her ridiculous, *as a woman*, who, unlike her male counterpart Joseph, is not committed to a political cause, and who commits a flagrant breach of responsibility for personal romantic reasons, in the futile hope of pleasing a man who ignores her. It is part of the suspension of disbelief demanded by this novel that Mary instantly regrets her act, lies to Amina that she "fell in love" with the baby, and becomes Saleem's ayah (137).

That said, Rushdie also calls attention to the subjections and gendered differences of servitude, manifested in the form of "the rivalry between the old bearer Musa and the new ayah Mary," as forces that lead to the revelation of Mary's secret (148). With remarkable astuteness, Rushdie highlights the micropolitics, the daily humiliations and deprivations of domestic servitude, which are differently gendered for Musa and Mary. When she becomes an ayah, Mary has to take the bus to the Sinai's house from the hospital, while Amina and Ahmed take the baby in their car (144); she "slept on a servant's mat" on the floor beside Saleem's crib, so that even at the end, when she is the rich owner of a successful pickle factory, she "is still unable to sleep on beds" (546, 547). But Mary still gets to sleep inside the employers' house, while Musa sleeps in grimy servants' quarters shared with other male servants. These details matter, Rushdie suggests, because they highlight the effects of servitude on human relationships, bodies, and psyches. As Mary gains importance in the household as the privileged caregiver of the firstborn son, and builds an amicable companionship with Amina through their shared pleasure in caring for the baby and working on feminine domestic tasks like making pickles, she arouses the jealousy and insecurity of Musa, who feels displaced.

Describing them as "quarrelling like aged tigers," Saleem asks, "What starts fights?" (170). Rushdie provides three possible answers as simultaneously operable: interpersonal dynamics and mutual aggravation; individual psychologies and histories; and systemic, material, social conditions:

> What remnants of guilt fear shame, pickled by time in Mary's intestines, led her willingly? unwillingly? to provoke the aged bearer in a dozen different ways— by a tilt of the nose to indicate her superior status; by aggressive counting of the rosary beads under the nose of the devout Muslim; by acceptance of the title mausi, little mother, bestowed upon her by the other Estate servants, which Musa saw as a threat to his status; by excessive familiarity with the Begum Sahiba—little giggled whispers in corners, just loud enough for formal, stiff, correct Musa to hear and feel somehow cheated? (*MC*, 170)

In this analysis, posed in the form of a question, yet unusually attentive to the nuances of microdynamics between servants, Mary is not exempted from responsibility for goading Musa, nor is Musa exempted from trying to preserve the privileges he has enjoyed due to his maleness, age, and length of service. Rushdie also suggests how Mary's provocation of Musa is itself provoked by her guilt for an act itself provoked by social inequality, and how Musa's territorialism is produced by the insecurities of servitude. Leaving the question open, as if it contained its own answer, Saleem proceeds to another concurrent possibility to elaborate on Musa's psychology:

> What tiny grain of grit, in the sea of old age now washing over the old bearer, lodged between his lips to fatten into the dark pearl of hatred—into what unaccustomed torpors did Musa fall, becoming leaden of hand and foot, so that vases were broken, ashtrays spilled, and a veiled hint of forthcoming dismissal—from Mary's conscious or unconscious lips?—grew into an obsessive fear, which rebounded upon the person who started it off? (170)

With self-fulfilling circularity, the aging, distracted Musa's growing resentment of Mary leads to his clumsiness, which then leads to a fulfillment of his insecurity and fear—incited by her—that he will be fired. With analogous circularity, Mary's guilt leads her, in a form of displaced abjection, to torment a fellow servant whose dismissal will lead to the disclosure of her secret. In this remarkable account of intra-servant interaction, Rushdie complements the individual psychological explanation with the sociological one, insisting that interiority cannot be separated from the material, social conditions that contribute to it:

> And (not to omit social factors) what was the brutalizing effect of servant status, of a servants' room behind a black-stoved kitchen, in which Musa was obliged to sleep along with gardener, odd-job boy, and hamal—while Mary slept in style on a rush mat beside a new-born child? (170)

No action or event has a single cause, Rushdie suggests: yet another possibility is "the injured pride of an abused old servant" whom the frustrated and drunk Ahmed Sinai repeatedly "insulted" and Amina failed to pacify (171). It is no small irony on Rushdie's part that Musa, who must share his sleeping quarters with other male servants, is jealous of a woman who sleeps on the floor next to their employers' infant.

To underscore the burdens that servants routinely endure, Rushdie includes—when the house is burgled, the police called in, and servants inevitably fall under suspicion—the contempt and callousness of the police inspector, who threatens torture and abuse to frighten them into confession. "These fellows have limited intelligence," he tells Amina. Yet this powerful episode has its climax not in the discovery of the burgled silver in Musa's room, but in the revelation, that prior to this discovery, Musa had taken an oath declaring his innocence: "It was not me, sahib! If I have robbed you, may I be turned into a leper! May my skin run with sores!" (172). In this moment of intense affect, calling for sympathy for this aging servant, it may be hard to see that what Rushdie gives with one hand, he takes away with the other. Rushdie's representation of Musa ultimately reinforces the servant stereotype: he steals, he lies, he over-protests, and, confirming inspector's contemptuous words, he does not even hide effectively the objects he has stolen. And, upon being discovered, he begs, abasing himself at Ahmed's feet: "Forgive me Sahib! I was mad; I thought you were going to throw me out into the street!" (171). Ironically, Rushdie suggests, the servant steals, not because he is dishonest, but as a form of restitutive justice, in anticipation of being fired.

But there is another important question, posed by the horrified Amina—"why did you make that terrible oath?"—to which Musa's answer is an eloquent, parting expression of feeling:

> The bearer's old face twists into a mask of anger; words are spat out. "Begum Sahiba, I only took your precious possessions, but you, and your sahib, and his father, have taken my whole life; and in my old age you have humiliated me with Christian ayahs." (172)

Musa's words are powerful in many ways. First, they brilliantly challenge the logic of bourgeois outrage, asking implicitly how the theft of a few objects can possibly compare to the theft of a human life and of human dignity. Having given a lifetime of daily service to the family, in an exploitative system that still leaves him at the end with nothing, what, asks Musa, does the theft of a few objects compare to what has been taken from him? Second, in this rare moment, before Musa leaves, he finally expresses his long-accumulated resentment, his rage at the humiliations he has suffered for years. And third, his words carry a curse, becoming material in the utterance: he leaves "a curse upon the house" and family whose fortunes will decline from here on. In the magically real world of *Midnight's Children*, even words carelessly uttered have a frightening habit of coming true, of creating reality. Musa himself contracts leprosy, making material the false oath he took.

Through this powerful episode, Rushdie showcases the indignities of servitude (and in particular, male servitude), to achieve a range of effects: to convey an indictment of class-based subordination and dehumanization; to emphasize the power of servants both to affect their employers' lives and, through their words, to curse, to cast ill will that hangs over their future as a dark cloud; and to convey the servant's interiority through his own voice, to communicate his humanness in his own articulation of his resentment of a lifetime of indignity and abuse. This latter aspect in particular is radical and new in South Asian English fiction, more overt than even in Markandaya or Sahgal's fiction. But at the same time, unfortunately, Rushdie undercuts it with the concomitant use of humor at the servant's expense. Clearly, Saleem, as an unreliable fallible narrator, deploys a mode of comic exaggeration, overstating Musa's importance, like his own. But Saleem alone cannot be faulted. Rushdie as author places Musa on a semi-allegorical plane: both Musa and Mary are rendered as at once poignant and absurd, real and unreal, literal and allegorical. Their very names, and their rivalry, even dubbed "the war of Mary and Musa," suggest a joking allegory of Christianity at war with Judaism or Islam (167). Musa is the Muslim name for Moses, and Musa is a devout Muslim; Mary is Christian, and Saleem often calls her "virginal Mary," so that Saleem, as her putative son, also becomes a kind of Christ (146, 457). At the literal level, the resonance, potential seriousness, and pathos of Musa's speech is undercut by the bathos and absurdity of its ending, "you have humiliated me with Christian ayahs," shifting focus from his humiliation to his prejudice against Mary's gender and religion (172).

Rushdie's portrayals of Musa and Mary also reveal a gender bias. Musa is presented as a relatively more poignant, even tragic figure, while Mary is merely comic. When Musa eventually returns, he is achingly decrepit, dying of the "self-inflicted curse of" leprosy, "the servant who robbed [Saleem's] father, [and] swore he was innocent," seeking to beg the forgiveness of Ahmed Sinai (336). But

Mary is still rendered as ludicrous, as she mistakes him for the ghost of Joseph, and, overcome by guilt, confesses the truth:

> Mary Pereira has begun to talk, gabbling out a secret which has been hidden for eleven years, pulling us all out of the dream world she invented when she changed name tags, forcing us into the horror of the truth. And all the time she held on to me, like a mother protecting her child, she shielded me from my family. (336)

Mary "gabbles" even when she reveals deeply unwelcome truths that change her employers' lives, even as she holds on to Saleem with love and shields him "like a mother" from his own family. In Western literary convention, from *Oedipus Rex* onward, lowly servants reveal life-changing truths at critical moments, because they are knowing witnesses to long-held family secrets.[7] Rushdie augments this tradition by making the servant the creator as well as the revealer of the truth. But rhetorically, he demotes Mary, casting her, through her demotic speech, as comic, uneducated, and foolish.

Throughout the novel, Mary speaks in an exaggerated, garrulous, ungrammatical, unpunctuated style, infused with Anglo-Indian Christian and Hindi rhythms and syntax. When, at the very end, she sees Saleem, long thought dead, she flies down the steps of her factory, "shrieking at the top of her voice: 'O my God, O my God, O Jesus sweet Jesus, baba, my son, look who's come here, arré baba, don't you see me, look how thin you got, come, come, let me kiss you, let me give you cake'" (545). Though she now owns a pickle factory, her speech is still that of a devoted servant, happy to lapse into her former role, offering love and cake, as if he is still a child. Saleem calls her "my erstwhile ayah, the criminal of midnight, Miss Mary Pereira, the only mother I had left in the world," at once expressing fondness and placing her below him (545). "I have forgiven Mary her crime," he declares grandiosely, though he is now her factory manager, beholden to her for his job: "Mary, with her ancient hatred of 'the mens', admits no males except myself into her new, comfortable universe" (548). Here not only Saleem, but also Rushdie, makes fun of her inadequate English, presenting her as asexual, virginal, now foolishly distrustful of all men.[8]

Late in *Midnight's Children*, after witnessing the genocide in Bangladesh (March–December 1971) and the Indian Emergency (1975–1978), Saleem discovers anger at all that he had been taught to take for granted, and recalls the misleading belief instilled in him by Mary Pereira: "Anything you want to be, you kin be, / You kin be just what-all you want" (457). This repeated refrain that Saleem has heard from childhood showcases (again) her poor grammar and pronunciation, the falsity of the hopes she infused him with, and, ultimately, her internalized servility. But Saleem's indignation emerges only on his own behalf. It is deeply ironic that no one applies her words to her—least of all herself. They are reserved for the privileged upper-class male child, not even for Jamila, Saleem's sister, and are certainly not imaginable for Mary herself. They emblematize Mary's function in *Midnight's Children*: she is there to enable Saleem and his narrative, not in her own right, nor for her own story.

Rushdie's treatment of servants, in addition to its peculiar contradictions, advances, and retrogressions, reveals a significant trajectory of development. In his next novel, *Shame* (1983), set in 1950s to 1970s Pakistan, Rushdie's heavy reliance on servants becomes almost obsessive, with new twists. Via the political allegory that constitutes this novel, Rushdie focuses overtly on the rivalry between two historical figures, the Pakistani heads of state Zia-ul Haque (martial law administrator and president 1977–1988) and Zulfikar Ali Bhutto (president 1971–1973, prime minister 1973–1977), respectively fictionalized as Raza Hyder and Iskander Harappa. The "peripheral hero" Omar Khayyam, scion of an affluent feudal family, is purportedly marginal (to history), but central to Rushdie's narrative (19). Again, servants are everywhere in *Shame*, though marginal (in every sense) to these three male figures. And here too Rushdie combines an unusual attention to a few named, individuated servant figures, in particular ayahs (split between the self-sacrificing older woman and the younger sexualized one) with striking references to unnamed servants. As in *Midnight's Children*, Rushdie again joins an unusual, critical attentiveness to the culturally accepted abuse of servants with a mode of humorous representation that borders on ridicule, diminution, and reinforcement of stereotype. However, in the postcolonial Pakistani world of abuse, violence, feudalism, and corruption, as Rushdie depicts it in *Shame*, servants become a benchmark to measure both the extent of the abuse of power, and the possibility of servant resistance or survival strategies.

Shame opens by calling attention to the extreme precarity of servants in contrast to the abusive power of their employers as a class. In the pre-Independence feudal mansion of Omar Khayyam's three mothers, "household servants" witness the obscene diatribes of the dying old patriarch (3); after his death they refuse to leave, "less out of loyalty than from the terror of the life-prisoner for the outside world" (7).[9] Yet such observations are coupled with a mode of exaggerated, humorous portrayal that undercuts Rushdie's progressive attempts. Rushdie also reinforces the implicit notion that an ordered world is one where women manage servants well, and servants do their work. In this disordered household, Omar Khayyam's three mothers fail to supervise the servants who are thereby "underoccupied" (29), and "[get] away with murder" (32). Because of their idleness, the narrator suggests, these servants become Omar Khayyam's "first willing subjects" to hypnotism and to homosexuality: "entranced, [three nameless male servants] happily confessed the secrets of their mutual caresses," so that their "contented three-way love . . . provided a curious balance for the equal, but wholly platonic love of the three sisters for one another" (29). This "trio of menservants" thus serves both to mirror Omar Khayyam's three mothers, and to become the target of a somewhat homophobic joke, as enabled by their mistresses who created the "circumstances" for their alternate sexuality (29).

Recurrent servant figures provide texture to the story Rushdie tells, across several generations and eras, from colonial Baluchistan to feudal Sind, to postcolonial Karachi and Islamabad. In the upside-down order of Iskander Harappa's feudal patriarchal home, his new bride Rani is terrorized by his aging ayah who now rules the roost: "in this house, it's still what Isky's ayah says," young Rani is told by insolent servant girls (99); young Rani can only win this power contest by "outliving" the "formidable" old matriarch (164). Indeed, Rushdie even implies that this nameless ayah's spoiling of Isky as a boy is partly responsible for his extreme misbehavior as a man and national leader. She minimizes his misdeeds even in adulthood: "'Went too far,' the ayah says, 'My Isky, such a naughty boy.... The little hooligan'" (104). Later, when Iskander Harappa decides to pursue his political ambitions, the narrator comments that he "gave up fooling around with the women servants in his city home" (implying that Isky could still continue exploiting women servants in his feudal village) (134). In the city, Pinkie Aurangzeb, the beautiful, pampered, upper-class woman desired by both Isky and Raza, is introduced "allowing a servant girl to oil and braid her hair" (111). Later, when Raza has become the commander-in-chief of the army, his daughter hires "an army of ayahs" to care for her endless stream of children (228); when she dies, the twenty-seven children barely notice, they are so well-cared for by their ayahs (275). When Raza becomes president, his wife's retreat into a black burqa and a "veil of solipsism" didn't matter, because "the house ran itself, there were servants for everything" (230). In such constant, casually dropped but telling references to literal servants, Rushdie calls attention to the pervasiveness of servitude in Pakistan as well, and uses it to highlight various aspects of its social ethos.

Beyond such references, in *Shame* Rushdie takes his usage of servants to new levels, linking the language and pervasiveness of servitude figuratively to national disarray. In a moment that becomes a major turning point, when Iskander Harappa, prime minister of Pakistan, has become so abusive, so carried away by his unchecked power, that he screams, spits at, and slaps Raza Hyder (his army chief of staff), this humiliation finally tips Raza into becoming Isky's implacable enemy, and eventually, as martial-law-administrator, to remove him from office and have him hanged by a secret jury (as Bhutto was by Zia). Raza's word choice is significant: "You have forgotten that we are not your servants, he says coldly" (231). Raza's response distinguishes between the domestic and the national realm, between what is considered acceptable in each. Domestic servants, he suggests, are normalized as the recipients of dehumanizing insult and abuse—it is culturally accepted that masters can mistreat them to such extreme degrees—but that is not how Isky can treat the head of the army of the nation. While Raza's language is meant to indicate, in contrast with actual servants, the army official's sense of dignity and consequent resentment, it surfaces the casual assumption that servants will tolerate what a man of higher class will not. For, as Rushdie's novel also indicates, though in very small moments, domestic servants also enact resistance, in such muted or covert forms that it is not easily registered as such.

Toward the end, "Asghari the sweeperwoman" grumbles about Omar Khayyam's thoughtless habit of eating pine-kernels and dropping the shells all over the floor that she is supposed to clean (279). She "muttered under her toothless old woman's breath which smelled strongly of the disinfectant *fineel*: 'That beast should come here and finish off all inconsiderate persons who won't let an honest woman finish her job'" (279). While giving her both name and voice, and noting the casual mistreatment she endures, Rushdie simultaneously puts her down, identifying her via her bodily odors, as if the smell of her decaying mouth has become one with the smell of disinfectant she uses for her work and has somehow become an emanation of her body. Yet Rushdie also suggests the power, knowledge, and agency of domestic servants, who have their ears (literally and figuratively) close to the ground.

Asghari is the first harbinger of the resurgence of the magical realist beast of *Shame*. When Omar Khayyam overhears Asghari's quiet grumbling, which is clearly not meant to be heard by him, he alarms her by asking what she meant, expressing his own anxiety about the beast. He then has to allay her (real) servant's anxiety that she will be fired for insubordination; when he convinces her that he will not, she "relaxe[s] and scold[s] him, in the manner of old retainers, for taking things too seriously" (279). Asghari is an important example of the servant who has the power to know, to keep, or to reveal her master's secrets, and the agency to abandon an employer she knows is doomed. Despite her reassurances, Asghari "spill[s] the beans" to the newspapers and is "the first of the servants to flee the terror, the first of them to guess what was likely to happen to anyone who stayed in that house" (288). Servants cannot be relied on for indefinite loyalty, Rushdie implies, they act on their own need for survival. Indeed, Asghari becomes the leader of other servants, the "bearers and hamals and sweeperboys, gardeners and odd-job men, ayahs and maids," whose "susurrations" or noises of departure Omar Khayyam also hears as the sure sign of their knowledge of imminent disaster (290). When he reaches Nishapur, his birthplace and childhood home, seeking a last refuge with his three mothers, he finds that that household too has been abandoned by its servants. To be servantless is a sure sign of decline for a family. "No servants anymore," his three mothers announce apologetically (298).

In *Shame*, as in *Midnight's Children*, Rushdie individualizes three servant characters, granting them some narrative space though not individual story lines. Each is present as a bit player who reveals something about the ethos of the major characters, for each becomes a victim of their masculine power: Gulbaba, an aged feudal servant in Isky's household, who is accidentally killed by Raza; the aged ayah Hashmat Bibi, who tends to Omar Khayyam and his mothers, and dies when she agrees to "go under" his hypnosis (30–31); and the young Parsi ayah Shahbanou, who volunteers to have sex with Omar Khayyam in lieu of her charge Sufiya Zinobia, Raza Hyder's developmentally disabled daughter. Of these three named servants, the aging male servitor, like Musa in *Midnight's Children*, receives more sympathetic treatment than the women. In a macho competition of toxic masculinity between Raza and Isky, Raza ties himself to a stake all night as a challenge. At dawn, naïve Gulbaba, on his way to perform pre-prayer ablutions, yet ever solicitous of the employer class, obsequiously creeps up behind Raza to offer comfort, and, mistaken for his employer, is "with one terrible blow, felled . . . like a twig" (118). "Old servants take liberties. It is the privilege of their years," comments Rushdie drily. Only old servants dare to nudge the hard line between servants and masters. Gulbaba literally falls victim both to his own servitude and to the murderous competition between the two principals in this novel, perhaps prefiguring the nation that would also fall victim to their rivalry.

Shahbanou is the servant with the most extended portrayal in *Shame*. She is introduced as complaining about her scalded hands when she bathes Sufiya Zinobia, whose preternatural blushing brings the water to "boiling point" (131). From this emblematic beginning, Rushdie casts Shahbanou both as having a voice, and as suffering the physical consequences of the dysfunctionality of her employer's family. With calm nonchalance, she defends Sufiya, and reprimands Raza's other daughter, Naveed, withstanding the latter's verbal and physical abuse: "Shahbanou, shrugging, impervious to Naveed Hyder's blows: 'You shouldn't talk so bad to your sister, bibi, one day your tongue will go black and fall off'" (148). The epitome of the selfless, caring ayah, and the loving mother that Sufiya lacks, Shahbanou attends devotedly to her charge, chaperoning her during her illness, adamantly refusing "to leave the girl alone with the male doctors" (155). Shahbanou even exerts power (indirectly) over the household when she persuades Raza to forgive one daughter (Naveed), and to accept Omar's proposal of marriage for the other (Sufiya). Sent to Raza as an emissary by Bilquis, who, "reduced to pleading with servants," recognizes this power, Shabanou uses her voice, at once placatory, deferential, and sensible: "Forgive my saying so, sir, but don't pile shame on shame" (182). She knows family secrets and saves the family from scandal and political ruin.

Yet Rushdie also presents her as a somewhat comical, absurd figure. In a typical exchange, as Shahbanou brushes her hair, Naveed Hyder both insults the ayah and shares her thoughts about her upcoming wedding: "Hey, you, . . . you know what marriage is for a woman?" "I am a virgin," replies Shahbanou calmly.

"Marriage is power," continues Naveed, "It is freedom," until it dawns on her what Shahbanou's words might mean: "Do you think I'm not a virgin also? You shut your dirtyfilthy mouth, with one word I could put you in the street," she threatens. "What are you talking, bibi, I only said," replies Shahbanou soothingly (169). While the humor in this scene clearly targets an over-pampered elite woman's abusiveness to a servant woman, it is intensified by Rushdie's mockery of the Parsi ayah's syntactically odd, slightly ungrammatical, ethnically marked speech. It is unclear whether Shahbanou intends to be subversive or merely prim, but her potential wit is undercut by Rushdie's rendition of her voice.

Moreover, Rushdie takes to absurd extremes the cliché of the self-sacrificing caregiver when he casts Shahbanou as willingly offering herself to Omar Khayyam, having sex with him secretly to protect the disabled Suifya Zinobia. On the wedding night, Shahbanou stands in the doorway connecting Omar's bedroom to Sufiya's, demanding with "fierce solicitude" whether he planned to have sex with his mentally disabled child-bride, threatening in an "outrageous breach of the master servant relationship" to kill him if he tried to consummate the marriage (232). Yet, shortly after, as Omar begins to gain weight, preternaturally inflated with unfulfilled desire, Shahbanou regards him with "grave sympathy" and offers herself as relief (233). Again, Rushdie's mode of representation of Shahbanou is problematic. She "solemnly" arrives in Omar's bedroom that night, "her hair loose, her bony body of a tilyar bird half-visible through her cotton shift," and in response to his surprise, explains matter-of-factly, "I don't want to kill anybody, . . . so I thought, better I do this instead" (233). Determined, practical, and self-sacrificing, yet again diminished by her mode of speech, and cast as stereotypically thin like a "tilyar" (a migrant bird, and a slur for immigrants from India to Pakistan), Shahbanou is made a somewhat ridiculous figure. Engaged in the act of sex, she is again described in animalistic terms, emitting "birdlike cries" (241). She is portrayed reductively as both witch and mother, a "shadow bride": "Under the spell of the Parsi ayah, [Omar] had diminished to remarkably normal dimensions" (233).

In this problematic representation, Rushdie suggests that the servant woman freely chooses to have sex with a male employer—as if the inequalities of power do not prevail—and obscures the fact of the sexual exploitation of women servants. He does point out the injustice that when Shahbanou is discovered to be pregnant, she is "dismissed on grounds of her immorality": "She left without a word, without attempting to apportion blame" (241). Rushdie gives her some dignity, but the narrative of *Shame* does not follow her beyond assuring us that Omar Khayyam paid for the abortion and sent her money afterward (241). While the main characters of *Shame* ask to be read not in terms of social realism but through the lenses of magical realism and allegory—Raza and Isky as political allegories, Sufiya as symbolic of women's rage—Shahbanou the ayah is neither.

She exists somewhere in-between, portrayed via a mode of comic absurdity, an instrument for Rushdie's critique of the hypocrisies of middle-class morality, gendered and classed inequalities, and abuses of power. Shahbanou remains ultimately a minor and ridiculous figure. She disappears, having played her role, as mere accessory to the main concerns of the novel.

Overall, Rushdie's fiction reveals a strange ambivalence, a self-contradiction regarding servants and servitude. On the one hand, he calls the servant out of the background and into the middle ground, overtly calling attention to servant intimacies, exploitation, destitution, and resistance. On the other, his modes of representation reveal unreconstructed notions that covertly reinforce the classist and sexist attitudes and assumptions he seems to push against. Rushdie's work manifests a continuing, marked preoccupation with servants, inside and outside the South Asian upper-class home, new to South Asian Anglophone fiction. These bifurcated patterns—an attentiveness to servants as exploited presences in wealthy and middle-class Indian homes; a focus on ayahs as caretakers of the vulnerable young; and a counter-tendency to render servants ludicrous—become more extreme and take yet different turns in his next two novels, *The Satanic Verses* and *The Moor's Last Sigh*.

The Satanic Verses (1988) focuses on migrancy and the South Asian diaspora in Britain at the end of the twentieth century, but servitude remains a powerful frame of reference, a marker at once of the India left behind, and of what continues to shape the South Asian migrant. Servants in this novel become increasingly more outlandish. Nameless servants proliferate around all the wealthy South Asians: Indian film star Pimple Billimoria is attended by a "dumbly distressed ayah" whose presence gives her employer respectability (12); Rekha Merchant, lady of leisure, commits adultery with Gibreel Farishta while her ayah fetches the children from school (26); the feudal landowner Mirza Saeed has lifelong servant women who can be relied on to "recall" the history of his village (217) and change his bedsheets three times a day (227). Servants are remembered by migrants in Britain, and their effects linger on the psyches of Saladin and Gibreel, the two main protagonists. The two servant characters who are named, Kasturba, Saladin's old ayah and Vallabh, her husband, his parents' bearer, are assigned peculiar individual traits, and reveal similar contradictions, exaggerated to even greater degrees.

In an odd episode, Saladin Chamcha returns from England to his parents' home in Bombay to find his old ayah, Kasturba, wearing his dead mother's *saris*, replicating her hairstyle, smoking a cigarette, literally stepping into her shoes. Casting her in the role of a mother, remembering resentfully how she failed to protect him from a child molester, Saladin nonetheless challenges her new position as a replacement for his dead mother, Nasreen (66). Kasturba has become a mistress, in both senses—Saladin's father's sexual partner and mistress of the house—and is supported by her servant husband. This bizarre adoption of the deceased Nasreen's identity is, all three claim, a voluntary arrangement, a way to "keep her spirit alive," because they all loved the dead woman (68). But Saladin is outraged both by what he sees as an insult to his mother, and by the ayah's prostitution by both men. Perhaps Rushdie's point is that women denied respect and sense of self will take to mimicry of their supposed social superiors. But again, it is undercut. Rushdie presents an ayah's sexual relations with the master as voluntary, and takes to fantastical exaggeration a dubious comic portrayal.

At the same time, Rushdie's fiction also carries stunning, extraordinarily astute moments that call attention to (and critique) how the South Asian system of servitude shapes the identities of the upper class, how it affects their sense of self and ways of being in the world. In an off-handed comment in *The Satanic Verses*, for instance, Rushdie notes how an ordinary man's sense of himself is changed by spatial relocation when he takes the privileged place of an elite and powerful employer of servants. When the Sarpanch Muhammad Din is invited by the feudal landlord Mirza Saeed to sit in the back of his Mercedes (which Mirza is driving himself since his chauffeur has deserted him to join the pilgrims' march), "as if [the Sarpanch] were the zamindar and Mirza Saeed the chauffeur, little by little the leather upholstery and the air-conditioning unit and the whisky-soda cabinet and the electrically operated mirror-glass windows began to teach him hauteur; his nose tilted in the air and he acquired the supercilious expression of a man who can see without being seen" (*SV*, 481). The psychosomatic effect of the accumulated luxury and position of being seated in the employer's seat is so powerful that it transforms the very body, bodily sensations, body language, and sense of self of the erstwhile humble village headman. He begins to act like the landowner. Elite behavior is learned, Rushdie suggests. Being driven by the zamindar while the villager sits in the zamindar's seat makes the Sarpanch feel, act, and see himself differently, even to the disposition of his body—it changes his sense of self, identity, and place in the world.[10]

This entitled mode of being, and habituated reliance on others such that even outside their homeland South Asians still expect others to serve them continually, becomes a problem when upper-class South Asian men form relationships with white women. In England, Pamela, Saladin Chamcha's wife, reflects on a reason for the failure of their marriage that she wanted him to know: "In bed, . . . you never seemed interested in me; not in my pleasure, what I needed, not really ever. I came to think you wanted, not a lover. A servant" (*SV*, 184). Saladin's unconscious expectation that others exist to serve him extends from the physical and material to the sexual arena. It becomes a benchmark of his self-absorption and obliviousness, his lack of solicitude or care for others, his failure of mutuality and relationality. Rushdie's critique suggests that it is specifically the habituation to domestic servants in South Asia, and even more specifically, his sense of South

Asian elite masculinity, that produces this failure on Saladin's part. (In an allusion to Richardson's novel, it is one of Rushdie's little jokes that Saladin's English wife is named Pamela: she is the wife who refuses to be a servant.)

Underscoring this as a pattern, in a remarkably similar moment, a disenchanted Alleluia Cone reflects on Gibreel Farishta, who acts as if he expects her to pick up after him:

> He wasn't housetrained. Used to servants, he left clothes, crumbs, used tea-bags where they fell. Worse: he *dropped* them, actually let them fall where they would need picking up; perfectly, richly unconscious of what he was doing, he went on proving to himself that he, the poor boy from the streets, no longer needed to tidy up after himself. It ... drove her crazy. (SV, 310)

Gibreel's class privilege is recently learned: having become a man accustomed to servants, he constantly needs it to prove, to himself, his successful class mobility, to affirm his new identity. From the perspective of his English lover, however, Gibreel's sexist, unthinking behavior takes gender inequality to intolerable levels. It is no accident that in this novel about migration and diaspora, about what can and cannot travel, it is white Englishwomen who find the domestic entitlement of South Asian men intolerable. Through this doubling of Gibreel and Saladin, Rushdie emphasizes that the South Asian culture of servitude and of the spoilt, self-absorbed masculinity that it enables, is unwelcome to women who are not South Asian and not inculcated into acceptance. Servitude does not travel as well, or, to be more precise, it is not as easily transferrable to upper-class white women who refuse the role of servant-wife to entitled South Asian men.

South Asian servitude thus works as a recurrent point of reference in Rushdie's novels, a way to explore a range of questions about upper-class socialization and psychology. His characters deploy the English word "servant" as a slur, as a mode of indicating contempt for individuals who (supposedly) surrender their autonomy, dignity, and self-respect, who submit to inferior status. In *The Satanic Verses*, the Bangladeshi restaurant-owner Hind Sufyan thinks contemptuously of her husband as servile. Once a schoolteacher, Mohammad Sufyan is unable to earn a living in England from his learning, and kowtows to their white customers. His wife, whose cooking is the source of the family's livelihood, reflects: "What was there for Sufyan to do? Take the money, serve the tea, run from here to there, behave like a servant for all his education" (248). From her perspective, Sufyan has failed as a man and husband. Like a servant, he has to please and ingratiate others while she runs the restaurant. Servitude—here racialized and neocolonial—is understood as incompatible with education and dignity; an educated man, Hind believes, should not act like a servant.

In a brilliant moment, the stuttering Sisodia comments on how religion has been hijacked by fundamentalists. But he uses the language of servitude: "religious fafaith, which encodes the highest ass ass aspirations of human race, is now, in our cocountry, the servant of lowest instincts and gogo God is the creature of evil" (*SV*, 518). Rushdie's humor mocks both religious "fafaith," (by implication the "ass . . . of the human race," and its mindless popularity) and the neocolonial nation (coco-country suggests a nation linked with commercialism and capitalism, Coca Cola perhaps, and coconuts, brown outside, white inside). Such comments reveal deeply embedded assumptions about servitude: in claiming that religion has become a "servant of [the] lowest instincts," Sisodia indicates that a servant is understood as one who serves without protest or independence of thought or action. Rushdie thus underscores how servants are seen as degraded within this dominant cultural set-up.

On other occasions, Rushdie seems to participate in the mindset he depicts and appears to deplore. In a powerful self-reflexive moment, Baal the artist, Rushdie's stand-in for himself, "stands on his dignity" and proclaims, "It isn't right for the artist to become the servant of the state" (*SV*, 98). These are brave words, and Rushdie himself, in his essays, frequently insists that writers must stand up to politicians. But the metaphor of the servant reinforces the widespread assumption that servants are mindless automatons, subservient to higher authority that they fail to question or contest. Even while living and writing in Britain (and later the United States), Rushdie calls on servitude as a figural and cultural marker, as constituting a terminology and way of thinking that continues to inform his writing.

The Moor's Last Sigh (1995) is the last of Rushdie's quartet of novels about the subcontinent. Here too, servants are ubiquitous, used to emphasize class inequality and unseen exploitation of the poor, and the power and privilege of the elite. But in the darker, more pessimistic vision of the *Moor*, we see both more overt satire of the injustices of servitude and a greater tendency to revert to stereotype. On the one hand, Rushdie calls attention, in seemingly casual references, to the mistreatment of servants in wealthy families. Early on, for instance, in early twentieth-century south India, Epifania, Aurora's grandmother, is horrified by the Japanese-style architecture that her husband has instituted in their new house: "at night one had to sleep on a mat on the floor with one's head on a wooden block, as if one were a servant," she thinks (16). Servitude becomes a reference point, and discomfort its defining feature, a discomfort for which Epifania has no compassion, or willingness to accept herself.

In a telling episode, Rushdie notes how the young Aurora Zogoiby becomes ashamed of the servitude practiced in her family. When valuable art objects begin to disappear, Aires, her uncle, gathers the servants in the courtyard "bellowing out his certain-sure conviction that one of them was a thief" (57).

Rushdie lists the various kinds of servants not by name but by the tasks they perform: "The domestic servants, gardeners, boatmen, sweepers, latrine-cleaners, all faced him in a sweating, terror-stricken line, wearing the ingratiating smile of their fear" (57). Rushdie's humor here heightens the grotesque horror of the servants' abuse, matched to their places in the hierarchy: Aires slaps the houseboys "Tweedlydum and Tweedlydee," pokes the gardeners, and ignores "the latrine-cleaners whom of course he would not touch" (58). This dark satire of the upper class highlights how servants as a group are denied individuality and humanity by their employers. Rushdie also emphasizes the distinctions of caste prejudice and untouchability, even among Christians: Aires' physical violence does not extend to the lowest caste, seen as polluted because they remove household refuse, and who therefore literally cannot be touched. This moment awakens the conscience of Aurora, the figure for the artist in this novel, evoking in her the courage to confess to the theft: "for the first time in her life the presence of the servants filled her with shame" (58).

Rushdie's narratives always begin with children growing up in elite or middle-class Indian homes, and hence return recurrently to the importance of the ayahs who shape those childhoods. The Moor, the narrator-protagonist, remarks on his paradoxical vulnerability as an elite child left to servants, "Children of the rich are raised by the poor, and since both my parents were dedicated to their work I was frequently left with only the chowkidar and the ayah for company" (193). The young Aurora is looked after by her old ayah, Josy, who enables her first art work and cares for her like a mother when she begins to menstruate (45, 58, 61). But Jaya, the ayah that Aurora hires for her children in Bombay, is more sinister.

Reflecting perhaps the darkening of Rushdie's vision after the fatwa, coincident with the rise of Hindu fundamentalism in the 1990s, servitude in *The Moor* takes a darker turn. Jaya turns out to be a petty thief, pilfering household objects and jewelry, while her husband Lambajan, the family's gateman, is revealed as a spy, involved in the underground crime mafia racquet, a "double agent at our [family's] gates" (345). Here Rushdie reinforces the stereotypes of servant criminality that his earlier work attempted to complicate. Servants' (justified) fear of employers' power and retribution in Rushdie's earlier novels now turns into the employers' fear of servants and their vengeful power to do harm: when the Moor gets Lambajan to stop Jaya's pilfering, Jaya takes revenge (217). This servant couple is more dangerous, and less funny than even the one in *The Satanic Verses*.

After *The Moor's Last Sigh*, affected no doubt by the rupture caused by the fatwa (February 1989) and Rushdie's enforced separation from South Asia through the long years spent in hiding under tight security, Rushdie's subsequent novels show more of a distance from South Asia, and less attention to servants or servitude. Servants retreat from the middle ground to the background in the novels of Rushdie's American phase—*Fury, The Ground Beneath Her Feet, The Golden House*—though they are always there in their transnational protagonists' South Asian pasts, having shaped those psyches in some way. *Shalimar the Clown* (2005), set primarily in Kashmir, India, and the United States, makes a notable comeback, where the Indian servant kills his American master (the man who serves as chauffeur is in fact an imposter who has taken on this role to exact his revenge on the man who stole his wife). Here, astonishingly, Rushdie fully reaffirms the stereotype of the violent servant that his earlier work attempted to undo, affirming that the proximity and intimacy of servitude poses danger to the rich, and the perfect opportunity for the poor and disadvantaged to take violent revenge.

After Rushdie, other transnational South Asian writers have also moved servants and servitude into the middle ground in their narratives, but unlike him, they do so with less self-contradiction, and with different tonalities and political purposes. Shyam Selvadurai from Sri Lanka, Mohsin Hamid from Pakistan, and Monica Ali from Bangladesh make manifest both the pervasiveness of servitude as an institution in South Asia, and the diversity of ways that contemporary writers address it. All three writers question servitude and its permeating effects, and suggest distinctive ways of giving servitude more prominence. They all call on the figure of the servant to perform new (if still subsidiary) roles or functions in millennial South Asian Anglophone fiction. Taking servitude more seriously than Rushdie, they present fresh angles of vision. In turning to these three writers in this chapter, I explore some of these new, different ways of addressing servitude in recent South Asian fiction, and suggest how they form an intermediate step toward the emergent fiction that offers a fuller critique of servitude as an institution and pulls it into the foreground.

Repudiating Instrumentalization: Shyam Selvadurai's *Funny Boy*

Sri Lankan Canadian writer Shyam Selvadurai's 1994 semi-autobiographical debut novel *Funny Boy* is acclaimed for its coming-of-age narrative of a Tamil Sri Lankan boy, Arjie, whose growing awareness of his own homosexuality develops concomitantly with his understanding of the Sinhalese-Tamil ethnic tensions that erupt into violence and civil war in 1983 and prompt the departure of Arjie and his family for Canada. Set primarily in 1960s and 1970s Sri Lanka, and focused on Arjie and his upper-class family, particularly the difficulties of cross-ethnic romance, this deceptively artless, first-person narrative calls in multiple ways upon servants. As a prepubescent child, Arjie secretly borrows forbidden "Sinhala love comics" from his grandparents' Sinhalese servant, Janaki, and is inducted through her into the structures of desire constituted by the dominant ethnic group's popular cultural production (43).[11] Arjie imagines romance in the heteronormative colorist terms constructed by Sinhala films and comics, and is later disillusioned when his aunt Radha, who is dark-skinned and Tamil, does not live up to the ideal created by lighter-skinned film stars like Malini Fonseka, "goddess of the Sinhala screen" (42). When Radha's romance with the Sinhalese Anil fails because of inter-ethnic strife, Arjie realizes how Janaki's comics have failed him by leading him to believe that "if two people loved each other everything was possible" (97). In Selvadurai's narrative, servants are thus both key to the construction of alternative desires, and liable to mislead. They provide both a non-hegemonic space and opportunity for queer desire and the occasion for a romantic idealism or sentimentality that realities of ethnic and power inequalities will correct.

In the opening chapter, "Pigs Can't Fly," it is in the liminal transgressive space of Janaki's room, hidden in the servants' quarters literally at the back of the house, that Arjie cross-dresses to play the game of "bride-bride" with his girl cousins, and looks at himself (or his alternative self, in his fantasized identity, made up as a girl) in Janaki's "cracked full-length mirror," itself indicative both of Janaki's lower economic status and of Arjie's fractured aspirations (5). In this novel, the female servant enables not male (hetero)sexual initiation, as in the codes of Victorian fiction, but the enactment, through play and performance, of a queer identity otherwise forbidden within the norms of the postcolonial upper-class Sri Lankan household, and the discovery of a proscribed self, temporarily actualized and legitimized among the community of Arjie's fellow players. Later, when Arjie has been found out and punished, he mourns the possibilities afforded by this servant mirror: "Never [would I] stand in front of Janaki's mirror, watching a transformation take place before my eyes" (39).

Janaki also serves other functions in this novel. Placed in-between employers and their children, she is empowered to discipline the children and ordered by her mistress to "keep the children quiet" (36). Like the servants we have seen in earlier narratives, Janaki thus also signifies the affluence and comforts of her employers' household where women can shunt their responsibilities onto servants. Through recurrent references, Arjie's narrative establishes the upper-class status of his Tamil extended family in which having servants is the norm. Arjie's own family servant, also Sinhalese, and to whom they speak in Sinhalese, is named Anula and described fulfilling various household tasks (15, 18, 57). But in *Funny Boy*, the normality of these inter-ethnic relations is established to highlight the disruption at the end when Tamils are attacked by Sinhalese mobs, Tamil houses set on fire, and inter-ethnic trust between employers and servants breaks down. In that later environment of fear, despite her years serving them, Arjie's parents send Anula back to her village (281).

Selvadurai's references to other unnamed servants with whom upper-class men have committed transgressions also serve to highlight the norms of desire that orchestrate Arjie's world. When Arjie fears the disgrace that he would suffer if his parents were to get divorced, for example, he thinks of a schoolmate whose parents had separated because the father had run away with "the next-door servant woman," and how even the abandoned wife and child had been mocked and humiliated (115). Or, when Arjie and his mother seek help from an old family friend, a retired civil-rights lawyer, Arjie recalls the "hint of scandal surrounding him and the servant boy" who worked as his aide (135). Through such seemingly minor details, Selvadurai points to both the existence of sexual transgression and intimacy between servants and (male) employers in Sri Lankan high society, and the social punishments that attend upon such violations of class-based sexual boundaries. Both cases serve at once as warning to Arjie himself, and as pointers to alternative possibilities.

Through a key episode, however, Selvadurai calls greater attention to the servant for a more significant purpose: to critique the instrumental use made of the servant by the higher classes. In the third chapter, "See No Evil, Hear No Evil," twelve-year-old Arjie meets "Daryl Uncle," a Burgher (the term for Ceylonese people of mixed European descent) who has returned from Australia to Sri Lanka as a journalist to uncover the truth about government and police abuse of Tamil insurgents. Daryl at first serves as an exemplum to reinforce yet again, for Arjie, the endogamous cultural dictum, "most people marry their own kind," that discourages inter-ethnic marriage: Arjie discovers that young Daryl was not allowed by their parents to marry Arjie's mother (53).[12] As Amma, in the absence of Arjie's father, renews her romance with Daryl, and Daryl disappears in Jaffna and is found murdered, he becomes a measure of the corruption and violence of the Sinhalese authorities. Arjie watches as Amma pursues a futile search for "justice" for her former lover (148). In a time of growing rumors of government-condoned torture and surveillance, Amma's determination seems naïve, endangering not only herself and her children, but also the servant boy, Somaratne, whom Amma wants to enlist as witness or source for further clues to the truth.[13] What she fails to understand, and what Arjie learns and tries to make her see, is how her class privilege blinds her to the unwittingly harmful use she wants to make of the servant and his family.

Selvadurai flags from the beginning how Somaratne, precisely because he is a servant, with access to Daryl's home, is used both by Amma, who sees him as a source of information, and the police, who scapegoat him. When Daryl fails to return from Jaffna after the library has been "burned by the police," Amma takes Arjie to investigate at Daryl's house (119). Arjie alone notices that the sixteen-year-old boy seems "afraid" when he answers Amma's questions, that the servant's silences and body language indicate an understanding of danger and vulnerability to which she is oblivious (119). When they find Daryl's rooms ransacked, Amma insists on going to the police, who inevitably blame the servant, apprehend him for "trying to run away," and disconnect the invasion of Daryl's property from his disappearance (126). Like many South Asian writers, Selvadurai highlights the irony that servants fear and try to flee the police because they (rightly) anticipate that they will be wrongly suspected of dishonesty or theft, and, in so doing, reconfirm the very suspicions they are trying to avert.[14]

Selvadurai calls attention to the servant boy's vulnerability, the implicit threat of physical and sexual violence, and his (learned) enactment of self-abasement to avert what he knows is coming. Somaratne begs Amma for help, throwing himself on the ground before her, and even trying to kiss her feet (118). But Amma draws away, in a moment that bespeaks her sense of class distance and (misplaced) trust in the police. As the police drag off the struggling boy, "his sarong came undone and fell to the floor, entangling his feet. The police lifted him . . . and dragged him naked" (127). Amma shudders and covers her face, but it is unclear if she realizes that it is she who has caused this disaster to befall the innocent boy, who, even though he is Sinhalese and not Tamil, is later tortured in police custody and his arm paralyzed (144). By contrast, Arjie "felt [his] legs become weak," suggesting greater empathy for the servant because of his closer sense of identification with a teenage boy (127). Or perhaps, Selvaduarai suggests, Arjie's own sense of otherness because of his non-normative sexuality induces a greater sensitivity to the servant, as also vulnerable to state and social power and violence.

Unlike Arjie, both the police and Amma use the servant for their own ends. The police cast Somaratne as "the culprit" (126) and use him to threaten Amma, insinuating that he would be able to provide testimony of her adulterous relationship with Daryl if she tried to continue her investigations into Daryl's death. "[T]hat servant boy was a real jobless character. He knew all the comings and goings of your friend," the ASP tells her (130). In a more benign but insensitive mode, Amma, though convinced of Somaratne's innocence, still wants to embroil him in her efforts to learn the truth. "I'm sure he saw something," she reflects, after being warned repeatedly of the risks she is incurring (138). Single-mindedly, she persists, using a ruse to get a neighbor's servant woman to reveal where he lives, and drags the unwilling Arjie with her to Somaratne's village. When Somaratne's mother refuses to tell Amma where he is, Amma enacts her accustomed sense of entitlement, expecting the poor to fulfill the needs of the rich. The scene explodes into a dramatic confrontation, as the Somaratne's mother finally speaks truth to power:

"Listen," Amma finally said, "a friend of ours lived where Somaratne used to work. He died and we are concerned . . ."

"And what about my son?" the woman said. "Are you not concerned about him?" She had raised her voice slightly. The other women began to come towards her hut. "What do you care?" She continued bitterly. "You rich folk from Colombo, what do you know about our suffering?" (143)

Where Amma expects the poor woman to share her desire for justice for Daryl, demanding that the servant's family serve her needs, not their own, the woman rejects her appeal, breaking the accustomed mode of servitude, talking back as to an equal, making visible Amma's own blindness. Echoing Amma's words back to her, the woman calls out Amma's self-involved self-indulgence, her callousness in not thinking or caring about the consequences to the servant or his family of her singular "concern" for Daryl. Upon Amma's insistence that she wants Somaratne to identify the murderer,

The woman laughed harshly. "So you want Somaratne to identify the murderer?" she said. "And what will happen to Somaratne then? Have you thought of that?"
Amma was silent.
"No," she said, "why should you? To people like you, we are not even human beings." (143)

Selvadurai emphasizes how, regardless of their ethnicity, the poor are more vulnerable to police and political violence, and how the rich are oblivious to this difference. The woman has already lost one son "killed by the army during the 1971 insurrection"; she makes it clear she does not want to lose the other to Amma's foolhardy enterprise (144).

As this powerful scene becomes more intense and the women's hostility more overt, Arjie persuades his mother to leave. As if to mirror Somaratne's bystander's experience of becoming a casualty to others' conflicts, Arjie is hit on the back so hard by a stone that he almost falls over. The "sharp pain" that makes him cry out seems to release something in him, as for the first time Arjie lashes out at his mother in a reprimand that echoes Somaratne's mother's: "We should never have come on this trip. . . . You're so selfish. All you think about is yourself. Thanks to you, we nearly got killed" (144). His words have a powerful effect: his mother looks at him "as if [he] had hit her" (144). Crucial to Arjie's coming of age, this experience teaches Arjie a great deal: the realities of police brutality, political violence, his own relative protectedness, the far greater precarity of servants and their families, the consequences that that disparity can unleash, and the wisdom of relinquishing a quixotic pursuit of justice for a dead man when that pursuit would cost harm to the living, in particular to socially subordinated others. He also discovers his own capacity for agency, his ability to speak truth to power, to shift from being bystander and beneficiary to participant and interventionist. Moreover, he finds, that he too can teach.

The figures of the servant and his mother are crucial in this scene, highlighting their concomitant proximity to and distance from power. Somaratne is vulnerable because he lives in his employer's home, making him the target of questioning, unfair suspicion, violence, scapegoating, and reprisal by state officials. Indeed, this proximity brings the danger home to his family. Despite his superficial affinities with Arjie, Somaratne is also more vulnerable because he is a village boy: he does not have the network of influence or safety nets of protection that Arjie does. But Selvadurai also highlights the voices and resistance of the poor and vulnerable. This crucial chapter marks a turning point, an awakening for Arjie to his privilege and to the unintended effects on less privileged others of even well-intended actions. Arjie both learns and is sorry to have to learn at expense of the servant boy and his family. And yet, I would contend, in Selvadurai's novel, the servant figure is not there merely to provide illumination for Arjie. Instead of focusing on Arjie's education, Selvadurai highlights instead, more broadly, the problem of instrumentalization. The episode reflects explicitly on the ethical problem of instrumentalizing the servant, by the mother, and asks implicitly how the novel might avoid doing the same. Self-reflexively, *Funny Boy* poses the question: how can fiction by and about the elite avoid making use of the servant for the benefit or elevation of the upper-class protagonist?[15]

Sevadurai brings the servant into the middle ground in a new way in this debut novel. On the one hand, clearly, neither this novel nor this chapter is centered on a servant. The narrative is told entirely from Arjie's perspective and provides no insight into the servant's interiority or inner life, even if the dialogue offers some access, in an important glimpse, into the thoughts and feelings of the servant's mother. It provides no solution or hope for justice for the servant. But, on the other hand, through the intensity of its emphasis on such a reality, the horror of Arjie, and the response of Somaratne's village, the novel offers an indictment both of the upper class and of the nation that fosters such injustice, marking the moment of emergence of the bourgeois self and fiction into self-awareness and ethical responsibility.[16]

Repudiating Servitude? Mohsin Hamid's *Moth Smoke*

In a scathing critique of 1990s Pakistan, *Moth Smoke*, acclaimed Pakistani writer Mohsin Hamid's debut novel (2000), charts the moral and socioeconomic decline of a bright, promising young middle-class man, Darashikoh Shezad (known as Daru), who turns to drug peddling, heroin addiction, and armed robbery after he loses his bank job and faces the difficulties of survival in the rigged systems of business, government, and feudal networks of power, privilege, and corruption in the city of Lahore. Threaded through the descent narrative of the main protagonist, the novel includes, in a minor strain, the ascent narrative of Manucci, Daru's servant boy. The novel uses multiple narrators, alternating between Daru, who narrates all the odd-numbered chapters, and various other characters who narrate the even-numbered ones: Murad Badshah, the lower-class drug-peddler with whom Dari robs a jewelry store; Ozi/Aurangzeb, Daru's childhood friend, son of a wealthy and corrupt ex-army official; Mumtaz, Ozi's wife and Daru's lover; and an unnamed narrator who addresses the judge hearing Daru's case as "you" (and who may be Mumtaz writing as a journalist under an alias).[17] Manucci, Daru's servant, does not narrate even one of the seventeen chapters. Manucci's social status seems to shape his narrative status: he is not given the importance of offering even one piece of testimony in a story told through multiple perspectives. This would have been a very different novel if the servant were given the opportunity to tell what he saw. However, like a dim shadow, Manucci dogs Daru's decline. Both like and unlike a double, Manucci's own story offers a chiasmic alternative to Daru's, as, by the end, their trajectories cross over and reverse: when Daru lands in prison, Manucci is adopted by Mumtaz, and promised a possible avenue out of servitude.

Hamid pulls Manucci into the middle ground of this novel for several reasons. At first, Manucci appears as the devoted servant who confirms Daru's middle-class status. With no parents or siblings, twenty-something Daru lives alone in a two-person household with Manucci as his cook, cleaner, and personal attendant, available at all times to be ordered to do all kinds of jobs. Like a mother or wife, Manucci wakes Daru when he is late for work, and serves him breakfast; like a servant, he addresses Daru as "Saab" (equivalent to "Sir") (18, 72). Like a master, Daru is peremptory in his tone, uses casual epithets like "you crook," and frequently "yells" for Manucci when he wants something (73, 72).[18] Yet, while maintaining master-servant boundaries, in the beginning they also have an almost affectionate homosocial relationship. Daru indulges Manucci, allowing him to watch TV with him, fall asleep at his feet, and sleep in his air-conditioned living room "because the servant quarters are too hot in the summertime" (42). When Daru's electricity is cut off, and, with as-yet unshaken faith in his master, Manucci smilingly assures Daru it will come back, Daru reflects, "The boy has no fear of me," as if that is abnormal, as if servants are supposed to fear their masters (72).

In *Moth Smoke*, Manucci also serves as a marker of the extreme precarity from which servitude offers a relative refuge, and of the failure of the supposedly democratic Pakistani state to provide the most basic protections or shelter for its most vulnerable populations. Set in 1990s neoliberal Pakistan, after the end of an eleven-year military dictatorship, the novel documents the rise of a new super-rich business class coincident with an existing feudal elite. Though we never learn how he acquires his Italian name, or what his real name is, we learn a little about Manucci's horrifying past: that he was a street urchin who lost a kidney to the "kidney-theft racket" and was "lucky [that] they only took one of his" (124); that he became a servant as a result of Daru's mother's benevolence when he tried to steal from her in the marketplace and she caught him by the ear and decided that "what Manucci needed was a home and some discipline" (110). Hamid twice overtly likens Manucci to Kipling's Kim: like that irrepressibly street-smart child of empire, Manucci also "sat, in defiance of municipal orders, astride the gun Zam-Zammah" (109). But unlike the "romantic" Kim, Manucci has no hope of access to higher status, no magical amulet or secret identity to enable recovery by imperial or governmental powers (124). And like Kim, Manuccu's adoption by a higher power is also self-serving, pressing him into domestic (not imperial) service. "It's difficult finding good servants these days," remarks Ozi tellingly (178). The upper classes, Hamid makes it clear, bring the poor into their homes not just as an act of kindness.

As the novel progresses, Manucci becomes a silent witness to Daru's growing misdeeds, and an example of servant loyalty as Daru's circumstances become more and more straitened. Remaining with Daru even when Daru cannot afford to pay him, Manucci continues to assure Daru of his class status even as Daru starts to lose that status. Indeed, Daru becomes more peremptory and makes more unreasonable demands of Manucci. When Daru witnesses his friend Ozi run a red light, hit a bicyclist, and flee, Daru takes the dying boy to the hospital and returns home to order Manucci both to clean his car and keep his mouth shut:

> When Manucci sees the blood on the back seat of the car, he just stands there with his lips pressed together like a kiss and questions ballooning behind his eyes. But I take one look at him and say "Clean it," and he jerks to attention, running for a bucket of water and cloth. (98)

Hamid's description of Manucci exceeds mere functionality as he presents the complex affective relationship between the servant boy and his master. (As we will see in Chapters 4 and 5, Gunesekera and Adiga recast such a relationship from the servant boy's perspective.) Hamid presents Manucci evocatively, as at once intelligent and self-controlled, innocent and knowing, querying with his body but not with his voice. Daru's account suggests how he reads but ignores Manucci's claims on him, "his lips" shaped "like a kiss," how he cuts off that wordless questioning to command Manucci both to stifle his curiosity and do his dirty work.

Manucci becomes more important in this narrative, however, when he becomes the moral voice of conscience, and objects, not to Daru's adulterous affair with Mumtaz, Daru's best friend's wife, but to Daru's heroin-taking and drug-peddling to minors. Daru's descent into moral monstrosity is marked most clearly by the decline of his relationship with Manucci. Hence an important role played by Manucci in this novel is as a measure of Daru's descent into darkness. In a key moment that gives the book its title, Manucci first refuses to do what Daru demands. Daru sees Manucci watching a "moth in love" circling a flame, and demands a fly swatter to kill it. When Manucci protests, "No, saab," Daru reports: "I hit him across the top of his head, not too hard and with an open hand, but forcefully enough to let him know that I won't put up with any impertinence" (137–138). In this first act of physical violence, when Manucci resists becoming an accomplice to Daru's casual destructiveness, Daru abuses his power, precisely because of his diminished and disgraced social status. But he also learns from Manucci, realizing that this is a metaphor for his own self-destructive tendencies as he observes the moth literally turn to smoke, burning itself to death in the flame it cannot resist.

Hamid accentuates how Daru's treatment of Manucci is a gauge of Daru's insecurity and deterioration, heightened by the fact that Daru is the narrator. Hamid thus uses Daru's own voice to reveal his decline. When Mumtaz comes to visit, he becomes jealous of Manucci's open friendliness toward her, and of the attention she pays the child, while both maintain the codes that signal mutual recognition of class and gender distance:

> Mumtaz is sitting on the sofa, legs crossed, with Manucci squatting on the floor beside her. He's chatting away, which annoys me, because I don't like it when the boy forgets his place. It makes me look bad, as though I've fallen so far my servant thinks there's no longer any need for him to behave formally. . . .
> "Is he telling you about his adventures?" I ask loudly, in the ringing tones of a master of the house making his presence known. Manucci falls silent. (164)

Daru feels the need to over-perform mastery precisely when he knows that it is slipping. Displacing his own abjection, he puts Manucci down, reinforcing well-known cultural codes of servitude.[19] When Mumtaz confronts him later, Daru gets angry and embarrassed that she might think he could be "jealous of his own servant" (for that in itself would diminish him), but after she leaves, and he finds out that Manucci has told her that he spends the day idling and taking drugs, he takes his leather belt to Manucci's "servant quarters" and threatens to "thrash" him "if he talks about [him] behind [his] back" (172). Again, Hamid presents Manucci's affective response through silence and body language, through what Daru sees: "[Manucci] pulls his bedsheet up around his eyes and stares at me. But he doesn't do it again," reports Daru (172). In an uglier moment, when Daru is embarrassed by the contrast between his own unkempt, unwashed self and the newly bathed, crisply clothed Manucci, he turns on the smiling boy: "Go clean my bathroom ... And scrub behind the toilet. It's getting filthy" (171). The politics of dirt, both physical and symbolic, are complicated here, as Daru vents his frustration upon the one person who depends on and has stood by him. Spitefully forcing Manucci to clean the toilet is no substitute, clearly, for Daru's failure to clean himself both morally and otherwise. Unlike the writers discussed in the following chapters, who explore servants' interiorities, Hamid gives his readers no direct access to Manucci's inner consciousness, thoughts, or feelings, except via Daru's reactions (though Hamid leaves no doubt that Manucci has that interiority). His focus remains on Daru, making his decline visible via Manucci.

The climax or turning point in this relationship occurs when Daru physically hits Manucci, lashing out with full force after Manucci begs him to stop selling drugs to a teenage boy. Again, Hamid does not give us direct access to Manucci's consciousness. Yet, through the narrative voice of Daru, who gives his own account of what occurs, Hamid uses Manucci to underscore the depths to which Daru has fallen. The power of Hamid's writing here humanizes Manucci even as Daru dehumanizes him, offering indirect indicators of Manucci's consciousness via Daru's observation of Manucci's body language:

> I hear Manucci come up behind me. He doesn't say anything.
> "What is it?" I ask.
> "Saab."
> Something in his voice makes me turn around. He's looking at the ground, and when he looks up, I'm surprised because he's so afraid.
> "What?"
> "Don't do this...."
> This is wrong, saab. You shouldn't sell charas." (178)

First, Daru reads Manucci's silence. The moment indicates how well they know each other, how Daru is able to pick up something unusual in Manucci's silent advance, and how even the tenor of his voice addressing him with the respectful title "saab" ("master"), has the power to make Daru turn around. Manucci performs servitude, looking at the ground, as if unable to meet Daru's eyes, unwilling to enact challenge. Yet Manucci's words bespeak a quiet assertiveness, a recognition on his part of a belonging that is ultimately repudiated by Daru's response. Manucci transgresses the role of the proper servant when he exerts moral authority over his master, as he tries to call on their deeper connection and the memory of Daru's mother to save Daru from himself. But Daru makes clear his need to retain his sense of self as master: "I feel the anger coming ... This will not happen. I won't permit it. My servant will not tell me what to do. ... I step forward and slap him across the face with all my strength" (178).

Hamid's presentation of this brutal moment of betrayal of this child who has come to depend on Daru, is in some ways more powerful because it is told in Daru's voice, making clear his extraordinary self-delusion and decline into monstrosity. The most we get of Manucci's inner world is via what Daru perceives. As Manucci's "head snaps to one side," and he falls to the ground and cries out, Daru reports, "Then he looks up at me, the fear gone from his expression, leaving only seriousness and a gleam in one watering eye" (178). The scene presents at least three levels of irony here: one, that Manucci shows fear before he speaks, and that though he speaks in spite of his fear, he loses that fear after he sees what Daru has become; two, that in asserting such a form of mastery, Daru makes clear that he no longer has mastery, either of himself or of Manucci; and three, that subsequent to this, Manucci enacts an important advantage of the servant over the slave, and leaves.

Here is where the trajectories of Daru and Manucci diverge, even as, in a telling moment, Daru recognizes their mutual interdependence:

> What am I going to do? I don't know how to cook or clean or do the wash. And I'll be damned if I'm going to learn. *The only people in my neighborhood who don't have servants are servants themselves.* Except for me. And I refuse to serve. I'm done with giving. Giving service to bank clients, giving respect to people who haven't earned it, giving hash and getting punished. I'm ready to take. (206; my emphasis)

I want to pull out three points from this telling moment. First, Daru again defines himself as master, clear about his lack of household skills and proud of it. Like women's labor, servants' work is both needed and demeaned. Daru is clear that he would not deign to learn to cook or clean, that what defines him, gives him his identity, is his sense of gendered and classed entitlement, his feeling that he is superior and therefore deserves to have someone else do these tasks for him. This is a matter of Daru's internal sense of self and status, not just of show. Second, Daru sees himself as placed in a curious state of in-betweenness in relation to his neighborhood, where everyone else has servants. What does not having a servant make him, he asks himself—a servant? And third, his thoughts turn by extension to his broader society, where, by the same binary logic, one is also either a servant or a master. His entire position as a member of Pakistani society is now seen via the lens of servitude. Either he is a servant in society at large or a taker of service from others. As he moves from the literal servant to the metaphoric, Daru (and Hamid as well) becomes very clear: in this world, the givers are servants; the takers are the servanted. Daru is determined not to be a servant.

Moth Smoke offers an unusual mode of making the figure of the servant necessary to the narrative: as the literal basis for the generalized malaise of Pakistani society in 1998. In Lahore in particular, where feudal landlords, businessmen, and army officials wield inordinate power over others, the public sphere of business and politics mirrors the domestic sphere of server and served. It is no small detail that the novel begins with Daru being fired from his bank job because he refuses to play servant to a feudal landowner. Daru's decline begins when he is punished for refusing to kowtow, to play sycophant in this system. He arrives at his office one morning to find a powerful client waiting for him, "rotating imperiously" in Daru's office chair, a man he describes as "a rural landlord with half a million U.S. [dollars] in his account, a seat in the Provincial Assembly, and eyebrows that meet in the middle like a second pair of whiskers. His pastimes include fighting the spread of primary education and stalling the census" (20). In Hamid's biting satire, Malik Jiwan is truly filthy rich, with ill-gotten gains from generations of indigent exploited peasants, from control of the government, and from the political clout to maintain his power by keeping the poor disenfranchised and uneducated.

When Jiwan demands whether his check has cleared, and Daru replies that it has not, Jiwan becomes irate. Their dynamic escalates because Jiwan expects not just unreasonable service, but servility; he wants Daru to abase himself, to show deference:

> "Didn't I tell you to take care of this personally?"
> "I don't remember your saying that, Mr. Jiwan"
> "Well I remember saying it."
> Good for you. "Next time you really ought to consider a cashier's check."
> "Are you making fun of me?" (20)

Jiwan can sense the implicit resistance in Daru's insouciant manner. "I'm not one of your serfs, bastard," thinks Daru, though he does not say it; "Your tone is disrespectful" says the angered Jiwan; "Do you know who I am" (20–21). (It is no small irony that Jiwan demands a respect that he does not give to fellow human beings.) To enhance his point, Hamid assigns these minor characters meaningful names. Jiwan's first name is "Malik" (meaning master, or lord), and he calls the bank manager by his first name "Ghulam" (meaning slave or servant). When Jiwan calls the bank manager and complains, Ghulam is predictably servile, and does not support Daru. It is then that Daru utters the life-changing words that get him fired. As he explains:

> I've had a bad day. A bad month, actually. And there's only so much nonsense a self-respecting fellow can be expected to take from these megalomaniacs. So I say it. "*This is a bank, not your servant quarters, Mr. Jiwan. If you want better service, maybe you ought to learn some manners.*" (22, emphasis added)

What Daru is fighting for is respect, and self-respect—he has more pride than his manager. But his medium is the language of servitude. Literal servitude provides the basis for what has become a metaphor for an operative binary in this society between the powerful and the disempowered, shaping the mode of interrelation between them. Daru loses his place, literally and metaphorically, because he refuses to enact the servant to this corrupt tyrant, and to participate in a system that only allows men to be one or the other. After this, he cannot find a job, even with the string-pulling of his friend Ozi's father. His decline is precipitated by his recognition of a system of obsequiousness where merit will achieve nothing, and where self-respect without influence will take him nowhere but down. Daru makes his own choices that escalate his downward spiral, but Hamid also makes clearly visible the real conditions that contribute to Daru's despair.

Afterward, when his uncle asks Daru about whether an influential friend of his had helped in Daru's job-search. Daru's response is telling: "'Butt saab,' I say, stressing the *saab*, 'told me other people were better connected'" (57). By using the word "saab" (a descriptor that signifies the speaker's deference, and that also means master, as used by Manucci for Daru himself), Daru sardonically underscores his understanding that his uncle's friend is no longer a social equal, but a superior to whom he has to kiss up, like a servant. With the pun on the name Butt, Hamid also suggests butt-kissing, confirming the extent to which a middle-class job-seeker like Daru, with no connections, must enact servility to beg for a job in this system.

With the figure of the servant boy, however, Hamid does something unusual: he suggests at the end a way out of servitude for Manucci, if not for Daru. After Daru has been sentenced to prison for the murder of a boy that Ozi killed, Mumtaz tells Daru that she will continue to look for evidence to exonerate him: "Manucci's been a big help tracking down witnesses. When I left Ozi he left with me. I've discovered he's a brilliant investigator. I might make a journalist out of him, once I've taught him how to read properly" (244). This is the last mention of Manucci in this novel, which remains focused on Daru. Even here, Manucci is mentioned in Mumtaz's narration as potentially useful for her own purposes. From that subsidiary place, it offers, on the one hand, hope that Manucci's life will change, suggesting an alternate future out of (at least literal) servitude, as a journalist, an uncoverer of truth, exposer of corruption, contingent crucially on his learning to read. On the other hand, it is relayed in her upper-class peremptory voice, conveying her plan for Manucci. She has not asked Manucci what he wants, nor given him agency in deciding his future, which depends on her whim, on her individual and exceptional beneficence, on what she "might" do if he continues to please her. There is no way out of servitude for him on his own.

In *Moth Smoke*, Hamid pulls the servant into the middle ground, but in different ways than Rushdie or Selvadurai. He presents an unusually attentive, detailed, affective relationship between master and servant, of emotional and practical interdependence. He humanizes the servant boy and highlights the failure of the postcolonial state to protect the vulnerable, specifically the street child. Manucci also becomes a way for Hamid to expose and track the moral decline of the protagonist, as seen in the privacy of his own home. With this close-up of literal servitude, Hamid makes clearer what it means to understand servitude figuratively as a generalized condition in this novel, as a descriptor of the relations between those with more and less power, in a system without any guardrails to prevent abuse. Servitude is what the middle class most fervently wish to avoid for themselves, and what they wish to maintain in their homes as a marker of their status. And finally, Hamid suggests, while servitude may be a midway refuge for the exploited underclass, a far better alternative and future remains to be imagined, not just at the capricious hands of the self-serving elite.

Repudiating Refuge: Monica Ali's *Brick Lane*

Bangladeshi British writer Monica Ali's debut novel *Brick Lane* (2003) focuses on the story of Nazneen, a young Bangladeshi village woman brought to London via an arranged marriage to a much older man. It charts how, from the mid-1980s to the early 2000s, Nazneen adapts to her new husband and home, suffers the death of her first-born son, raises two daughters, has an adulterous affair with a younger man (a British Bangladeshi Islamicist), and belatedly develops a sense of her own independence and agency strengthened by female friendship and solidarity.[20] Ali explores, among other things, the disabling internalization of fatalism (the belief in fate) or passivity inculcated in Nazneen by her mother, the gendered problems faced by impoverished Bangladeshi women in Bangladesh and Britain, racism and xenophobia in Britain, the rise of Islamophobia and Islamicist movements among disenfranchised and impoverished immigrants, and the consequences of 9/11 on these marginalized populations. Intertwined with the immigrant narrative of Nazneen in London, however, is the relatively minor but important contrasting narrative of Nazneen's younger sister Hasina in Bangladesh, who runs away from home at age sixteen to carve her own life, and for a significant period, becomes a domestic servant.[21] Female servitude is thus a key part of this novel in at least two ways: for the poor, uneducated village woman in Bangladesh, it is presented as both a welcome refuge from worse alternatives, and eventually, as not enough; for the immigrant woman in Britain, servitude offers comparison in that Nazneen, though married to a man who provides for her, also effectively functions as a domestic servant in his house.

Unlike Nazneen, who silently accepts and endures, Hasina refuses both fate and fatalism to exercise agency even in the face of rapidly worsening conditions.

Seeking alternatives—to an oppressive and patriarchal father, an abusive and violent husband, sweatshop work in a garment factory, forced prostitution, and betrayal by numerous men in the city—Hasina finds refuge in domestic service as a maid for an affluent family. At the end, however, she flees servitude, eloping with the household cook, for an uncertain and unknown future. Hasina's narrative clearly serves to demonstrate the relative advantages that the poor Bangladeshi emigrant married woman in London has in contrast to the poor internal migrant and single woman in Dhaka. But Hasina's narrative also serves to compare unfavorably the acquiescence and defeatism of Nazneen versus the strength, irrepressibility, and will to live of her sister Hasina. It is therefore ironic, Ali suggests at the end, that Nazneen, despite her submissiveness, has better opportunities, support system, and outcome in Britain than Hasina, despite Hasina's feistiness, does in Bangladesh.

I want to focus here on the sections of the novel that address Hasina's experience as a maid. Servitude is not a central concern in this diasporic millennial novel. Hasina's story, of which servitude is a part, occupies a fraction of textual space compared to Nazneen's. Nor is it a permanent marker of Hasina's identity. But servitude is crucial both to Hasina's story and to the contrast it creates for Nazneen's. At first, domestic service is a welcome refuge for Hasina when she is rescued by Christian missionaries from destitution and prostitution, taken to the "House of Falling Women," and then employed as a maid by a "charitable lady" (179).[22] Hasina's first account of servitude is joyous; she perceives it as a fresh start, an opportunity, a safe haven from her experience of life on the streets:

Everything I am putting out of mind now. They have taken me in and I am maid in good house. All are kind. Children are beautiful. My room is solid wall room. Clean place. Nothing here for making scared of. Mistress is kind. Mister is kind. They give plenty of food. (141; italics in original)[23]

Hasina clearly values, in fact takes pleasure in, the physical safety, the creature comforts (the wood furniture that glows, the "electric light" in her room, the children's toys, the space provided by multiple rooms), and, most importantly, the expectation that she does not have to pay for food and lodging with coerced sexual labor (179). Though she is assigned multiple menial tasks (normally distributed among a variety of servants) that even include gardening, she sees herself as highly fortunate:

My duty in house is for care the children cleaning wash plate wash clothes shopping and errand and thing. That is all. There is man for cooking and he also take heavy work in garden and I only do is bit watering weeding and grow some special few vegetable behind house. You see how is. Very good position. (180)

In describing Hasina's experiences as a maid, Ali offers an unusually detailed, complex portrayal of gendered domestic servitude, as experienced by a young and beautiful woman. Given the brutal exploitation and abuse she has experienced, Hasina finds in servitude psychological relief and emotional sustenance as well as material comfort. She grows to love the infant girl she has to look after, and savors the unprecedented offering of uncomplicated love and dependence from the child.

> Baby Daisy always want her face to me and she sit on my hip all day if only no work to do. When she smile she put her head back and show all her teeth. All my life I look for one thing only for love for giving and getting and it seem such a thing full of danger can eat you alive and now I stop the looking it come right up to me and show all it tiny little teeth. (185)

Despite her awkward language, Hasina's sincerity, tenderness, and poetic sensibility come through as she articulates her own desires, her yearning for love, and her surprise at finding it unexpectedly with the child of her rich employer. Repeatedly, Ali presents Hasina's servitude as a preferable contrast to other catastrophic narratives of poor women's suffering. After she sees a hospitalized woman friend whose husband has subjected her to a vicious acid attack, Hasina returns to find relief in her job and comfort in her charge. Servitude again provides the physical intimacy and attachment that she has not found anywhere else: "*Baby Daisy poke me in cheek and rub nose on my nose and I give thanks to Allah for this love which come at last*" (221).[24]

Ali also takes a risk in presenting all this from Hasina's perspective. Her representation of Hasina's ungrammatical English has been a subject of critical controversy, in no small part because the implausible discursive conceit unnecessarily diminishes the sister in Bangladesh, rendering in an artificially created, broken English an approximation of what would be Hasina's unschooled written Bengali. Though both sisters purportedly write to each other in semi-literate Bengali, equally unable to write or speak in English (these letters are not a literal representation of their writing), Ali's third-person rendition of Nazneen's consciousness, thoughts, speech, and letters in fluid English casts her by contrast as a more coherent and sympathetic character. Though the choice of first person would seem to give relatively more direct access to Hasina, paradoxically, the incoherence and sense of impediment created by her inarticulate language arguably create a filter, an unnecessary stumbling block for readers, whereas the relative clarity and reliability of third-person free indirect discourse offer more direct access to Nazneen as more knowable, understandable, and trustworthy. It makes Hasina more of a remote, pitiable, disadvantaged, and subaltern figure than Nazneen.

However, Hasina's first-person voice in her letters does offer the advantage of apparently offering her own story, as she experiences it, and gives space to her interiority.[25] In a rare moment in the novel, Ali partially explains her technical choices as indicators of Hasina's energetic, vivacious spirit, of her blithe disregard of rules and regulations. Through free indirect discourse, Ali conveys Nazneen's reflections on the contrast between the sisters' letter-writing: "Nazneen composed and recomposed her replies [in Bengali] until the grammar was satisfactory, all errors expunged along with any vital signs. But Hasina kicked aside all such constraints: her letters were full of mistakes and bursting with life" (72). Hasina, the narrator suggests, maintains a vitality and integrity in her voice, whereas Nazneen's efforts at self-correction crush the life in her writing. If we take Hasina's letters to be broadly veracious, her accounts convey both her naiveté and her extraordinary resilience and will to continue. Despite their nonstandard idiom, her letters also convey her imaginative sensibility, her sensuous appreciation, and joy in life, all of which come through in her poetic language. She describes herself gazing at Baby Daisy's curls and delicate face. "*I kiss her with very care. I feel like holding the breath sometime when I look at Baby Daisy. Is like have soap bubble on the hand catch light with thousand beautiful color*" (277). Highly unusual for English-language fiction, Ali's technique emphasizes a servant woman's interiority and subjectivity as itself powerful and coherent despite its awkward expression.

While servitude clearly provides Hasina with basic necessities, relative dignity, and most crucially, the sense of physical safety of which she has been deprived, her letters also show a gradual sense of doubt, of growing dissatisfaction and critique. She loves the children she is hired to care for, builds solidarity and community with other servants—particularly women servants in the neighborhood—and even likes her employer, Lovely the shallow socialite. But she is clear-sighted enough to see Lovely as self-absorbed and myopic, engaged in charitable activities for self-advancement rather than altruism. Through Hasina's letters, Ali also provides a glimpse of the lives and voices of other servants, of the gendered differences and varied experiences of forms of servitude that Hasina begins to understand. Though (like Mary Pereira in *Midnight's Children*) Hasina sleeps on the floor of the baby's room to attend to the baby at night, she sees that she is relatively privileged compared to the male cook Zaid, who (like Musa) does not have his own room or a "*proper servant quarter*" and has to sleep on the kitchen table (181). We also learn from Hasina of maids in neighboring homes, though we do not know what pasts have brought them to their present conditions: Syeeda, who smiles, says nothing, but seems content with her lot; the unnamed child-maid who looks "*frighten*" (sic) and runs away when Hasina calls to her (218). Hasina's servitude thus suggests both protection from much worse realities—she witnesses a bank robbery where the robbers are burned alive by an angry vigilante mob in the absence of state provision of public security, for instance—and affirmation for Nazneen, the recipient of her letters, that despite Nazneen's unhappiness, her life in Britain is relatively better. Hasina explicitly cautions Nazneen against the nostalgia and growing desire for return expressed by Nazneen's husband.

Hasina learns most, however, from Zaid the cook, her fellow servant, as she begins to see his dissatisfaction, and his awareness of the broader politics of servitude as a systemic form of exploitation of the underclasses. When Hasina is grateful for her own room, she reports, he points out how tiny it is: "*'Room?' He say. 'What room? I see cupboard. I see shelf. I don't see bloody room'*" (181). When their employer James complains loudly to his wife about corrupt politicians and how they damage his business, Zaid stands behind the dining room door and listens. He then voices his skepticism and alternative analysis to Hasina in the kitchen: "*this people is all the time shitting and say stink is not come from own behind*" (220). He is vigilant and actively alert to what is going on in the home and the nation, understands the connections between them, and implicates the employer in the system that ultimately benefits the upper classes. In sharing his ideas with Hasina, he begins to educate his co-servant in skepticism and covert resistance. At first Hasina is baffled by his words, but she begins to respect him. "He look pretty smart," she notes (220). When he sees Hasina kissing the baby, he warns her against the trap of emotional binds, of forgetting that she is a servant: "Don't make mistake. She is not for you" (278). A servant, he reminds Hasina, will never be family: she can be kicked out at any time.

A turning point occurs when Hasina reports Zaid's response to their wealthy employers' discussions about the different political parties running for election: "*The cook say do you hear them how they talk? Politics is this. Politics is that.... All strike and violence and guns and stabbing... Like as if had nothing to do with them. But this is system. And who has made the system? Is not the laborer. Is not the beggar*" (279). Zaid's political analysis astutely identifies the nation's problems as *systemic*, not due to any one individual or political party, but maintained by the ruling class. When Hasina asks him "which (political) side" he supports, his answer is "*My side*" (279). None of the rival parties, he suggests, look out for the underclasses; though, he asserts, he will support "whoever give pay," or whichever party will economically benefit the poorest of the nation (279). It is after this that Hasina begins to speak up and challenge her employer's pretensions. When Lovely announces that she plans to start a campaign to end child labor, Hasina sees through Lovely's self-advertising. She knows that Lovely's real motivation is to best her rival, and calls out Lovely's obliviousness: "*Lovely tell me she will start Charity for stopping the child worker. Which ones you will stop I asking to her. Oh she say all of them. The maid next door? I asking her this. She look surprise*" (301). Lovely is surprised presumably by Hasina's pertness and by her own ignorance of the child who works as a maid literally next door. Hasina is clearly more aware of the realities, proximity, and pervasiveness of child labor, and of how Lovely is a beneficiary of the very system she claims to deplore.[26]

It is also after this encounter that Hasina becomes dissatisfied with servitude. She gives in to her desire to be like Lovely, able to "wander around" in her own house (301). She breaks the boundaries of servitude: when the employers are away, Hasina goes into the guest room, lies on the clean bedsheets, and revels in their luxurious sensuousness; she puts on Lovely's make up and finds Zaid watching her. They understand each other and each other's desires: "*He look at me and I know this look*," she writes (302).[27] In her last letter to her sister, before she disappears, Hasina describes her "unquiet mind," but voices most clearly why she cannot remain a servant: "*Big house it good house. But one room house feel big if belong in fact to you*" (365). What she wants is a modest place of her own, where she is not a servant, not dependence and subordination in someone else's grand house. Hasina refuses her mother's code of inculcated helplessness and passive suffering. She teaches Nazneen likewise to reject that gendered philosophy of acquiescence, revealing, finally, that their mother violated her own philosophy of acceptance and committed suicide, that ironically, their mother's only act of agency was to repudiate her circumstances through self-annihilation: "*Amma always say we are women what can we do? . . . But I am not like her. Waiting around. Suffering around. She wrong*" (365). Hasina is very clear that she prefers to take risks, to craft her own life. Servitude is for her an important intermediate stepping-stone, not an end-point in her life's journey.

At the end, when Hasina runs away with Zaid, we hear about it indirectly from Chanu, Nazneen's husband, who telephones Nazneen from Bangladesh with the "terrible" news (412). Condemning it as yet another foolish move on Hasina's part, Chanu views it as improvident and risky to give up the security of servitude with a "respectable" family (411): "Why did she do it? Why does she do these things?" he says with exasperation (413). As a middle-class man, he cannot understand why a woman would give up the (relative) safety of servitude. Nazneen, however, sees it differently. "Because . . . she isn't going to give up," she replies (413). For Hasina, as Nazneen understands, accepting servitude for life is to give up (or give in), to accept fatalistically what life has doled out. Earlier, Nazneen recalls a childhood memory of Hasina calling to her, inviting her to jump with her sister into a deep body of water. But, emblematically, Hasina "never waited. She ran and jumped, disappeared and resurfaced. Her hair streamed behind her, catching little gems of water and sunlight" (357). It is a moment deeply characteristic of Hasina, who, again at the end, jumps without waiting, without caution, willing to dare, to go all in. This memory suggests that though she has disappeared again, Hasina will again resurface, "unbroken" as Chanu earlier describes her, living life to the full (411). To remain a servant, Ali suggests, is to settle for less. Both Zaid and Hasina have greater aspirations. And yet, as the novel also reminds us, Hasina's past experiences also indicate how gender differences magnify the risks that Hasina has taken. Her choice to leave servitude carries with it far greater danger for her than it does for Zaid. It is therefore telling that Hasina, knowing this, is still willing to take the risk to leave servitude behind.

Servitude functions in *Brick Lane* as a condition of in-betweenness, as clearly a better option and refuge for the unprotected indigent woman from the dangers of commercial and sexual exploitation awaiting her in the postcolonial city, but also as insufficient, as ultimately degrading, stigmatized, and unfulfilling for the very woman who has suffered worse and yet wants more. Servitude in this novel is both a refuge, and eventually not enough to those who aspire for more from their lives. It is crucial not only to Hasina's story but also to Nazneen's, because it serves to locate Nazneen as effectively a servant in her marriage to Chanu. Like Mohsin Hamid, Monica Ali is unusual among South Asian English writers in her attempt to imagine ways out of servitude, and to cast it as not a permanent or inevitable condition.

At a climactic moment in *The Moor's Last Sigh*, when an unimaginable betrayal destroys the protagonist's family, the banished Moor imagines his devastated parents and household as follows: "*through a shadowed doorway a glimpse of frightened servants, fluttering like trembling hands at the edges of the frame*" (*Moor*, 321). In this arresting phrase, Rushdie captures the condition of servants in his fiction: they are always there, on the edges of an upper-class family's story, affected by what happens, noticed as fragile and vulnerable, "trembling" on the margins, "hands" but not whole, apart and yet part of a picture that seems static. But that picture quickly becomes dynamic, "fluttering" in an eye-catching movement, on the cusp, beginning to break in through the frame. As I show in this chapter, Rushdie moves servants from the edges of the frame to the middle ground, though with notable self-contradiction. Rushdie's pivotal, game-changing work from the 1980s to 1990s brings a startling new visibility and importance to servants, and calls attention to the injustices of servitude in new ways, even as it simultaneously diminishes the servant figure through a reductive comical lens, as the butt of comic humor. After Rushdie, many (though by no means all) transnational, diasporic South Asian fiction writers—such as Shyam Selvadurai, Mohsin Hamid, Monica Ali—also pull the servant into the middle ground, and also attend critically, if briefly, to servitude, but differently, for diverse purposes, without Rushdie's self-contradictions. In so doing, they create a midpoint in the trajectory of South Asian English fiction this book charts, and a point of comparison and departure for the emergent servitude fiction to which we can now turn.

PART TWO

3
Foregrounding the Servant
What's New About Daniyal Mueenuddin's Interlinked Short Stories

In 2009 Pakistani-American writer Daniyal Mueenuddin published his debut collection of interlinked short stories, *In Other Rooms, Other Wonders*, to strong acclaim. Many Western reviewers noted that the freshness of Mueenuddin's writing came from his sympathetic and unusual focus on servants. Amy Rosenberg, for instance, wrote in *Bookforum*:

> Daniyal Mueenuddin, a half-American, half-Pakistani writer, has crafted a chronicle of poverty as detailed and revealing as any by Steinbeck, with the same drive to humanize his subjects. Mueenuddin's collection of linked stories does for the servants of Pakistan what Steinbeck's fiction did for the laborers of America, capturing the lives of individuals whose suffering stems from their class situation.... Mueenuddin's sympathy lies not with Harouni ... but with the workers, managers, and servants who sustain his farm, city mansion, and weekend home and whose lives are destroyed by the failure of the old system.

In *Bookslut*, Jacob Silverman found Mueenuddin's many servant stories "brilliantly" successful, "vividly drawn," even "heart-rending," in comparison with the few about Pakistan's elite. Richard Murphy, in *The Daily Beast*, praised Mueenuddin as "a prodigiously talented writer, capable of imagining the inner lives of Punjabi aristocrats and their servants with *equal* sympathy, precision and power," and likewise noted Mueenuddin's unusual attention to those who suffer from Pakistan's stark social and economic inequalities: "[His] characters inhabit a profoundly unequal world in which a destitute majority toils to provide comfort for the privileged few." Though Mueenuddin belongs to an "accomplished crowd" of young Anglophone Pakistani writers like Mohsin Hamid and Kamila Shamsie who address "a global literary audience," wrote Murphy, he also "stands apart" because "his characters span the entire range of Pakistani society, rather than focusing mainly on the urban elite." Indeed, Murphy argued, Mueenuddin is distinctive for "his preoccupation with social justice," enabling readers to understand "contemporary Pakistan" in new ways.

Most Western reviewers were quick to compare Mueenuddin to Western male writers they knew, like Gogol, Chekhov, Turgenev, Faulkner, and Truman Capote. But apart from some obvious comparisons to Mohsin Hamid, another internationally successful young Pakistani male writer with Ivy League credentials, almost none attempted to link Mueenuddin's writing to other South Asian or postcolonial writers (which is rather odd, given the detailed texture of Mueenuddin's work and its setting in Pakistan).[1] In this chapter, I locate Mueenuddin's work in relation to that of other South Asian writers, and explore how his fiction both does something new in the context of South Asian literature in English, and belongs within an emergent wave of global and transnational or bicultural millennial South Asian fiction that has begun to focus anew on servitude as a system. This servitude fiction, I argue, brings servants as characters into the foreground and tries to change, as it makes visible, habituated and acculturated South Asian ways of seeing, treating, and representing domestic servants.

Unlike the Anglophone South Asian writers discussed in the previous two chapters, and unlike his Pakistani contemporaries (such as Hamid or Shamsie) who write about and from the perspective of Pakistani elite or middle classes, Mueenuddin is the first among Anglophone Pakistani writers to give empathetic attention to the experience and interiority of the domestic servants who work in upper- and middle-class homes. Indeed, Mueenuddin's delicate, nuanced short stories move back and forth between the psychic inner worlds of various servants and the systemic outer world of power and hierarchy that constitutes them and their complex relationships with their employers and other servants. Mueenuddin is moreover distinctive even among the servitude fiction writers discussed in this book in his use of the *form* of the interlinked short story, which, unlike the novels I discuss in Chapters 4 and 5 that focus on a single servant protagonist's perspective, instead allows for an intra-textual comparative exploration of multiple and diverse servant subjectivities and experiences. Unusual both for the variety of servants he presents in his collection through the short-story form, and for his interest in the intersection of late feudalism and gendered servitude in Pakistan, Mueenuddin focuses in over half his stories on servants as protagonists that are central, not marginal, to the narrative.

Focusing on Mueenuddin's servant stories, I argue in this chapter that his most significant interventions inhere in his evocation of the psychic *interiority* of servitude and his exploration of the effects on diverse servant subjectivities of daily indignities and habituation to a culture of humiliation and subservience. He asks how such a system affects relations among servants as well as between servants and employers, as well as how it is gendered, sexualized, or inscribed on the body. A major goal of his stories, I suggest, is to re-humanize those who are regularly dehumanized; to build an understanding of different subjectivities through techniques of detailed observation and beautifully written, sensitive, nuanced representation; and to carve a space for the articulation of desire for those otherwise rendered as (and who come to see themselves as) abject or merely instrumental. He is interested less in what servants can tell us about the constitution of the upper classes or how elite subjects are formed or understand themselves, and more in interrogating a system that is taken as normal in postcolonial Pakistan, in de-normalizing it, in making visible and questioning what is usually taken for granted. Another goal for Mueenuddin, however, is to understand how those empowered to command or abuse servants are *systemically* enabled to enact such power. His stories ask us to focus, with an important duality of vision, on servant and employer interiority and interaction as well as the interlocking social, political, historical, legal, gendered, and cultural frameworks that necessarily constitute servant subjectivities and interrelationships—in other words, on the *systems* within which individuals are placed and that shape who they become. Hence, these are not short, compact, or rushed short stories. These stories are long, leisurely, and capacious, including, as they gradually unravel over lengths of time and changing circumstances, explorations of the inner consciousnesses of various characters, their shifting relationships, the nuanced micropolitics of various interactions, and elucidating the stratified yet complicated worlds these individuals inhabit.

Born in 1963 to an American journalist mother and a Pakistani father who was a feudal landowner and government official, Mueenuddin grew up in Lahore, Pakistan, and Elroy, Wisconsin. He majored in English at Dartmouth College, earned a law degree from Yale University, and worked as a corporate lawyer in New York City before returning to manage his father's farmlands in southern Punjab, where he began writing fiction. Of the eight stories in *In Other Rooms*, three were first published in *The New Yorker*, one in *Granta*, one in *Zoetrope*, and one was selected by Salman Rushdie for *The Best American Short Stories of 2008*. *In Other Rooms* was a 2009 National Book Awards and Pulitzer Prize finalist and was named one of the top ten books of the year by *Time Magazine*, *Publisher's Weekly*, *The Guardian*, and *The Economist*, among others. Mueenuddin acknowledges that, like many transnational writers, his perspective is that of a privileged insider-outsider, not solely Pakistani or American, but hyphenated or multiply affiliated: "Half-Pakistani and half-American, I have spent equal amounts of time in each country, and so, knowing both cultures well and belonging to both, I equally belong to neither, looking at both with an outsider's eye. These stories are written from that place in-between, written to help both me and my reader bridge the gap."[2] He is thus well able to see as insiders might not, to translate (as attested by his success in prestigious American and British venues), and to render with stunning empathy, acuity, and precision the lives of Punjabi Pakistanis ranging from humble villagers, middlemen, and hangers-on, to the most aristocratic and cosmopolitan of elite jet-setters. Taking place mostly in 1970s and 1980s Pakistan, the stories in *In Other Rooms* are loosely linked through the figure of K. K. Harouni, an aging feudal landlord challenged by the rise of a newly rich and powerful industrialist class, and revolve around this feudal world in transition. They shift perspectives, zooming in to concentrate on different individuals and their intricately related lives that are yet disjunct from one another because of different social locations, intersectionally constituted by class, gender, age, and so on. In an important decentering move, Mueenuddin refrains from making the employer/landowner Harouni the focus of even one story: over half of the stories zero in on domestic servants—male and female, rural and urban, young and old—with an attentiveness, complexity, and diversity unprecedented in earlier Anglophone South Asian or diasporic writing.

The seemingly independent stories in this collection are interlinked, offering different dimensions of intersecting lives that all occupy Harouni's world without necessary interaction, playing off one another. The arrangement of the stories reveals two arcs: one, a movement from exterior to interior spaces and then back to exterior spaces; and two, a movement that begins with servant stories, shifts to higher and higher classes, and then back to a villager whose life is destroyed after he becomes a servant. Servants thus both frame and centrally occupy the collection. Beginning with "Nawabdin," about an electrician who acts like a domestic servant at the outer edges of the feudal household, the collection shifts to male-female intra-servant sexual relations ("Saleema"), male employer–female servant sexual relations ("Provide, Provide"), to male-male employer-servant relations ("About a Burning Girl"), and finally, female employer–male servant relations (A Spoiled Man"). The title story, "In Other Rooms, Other Wonders," placed in the middle of the collection, concerns a lower-middle-class girl caught between servants and elites, who tries to improve her lot by having sex with her wealthy old relative, Harouni. The servants in this story become guardians of social and moral codes, enacting resentment or servility toward the girl, whose transgressive sexual labor by comparison both lowers and elevates them in relation to her. The only story in the collection with no mention of servants at all ("Our Lady of Paris") is tellingly *not* set in Pakistan; in which an upper-class Pakistani couple visits Paris to manipulate their son's American girlfriend into leaving him. Even "Lily," about a disintegrating marriage between a young socialite and wealthy landowner, teems with various nameless servants as minor figures, whose constant presence both enables their employers' freedom from labor and limits their privacy.[3] The collection is thus carefully shaped as a whole, with an intricate thematic and formal design.

While my primary method is intensive close analysis of Mueenuddin's stories, with the aim of identifying their innovations and interventions and unfolding the implicit arguments they make, I also draw on broader interdisciplinary frameworks. These include the historical contexts of Pakistan's postcolonial feudal system, a socio-cultural understanding of abjection and power relations in Pakistan's contemporaneous culture of servitude, and intersectional feminist analysis of various interlocking dimensions of identity, such as gender, class, or age. I emphasize Mueenuddin's narrative techniques to highlight the modes by which he evokes the inner lives or interiority of the servants in his fiction, and to explore how his pioneering fiction calls attention to, and seeks to represent and evoke empathy for, figures who may seem remote or whose oppressive conditions of exigency may not be visible to international readers, and who may be so familiar to South Asian bourgeois ones as to be habitually overlooked. I examine how these stories dissolve the boundaries between the private (sexual and emotional interactions among servants and employers) and the public (the intrusion of state violence, law, and corruption in servant lives) and underscore their imbrication. I am interested in what cultural assumptions and social failures these stories seek to expose as well as what attitudinal shifts they exemplify and seek to effect in their readers.[4]

In contrast to the types of representation exemplified by many of the writers discussed in Chapters 1 and 2, Mueenuddin eschews instrumental usages of servant figures that would elevate or help educate the bourgeois (post)colonial subject, or perpetuate servant stereotypes. In Mueenuddin's servant stories the third-person narrator effaces himself (with one important exception), directing readers' attention unobtrusively and empathetically to the servant's interiority. However, unlike his contemporaries Aravind Adiga or Romesh Gunesekera, Mueenuddin does not attempt to narrate a story in a servant's voice.[5] Nor does he attempt to explore relations among women, as do Attia Hosain and Thrity Umrigar. Mueenuddin's stories, whether they explore intra-servant sexuality, or the sexual exploitation of women servants by their male masters, or the struggles of various servants to ameliorate their lot, focus on the complex emotions, intimate relations, and choices of individual servants. If he explores an employer's perspective, as in "Provide, Provide," or "About a Burning Girl," it is to unravel the employer's ethical failures and negative effects on servants.

At the same time, Mueenuddin also evokes a complex and diverse world of servants that constitutes and is constituted by each servant character. In Mueenuddin's fiction, servants do not serve as learning devices or reflective foils for an upper-class protagonist. Nor are they cast as helpless victims. Mueenuddin gives them agency, and the capacity for limited forms of resistance, presenting them as complex human beings located in a thickly described mesh of social and cultural conditions that are shown to shape their subjectivity and actions. Moreover, as the stories build, the accretion of perspectives creates a multidimensional kaleidoscopic effect. Hence, I want to emphasize Mueenuddin's choice of the interlinked short story form, and how that form affects the story and storytelling. Each short story is both stand-alone and connected to others; thus, its meanings multiply relationally, building a cumulative, kaleidoscopic effect, as each story plays off and enhances adjacent ones, and reflects off and adds to many others.

The short-story form in itself, perhaps because of its brevity, its capacity to provide a glimpse as opposed to a life trajectory, has often been regarded as more conducive than the novel to the exploration of social marginality. In South Asia, for pragmatic, even commercial reasons, many middle-class writers have found the shortness of the short story more amenable as a medium for the exploration of social marginality than the novel because it demands less investment of readers (of time or identification) and of publishers (of money). (Anand's difficulty finding a publisher for his first novel *Untouchable*, which focuses on a day in the life of an untouchable, is a case in point.) In his introduction to his short story collection *Under the Banyan Tree*, R. K. Narayan comments that the short story form allows for a brief, intensive exploration of marginal figures from all walks of South Indian life, whereas the longer form of the novel calls for protagonists that may better sustain the interest of middle- and upper-class readers:

> I realized that the short story is the best medium for utilizing the wealth of subjects available. A novel is a different proposition altogether, centralized as it is on a major theme, leaving out, necessarily, a great deal of the available material on the periphery. Short stories, on the other hand, can cover a wider field by presenting concentrated miniatures of human experience in all its opulence. (Narayan, 1992, viii)[6]

Where Narayan suggests that the short story's brevity gave him more leeway to explore marginality than the constraints imposed by cultural and length expectations of the novel, the Irish writer Frank O'Connor offers another explanation. In his quirky, still widely read book *The Lonely Voice* (published in 1963, the year Mueenuddin was born), O'Connor suggests another link between the short story and its interest in marginal figures, inherent in its very form: "the short story has never had a hero. What it has instead is a submerged population group, ... always dreaming of escape.... Always in the short story there is this sense of outlawed figures wandering about the fringes of society, superimposed sometimes on symbolic figures whom they caricature and echo—Christ, Socrates, Moses" (18–19). For O'Connor, this new nineteenth-century form of the realist short story was exemplified by Gogol's "The Overcoat," a form that enabled a focus on "the Little Man" and could render with both sympathy and distance the socially marginal figure as narratively central, as neither superior nor inferior, demanding of the reader not identification but an understanding of both the absurd and the horrific (15). O'Connor argued that the short story could eschew both the bourgeois hero form and the epic. It could instead use the "mock-heroic ... to create a new form that is neither satiric nor heroic but something in-between—something that perhaps transcends both" (15). Mueenuddin's servant stories produce precisely this effect of transcendence, of forging a complex affect that is unblinking in its portrayal of a servant's calculation or unfeelingness, and also compassionate and assiduous in evoking the servant character's limited choices and inner world.

O'Connor argued that the short story form created a powerful focus, shifting its affect and tonality: "since a lifetime must be crowded into a few minutes, those minutes must be carefully chosen indeed and lit by an unearthly glow, one that enables us to distinguish present, past, and future as though they were all contemporaneous" (22). Narayan makes a similar point when he identifies the capacity of "the concentrated miniature" to zoom in, and to provide variety. However, where Narayan's servant stories are invariably told from the perspective of an upper- or middle-class employer, and where Narayan still sees the subject of the short story as relatively minor, not "major," Mueenuddin uses the short story form to make the interest in marginality its central theme.[7] For O'Connor, the short story that succeeds is the one that is "told from the inside" (33). In their writing about peasants, he asserts, the less well-known Leskov succeeds better than Chekhov, who, in "trying to help them from without, simply has no clue to the workings of their minds" (33). Mueenuddin's stories bear this out. Although he uses a third-person narrator, Mueenuddin shifts the focalization to the servant at the center of his stories, so that readers are asked to understand that character from within, to see both what and how that character sees his or her world. At the same time, Mueenuddin's stories bespeak a tact that does not presume total insight into the "other" (not that anyone has total insight into the "self" either).[8] He avoids creating a first-person servant voice or narrator, and deploys a carefully constructed third-person narrative voice and tone that maintain a respectful distance from the subaltern subjectivities he portrays. Moreover, as if in contrast to his own enterprise, his stories dramatize the disastrous consequences when those in power—the satirically presented self-absorbed judge, Jaglani, or the police—*fail* to empathize, to imagine the interiority of, or care about those over whom they have power. And, as we will see, Mueenuddin situates this servant interiority within a carefully delineated cultural, social, economic, historically specific context.

Feudal Servitude in Postcolonial Pakistan

In his review, Richard Murphy provides the following contextual explanation to help Western readers understand the feudal set-up of Mueenuddin's stories:

> Like Mueenuddin's father, Harouni belongs to what Pakistanis call the "feudal" class. In the West, the term "feudal" has a rather musty resonance: it evokes

medieval European barons and, more recently, Marxist invective. In Pakistani English, the term connotes a great landowner who wields political power because he commands the votes of the peasants who work his farms. Pakistan's feudal grandees belong to the old, tightly connected Anglophone elite that dominated Pakistan's three ruling institutions during the decades after Partition: the army, the civil service, and the elected government. With power came prestige: when I worked in Lahore as an anthropologist in the mid-1990's, a local tailoring shop proudly displayed the following sign, "Ossian Tailors, Stitched and Stitching, for Elites and Feudals."

What Murphy impugns as "Marxist invective," we might more usefully understand as Marx's historical framework for understanding successive stages of European economic history as organized by different modes of production (with obviously different social, cultural, and political ramifications). In Marx's theory, feudalism was the pre-industrial stage (based on land ownership), succeeded by capitalism (based on private ownership of capital), in turn to be overthrown by socialism/communism (collective ownership of resources and equal distribution of resources). (Capital is defined as resources that are not consumed for themselves but generate further wealth by producing goods and services that are consumed.) In postcolonial Pakistan, however, feudalism has continued, and coexists with late capitalism. To understand what may seem like a strange anachronism in comparison to the trajectory of development of Global North economies that have left feudalism behind, necessitates more socio-political and colonial historical context than Murphy provides. Great landowners in Pakistan do command the votes of their peasants, making "democracy" a meaningless term, but they also command a lot more entrenched power over the nation because of their connections to the government, army, and judiciary.

At the time of independence in 1947, both Pakistan and India inherited a feudal landlord tenant-farming system of private land ownership that was partly created and partly formalized by British colonial rule. In order to consolidate colonial power after the Sepoy Rebellion of 1857, the British instituted a system of indirect rule (particularly in the northern agricultural belt in Punjab, Sindh, and Bengal) via *zamindars* or *jagirdars*, many of whom were originally revenue collectors without legitimate or ancestral claims on the cultivators' lands. They were rewarded with land ownership for their loyalty to the British government and for their reliable collection of land revenue from tenant farmers (Rahman 159–164; Cheesman 12–13). Mueenuddin's stories depend on and allude to this formative history: the landowner K. K. Harouni's "family consolidated its lands and amassed power under the British, who made use of landowning gentry to govern" (114). This system of land (re)distribution, mutually beneficial to the British and to the new landowners, produced a ruling class of absentee landlords who wielded an inordinate amount of social and political power both locally and nationally. As Mueenuddin attests in his memoir essay in *The New Yorker*, his own ancestors benefitted from such an arrangement: "in the eighteen-thirties and forties, . . . as the British chronicles tell it, Kashmir groaned under the exactions of my ancestors, who were sent there as overlords by Ranjit Singh, ruler of all Punjab . . . On his death, the British usurped his domains, and my family silkily changed allegiances and flourished under their rule, being rewarded with more lands and small honors, suitable for small gentry" ("Sameer and the Samosas," 64).

After Independence, both Pakistani and Indian governments tried to curtail the power of this landowning class by passing various land reforms. Scholars even with different agenda and national origins agree that these reforms failed in their promises, though they were more effective in India than in Pakistan (Raj, 131–141; Herring, 125; Naqvi et al., 28–29). In India, the system of *zamindari* or feudal landownership was legally abolished (as documented in Attia Hosain's novel *Sunlight on a Broken Column* and symbolized in the title's phallic "broken column"). In Pakistan, however, that system was not abolished. Two different presidents passed reforms that imposed ceilings on land ownership, Ayub Khan in 1959 and Zulfikar Ali Bhutto incrementally in 1972 and 1977. But even the most radical of these reforms were full of loopholes, designed at best to limit but not eliminate the monopoly of feudal families, and were easily circumvented by a ruling class that controlled the government, the legal system, and the army (Herring, 85–125).[9] (It is worth recalling that Pakistan was founded in 1947 as a secular parliamentary democracy, a "Dominion" of the British Commonwealth. In 1956, Pakistan declared itself an Islamic Republic, with a new constitution. With the suspension of this constitution in 1958, and the beginning of martial law under Ayub Khan, Pakistan has experienced years of alternating military and democratic rule, multiple changes to the constitution, and the increasing political power of the religious right.[10] After the 1971 civil war, which resulted in East Pakistan becoming Bangladesh, and West Pakistan becoming modern-day Pakistan, the power of the feudal landowning class became more, not less, entrenched.)

Subsequent to Bhutto's death in 1979, the period in which Mueenuddin's stories are mostly set, the power and wealth of this very male-dominated, feudal landlord system remained entrenched, though rivaled by a rising industrial class. The social, political, and economic changes of the 1980s—following upon the 1979 Soviet invasion of Afghanistan, the consequent economic and political support by the United States of the military dictatorship of Zia-ul-Haque in Pakistan, and the rise of Islamic fundamentalism—were not enough to ameliorate the life conditions of Pakistan's rural landless peasants, many of whom shifted to domestic service either in the homes of their feudal landlords or in middle-class urban homes by moving to cities as migrant workers.[11] Pakistan's current systems of landownership-based feudal power, and consequent extreme inequality, lack of educational or employment opportunities for displaced agricultural populations, farmer poverty, and the consequent pervasiveness of domestic servitude in Pakistan, owe their origins to British colonialism, which has cast a long shadow in the form of its powerful colonial legacies, though doubtless the instability of Pakistan's successive governments and the rule of the military are also responsible for the lack of positive change. Accordingly, I would argue that the feudalism-based servitude described in Mueenuddin's stories is "postcolonial" not only in the looser sense of being part of a postcolonial nation's sociocultural fabric, but also in the more specific sense of being a direct product of British colonization.

Among Pakistan's emergent and elite Anglophone writers, a certain scorn is sometimes voiced for the idea that their writing might be designated "postcolonial" or that it might have to do with postcolonial "problems." Kamila Shamsie, for example, has stated that she finds the term "postcolonial" irrelevant to her concerns. "It might have been relevant to my parents' lives, but we're a completely different generation now. Our vexed relationship with subaltern positions or with English is just not an issue. That makes you feel . . . impatient with postcolonial discourse."[12] This rejection of the term stems, I would contend, from a basic misunderstanding of what postcoloniality is, as if "postcolonial" writing could be limited only to that which addresses Partition or direct experiences of colonization, and as if post-Independence writing about a nation deeply structured by colonial legacies is not postcolonial. I identify Mueenuddin's work as postcolonial (as well as transnational in its address to multiple audiences and anticipated global circulation) in the broader sense of addressing the long-lasting consequences of colonial actions and policies. Pakistan is postcolonial not only because it was once colonized (as if that past were past and not formative of the present), but also because of the way it was hastily partitioned, with the lasting consequences of ongoing hostility with India, and because of the economic and political legacies that have continued to shape its history. The very use of English itself, not only among the elite educated class, but more broadly, in the judiciary, army, government, journalism, and education, and enshrined in the 1962 constitution, attests to this lingering colonial legacy. Moreover, I would add, Mueenuddin, unlike Shamsie, to his credit, also sees ongoing "subaltern positions" such as servitude as indeed a postcolonial "issue" that is very much his concern.[13]

The colonial past is always present, as Mueenuddin makes clear through the carefully placed details that add texture and meaning to the world of his stories. "The British built the large but run-down house in which I am quartered," notes the sardonic narrator of "About a Burning Girl" (97–98). This corrupt judge literally inhabits the structures that he has inherited from British colonialism—Lahore and Karachi are in fact littered with such houses—that enable him to operate in a judicial system also inherited from the British. In "Lily," a "retired English brigadier, an old colonial" still living in postcolonial Pakistan, takes Lily and her father fishing for trout in the beautiful Kaghan valley, suggesting the ongoing links between the past and present powerful elite (170). When Lily's husband, a feudal landowning farmer, has a bad day, he expresses his frustration by wishing for the return of British discipline and order: "I swear, it's impossible to get anything done in this country. We just sit around scratching our fleas and telling lies. The British should come back" (215). This is not an uncommon sentiment expressed among the elite, who wish for yet more power over the working classes.

These feudal landlords, as continuing beneficiaries of colonialism, clearly still exert enormous control in the new nation: "At that time, in the 1980's, the old barons still dominated government, the prime minister a huge feudal landowner" (120). Mueenuddin also frequently references the links between these feudal landlords and other upper echelons of power: the army, the politicians, and the rising industrialists, who often share family or social networks. The doctor who attends on old Harouni, for instance, is an army general, trained by the British, described as "a tall anglicized officer, his trimmed moustache and even the cut of his slightly military clothes reflecting purpose" (137). Sohail Harouni, who appears in multiple stories, borrows an apartment in Paris from a friend who is described as "also a Pakistani industrialist's son" (145). This rising industrialist class that potentially threatens the power of the feudal landlords is in fact also connected to them. Sohail's father, a relative of K. K. Harouni's, has, we are told, a "sprawling business—a sugar mill, farmlands, and much else," indicating a continuation, and not a break, between the feudal owners of land, and the new owners of postcolonial capital (143). With both the older and newer properties and the unspecified "much else," Sohail's father is one of the super-rich, able to send his son to Yale Law School and enable his wife and family to move comfortably and frequently between Asia, Europe, and America.

This postcolonial feudal world that Mueenuddin's stories elaborate is hence vastly different from the early twentieth-century pre-Independence aristocratic feudalism of Attia Hosain's short stories. Although there are some surprising connections between Hosain's and Mueenuddin's servant stories (Hosain's "Street of the Moon" and Mueenuddin's "Saleema" are both about the sexual relationship between an older male servant and a young female servant, and both writers are concerned with the power play and hierarchies among a collective of servants in a feudal household), there are some important differences. For one, where Hosain's stories restrict themselves to the dominant point-of-view of an upper-class character-narrator, Mueenuddin's, in omniscient third person, attempt to evoke the servants' interiority. For another, the feudal world of Hosain's stories, which are mostly set in pre-Independence urban Lucknow or Delhi, and which all concern Indian Muslims as a minority in predominantly Hindu British India, carry a very different ethos of multigenerational servitude, *noblesse oblige*, and mutual care than the more precarious world of Mueenuddin's servant stories, all set in rural or semi-rural Pakistan's post-Partition Punjab, where Muslims are not only the majority, but where non-Muslims are barely present, and where other forms of difference prevail. Despite the obvious hierarchies that separate employers from servants in Hosain's stories, her employers are obligated to care for the servants whose families have served theirs for generations. In Mueenuddin's dog-eat-dog, late twentieth-century world, feudal servants have a far more tenuous, unstable hold on their employment; for many, especially young women like Saleema or Zainab in "Provide, Provide," the descent to prostitution and destitution is immediate, with no support from either a network of ancestral familial connections or state institutions.

Nawabdin and Male-Male Dynamics: Balancing Interiority and System

In an interview with *BookBrowse* in 2010, Mueenuddin notes:

> In Lahore I was closer to the old servant who brought me up than to anyone else—thirty years after his death I still wear the bracelet he gave me when I went off to school in America. Because I was a child, the servants and the villagers were not guarded against me, unaware that I was watching: and therefore I learned the rhythms and details of their lives in a way that I never could as a grownup. I heard the women in the village calling to each other over their common walls, walked out with boys when they took their buffaloes to be watered at the canal. These people, their gestures and intonations as I observed them in my childhood, appear throughout the stories in *In Other Rooms, Other Wonders*. (Mueenuddin, interview with *BookBrowse*)

Mueenuddin here testifies to both the emotional attachments and the distances between himself, a privileged employer's child, and the male servant hired to care for him, and suggests how the contact zone of servant-child interactions continues to shape him and his writing.[14] It also indicates how his liminal position as a feudal landlord's child gave him access to a village community un-self-censored in his presence, to a world of human relationships and hierarchies that he is now invested in describing, in their complexity. Anything but nostalgic, Mueenuddin's stories offer a double vision: they ask us to understand both the interiority of vulnerable individuals situated within corrupt dehumanizing systems, *and* the systems that induce actions that resist easy judgments based on universalist or liberal humanist ethical codes.

Mueenuddin's collection opens with "Nawabdin Electrician" (originally published in *The New Yorker*), presenting Nawabdin, an engaging villager whose success working at the farm of Harouni, his patron, hinges on his unique ability to cheat the electric company by "slowing down the revolutions of the electric meters" (13). But Nawabdin is also shown from within as a man of determined enterprise, an adoring husband and father of twelve girls, well aware of and spiritedly facing the challenge of providing for twelve dowries: "Another man might have thrown up his hands—but not Nawabdin. The daughters acted as a spur to his genius, and he looked with satisfaction in the mirror each morning at the face of a warrior going out to do battle" (15). For the likes of Nawabdin, the story makes clear, daily existence is indeed a war, and only those most adept at reading and manipulating a corrupt system will survive it. Hence, though not strictly a domestic servant, Nawabdin adopts the identity of a feudal servant through performance (in Judith Butler's sense), *acting* like a servant, *performing* servitude through servility and obeisance—as servants in subsequent stories do. Moving between the "servants' sitting area" and the house, Nawabdin tends to farm and "household machinery" such as air conditioners, and thereby gains proximity to his employer (15). "Harouni ... became familiar with this ubiquitous man, who not only accompanied him on his tours of inspection, but morning and night could be found standing on the master-bed rewiring the light fixture or in the bathroom poking at the water heater" (15–16). Then, "gauging the psychological moment," Nawabdin presents his humble supplication, a carefully modulated request for a motorcycle.

> "Sir, as you know, your lands stretch from here to the Indus, and on these lands are fully seventeen tube wells, and to tend these seventeen tube wells there is but one man, me, your servant. In your service I have earned these gray hairs"— here he bowed his head to show the gray—"and now I cannot fulfill my duties as I should. Enough, sir, enough, I beg you." (16)

This scene illustrates the male-male dynamics between feudal master and servant on which subsequent stories in the collection elaborate. With humor, gentleness, and understanding of the effects of systemic disempowerment, Mueenuddin portrays Nawabdin as a likeable opportunist. The subordinate has to learn to read his master with a care that the master's privilege does not require him to reciprocate. Nawabdin must flatter and appease, literally bow and "beg" for what he needs by casting it as a way to do better service, even though both understand that what drives each is self-interest.

In an important shift of perspective, Mueenuddin takes us into Nawabdin's consciousness, his attachment to his wife, his anxiety about providing for his offspring, his desultory thoughts when he relaxes at home. "'Hello my love, my chicken piece,'" he greets his wife, before inviting her with playful ardor to search for the surprise (raw sugar) he has hidden in his pockets for his family (18). "I wonder what the moon is made of?" he ponders as he relaxes after dinner (19). When Nawabdin acquires his motorbike, it brings him status, business beyond his employer's farm, and the attention one night of a robber who shoots him six times in the groin. Able to call for help, Nawabdin survives—thanks to his new ability to pay those who attend him. The story suggests that in such a system of structural inequality, Nawabdin's mild dishonesties call for compassion, not easy condemnation. It focuses not on the hardened old feudal landlord Nawabdin serves, nor on the robber, but on Nawabdin. Mueenuddin uses an unobtrusive third-person voice to invite us into Nawabdin's interiority. The narrator is present not as a character, but as a quiet voice that moves almost unnoticeably from the world outside to that inside Nawabdin. This self-effacing, non-judgmental quality of Mueenuddin's unnamed narrator is a strategy, I would argue, that exemplifies what Black describes as border-crossing fiction (60).

It is on Nawabdin's pain and thoughts that we are asked to focus as he lies on the road expecting to die, ("Nawab lay on the road, not wanting to move"; 24), on his perceptions, such as "the blood [that] felt warm in his pants" (24), and the "smell of frying fish" that he remembers as the pain gets worse (25). Mueenuddin grounds us in Nawabdin's body and mind. Through free indirect discourse, he conveys Nawabdin's attachment to his motorbike, the source of his livelihood, to explain his determination to resist the robber, "Nawab couldn't let him get away with this. The bike belonged to him" (24). This is not just selfish territoriality. Nawabdin's bike embodies his fatherhood, his needs, desires, hopes, and fears for his children. When he gets to the clinic, it is the blood on the unwashed sheets that Nawabdin observes, and the disinfectant that he smells, to which our attention is called (26).

Consequently, though this story is based on an actual fraudulent employee of the author's,[15] it draws sympathy toward Nawabdin, encouraging its readers to desire Nawabdin's survival, and his return to his family.[16] In the closing scene, as the robber lies dying, callously unattended, in the bed next to Nawabdin's, and abjectly begs forgiveness, we are asked to understand Nawabdin's refusal: "Never. I won't forgive you. You had your life, I had mine. At every step of the road I went the right way and you the wrong. . . . My wife and children would have begged in the street, and you would have sold my motorbike to pay for [drugs]" (28). Mueenuddin locates Nawabdin in a complex code of ethics. As Nawabdin sees it, he does not victimize the vulnerable nor seek personal pleasure; in the total absence of safety nets or social support, and placed in a system riddled with corruption, his actions are, and must be, geared exclusively by a responsibility for his dependents' survival. While doubtless, in an ideal world, the pharmacist would help and Nawabdin forgive the dying man, such expectations, Mueenuddin suggests, arise from a world out of touch with the realities within which they live. This is not to argue for ethical relativism, but to recognize how the story asks us to *situate* both judgments and actions within their specific contexts and networks of power.

Women Servants and Sexual Exploitation

As in "Nawabdin," in all his servant stories Mueenuddin maintains this dual focus, asking us to rethink and resist easy moral judgments as he emphasizes a character's individuality, interiority, and agency, and elaborates on the systemic forces that affect that individual. In this section, I compare and examine closely two stories, "Saleema" and "Provide, Provide," which center on young servant women who transgress sexual cultural mores by using their bodies to access power. In the next section, I place these two stories in dialog with two others, "About a Burning Girl" and "A Spoiled Man," which center on male servants (young and old), and their interactions with employers (respectively, male and female) and systems of law enforcement. These two pairings also cross over: "Saleema" and "A Spoiled Man" focus on the interiority of subordinate servant figures, while "Provide, Provide" and "About a Burning Girl" critically examine the perspectives of employers. Though the shift to an employer's consciousness may seem to turn away attention from servants to evoke sympathy for employers, I would argue that this choice of technique is designed to explore the effects of the employers' evident corruption and callousness on the servant toward whom our sympathy is ultimately directed. This perspectival shift also encourages us to examine how the empowered are enabled to subordinate the disempowered, and how they see it themselves. All four stories also explore the positioning of individual servants within systems of power (patriarchy, law, police) that constitute and ultimately threaten them. Each story is interested in the different forms of vulnerability and agency of those who inhabit a particular feudal culture of servitude within a contemporary postcolonial state, and each uses different techniques as it builds on the linkages to other stories to expand its range of meaning.

"Saleema" opens with a calm reflective voice that makes no attempt to draw attention to itself and takes us straight to the title character and her history: "Saleema was born in the Jhulan clan, blackmailers and bootleggers, Muslim refugees at Partition from the country northwest of Delhi" (29). From the start, we understand, she and her family are outsiders, casualties of the colonial division of British India into modern Pakistan and India, displaced and dispossessed migrants with no ancestral connections to the land. This narrative voice sweeps over place and time, quickly describing Saleema's village, impecunious childhood, and sexually exploited youth, and arrives, in two paragraphs, at the present moment in which Saleema, now a servant, is found: in her "cramped servants' quarters" in K. K. Harouni's Lahore household and the dissatisfied wife of a drug-addict (30). This voice then pulls us deftly into her inner life, as she ponders her next move now that the cook she has slept with has dumped her: "She picked at the chipped polish on her long slim toe, feeling sorry for herself" (30). "Saleema" alternates between what Mieke Bal calls "character-bound internal focalization" and anonymous "non-character-bound external focalization" (105), reporting what Saleema sees or feels, as well as what the narrator wants us to see. However, since the story provides no access to what any other character sees or feels, and only to how Saleema *reads* others acts or feelings, her consciousness is the one to which the story grants the most importance, upon which it centers and to which it pulls our empathy. As Bal notes, "focalization is ... the most important, most penetrating, and most subtle means of manipulation" and technique for embedding ideology in a text (116). Readers are drawn into seeing through the lens provided by the focalizer, even when there are clues to suggest that that focal perspective is flawed or unreliable.

Mueenuddin's narration shifts between these kinds of focalization so that *what* Mueenudin tells us of Saleema's machinations blends with *how* Saleema sees and understands her world, and why. "She had been a maidservant in three houses so far, since her husband lost his job ... and in every one she had opened her legs for the cook" (30). The crudeness of this formulation emphasizes Saleema's consciousness and ethos, for, as the only female servant in a large feudal household, subordinate to all the senior male servants, she has learned how to access food and indirect power among servants via sex with the "lord" of the kitchen (30). "Why are cooks always vicious?" the narrator asks, as if relaying her frustration (31). Soon after, we are told what Saleema "knew" almost as if she needed to remind herself: "Saleema knew that he [Hassan the cook] was through with her, would sweeten up and try to fuck her now and then, out of cruelty as much as anything else, to show he could--but the easy days were over, now she had no one to protect her" (31). The gender and age-based hierarchy among servants that enables this capricious exertion of power by an older male servant over a younger female one is confirmed by the narrator, whose voice merges with what Saleema "knew": "In this household a man who had served ten years counted as a new servant. Hassan had been there over fifty, Rafik, the master's valet, the same. Even the nameless junior gardener had been there four or five" (31–32). Then gradually the narrator's voice emerges to add what Saleema probably also knew: "With less than a month's service Saleema counted for nothing. Nor did she have patronage. She had been hired on approval, to serve the master's eldest daughter, Begum Kamila, who lived in New York.... Haughty and proud, Kamila allowed no intimacies" (32).

Thus the story also begins by establishing Saleema's knowledge of her isolation and outsider status. Unlike fiction by women writers (Attia Hosain, Bapsi Sidhwa, Moni Mohsin) that explores intimacies and bonds between women across the servant-employer divide, this story presents Saleema as a new, temporary maid in a male-run household, alone and vulnerable, without "patronage," unsupported even by the woman she is hired to serve. Saleema is clearly an opportunist, not unlike Nawabdin, but Mueenuddin emphasizes how defiantly she struggles against the odds on a playing field tilted heavily against her. Suzanne Keen identifies two narrative techniques that narrative theorists and empirical researchers believe evoke reader empathy: *character identification*, which includes "naming, description, indirect implication of traits, . . . [and] depicted actions"; and *narrative situation*, "the nature of the mediation between author and reader, . . . the person of narration, . . . the internal or external perspective on characters, . . . the style of representation of characters' consciousness" (92–93). Moreover, authors themselves frequently nominate empathy (feeling *with* and *for* their characters) as crucial both to their own acts of creation and to the effects they seek to inspire in readers (Keen, 123–131). Meenuddin's use of these techniques, in presenting though free indirect discourse Saleema's memories of her sexually abused and impoverished childhood, her mother's callous mistreatment, her escape via marriage, as well as her own feelings and consciousness, or her gutsy actions and reactions to her world, in a non-judgmental third-person voice, seem designed to invite diverse readers to empathize, if not identify with her as protagonist, to care about her, and to understand her struggles for agency in a context that gives her few options. Saleema's opportunism is not something we are asked to condemn. Instead, Mueenuddin invites understanding as we see her disempowerment and struggle against humiliation and exploitation.

Mueenuddin thus also elucidates the iniquitous systems in which Saleema finds herself, and her awareness of her vulnerability. Through dialogue and carefully observed detail, Mueenuddin presents the oppressive gendered culture of feudal servitude—the crass sexual slurs of male servants in their Punjabi villagers' speech toward a woman they can insult with impunity, the daily indignities and disrespect, and the physical conditions, such as the limited facilities, that Saleema has to cope with. Carefully, almost unobtrusively he drops in telling details, such as the "furry walls in the [servants'] dank bathroom" (33), the "dirty white metal chairs" in their courtyard (33), the separate "servants' crockery," the "chipped cups" servants use even in this lavishly wealthy household (35). Subjected to sexual harassment, given no privacy, reduced to weeping in a filthy toilet she is forced to share with male servants, Saleema is, however, not presented as a mere victim (32). Like all of Mueenuddin's servant protagonists, Saleema makes choices within her limited options, choices we are asked to understand within specific contexts. Without education, money, family, or social support, she has to rely only on herself in a world set up to exploit her. Determined to find another "protector," knowing that only another male servant can deflect other male predators, she chooses Rafik the valet, three times her age, whom she accurately reads as having a rare decency.

Mueenuddin invites us to see her as she cannot see herself, as designing and manipulative, but also repeatedly brings us back to her inner world, as Saleema rides in a private car for the first time to follow Harouni and his daughter on a visit to the feudal farmlands (36–38), holds her mistress' emerald ring left by the bathtub "feeling the heft of the stone, guessing what it must be worth" (39), hand-washes Kamila's clothes, and enjoys rare physical pleasures like sitting in the sun (40) or taking a shower (33). By contrast, we are not given access to the feelings or thoughts of even the other major character in the story, Rafik, except as Saleema reads him, for Mueenuddin maintains our focus on Saleema's attempts to orchestrate what she can of her life. It is her perspective we are invited into when she is amazed at the size of Harouni's property, "My village would fit in a corner of this garden, and we were thirty families" (39). When Rafik as loyal servant denounces the estate managers who cheat his feudal master, we understand Saleema's disagreement, "At least their bellies are full," she replies (40). Her sympathies are with those who violate the expected feudal allegiance, because she understands well their desperation to survive.

The story grows in emotional power with the slow accretion of details, showing how Saleema's growing love for Rafik is inextricable from her need for security and a slight amelioration of status. Mueenuddin gives Saleema unexpected depths of feeling that surprise even herself as she is drawn to Rafik. "I can get him, she thought, and it sent a shiver of happiness through her" (35). When he smiles at her "like a child," she feels an unwarranted connection, "He smiles all over, the same way I do," she thinks (35). She is shown as capable of growth. She learns a discretion and "delicacy" new to her, as she pursues Rafik (36). There is a tenderness and reciprocity in their relationship, a lack of haste or disrespect. She is grateful when Rafik speaks up for her when the cook pinches her, effectively providing that protective support she had needed (41). When Harouni's daughter leaves, and Saleema is "kept on, through Rafik's intervention" (44), Moinuddin includes an ironic self-reflexive moment, commenting on how carelessly Rafik's master grants Rafik's request, "The old man did not merely lack interest in the affairs of the servants—he was not conscious that they had lives outside his purview" (45). It is this unthinking attitude that Mueenuddin's stories attempt to identify, puncture, and change.

Thus Mueenuddin grants priority to the fact and articulation of a servant woman's complex desires, to her efforts to exercise agency within a densely textured socio-economic, gendered cultural fabric. "Saleema" reaches crisis, not with Saleema's pregnancy or the birth of her illegitimate son, but with a letter from Rafik's aging wife, rupturing the months of happiness that Saleema has enjoyed with Rafik. Against stereotype, Mueenuddin renders Rafik's rejection of Saleema as an ironic exercise of the very decency that drew her to him. We see Rafik via Saleema's reading: "she could tell that the letter had shaken him, as a man of principle. The baby and her love had made him gentler . . . but the same gentleness would bend him toward his duty, which always would be to his wife and grown sons. He would punish himself and thus her for not loving his wife and for loving Saleema so much and so carnally" (55). Mueenuddin's writing is also notable for the crafted, deceptively simple cadence of each sentence, as exemplified here.

Unlike her previous lovers, Rafik rejects Saleema not from callousness but in response to a cultural system that gives him both the power to renounce her and the duty to honor his wife. But while interested in the complex, differently situated, gendered subjectivities of both the older male servant and the younger female one, this story remains centered on Saleema and her disempowerment, focusing on her feelings as she moves from "panic" and "jealousy" to "a strange pride" that she could occasion so much turmoil (55), on her understanding of Rafik's decision because she understands the system that they both inhabit (57). In gorgeous sentences, Mueenuddin renders Saleema's feelings when she moves back to her husband's room, giving her a complexity unprecedented in South Asian writing about servants: "Lying and staring at the ceiling, nursing the baby when it woke, she felt her love for Rafik tearing at her breast, making her a stranger to herself, breaking her" (56). With remarkable percipience, she gauges Rafik's inner world based on his body language: "she saw from his broken and haunted look that he missed her as she missed him. Yet she also saw how resolutely he had turned from her" (57). When he appeals to her for understanding, she understands the system within which he sees her, given her history, and forgives him: "The well inside her stirred, all the sorrows of her life, the sweet thick liquid in that darkness, which always lay at the bottom of her thoughts, from which she pulled up the cool liquid and drank. 'I know.' And [Rafik and Saleema] knew that she forgave him" (57). With this stunning metaphor of the well, Mueenuddin renders not only Saleema and Rafik's depth, complexity, and turbulence of feeling, but also the intricacy of their mutual comprehension of each other and of each other's circumstances, and Saleema's generosity in accepting what Rafik does to her and her child, habituated as she is to expecting nothing else.

However, Mueenudin also asks readers to see what Saleema does not understand, while maintaining her as the subject of the story (and of the sentence). *She* is the one to whom Rafik turns for comfort, when Harouni their master dies. "She couldn't understand what [Rafik] said, except that he repeated how he had fastened the old man's shirt the last evening in the hospital; but he kept saying *butters* instead of *buttons*. He couldn't finish the sentence, he repeated the first words over and over" (58). Mueenuddin alludes, perhaps, to the end of *King Lear* ("Pray you undo this button") to focus on the grief, not of a king mourning his dead daughter, but of a servant whose very sense of self depended on the master he had served daily over fifty years, and without whom he is literally bereft of himself. Psychically as well as literally, what he has lost *was* his bread and butter. In the contact zone of a feudal household where servants' interactions with each other are dependent on their mutually constituted identities as their master's servants, where even the master's illness "weakens the bond among servants" (57), Rafik's broken speech reflects his broken sense of self. This attachment is something that Saleema, as a newcomer to this system, cannot fathom.[17]

Nor can Saleema entirely share in the sense of bereavement the household servants experience when called in by Harouni's daughter to learn their fates. Long-term servants like Rafik and Hassan are retained, and newcomers like Saleema turned away with compensation proportionate to the duration of their "service" (58). In a moment exemplary of Mueenuddin's spare, deliberate style—his balanced, measured sentences, and precisely selected words—we get the older servants' collective perspective: "Crushed, they all left. They had expected this, but somehow hoped the house would be kept. . . . Gone, and they the servants would never find a berth like this one, the gravity of the house, the gentleness of the master, the vast damp rooms, the slow lugubrious pace, the order within disorder" (58–59). As a result, Saleema's identity and sense of self changes, as she sees herself as she is seen: "[Rafik] had raised her up, but Hassan had degraded her. . . . Again she became the stained creature who threw herself at Hassan, for the little things he gave her" (59).

The end of the story can be shocking to many readers, for its style as much as its content, as the narrator suddenly pulls back from Saleema's perspective, to conclude crisply, in one paragraph, with her decline and death. "Within two years she was finished, began using rocket pills, . . . lost her job . . . And then, soon enough, she died, and the boy begged in the streets, one of the sparrows of Lahore" (60).[18] Why, after the lengthy immersion in Saleema's interiority, would Mueenuddin jerk us out of it so abruptly, without explaining why a woman who struggled against the drug addictions of her father and husband should finally succumb herself? The story creates this film-camera effect of zooming out at the end to contrast its assiduously created interiority and humanity with the dehumanizing reality that Saleema and her child experience, the brutal lack of safety nets or social support systems. It invites us to view instead the exterior lens through which they are usually seen, as the nameless indigent unwanted. It is perhaps precisely because she was a fighter that Saleema is defeated, for she goes into a downward spiral when finally faced with the impossibility of changing her lot. No one will save her from the streets, as she learns: not the employers who dismiss her, nor the husband or lovers who abandoned her. It is by immersion in her interiority that the story creates its intense affect, highlighting the callousness of systems—both social and representational—that see her only from the outside. What Mueenuddin's story achieves, finally, in addition to the cultural work of protesting such systems of social, economic, and gendered in justice, is a shift in ways of seeing, and indeed foregrounds and contrasts those ways of seeing.

At thirty-two pages, "Saleema" is a long short story. It takes time to explore the shifts and changes in the eponymous character's inner and outer worlds. But the next, "Provide, Provide," at thirty-six pages, is even more expansive. Placed third in the collection, "Provide, Provide" explores how a village servant woman named Zainab is similarly picked up as a sexual toy and then ruthlessly abandoned, in this case by Jaglani, her employer (who is also Harouni's estate manager). However, this story presents a different angle of vision, alternating focalization between the narrator and Jaglani, so that we do not get direct access to Zainab's consciousness. This story's placement directly after "Saleema," however, encourages us to read it differently than we otherwise might. Having been sensitized by "Saleema" to a woman servant's vulnerability and interiority, readers are cued to interrogate Jaglani's ways of seeing, alerted to read between the lines, to notice the ways he fails to understand the woman who serves him. Through the indirection of his clouded understanding, and her reported dialogue, Mueenuddin conveys Zainab's complexity and unexpected depths. These two stories thus work as a pair: both explore a servant woman's exploitation and agency, but one proceeds from the inside-out and the other from the outside-in.[19] Mueenuddin's choice to tell this story primarily from Jaglani's perspective does not, I would argue, render Zainab less significant than Jaglani, but rather, while keeping our focus on Zainab, highlights how insignificant she is rendered by the very men—her brother as well as her master and eventual husband—to whom she is closest and on whom she is forced to depend. The technical challenge Mueenuddin sets himself here is the opposite of "Saleema": how to maintain sympathy for Zainab while giving interiority to Jaglani.

"Provide, Provide" opens by presenting a series of layers or concentric circles of male hierarchical power in the feudal landowning system in which Zainab is located. Harouni, the aging landlord, is clearly at the top or center, though threatened by the rise of a new industrialist class. Jaglani, his estate-manager, has taken advantage of his master's ineptitude to line his own pockets, and is next.

Below or beyond him is Mustafa, Jaglani's personal chauffeur, who recommends his sister to Jaglani as cook for his house in the village. Jaglani thus occupies a middle position as both master (to Mustafa) and subordinate (to Harouni). The story consequently explores nuanced relationships of servitude and subordination between men as well as between men and women. In two parallel scenes, we see how Jaglani and Mustafa have both learnt to gauge the psychology of their respective employers, to devise ways to better their positions within this feudal system.

First, in an exclusively male-male interaction, Jaglani both soothes and cheats his master, whose implicit shame at having to sell ancestral land he intuits and adroitly manages: "They spoke for a minute about a murder recently committed by one of the tenants, a matter of a girl. Jaglani knew to do this, in order to paper over the embarrassment his master must feel at having to sell land held by his family for three generations" (62–63). The instrumentally mentioned, unnamed girl, possibly the victim of an honor killing, remains notably irrelevant to both men. Second, in a similar scene, Mustafa asks Jaglani for employment for his sister Zainab, who has left her husband. As the servant of a subordinate, Mustafa also knows how to enact and perform servility according to implicitly understood codes between them. He has "earned Jaglani's confidence by his discretion.... Although they spoke frankly and easily on long drives to Lahore, Mustafa became mute in the presence of others, stone-faced as a chauffeur should be" (63). Mustafa too knows his place and how to make the most of it, proportionate to his status. He had "always managed to ask favors in a way that made Jaglani glow, choosing moments when his master felt satisfied, with work or with politics, the moment when the day seemed sweetest" (65).[20] The ironic title "Provide, Provide" thus suggests the pressures upon men of all classes as sole providers for their extended families and dependents. It applies to Jaglani, who must provide for his wife and sons in the city (and all their dependents), as well as to Mustafa, who provides for Zainab in the village by offering her to Jaglani as cook, and for his own family by using his sister's sexual services as leverage.[21]

Having set the scene, Mueenuddin shifts to Jaglani's perspective, as Jaglani first sees Zainab, crouched over the stove, when he returns to his house in the village. She greets him with deference and modesty as she "covered her head, turning her face away" (66). As a new female servant in his house, she becomes the target of his interest; when she comes closer to serve his food, "he looked up at her suddenly, wanting to find out what kind of woman she might be" (66). This open, unabashed, aggressive intrusiveness and sexual predation is quite different, Meenuddin makes clear to his international readers, from the world of liveried British servitude as represented in films like *Gosford Park* (2001) or television shows like *Upstairs Downstairs* (1971–1975) or *Downton Abbey* (2010–2016), where the distance between employers and servants is highly formalized.

Jaglani need make no pretense of distance. It is clear from the beginning how much asymmetric power he has over Zainab. Upon first meeting, having inspected her and eaten her food, he relaxes, smokes his hookah, listens to the animals "bedded down," and decides "to keep her on," as if she were indeed part of the livestock (67).

As with Saleema, however, Mueenuddin presents Zainab not as a passive victim, but as capable of initiative. Jaglani's first impression of her is of an outlaw toughness: "she had a hard pale face, angular, with high cheekbones, almost beautiful but too forceful, reminding him of a woman who had been caught years ago on the banks of the Indus, a cattle thief" (66). There is something both vulnerable and defiantly determined about her. Alone with Jaglani in his village house (since his wife and family reside in the city), Zainab is careful of decorum as she serves Jaglani food and drink. Then one day she offers to massage him, building a "routine" that extends her solicitous care of his bodily comforts to sexual needs (68). Because the narrator focuses on how Jaglani sees Zainab, we do not know at first why she acquiesces to him, whether she feels she has a choice, or whether she has calculated upon some instrumental gain, for these are not questions that occur to Jaglani as he becomes besotted with her. "As he drove around the farm, or in the city, the vision of her giving herself so trustingly would come to him" (69). Although he cannot understand her, he is perceptive enough to realize that for all her sexual responsiveness, she remains emotionally remote: "She did not caress him, and he felt that she herself was not touched to the core.... Although she massaged him, cooked for him, cleaned his house, and made love to him, he found that after two months she still had not come any closer" (70).

Via dialogue, however, Mueenuddin provides glimpses of Zainab's interiority, and invites readers to understand her as Jaglani cannot. After a quarrel, for instance, Jaglani tries to reconcile by inviting her back to bed and offering her money. She refuses:

> "You buy me things and then later you'll think you bought me. I was never for sale," she replied, standing up [from his bed].
> "Stop," he called. He spoke in the voice he might have used with a servant.
> She left, quietly closing the door behind her. (69)

With dignity, she implicitly draws a line between servitude and servility, between the domestic work for which she is paid and the sexual labor for which she refuses payment (even though she submits to sex with him because she exists in a gendered relation of feudal, subservient employment). When Jaglani crosses that line, she resists. She refuses to touch the money he leaves by the bed. Given the harsh world of gendered injustice and sexual surveillance she inhabits, we can see why she does not trust him, or stay the night. With cynical clarity, she lets him know that she understands the differential created by their respective ranks and gender, that though he is exempt from the villagers' opprobrium because they are "afraid" of his power, she is not: "If you dropped me, they would call me a whore out loud as I walked down the street" (70). She is capable of fine distinctions, and understands the need to maintain the appearance of respectability. If she stayed the night, she tells Jaglani, "Then I *would* be your whore. At least now we pretend. Leave it alone" (70). Through such indirect moments of dialogue, Mueenuddin enables readers to understand her thinking.

Yet despite these moments of Zainab's resistance and exertion of agency, Mueenuddin leaves no doubt of her systemic disadvantage and Jaglani's abuse of power. The subtle shifts between the narrator's commentary and Jaglani's perspective direct us to examine Jaglani's actions, motivations, obtuseness, and the social framework and structure of feeling that constitute them. We are shown how Jaglani uses his power to bully Zainab's husband into divorcing her and to intimidate the village *maulvi* into performing a second marriage that Jaglani keeps secret from his first wife and sons (75–76). (Polygamy is legal in Pakistan, but Jaglani keeps his first wife and family in the city separate from and unaware of his second "wife" in the village.) Zainab remains subject to Jaglani's moves, caught in a legal and cultural system controlled by men ruthless and unscrupulous about how they position her. She is even kept ignorant of the fact that her marriage to Jaglani is technically incomplete, that she cannot make any legal claims on him or his property. For Jaglani, the "marriage" is only a cover to induce her to live full-time in his village house, by giving her some respectability within the village. Jaglani takes care of the paper work, so that the legal documents to which illiterate Zainab "affixed her thumbprint" and that are signed by only one male witness ("the other three required witnesses would sign later if the need arose"; 76) enable him to claim her whenever he wants, but not vice versa. She is left thus legally unprotected when he dies.

Mueenuddin presents Jaglani's feelings for Zainab, early in the marriage, as not uncomplicated, as mixed and intense. There is something indomitable and unfathomable about her, as Jaglani sees her: "He wanted to take care of her, but often she would not allow him to. He feared Zainab, strangely enough, although he had made a career of fearing no one and of thereby dominating this lawless area. Sometimes he thought that it would be a relief to be rid of her, and yet his love kept increasing" (78). As long as Jaglani remains healthy, he stays in love with Zainab. Mueenuddin gives Zainab unusual depths and determination. When Jaglani discovers her moping, a year into their marriage, because she has not yet conceived, it crushes him to learn that she married him, not for himself, but for her own reasons: she wanted children. "She almost began to cry, but then stopped herself. Her face became hard. 'I only married you because of that'" (79). What she wants desperately, she reveals, is not money or wealth or power, but a child, something to love. She left her first husband because she thought he was infertile. Despite her "hardness," she begs Jaglani to bring her one of his grandchildren to raise: "I never begged, but now I'll beg from you," she says (79).

Mueenuddin casts Jaglani too as complicated, as torn by conflicting loyalties. He succumbs to Zainab's pleas for a child, yet he is enabled to do what he does by a patriarchal feudal system's ethos. "No one thought anything of it, he ruled his area in the old way, with force. He had the prerogative of taking a second wife, a chosen wife. Flushed with his power, Jaglani went further. He brought his son's infant daughter to Dunyapur and gave her to Zainab" (80). (The minimalism of this sentence strikingly emphasizes how autocratically Jaglani can behave— parceling off his own granddaughter without consulting his son, let alone the child's mother.) It seems to me a mistake to see this story (as some of my students have done) as inviting empathy for Jaglani and condoning his treatment of Zainab just because it gives us Jaglani's perspective and not hers. A phrase like "Flushed with power," for instance, implies negative judgment and asks us to see Jaglani as he cannot see himself. Yet the story complicates both the roles of oppressor and oppressed. It asks us to see how a man like Jaglani can feel for and yet treat Zainab the way he does within a system that empowers him at her expense, as well as how Zainab responds within this severely limiting framework. I would contend that it is not lack of concern for disempowered women, but rather an effort to investigate how *systemically* such women are rendered powerless that mobilizes Mueenuddin's shift of perspective in this story. Jaglani is presented as *both* powerful and susceptible, as perceptive and self-absorbed, infatuated and yet able to repudiate her when he learns he has terminal cancer.

Once impelled to marry Zainab to ward off his fear of death (he decided to marry her after seeing a village boy die of snakebite; 72–73), now, with death at his door, he is repelled by her servant status:

> He minded very much that he had given his sons a stepmother of that class, a servant woman. He minded that he had insulted his first wife in that way, by marrying again, by marrying a servant . . . He reproached himself for taking his eldest son's daughter and giving her to Zainab, transplanting the little girl onto such different stock. (86)

Unlike "Saleema," in which the text's focus on the consciousness of the title character directs readers' empathy toward her, the focus on Jaglani's consciousness in "Provide, Provide" *averts* readers' empathy and directs us to experience the magnitude of *his* final lack of empathy for the woman with whom he was once infatuated, and whose life he controls. The difference between Mueenuddin's treatment of Jaglani and Saleema lies in the fact of Jaglani's power and abuse of power, as well as in the way that the narrative voice directs us to scrutinize

Jaglani's change of heart and criminal negligence, and shows how they are fueled by a system that grants him such extraordinary privilege and impunity. Even as he knowns he is dying, Jaglani postpones doing "something for Zainab" materially, making a promise that both know "meant nothing" (90), leaving her as unprovided for as Rafik leaves Saleema. When she tries to see him before he dies, she is barred from his city house (92–93). The last image we have of Zainab is of her being led away by her brother, weeping and bewildered, "saying to herself, 'And they didn't even offer me a cup of tea'" (93).

As with "Saleema," Mueenuddin ends "Provide, Provide" with a sudden shift of perspective. After Jaglani's death, he returns us to the wider circles of male power within which Zainab is located, along with a brief shift to the perspective of Shabir, Jaglani's son and heir. Shabir turns his fury upon Mustafa, now his driver, whom he plans to fire for witnessing his political humiliation. Zainab is not even mentioned by either man. But her astonishing absence points precisely to the ways she is disregarded in this chauvinistic, macho world. Mueenuddin thus exposes the ways of seeing of those with power, and highlights the deployment of that power over servants who have literally become family. Zainab's brother, also a servant, will be punished not only for having seen Jaglani's son "shamed," but for his (shaming) link with the woman Jaglani secretly married (96). By sacking Mustafa, Shabir paradoxically comes closest to acknowledging the unwelcome existence of his father's servant-wife: in his repudiation or disavowal of that connection.

Male Servants and the Law

"Saleema" and "Provide, Provide," are new to South Asian Anglophone fiction in their sustained focus on and humanization of young female servants as they face inevitable and constant sexual predation under systems of postcolonial feudalism and patriarchy. In other stories, Mueenuddin also explores the differently gendered consequences of male servitude. I explore, in this section, how "About a Burning Girl" and "A Spoiled Man" unravel the intricate mesh of corruption and police violence that inevitably threatens a male servant who falls under suspicion of any crime.[22] "About a Burning Girl," the story that follows "Provide, Provide," similarly invites scrutiny of an employer's perspective to explore the self-interested callousness that servants are subject to within systemic forms of power. This humorous and satiric detective story explores further the vulnerability of servants to both the vagaries of the criminal-justice system and the amorality of employers. In depicting the warped perspective of such an employer, Mueenuddin turns the self-absorption of a middle-class male narrator into the butt of comic satire, making even clearer than in "Provide, Provide" how a focus on a corrupt perspective can invite not sympathy or identification but critical distance. This is the only story in the collection narrated in the first person, as if to expose, through his own sardonic voice, a disillusioned "sessions judge in the Lahore High Court" who has cynically accepted the failure of the judiciary and of his own ambitions, as well as the rampant pervasiveness of bribery and corruption in Pakistan. "[D]espite my profession I don't believe in justice ... I render decisions based on the relative pressures brought to bear on me," he announces from the start (97).

Mueenuddin thus quickly establishes the moral unreliability of this persona, as well as the clarity of his self-knowledge. His wife is a "shrew," the judge tells us unabashedly (97), "a poor man's Lady Macbeth" with networks of influence that have secured him his house, salary, and servants (104):

> There are three servants in my house, a cook, a sweepress, and a bearer. All three have the mute expression of servants in a modest household such as mine: lordly dishonest valets, the sort who are immune to colds but are martyrs to dyspepsia, work for ampler men than me.... The bearer, named Khadim, is a boy of twenty, from one of the villages near Abbotabad. He has no personality whatsoever. He cleans, takes care of the children, washes the car, waters the few plants arranged along the driveway, brings lunch in a tiffin carrier to my office, lays out my clothes, and does all this with a lugubrious expression consistent with the tone of the house... The bearer is gentle in a bovine sort of way and he works at half speed but consistently. He has no opinions and no dissipations, at least that I know of, although as a judge I am often amazed by the behaviors of seemingly mild people. In short he is the ideal servant. (98)

The story thus begins by asking us to notice the list of servants with different roles even in a "modest" urban middle-class home, the assorted domestic duties that Khadim the odd-job "boy" performs, and the hierarchies among servants that parallel the hierarchies among their masters. This middle-class judge can only afford three servants, and has to do without the "lordly" valet attendant on "ampler men." This passage also reveals the multiple levels of subtle irony and humor that operate in this story. The judge, despite his middling status, is well aware of his class privileges, which he exercises through his cultivated obliviousness to the world of servants, the people who ensure his everyday comforts and are entrusted with his children. He self-servingly declares Khadim an "ideal servant" with "no personality whatsoever" because casting Khadim as a nonentity, with no inner or other life than that of servitude, allows the judge to not have to think about the man who serves him. (It is no small irony on Mueenuddin's part that Khadim's name refers exclusively to his servant role, for in Urdu it signifies an obeisant server, who does *khidmat*, or service.) Yet, though clearly selfish and dismissively contemptuous of lower-class people, he has a detailed knowledge of Khadim's daily tasks, and awareness of the surprises that apparently "mild" people can produce.

Such a surprise awaits the judge when, on a visit to his village, Khadim is arrested for burning his own brother's wife to death. The "facts" are impossible to ascertain, both for us and for the judge, except for the information that kerosene was poured over the woman and set on fire, and that, before dying, she named Khadim as the perpetrator (99–102). Uncaring of the truth, the judge's wife demands her servant back: "Good servants are impossible to find," she declares (104). Though the judge believes Khadim to be guilty of murder and theft, he sends a functionary who eventually bribes the police and the medical personnel who recorded the dying woman's testimony, and frees this servant whose culpability the story ultimately leaves unclear. "In Pakistan all things can be arranged," the judge announces (110). By highlighting the judge's unreliability as a narrator, his disregard for justice as well as for a girl who dies a brutal death, and his willingness to manipulate the legal and medical systems for the judge's own convenience, Mueenuddin asks us to judge both this "judge" and the system that he (over)sees, and to assess the amorality of a bourgeoisie that finds indispensable the routine comforts it demands of servants whose lives and ethics it regards as having no connection to its own.

It may seem as if the story confirms the servant's guilt, and reconfirms stereotypes of the male servant as violent, unreliable, criminal. But I would argue that the story emphasizes more the criminality of the judge, and of the system in which he operates, which are certain, and less the criminality of Khadim, which remains unproven.[23] Mueenuddin presents both a mystery to be solved and the impossibility of finding the truth in this corrupt system, given the malleability of evidence in the hands of those in power, and the ease with which lower-class individuals can be implicated or freed. What does become clear is how all those involved (the girl's family, Khadim's family, the police, the doctors) are out to fleece each other, to exploit the changing situation to get what they can, to change their story and take or offer bribes to serve their own interests. What disappears altogether, in the judge's narrative, is the subjectivity of the girl who is murdered, and of Khadim, the servant accused of her murder.

Through its form and title, however, the story calls attention to this disappearance. The judge receives at least three different versions of what (may have) occurred. First, he describes how he received a visit from Khadim's brother, who claimed that his father's life earnings were stolen by his wife and her brother, and that after police questioning, she lost her nerve and committed suicide (101–104). The judge is openly contemptuous of Khadim's brother, whom he describes as "a useless sort of fellow" not even clever enough to tell plausible lies (99). Perspicaciously pointing out the inconsistencies in Khadim's brother's story, the judge quickly dismisses this version. Second, the judge is visited by Khadim's father, who confirms the loss of his savings and insists that the girl "became insane" and "killed herself" (107). Before dying, he says, prompted by her family, she falsely accused Khadim. This pathetic "old man standing by the portico with the timeless patience of peasants and old servants," turns out to be a lifetime servant of the feudal Harouni family (106). For him, and his fifty-eight years of service, his "master" Sohail Harouni is willing to pay good money (107). Aided by the promise of this cash, and unexpectedly moved by the sobbing old man who reminds him of his own old servant who raised him, the judge promises to help: "Don't cry, Baba, don't cry," he finds himself saying, to his own embarrassment (107).[24]

The judge next meets with Mian Sarkar, his legal assistant, and sends him to Khadim's village to sort things out. Upon his return to Lahore, Mian Sarkar offers the judge a third version of what happened. The girl, he reports, was in fact "killed" by her own husband and Khadim, because she would have given away the brothers' theft of their own father's money (108). But the girl's evidence only implicated Khadim. As the girl's family wanted "blood," and the older brother tried to implicate the younger, Mian Sarkar's "solution" was to bribe the police and the attending doctor to get the girl's testimony dismissed (110). While it remains unclear what would happen to the older brother (the judge plans to use his influence with the judge who would preside over the case), it is clear that Khadim would be released, freed to return to work in the judge's home. That is all that matters to the judge.

However, by establishing how conveniently officials at all levels can be made to change their stories, Mueenuddin throws even this final "solution" into question. The title, "About a Burning Girl," is heavily ironic, for the story circles *about* the girl—a mere relative of a servant—who never actually appears in it, marking her devaluation in this system. As in the preceding story, the nameless girl who suffers a brutal death is rendered immaterial. Even her dying words are lost in the miasma of fabrications produced by different men. Like Zainab's, Khadim's sister-in-law's disappearance from a narrative recounted by a man inured to this gendered feudal system only emphasizes the moral degradation of a judiciary and society that in multiple ways refuse her justice even in death.

The critique of the ruling class that this story makes obvious gains yet more clarity when read together with the last story of the collection, "A Spoiled Man," which also turns on the disappearance of a poor village girl, and a male servant's encounter with the police. Having established the limitations of the first-person employer-narrator, Mueenuddin returns to third-person narration in this story to contrast the interiority of the male servant with the naive perspective of his female employer, and to make clear, with powerful affect, the servant's innocence and the abusiveness of the system the employer (unwittingly) unleashes on the servant. "A Spoiled Man" takes us outside the strict boundaries of domestic servitude to focus on an aging watchman who exists literally on the fringes of Harouni's nephew's "weekend home" in Islamabad (221). Oddly self-contained and the inhabitant of a "portable cubicle" (225), Rezak, a humble villager dispossessed of his lands by conniving step-brothers, described as a "small bowlegged man with a lopsided battered face," is hired as an outdoor servant by Sonya, Sohail Harouni's American wife (221). "Once he had happened to be walking past as she was driven through the gate, and she had waved" (221). Her casual act, ignorant of class and gender decorum, prompts his disproportionate devotion; he begins to hover, waiting for "hours to receive this recognition from her" again, offers his labor, and is granted the task of guarding her orchard (227). Low though he remains in the hierarchy of her army of servants, he gets a high salary, for "it made her happy to think of spoiling him in his old age" (227). This story hence explores the cross-gender and cross-racial dynamics between an aging Pakistani male servant and a young American female employer. A random beneficiary of Sonya's intermittent attention as she struggles to adapt to upper-class wifehood in a patriarchal feudal system, Rezak becomes "spoiled" (in the dual sense of being over-petted, and destroyed, or ruined): a fellow villager offers him a disabled child-wife who vanishes; when Sonya tries to help by getting a powerful friend in the police to intervene, the local constabulary, whose first impulse is to blame and abuse the servant, end up apprehending and torturing the distraught Rezak, who dies from his injuries, abjectly grateful to the end to the Harouni family. With unmistakable irony, Mueenuddin gives us a last glimpse of the unknowing Sonya "musing by the fire on having done the right thing for a lonely old man" (246).

This story clearly indicts the self-satisfied insularity and naiveté of a feudal landowner's pampered white American wife who fails to understand both the horrible system of power and crime in which she embroils Rezak, and the tidal consequences (for him) of her well-meaning intervention.[25] More significantly, it renders Sonya peripheral, and attends much more solicitously to the interiority of a man regarded as worthless trash by those in positions of power, such as the district superintendent of police (243). It also leaves unexplained the horrifying disappearance of the mentally disabled, speechless girl who, the story suggests, may have been kidnapped and trafficked into sexual slavery, thus emphasizing how the weakest are preyed upon. We are invited instead to focus on how Rezak thinks and feels, and to see him not merely as victim but as a spirit of independence and perseverance. Mueenuddin's quiet narrative voice and careful details evidence Rezak's initiative in volunteering his labor, devotion, and creativity in planting a vegetable garden to bring offerings to the big house, his artistry in building and decorating his tiny wooden hut, his tenderness toward the girl given to his care, his incomprehension of the rich and arrogant, and his desire to be buried in the orchard he felt privileged to tend.

While overseeing arrangements for an outdoor party, Sonya passes by Rezak and throws him a casual greeting. Mueenuddin focuses on Rezak's reaction:

> His heart, his soul melted, as if a queen had spoken to a foot soldier. She had given him charge of the garden, of the trees that she brought from her homeland, and now she was seeing the results of his husbandry for the first time. (228)

We are invited to see Rezak as he sees himself, as a devotee, as a "foot soldier" overwhelmed by the gracious notice of a queen far above him. But he also sees himself as providing, in response, a crucial service to her, making her a home away from home, transplanting in Pakistani soil the trees she had brought from America, "her homeland." He sees himself as carrying an important responsibility, as engaged in "husbandry," husbanding her garden, and, by implication, her. And yet, Mueenuddin, adds, while confident of his gardening skills, Rezak also feels out of place, not sure of his role among "the other servants" who all "knew what to do" (228). As the guests arrive and are attended to by the butler, the cook, and the guards, Rezak sits apart, hoping to be noticed. "He squatted under an apple tree, trying not to look at the sahibs, pulling up sprigs of grass, tying them into figures and knots, hoping to be summoned" (229). It is Rezak's unspoken desire to which we are alerted, his desire to be included and appreciated, even as he recognizes fully his lowly status.

As the story continues, through carefully built, poignant, measured sentences, Mueenuddin conveys first Rezak's joy at acquiring a young wife, then his despairing concern when she vanishes, and his thoughts as he stoically accepts what has happened: "Imbecile, chattering—but she was gone, stolen, dead or stolen, taken to the brothels of 'Pindi or Karachi. He prepared himself to bear the loneliness again" (236). It does not occur to him to go to the police. He has not learned to expect or rely on help from any state institution. When Ghulam Rasool, the majordomo of Sonya's household, takes it upon himself to request the influence of Sonya's powerful friend, the "son of the inspector general of police" (237), we are invited to read Rezak's self-abjection, as he humbles himself before Sonya's friend, inordinately grateful for a moment of the great man's attention: "Rezak, who understood none of the conversation, which had been conducted in English, crouched and touched Bukhari's knee with both hands, began to speak and then fell silent, bowing his head" (239). Through Rezak's body language, Mueenuddin conveys the psyche that has internalized humility, inferiority, and helplessness. Later, in a powerful moment, entering more explicitly into Rezak's mind, Mueenuddin elucidates how, even after his naïve trust in those in authority is broken, after he is horrifically brutalized by the police, Rezak is unable to blame them. Instead he blames himself for having attempted to rise above his station:

> His mind whirled—without touching on any one thing for a moment, the wife he married when almost still a boy, who died so many years ago, then his second wife, the little mentally disturbed girl. . . . His things, his television, the day he went to the store and bought the bright red plastic television. . . .
> "Why should I complain? The policemen did as they always do. The fault is mine, who married in old age, with one foot in the grave. God gave me so much more than I deserved, when I expected nothing at all." (244)

We see what is precious to Rezak, even in the blur of pain and imminent death. We hear him thinking. We see the sweetness of his approach to life and death, the unassuming humility and gratitude for the unexpected lift he has had in life, despite the crash it subsequently induced.

Mueenuddin leaves no question of the complexity of Rezak's inner world, mistaken though Rezak's perceptions might be:

> After he recovered, he was left with one last wish. In Rezak's mind good fortune and grace were wound together, so that the Harouni family's connections and wealth established not simply the power of the household but also its virtue. . . . when he lost the girl, their instruments punished him for having dared to reach so high, for owning something that would excite envy . . . Now he belonged to the Harounis. This was how he understood justice. (244)

This is a picture of the internalization of feudal servitude, when a man accepts his own subordination and the order of things as the way they must be. What Rezak wants in the end is not revenge, nor compensation, nor even the return of his wife. He accepts what comes to him. What he wants simply is burial in a corner of the Harounis' land, and a marble gravestone for which he pays from his accumulate savings. This is his only "dream and his consolation" (245).

But Mueenuddin's narrative also moves us out of Rezak's consciousness to highlight the networks of power and greed that make Rezak so vulnerable, the rapaciousness that runs rife in a system with no checks or balances. We see the interactions among the rich and powerful, and between the various levels of power that lead to the multiple betrayals of Rezak's trust. In the end, Rezak gets part of his wish—he is buried in the orchard that he tended—but is cheated out of the permanent markers on which he spends all his money. When Sonya visits his grave, she is surprised by its "smallness," by the "mound decorated with tinsel," with a few "marble stones" stacked beside it (246). She does not know, as readers do, that this is not the fulfillment of Rezak's dying wish.

The conclusion to "A Spoiled Man" thus serves also as a conclusion to Mueenuddin's story collection and suggests symbolic overtones that apply to the many servant figures that are subjects of earlier stories. With an echo of the "unhonour'd dead" who lie in "many a mouldering heap" in Thomas Gray's *Elegy Written in a Country Churchyard* (1751), Mueenuddin leaves us with an image of Rezak's impermanent, soon-forgotten grave in a corner of Sonya's orchard, covered by falling autumn leaves. This image can be read as a complex emblem of postcolonial servitude, of those who live and die, but remain (as do Rezak's remains) on the peripheries of feudal power. At the same time, his body mingles with the soil that produces the orchard fruit, and literally fertilizes what the feudal owners absorb into their bodies, inextricable from the land they possess. Servants, it suggests, remain in relations of enforced distance and proximity, intimacy and exploitation. It emphasizes the obscurity of the spoiled man, whose last remnants are absorbed by an order that erases him and his humanity. His handmade habitation, the makeshift hut, is slowly plundered and depleted of its carefully gathered possessions, "Even the filthy mattress pulled out and put to use, taken by the sweeper who cleaned the toilets in the big house. The door of the little cabin hung open, the wind and blown rain scoured it clean" (247). Mueenuddin closes with this reminder both of extreme poverty (Rezak's belongings are used by those even lower than Rezak in the hierarchy of servitude), and of the erasure of the human beings that Mueenuddin's writing asks us to see not as curiosities, but as figures of resilience and agency, however minor, in broader national and global systems that we are invited to scrutinize, understand, and deplore.

Mueenuddin's interlinked short stories focus on servants as central characters with complex interiorities, shaped by the complex systems within which they are located, and build a cumulative multi-perspectival effect with the connections and comparisons set up among the stories. I turn now to servitude fiction writers who use the form of the novel instead of the short story. If the novel with a servant protagonist foregoes the multiple servant perspectives that Mueenuddin's story collection offers, it takes on some different challenges. First, the servant novel must sustain its readers' interest in a longer narrative, engaging global and local readers who (at least in South Asia) are unlikely to be from the lower classes, and who are unlikely to identify automatically with a servant protagonist. Second, the servant novel will have to contend with a tradition, at least in South Asia, where servants are not protagonists of novels. How Gunesekera, Adiga, Umrigar, and Kiran Desai address the formal and other challenges posed by these factors is a question explored in the chapters that follow.

4

From Periphery to Center

The Male Servant as Narrator and Protagonist in Romesh Gunesekera's *Reef*

Sri Lankan British writer Romesh Gunesekera's *Reef* (1994) and Indian Australian writer Aravind Adiga's *The White Tiger* (2008) are the only South Asian English novels to reach Booker Prize acclaim that have a male servant as the sole narrator and protagonist. (*Reef* was short-listed for the Booker in 1994; *White Tiger* won in 2008.) Both invert the tradition of backgrounding the servant by making him the single center of attention, unrivaled by other narrators or perspectives. Both novels have, for different reasons, drawn significant critical attention, but scholars have not, so far, compared them to each other, or explored the significance of their remarkable congruencies. Both novels construct the fictive voice of a male domestic servant and present his first-person account of his world and of the evolving relationship between himself, a migrant village boy, and his urban upper-class male employer; both therefore invite scrutiny of that servant's perspective in itself, and of how it has been shaped.

Reef and *The White Tiger* both trace how the servant's sense of self and identity changes and develops in relation to his strong, even homoerotic attachment to his master; both explore his desire for the master and his desire to emulate or mimic that master (through clothing, gestures, the use of the English language). In both, the servant narrator expresses initial jealousy, even resentment, of the women (the master's wife or mistress) who threaten to break into their servant-master homosocial intimacy and space, and for whom the servant then develops a triangulated desire; in both, the servant eventually breaks free of his (psychological and emotional as well as economic) dependence on the employer to become his own person with the master's death. Both emphasize the importance of education, enterprise, and independent thinking as a route to material independence and ways out of servitude. And both choose the same form of narration—a servant's first-person monologue—for the entire novel. Unlike Thrity Umrigar and Kiran Desai, the women novelists I discuss in Chapters 6 and 7 (who alternate the perspectives of servants and employers to bring out their connections and disconnections), Gunesekera and Adiga maintain throughout these novels the perspective of a single narrator who monopolizes the narration. Thus, both also pose the challenge of reading between (and beyond) the lines of this single and necessarily partial perspective.

Reef and *The White Tiger* are, however, also importantly different from each other. Indeed, their similarities serve to highlight the significance of their differences. Gunesekera presents, from a distanced, somewhat vague perspective, the growing turbulence of the young postcolonial state (Sri Lanka) and arguably idealizes the benevolence of the master who educates his servant, Triton, and helps him escape their violence-torn country to build a new self and future in England. Adiga focuses on a fine-grained, searing critique of the nation-state (India) and its failures, of the widespread societal corruption and systemic failures that interlock to crush the poorer class, and highlights the master's (and master class's) brutal exploitation of the servant (and his class), where the servant protagonist, Balram, has to kill his master and sacrifice his family in order to build an alternative life. Gunesekera is more interested in memory, in exploring how a diasporic, exilic, lower-class sensibility might remember, possibly nostalgically, a pre–civil war era of relative peace, and how a male subordinate's devotion to even a benign master is gradually eroded and replaced by a growing independence, a need for separation that is built, paradoxically, on imitation (or even mimicry) of that from which he seeks freedom. Adiga is more concerned with globalization, neoliberalism, corruption, and deeply entrenched social inequalities in modern India, and their compounded effects on an impoverished, disenfranchised male psyche. And, though both servant protagonists are assigned a variety of domestic tasks, Gunesekera's protagonist Triton is primarily a cook, with the kitchen as the heart of his domain, while Adiga's Balram is primarily a driver. In Adiga's important innovation, the car becomes a no less private, restricted domestic space, a mobile extension of the employer's home. *Reef* remains more restricted within the strict boundaries of the bourgeois house, and the depoliticized, interpersonal dramas located within it, while *The White Tiger* extends the home into the larger sphere, to suggest the intersections between the two, and broadens its reach to the connections between national and domestic politics.

I focus on *Reef* in this chapter, and on *The White Tiger* in the next. In looking closely at these two novels side by side, I am interested, not in mapping influence, the unidirectional flow from a predecessor author to successor, but in intertextuality, in the multidirectional, mutually illuminating relations between texts placed in conversation with each other. I want to explore how these texts speak to, and cast light on, each other and the issues they address, as well as the broader contexts of which they are symptomatic. Ultimately, I am interested in asking what conditions—cultural, political, other—produce the similarities (as well as differences) between these two novels. Both novels suggest that it is heightened economic injustice—not just poverty but the intense *disparity* between rich and poor, and the disparities of power, brought to the fore by the close proximities of servitude relations—that lies at the core of the violence and political troubles of both postcolonial South Asian nations. And both novels originate in diasporic male responses to male servitude: both are interested in exploring the (masculine) gendered condition of postcolonial servitude and the subjectivity it creates.

My main question—how these texts address postcolonial servitude—opens up many others. How does Adiga's corrosive irony and denunciation of India's neoliberalism and failure to care for its most vulnerable citizens compare to Gunesekera's more meditative, even nostalgic tonality in his account of Sri Lanka prior to its twenty-seven-year civil war? How (and why) does each construct the speaking voice of a subaltern male figure as a lens through which to view the nation's past, present, and future? What are the implications of *Reef*'s turn to Britain (reaffirming the centrality of the former colonial power), and *The White Tiger*'s to China (denying centrality to the Global North), as each imagines another nation as a site of refuge, alternative, or ironic mirror to its own?

Servitude is foregrounded in both novels as a literal condition, but carries metaphorical implications. Both deploy a form of social realism, where the servant narrator-protagonist and his condition are very much literal. Adiga's novel, as we will see in Chapter 5, also carries elements of deep satire, deploying the modes of exaggeration, hyperbole, parody, and almost surreal symbolism. Both novels highlight how domestic servitude is the site (or contact zone) at which individuals from widely disparate socio-economic groups—the rich and the poor, or what the Victorian Prime Minister Benjamin Disraeli called the two nations within the nation—come into close and intimate contact.[1] Both novels explore and highlight the gender and power dynamics and peculiar intimacies of servitude—the homosocial and homoerotic relations between male servant and male employer in the intimate space of the home (and in the case of *The White Tiger*, the car as well as an extension of the home). Both also use the perspective of the male servant as a fresh, unusual, but revealing angle to look at the condition of the postcolonial nation a few decades after independence. And both suggest that servitude indicates more: the poor of this postcolonial national are metaphorically all servants of the rich, suggests Adiga, while Gunesekera suggests an analogy between the servitude of the poor within the nation to the servitude of the postcolonial Third World nation in relation to the more powerful nations of the Global North. Gunesekera thus expands the compass of servant-master relations to a global scale. Yet how each goes about exploring these questions or making these comparisons is strikingly different.

Looking closely at each novel, I focus on three main questions. First, how does each explore the gendered psychology of the male servant in his relationship (from his perspective) with a master whom he both admires and ultimately seeks distance from, and thus how assumptions of gender (primarily masculinity but also femininity) and sexuality intermesh with notions of servitude? Second, how does each chart the servant narrator-protagonist's growth from adolescence to adulthood and gradual disenchantment with servitude until he reaches psychological and economic independence? And third, what does each narrative, through its dominant tropes and trajectory, suggest about the relation between servitude and the postcolonial nation? I argue in this chapter that *Reef* pioneers a mode of centralizing the servant, but offers a somewhat depoliticized, muted assessment of domestic servitude. With that caveat, I also argue that *Reef* at the same time provides a remarkably knowing portrayal of a young boy's experience of and emergence from servitude, both actual and psychological.

Reef as Fantasy?

Most of the short stories in *Monkfish Moon*, Romesh Gunesekera's first collection, published in 1992, are concerned with how everyday Sri Lankan lives, rich and poor, resident and diasporic, are impacted by the violence of the civil war (1983–2009) that was then raging with no end in sight. Many are also interested, if peripherally, in the dynamics between domestic servants—male and female, young and old—and their upper-class employers. None, however, focus on or are narrated from the point of view of the servant. In "Ranvali," for instance, the first-person narrator, a young upper-class woman, describes her return to her family's beach house, where she sees an old family servant, Carolis, who inspires her memories of her childhood and revelations about her now deceased Communist father. Carolis addresses her as "Missy," takes care of her, and brings her tea and meals, but, though she mentions his lifelong servitude, he remains peripheral to her story: "He was small and stooped and dug out. Practically his whole life had been tied to Ranvali. Father had brought him to the bungalow before I was born and he had stayed on," she reports (91). She recognizes the distance between them as he refuses to answer her questions about the "disturbances in the area" (91) and guiltily worries about his greater vulnerability: "I felt awful about the dead children in the river, about Carolis, his life, and the boy [Carolis's son] who cut the *thambili* [coconut]. I felt awful about my own life" (99). But after this brief and awkward announcement, she leaves Carolis behind, knowing she cannot provide him with the protection that she herself, as an upper-class woman, enjoys.

Likewise, in the opening story, "A House in the Country," a third-person omniscient narrator describes how Ray, a diasporic returnee from Britain, wants to change the culture of servitude, to offer support and protection to his young male domestic servant, Siri, but cannot. Siri, whose name suggests Sri Lanka, and is perhaps an emblem for the vulnerable working class to which the privileged diasporic male subject longs to reach out, is a village carpenter whom Ray hired at first to renovate his family house. As an enlightened and benevolent modern master, Ray has built a fragile, uneasy relationship with Siri, a willing servant mired in "antiquated" ways (15):

> [Ray] didn't quite know how to develop their working relationship. To him it should have been simply a relationship of employment. The old conventions of Colombo serfdom died years ago, but Siri kept saying "Sir" and circumscribing their roles. He developed his job from artisan, to supervisor, to cook, night-watchman and, in effect, the servant. Ray felt things had to change incrementally: he acquiesced and played the roles Siri expected. (14)

Notably, Gunesekera here presents Siri as the one who redefines the relationship. Siri exceeds his original role as carpenter and voluntarily takes on the role of domestic servant, insisting on maintaining traditional codes of subservience and distance, standing while Ray sits even when Ray offers him companionship and a beer (15). However, the narrator does not give us access to Siri's thoughts or feelings, except as Ray imagines them, focusing instead on Ray's shock and sensations when he discovers that Siri's brother has been lynched and his "mutilated" body hung on a lamp-post, on Ray's disconsolate helplessness and speechlessness when Siri voices his futile desire to leave Sri Lanka ("I want to go away. . . . you, Sir, have seen the world. Tell me where. Where is a good place?") and retreats silently to "his room in the servant's quarters" (23–24). The story ends inconclusively without indicating whether Siri will in fact disappear into the unknown, leaving Ray to "drink alone on his incomplete veranda," or whether Ray will find another "place" for Siri, a way to enable Siri to flee the violence (25).

Almost as a counter-story, *Reef*, Gunesekera's 1994 debut novel, seems to pick up where "A House in the Country" leaves off, as if enacting the fantasy, unrealized in the short stories, of the employer's rescue of the lower-class servant. Indeed, the fantasy seems enhanced by Gunesekera's choice to present the entire narrative in the grateful servant's own (imagined) voice. While Gunesekera is here arguably the first modern South Asian Anglophone writer to craft the voice of a servant narrator and make him the protagonist of a novel, such an effort may at times come across, unsurprisingly for pioneering work, as disingenuous or ideologically problematic.[2] The question I want to pose about this novel is what the novelty of this focus on a servant protagonist-narrator actually achieves, or seems designed to achieve. Even if it started out as a fantasy, *Reef* becomes a far more complicated novel as it explores the psychology and intricacies of male-male servant-master relations and interdependence. I suggest that, as servitude fiction, *Reef* is ambiguous and ambivalent: it centers on the servant boy's perspective, consciousness, and experiences, yet glorifies the benevolence of the master who makes possible this boy's escape from servitude; it emphasizes mutual interdependence yet provides no access to the perspective of the employer who remains thereby distant even to the servant who idolizes him; it minimizes the vicissitudes of servitude, yet shows how even this happy-to-cook, well-treated servant is glad, at the end, to be rid of both servitude and benign master; it reaffirms elitist stereotypes of the lower-class male servant in its portrayal of Joseph, Triton's co-servant, and casts Triton as the exceptional good servant, yet affirms at the end Triton's resistance to the elite upper class and desire to be independent and free of the entire system. *Reef* is nonetheless an important work of servitude fiction in its centralizing of the servant boy's consciousness, its portrayal of his gradual emergence from literal and psychological servitude, and its emphasis on his agency in his trajectory toward freedom.

Set primarily in the historical context of Sri Lanka's growing political and ethnic tensions in the 1960s, *Reef* is structured, after the brief prefatory opening, as a self-told postcolonial Bildungsroman in four chapters.[3] Chapter 1, "Kolla," presents the eleven-year-old Triton's arrival at Salgado's house in 1962, the moment that he becomes a servant, his initial exhilaration at escaping his village, his fear of Joseph, and his release from Joseph's menacing presence by 1963. Chapter 2, ironically titled "Cook's Joy" (since Triton both finds joy in cooking and realizes that he does not enjoy being a servant), details Triton's growth into adolescence, as he comes into his own, learns about Salgado's interest in oceanography and coral-reef preservation, witnesses the growing romance between Salgado and Nili (the woman who becomes Salgado's lover), and becomes infatuated with her himself.[4] The chapter ends in December 1969, on the brink of upcoming changes in the household and the nation, as Triton turns eighteen, Nili moves in, and violence begins to erupt in the country. Chapter 3, "A Thousand Fingers," details Triton's coming of age: his double disillusionment as he learns of the growing violence and political unrest in the country, watches the disintegration of the Salgado-Nili romance, and develops his own growing dissatisfaction with servitude. It ends in late 1970 with Salgado's decision to depart for England and take Triton with him, effectively initiating Triton's escape from both nation and servitude. In the very short epilogue-like Chapter 4, "Strandline," Triton, looking back from the vantage point of the early 1990s, describes briefly how this English sojourn has enabled, with Salgado's help, his emergence from servitude into economic and psychological independence, a refuge both from Sri Lanka's civil war in the present and his subordination in the past.[5]

In charting this narrative through Triton's voice, Gunesekera explores the gendered aspects of male servitude (highlighting specifically the same-sex dynamics between Salgado and Triton), and Triton's gradual disenchantment with servitude despite his continued devotion and attachment to Salgado. These form two intertwined strands of Triton's narrative: one, the intensification of Triton's dyadic attachment to Salgado, his close observation and knowledge of Salgado's doings and private life, his desire to serve and be like Salgado, his fascination for Nili; and two, his gradual realization that though he loves being with Salgado, and loves being a chef, he does not love being a servant. Triton takes great pride in his inventive cookery and presentation, but it is the pride of an artist, distinct from the subordination of being a servant. In what follows, I trace the ways that Gunesekera presents the development of these dual strains: the psychology of Triton's attachment to Salgado, and Triton's gradual disenchantment with servitude.

Literary scholars have taken a variety of approaches to *Reef*, including some that have produced controversy. In an early assessment, Walter Perera argued that Gunesekera was an expatriate "white-washed elite" Sri Lankan whose distanced representations of his homeland and its troubles distort reality and echo colonialist discourses (63).[6] In her important book, *Writing Sri Lanka*, Minoli Salgado pushes back against such "reductive" readings of fictional representations that are based on assumptions of "mimesis, authenticity, and truth-telling," calls attention to other critics who laud Gunesekera's style and use of metaphor and *Reef's* "elegiac lyricism and formal complexity" (149), and emphasizes the novel's interest in interiority, memory, loss, and imaginative recreation.[7] Others have attended to various themes and their implications: Anita Mannur notably explores food and culinary creation and consumption in the novel; Edward Mallot explores the question of healing and history versus memory; Gerd Bayer and Melanie Murray, among others, take an ecocritical or environmental studies approach to examine, respectively, the epistemology of science, or the significance of *Reef's* tropes of the marine and oceanic.[8] Few, however, have attended to servitude as an issue or a theme.[9] While indebted to these readings, I take a different approach, centralizing the question of servitude and the novel's exploration of the narrator-protagonist's complex, shifting affective relations and gradual emotional and psychological decolonization.

Beginning Servitude: Triton's Arrival at Salgado's House

Reef opens with a brief prefatory section, titled "The Breach," set in the present, where Triton, the now adult narrator, describes a chance encounter with a gas-station attendant, a fellow Sri Lankan, who has recently arrived in England and who speaks little English. In a curious mirror moment, the narrator sees a face in the window that is "almost a reflection of [his] own" (11). As both realize that they share the same country of origin, the "young refugee" asks Triton, the older refugee, for help with the cash machine. Ironically, they find they can only communicate in English: they are from rival ethnic groups; Triton speaks Sinhalese and the cashier Tamil. More ironically, the civil war that is splitting their country apart and that has brought them here now becomes distanced as they recognize, as diasporic migrants, their bonds to each other, as one asks for help and the other gives it. It is this moment of connection that becomes a trigger of memory, breaching, as the title suggests, Triton's self-protective defenses against the emotions and longing for home that he has locked away. The novel thus begins with the language of sea imagery, as Triton narrates, and is swamped by, the flood of memories of the past that breaks in.

Triton's memories (and hence his narration) begin with the moment of his arrival, as an eleven-year-old, at Mister Salgado's house in Colombo, as if that is the origin point for his journey toward who he has become, and that carries the emotional heft of his story. Unlike *The White Tiger*, which provides much more detail about the childhood of its servant-narrator, to elucidate the historical and structural conditions that form him, *Reef* offers very little of the conditions of Triton's childhood, family, or early formation. Replicated almost exactly in the opening of Chimamanda Adichie's later novel *Half of a Yellow Sun* (2006), the main narrative of *Reef* opens with the self-narrated arrival of a young village boy at his new master's home, escorted by an older relative who instructs him on how to be a good houseboy.[10] " 'Mister Salgado is a real gentleman. You must do whatever the hell he tells you.' My uncle pulled my ear" (15). Inaugurated with physical violence, servitude is thus presented to young Triton as an opportunity and a privilege for which he must relinquish his agency. This servitude is a refuge, Triton hints, from the violence of his village, an escape from his alcoholic widower father after Triton has "by accident" incinerated a schoolyard hut (17). And yet, from the start, Gunesekera also implicitly calls attention to class injustice, to how this employment and "new life" are bought for Triton in an unfair system where the poor must kowtow to appease the rich: Triton's elderly uncle, a truck driver, brings an offering of "a bag of green mangoes" for the wealthy and younger Mister Salgado, who is described as "a product of modern feudalism," a beneficiary of inherited wealth and education (16–17). Not only must Triton learn to serve, to be self-abasing, he must be grateful for the opportunity to do so.

Compared to *The White Tiger*, *Reef* casts servitude and the master-employer as far more benign, though in both servitude is unquestionably preferable to the village life left behind. Triton presents Ranjan Salgado from the beginning as unusually benevolent, as somewhat eccentric, absent minded, and vulnerable, yet able to provide for his young charge a sense of safety, an escape from the violence and poverty of Triton's village, and from the dangers of the world beyond Salgado's garden gates: "He was thin and had a curved spine. . . . The sad expression of a hurt heron would struggle in his face. He spoke slowly, almost hesitantly, politely changing the subject, and asking my uncle about the failed coup [of 1962] as if it were some unseasonable rain" (17). The turbulence of 1960s Ceylonese politics (which eventually lead to the civil war) is mentioned but kept at arm's length, softened by Salgado's conversational mode of gentle consideration. Triton quickly begins to idolize his master, who offers a contrast even to his uncle, an alternative model of civility and kindness embodied early on in his voice:

> I had never heard language so gently spoken [reports Triton]. My uncle's speech, in comparison, was a strangulation of the spirit. . . . I could lose myself in [Mister Salgado's] voice; this happened not only on that first day, but frequently over many years. (17)

Likewise, Salgado's house, for young Triton, becomes a better home, an idyllic, protected space that, from his child-perspective, seems "the center of the universe":

> . . . everything in the world took place within its enclosure. Even the sun seemed to rise out of the garage and sleep behind the *del* tree at night. Red-beaked parrots and yellow-eared *salaleenas* came and sang in the garden. Bullfrogs croaked by the gate. On Monday the greengrocer turned up with his basket of okra and beans; on Tuesday the butcher . . .; on Wednesday the fishmonger . . . (27)

The safety, soothing routines, rhythmic regularity of time, provision of a variety of foods, all conveyed through Triton's sensuous descriptions, make Salgado's home seem like paradise, with Salgado as its benevolent presiding god.[11]

In an unobtrusive, seemingly off-handed way, Salgado also takes care of Triton and supervises his (informal) education. Did Triton go to school in his village, is Salgado's first question. Triton had to leave school after "Fifth Standard," we learn, but "can read and write" and "even learned some English" from the "tormented schoolmaster" whom Triton found (as he reveals elliptically at the end) in a ditch with his legs broken by some older boys in "that unsettled month" before Triton came to Salgado's house (16, 189). Though Triton is set to work as an underling to be trained by two other house servants, Salgado himself assigns Triton "counting jobs," instructing him "like a teacher—a *gurunanse*" in his various tasks (32). Yet, although the novel clearly casts Salgado as an unusual employer, almost godlike, minor cues suggest that Triton's education is in fact from the start the result of a partnership, the joint effect of Salgado's unobtrusive kindness and Triton's own initiative and enterprise. Gunesekera thus underscores Triton's agency in his self-fashioning. Though Triton describes himself as "ensnared" by Salgado's voice, as feeling "guilty" about his "furtive attempts to emulate Salgado and better [him] self," the details suggest that it is Triton who aspires and desires, who takes action to teach himself to write, inspired by Salgado (32–33).

Gunesekera also suggests a muted homoerotic sexual interest on the young servant's part for his master. Early on, assigned the task of serving bed-tea, Triton enters Salgado's bedroom early one morning to find him snoring: "The over-sheet was crumpled up on a side, and his sarong lay sloughed off his slim hips. His banyan revealed a few strands of black hair on a narrow boyish chest" (22). Servitude enables (or necessitates) proximity, intimacy, and glimpses into privacy, whether welcome or not to either servant or master, but Triton's focus on the details of Salgado's sleeping, exposed body suggests an interest that borders on the physical (his uncovered "slim hips," his chest-hair). As a yet-untrained servant boy, Triton has already learnt how to read his master's body language. Having woken Salgado by announcing the arrival of tea, Triton knows not to disturb him, to understand that he wants "privacy," for thinking time: "He was awake but he kept his eyes closed. He pretended to be asleep so that he did not have to acknowledge me.... His *Einstein-time*, as he would call it later" (22). The scene emblematizes the asymmetry or inequality of their interdependence: Triton has to understand, by learning to interpret bodily signs, Salgado's desires, often wordlessly, and fulfill them, while the latter does not need to reciprocate. Later, Triton's dependence on Salgado (who occupies at once the role of father, mentor, and beloved) becomes emotional as well as material, whereas Salgado's dependence on Triton is only practical, or at most psychological, in the peace of mind it affords the employer to know the servant will fulfill his responsibilities.

Unlike *The White Tiger*, *Reef* offers little sense of the dehumanization or demeaning aspects of servitude. The only trouble, threat, or fear that Triton experiences working as a servant in Salgado's house comes from his fellow servant and supervisor, Joseph, the proverbial serpent in paradise. Joseph emerges early on as a villainous tyrant. Having been given a broom that was dangerously long for him, young Triton cuts the handle short, demonstrating the enterprise and intelligence that make him (almost) as exceptional as Balram, the eponymous white tiger of Adiga's novel, and earning the ire of Joseph, who accuses him of wastage and destruction of (the master's) property. Mister Salgado, by contrast, appreciates the reasons for Triton's act and stands up for him, earning Triton's gratitude and devotion: "Then I knew I was in the right place; *he*, at least did not think I was stupid" (20).

Triton's comments about Joseph, moreover, suggest a somewhat dubious politics on Gunesekera's part:

> I was meant to help Joseph, but he resented me right from the beginning. Perhaps because, despite my circumstances, *I was not of his kind.* . . . He had

been born with the moral equivalent of a sweet tooth—no temptation was too small. I despised him for this defect: I felt he sullied Mister Salgado's house. (19; emphasis added)

Triton's suggestion that Joseph's decadent, corrupt tendencies are innate, not acculturated, indicates an assumption of inborn degradation and inferiority, and perhaps, an equation of moral with class inferiority. Reinforcing an elitist ideology, it suggests Triton's internalization and reiteration of negative stereotypes of the male, lower-class servant. (Unfortunately, Gunesekera's orchestration of Joseph's subsequent monstrous behavior confirms these stereotypes.) And yet Triton's remark is not as clear-cut as it seems, for it does not necessarily equate Joseph's moral culpability with his class status. An alternate reading would suggest that Triton distinguishes between his "circumstances" (the poverty and lower-class, villager status that he shares with Joseph) and his "kind" (the moral depravity that Joseph supposedly was "born with" and from which Triton, despite his circumstances, is exempt). Nonetheless, both author and servant narrator concur in marking Joseph as *inherently* inferior and contemptible, as unworthy of belonging to the house of Salgado. Triton here becomes a complicated tool for the upper-class author: he serves both as a lower-class voice to promulgate an elitist or essentialist ideology, and as a counter-example of that lower-class. Bifurcating the portrayal of the male servant into two extreme types, Gunesekera casts Triton as the exceptional good servant to contrast with Joseph the bad one, or as Ariel to Joseph's Caliban, in a (homoerotic) replay of Shakespeare's *Tempest*, with Salgado in the role of Prospero.[12]

This Caliban, however, tries to rape Ariel, not Miranda. Or, Triton occupies at once the position of both Ariel and Miranda, both servant and child. Triton describes how Joseph repeatedly terrifies him until one day, when Salgado is away, and the two male servants are left alone in the house, Joseph, in a fit of drunkenness, attempts to sexually assault Triton. Triton emphasizes both his voicelessness, and his ability to escape: "I wanted to scream but I couldn't. I had no voice. I jumped up and ran out of the house" (46). When Salgado returns, Triton does not tell him what happened, but Salgado seems to sense something is wrong. When Joseph turns up drunk, Salgado summarily fires him. In casting Salgado as the discerning, benign rescuer who restores Triton's paradise, Gunesekera, through Triton's account of the Joseph episode, also establishes two more points. One, Triton sees, and understands the precarity of servants who, like himself, can be dismissed and lose their livelihoods without warning; he finds it possible "to feel sorry for Joseph even though [he] hated him" (51). Second, Triton's attachment to Salgado is such that he suppresses the truth about Joseph because he wants his relationship with Salgado to continue unaffected by the memory of Joseph:

> I wanted to tell him exactly what I had seen and what had happened. But the words were impossible to get out. I did not want to be tarnished by telling—by putting into words—what had gone on. It would have spoiled everything. We would have had Joseph between us forever. It was not what I wanted. It was better, I thought, to leave it untold. (49)

What Triton desires is a purely dyadic relation with Salgado, not triangulated or shaped by Joseph.

It is therefore not difficult to read *Reef* as ideologically questionable, as glorifying servitude, and to view Gunesekera's use of Triton's servant voice as a disingenuous, self-serving device that promotes elitist or other problematic ideologies. I would argue, however, against such a reading, for at least two reasons. First, young Triton's endorsement of such ideologies, can also be understood in terms of psychological realism, as the result of his absorption and internalization of dominant societal classist and essentialist assumptions and ways of seeing. Hence Triton's comments and ways of seeing could instead be seen as Gunesekera's critical exposé of the way that Triton has been formed. (That said, Gunesekera's own choice to represent Joseph, as confirming those assumptions, remains a problem, indicated by the novel's mixed approach toward servants.) Second, even though Triton idolizes his master, Triton later comes to awareness of the undesirability of servitude and outgrows his desire to be a servant as he feels the sting of condescension or disrespect from Salgado's visiting friends, protected though he is by Salgado. After the first chapter, and the banishment of Joseph, *Reef* provides many subtle hints of Triton's growing unease with the position of servant that he was initially so happy with. An alternative way to read *Reef* then is as a self-revealing disclosure of Triton's gradual coming to awareness, as he develops and then grows out of his dependence on Salgado. Such a reading would affirm the novel as a critical exploration of the psychological effects of servitude, tracing the disenchantment of a hegemonized servant even to a benign master. I want to propose a reading that combines both approaches, that takes a both-and rather than either-or approach, to suggest *both* that *Reef* carries dubious elements that suggest an insufficiently critical approach to domestic servitude and the power relations that constitute servant-master relations, *and* that it is a canny exploration of the process of gradual psychological emancipation or (self-)liberation, as Triton eventually comes to recognize the problems of servitude, value his independence, and leave servitude behind. *Reef* thereby offers a complex understanding of the psychology of male-male relations within servitude.

Toward the end of the novel, Triton meditates on how he learned to cope with Salgado's moods, on how he could not tell what Salgado was thinking or feeling, as he watched how Salgado coped with what life brought him: "it takes time, years, to learn how other people cope with themselves, how they come to terms with the changes that happen, always happen around them" (142). Triton here describes how he learned by watching Salgado, how Salgado coped with himself and with the changes around him, and how long it took Triton to understand, and grow by watching. Yet this comment also applies to Triton himself: it could be an epigraph for the novel itself, which takes time to trace how Triton coped with himself, how he came to terms with the changes that took place around him, and how, as a result, they changed him.

Given how positively Triton portrays his master throughout the novel, and how much he emphasizes his pleasure in becoming Salgado's "cook as well as everything else" (18), it may come as a surprise to most readers that at the end, Triton is glad to be rid of Salgado's shadow. Living in England in 1983, no longer a servant or child but a restauranteur and adult (190), yet still beholden to Salgado, who "invested the last of his savings in [Triton's restaurant]" (188), Triton realizes that Salgado's plan to return to Sri Lanka, during the civil war, to help his ex-lover Nili (who has been attacked by violent mobs) meant that Salgado could die:

> I knew he was going to leave me and he would never come back. I would remain and finally have to learn to live on my own. Only then did it dawn on me that this might be what I wanted deep down inside. What perhaps I had always wanted.... It was the only way I could succeed: without a past, without a name, without Ranjan Salgado standing by my side. (190)

The slow cadence of Triton's sentences suggests his own belated, reluctant recognition of a subterranean desire that has been hidden even from himself: "what perhaps I had always wanted." Perhaps this is only a rationalization of grief, knowing that he cannot save or stop this beloved man to whom he owes his life and his self. But mingled with that grief is a sense of relief at the separation, at being forced into a welcome self-reliance, an unforeseen, unprecedented independence. How does the grateful, subservient Triton, initially incredulous at his good luck in becoming Salgado's servant, change into the self-aware man who recognizes, slowly but surely, his desire for independence even from the most benevolent, generous, and ultimately egalitarian of masters? This, ultimately, is the trajectory this novel attempts to chart.

Gunesekera plants many hints of this trajectory and its final turn, right from the start. In a key moment, after firing Joseph, Salgado decides not to hire another adult servant, and asks Triton to take over Joseph's responsibilities. Both thrilled and trepidatious, twelve-year-old Triton is reassured by Salgado's assurance that he is a "smart *kolla*" (boy), that he will have to learn to cook (from Lucy the elderly woman who has served Salgado's family for decades and is about to retire) and to manage the household (as Joseph did) by himself (52). It is important that when Salgado briefly considers an alternative future for Triton, saying "Really you should go to school," Triton refuses:

> "No, Sir." I was sure, at that time, that there was nothing a crowded, bewildering school could offer me that I could not find in his gracious house. "All I have to do is watch you, Sir. Watch what you do. That way I can really learn."
> He sighed, slowly releasing us into the future. "Let's see."
> So I watched him, I watched him unendingly, all the time, and learned to become what I am. (52–53)

Looking back, however, the adult narrator notes that "*at that time*" Triton could see nothing better than the privilege of having free run of Salgado's house, of being a servant in that house. He chose to "watch" and "learn" from Salgado as his model. The slow, sinister repetition of "I watched him" suggests something ominous, something troubling about the single-minded mimicry of master by servant, the total absorption of the boy servant in that master. It produces an expectation subsequently fulfilled by Triton's unusual word choice in describing himself as "what" and not "who" he has become. The novel thus poses the question of what exactly Triton is—a person, a creature, or a thing—and how his sense of self and identity are created by his experience of this servitude. Perhaps that is what Triton's name suggests, the name he wants at the end to forget.

We do not know if Triton, originally the Greek name of a mythical creature, the son of Poseidon and Amphitrite, is a nickname and whether Triton has another real Sri Lankan name. Chapter 1, in which the narrator remains unnamed, is simply titled "Kolla" (boy), which is what Triton is called when he arrives at Salgado's house, as if that is the extent of his identity in this chapter. Triton is named for the first time in the second chapter, after Joseph and Lucy have left and he is fully in charge of Salgado's household, as if that is when he comes into himself, or acquires a Western nickname under Salgado's aegis. The text provides no indication of how he comes by this name.[13] "Triton" suggests a hybrid, something in between land and sea, half-fish half-human, a herald with a trumpet, traditionally associated with the trident that gives him his name. "Triton" also denotes the symbol for psi, the psyche, as well as control over the three aspects of time—past, present, and future. It therefore apt that in this novel Triton narrates his own story, showing how his own past, present, and future are connected. In so doing, Triton both explores and reveals the psychology of his servitude, the slow unraveling of his initial subservience, and shift to the desire for independence.

As Triton grows into adolescence, he replaces both Lucy the cook and Joseph to become the single servant entirely responsible for all tasks in Salgado's household, as manager, housekeeper, cook, errand boy, gardener. As the mutual dependence between Triton and Salgado grows, so does Triton's adulation of

Salgado. Triton both desires Salgado and desires to be him (or like him), to the extent that he begins to desire what Salgado desires. Triton's initial investment extends to what becomes Triton's attempt to foster Salgado's new relationship with Nili, the woman who becomes Salgado's lover, and to Triton's own somewhat sublimated, triangulated desire for Nili. Triton also takes pleasure in becoming a cook, in producing mouth-watering, inventive, inspired, hybrid food that combines local ingredients with Western cuisine, as he strives both to please Salgado and his guests and to find fulfillment in his own creativity.

From a psychoanalytic perspective, echoing Freud's famous question (what does a woman want?), one might ask, what does a servant want? That is not a question possible within the frameworks of traditional Freudian psychoanalysis, which is premised on the (nuclear) family romance. But it is certainly a question possible to consider under a broader psychoanalytic framework that includes unconscious ambivalences, structures of desire, disavowal, and dialectics of sameness and otherness. Why does the servant want to mimic his master, in both *Reef* and *The White Tiger*?[14] While I certainly would not equate servant-master dynamics with colonizer-colonized ones (since in these postcolonial texts both servant and master occupy the position of the colonial subject, though differently), I find that Bhabha's concept of colonial mimicry, which similarly concerns intimate and unequal power dynamics, is highly pertinent as a lens to understand servant-employer dynamics in servitude fiction. Repeatedly, we see the servant desiring to emulate the employer, and the employer (like the colonizer) wanting the servant to approximate his notion of civility or upper-class modes of decorum, without becoming the same. In his powerful meditations on colonial mimicry, Bhabha does not explore what the colonized might want, but focuses on what the colonizer wants, which, he argues, is approximation not sameness, that the colonized become like, but not fully like, the colonizer, "*a subject of difference that is almost the same, but not quite*," or "*almost the same but not white*" (*Location*, 86, 89). In exploring the structure of desire of the servant who mimics his master, watching him, wanting to be (like) him, Gunesekera (and Adiga too, as I will discuss in the next chapter) shifts focus to mimicry from the point of view of the servant. Mimicry is not "subservience," as John McLeod points out (67); it is also, as Leela Gandhi notes, "the sly weapon of anti-colonial civility, an ambivalent mixture of deference and disobedience" (149). Triton is not consciously subversive of his master, whom he adores, and who encourages him to learn, to improve himself. Gunesekera casts Triton's mimicry as not disobedience but agentive and willing emulation. But unconsciously, Triton's gradual shift toward approximation of his master brings him to a point where, to become (like) him, he can no longer be a servant or enact servility, and where, in a necessary separation, he must disinvest from the relationship itself.[15]

"Your Life, Your Everything": Mimicry, Desire, and Triton the Adolescent Servant

Triton's hunger for education and his efforts to better himself stem not so much from pecuniary or social ambition as the desire to become like Salgado. Picking up after Joseph's departure, Chapter 2 begins with Triton's account of how he taught himself to read and learn English by making a deal with Salgado's neighbor's son: "In return for my playing dead and other minor exorcisms, he let me devour his school primers and English readers" (55). It is thus again not Salgado who educates him, but Triton who takes the initiative, willing to sacrifice his dignity and play the subordinate role in these boyhood games to advance his own project of self-making. Alone in the house with Salgado, Triton watches Salgado closely and notes how he sits reading "cross-legged" at a low table in the library after his bath:

> I could feel the air move when he turned a page, each one catching the lemony light slice by papery slice. I too liked to sit unfettered in a room of my own, emptied of the past, nothing inside, nothing around, nothing but a voice bundled in paper, a pattern of marks entering my own stillness. (61)

In this gorgeous evocation of the power of reading, Gunesekera suggests how watching Salgado produces in Triton a yearning to do and be the same, to extend his mind beyond the immediate, to heal as he relishes the safety and peace afforded by their quiet, dyadic existence. It initiates his project of self-making, in the mirror-image of his master. Does this mean that the novel implies that servants can escape servitude via their own initiative? As I discuss below, *Reef* emphasizes individual action on the part of *both* servant and master as needed to end servitude. It does not, however, carry a sense of the necessity of broader systemic change.

As the sole remaining servant in Salgado's house, Triton also likes no longer being at the bottom of the hierarchy of servants. He enjoys growing out of the subordinate position he started with, being treated with more respect by vendors now that he "ran the place" (56). He starts to develop a stronger sense of self. Taking pride in his new expertise, he likes anticipating what Salgado and his friend Dias might want, and the pleasure his food will provide: "I had become an expert in the kitchen. . . . I was also pretty good at a curry in a hurry. A nice red salmon dish could be on the table in twelve minutes flat, and they would both love it" (59). What "they" take for granted—the appearance of ample, freshly cooked meals with delicately balanced flavors—are the result, Gunesekera highlights, of the servant's careful planning and ingenuity.

Yet even at this relatively early stage, as a teenager, Triton is aware of and expresses some resistance to their perception of him as an uneducated houseboy with the supposed superstitions of the underclasses. On Triton's first car trip to the coast with Salgado and Dias, they hit a cow on the way. While the upper-class men laugh, to Triton the near-accident seems inauspicious since the cow, though not seriously injured, was revered as "the source of milk and labor" (65). At a traffic stop Salgado allows Triton to donate ten cents to appease potentially angry gods, though Triton can sense the upper-class men's condescension. But while he can read their minds, he notes, they cannot read his:

> They were both indulging my unenlightened habits, they thought, but I was not a believer. In my own way I am a rationalist, same as Mister Salgado, but perhaps less of a gambler; I believe in tactical obeisance, that's all. If there is a possibility that the temple exerts some influence, that there is some force or creature or deity or whatever that is appeased by ten cents in a tin box, why take a chance? At worst the ten cents will help keep the place tidy, or fill the belly of a monk... So I dropped the coins in the box thinkingly, not unthinkingly as I am sure Mister Salgado and Mr. Diaz thought I did. (65)

As a servant, Triton cannot tell Salgado and Dias that they are wrong to make assumptions about what he believes, but he articulates it for himself, and for us. He knows that because he is lower class, they think of him as ignorant, irrational, and superstitious. But Triton is more knowing, both of what they think and what he thinks. (He is also more knowing than them and more knowing than they think he is.) His startling point is that he is actually more rational than they are. Since no one really knows if there is a deity to be appeased or not, he reasons, why risk bad luck? Gunesekera presents Triton as effectively arriving autonomously at Pascal's wager: if there is a god to be appeased, he argues logically, this will do it; if there is not, the money will help those who need it. Moreover, unlike these entitled men who live in what proves to be a false sense of security, Triton's awareness of precarity sensitizes him to the greater risk of harm (to himself and to Salgado), and to the effect even a small donation would have on others (those less fortunate). In tracing a young servant boy's psychology as it changes, Gunesekera presents Triton as almost never critical of Salgado, but also, as in this important early occasion of servant pushback, showing "thinkingly" an independence of mind that will develop into a fuller rejection of servitude and dependence.

When Nili enters their lives, disrupting the Triton-Salgado dyad, Triton's reactions are significantly mixed.[16] On the one hand, he is eager to please Salgado, to welcome her, and do what he can to foster the romance and make Salgado happy. On the other hand, his language suggests a suppressed jealousy, even possessiveness of and desire for Salgado, a proprietariness about their home, and protectiveness in assessing whether she is a fitting partner for Salgado. To foster his master's new romance, Triton does what he knows best: he cooks. When she first visits their house for tea, he makes his "richest, juiciest love-cake," in addition to a variety of other mouth-watering offerings—several kinds of sandwiches, patties, and "little coconut cakes" (74). He describes with pride how he created these confections, emphasizing his artistry in combining Eastern ingredients with Western recipes to produce innovative, hybrid foods: "I had made mutton patties that day and put green coriander in them; unheard of anywhere else in our country at that time" (76). His food is a big hit, she devours it all, he reports proudly, especially the love-cake, the magical concoction that seems to cement the romance: "I had used ten eggs instead of the regulation seven that day, because of her. And real yellow butter creamed to perfection. And *cadju*—cashew nuts—fresh from the countryside" (75).

And yet, though thrilled with Nili's reaction and Salgado's approval, Triton also disapproves of Nili: "She made a lowing sound between bites. It made him happy, and although I didn't approve of her being quite so uninhibited so soon in our house, I was touched too" (74). While taking pleasure in Salgado's pleasure, and in Nili's, Triton is still cautious, proprietary, rivalrous. His expression, "our house," indicates that he sees their home as not yet hers in which to make herself at home. He wants to wait and see if she is indeed right for his beloved master, and he does not like her unladylike unrestraint in expressing her physical pleasure, even in his cake, before two strange men. His criteria for her reflect a learned form of classed and gendered traditionally feminine social decorum; he wants her to have more reserve, to hold back, not to let herself go in this unselfconscious performance of bodily pleasure. So far, these reactions manifest the not unexpected acculturated responses of a devoted boy servant to the intrusion into his all-male terrain of a new and powerful female presence. But another remark complicates even further Gunesekera's portrayal of young male servitude.

When Nili asks Salgado where he obtained the heavenly cake she cannot stop eating, and Salgado responds, "Triton made it," Triton reports the thoughts that he cannot express:

> *Triton made it*. It was the one phrase he would say with my name again and again like a refrain through those months, giving me such happiness. *Triton made it*. Clear, pure and unstinting. His voice at those moments would be a channel cut from heaven to earth right through the petrified morass of our lives, releasing a blessing like water springing from a river-head, from a god's head. It was bliss. My coming of age.
>
> "Your cook?"
>
> *Your life, your everything*, I wanted to sing pinned up on the rafters, heaven between my legs. (74–75; italics in original)

I want to highlight some key points about this remarkable passage. First, even Triton's pride in his cookery, his eventual basis for independence, is not independent of Salgado, but derived from, and motivated by, Salgado's pleasure and pride in it. His repetition of Salgado's laconic sentence "Triton made it" suggests a sense of achievement, belonging, and need for affirmation from Salgado. Instead of rendering him invisible, Salgado has actually referred to him, and voiced their connection, as if Triton were an extension of Salgado himself. Second, in describing his own response to Salgado's approval, and to his voice, Triton's joyful excess—his euphoric, ecstatic language and use of an almost orgasmic image—simultaneously eroticizes and deifies his master. It more fully reveals Triton's desire, his wish to be all for Salgado in every sense, his own erotic investment in Salgado, confirmed by his self-knowing yet self-censored desire to be Salgado's "life, his everything," and his longing to sing, with clear (homo) erotic connotations, "pinned" above, "heaven between [his] legs" (75). As if mirroring the dual position of Triton as autobiographical narrator looking back to his younger self, and inhabiting that self, here in this moment Triton seems to look down from above as an observer upon himself as participant in his household drama, as desiring agent both outside and within this triangle, at once enviously looking in on and constitutive of this budding romance. Perhaps it is not surprising, Gunesekera suggests, that a young boy, isolated from the rest of the world, dependent emotionally as well as materially on the man who constitutes his world, should become imprinted by him, and regard him as the center of his emotional world, as at once father, lover, teacher, mentor.

And yet, third, this desire, this affective intensity, is always suffused by Triton's awareness of himself as Salgado's servant. After Nili leaves, when Triton tries to tell Salgado in too much detail how he made the food, Triton realizes that Salgado does not share his interest in gourmet food-making, that Triton's desire for more affirmation is a sign of his own emotional dependence: "however confident I was about the perfection of what I produced, like everybody else, I needed praise. I needed his praise and I needed her praise. I felt stupid to need it, but I did" (76). Anticipating the end, when he seeks to overcome his deep dependence on and need for Salgado, here Triton becomes aware of his unreciprocated need, his sense of inadequacy: he cannot just make the food and watch it be eaten; he needs reassurance, recognition, appreciation.

Triton's response to Nili likewise suggests these mixed feelings. Triton begins to connect with Nili when he realizes that they share an interest in Salgado. Arriving one day at Salgado's house in his absence, she draws Triton conspiratorially into her secret plan to borrow one of Salgado's shirts to have a new shirt tailor-made for him as a Christmas present. Triton is torn between loyalty to his master, unsure about lending Nili his master's favorite shirt without his knowledge, and the desire to please his master by accommodating her. He agrees, he says, because she treats him well as a servant: "I liked Nili. She had no airs. She treated people—everyone, top and bottom—as real people. Not like other ladies—the *nonas*—who screeched *chi, chi, chi* at their servants" (82). Clearly, Triton is well aware of how other servants in Sri Lankan society are normally treated, and how lucky he is by comparison. He implicitly aligns her with Salgado: she treats Triton well, which makes her a good match for Salgado. Yet Triton's awareness is highly gendered: as a male servant, he thinks of women employers misogynistically as "screeching," as exerting wrongful power, unlike male employers, who rightfully command more authoritatively.[17] Implicitly, Triton challenges women's power over male servants, as if women were more likely to abuse servants, and were more culpable when they did.

Gunesekera's evocation here of an isolated servant boy's emotions and psychology in a situation of same-sex dyadic dependence takes, however, a yet more complicated turn. For this is not only a story of a servant's homoerotic desire and yearning to emulate his master. Triton also becomes infatuated with Nili himself, learning to desire what Salgado desires. In his classic book, *Deceit, Desire and the Novel*, Rene Girard famously introduced the concept of mimetic or "triangular desire," to explain how often a subject's desire (for an object) is mediated through another person, whose desire for that object is imitated and internalized by the subject who holds the "mediator" in a relationship of conscious or unconscious rivalry or admiration (4). Hence, in this (heteronormative) model, male desire for a woman is catalyzed through and magnified by the admired other male (as in *Don Quixote*'s tale of Anselmo and Lotario). In a perfect example of such triangulation, Triton finds Nili desirable because he looks up to Salgado so much that he sees her via Salgado—she becomes more exciting through, and because of her relationship with, Salgado. But Gunesekera further complicates this model of desire as he explores how servitude inflects this triangulation.[18]

In a central episode at the heart of the novel, Triton single-handedly prepares a Christmas dinner at Salgado's house in honor of Nili, who is Christian, though Salgado is not. The dinner party also affirms the Westernized, secular, cosmopolitan ease of the Sinhalese Salgado as a member of late 1960s upper-class Sri Lankan society before ethnic tensions split it apart. In expecting Triton to produce this enormous meal, without help or instruction, and serve eight to nine people, Salgado does not seem to realize what a huge demand he makes of this young boy. Rising to the challenge, Triton executes it with triumph, roasting a gigantic turkey by himself for the first time, making accompaniments, carefully setting the table, serving drinks and homemade appetizers, acting at once as chef, footman, and butler. In a rare description of Triton's physical appearance, Gunesekera calls attention to Triton's servant status via his clothing, which contrasts with the formal Western clothing of the guests, as Triton reports with unwitting pride: "I wore my white sarong for the occasion" (89).

Excited by the guests and the conversations Salgado is engaging in, eager to listen and regretful that he has missed much of it as he shuttles between kitchen and sitting room, Triton begins to show a heightened awareness of Nili and her physicality throughout the evening. He notices her "infectious laugh," which "started at her lips and seemed to slither down her throat with a sucking sound" (90). Despite a hint of residual resentful territoriality, when he notes how she behaves "as though she were the hostess instead of the chief guest" (98), he describes in sensuous detail what he sees, smells, and touches of Nili when he serves the potatoes and vegetables to the seated guests, bending over them from behind:

> The nape of her neck was bare. Her dress hung suspended by two thin black straps. She had pinned her hair up at the back with a silver clasp. Some of the hair had slipped out, but I could still see a swollen red lump like a mole, or a bite, on the left side of her neck along a downy tendon. . . . My sarong, tight around my hips, brushed her arm. (98–99)

The demands of servitude necessitate the close proximity that enables Triton's observation of such intimate bodily details. Gunesekera here reveals how a servant's perspective literally enables Triton to see what others at the same social and physical level, such as the other guests, cannot see, and indeed what Nili herself cannot see. But his attentiveness is not neutral; it is sexual as he lingers over the back of her neck and her bare skin, as he notes the thin shoulder straps, the suggestive flimsiness of her clothing, and focuses on the almost microscopic details of her body, from red spots to down. Is this physical interest in Nili a form of rivalry with Salgado, or an extension of Triton's interest in and admiration of Salgado and all that is his, or, a triangulated desire for her produced and intensified precisely by his knowledge of Salgado's interest in her? I would suggest that it is a combination of all three, that Gunesekera's point is that this is precisely the psychological consequence of Triton's closeness to Salgado, produced by his servant position in relation to his master.

Triton's next remark confirms that this intensity of focus on Nili has something to do with his deep affective connection to Salgado, and is tied to Triton's servant status, which makes her at once so close and yet utterly unattainable. Still looking at her from behind, as he serves her food, he focuses on her ears, comparing them both to a poppadum (something perfect and delectable to eat that he can cook), and to a conch shell (an enticing, sexually suggestive, vagina-like opening to the body that can be entered):

> Her ears moved too when she spoke. They were larger than I expected. Each with two symmetrical wrinkles where they joined her neck and the outer edges

curled in like the edge of a puppadum when it hits hot oil. My instinct was to press the ears back with my hands and keep the entrances to her soul open like the lips of a glazed pink conch. (99)

This extraordinary focus on Nili's ears, moreover, associates her with Salgado, as it harks back to an earlier occasion when Triton, seated in the back of the car while Salgado was driving, looked closely at the back of Salgado's head and similarly examined his ears, comparing them to Dias's:

> Looking at them from behind, I discovered a tremendous difference between them, especially between their ears. Of course they were both intelligent educated men, but Dias' ears were small and firmly pinned to [his] skull . . . His ears were hardly distinguishable from the rest of the head, still forming: a foetus ear, a bud insensitive to the calls of nature—my earlier calls for a piss-stop, "Sir, *su-barai!*"—whereas Mister Salgado had such a clearly articulated pair. Each an elegantly cupped, long slender hand attached by a flared stem to the side of the head, exactly midway between top and bottom, and shrouded by his black hair; the lobes divinely long. (66)

Triton's almost scientifically minute observation is charged with affect and meaning: he reads each man's ears as symptomatic of his character. Where Diaz's "foetus"-like ears, or "buds," bespeak arrested growth, his moral and literal failure to attend to the call of the child servant's needs from the back of the car, Salgado's large yet delicate ears, almost like tactful hands, emblematize his greater solicitousness, attentiveness, and care, his higher moral almost god-like status. Indeed, young Triton both likes and wants to be like Salgado, as he pulls his own ear lobes downward in an effort to lengthen them to resemble his master's "divine" ones. Likewise, Triton's fascination for Nili's ears suggests a similar affective charge, an unseen adoring gaze from behind. But in Nili's ears he sees sexual desirability, not greater moral stature. In all three cases, Gunsekera suggests how Triton's servant's perspective (literally looking at the back of upper-class heads) enables him to see from a strange, unusual angle, and to read what he sees as symptoms of character. Each individual's ears suggest the extent to which they can literally and figuratively hear him, or are sensitive to his presence. Hence part of the point of Triton's interest in their ears is a way to gauge whether they are or are not listening to him. To Nili, as it soon becomes clear, he is just a servant, a sexless being to whom she can be kind, but whom she cannot see as having sexual desires or responses to her actions, gestures, or physical presence.

Triton's sexual interest in Nili as he bends over her at the Christmas dinner table is further confirmed by his subsequent suggestive comments, as he breathes in her perfume, "as it rose up from below her throat down inside her flapping dress" (99). But she is oblivious to his proximity, or to her effect on him. As she raises a hand to stop him ladling more potatoes on her plate, they accidentally touch: "My sarong, tight around my hips, brushed her arm. She didn't notice" (99). Triton notices that she does not notice him, that what he sees as potentially sexual contact, as she brushes against his sarong, which covers him from the waist down, is to her nothing. This asymmetry is repeated and magnified in many subsequent interactions, as Nili, oblivious to how her uninhibited actions may arouse or impinge on Triton, fails to see him as a sexual being, or as someone who might see her as a sexual being.

At the end of the Christmas party, Nili visits the kitchen to thank Triton for his efforts and to give him a present: a book of recipes from around the world, with a hundred-rupee note tucked inside. While she touches his hand as if he is so far below her that she does not need to be careful about sending the wrong message, Triton's response to her is unquestionably sexual: "I could see . . . the tip of her tongue—a piece of red, warm, inner flesh—move between her lips. . . . I felt her hand touch mine" (108).[19] But it is also deeply emotional. At first amazed and touched to receive a present at all, Triton experiences it as a form of emotional and human connection that he wants to reciprocate. He wishes he had thought to get her a present as well—telling in itself, because servants do give gifts. But the money he finds the book inside introduces a negative note. It reminds him of his place as a servant: "'What is this?' I asked, but she had gone. *Missy*, I wanted to call out and bridge the gulf between us. I was only a servant but I wanted there to be more than money between us" (109). Unable to bridge the gap himself, habituated to addressing her in forms of deference (he still calls her "Missy"), Triton yet knows that he wants more of a connection, whether human or amorous, between them, than that of the cash nexus, and that the money somehow tarnishes that desired connection.

Moments earlier, as if forgetful of his servitude, Triton had expressed his pleasure in giving, in producing this extraordinary feast, which he thought of as an act of generosity, a celebration of the end of the year. Comparing himself to his father, who gave alms on alms-days, and to Salgado, who seems to be reveling in successfully hosting this party, Triton comments: "[In Salgado's case] it was not charity, but it was an act of giving. In my case, the giving was in transforming the intention into something edible. I gave by cooking and it gave me pleasure in return" (102). Triton prefers to think of his work as generosity, as service, not servitude. Nili's money dissipates that feeling. Whereas he interprets the recipe book as a token of interest, a way to further his talent, the cash is a let-down—it reaffirms the distance between them, telling him that she sees him only as a subordinate. "Her perfume had filled the whole [kitchen] at first, overpowering the giddy smell of turkey; but now it seemed only to have left a trace of sourness in me" (109). Triton wants a different connection with her and with Salgado. His let-down with Nili is intensified by his knowledge that Salgado knows about and has approved Nili's present ("'Mister Salgado said you would like this [book],' she tells Triton"; 105). Nili's actions suggest that to her Triton is only a servant, as even her gift indicates: the cook can only be given recipes to help him cook even better. Triton's remarks make clear that his interest and investment in Nili, cathected as it is through his investment in Salgado, is both sexual and deeply emotional: they bespeak both his intense affective need and the lack of fulfillment of both those needs.

Later, Triton describes a subsequent encounter with Nili that occurred when she was becoming disillusioned Salgado, and when Triton was again alone in the kitchen with her, in that quintessential domestic space of interaction between servant and mistress:

> She was so close I could smell her hair. She said, "You don't really belong here, Triton." It was not what I felt. There was nowhere else I belonged. I didn't know what she meant. "We've all been put in the wrong place. We will never really produce anything here," she said and touched my face with her hand. "Only our grotesque selves." Her hand was soft with a light oily sheen. I wanted to kiss it. I felt the impossible rise inside me: to be anything but invisible. (168)

This rich scene again begins with Triton's intense awareness of her femaleness, her physicality, as he smells her hair in a proximity where she again treats him like a sexless child. But now she seems to understand something that he as yet does not, that there is a link between them, one of shared disadvantage. She is disadvantaged among upper-class men by her gender and unmarried status, whereas Triton is disadvantaged because of his class. (Triton recalls this memory right after he describes how she got angry with Salgado, and accused him of assuming he "own[ed]" her just because she slept with him [166]. She was also upset that Salgado's male friends view her as merely a mistress.) But while Triton cannot see this connection, that they are both devalued in a masculinist and classist system, she cannot see how Triton feels he does belong with Salgado, the only man who has given him a home and a refuge. Her gentle touch on Triton's face suggests again her sense of him as a child, whereas his response is the intensified yearning to be seen—as more. Subsequently, he notes, she "stroked" his face as if she was "rubbing" him out, erasing him from existence by her very act of seeming empathy (168). Her attempt to reach out to Triton only serves to intensify the gap between them. This gap, however, is less than that between Triton and Salgado, who, secure in his male privilege, seems oblivious to them both. Gunesekera thus further complicates Girard's model of triangular desire by showing how servitude and gender differences add further tension and layers to the relation between a servant boy and his master's lover.

Increasing Discontent: Triton as Young Adult

Gunesekera's complex evocation of Triton's psychological and emotional responses to his solitary servitude in Salgado's home thus also requires the figure of Nili to underscore how these experiences of servitude are deeply gendered, and how they change traditional gender roles or assumptions of masculinity for the male servant. As Triton grows older, in Chapter 3, when Nili moves in with Salgado, Triton's feelings are notably mixed. He overtly welcomes her arrival: "I was pleased that she was coming to live with us" (114). But his language suggests a certain reluctance, a sense of invasion and trepidation about how things would change, now that he would no longer be in charge of the house. He is glad to note that, when she arrives, Salgado offers her coffee as to a guest: "She was still a guest; in that sense nothing had changed yet" (114). Triton's infatuation continues—"I took in her words like honey"—but he also expresses a sense of loss and unwelcome change: "He was a man's man once; now he had become a woman's man" (115). Triton's response suggests a certain rivalry, a possessiveness over Salgado, a concern for how Salgado will change. But it also reveals how Triton himself has been operating in the position of a woman or wife: he has looked after Salgado's clothing and appearance, responsibilities for bodily needs that he now has to relinquish to Nili. The situation creates a triad, where Triton now has to share Salgado with her.

Yet when Triton is asked to unpack and wash her clothes as he does for Salgado, the difference of her femaleness occasions a shift in his sense of his own gender and sexuality. "I had never touched women's clothes before" he notes (116). He has to suffer the intimacy of handling her lingerie, and handwashing her soiled underwear, which includes "knickers stiffened in the middle with what seemed like dried milk" (117). On the one hand it is arousing for him, as he learns about the female body, from the shape of her bras and the remnants of her vaginal excretions, intensifying his sense of his masculinity. But on the other hand, at the same time, it also feminizes, or de-masculinizes him (like Zirigu in Aidoo's story) as he has to do what is traditionally women's work. Where Nili would conceal her intimate clothing from most men, she hands it over to Triton with such unconcern precisely because she sees him as non-sexual, as merely a servant, not fully a male person. In assigning him this intimate task she denies his gender, and diminishes his sense of his masculinity and personhood.[20]

Triton's experiences with Nili also contribute to his awareness of and growing dissatisfaction with his servitude. He begins to change, partly because he becomes more aware of the world around him, and partly because of his interactions with Nili. When Salgado takes Nili to the beach house for the first time, with Triton to accompany them for the housework, Triton has a dissonant experience with Wijetunga, Salgado's research assistant. When Triton mentions that Nili runs a hotel for tourists in Colombo, Wijetunga's response is dismay: "'Tourists? ... Don't they realize what will happen? They will ruin us. They will turn us all into servants. Sell our children ... You know, brother, our country needs to be cleaned, radically. There is no alternative. *We have to destroy in order to create*. . . . Like the sea'" (121). Wijetunga sees Nili and her upper-class cohort as complicit in class exploitation within as well as beyond the nation, as the beneficiaries of a global game in which the underclass are the victims and losers. When he says "they will turn us into servants," he refers both to the Global North and to the upper class who relegate the poor of the Global South to servitude, both literally and figuratively, in the political-economic system where postcolonial nations like Sri Lanka become abject subordinates of their former colonial masters. (Here Gunesekera also suggests an analogy between domestic and geopolitical servitude.) Enjoining Triton to conspiratorial silence, telling him not to speak of it to Salgado, Wijetunga instructs Triton in class war and revolution. But Triton is not ready to hear this, nor to be separated from Salgado. "But I am only a cook," he replies evasively, refusing to be politicized, unable to voice his feelings for his employer (121). As yet, Triton regards his microcosmic world of emotional connections and domestic labor as separate from the macrocosmic public world of politics, socialism, and social movements. However, when Wijetunga replies, "one day ... we will be able to live for ourselves," Triton, though not welcoming this critique, breathes in the air that has "turned sour" and recognizes that, as a domestic servant in Salgado's house, he is not living for himself (121).

Soon after, Triton begins to enact what he is learning. Seeing Nili gazing at the ocean, he imitates her and for the first time allows himself release from housework. "A beach house requires very little day-to-day housework. The sand got everywhere whatever you do. It was a holiday, in a way, for me also." (125). He still has to make beds, do shopping, and cook, but he likes buying fresh fish from the fishermen at the beach, because he is perceived as more than just a servant: "'How much?' I asked, nodding at [a blue-striped fish]. I thought Nili would be impressed." Nili becomes his measure as he tries on a new identity brought about by his new surroundings. He lets the village fishermen think that he is above them, a city boy who does not do dirty work: "I think they thought I was a real city *mahathaya* because when I got my money out, one of the men said he would clean the fish for me. . . . I liked the idea of them thinking of me like that, it was worth the extra money" (124–125). It is a novelty to Triton to be treated like this, and he enjoys his heightened status among the country folk. It begins to shift him out of his servant identity as he realizes he likes not being thought a villager and servant. Inspired in part by Nili, it prompts his desire to leave behind his servant identity. But unlike Wijetunga, Triton wants to join the ranks of Salgado, not turn against them.

When things go wrong between Nili and Salgado, Triton also becomes tinged by her anger and discontent, evoked perhaps by her comment that they share a similar position of structural disadvantage in relation to upper-class men. As a servant, Triton occupies the position of a fly on the wall, unobtrusively able to observe, to sense the atmosphere in the house, to see what the actual participants often cannot. He is invested in knowing about the changes of emotional temperature, because they affect him emotionally as a member of the household. He can see that Nili is becoming upset with Salgado when Salgado, now used to her presence in the house, yet strangely inconsiderate and inattentive to her feelings, casually invites his male friends over for Sunday. Triton listens to their conversations, hearing how Salgado fails to hear her when she tries to tell him that she does not like them: "I don't want to spend the whole day and night with you in a poker game, drinking. I want to go out" (149). Triton senses her "bad mood" and tries to distract her with offers of a "special" breakfast (150–151), and hears her "arguing" with Salgado as the men get boisterous (156). He understands when she leaves the house with Robert, a visiting American who is interested in her, though he cannot explain it to the "puzzled" Salgado (158).

As if catching Nili's discontent, Triton also becomes irritated with Salgado's over-privileged, chauvinistic friends, though not with Salgado himself. Without Nili's feminizing presence, the ethos in Salgado's house seems to become now too male for Triton, as it positions him alone in the role of subservient housewife. "Without Nili the place was full only of men," he notes (161). For the first time, he expresses irritation at their demands, noting their peremptoriness and lack of appreciation. He describes his work—preparing the lunch, cooking a chicken curry with accompaniments, setting the table, getting the cards, making the tea—while they loaf about, laughing and playing. He notes how Tippy, who has been "drinking heavily," orders him about without even acknowledging his presence: "'Pour the tea, *kolla*.' He didn't even look at me when I served him his cup" (162). Triton is no longer just a boy, and the insulting treatment gets to him. "I wanted to get away from all of them," he says, as if to replicate (unconsciously) Nili's action (162). Literally and figuratively looking for a breath of fresh air, Triton goes outside the house, into the garden, and refuses to answer when Tippy calls him for a beer. "If he wanted it so much he could fetch it himself," he thinks (163).

This is Triton's first act of resistance. He refuses to enact the obliging, willing servant. Something has changed. To the more insistent call, "Where the hell is that bugger, Triton?" Triton's new response is anger, perhaps also a response to the casual homophobia associated with his status as a male servant, the suggestion that a man who serves men is a "bugger":[21]

> I shoved my arm in the air and swore at them under my breath. *Kiss the sky!* Something in the night air infected me too. Too much was going on. Wijetunga

on the beach had worked it all out. I wished I *had* finished my school certificate.... Inside me, everything was burning up. (163–164)

Triton attributes to Wijetunga this dissatisfaction as political, this desire for the education that would provide an alternative to servitude and class oppression. But Triton is also prompted by what he has learned from Nili. Though he still perceives it as an infection, Triton is starting to see, and is less willing to tolerate, this entitled, self-absorbed, abusive male behavior, the real infection that pervades both his home and nation.

As a servant Triton sees from different angles, and sees more of what happens in the house than outsiders or his employers can. But as a servant he also sees less of what happens between the principals, limited necessarily by what he cannot access. He cannot see into the privacy of his employers' bedroom, or what is said or done behind closed doors.[22] He is thus aware that he occupies an in-between position, both insider and outsider, when he recounts what he sees of Salgado and Nili's story with the inevitable gaps that he has to fill in by reading signs and clues. He gauges their sex lives from what he finds when he changes their bedsheets; he knows about their friction when he sees what they do or do not eat; he senses Robert's interest in Nili and her gradual responsiveness from their body language as he stands by serving them; he learns about the violence of Nili and Salgado's last argument when he finds the plate of his homemade lasagna smashed against the wall. Triton's narrative is neither a simple autobiography, with himself at the center, nor simply the witness-testimony of a servant narrating his employer's story: it is both at once. His narrative interweaves his story of his own life (what he experiences, how he feels, how he grows and changes in response to what he sees, with its own incompleteness, omissions, and interruptions) and his story of what he sees of Salgado's life. And yet, in Gunesekera's presentation, in Triton's desire and effort to observe and learn from and about Salgado's life, we learn more about Triton and his life than we do about Salgado, about what matters to Triton and what shapes him and his future.

In a revealing moment, Triton becomes anxious about the growing acrimony between Salgado and Nili. He picks up her anxiety about her social status when she asks Salgado if she really is invited to a party, given that she is not a wife or "pedigreed bitch" (131). When they return, he overhears them talking about servant violence, about a driver (like Balram in Adiga's later novel) who unexpectedly pulled a knife on his employer. "Why did the bugger attack Bala?" he hears Salgado echo Dias's earlier homophobic epithet for a male servant (135). Worried about what is happening inside and outside their house, Triton creeps into their bedroom, pretending to bring in towels, and finds Nili naked in the bath. Stunned, he gazes at her exposed body, focused on her breasts and nipples, until she looks up, and then, terrified and embarrassed, feeling as if he "was going to burst," drops the towels and flees to his room (136). "My chest hurt. She had said nothing. She must have seen me standing there staring at her, yet she had said nothing. The blood pumping inside made me deaf" (136). Nothing further happens, but for Triton it becomes a moment of self-realization, as he acknowledges his own emergent sexuality. Gunesekera makes it clear that Triton's presence in Nili's bedroom is fundamentally connected to his precarious position as a servant. As a dependent in this household, Triton needs to know what Salgado and Nili are saying and thinking about growing inter-class violence and mistrust, all of which would then impinge upon him and his relationship with them. Later, when he hears them fighting, he peers past the "slightly open" back door, unable to keep away (166). Gunesekera is thus also interested in the dynamic interplay between what Triton does and does not see, and how that affects him: he does not know what his employers are thinking or feeling, about each other or about him, and in trying to find out he sees more than others can, or than he should. As he tells their story and his own, the two become inextricable. He is not a mere separate witness to their lives as nineteenth-century servant narrators are to the lives of their employers.

And yet, for all his infatuation with Nili, and what his encounters with her teach him, Triton's attachment to Salgado remains his primary affective connection. After he hears her shouting at Salgado, he becomes disillusioned, not with Salgado, but with her. Though she contributes to his awakening, as when she challenges Salgado for thinking he "owns" her, and accuses him of devaluing and not prioritizing her, Triton's reaction is disenchantment with Nili: "It was only then I realized how much I had moulded her in my imagination. How little I had seen of her, really" (166). Triton's responses to Nili continue to be filtered through his primary attachment to Salgado. In his retrospective narration, the older Triton juxtaposes another significant memory with this memory of Nili. As he recalls her calling Salgado names, and Salgado accusing her of infidelity, Triton recalls a formative moment from his boyhood, when, practicing with a catapult, he had killed a bird in the garden and Salgado taught him otherwise:

> He held my wrist and said, "You know, you must not take life. To destroy is easy, but you do not have the gift to make life so easily." Shame filled every vein in my body. I wished I were dead. (167)

It is significant that Triton recalls and places this memory immediately after recounting the ugliness with Nili, as if to offer a testament to Salgado's gentleness, his kindness, his almost sage-like role in having taught Triton to abjure violence and harm to fellow beings. The memory seems designed to counter, for both Triton and his readers, Nili's harsh accusations, to prove her wrong, to attest that as servant boy, raised by Salgado in Salgado's household, he knows Salgado better. Triton takes Salgado's side, insisting as a witness that he saw and learnt from Salgado how to act ethically toward others, with restraint, respect, and empathy.

Nonetheless, the cumulative effect of Triton's experiences with Nili changes him. When she leaves, Triton cannot return to his former self or restore the old twosome. At first, almost exactly like Balram in *The White Tiger*, Triton as devoted servant steps in to comfort and care for his devastated master, taking on the feminized role of the absent wife or mistress. Tactfully, he acts as if he does not know about Nili's departure: "I cleaned the place and pretended nothing was wrong" (169). As a household servant, he both knows and has to pretend not to know, so as not to intrude upon his employer's privacy, or to let him know that he knows. He produces tempting foods, but doesn't "dare go into the bedroom" (169). He does extra work—more dusting, cleaning, polishing, shaking rugs, while watching over Salgado—as if to distract himself and Salgado, or compensate for her actions. However, when it is clear that Nili is gone for good, and Salgado rejects yet one more carefully concocted special offering—Triton's "own mixture of high grown coffee, cocoa, raw egg, vanilla and brandy whisked with hot milk and butter and stirred with a cinnamon stick, sprinkled with ground nutmeg"—Triton's reaction is new (172). Upon Salgado's second rejection, Triton reports, "I drank it myself" (172). Triton retains his former devotion, but not his subservience. Earlier, after the Christmas dinner, Triton reported that he would not eat until his master had eaten, regardless of how tired and hungry he was. Since Salgado often deferred eating, so did Triton: "It was always awkward for me to eat his food before him. Sometimes when he didn't eat, I also had not to eat until the next day.... Otherwise he would be eating my leftovers. It was not right" (104). Then, Triton acted in accordance with a mentality that accepted servitude, that saw his own touch, or partaking of food he had cooked for his master, as polluting or tarnishing his master's food. Now, he sees himself as more deserving, less of an inferior, less willing to waste his labor. In consuming that comfort drink himself, Triton is effectively coming into his own, claiming it as a reward for himself, willing to put himself in the position of the one who does not only serve.

Chapter 3 ends somewhat abruptly, as does the main narrative of the novel, with the sudden shift into national turbulence as Sri Lanka erupts in interethnic and inter-class violence. As a servant, Triton focuses on his domestic domain, able to ignore what is happening in the world outside the house. The older Triton looks back at his younger self who responded to changes in his "house" when Nili moved in with Salgado, but ignored the similarly "unorthodox changes" in the country:

> The rest of the country ... girded itself for change of a completely different order: a savage brutalizing whereby our *chandiyas*—our braggarts—would

become thugs, our dissolutes turn into mercenaries and our leaders excel as small-time megalomaniacs. *But in those days I had no real interest in the politics of the countryside*: we each have to live by our own dreams. The changes in our house were momentous enough for me." (118; emphasis added)

And yet, as a servant, Triton was more aware than the educated upper-class Salgado of political unrest and brimming discontent among the underclasses. At the Christmas party in 1969, Triton listened to Salgado chatting with the guests, and saw that Salgado was living in a fools' paradise, that he, Triton, had picked up more hints of ominous changes:

I was happy for him, even though the politics of the day ruled against such emotions: his new world was one that had no place in the future, as ordinary people saw it then. It was a bubbly world of gaiety seemed to belong to a previous, more frivolous generation. At the *kadé* on the main road the talk was on the need for revolution, or for a return to traditional values. (93)

Despite his relative isolation in Salgado's house, Triton hears street talk, he knows that "ordinary people" are growing less accepting of this social order, more impatient with the systemic inequalities of which Salgado and his guests are beneficiaries. Perhaps this discrepancy also affects Triton, despite his attachment to Salgado, as he too grows less accepting of the demeaning aspects of his own servitude. In such moments, Gunesekera creates a parallel between the domestic microcosmic world of the home and the public macrocosmic world of national politics. Though Triton is focused on changes in the home, not in the country, the two intersect. It also suggests that literal servitude is connected, or analogous to, the more figurative servitude of the lower to the upper classes that produces national unrest.

What seems to push Salgado into leaving Sri Lanka is the sudden death of his friend Dias.[23] Oddly, Salgado turns to Triton for comfort, asking him to retell the demotic legend of *Anguli-maala*, as if to explain this violence. The story, as Triton obligingly tells it, is of a prince who, prompted by injustice, becomes a "monster," spreading terror in the countryside until the bodies he has killed rise up as silent witness to his misdeeds (177). In the context of the 1970–1971 uprisings, the story points allegorically to the underclasses that, also as a result of injustice, have turned into a killing machine, spreading havoc in the nation. Perhaps Salado asks Triton to tell this story because he assumes Triton, as a lower-class person, has better knowledge of the story, or better understands this violence. Gunesekera's odd placement of this story here suggests the multi-causality of and dispersed responsibility for the violence of the civil war, an explanation perhaps, through ancient local legend, of what is about to pervade the nation. Here the servant seems to reverse roles with his master, to provide instruction, and suggest the consequences of injustice: "Mister Salgado watched my lips like a little boy, listening" (177). But, as if unable to wait for the reassuring end where the monster-prince repents and turns into a saintly monk, Salgado abruptly walks away: there is no comfort to be had in their reality.

Salgado does, however, enact a partial rescue for Triton. As the violence grows, Salgado, departing from the script, seems to decide that he cannot leave Triton behind, as if he recognizes some kind of belonging or guardianship. "Triton, we are going away," he announces, without asking if that is what Triton wants (179). Triton offers no objection. "He said I should go with him, fly to England. Maybe I too would be able to study; learn something and make a real life for myself" (179). Salgado's language suggests that being a servant is not "real life." Both agree that education is the way out of servitude and dependence. To leave (postcolonial) servitude, the novel suggests ironically, is to leave Sri Lanka for England. The colonial metropolis has become, ironically, the site of refuge from the disastrous failures of the postcolonial nation.[24]

The End of Servitude

How, then, does this novel suggest that servitude can be left behind? In the brief, epilogue-like final chapter "Strandline," Triton recounts, with extreme minimalism, his departure with Salgado from Sri Lanka in 1971, and resettlement in England, which, the title suggests, is a "strandline," a border zone, an edge, a refuge between land and sea, between peace and forces of destruction, but not, perhaps, a final home in itself. It skips over, in a few short sentences, how Triton became a new person, and learned to live in England: "I read all Mister Salgado's books, one by one, over the years" (185). Salgado contributes to this process, strategically leaving particular books lying about in unobtrusive places. And Triton reads them. Physically more proximate in a smaller apartment, as opposed to the large house they left behind, they share communal spaces and become more egalitarian, using the same bathroom, eating at the same dining table, drinking beer together in the same sitting room. This final chapter seems to fulfill the dream from Gunesekera's early story "A House in the Country. "I went to classes and other libraries, night and day, for almost all the years we spent in London together; broke all the old taboos and slowly freed myself from the demons of our past" (185–186). Triton does not explain what those taboos were—Gunesekera glides too smoothly over this process of becoming. Triton drops a few details: Salgado teaches him to drive and takes him on tours around the country, showing him how to live in England (188). Finally, Salgado uses "the last of his savings" to buy Triton the snack bar at the end of their road, to turn into a restaurant (188). Leaving Triton his spare keys—for his house and his car—Salgado departs, effectively making Triton his heir.

If *Reef* started out as a rescue fantasy, by the end it has shifted into a minute, perceptive exploration of the interplay between the servant's agency and the employer's kindness, and of the gendered micropolitics of power in interactions between servants and employers. It is not an account, like *The White Tiger*, of a lone servant's struggle to fight off, with no help, the manacles of poverty and servitude. *Reef* is a much more muted assessment of servitude, poised between an understanding of servitude as a refuge from far worse, and an account of how, despite its relative benefits, the servant may grow to need something more, enabled by the joint exceptionality of both servant and master. Ironically, of course, as Triton seems aware, he can never shake off his history with Salgado, to whom he remains permanently indebted. But he does shake off his continuing dependence. Moreover, as his narrative insists, Triton is also responsible in part for his own education and future; he has enterprise and agency in his own self-fashioning. Imagining a conclusion that requires both a benevolent master and an enterprising servant, Gunesekera presents a model of a joint partnership that enables the end of servitude, in a space other than that of a postcolonial nation bent on self-destruction.[25]

As the next chapter reveals, both male writers, Gunesekera and Adiga, imagine an end to (male) servitude, whereas women writers, Umrigar and Desai, as we will see in the Chapters 6 and 7, do not.[26] What the implications are of these narrative choices, and whether they are gendered, are questions I address in the conclusion. For now, let me note that the solutions offered by Gunesekera and Adiga, though with reservations, are imagined as individual or private enterprise under capitalism, not as collective, public, or systemic change.

5

In the Driver's Seat?

Aravind Adiga's *The White Tiger*

On the last page of *The White Tiger* (2008), at the very end of his narrative, Balram, the eponymous servant-narrator-protagonist, reflects on both the story he has just finished telling, and on its implications for servitude:

> Yet even if all my chandeliers come crashing down to the floor—even if they throw me in jail . . . —even if they make me walk the wooden stairs to the hangman's noose—I'll never say I made a mistake that night in Delhi when I slit my master's throat.
>
> I'll say it was all worthwhile to know, just for a day, just for an hour, just for a *minute*, what it means not to be a servant. (276; italics in original)

The fervency of Balram's repetitions, "even if . . ." and "just for . . . ," powerfully conveys how ardently he desires escape from the dehumanizing debasements of servitude, how willing he is to accept punitive consequences for the exhilaration of experiencing, for as briefly as a minute, release from that yoke. Given that readers know by this point how reluctant Balram was to "slit" his "master's throat," how intensely ambivalent was his attachment to that master, and what it took for him to reach the point of murdering Ashok, this concluding statement offers the novel's culminating indictment of the system of contemporary Indian servitude that it has delineated, compounded by entrenched feudalism, political corruption, and the failures of the neoliberal postcolonial state. If Balram comes across as a bitter cynic and cutthroat by the end (though, as we will see, with a significant ethical register of his own), the work of the novel is to show just how such a psyche is produced, and to call upon its readers to understand the conditions that create such desperation.

The White Tiger (henceforth *WT*) is a corrosive and deeply ironic satire, tonally and thematically quite different from *Reef*. Where *Reef*, even while centralizing a male servant-protagonist, offers a more subdued, intermittent, implied indication of some problems of servitude, *WT*, by contrast, is flagrant, in-your-face, designed to shock, with its gritty, unflinching, excoriating depictions of the degradations and dehumanization of servitude, unequivocally thrusting not just the servant, but servitude, as an issue, into the limelight. Indeed, as I argue in this chapter, Adiga's novel makes servitude a central focus as a literal, pervasive, and overlooked contemporary postcolonial condition. Much more than *Reef*, *WT* is interested in exploring the damaging psychological consequences of servitude on the gendered subjectivity, sense of self, and world view of the male servant, as well as the contorted micropolitics and affective dynamics of the master-servant relationship as experienced from the servant's perspective. But, where *Reef* suggests that servitude is a private or social, not a political, issue, suggesting at best an analogy between servants in the homes of postcolonial elites and the underclasses of Global South nations in relation to the elite of the West, *WT* makes a more literal and powerful connection, showing overtly how the horrors of servitude it depicts are indeed political, and the direct consequence of (and consequential for) the failure of the postcolonial state and the abysmal corruption of its promises. *WT* is the servitude novel par excellence.

The White Tiger hence also devotes far more attention than *Reef* does to its eponymous narrator-protagonist's history and formative experiences and what they reveal, not only about him but about the world that shaped him before he became a servant. In giving us much fuller detail about Balram's childhood and family, Adiga calls attention to the *systemic* problems that cripple the life-chances of the young village boy: the joint family system and its bloodsucking demands, embodied in the sinister figure of Kusum, Balram's grandmother; the obscenely tyrannical, exploitative feudal landlords who terrorize villagers like his father and brothers; the political system riddled by corruption at all levels, and the neoliberal postcolonial government that utterly fails its most precariously located citizens.[1] Balram's narrative (unwittingly) elaborates how these three systems—feudalism, family, and failed democracy—interlock to entrap, in particular, poor men. The joint family system makes emotional and economic demands, sinking generations in debt, especially via the dowry system; feudal landlords with limitless power exploit and destroy those families, enabled by deep levels of corruption of the political system; and the state fails to provide basic necessities—food, education, healthcare, employment—to its most vulnerable, especially children. *The White Tiger* hence offers a far more clear and powerful indictment of the postcolonial state and shows how the vitiation of all possibilities of opportunity for its protagonist leads an exceptional, enterprising individual to the path of resistance that Balram eventually carves for himself.

An important difference between *Reef* and *WT* is that where Triton is primarily a cook, Balram is primarily a driver, or personal chauffeur. One of Adiga's great innovations in this servitude novel is his elaboration of the car as a modern, mobile extension of the home. Where other servitude fiction shows powerfully how the private space of the employer's home, which is the servant's workplace, becomes a site of unobserved abuse or intimacy, Adiga emphasizes how that space can be extended to the yet more tightly enclosed, more isolated, more physically proximate space of the car. Noting the contrast between the life-shortening, polluted air outside the car, and "the cool, clean, air-conditioned air" inside, Balram describes, in a striking and repeated image, "the cars of the rich [that] go like dark eggs down the roads of Delhi" (112). Occasionally this dark egg "crack[s] open," so that its rich occupant can fling some trash out on the road and is then "resealed" (112). Yet what else is being hatched inside this egg, literally beside the rich, is a dark twin, the driver, who, present in the car as a worker, minion, and outsider to the family, becomes an intimate, inevitable observer, a secret sharer, sometimes participant, to interactions between his employer and his employer's wife, brother, or business associates. The private space of the enclosed car thus intensifies the bond between male servant and male employer as the driver is forced to know, and often to serve as accomplice to, whatever nefarious acts occur within that insulated space, from sexual misdeeds to violations of the law. Paradoxically, therefore, that space inside the car also gives the servant intimate knowledge, and hence power, over his employer. For Balram, as I elaborate below, it also affords an occasion to learn from and mimic his employer, via the crucial image of the rearview mirror, through which each can observe the other, and which enables the servant to refashion himself in the image of the master.

Adiga's novel thus puts under pressure the meaning of the idiom "in the driver's seat," normally understood as indicating a position of control, being in charge, in a dominant or influential position, having authority or power. But that meaning reveals its late twentieth-century Western cultural orientation, for it assumes an absence of servants, where the driver is the one who controls the vehicle. Who is in control, however, when the driver is a literally a servant, and must obey the employer seated behind him? In South Asia, even the different architecture of cars reflects the powerful effects of a culture of servitude, where rear passenger seats are designed to be cushier than the driver's seat designed for the servant—the opposite of cars in the Global North. *WT* raises the question: to what extent is Balram in charge—or can he be—of his life or of the car? To be in the driver's seat, for the South Asian driver, is in fact to be subject to command, a factotum: to take charge, he has to fight, to break out of the system.

I want to begin by identifying some distinctive features of *WT* that, despite the similarities, mark its distance from *Reef*. First, *WT* is notably different in its plot structure. Unlike *Reef*, which presents no central crisis, nor any real conflict for the servant, *WT* pivots on a crucial turning point for Balram. One may identify at most a minor shift in the trajectory of *Reef* when Nili leaves and Triton realizes he was wrong about her and reaffirms his loyalty to Salgado, or when Salgado is shocked by the growing violence and decides to leave Ceylon. But none of these occasions a soul-altering change in Triton. *WT*, however, is structured around a major crisis that precipitates a series of disillusionments and internal conflicts for its servant-narrator-protagonist: when Balram's employer's wife Pinky, in a drunken fit, grabs the car from Balram and kills a child on the street, and the feudal landlords force Balram to take the blame, Balram begins to see Ashok as ultimately no different from Ashok's evil father and brother, and realizes gradually that he has no choice, if he wants to escape and survive the trap he is caught in, but to steal from and kill his master. (To borrow from the title of another contemporary attention-garnering South Asian novel, Balram could well be titled, not a reluctant fundamentalist, but a most reluctant murderer—driven to murder.)

Thus, to emphasize a key second point of difference: while Adiga, like Gunesekera, also focuses on the dyad of male servant and male employer, he presents Ashok as a very far cry from the benign Salgado. Adiga's presentation of servitude, the servant, and of the servant-master relationship is thus notably different. When Balram, also an unusually smart, feisty boy like Triton, finds his way, without help, and without an education, to the city and becomes a servant—as a driver—he is employed by his feudal landlords' family to serve Ashok, who seems at first less malign than his vicious father and brother. Balram's initial fascination with Ashok, his gradual disenchantment, and, final decision, despite continuing ambivalence, to kill his employer in order to escape, thus carry a very different timbre than Triton's continued idealization of Salgado. Triton is never disillusioned with Salgado, only with the position of being a servant. But Balram's discovery that Ashok is no different from his brother Mukesh— "they were both their father's seed"—enables him to detach from Ashok, and to see the feudal-political system as even worse than he had thought (206). Hence, by comparison to *Reef*, *WT* also presents the male servant as having far greater autonomy, agency, resistance, and ingenuity in breaking out of his shackles, in spite, and not because, of his employer.

Third, the dominant tropes of *WT* are very different from *Reef*'s and form a much more powerful imagistic web that structures the tone, mood, and figurative world of the novel. Unlike *Reef*, which draws evocatively on metaphors of sea, coast, and oceanography, *WT*'s sustained recurrent metaphoric web draws heavily on the animal world, or the laws of the jungle, to convey the inhuman and dehumanizing forces that oppress its servant-protagonist-narrator.[2] "Animals," when capitalized, represent the corrupt oppressor (the feudal landlords the Stork, the Buffalo, the Wild Boar, the Raven, and the Mongoose; 20–21, 88) and, when lowercase, the helpless oppressed (the chickens in the Rooster Coop; 147–150), or the (imagined) cartloads of buffaloes with "dead skinned faces" that Balram envisions as he anticipates what will happen to his family members if he kills his master (219). Animal images and poetic repetition also convey the routine cruelty and systemic degradation and dehumanization to which impoverished humans are subject, as when Balram describes the men who work with him in his first job at his village tea-shop: "men, I say, but better to call them human spiders that go crawling in between and under the tables with rags in their hands, crushed humans in crushed uniforms, sluggish, unshaven, in their thirties or forties or fifties but still 'boys'" (43). Such "work" has literally bent the bodies of these supposedly erect, two-legged vertebrates, into the shape of crawling invertebrates, who crawl both literally and figuratively because they must.

As the title suggests, the framework of the law of the jungle is central to this novel, where the white tiger signifies the exception, the rarity, perhaps the mutation, which nonetheless has to operate within that law to survive. And like his namesake, the caged animal that Balram sees in the Delhi Zoo, both prey and predator, Balram knows that when he flees the cage (or Rooster Coop) of servitude, he too will have to operate within the law of the jungle to survive in early twenty-first-century India. If the hope of satire is to critique in order to make what it critiques better, to posit alternatives and ideals, then Adiga's figurative use of the animal world suggests that humans are capable of and can aspire to more, to build societies based on higher values than the law of the jungle. "Amazing how much money they have, . . . yet they treat us like animals" (176), remarks Balram to an indigent bookseller and fellow caste-member with whom he bonds "servant-to-servant" and "man-to-man" (174). Balram's guiding aspiration and motivation ultimately are simply to be treated like a human being. "Let animals live like animals; let humans live like humans. That's my whole philosophy in a sentence," he says, right before he decides to kill Ashok, in order, ironically, to reclaim that humanity.

WT also deploys allusively the language of Light and Darkness (both capitalized), not to replicate the colonial discourse of Conrad and Naipaul, but rather, I would contend, to emphasize, with heavy irony, the Darkness as a space that represents misfortune, disempowerment, and deprivation, versus Light as the place of the exploitative, privileged, and powerful.[3] The opposition of Light and Darkness in this novel becomes a multivalent and metaphorical shorthand for the chasm between the nation's haves and have-nots. "You see, I am in the Light now, but I was born and raised in the Darkness," Balram announces as the novel opens (11). "India is two countries in one," he insists, "an India of Light, and an India of Darkness" (12). The geography of these two countries is not physically separate but proximate, he adds later: "Delhi is the capital of not one but two countries—two Indias. The Light and the Darkness both flow into Delhi" (215). Alluding to Disraeli's famous statement about two separate nations within England, the rich and the poor, and to the title of Naipaul's infamous first travel book about India, *An Area of Darkness*, Adiga rejects Naipaul's neocolonialist attitudes to make clear that it is not India itself that is the area of darkness, but the deprived segments within it that are wantonly deprived of opportunity and hope, and controlled from the same center.[4]

Early in his narrative, Balram reflects on the difference between Bangalore, a place of Light, where he now lives, with its plethora of (high-tech) job opportunities (45), and the Darkness of the north (his village Laxmangarh and its nearest city Dhanbad), where "smart" men idle, having "given up the fight," and "stupid ones" crowd to beg for menial laboring jobs from which they are literally beaten back (46).[5] But the opposition between Darkness and Lightness grows into something far more than a reference to a geographical place, and becomes a state of being. What characterizes Darkness is the futility of efforts to leave it; what characterizes Light is the determination of those in the Light to keep the Darkness out: what connects and unites both is inhumanity. When he can find no job in the city until he becomes a driver for his feudal landlord's family, Balram looks at the buses full of hopeful villagers heading to the city to look for work: "They were all headed from the Darkness to Delhi. You'd think the whole world was migrating" (94). Part of Adiga's irony is that these men fleeing poverty, seeking opportunity, hanging off the doors and roofs of buses, getting literally crushed in the process, are heading into a different darkness and denial of opportunity in the city. In fact, as Balram explicitly notes, Delhi also contains darkness: "these poor bastards had come from the darkness to Delhi to find some light—but they were still in the darkness" (116). When Balram has finally escaped this darkness and become an entrepreneur, he obsessively surrounds himself with chandeliers, not only because he craves the literal light, but also because it carries deep ironic and symbolic value: "the police searched for me in darkness: but I hid myself in light" (98). Balram has both arrived in the light, and cannot be found because he is in the light—the light is his space of opportunity and release, to which he has escaped from the condition of abjection, darkness, in which state power expects to apprehend him.

Another key trope for *WT* is the mirror. Balram, as the driver seated in the front of the car, frequently observes his master, seated in the back, through the rearview mirror. This mirror becomes a critical site where master's and servant's eyes can surreptitiously meet, the intimate space where they frequently observe each other and exchange glances in silent forms of communication, enabling a connection where they may acknowledge (or reject) their sameness or connection. It also suggests the mirroring between servant and employer, as Balram deliberately starts to eavesdrop, to imitate Ashok, not only to like, but to be like him, to model his behavior and appearance on Ashok in order to appear less like a servant.[6] It enables his realization that they are in fact not unalike. The rearview mirror of the car therefore becomes an overdetermined trope. Indeed, it becomes a way to represent mirroring itself. Through a visual ricochet, the rearview mirror also enables mutual surveillance, as, both facing the front, passenger and driver can watch each other. And eventually, it serves as the tool that enables the servant to displace and replace his master.

Balram first mentions this mirror as he begins to recall his employer's face: "Mr. Ashok's face reappears now in my mind's eye as it used to every day when I was in his service—reflected in my rearview mirror" (38). This literal view becomes a metaphor for Balram's retrospective narrative, as he looks back in "memory's mirror" (38). It also becomes a powerful trope for a way of seeing and being seen, for an indirect gaze between servant and employer that at first builds a bond between them. After he becomes Ashok's driver, Balram, while driving, cannot help overhearing Ashok reassuring his suspicious brother Mukesh that Balram can be trusted; catching Ashok's eyes in the mirror, Balram for the first time sees in them an "unexpected emotion: . . . pity" (102). This silent communication between servant and employer undercuts the instructions Mukesh is giving Ashok. Another time, Balram watches Ashok in the back feeling up Pinky's thigh and realizes Ashok can see him watching: "I watched one second too long. He caught me in the mirror" (135). The mirror works both ways, where the servant can observe the master, and the master can catch him at it. "This little rectangular mirror inside the car" then also becomes a basis for a mutual recognition of sameness, as Balram and Ashok catch each other leering, both aroused by the same girl crossing the road: it provokes a startled intimacy between the two men, as they "find each other's eyes in this mirror," embarrassing them both as if they have "suddenly caught each other naked" (169).

The significance of this mirror changes as the relationship between master and servant turns more sinister. Each uses the mirror to surveil the other. Balram calls it "the spy mirror" when he looks through it to see Ashok preparing the cash bribes he will offer a corrupt minister (180), and to see what else Ashok keeps hidden in the back of the car. Through this mirror Balram first views the blonde Ukrainian woman Ashok picks up (185), and the red bag full of cash that Balram will later steal, which he describes as "sitting at the center of [his] rearview mirror, like the exposed heart of the Honda" (210). (Later, in mimicry, this glimpse through the mirror inspires Balram to steal money and hire a blonde prostitute.) It is also through this mirror that Balram knows he is under suspicion, when Mukesh, Ashok's brother, "pointedly" watches him from behind via the mirror, letting him know that he is watching (206). And finally, Balram knows that Ashok is planning to replace him when Ashok avoids looking at him in that mirror "eye to eye, man to man," symbolic of their broken connection (229). Right before the murder, through the rearview mirror, Balram watches Ashok and sees him "paying attention to nothing but his cell phone" (241). Finally, the mirror becomes a tool for murder, telling Balram when Ashok is distracted, unsuspicious, a ready victim. It confirms both Balram's resolve and reason for the murder, reaffirming their disconnection, for now Ashok is no longer looking at Balram.[7]

Balram has often been read as the villain of this novel, as an unrepentant, hardened criminal. Such readings, I contend, tend to reveal an implicit bias against the servant character, a tendency to see him as innately or stereotypically criminal. They ignore the novel's urgent push to provide an explanation for Balram's actions, for the lack of choices that leads to his decision to kill as the last desperate resort of a man dehumanized but determined not to be crushed into the mud.[8] In this chapter, I offer a more sympathetic reading, which I suggest is more accurate and in alignment with the text. As in the previous chapter, I follow two strands or trajectories. One, Adiga's exploration of the gendered *psychology* of servitude, of the fascination and attachment a young male servant develops for an older male employer, and in particular, of an erotics of inequality built on the dynamics of masculinity, homosociality, and triangulated desire. Like Triton, Balram both desires to be like Ashok and learns to desire what he desires. Two, I examine how Adiga charts differently the servant protagonist's *growth* from adolescence to adulthood, and more specifically, Balram's initial desire for servitude, and then his dawning realization that escape is a necessity that requires a high-cost sacrifice that he becomes willing to pay. In so doing, I push back against readings that fail to see Adiga's careful delineation of this complex and gradual trajectory to Balram's final decision, and that miss altogether Balram's extreme reluctance to turn criminal.[9] Moreover, I show how, in contrast to Gunesekera, Adiga locates the male servant's desires and developments firmly within a complex matrix, the systemic interlocking factors (feudalism, pseudo-democracy, economic inequality, family, religion) that interact to produce such problems and exact such a cost. I argue that, in thus highlighting these connections between servitude and the postcolonial nation, Adiga offers a more damning indictment than Gunesekera of both servitude culture and of the nation that promotes it. *WT* unambiguously puts servitude at the center of its narrative and more clearly denounces postcolonial servitude and the political systems (feudalism, corruption, failure of public education and health services) that produce and maintain it.

Adiga takes on a greater challenge than Gunesekera: he makes his protagonist much less attractive, but proceeds to show how that psyche is formed and deformed. In so doing, Adiga argues for a need to rethink ethical and national systems that criminalize a servant for theft and murder while not scrutinizing those who routinely do worse with impunity, and who thereby induce such desperate efforts at freedom. In fact, as I will also argue, Balram's *ethical* dimensions become clearer at end. In the absence of ethics in the world around him, Balram is forced to do what he does, but he nonetheless develops his own private code of ethics, a form of honor among thieves. Pushing back against what is read as Balram's irrepressible criminality, I suggest that the novel poses the cliché of the servant as violent and dishonest only to undo and complicate it, to show how that putative thief and murderer is formed by a society that is far worse, motivated by greed and power, and not, as in Balram's case, the need to survive or live like a human being.

The White Tiger won the Booker Prize in 2008, but its very acclaim seemed to prompt a backlash, especially among Indians. Akash Kapur noted in the New York Times both that "some in India lambasted it as a Western conspiracy to deny the country's economic progress," and that the novel "correctly identifies—and deflates—middle-class India's collective euphoria" as it reveals how "the social compact is [of the nation] is being stretched to the breaking point." Unfortunately, many scholars have too easily (mis)read as self-aggrandizement or an attempt to diminish India in Western eyes (what I see as) Adiga's altruistic, progressive aim to better the conditions of extreme inequality, exploitation, and brutality he describes. Such facile readings fail to recognize how Adiga's critique belongs in a long postcolonial tradition, from Armah to Rushdie, of satire and critique of the failure of the postcolonial nation-state to which the writer belongs and claims belonging. Many of these attacks on Adiga stem from a beleaguered defensiveness. They charge Adiga with inauthenticity on two counts: one, dismissing him as an outsider, suggesting he is not truly Indian because of his Western education; and two, dismissing him because he is not of the servant or subaltern class. Both are problematic. To claim, for one, that only putative insiders can mount social critique is to construct a false dichotomy, and to refuse to see how the putative outsider can sometimes see or expose what the insider cannot. Such notions of authenticity can thus also serve as a means of enforcing an in-group's notion of who or what fits with some self-constructed, self-serving, and invented notion of Indianness. And two, the issue of who can speak of or for whom, as I discuss in my Introduction, becomes an easy way to dismiss intervention on behalf of the socially marginalized, to not see how speaking for those disenfranchised can itself be an ethical act.

Others have questioned not only the novelist's but also the novel's and narrator's authenticity. In an early review essay, for instance, Amitava Kumar accused Adiga of "being inauthentic" (3) in the sense of failing at verisimilitude in his presentation of Balram's voice and of the "ordinary people" and "emotional truths of life in Bihar" (4). In my view, such deployments of notions of authenticity rest on a misreading of the novel as literal, social realism, as if fiction does not require any suspension of disbelief. The White Tiger clearly signals other generic and rhetorical modes: satire, comic exaggeration, farce, bathos, to name a few.[10] While I too might, in the case of social realist fiction, expect accuracy or plausibility (rather than authenticity), it seems a category mistake to measure fiction that is clearly written in another idiom, in terms of its ability to mirror a putative reality. Certainly, a working-class man like Balram would not speak English, but the novel sets up Balram's narrative as a literary fiction or imagined translation for larger purposes than mere verisimilitude. This early controversy over authenticity hijacked discussions of the novel and framed, even subordinated, other issues to which it calls attention. In an interview, as Adiga himself has explained, as a former journalist, he sees his fiction as *"neo-realist,"* not realist in the sense of mimeticism, but as imaginative work that does something different from documentary: "What fiction can provide, which reportage often cannot, is narrative, ambiguity, and moral complexity. There should, ideally, be no 'message' or 'point' to a novel; it should keep you thinking and entertained and disturbed years later too."[11] It is in this spirit that I approach this important novel.

Scholars have approached *The White Tiger* from a number of angles. Many have addressed the novel as a critique of neoliberalism, though some also claim that Adiga is either insufficiently critical of, or actually reinforces, neoliberal ideologies.[12] I read *The White Tiger* as highly critical of both neoliberalism in post-1991 India and of systems that pre-date neoliberalism and work in conjunction with it, like feudalism and the corruption of democratic socialism. Others have explored issues such as humor, animalization, precarity, justice, and human rights in the novel.[13] Still others have explored connections between *The White Tiger* and other texts, from postcolonial to American.[14] While indebted to the work of these scholars, I take a different approach. As many of the titles of these essays indicate, scholars tend to focus on subalternity, but not servitude, and thereby miss some of the nuances and specificities that servitude entails.[15] Focusing on servitude, and the peculiar intimacies and psychologies it produces, enables both a sharper focus on the problems and dynamics that Adiga highlights, and changes the lens by which we can understand many of the broader questions it poses, such as the relation between nationhood and citizenship, neocolonialism and global neoliberalism, violence and oppression, desire, affective relations, and domesticity.

Telling the Truth: How a Half-Baked Fellow is Produced

Like *Reef*, *WT* opens with an adult narrator in the present, looking back to his past, initiating a retrospective narrative of his life as a servant who eventually found independence. But unlike *Reef*, *WT* is explicitly addressed to a narratee, a fictive imagined audience within the text, taking the form of a letter to Wen Jibao, the premier of China, who is on a visit to Bangalore to learn from "Indian entrepreneurs" how they achieved their success (1–2). Adiga dramatizes, more than Gunesekera, and like Rushdie in *Midnight's Children*, the process of telling. Older Balram, unlike Triton, repeatedly addresses his narratee, telling his story not as a nostalgic reverie, but to justify and explain what he has done, and show what has gone into the making of what he has become. "The story of my upbringing is the story of how a half-baked fellow is produced," he announces, right from the start. (8). Like Gunesekera, Adiga avoids attempting to create the verisimilitude of an unlettered servant's voice, but he maintains the fiction of orality in emphasizing that Balram is "dictating" his missive (presumably recorded on Balram's laptop) (3).[16] Readers are thus asked to suspend their disbelief, to understand that this Anglophone novel written by an upper-class writer in the voice of a lower-class man, is constituted as an imagined, mediated, aural text, to be translated from one language and idiom (presumably Bihari or Hindi) to Chinese, since Balram, as he informs us, cannot "speak English" (1).[17]

The impetus for this narrative, as Balram sees it, is his urgent desire to tell "the truth about Bangalore" (and hence India) by telling his "life's story" (4), to counter the lies purveyed by Indian officials about their nation as "moral and saintly" (2).[18] "*What a fucking joke*," his favorite English phrase learned from Pinky, his ex-employer's wife, conveys Balram's radical dissent (5). Telling his story is thus not an exercise in memory or memorialization, as it is for Triton, but an ethical imperative, a moral corrective and counter to nationalist propaganda and self-congratulatory rhetoric. For Adiga, Balram's narrative enables a critique of India's neo-liberal capitalism and failed postcolonialism: it is no accident that Balram's story is addressed to a Chinese premier who wants to learn about entrepreneurs. The neoliberal preoccupations of speaker and addressee ironically highlight the displacement of the earlier aspirations of both Indian socialism and Chinese communism by narrow-minded self-interest and greater economic and social inequities. In this India, Balram's life story shows satirically, it takes literally a cutthroat to survive and succeed.

Like an overture, the first chapter sets up key concerns of the novel and introduces us to Balram as a character, to his jaunty, sardonic voice, and to the early experiences and conditions that formed the person he has become. It also emphasizes the conditions that lead to and maintain servitude, and the ways that servitude still pervades Balram's thinking and sense of self. With pride, he introduces himself as a "white tiger" (a rarity), a "thinking man," and an "entrepreneur" (1). Balram does not call himself an ex-servant, at first, but it soon becomes clear how scarred he still is by that former identity, by the experience of domestic servitude, how much his sense of self is still defined by what he has resisted and yet cannot fully escape. "Once a servant, always a servant; the instinct is always there, inside you, somewhere near the base of your spine," he notes at the end (256). It is because of their putative freedom from servitude that, he reveals, he desires to connect with the Chinese. "You Chinese are great lovers of freedom and individual liberty. The British tried to make you their servants, but you never let them do it. I admire that, Mr. Premier. I was a servant, once, you see," he announces at the start (3). Here Adiga links private, individual domestic service with collective, colonized status as both forms of servitude and subjection. Indeed, Balram implies that the Chinese were better than Indians at warding off colonialism and suggests how important putting up that resistance is to his own sense of self: the only three nations he admires, he declares, are China, Afghanistan, and Abyssinia, because they "never let themselves be ruled by foreigners" (3).[19]

It is this urge to resist, to refuse to submit to dominance and oppression, to demand dignity and self-determination in the face of powerful systemic forces (colonial, social, familial) that Balram also cherishes as a lasting legacy from his (deceased) parents. In describing his mother's untimely death, he remembers how, as a child of six or seven, he watched how her foot would not burn in the pyre, how her toes seemed to be "offering resistance to what was being done to them," and how he read this action of her body in death as epitomizing her fighting spirit: "My mother wasn't going to let them destroy her" (14). Balram's mother is ultimately overcome, both (literally and figuratively) by the "black mud" of the holy river Ganga that "was sucking her in" (14), and by the gender-based systemic oppression of the joint family system, exerted in particular by her mother-in-law, Balram's evil "Granny," who had made her life extraordinarily "miserable," and who exerted "control" over all the household, terrorizing the sons and daughters-in-law who "lived in fear of her" (12). Indeed, in a key moment, Balram reveals that the first time he ever fainted was at his mother's funeral, when he realized that the powerful, emblematic black ooze of the Ganga was "the real god of Benaras— ... into which everything died.... Nothing would get liberated here" (15). It is this impossibility, as he sees even his stalwart mother succumb, this despairing knowledge that for those born into his circumstances, struggling was futile, that paradoxically forms the determination in the child to escape.

Likewise, Balram remembers his father also as a fighter eventually subdued, a rickshaw driver who died young of tuberculosis, in horrendous conditions in a government hospital that utterly failed the poor who had the misfortune to land up there. Demanding respect for his father as "a man of honor and courage," adding the honorific "*Mr.*" to his father's name, Balram recalls how his father refused to crouch like a servant, how he desired dignity, if not for himself, then for at least one of his sons (19). Outside the tea-shop that "was the central point of [their] village," Balram's father would wait for customers: "The rickshaw pullers ... were not allowed to sit on the plastic chairs put out for the customers; they had to crouch near the back, in that hunched-over squatting posture common to servants in every part of India. My father never crouched—I remember that. He preferred to stand ..." (20). Balram's astute observations suggest that servitude—signified by bodily degradation and obsequiousness—has become a recognizable, generalized, pervasive condition India's poor, not just for domestic servants, as if all the poor are servants of the rich. He emphasizes how servitude is marked on the body, literally re-shaping it, and how servitude enforces a politics of space even in the public sphere, dictating where the poor worker is allowed to sit. "My father's spine was a knotted rope... The story of a poor man's life is written on his body, in a sharp pen," Balram notes (22). From the beginning, Adiga includes such trenchant observations, alerting readers to the insidious and pervasive ways that the politics of servitude infiltrate daily, affective, and social life, and touch every aspect of human relations, from an individual's inner sense of self to interpersonal relations even among strangers. Unlike Gunesekera, Adiga recurrently points out the demeaning, dehumanizing, degrading aspects of servitude and emphasizes the agency of the servant-protagonist who eventually exerts himself to escape.

Balram is clearly shaped by his father's efforts to fight the system he was trapped in, to the extent he could. He refused to work the land under the monopoly of the extortionist feudal landlords: "My father could have worked... with the landlords' mud, but he chose not to. He chose to fight it" (23). Recognizing that education was the only hope, he aspired to give Balram, his smartest son, a way out, and to honor Balram's mother's dying wish. "Munna *must* read and write!" he insisted, despite Granny's selfish demands and scornful opposition (23). After his father's death, when he is pulled out of school to help pay for a female cousin's dowry, Balram remembers his father's one heartfelt wish: "My whole life, I have been treated like a donkey. All I want is that one son of mine—at least one—should live like a man" (26). Inspired by these memories of his father, Balram strives in his life to fulfill this desire for human dignity.

Yet it is important to note that this mantra, "to live like a man," while suggestive of positive aspirations—to live and not merely to exist, like a human being, not a tormented animal, a beast of burden for others—nonetheless also carries its own gender privileges. Balram's father does not claim any such desire for a daughter, nor does Balram extend this desire for humanity or dignity to women. Indeed, as we will see, his goals are shaped by notions of toxic masculinity, a poisonous sense of manhood as defined by violent sexual supremacy. To "dip his beak," for instance, is a crude idiom that Balram frequently uses to indicate what a man does to a woman when he has sex, which is understood only as a form of animalistic victimization, a one-way taking of pleasure. It means, figuratively, to screw someone. Balram then uses the same idiom to convey what powerful men also do to men subject to them. Balram's understanding of what it means to be a man is thus both shaped and threatened by the demeaning positionality of servitude. Balram's notion of his own manhood is constituted as a form of overcompensation for his servitude, where manhood or manliness is understood in deeply sexist, gendered, and sexualized terms as having dominance over others seen as weaker (women, prostitutes, servants). Balram's memories of his parents' failed efforts to secure freedom from entrapment become crucial guides for him, both positively, signifying the aspiration to strive, to resist, to seek dignity, and negatively, making him realize what is the extra mile he must go to succeed, the ruthlessness he must harden in himself, in order to obtain that freedom. They shape his understanding of his masculinity.

From the very beginning, Adiga takes an enormous risk in making his protagonist appear not endearing or likeable (to most readers), but often misinformed, bigoted, and prejudiced. Despite his astonishing independence of mind, Balram displays a curious mix of the savvy and the ridiculous, of knowledge and ignorance. Frequently he repeats deeply reactionary, chauvinistic, sexist, and racist ideas, reflective of the harmful ideologies and propaganda he has internalized, and that are intensified by his ruptured schooling. Early on, for example, he exhibits a paranoia that exceeds understandable suspicion of Western colonialism, technology, and globalization: "I don't keep a cell-phone, for obvious reasons—they corrupt a man's brains, shrink his balls, and dry up his semen, as all of us know—so I have to stay in this office. In case there is a crisis" (33). Understanding masculinity and independence exclusively in terms of sexual prowess and fertility, Balram is mentally trapped, just as he is trapped literally in a cell of his own making, from where he runs his business.[20] Quite unselfconsciously, he addresses his Chinese audience as "you yellow-skinned men" even when he is trying to be earnestly friendly (79). Or, with less amity, having absorbed the logics of rightwing Hindu nationalism, he casts Muslims as invaders, outsiders to India (as if ancient Indo-Aryans, who brought Vedic Hinduism to India, were not likewise invaders or, more accurately, migrants): "For this land, India, has never been free. First the Muslims, then the British bossed us around. In 1947 the British left, but only a moron would think that we became free then" (18). His internalization of the desire for (political) independence and self-determination precludes the possibility that "us" might include Muslims, who are also South Asians colonized by the British.[21]

Balram's fallibility is in part a source of the book's humor, in that such attitudes are clearly rendered as absurd. Yet this humor does not work merely at Balram's expense. Adiga's mode of representation of this servant-protagonist calls at once for sympathy and understanding even as it creates a certain distancing effect for readers who would necessarily be of a higher class. Adiga's humor is complicated, for it does not work merely to produce a sense of superiority for the reader. Rather, as we will see, Adiga's (and Balram's) grim, even black, humor is a way of alleviating the horror of what Balram experiences, of making the unbearable bearable. It also suggests Balram's own capacity to cope, as he recounts, in his insouciant, offbeat, colloquial style, some of his more searing experiences. As in the form of a dramatic monologue, Adiga's narrative choices give Balram the occasion to reveal both his fallibility and the reasons that produce that fallibility.[22]

Adiga provides context for the less endearing aspects of Balram, educating his readers to understand how Balram has been denied an education, a chance of better life opportunities, or of the capacity to develop breadth of mind or a critical framework to understand history, or deeper contexts that might enable him better to assess what he sees.[23] He describes how his extended family pulls him out of school to repay their landlord's loan, how the supposedly free government education system is compromised:

> There was supposed to be free food at my school—a government program gave every boy three *rotis*, yellow *daal*, and pickles at lunchtime. But we never saw *rotis*, or yellow *daal*, or pickles, and everyone knew why: the schoolteacher had stolen our lunch money. The teacher had a legitimate excuse to steal the money—he said he hadn't been paid his salary in six months.... No one blamed the schoolteacher for doing this [selling the children's school uniforms sent by the government]. You can't expect a man in a dung heap to smell sweet. (28)

This wanton deprivation of opportunity is clearly gendered: this village school where resources are stolen is for boys, but there is no mention of even a pretense of schooling for girls. When a surprise inspector arrives and notes the problems—the "holes in the wall," "the red discolorations," the missing duster and chairs in the classroom, the boys' illiteracy—the teacher's malfeasance is taken in stride. Balram proves to be, however, the only boy in the classroom who can read, earning him the sobriquet of the "white tiger," "the rarest of animals— the creature that comes along in only in a generation" (30). Hence, as Balram tells us from the start, he is "self-taught" (4), his "formal education" having ended soon after, when he was forced to leave school to break coals in the village tea shop (32). It is through his innate smarts, his enterprise, and refusal to be pushed into the mud, that Balram has made the most of what he ironically calls his informal education. "I used my time at the tea shop in Laxmangarh to spy on every customer at every table, and overhear everything they said. I decided that this was how I would keep my education going forward—that's the one good thing I'll say for myself. I've always been a big believer in education—especially my own" (43). Balram thus shifts (or distorts) the idea of education from formal, public, collective, to informal, individual, self-propelled, as what enables individual economic success. Balram has no concept of education in the broader, liberal sense as that which opens the mind and teaches us how (not what) to think.

Adiga thus establishes, from the start, the accumulated systemic disadvantages, the multiple conditions that together lead to Balram's servitude. Like Triton, Balram becomes a domestic servant to escape the greater horrors of village peasant life. In Balram's case, these include being trampled underfoot and bled by the feudal landlords who reign there with impunity. He explains why men from his village leave for the city: "the Animals stayed and fed on the village, and everything that grew in it, until there was nothing left for anyone else to feed on" (21). The Buffalo, Stork, and their brothers not only own all the resources, and fleece the helpless villagers, they also rule through lawless terrorization. When the son of one landlord is kidnapped and killed by the Naxalites, his domestic servant is blamed for it and made an example of; not only is he tortured and shot dead, but so, Balram reports, are all the members of his family, including women, who are also raped and "finished off," and their house burnt to the ground (57).

Adding to the stranglehold of the feudal and political system is the power of religion. Adiga's opening chapter emphasizes both the material conditions that push poor villagers into servitude, and the cultural conditions that foster acceptance of it. Early on, Balram notes how Hinduism as a religion has inculcated acquiescence and servility in the supposedly lowly toward those ranked as higher born, how religion works hand-in-glove with other oppressive systems—feudalism, family, economic injustice—against the underclasses. Inside his village temple is the statue of the god Hanuman, whom Balram describes as follows:

> a saffron-colored creature, half-man, half-monkey: . . . Hanuman, everyone's favorite god in the Darkness. . . . He was the faithful servant of the god Rama, and we worship him in our temples because he is a shining example of how to serve your masters with absolute fidelity, love, devotion.
>
> These are the kinds of gods they have foisted on us, Mr. Jibao. Understand, now, how hard it is for a man to win his freedom in India. (16)

Balram's irony veers into sarcasm here, as he suggests how religion works as a system not only to drug the masses, but also to induce their cooptation into their own exploitation, where servitude again becomes a frame of mind, and a pervasive condition for the poor. The temple in their village upholds the servant god Hanuman as a model for the underclasses. Later, following this template prescribed by religion, when Balram gets a job driving his feudal landlord's son Ashok and Ashok's wife Pinky in their car in Delhi, he sees himself as such a Hanuman figure, a hybrid creature, elevated to semi-divinity but still part-animal, a servant to the greater gods: "I would drive them wherever they wanted, as faithfully as the servant-god Hanuman carried about his master and mistress, Ram and Sita" (38). (Balram's self-connection to the monkey-god later is linked to his mimicry of Ashok—he sees himself as a monkey.) Religion here becomes clearly an accomplice to the interlocking systems of feudalism, politics, and corruption that maintain a stranglehold of oppression on the poor, inculcating attitudes of acceptance and acquiescence, helping to stamp the underclasses harder into the proverbial mud.

Balram's urge to resist these forces is linked, interestingly, to his capacity to recognize beauty, a capacity he associates with his mother. Throughout his narrative, Balram refers jokingly to "the four best poets in the world, . . . [Iqbal], Rumi, Mirza Ghalib, and a fourth fellow, also a Muslim, whose name [he has] forgotten" (34).[24] It is no small irony on Adiga's part that this sadly mis-educated man with strong anti-Muslim prejudices continually gives tribute to and finds pleasure and guidance in the poetry of four Muslim South Asian poets. (The fourth is likely Faiz Ahmed Faiz, acclaimed for his Urdu poetry of postcolonial resistance.) To begin with, Balram quotes Iqbal on slavery (as a metaphor for colonialism) and links the capacity to see beauty with the capacity to aspire, to seek more than what one is given, and to thereby fight to rid oneself of the shackles of oppression: "*They remain slaves because they can't see what is beautiful in this world*" (34). Taking this to imply that the oppressed are partly at fault for their own oppression, for failing to resist, Balram inverts Iqbal's line to suggest as a corollary that the capacity to appreciate beauty enables the capacity for resistance. Applying this insight to himself, Balram states: "Even as a boy I could see what was beautiful in the world: I was destined not to stay a slave" (35). Faulty though his logic often is, Balram's boyhood desire to see his own village from a distance, literally looking down from the height of a nearby ruined fort, is important. It is, he indicates, inherited from his mother, and is equally disapproved of by his Granny, the family matriarch: "He just stood there gaping at the fort—just the way his mother used to," she complains to Balram's father (35). To Balram, when he finally musters the courage at age twenty-four to leave the village behind and go up the hill to the fort, the view from above of his own village is "the most beautiful sight on earth," perhaps because it confirms what he has left behind (and below) him; it literally gives him a different sense of perspective (36). What those in the village like his grandmother cannot understand, he suggests, is that the capacity to aspire for something more, to see differently, and from another angle, gives him the strength to fight, even to the extent of being willing to kill for the sake of freedom.

At the same time, from the beginning, Adiga also makes clear that such servitude is not merely an individual or private problem, but is absolutely linked to the breakdown of democracy, and indeed to forms of fascism. It is both caused by, and causes, failed democracies. The story of Balram, who escapes his village to become a driver, then a successful businessman and hunted criminal, also reflects on the nation, on the condition of Indian postcolonial democracy for some of the most downtrodden and disenfranchised of its citizens. As a "statutory warning" before telling his story, Balram describes an incident when, while driving his employer, Ashok, and his wife Pinky, he was unexpectedly told to pull over. Ashok then quizzed Balram on some basic questions. "How many planets are there in the sky, . . . Who was the first prime minister of India, . . . what is the difference between a Hindu and a Muslim, ... what is the name of our continent?" (7). Balram does not tell us how or what he answered, but he reports Ashok and Pinky's responses, as she giggles in derisive disbelief, and Ashok says (to her) with calm superiority, as if Balram was not present:

> "he probably has, ... what, two, three years of schooling in him? He can read and write, but he doesn't get what he's read. He's half-baked. The country is full of people like him ... And we entrust our parliamentary democracy"—he pointed at me—"to characters like these. That's the whole tragedy of this country." (8)

Ashok uses this interrogation and Balram's answer to demonstrate a point with Pinky—that the uneducated and poor cannot and should not participate in a democracy. Balram remains merely instrumental to Ashok.

This scene is reminiscent of an equally important moment in Kazuo Ishiguro's *The Remains of the Day* (1989), when Stevens, the butler to the pro-Nazi Lord Darlington, is likewise summoned before "three gentlemen" to answer a series of questions that he is likewise unable to answer (194). In this case a guest conducts the interrogation to establish the same point. Stevens' inability becomes both an occasion for contemptuous laughter by these members of the English elite, and used as proof of the inability of the lower class to participate in democratic politics. In the context of Hitler's rise to power, Lord Darlington allows his guest to use (and abuse) Stevens, to demonstrate Stevens' lack of detailed knowledge of current affairs before his guests in order to confirm his (and their) shared fascist views: "Democracy is something for a bygone era. The world's far too complicated now for universal suffrage. ... Look at Germany and Italy, ... See what strong leadership can do if it's allowed to act" (198). (Darlington later apologizes to Stevens for the humiliation, but maintains his views.) As a proper servant, Stevens the narrator adopts and parrots these views himself, insisting, even in retrospect: "a butler's duty is to provide good service. It is not to meddle in the great affairs of the nation. The fact is, such affairs will always be beyond the understanding of those such as you and I" (199).

Adiga's clear allusion to this scene in a novel which also explores the formation (or de-formation) of a servant sensibility (in Ishiguro's case as an index to national politics and the history of British appeasement of Nazis in the 1930s) suggests how Balram's encounter with Ashok is also an index to questions of nationhood and participation in the political process (in 1990s India).[25] In both cases, an upper-class man humiliates his servant, highlighting his ignorance, in order to prove that the lower classes are not fit to participate in a democracy. Unlike Stevens, however, Balram responds with anger and rueful irony, agreeing with Ashok's diagnosis but resisting his conclusion. Balram reflects instead on the system that has denied him education and vitiated his capacity to become an informed (let alone well-informed) democratic citizen:

> I didn't like the way he had spoken about me, but he was right.
> "The Autobiography of a Half-Baked Indian." That's what I ought to call my life's story.
> Me, and thousands of others in this country like me, are half-baked, because we were never allowed to complete our schooling. Open our skulls, look in with a penlight, and you'll find an odd museum of ideas— ... all these ideas, half-formed and half-digested and half-correct, mix up with other half-cooked ideas in your head ...
> The story of my upbringing is the story of how a half-baked fellow is produced. (8)

Balram's imagined title for his autobiography alludes to Nirad Chaudhuri's well-known 1951 memoir of his upper-caste and upper-class life and education under British colonialism (*The Autobiography of an Unknown Indian*), implying, by contrast, how even less known are the trials and tribulations of a lower-caste villager's life after decolonization. Balram's reflections become an indictment not only of India's education system, but also of its putative democracy, as the novel continues to expose the horrifying mockery of the electoral system that rests on bribes, bought and rigged elections, and the constrained votes of the poor. Balram concludes that he did not need an education or democracy, since his out-of-school education enabled him to do better than the "fully formed fellows" who finish their formal schooling but end up taking "orders from other men for the rest of their lives" (9). "Entrepreneurs are made from half-baked clay," he jokes (9).[26] Both Ishiguro and Adiga link servitude (and the attendant issue of education for its citizenry) to the broader question of participant democracy in modern nations: in a vicious cycle, they suggest, servitude both results from defective systems of education, and is maintained by illiberal, unegalitarian, unjust governments; and servitude (both literal and figurative, material and mental) produces failures and negations of democracy.[27]

Becoming a Servant: Balram's Attachment to Ashok and Desire for Servitude

Structurally, *The White Tiger* is divided into eight chapters, each titled for a time during the week when Balram narrates how he became a successful entrepreneur ("The First Night" to "The Seventh Night"). Intertwined with the primary narrative of Balram's past is thus a secondary strand, the timeline in the present, over the seven days that it takes Balram to tell his story, which includes Balram's own interjections or interruption by events in the present. The intertwined trajectory of both narrative arcs can be grouped into three segments: (i) the set-up and account of the experiences that lead the village boy from Laxmangarh to become a driver in Dhanbad, and build his relationship with Ashok (chapters 1–3); (ii) the pivotal crisis when, after their move to Delhi, Pinky kills a child and Balram is forced by the landlord family to sign a false confession admitting to the car accident (chapter 4); and (iii) the gradual, painful process of Balram's disillusionment with Ashok, the murder, Balram's departure for Bangalore, and eventual escape from servitude (chapters 5–8).

The first segment of *WT* presents, as in *Reef*, the young Balram's desire to become a servant (since servitude is a better alternative than the conditions of his village), and his growing attachment to and desire to serve his master Ashok. At the same time, unlike *Reef*, *WT* also details the grotesque abjection and deprivations that servitude entails, and Balram's agency in shaping his life trajectory. Balram is neither as young nor as naïve as Triton when he starts working for Ashok. Like Triton, Balram tells the story of his entry into servitude, his fascination to his employer, and their changing relationship. Unlike Triton, however, Balram highlights graphically the degradations of servitude, and his initial willingness to accept them. In elaborating this stage of Balram's servitude, Adiga explores the psychology of servitude and underscores both the horrific conditions of servitude, and the reasons why so many are willing to accept them. In this section and the next, I want to pull out two main threads of this text: one, what Adiga shows about servitude through Balram's experience of it; and two, how Balram's intense, near-obsessive, homosocial (and almost homoerotic) attachment to his employer Ashok develops and changes. I use the conventions of life-writing scholars (since this autobiographical fiction), and distinguish between the older (experienced) Balram who narrates and reflects on the past from the younger (naïve) Balram who experiences what is described.

Older Balram's reflections, as he begins his narrative proper, are guided by the memory of his employer Ashok, whom he dubs his "ex," "the other important man in [his] story" (38). Emphasizing Ashok's importance to his life and story, Balram's language hints at a homoerotic relationship ("ex" suggests both past employer and former lover):

> Mr. Ashok's face reappears now in my mind's eye as it used to every day when I was in his service—reflected in my rearview mirror. It was such a handsome face that sometimes I couldn't take my eyes off it. Picture a six-foot-tall fellow, broad-shouldered, with a landlord's powerful, punishing forearms; yet always gentle (almost always—except for that time he punched Pinky Madam in the face) and kind to those around him, even his servants and driver. (38)

Balram's description indicates his own learned and internalized values: his admiration for the manliness of Ashok, as defined by Ashok's propensity for violence (when deemed necessary to control either his wife or his social inferiors, if either got out of hand), and his capacity to exert power unhampered by his surface charm.

In recalling this propulsive memory of Ashok, Balram also introduces the central motifs of the monkey (an emblem for himself), and of the rearview mirror (through which Balram, as driver, observed his master and started to mimic him).[28] Describing Ashok and Pinky as gods, Ram and Sita, he imagined himself as the (lesser) monkey-god Hanuman, "who carried about [the greater gods] his master and mistress, Ram and Sita" (38). Presenting his younger self as both servile accomplice and desirous aspirant, eager to be more like his master, Balram describes how he deliberately eavesdropped, learning secrets and information that enabled him to model himself on Ashok. "I owe him so much. He and Pinky Madam would sit in the back of the car, chatting about life, about India, about America—mixing Hindi and English together—and by eavesdropping on them, I learnt a lot about life, India and America—and a bit of English too. . . . I am not an original thinker—but I am an original listener" (39). In this project of self-betterment, driving enables a form of one-way osmosis, as Balram actively listens and absorbs what happens in the car. As a driver, while disregarded and non-participant, he hears everything said in the car. Like the monkey-god, he transports his master and mistress from place to place, but unlike Hanuman, Balram is also learning for his own sake.

Even when he announces that he has murdered Ashok, older Balram insists on this lasting attachment. Revealing in the dramatic close to the first chapter that after eight months as Ashok's driver he "slit Mr. Ashok's throat" (36), Balram hastens, in the following chapter, to assure his readers that he is no monster, that he in fact loved Ashok, and that, in a sense, murder produces an even deeper intimacy than the one they shared as master and servant: "Here's a strange fact: murder a man, and you feel responsible for his life—*possessive*, even. You know more about him than his father and mother; they knew his fetus, but you know his corpse. Only you can complete the story of his life . . . " (38; italics original). Balram's language again suggests a deep, even homoerotic connection, a physical knowledge of and sense of ownership over the body he has both served and killed. Like Triton, who continues to love Salgado, even though he recognizes the need to separate from him, Balram exhibits a rueful sense that the murder was a regrettable necessity: "Now even though I killed him, you won't find me saying one bad thing about him. I protected his good name when I was his servant, and now that I am (in a sense) his master, I won't stop protecting his good name. I owe him so much" (39). Sitting in a room full of light shredded by darkness, Balram insists that he is now the master of his former master, but exhibits the devotion of the loyal servant he cannot erase within himself. Indeed, the identity of servant is embedded in him even through his name: he was named by a schoolteacher who reminded him that, according to Hindu scriptures, "Balram was the sidekick of the god Krishna" (11). Balram knows no other name. His lifelong effort is to live down this name (as he does at the end by taking Ashok's name), to become a central protagonist, not subordinate, secondary, or sidekick to another's story, to be both socially and narratively major, not minor.

And yet despite these passionate tributes to Ashok, the story that Balram tells of his lone struggle to get training and employment in fact demonstrates his own initiative, determination, and drive, his desperation to escape, and hence his desire to become a servant. Unlike Triton, whose uncle helps him get the job with Salgado, young Balram has to rely entirely on his own enterprise, in the face of family opposition. After his father's death, and a move to another dead-end job in Dhanbad, where his brother Kishan shows "no entrepreneurial spunk," and is "happy to let [Balram] sink in the mud" with him, Balram refuses to acquiesce (45). But, Adiga makes clear, what Balram learns as a way to succeed is an uncritical embrace of neoliberal capitalist ideology, of unscrupulous individual self-advancement at the expense of others: "I did my job with near total dishonesty, lack of dedication, and insincerity—and so the tea-shop was a profoundly enriching experience," he notes sardonically (43). Balram eavesdrops with the intentional goal of learning what he can by chance from customers' conversations and, discovering what drivers get paid, determines to pay to learn to drive. Despite his caste, multiple setbacks, and swindlers along the way who fleece him, Balram invests in acquiring this crucial skill that enables one step out of the mud of the Darkness in which he lives.[29]

However, Adiga suggests, there is no escape from the strangleholds of feudalism and family even for the enterprising young Balram. Upon finding that he still could not get a job without "know[ing] someone in the family," Balram gets his first job in the nearby city of Dhanbad ironically precisely because of his family, with the very feudal landlord he sought to escape from in his village (50). Ashok's father, the "Stork," the rapacious feudal landlord who has Balram's village in thrall, agrees to hire him only because he knows that he can hold Balram's family hostage. Recalling the rapes, torture, and killings that befell the entire family of a domestic servant who incited the landlord's wrath, Balram notes grimly, the "Stork and his sons could count on [his] loyalty" because they knew how to get to his family (57). And yet, to get even this job, Balram has to perform servility, enacting obsequiousness and gratitude: "You should have seen me that day—what a performance of wails and kisses and tears! You'd think I'd been born into a caste of performing actors!" (51). That young Balram is fully aware that this is a performance, insincere but necessary, is clear: "And all the time, while clutching the Stork's feet, I was staring at his huge, dirty, uncut toenails, and thinking, *What is he doing in Dhanbad? Why isn't he back home, screwing poor fishermen of their money and humping their daughters?*" (51). Balram knows well how this feudalist exploitation is gendered in its many manifestations, and what different types of violence are visited upon different bodies.

Clear thinking though he is about the Stork, young Balram at first sees Ashok as somewhat different, as Balram's hope for advancement. Returning to the language of romance, Balram describes their first meeting as fated, almost as (one-sided) love at first sight. Just as he is being turned away by the Stork, he catches sight of Ashok: "I swear by God, sir—I swear by all thirty-six million and four of them—the moment I saw his face, I knew: *This is the master for me.* Some dark fate had tied his lifeline to mine, because at that very moment he looked down. I knew he was coming down to save me" (50). Balram's melodramatic style is coupled with his recognition of some weakness in Ashok, a chink in the wall of feudal power and monopoly, that spells an opening for Balram.[30] Adiga's comic exaggeration also suggests how the young Balram is mistaken: Ashok is not going to save Balram—nor is anyone.

Adiga underscores, through carefully delineated detail, the intensified degradations of servitude to which Balram is subject because of the yet greater servility demanded by a feudal landlord. Though he is hired as the "number two driver," assigned to Ashok, and delegated to do the lesser tasks of the household in a lesser car while the "number one driver, Ram Persad" drove the masters around town in the more expensive car, in reality (58), as a servant, Balram is required and willing to do whatever tasks are needed in the household:

> Now, as I say they took me on as their "driver." I don't exactly know how you organize your servants in China. But in India—or, at least, in the Darkness—the rich don't have drivers, cooks, barbers, and tailors. They simply have servants.
>
> What I mean is that anytime I was not driving the car, I had to sweep the floor, make tea, clean cobwebs with a long broom, or chase a cow out of the compound. (58)

Adiga's irony suggests that it is unimaginable to Balram, living in India's "Darkness," that any society might be organized without servants and a culture of servitude. The most he can stretch is to imagine the possibility of clearly differentiated tasks. In Balram's world, drivers do not only drive. After every ride, Ram Persad, the senior driver, has to wash and clean the streaks of *paan* that the Stork (Ashok's father) regularly spat all over the car and spittoon (a habit Ashok denounces as "disgusting"; 58); Balram has to soak the old man's feet daily in hot water, massage them, and cut his toenails. Adiga does not spare his readers the grotesque physicality of this task:

> After half an hour, he would say, "The water's gone cold," and then I had to lift his feet out, one at a time, from the bucket, and carry the bucket in to the toilet. The water in it was dark—dead hair and bits of skin floated on it. I had to fill the bucket with fresh water and bring it back (60).

As if to evoke readers' disgust, Adiga emphasizes the reality and outrageousness of demands to which a domestic servant is subject. A feudal landlord can make such intimate physical demands of a servant who does not have the option of refusal. Balram's response makes clear how that disgust is not just restricted to the bourgeois or upper class, but is fundamental to what makes him also human and worthy of dignity:

> I washed my hands for ten minutes, and dried them, and washed them again, but it made no difference. No matter how much you wash your hands after you have massaged a man's foot, the smell of his old, flaky skin will stay on your skin for an entire day. (61)

Reminiscent of Lady Macbeth who cannot wash off her guilt, what Balram cannot wash off from his psyche is the degradation of servitude, which seeps into his very body.

And yet consequently, Balram turns even this degradation into an opportunity. Because of this proximity, he is able to listen in on conversations between the old man and his sons, like a fly on the wall, to continue to "absorb and grow"—until he receives a "sharp blow" on the head for his pains (60–61). The scene serves not only to exemplify the routine physical violence that is also a servant's lot, but more importantly, to dramatize the difference between the feudal landlord and his America-returned son:

> "Do you have to hit the servants, Father?"
> "This is not America, son. Don't ask questions like that."
> "Why can't I ask questions?"
> "They expect it from us, Ashok. Remember that—they respect us for it." (61)

Easily dismissive of Ashok's new-fangled American notions, the Indian father counter-trains his son, reinforcing his ideas with the weight of dominant cultural practice. Adiga's point is that the new generation does not necessarily escape this toxic culture of servitude: the father is successful, as we see later when, under the stress of Pinky's accident, Ashok's thin patina of modernity quickly wears off.

For young Balram, so far, this scene manifests Ashok's difference, his superiority to his vile father and brother. But even at this early point in the narrative, it is clear that Ashok is no Salgado. Ashok uses the rhetoric of family to cover up his preference for the comforts of servitude in India. Rejecting Pinky's demand that they return to the United States, Ashok responds, "I like it better here. We've got people to take care of us here—our drivers, our watchmen, our masseurs.... [Ram Bahadur] has been in my family for thirty years—we call him servant, but he's part of the family" (77). But the servant is not family, not even for Ashok. He silences Pinky when she swears in the car, rebuking her not for swearing but for swearing when a driver is present: "There's a driver in the car, Pinky," he reminds her of the outsider, clearly not a member of the family (68).

At first, while working for the landlord's family in Dhanbad, Balram views Ashok as a benign master, with whom he begins to develop some intimacy. In a telling scene, Balram describes a complex interaction between servant and master when Ashok comes unexpectedly to Balram's room (shared with Ram Bahadur, another male servant) to ask him to drive him and Pinky to Laxmangarh. Ashok is embarrassed to see, for the first time, Balram's filthy, cramped servants' quarters, the lodgings he is provided within his family mansion.

> Mr. Ashok was standing outside my room.
>
> I ran up to him and bowed low. He went into the room; I followed, still crouched over. He bent low to make his way through the doorway—the doorway was built for undernourished servants, not for a tall, well-fed master like him. He looked at the ceiling dubiously.
>
> "How awful," he said.
>
> Until then I had never noticed how the pain on the ceiling was peeling off in large flakes, and how there were spider webs in every corner. I had been so happy in this room until now.
>
> "Why is there such a smell? Open the windows." (67)

As Balram practices the self-abasement and self-effacement expected of him as a servant, Adiga also signals how the very architecture of Indian homes is designed differently for servants' bodies: the very doorway is lower for the undernourished servant, so that Ashok has to bend, literally and figuratively, to enter the servants' space. Ashok's reaction is also deeply revealing: while implicated in the meanness of the space provided for his servitors by his family, in their family mansion, his curt, imperative demands address his own needs, not Balram's. When the smell offends him, he orders Balram to open the windows. But Balram appreciates Ashok's visible embarrassment—"He looked in my direction but avoided my gaze, as if he were guilty about something"—and his promise that Balram and his fellow servant would get "a better room," "separate beds" and "some privacy" (68).

More revealing however, is young Balram's own reaction, as he begins to see this room not through his own eyes, but through Ashok's. First, to alleviate Ashok's evident discomfort, he engages in emotional labor, to make Ashok feel better.[31] Knowing that guilt can rebound negatively on the one who triggers it, Balram tries to reassure Ashok: "This place is like a palace for us," he insists (68). But second, with yet more complex psychological insight, Adiga shows how Balram begins to perceive his own world as Ashok's perceives it, through Ashok's senses: "And so I saw the room with *his* eyes; smelled it with *his* nose; poked it with his fingers—I had already begun to digest my master!" (67–68). Such an extraordinary shift suggests not only, on Balram's part, a peculiar empathy— literally in the sense of feeling what another is feeling—but also a capacity to shift sensation, to get outside his own skin to see, imagine, through the other. Balram's language suggests that he takes over Ashok's body, as if internalizing his master to become him. This is a retrospectively prescient moment, prefiguring the later act by which Balram actually kills Ashok and takes his name, his suitcase, and in a sense his identity, donning similar clothes, as if consuming Ashok, internalizing his master to become (like) him. It represents an early step toward Balram's subsequent efforts to mimic and become Ashok, in a man-to-man identity takeover, as he starts to use Ashok as a model, having had no other models in his life so far. But the scene also suggests the overpowering presence of Ashok, and his power to influence Balram, to make him see and feel not as himself, but via his master. In fact, it is Ashok's mode of being that has taken over Balram, so that Balram can no longer sense—see, touch, smell—with his own senses.

At this stage of his career, pleased though young Balram is with Ashok, Balram is also very clear about the dehumanizing degradations of servitude, and the damage it does to individual psyches and communities. Adiga calls attention to the effects of this culture of servitude on servant-to-servant relations, as a system that induces not solidarity, but disabling rivalry among differently oppressed servants. "Is there any hatred on earth like the hatred of the number two servant for the number one?" reflects Balram ruefully about his younger self (66). The hierarchy among servants, and the effects of extremely scarce resources for which each servant must compete with other servants, pit the servants against one another, inciting hatred of fellow servants rather than of the employers who mistreat them all. The two senior servants of the Stork's household treat Balram with contempt and incite in him the desire to better them. But Adiga provides a complex psychology for these men as well. It is precisely because they are denied respect by those they serve that they demand it more of those below them. "Servants, incidentally, are obsessed with being called 'sir' by other servants," remarks Balram about Ram Bahadur, the Nepali watchman who initially tries to throw him out (89). Hence, as a good student of cutthroat neoliberal capitalist ideology, and of the law of the jungle where only the fittest can survive, and the weak are uncared for, Balram learns how to survive and advance himself in this dog-eat-dog system. Adiga's goal is to make Balram not likeable but understandable, as determined to find a way for himself within the grotesquely impossible conditions that Adiga elaborates and excoriates.

As in *Reef*, where Triton replaces Joseph, in *WT*, Balram also displaces a senior servant in the household hierarchy. But unlike Triton, Balram moves up from being "number two" driver to "number one" not because he is more deserving and the man he displaces is villainous, but because Balram discovers his sad secret and threatens to expose it. Thanks to his sharp wits and percipience, Balram discovers that Ram Persad, the senior driver, is actually a Muslim pretending to be a Hindu. Because he shares a tiny, filthy, windowless room with Ram Persad, Balram is forced into the close proximity that enables him to notice that the other man's breath has begun to smell different, and that he is acting differently (90). Upon discovering that Ram Persad is secretly fasting for Ramadan, and visiting a mosque, Balram confronts his erstwhile superior and effectively intimidates him with verbal and physical violence:

> Before he could run, I caught him by the collar. Technically, in these servant-versus-servant affairs, that is all you need to do to indicate: "I have won." But if you're going to do these things, it's better to do them in style, right? So I slapped him too.
>
> I was servant number one from now on in this household. (92)

Balram's humorous, self-knowing account reads almost like a tongue-in-cheek manual on how to ascend the ladder of servitude. Adiga both highlights the ruthlessness necessitated by such a system and complicates his portrayal of Balram's psychology. Balram is torn between pity for his victim (the man he has jockeyed out of position), and the need to get ahead. He both wins the game and regrets that he has to play it. He demands and gets the perks he wants (the more comfortable bed, tea and biscuits, a better uniform) and wishes he could apologize to the Muslim man he has ousted from his job: "Part of me wanted to get up and apologize to him right there and say, . . . '*You never did anything to hurt me. Forgive me brother*'" (93). But he does not apologize, knowing that to keep his top-dog position he has to maintain the performance of ruthless masculinity that he has had to learn. And yet this moment of regret, this empathy for a man who has had to conceal his religious identity in order to retain this ultimately horrible job, demonstrates from this early stage not weakness, but an ethical side to Balram, a generosity toward the downtrodden that he has to suppress, and will only allow himself to exercise when he has more power.

It is very clear from the start how much, unlike Triton in *Reef*, Balram abhors servitude and the interlocking forces that place him in it, and how glad he is to have escaped it. In a key moment of reflection from the present as he looks back to this stage in his life, the older Balram reflects bitterly on servitude, addressing his Chinese audience directly as he recalls a poem he loves:

> You are familiar already with my love of poetry—and especially of the works of the four Muslim poets acknowledged to be the greatest of all time. Now, Iqbal... has written this remarkable poem in which he imagines that he is the Devil, standing up for his rights at a moment when God tries to bully him. The Devil, according to Muslims, was once God's sidekick, until he fought with Him and went freelance, and ever since, there has been a war of brains between God and the Devil....
> God says: *I am powerful. I am huge. Become my servant again.*
> Devil says: *Ha!*
> When I remember Iqbal's Devil, as I do often, lying here under my chandelier, I think of a little black figure in a wet khaki uniform who is climbing up the entranceway to a Black fort. (74–75)

In this very Miltonic, or rather Blakeian, understanding of Satan/Lucifer as a Romantic hero, fighting against an oppressive tyrant (God), what Balram sees is a battle of brains, not brawn, cast in terms of servitude. (Incidentally, given this highly intertextual intercultural allusion, it is worth recalling that Iqbal's poem was very much shaped by this Romantic heritage.) God's language, "be my servant again," suggests that servitude is more broadly a cosmic condition of the oppressed, that to submit to a tyrant and do his bidding is to be a servant. Balram identifies himself clearly with the Devil, or imagines the Devil as a figure like himself, and recasts the Devil as a falsely maligned, misunderstood figure of resistance. Adiga here casts Balram indubitably as a sympathetic figure, struggling against impossible odds. He too, Balram suggests, is such a Devil, a "sidekick" refusing to be a sidekick, cast as evil by the oppressor because he has dared to resist his circumstances and oppressors. Invoking the overdetermined language of darkness and light, he is that "little black figure in a wet khaki uniform," struggling to climb out of the oppressive mud of his village and family's poverty and dependence into the light, and sees himself as "spitting at God again and again" (75). In the present, that light is still shadowed by the dark, literally "sliced" by the shearing "black blades of [his] midget fan" (75).

Balram remembers this moment, however, not when he is decrying the horrors of servitude, but when he is recounting the stranglehold of his extended family, the demands his grandmother makes on him to marry so that he will be bonded even more tightly to his family, so that she can command a dowry from the bride's family, and so that he can have children who can be held as ransom, making him yet more vulnerable to the coercive brutality of the feudal landlords.[32] Ultimately, Balram seeks escape not only from domestic servitude, but from the interlocking systems that necessitate his turning to servitude, the combination of feudalism and family that he must escape altogether to secure his freedom.

Unbecoming a Servant: Balram's Move to Delhi, and the Impact of Pinky

Pinky's drunken hit-and-run accident in Delhi, when she kills a child and Ashok's family forces Balram to take the blame for it, is a critical turning point, precipitating the changes that lead Balram to murder Ashok. Consequently, young Balram's view of his servitude changes, as does his relationship with Ashok. However, prior to this event, the move from Dhanbad to Delhi itself brings about significant changes, as Balram, promoted to primary driver, is now alone with Ashok and Pinky, in a new relationship of proximity and intimacy. Like Nili in *Reef*, Pinky becomes more prominent in this part of the story, a significant third to the male duo, evoking in Balram a similar triangulated desire. He also begins to be ashamed of his servant identity, and more critical of Ashok, even he also desires increasingly to emulate his "master."

In an important scene, on their way to Delhi, as Balram drives Ashok, Pinky, and Mukesh in their air-conditioned car, and rejoices in having achieved his dream, comparing himself to the impoverished men hanging off the buses they pass by, Ashok taps Balram on the shoulder, in an unspoken command, indicating that he wants to take over the wheel. Young Balram's reaction is that of devoted, gratified servant, as he likens himself to a faithful dog:

> From the start, sir, there was a way in which I could understand what he wanted to say, the way dogs understand their masters. I stopped the car, and then moved to my left, and he moved to his right, and our bodies passed each other (so close that the stubble on his face scraped my cheeks . . . and the cologne from his skin . . . rushed into my nostrils for a heady instant, while the smell of my servant's sweat rubbed off onto his face), and then he became driver and I became passenger." (94)

As yet, Balram is content to be servile, to understand and obey his master's wordless commands. Yet his description of the switch also suggests a homoerotic, physical closeness between servant and master, even as it highlights their differences: as their bodies brush against each other, Balram breathes in the smell of his master's cologne, while Ashok is literally smeared with his servant's sweat. Mukesh, "an old-school master," orders his younger brother to switch back, to reassert the hierarchical order of things, where a driver is a servant, and a master is driven (94). For Balram there follows another gratifying exchange of intimacy, reversing the momentary switch: "The car came to a stop. Our bodies crossed once more, and I was again the driver and servant, and Mr. Ashok was again the passenger and master" (94). This brief double exchange both underscores the intimacy between master and servant, and makes real the possibility of exchanging positions that Balram will later realize. It prefigures what will come.

Upon arrival in Delhi, Balram notes how being a servant in the big city and nation's capital brings no change in terms of degradation. The architecture of residential buildings is designed both to house and hide servants:

> ... in India every apartment block, every house, every hotel is built with a servants' quarters—sometimes at the back, and sometimes ... a warren of interconnected rooms where all the drivers, cooks, sweepers, maids, and chefs of the apartment block can rest, sleep, and wait. When our masters wanted us, an electric bell began to ring throughout the quarters—we would rush to a board and find a red light flashing next to the number of the apartment whose servant was needed upstairs. (108–109)

Repeatedly Adiga underscores how the culture of servitude structured the very physical, built environment of India. In Ashok's family's luxury apartment building, this dehumanizing system creates a paradoxical community of servants, but no solidarity, as established servants mock the uninitiated newcomer: "Servants need to abuse other servants. It's been bred into us, the way Alsatian dogs are bred to attack strangers. We attack anyone who's familiar" (109). Coping with infestations of mosquitoes and cockroaches, no privacy, a shared toilet and bathroom, Balram is, however, befriended by another chauffeur from "the Darkness," an unnamed man identified by his skin disease as "Vitiligo Lips," who gives Balram "a course on how to survive Delhi" (102–105).

In Delhi, Balram is not as alone as in Dhanbad. He meets and talks to many other members of the underclasses—servants, a bookseller—men in whom he finds a shared anger and resentment, and an odd reluctance to resist the system. In a powerful episode, "Vitiligo-Lips" introduces Balram to *Murder Weekly*, the cheap, lurid, commonly available pulp fiction that is supposedly popular reading material among servants, and speaks to their secret desires:

> Of course, a billion servants are secretly fantasizing about strangling their bosses—and that's why the government of India publishes this magazine and sells it on the streets ... the murderer ... is so mentally disturbed and sexually deranged that not one reader would want to be like him—and in the end he always gets caught by some honest police officer (ha!) ... (104–105)

In this very clever move, Adiga at once evokes the widespread employers' fear that servants will kill them, because servants have access to the privacy of their homes. But, he also suggests, through this cheaply disseminated propaganda fiction, the Indian government deliberately seeks to indoctrinate servants not to kill, using cautionary tales to instill fear in the servant instead, representing killer-servants as pathological villains coming to such bad ends that no servant would want to be like them. In this self-reflexive meta-fictive trope, Adiga also suggests the potential of fiction to be used as a political tool to control the abused underclass, to manipulate and redirect human desire through disidentification. With irony, Balram (and Adiga) suggests, employers need not fear that servants read such materials; far more dangerous and potentially subversive of the status quo are other kinds of reading (like Adiga's own novel) or ideologies of social justice that foster resistance instead of acquiescence: "It's when the driver starts to read about Gandhi and the Buddha that it's time to wet your pants, Mr. Jiabao" (105).

It is perhaps because of such encounters in Delhi that Balram starts to become impatient with Ashok, to see his clay feet, and to feel, in contrast with Ashok, an empathy and connection with others outside the circle of privilege. As he drives Ashok around Delhi inside his air-conditioned car, Balram is very aware of those outside, the "multitudes of small, thin, grimy people squatting" at bus stops or sleeping on pavements, the "poor bastards" who came to the city looking for betterment (116). When Ashok criticizes a rickshaw driver whose racking cough casts some spit on their clean Honda, Balram remembers his father, who died of the lifetime of toxins he inhaled as a rickshaw driver: "*if you were out there breathing that acid air, you'd be spitting like him too, I thought*" (116). More intensely than Triton in a similar moment in the car with Salgado, Balram's reaction suggests how even devoted servants can become critical and resentful of the disregard of the rich for the ordeals of the poor. "We were like two separate cities—inside and outside the dark egg" (116). His father would be outside on that pavement, thinks Balram. But it is in the position of a servant that inside meets outside. As a driver, Balram is positioned at once inside and outside, feeling connected with those outside while himself physically inside: "So I was in some way out of the car too, even while I was driving it" (116). This becomes an emblematic moment, as we will see, for it is an indicator of Balram's capacity for empathy with those downtrodden, less fortunate, more exploited, and that incites his rage against the ruling class, not just from self-interest, but on behalf of such others. This is a key aspect of Balram completely overlooked by critics who see him as simply a self-centered, unregenerate criminal.

Hence, for example, Balram notices how the "homeless" or male "servants like night watchmen and drivers" are forced to wait outside for hours in freezing winters, and resort to burning plastic to keep themselves warm (133). "One of the best things to put in the fire is cellophane ... the only problem is that while burning, it gives off a white smoke that makes your stomach churn" (133). The body knows that these fumes are carcinogenic, even though consciously the indigent do not. In this horrific eco-critical moment, Adiga uses the narrative device of the servant narrator to tell his readers more than what the servant narrator knows, conveying both the servant's greater vulnerability because he is kept uninformed, and the servant's victimization by the rich who know of and can avoid such bio-pollution and environmental harms.

In Delhi, Balram's relationship with Ashok also becomes more complicated and is triangulated by Pinky (as for Triton, with Salgado and Nili). In Delhi's permissive environment, free from the surveillance of Ashok's father and brother, Pinky's skirts become shorter, and her necklines plunge. Now, instead of looking at Ashok through the rearview mirror, Balram is sexually aroused by what he sees of Pinky through that mirror. Voicing confusion, split between what he understands as masculinity and servitude, since his reaction as a man is inappropriate for a servant, Balram remarks: "This put me in a very bad situation, sir. For one thing, my beak was aroused, which is natural in a healthy young man like me. On the other hand, as you know, master and mistress are like father and mother to you, so how can you get excited by the mistress?" (120). Adiga presents Balram as having internalized the rhetoric of servitude that subordinates the servant, and relegates him, via the fiction of family, to the position of infantilized child. When servitude conflicts with the ideology of toxic masculinity that he has also internalized in a deeply patriarchal, misogynist culture, Balram's (almost comical) solution is to choose propriety over physical safety, the decorum of servitude over the responsibility of driving. He avoids looking in the rearview mirror: "If there was a crash, it wouldn't be my fault," he states (121).

Yet it is a subsequent encounter with Pinky that precipitates Balram's desire to change himself, as her feminine bourgeois disgust prompts him to look at himself for the first time in a real mirror, to see himself as she sees him, and then, because of her, to desire to look more like Ashok.[33] Summoned by her to serve in the kitchen, Balram is startled by her furious outrage at what he does not even realize he is doing: "Stop scratching your groin with your left hand!" she shouts as she tells him off for his "disgusting" appearance and throws him out of the apartment. For the first time, we get a view of Balram's physical appearance—reflected via Pinky. "You're so filthy! Look at you, look at your teeth, look at your clothes! There's red *paan* all over your teeth, and there are red spots all over your shirt" (123). And Balram looks: "I got in front of the common mirror and opened my mouth. The teeth were red, blackened, rotting from *paan*. I washed my mouth out, but the lips were still red" (123). In this key moment, at the center of the novel, the male servant's gaze is directed toward an image of his own self and sees how he is seen. It is a moment of both recognition and unrecognition, prompting readjustment of identity and selfhood, because Balram now sees himself through what Fanon has called a "third person consciousness," via the redirecting, abjecting gaze of a dominant other, in this case, his master's wife.[34] Even his language suggests his alienation from himself, as he describes "the teeth," as if unable to say "my teeth," to claim what he sees in this mirror as his own self. It is after this experience that Balram begins to emulate Ashok, to look at him literally as a model, in order to refashion himself in his master's image. Through the rearview mirror again he observes closely what Ashok is wearing, a plain white shirt, and begins to adopt outward signifiers of higher class: he buys toothpaste and inflicts pain on himself to stop his unconscious habit of rubbing his groin (126–127).

At this point in his trajectory, however, Balram still remains the faithful, obedient servant. When driving a drunken Pinky and Ashok one night, putting up with her contradictory commands and mockery, he stops the car and hands it over to her when she demands it and is left stranded on the road. When she returns to pick him up, he gets in quietly into the back. Even when she drives at "top speed" through a red light and hits "the small black thing" that he cannot bear to describe as a little girl living on the street, knowing that it is not a dog that has been "crunched completely" by the wheels, Balram acts in concert with Ashok (138): "Without a word between us, Mr. Ashok and I acted as a team. He grabbed her, put a hand on her mouth, and pulled her out of the driver's seat; I rushed out of the back . . . and drove the car at full speed all the way back" (139). In this gendered and classed economy, Balram and Ashok act together as men who protect not the impoverished child victim, but the pampered rich woman from her crime, against her protests, against all ethical and legal obligations to the contrary. And, as the perfect servant, like Manucci in Hamid's *Moth Smoke*, Balram literally washes out the evidence, scrubbing "every bit of blood and flesh" from the car (139). Enjoined to silence, now aware that he shares a powerful secret with Ashok, but unaware of the danger that this secret poses to himself, Balram goes to sleep that night with "the big contented smile that comes to one who has done his duty by his master even in the most difficult of moments" (141).

Adiga thus emphasizes how long it takes, and what extreme oppression Balram experiences before he begins to see the light, or before, so to speak, the worm turns. It is not until the next morning that Balram begins to understand better, when the "Mongoose," Ashok's brother, arrives and both praises him for proving himself "part of the family" and forces him to sign a false confession to the hit-and-run, under duress of threatened vengeance upon his family (141–144). Recognizing the blatant hypocrisy and manipulativeness of this rhetoric of family, and knowing that he has no recourse to the law, that the judge has been paid off, Balram now realizes the trap that he is in, the pervasiveness of what he will call the Rooster Coop:

> The jails are full of drivers who are there behind bars because they are taking the blame for their good, solid middle-class masters. We have left the villages, but the masters still own us, body, soul, and arse.
> Yes, that's right, we all live in the world's greatest democracy.
> *What a fucking joke.* (italics in original; 145)

That this is a matter not just of interclass exploitation, but of national injustice, becomes clear with Balram's comment about India's democracy. His lasting anger and bitterness spurt out, at the retelling of this memory in the present: "Even to think about this again makes me so angry I might just go out and cut the throat of some rich man right now," he concludes (145).

Colored Wires Twisting: The Rooster Coop, and How Balram's Thinking Changes

What is actually surprising about Balram's story, contrary to how it has been read, is how *long* it takes Balram, even after the accident, to turn on Ashok, and how difficult a process it is for him. In a compelling image, Balram notes that like the "mysterious and magical... colored wires twisting" in the "entrails" of the car engine, he cannot himself understand the intertwined causes of what happened after Pinky's accident (95). He cannot say "how I went from thinking *this* about my master to thinking *that*," but, he warns forebodingly, "the story gets much darker" (95). Adiga's meta-fictive metaphor conveys the multi-causality and twisted, intertwining forces that convert this servant into a killer. Indeed, Adiga's narrative here onward emphasizes how much more difficult it is to *unbecome* a servant than to become one, and how hard it is for Balram to turn on Ashok, despite multiple reasons for doing so. What follows then is the process of Balram's extremely slow awakening. "The door was always open," as he says later (216). What is astonishing is what takes him so long to see it, for the scales to fall from his eyes.

It is important that even after the accident and forced confession, Balram still believes in his bond with Ashok. But Ashok betrays him. In fact, it is Pinky, not Ashok, who exhibits a semblance of ethical responsibility when she insists that someone should tell Balram that he does not have to go to jail, that no witnesses to the accident have emerged. None of the men in the family see any need to allay Balram's terror. She was the only "one with a conscience," Balram realizes (153). Adiga underscores how deeply embedded the ideology of servitude is in someone like Balram, and how it messes with his emotions as well as his sense of self. When Pinky leaves, and Ashok falls apart, Balram's reaction is a complex mix of devotion and self-abnegation to the point of self-emasculation. He devotes himself to Ashok, even though Ashok blames Balram for not trying to stop her and subjects Balram to physical violence: "Now that she was gone, I knew it was my duty to be like a wife to him. I had to make sure he ate well, and slept well, and did not get too thin" (157). Like Triton when Nili leaves, Balram pampers his master, taking on the feminized role of servant as surrogate wife-mother. But Balram knows that he does so partly out of self-interest, because his livelihood and survival depends on Ashok: "when the master's life is in chaos, so is the servant's" (158). To offer comfort and distraction, Balram plays the clown, offering clichés he does not believe in himself, while thinking, "*if you die, who's going to pay me three and a half thousand rupees a month?*" (159). But there is an emotional piece to this as well, for upon witnessing Ashok's misery, Balram softens and forgives: "He was so powerless, so lost, my heart just had to melt. Whatever anger I had against him for trying to pin Pinky Madam's hit-and-run killing on me passed away that evening. That was *her* fault" (159). Misogynistically blaming Pinky, Balram forgets that it was Ashok who was responsible for the cover-up, who aided and abetted her drunken car-snatching, and who went along with his father and brother's coercion and intimidation of Balram. As a servant, Balram is emotionally and not only financially dependent; his feelings oscillate so wildly in this asymmetric relationship that finally, in a retrospective moment of extraordinary self-knowledge, Balram confesses paradoxically to the impossibility of self-knowledge that servitude entails:

> I put my hand out and wiped the vomit from his lips, and cooed soothing words to him. It squeezed my heart to see him suffer like this—but where my genuine concern for him ended and where my self-interest began, I could not tell: no servant can ever tell what the motives of his heart are.
> Do we loathe our masters behind a façade of love—or do we love them behind a
> façade of loathing?
> We are made mysteries to ourselves by the Rooster Coop we are locked in. (160)

In this brilliant moment of insight, Balram demonstrates self-knowledge about the lack of clear self-knowledge entailed by servitude. Adiga highlights how a servant's inner sense of self is (re)constituted by servitude, where caring for another (in both senses of looking after, and having feeling for) becomes inextricable from caring for oneself.

The Rooster Coop is Adiga's brilliant metaphor for the power of ideology in the Althusserian sense, for that interpellation of the underclasses that functions systemically, through fear and psychic rewiring, to indoctrinate and inculcate submission to power, and that hence enables the hegemony of the ruling class. Drawing on the reality he sees of chickens in a cage waiting to be butchered, "terrified, feathered flesh" tormented and bunched together, creatures that yet "do not rebel" or "try to get out of the coop" (147), Balram builds the comparison to human beings, to domestic servants trusted to handle suitcases full of diamonds or millions of rupees while themselves paid a pittance: "A handful of men in this country have trained the remaining 99.9%—as strong, as talented, as intelligent in every way—to exist in perpetual servitude; a servitude so strong that you can put the key of his emancipation in a man's hands and he will throw it back at you" (149). That this pertains to the nation, and not just to the home, that the arena of the domestic connects the home and the nation, is made clear by Balram's term for this system: "the Great Indian Rooster Coop" (149). At this point, Balram asks two crucial questions: one, what maintains this trap; and two, what does it take for one entrapped to get out? His answers are clear: for the first, it is "the Indian family," held at ransom should any servant betray his trust; and for the second, it takes a rarity, a white tiger, "a man" willing to sacrifice that family, "prepared to see his family destroyed—hunted, beaten, and burned alive by the masters" (150).

If it is not the accident, nor his treatment thereafter, then what brings Balram to this point? Adiga eschews single causality, presenting instead a chain that begins with two betrayals by Ashok. Balram thinks that his efforts caring for Ashok in his time of need, acting as a wife-substitute, will cement their bond. However, when Ashok's brother comes to visit, first, Balram realizes that the "intimacy" he thought he had with Ashok did not exist. Balram overhears Ashok talking to "the Mongoose": "[in India,] without family, a man is nothing. Absolutely nothing. I had nothing but this driver in front of me for five nights. Now at last I have someone real by my side: you" (161). Balram now understands that Ashok considers him a complete outsider, "nothing," certainly not family. The rhetoric of family is maintained only as an emotional ploy to manipulate servants. Second, when after cooking, cleaning, and serving the two brothers, Balram finds Ashok soaking his feet in a bucket of water, and, as a devoted servitor, eagerly puts his hands in the "dirty" water to massage Ashok's feet, Ashok spurns him:

> Mr. Ashok kicked the bucket, and the water spilled all over the floor.
> "How *stupid* can you people get? He pointed to the door. Get out! Can you leave me alone for just five minutes in a day?" (164)

What seem like trivial domestic acts of ingratitude or churlishness speak in fact to deeper realities of callousness, dehumanization, and emotional betrayal. It is multiply ironic that Balram has to clean what Ashok spills, and that Ashok's desire for privacy is voiced right after he and his brother read Balram's grandmother's letter to Balram and declare that poor villagers have "no sense of privacy" (162). But what stings most is Ashok's generalizing, othering language: "you people," a phrase only used to lump individuals with a group understood as inferior. It is a shock for Balram to see the enormous disparity between his perceptions and Ashok's, to discover Ashok's blindness to what Balram had offered as companionship and care, far beyond the call of ordinary servitude, to find that for Ashok too the servant exists merely as a dispensable object, a convenient, passive receptacle upon which to vent his frustration.[35] Adiga's remarkable attempt to understand the complex psychological effects of India's culture of servitude here takes a deeper dive into yet more unplumbed levels.

For Balram, Ashok's rejection occasions deep self-scrutiny, and self-realization:

> Why did I feel that I had to go close to his feet, touch them and press them and make them feel good—why? Because the desire to be a servant had been bred into me: hammered into my skull, nail after nail, and poured into my blood, the way sewage and industrial poison are poured into Mother Ganga. (165)

Coming to consciousness, becoming aware of how one is entrapped, is a key step toward the struggle for freedom. One cannot fight to leave a cage if one cannot even see it. Balram's language suggests the violence that has been done to him, through the inculcation of a psyche of servitude so deeply ingrained that it destroys a sense of one's own humanity. And to change that, Balram also realizes, involves a turning upon that self as it has been formed, in order to re-form it. What inspires him to resist, at this point, is the memory of his dead mother's foot, "pushing through" the fire (165). His resistance to servitude emerges concomitantly with his resistance to the demands of the extended family system, as inextricable from each other, because to refuse to be a servant is to be willing to relinquish his (existing) family and forego the future family that would only perpetuate the cycle of entrapment: "I was like that ass now. And all I would do, if I had children, was teach them to be asses like me, and carry rubble around for the rich" (165). Now, in a more metaphorical sense, Balram looks in a mirror (at himself), in a process of self-discovery. Though Balram takes Ashok as a model, this is no longer mimicry, but a project of self-dismantling in order to reconstitute and re-create a new self of his own.

However, astonishingly, Balram still does not think of killing Ashok. That takes a number of further betrayals. And, until the very last minute, Balram waits, hoping for a sign, a reason to change his plans. A key contributor is Ashok's sharp moral decline after Pinky's departure. Describing (with comic irony) how he was "corrupted from a sweet, innocent village fool into a citified fellow full of debauchery, depravity, and wickedness," Balram states, "All these changes happened in me because they happened first in Mr. Ashok. . . . life in Delhi corrupted him—and once the master . . . becomes corrupted, how can the driver stay innocent?" (167). Reappropriating the employers' rhetoric of servant-as-family, speaking with ironic deliberateness of Ashok as his father and role model, Balram now justifies his own degradation as a mirror of Ashok's. In alluding to Shelley's famous conclusion to "Ode to the West Wind," "O Wind, / If Winter comes, can Spring be far behind?" Adiga (not Balram) suggests not only that the servant follows the master, as naturally as spring follows winter, but also that a revolution may be imminent, that the servant's uprising could likewise bring change and renewal.

The dramatic acceleration of Ashok's deterioration (and Balram's disillusionment) is signaled, and symbolized, by Ashok's change of clothing, from white to black. Balram is horrified, first by Ashok's adulterous involvement with other women, and then by Ashok's willingness to do his father's and brother's dirty work and bribe a minister. At first, Balram thinks that the Nepali girl Ashok brings into the car is a mere "pickup" until he discovers that she is Uma, a former girlfriend Ashok was not allowed to marry (178–179). But then Ashok is pressured by the corrupt minister into having sex with a high-class prostitute, a blonde Ukrainian: "They corrupted him" he insists (185). Balram is actually forced to serve as a barman in the car, to pour whisky for this man while driving Ashok around with the minister's evil "sidekick." "The skills required of an Indian driver!" he remarks, satirically (183). However, it is Ashok's failure to resist, his inability to refuse, to be faithful even to Uma, that upsets Balram. He takes the car to drive around Delhi by himself at night, feeling as "if something is burning inside me as I drive," as if "she will burn with the same thing," that both he and "*she*," the city, were equally "bitter" (188). Later, Balram tries to copy Ashok, to buy a blonde woman, and finds, to his dismay, that a copy can only obtain a copy, that the rules are changed for the lower-class servant, and the only prostitute he can hire is a fake one, a poor Indian woman dyed blonde, leading to his further sense of outrage and injustice.

Another key factor is Balram's realization that, even as a full-time servant to an extremely wealthy man, he has no security for his future. "What happens to old drivers?" he asks his friend of the "diseased lips" (170–171). The best-case scenario, his friend answers, if he is thrifty, is a "house in a slum, a kid in college" (171); worse scenarios involve losing his job from illness, accident, or getting sacked "for no reason" (172). Balram's sudden awareness of his precarity, just when he thought himself fortunate, feeds his growing resentment. But that resentment still does not turn murderous—as yet. He begins to see that what he had gratefully viewed as generosity was in fact stinginess, that when Pinky gave him money for helping her flee to the airport, she in fact withheld much more, just like Ashok and his brother, that in fact Balram's entire framework of vision is based on his inculcated, internalized sense of his own worthlessness, that his gratitude for a pittance was in fact a result of his failure to see what had been taken from him. He begins to pilfer, siphoning petrol, charging Ashok for fake repairs, aware that he is very minimally rectifying an enormous injustice, feeling not guilt but a growing rage: "The more I stole from him, the more I realized how much he had stolen from me" (196).

However, it is not until Balram opens Ashok's red briefcase and sees how much money is in it, money to bribe a minister for the landlords' tax evasion, that he sees the larger scale and understands for the first time that this is in fact money stolen from the poor of the nation, a systemic form of theft where the rich further deprive those already deprived. It is a moment of illumination, conveyed in a mode of comic magical realism, to suggest the intensity of Balram's epiphany: "all at once, the entire stairwell filled up with dazzling light—the kind that only money can give out" (208). He begins to connect all the deprivations he has himself experienced, the collective lack of resources for state institutions, with this corrupt recirculation of wealth at the highest levels, which explains why the state has no money to spend on hospitals like the one where his father died, or on the schools like the one where Balram received no food or education:

> *See—Mr. Ashok is giving money to all these politicians in Delhi so that they will excuse him from the tax he has to pay. And who owns that tax, in the end? Who but the ordinary people of this country—*you*!* (208; italics in original)

Addressing himself as "you," Balram is split, torn between selves, as he now looks at himself in the rearview mirror:

> At a red light, I looked at the rearview mirror. I saw my thick moustache and my jaw. I touched the mirror. The angle of the image changed. Now I saw long beautiful eyebrows curving on either side of powerful, furrowed brow muscles; black eyes were shining below those tensed muscles. The eyes of a cat watching its prey. (208)

In this crucial moment, Balram is looking no more at Ashok, but at himself. As he touches the mirror, he changes its angle, showing him a new self, no longer subordinate, but powerful, a potential predator, biding his time. And now he literally begins to see red—from the "red bag" to the "red light" (208), "the red wall of Parliament House" (209), a neighboring driver's "vivid red puddle of expectorate splashed on the road [that] festered there like a living thing" (209), evoking blood, and then, as the driver spits again, as if silently encouraging him in servant solidarity, "two puddles of red, spreading spit" (210). These red images externalize, or bespeak, Balram's rising fury, turning murderous.

Adiga presents Balram's insight as based on infallible logic, that the money he steals is in fact stolen from the poor. (Unlike Robin Hood, Balram, having learned self-interest as the only mode of survival, takes it for himself.) But Adiga also highlights the intensity of emotional and psychic disorientation that Balram undergoes, emphasizing that this is no mere emotionless calculation, that it involves a kind of derangement, a self-alienation, as Balram struggles with himself, or, more accurately, with his split self. Balram has to talk to himself, or talk himself into going where he is has not dared to go before, as he refers to himself not as "I," but as "the creature in the mirror" (208). As he contemplates doing what he is contemplating, Balram in fact begins to lose his mind. The text makes it unclear whether he actually sees, or thinks he sees, "paw prints" in the cement pavement, small dark marks that vanish, as if he is seeing himself, or an animal incarnation of himself, mirrored everywhere in the environment (221–222). A little later he squats in a slum, and sees "a thin black fellow . . . grinning back at [him]," who echoes Balram's words, shouting and laughing at him—"We'll even fuck your wife for you, Balram"—until he falls "face-first into the ground" (223). When Balram goes to wash his face, it becomes clear that this "fellow" was Balram himself, shouting and laughing at himself, split between his old self, the faithful servant, and the new self, the angry rebel. Already traumatized, Balram is now struggling with self-recognition. Or rather, the self he must become in order to save himself is unrecognizable to him. That in itself induces a form of trauma, of psychic disruption, involving cognitive and emotional dissonance. Adiga's brilliance at unraveling the psychology of Balram unraveling has not been fully recognized.

And yet, despite this breakdown, this searing, consuming rage, again and again, even now Balram is ready to give up the idea of stealing from and killing his master, if prompted by any proof of humanity, or evidence that he is wrong. (He knows he cannot merely steal and get away without killing Ashok as well.) What is astonishing is not that Balram kills, but that it takes him so long. One morning, he turns hopefully to look at Ashok: "I swear, I was ready to make a full confession right there . . . had he said the right word . . . had he touched my shoulder the right way. But he wasn't looking at me. He was busy with the cell phone" (219–220; ellipses in original). Balram marvels at Ashok's obliviousness, his sense of entitlement and lack of sense of danger: "To have a madman with thoughts of blood and theft in his head, sitting just ten inches in front of you, and not to know it. . . . What *blindness* you people are capable of" (220). Ironically, Balram now reverses the use of that painful phrase, "you people," turning it on Ashok. He is now the one in power, who can use it on the other. Unwittingly, Ashok aids Balram by demonstrating again his own meanness, as he takes out a thousand rupees and, under guise of generosity, gives Balram a mere hundred as a bonus—another sign of Ashok's holding back from the poor in stark contrast to what he gives to the rich (221). (Balram later throws away that money into the gutter; 222.)

Yet Balram *still* continues to yo-yo. When his nephew Dharam arrives from the village, Balram sees it as an occasion to jolt himself back into the old form of sanity: "I had come to the edge of the precipice. I had been ready to slay my master—this boy's arrival had saved me from murder (and a lifetime in prison)" (225). But then Balram overhears Uma persuading Ashok to fire him and hire another "replacement driver" (229), and sees Ashok secretly interviewing another man for the position, a "small dark man of the servant class" who "bowed" before he left (235). Balram knows how to read his master—Ashok's expressions and body language tells him that Ashok had "just concluded a deal" (235).

It is not until he visits the zoo with his nephew and, in another mirror moment, meets the eyes of the caged white tiger, just as he had met the eyes of his master "in the mirror of the car," that Balram actually makes his decision (237). Ironically, at this final point of decision, his former connection with Ashok is now replaced with a sense of connection with the tiger, a moment of (self-)identification so intense that Balram actually passes out. It is after this that he writes his final letter to his grandmother, effectively telling her that he has chosen to sacrifice the family: "*I can't live the rest of my life in a cage, Granny. I'm so sorry*" (239; italics in original). And yet, still, even at the last moment, in the final car ride before he kills Ashok, Balram waits, willing, at a sign from Ashok, to change his plan. It is Ashok who fails Balram. When Balram looks at Ashok in the rearview mirror for the last time, and stops the car, Ashok does not even look up from his cell phone, emblematizing the completeness of their broken connection (242).

Balram as Different from Ashok in the End: Empathy and Ethics

Unlike Gunesekera, Adiga gives much more space in his novel to the process of the servant's emergence from servitude, to Balram's efforts to build that independence, both material and psychological. Adiga thus brings to a close, and ties together, the dual narrative threads that explore the gendered psychology of servitude and Balram's growth from adolescence to adulthood, or, more precisely, from entrapment to a kind of freedom. I want to conclude this chapter therefore with some key elements that Adiga uses to underscore how Balram chooses, in his moment of freedom, in fact as a sign of his freedom, to be *different* from Ashok. Even though he learns from Ashok and (superficially) imitates him, even to the point of commemorating him by taking his name, Balram also learns and decides what *not* to be. In other words, I suggest, Balram *changes* over the course of the novel, and ironically, at the end, when he has the opportunity, is a better employer than Ashok. Hence, I would emphasize two points about the last section of this novel that critics seem to overlook: one, that despite leaving servitude behind, having built a successful business in Bangalore with the money in the red bag, Balram still cannot be completely free of servitude, which leaves deep, lasting imprints in his psyche; and two, that despite what he has done, Balram exhibits a capacity for empathy and ethical behavior that suggest something very different from what he has learned from Ashok.

First, as he tells his story, and as he reaches the end, Balram occasionally catches himself slipping into the habits of servility. At one point, he finds himself wheedling when he meant to be assertive: "I couldn't believe I had said that. Once a servant, always a servant: the instinct is always there, inside you, somewhere near the base of your spine" (256). He notes his own ingrained habits of performing servitude, that are learned, not instinctive, and that, despite his efforts at self-(re)fashioning, he can never fully eradicate. But second, now that he is an employer, he makes an intense effort to enact power in ways very different from the models he has seen, to demonstrate a different and intentional ethic. Proudly, he says:

> Once I was a driver to a master, but now I am a master of drivers. I don't treat them like servants—I don't slap, bully, or mock anyone. I don't insult any of them by calling them my 'family' either. They're my employees, I'm their boss, that's all. (259)

If he began by mirroring Ashok, now Balram refracts instead of reflecting the image of his former employer: "Here, if a man wants to be good, he *can* be good. In Laxmangarh, he doesn't even have the choice. This is the difference between this India and that India: the *choice*" (262). Here Balram (and indirectly through him, Adiga) makes a key point about subaltern ethics and the constraints that interfere with acting as autonomous ethical agents. The person trapped in Laxmangarh, in the "Darkness," ground into the mud, forced to behave like an animal, has very limited choices, and limited room to be good. How then can he be judged by the same rules as someone with more privilege and power? To be fully human, suggests Balram, is to have the option to act ethically.[36]

Even when he was a servant, Balram had moments where he showed an unexpected empathy for those in tougher situations than himself. As we have seen, even though he bullied and supplanted Ram Persad, the senior servant who bullied him, Balram felt bad about it. Or, in a rare moment of feeling for women, when he went to the red-light district, he could not bring himself to exploit the women he could see literally trapped behind barred windows. "*They're like parrots in a cage. It'll be one animal fucking one another,*" he thought, as he repudiated the pimps calling to him (214).³⁷ But Balram behaves very differently when he has more power, a point that Adiga emphasizes through two key episodes at the end: first, after the murder, Balram's risky decision to take his young nephew, Dharam, with him as he escapes to Bangalore; and second, Balram's conduct when one of his drivers kills a bicyclist in Bangalore.

After Balram kills Ashok, he plans to flee Delhi as fast as possible. But, at the railway station, he realizes that though he is willing to sacrifice the rest of his family in the village, he cannot bring himself to leave Dharam behind in Delhi. Balram recognizes a different claim from the nephew in his charge, knowing what would happen to a young boy both at the hands of the police and in jail among "a bunch of wild men" (246). At risk to himself, increasing the chances of being captured, Balram returns to get Dharam and takes the boy with him to Bangalore, where, after he sets up his business, Balram pays to educate Dharam in an English school. Proud that his nephew will have the chances he did not himself have (271), Balram extends this altruism and sense of responsibility to more of the next generation from the "Darkness" in Bangalore: he plans to "start a school—an English-language school—for poor children in Bangalore," to give the downtrodden a leg-up when he can (275). (Darkness here clearly represents the generalized condition of poverty, deprivation, and disempowerment, not Bihar.) He knows, as most servitude fiction writers emphasize, that the only hope of escape from servitude is through education. Balram's plan, in fact, is for a social revolution: the school he will found will be "full of White Tigers, unleashed on Bangalore!" (275).

Second, even more significantly, Adiga includes an episode that contrasts pointedly with the earlier hit-and-run episode when Pinky kills the street child. In Bangalore, Balram sets up a night-time taxi service, and when one of his drivers accidentally runs over and kills a young boy on a bicycle, Balram does the opposite of what the feudal landlords did to him. Instead of making the innocent and powerless take the blame, Balram takes the blame himself. (The degree of responsibility of the driver here is questionable, as I elaborate below.) Instead of firing the driver, or allowing him to be arrested by the police, Balram voluntarily takes the greater responsibility as owner of the taxi service. Still no unmitigated hero, Balram first bribes the police to get the driver off, then visits the dead boy's parents, apologizes, and offers both monetary compensation and a job in his company for the brother of the deceased boy. As he says to the parents: "The police have let me off. That is the way of the jungle we live in. But I accept my responsibility. I ask your forgiveness" (268). Balram makes clear that he does what he has to do to survive in a hornets' nest. No one chooses to live in the jungle they live in. (And given that they do, he has learned what he must do to survive.) Nonetheless, he also makes clear, he will not do so gratuitously at the expense of vulnerable others. He makes it clear to the mother that he is offering her money not because he has to but because he "wants to" (268). He cannot live, he explains to Jiabao, like the feudal landlords: "I had to do something different.... I am in the Light now" (269). Even at the risk of being thought weak and therefore cheatable by his own employees (269), Balram feels he has to operate differently, with a different code of ethics, to differentiate himself from the real rogues, the bloodsucking men who abuse the powerless to gain more power than they already have. He does what he does out of necessity, and he maintains a code of honor (as if among thieves). His last sentence, "I am in the Light now," is key. With power, Balram recognizes, comes responsibility. He is no longer in the "Darkness" of poverty and exploitation, but living in a state of relative privilege, which brings social responsibility. That recognition and action distinguishes him from the real beasts of that jungle. Here the meanings of Light/Dark shift from signifying economic polarity to the opposite ends of a moral spectrum, where those living in the Darkness are the landlords who extort and brutalize, and those in the Light are those who operate with a greater sense of social justice.

But Adiga is interested not only in individual responsibility as a code of ethics. Balram also directs our attention to the greater systems of capitalism, neoliberalism, and globalization, to the cost-cutting pressures of fast money-making, so that drivers are ordered to drive fast, regardless of those they literally run over: "It was not his fault. Not mine either. Our outsourcing companies are so cheap that they force their taxi operators to promise them an impossible number of runs every night. To meet such schedules, we have to drive recklessly; we have to keep hitting and hurting people on the roads. It's a problem every taxi operator in this city faces. Don't blame *me*" (266–267). Adiga makes it clear that it is a transnational system of economic globalization, where, under pressure from the Global North, those in the Global South are forced into this cutthroat race for more and more profit, at no consideration of costs to others, that literally and figuratively runs poor human beings over. (Unlike Balram, who was forced to take the blame when it was Pinky driving the car, here the driver was driving the car, but under conditions over which he had no control. Balram thus shifts the responsibility from the driver to the greater forces that drove him.) Hence, at the end, Adiga, like Gunesekera, also suggests how, though Balram's domestic servitude has ended, he is still part of a larger system where nations in the Global South remain subject to those in the Global North, in an international system of servitude: "men and women in Bangalore live like animals in the forest do. Sleep in the day and then work at night, ... because their masters are on the other side of the world, in America" (255). Neoliberalism and globalization have expanded servitude into a worldwide, global system of transnational outsourcing. Poor countries serve the rich, the have-nots the haves, and the Eastern Hemisphere bends to the convenience of the Western, like the dark side of the moon in Rushdie's *Haroun and the Sea of Stories*, whose inhabitants grow resentful because they never see the sunlight monopolized by those on the fortunate side.[38]

At the end, Balram, in his "final word," is well aware of the darkness of murder (272). "It has darkened my soul," he reflects grimly (273). But he asks his readers to place his actions in relation to others': "isn't it likely that everyone who counts in this world, . . . has killed someone or other on their way to the top?" (273). Is this ethical relativism (on Adiga's part)? Or a justification of a mode of survival in the jungle created by others? Balram still dreams of a day when "humans can live like humans and animals can live like animals" (273). He thinks that the Rooster Coop can be broken, but, he adds, it needs "exceptional servants . . . like [Balram] to break out of it" (275). Ironically, Balram here changes the meaning of the term "exceptional servant," which, from an employer's perspective, has long signified the good servant. But from the (liberated) servants' perspective, what Balram values as exceptional and good is the servant who has the guts to break out, to resist the system (what masters would consider the exceptionally *bad* servant). Balram quotes the Buddha, "I have woken up, and the rest of you are still sleeping, and that is the only difference between us" (271). Clearly, Adiga does not present this as an ideal solution, as some critics have thought.[39] Its very failure or limitation is an indictment of the system that prevents a greater reordering of society or imagining of justice. What *The White Tiger* offers is not a solution, but an incitement and provocation to readers to help produce one.

The White Tiger constitutes an achievement and benchmark against which all other servitude fiction might be measured. Infused and enriched by a tonality that combines satiric humor, irony, and wit, it offers a deeply serious psychological exploration of the harms effected by a gendered culture of servitude upon vulnerable individuals, families, and communities. But it also emphasizes how such a system of abjection is enabled by other interlocking systems: feudalism, religion, political corruption, betrayals of promises of postcolonial democracy, and global neoliberalism. And yet, instead of offering what could easily become an account of helpless victimization, *WT* also suggests possibilities of resistance, agency, and ethical action, while making clear the limitations and constraints on individual efforts to resist. In so doing, it suggests the necessity of thinking otherwise, of imagining alternatives for systemic change.

6
Sharing Space: Alternating Female Servant-Employer Narratives in Thrity Umrigar's *The Space Between Us*

In 2006, *The Inheritance of Loss*, Kiran Desai's second novel, won the Man Booker prize and subsequently, much critical acclaim. Exquisitely written, empathetic yet unsentimental, astutely analytical, and laced with a diabolic sense of humor, it has been hailed by scholars as a major work that addresses a range of pressing contemporary issues: the powerful legacies of colonialism; the rise of separatist (neo)nationalisms in postcolonial nations; the effects of neoliberalism and globalization, migration, and diaspora; and local and global class divides, among others.[1] Few, however, have addressed its exploration of domestic servitude, channeled through the key figure of Panna Lal the cook (who remains carefully unnamed until almost the last page), or the implications of its alternation of the narratives and perspectives of the cook and his son Biju with those of the cook's upper-class employers. In 2005, Parsi Indian American writer Thrity Umrigar published *The Space Between Us*, a novel that has received comparatively very little attention, and that centrally focuses on female postcolonial servitude and relations between women servants and employers and the complicated nexus of cross-class relationships thereby entailed for their respective families.[2] *Space* also alternates between the perspectives and narratives of a servant and an employer in India—Bhima, an indigent sixty-five-year-old Hindu woman who works as a daily maid-of-all-work for Sera, a middle-class affluent Parsi widow—and explores both how servitude can provide an escape from extreme indigence and how individuals who spend their lives as servants may seek escape from servitude for their children and future generations.

In this chapter and the next, I compare these two novels with each other and examine how these two Indian diasporic transnational millennial women writers make importantly different formal and thematic choices from the two male writers discussed in the two previous chapters, with very different consequences. I focus in this chapter on *Space*, and in the next chapter on *Loss*, to show how both Thrity Umrigar and Kiran Desai *share* narrative space as they alternate between the narratives of servants and employers. Where Gunesekera and Adiga, as we have seen, *center*, in a formal reversal, a single male servant as the sole narrator and protagonist, and invert, or turn on its head the usual novelistic practice of casting members of the employer classes as protagonists and centering on their perspectives, Umrigar and Desai choose a different tactic: instead of focusing exclusively on the perspective and psyche of a servant protagonist, they divide narrative space between the employer and employed, alternating between and contrasting their perspectives. In so doing, they create not one but two or more protagonists for each novel.

Moving back and forth across what Desai calls "both sides of the great divide" between classes, Umrigar and Desai interweave narratives of servants and their employers (75). Both women writers thus build a formal structure of (relative) narrative equality, disallowing the prevalence or monopoly of a single narrative or class perspective. These narrative choices reflect a certain egalitarianism, and enable contrast, comparison, and mutual corrective of each perspective. Umrigar focuses on the relations between women employers and servants, where both the servant and the employer are older women, and on the effects of servitude on mothering. Kiran Desai explores the criss-crossing dynamics of power between a young upper-class woman and an older male servant, the cook who has helped raised her from childhood. While Gunesekera and Adiga center the predicaments of young male servants who are alone, with no immediate family, Umrigar and Desai address the complications of aging and familial responsibility under servitude, as their older servant protagonists contend with lack of security for their own futures and seek better, different futures for their children, or mitigation of the intergenerational legacies of servitude.

Umrigar's alternating narration suggests both connections and disconnections between the histories and present-day dilemmas of two older women living in 1990s Bombay—Bhima and Sera, one Hindu, one Parsi, one poor and illiterate, one affluent and educated—as it explores their complicated, decades-long relationship as servant and employer. Umrigar focuses on their interpersonal dynamics, structured by inequality, their separate yet entangled pasts and present, and, despite their obvious distances, their complex emotional and material forms of interdependence, intimacy, sense of mutual obligation, concomitant attachment and antipathy, trust and distrust, and conflicting allegiances to their own families, that build to an inevitable crisis. Kiran Desai, through a more complicated narrative structure, explores the cross-generational and cross-gender interdependences, connections and disconnections among four individuals (Sai, an orphaned girl living with her wealthy grandfather, a retired judge; Jemubhai, her grandfather; her grandfather's aging male cook; and Biju, the cook's son, who has migrated to the United States to become an undocumented restaurant worker), the first three of whom inhabit literally the same house, domestic space, and political environment in Kalimpong, a small town in the foothills of the Himalayas, near India's border with Nepal. Where Umrigar focuses on one dyadic relationship between two women, formally alternating between their narratives and perspectives chapter by chapter, Desai creates a quadrangular dynamic, formally alternating between Biju in New York City and the narratives and flashbacks of the other three in India, structurally extending the triangle into a quadrangle.[3]

In a telling moment in *Loss*, Noni, the judge's neighbor in Kalimpong, an affluent Anglophile widow, reflects:

> It was important to draw the lines properly between classes or it harmed everyone on both sides of the great divide. Servants got all sorts of ideas, and then when they realized the world wasn't going to give them and their children what it gave to others, they got angry and resentful. Lola and Noni constantly had to discourage their maid, Kesang, from divulging personal information, but it was hard, Noni acknowledged, to keep it that way. (Desai, 75)

Noni justifies maintaining the boundary between servants and employers, even among women, by convincing herself that it is mutually beneficial for both sides *not* to bridge the gap, even as she recognizes the difficulties of maintaining it. Through her ironic use of free indirect discourse, Desai critiques the self-serving rationalization of the class to which Noni belongs. Desai's novel itself seeks to cross that divide through the structural organization, mode of narration, and thematic concerns of its narrative. Likewise, Umrigar renders the inner consciousness and perspectives of both upper- and lower-class women, alternating between the two protagonists, building up their contrasts and similarities throughout the novel.[4] Only at the end of *Space* does Umrigar break her own pattern and shift, significantly, entirely to Bhima's perspective. At the end of *The Inheritance of Loss*, Sai has an important realization:

> The simplicity of what she'd been taught wouldn't hold. Never again could she think there was but one narrative and that narrative belonged only to herself, that she might create her mean little happiness and live safely within it. (355)

The form of Desai's and Umrigar's novels underscores this insight as both put in play multiple narratives that jostle against one another, that compete with, challenge, amplify, or augment, others. Like any other, Sai's narrative—the story she tells herself about herself, or the way she connects her experiences—cannot be hers alone because others impact it, share in it, lay claim to it, have their own narratives. Nor, as a result, can any one narrative provide the pseudo-safety of self-insulation. The form of Umrigar's novel similarly insists on multivocality, as it toggles between the narratives of two main characters, and in its own narrative mode reinforces the importance of not allowing one perspective or story to dominate or drown out others.

When we look at them together as servitude fiction, *The Inheritance of Loss* and *The Space Between Us*, though not obviously similar, reveal some important congruencies. Both novels present as a central character an aging servant who has spent decades in the service of one family, and who, in addition to parenting his or her own biological children (or grandchild), sees herself or himself as parenting that family's young child, even though the employer does not see or recognize this care work, or the conflicting (and different) mutual attachments that ensue. Both emphasize the interiority—the memories, thoughts, and feelings—of the servant characters, especially as they struggle painfully with the conflicting needs of their own families and the demands of the families they serve. Both explore the emotional labor that falls upon the servant who must enact servility within the household, and whose identity and sense of self are structured by his or her work. Both explore with careful nuance the intricate micropolitics of the interactions and relationships consequently built between servants and employers over the years. Both are concerned with the future of an aging servant who, after decades of service, cannot rely on any provision for their old age or their families. Both build up to the crisis at the end induced by the employer's betrayal—Bhima is fired for speaking an unwelcome truth, and the cook is violently beaten—in scenes of horrendous abjection of the servant and abuse of power by the employer when the servant is torn between the affective ties to their own families and to those of their employers.

Hence both novels pose questions about employers' ethical obligations to those on whose menial labor they depend, and over whom they have such asymmetric power, and about the conflict imposed on servants by competing claims.[5] More specifically and distinctively, both novels engage in a sustained investigation of how parenting by the poor is shaped and complicated by servitude, what disjunctions are implied between servitude and parenthood, and what are the cross-generational effects of servitude. Both explore modes of escape or release from servitude for the next generation. We do not often think about servants in literature (if we think about them at all) as mothers or fathers, as providers, torn between and often attached to both their own and their employer's families. Unlike *The White Tiger* and *Reef*, which both focus on a young male servant-protagonist's growth into manhood as he gains freedom from servitude, both Umrigar and Kiran Desai focus on the servant in old age, looking back to a life of servitude, and worrying about the future of their children or grandchildren. For the elderly servants themselves, both Umrigar and Desai suggest, independence or escape from servitude is not a real possibility—as yet.

The differences between Umrigar's novel (hereafter *Space*) and Desai's (hereafter *Loss*) are therefore also revealing, as are the implications of those differences. Umrigar emphasizes education as a route to release from servitude, women's sexual vulnerability in situations of domestic servitude, the ethical responsibilities of the employer, because of their greater power, and more broadly, changes to the entire system of servitude. Less directly, Desai also suggests education as a form of escape from servitude, and less optimistically, indicates why servants, who are servants because of their lack of education, do not emphasize education for their children, and instead choose less effective means, such as migration, or material accumulation. Umrigar's novel tends often to be sentimental, in its tone, ethos, and plot, whereas Desai's eschews sentimentality, offering instead both a powerful empathy and gritty understanding, distanced by a certain humor.

Umrigar's structure and priorities are clearer, as she alternates between Bhima and Sera and their standpoints to highlight the intersecting problems of gender and class inequalities, sexual exploitation of female servants, domestic abuse, and the importance of women's education. The complexities of servitude and its long-reaching effects on others, particularly families, become the center-point of the novel, as Umrigar also focuses on the relationship between Bhima and her granddaughter Maya to explore the cross-generational impacts of servitude, and how the experience and identity of being a servant affects Bhima's ability to function simultaneously as a parent (or grandparent). Bhima's perspective and story eventually outweighs Sera's, as Umrigar ultimately gives more moral weight, respect, and sympathetic treatment to Bhima. Despite the alternation, Bhima's narrative by the end takes literally more space in the novel than Sera's. Bhima is given more character space and emerges at the end as the real protagonist of this novel.

Desai's structure and priorities are more subtle and complex. The alternation in *The Inheritance of Loss* is twofold. In a clearer spatial and geographical divide, Desai's narration moves back and forth between chapters on Sai, the judge, and the cook in India and separate chapters on Biju in the United States. Biju's narrative is thus set apart, as running parallel to those of the other three, which are often combined within a single chapter. This structural feature of *The Inheritance of Loss* poses comparisons and thematic connections between the domestic dynamics of these characters in India and the migrancy narrative of Biju. An obvious comparison, for example, is set up between the judge Jemubhai's journey to England to study law, under the colonial/racial system, and Biju's journey to the United States to work as an undocumented cook's helper, under the imperialist/racial neoliberal system. The more overt form of alternation (between the characters in Kalimpong and Biju in New York) calls attention to comparisons between India and the United States, between the past and the present, and hence between colonialism and postcolonialism, between globalization across nations, and nationalism, or separatism and ethnic/racial discrimination within nations. Within the India chapters, however, Desai also sets up an internal alternation among Sai, the judge, and the cook, whose inextricable, interconnected stories and perspectives both imperceptibly merge and diverge. This less overt form of alternation among the cook, Sai, and the judge also calls attention to the internal divides, connections, and disconnections literally within the domain of the domestic. Scholars have focused on the comparison the novel sets up between Biju, the impoverished undocumented immigrant, and Jemubhai the judge, privileged scion of a mercantile family, and hence the comparison between twenty-first-century American imperialism and globalization and twentieth-century British colonialism. But they have not noted that what connects these two key parts of the novel is the cook.

As I will elaborate in the next chapter, in *Loss*, the cook's narrative (though seemingly muted) and Biju's together constitute a significant portion of the novel, making servitude and its wide-ranging effects a central theme or concern, connecting the postcolonial servitude of the cook with the millennial migrancy of his son. Though it may seem as if the issue of domestic servitude is restricted to the cook and his interactions with Sai and the judge, I will argue that in fact Desai's exploration of servitude extends to the story of Biju, who experiences a second-hand servitude, suffering the ill effects of the toxic cross-generational consequences of his father's servitude, and the limited chances or possibilities it entails for him. Biju's narrative of abasement, exploitation, and underpayment working in the United States as an undocumented restaurant worker also calls for direct comparison with the domestic servitude of his father in India from which Biju seeks escape. Thus, like Umrigar, Desai focuses both on the gendered micropolitics between employers and servants, and on the intergenerational effects of servitude, and particularly on relationships between servants and their children. Both explore how servants become servants to provide for their children, and to find a way out of servitude for them, as well as the opportunities or lack thereof thereby created for servants' children and grandchildren.[6]

In this chapter and the next, I explore the implications of both writers' formal space-sharing in their use of alternating narratives, and their construction of servant-employer relations as embedded in broader contexts of geo-political turmoil or economic and social inequality. Indeed, I argue that the formal narrative technique of alternating perspectives enables both novelists to craft a more meaningful account of the complexities of those servant-employer relationships. Instead of narrating from a single perspective, as Gunesekera and Adiga do, this shifting back-and-forth between perspectives allows Umrigar and Desai to compare servant-employer perspectives, to reveal both the connections and disconnections in their points of view and ways of seeing, to reveal the gaps as well as the congruencies, and to explore the ways that power and positional asymmetries affect what and how we see. This technique also produces complicated affects. Instead of directing sympathy to only one main protagonist, I suggest, Desai and Umrigar attempt something more complicated.

Alternating between servants' and employers' stories and perspectives asks readers not only to understand both sides, but also to understand the effects of power on perception. Instead of inviting readers to identify with one character or the other, the constant shift of perspective nudges readers into a curious disidentification, as the novel shuttles us from one to the other. This shifting enables a double vision, encouraging readers to see the servant and the employer both from within and without, to understand each *relationally*. Eventually, Umrigar tilts us toward the servant, validating her perspective over that of her employer, inviting more sympathy for the servant woman, as if to demonstrate the feminist truism that we can see better from the margins than from the center, and using the contrast to show what the employer misses despite her unusual perceptiveness.

Desai, by contrast, does not make such a clear choice visible through formal techniques—her third-person limited narration continues to toggle between servant and employers, and reveals the limitations of each perspective. Unlike Umrigar, Desai inserts a distance between readers and characters, forestalling uncritical sympathy, an effect augmented by the ironic tonality of the narrator's voice. But, I would argue, through her use of plot and description, highlighting the intense abjection of the cook and his son, in the end Desai also calls for greater sympathy for the cook and his son than she does for any of the upper- or middle-class characters. There is a freshness to the narratives of the cook and Biju, thrown into relief by the contrast with the more recognizable perspectives of Sai and her grandfather the judge, the Naipaulian mimic man. Ultimately, both writers use alternation to suggest the concomitant proximity and distance between servants and employers. This comparative technique provides an inside glimpse of each subjectivity and of their asymmetry, pushing readers who would normally identify most automatically with the employer characters toward a transformative shift in their own perspectives, across lines of social division.

Thus the very form both writers choose—intertwined narratives of servants and employers whose lives intersect yet remain apart—creates a comparative framework that calls attention to different perspectives and their asymmetry, and arguably pushes readers toward a transformative shift of their own perspectives, toward understanding, caring, and desiring change across lines of social division for individuals toward whom they may not at first be inclined to gravitate. Indeed, it is through the alternation of perspectives that we are enabled to understand the micropolitics of servants and employers better.

In the following discussion of each novel, I focus on three main questions. First, how does each writer elucidate the nuances of the relationships—the microdynamics and micropolitics—between employers and servants who work in the employers' homes? How do they present the interiority or inner lives and subjectivities of each and the limitations of how and what each side sees? Second, how does each novel present the relationships between servants and their children (or grandchildren) and how those are impacted by servitude? What are the problems of intergenerational servitude and how does the aging servant attempt to construct an alternative future for their children or grandchildren? And third, how does each novel approach the crisis at the end where the employer betrays the servant, and imagine a future, in or outside servitude, for the servant and his or her children?

Inner Worlds and Microdynamics Between Women Servants and Employers in *The Space Between Us*

The Space Between Us opens by plunging us into the inner world of Bhima, torn between her "milky maternal" love for Maya, her seventeen-year-old granddaughter and sole remaining kin (5), and her "hard merciless . . . rage" at unmarried Maya's pregnancy (6). In an intense and yet complex depiction, Umrigar presents Bhima as wanting both to punish and protect Maya at the same time: "[E]ver since she has learned of her granddaughter's shame, she has been waking the girl up early," refusing to pamper her anymore; but she also "does not want the lewd young men who live in the slum to jeer at her sleeping granddaughter as they pass by" (6–7). Very soon Umrigar supplies the deep context and history that presents Bhima more sympathetically. Having lost her only daughter, Pooja, Maya's mother, to AIDS, and her only son, Amit, to an absconding husband, Bhima has built her hopes on Maya's college education, funded by her work for Sera, to break a familial cycle of illiteracy, poverty, and servitude. What Bhima most wants at this point in her life is that Maya should "continue going to college and choose a life different from what Bhima had always known" (6). Bhima has lived all her life in Bombay as a domestic servant, the daughter and granddaughter of servant women, though she belongs to the indigent class of rural intra-nation migrants like her husband who arrived more recently to seek work in the city. She, and her desires, are thus shaped by that heritage of servitude: "she would have to go back at least to her great-grandmother's time, . . . how every female member in her family has worked as a domestic servant in someone else's home"; she remembers the pain of being shunted as a child "when her own mother left her home sick to go take care of other people's homes and children" (290). Her one aspiration is to enable her grandchild to escape that cycle of constant, crushing humiliation, and rise via education into the Indian lower-middle class. Hence Maya has become "the golden focal point of all of Bhima's fantasies and daydreams," and Maya's pregnancy a blight to all Bhima's late-life hopes (37).[7]

Umrigar does not attempt to approximate Bhima's voice, but her third-person narration is focalized through Bhima's consciousness, so that we are invited to understand from within Bhima's fierce protectiveness of Maya, her sense of their vulnerability as single women living in a "basti" (slum) without access to running water or a private toilet, her knowledge of cultural stigma, and her equally ferocious desire to end Maya's pregnancy with "one swift kick" (6–7). "They will know about the disgrace Maya has brought upon herself soon enough, and then they will attack her like vultures," she thinks, both blaming Maya and attempting to postpone the inevitable (12). What we are not asked to probe, yet, is Bhima's fury at Maya, or her oddly untenable assumption that this pregnancy must be the result of Maya's promiscuity.[8] What Bhima manifests is a deeply misogynistic, victim-blaming mindset, yet one that, Umrigar makes clear, is absorbed from her social environment (not unlike Adiga's representation of Balram). Umrigar's use of the present tense places us with Bhima in the immediacy of her present moment, engaged in the acts of daily living, and the urgency of the decisions she must make now, without the distance of retrospection. This use of present tense alternates with the past tense when Umrigar provides Bhima's backstory or memories, to give context to this present, when Bhima remembers or later tells Maya about the history that has shaped her and the present situation that affects them both.

From the first chapter, Umrigar thus calls upon her readers to focus on Bhima's interiority, to enter into her conflicted emotions and thoughts, calling attention to her physical sensations of pain and discomfort as an emaciated sixty-five-year-old woman with an unstable knee and dislocated hip, enduring the trials of daily life in a filthy slum (7). Before we see her as a servant in Sera's home (which is Bhima's workplace), we see her as a tough, resilient human being in her own home, and understand why she is frequently late to work. Bhima has to stand in line every morning to get water from the single communal tap, then line up again to "walk between the tidy piles of shit that the residents of the slum leave on the mud floor of the communal toilet" (8). Not sparing us the graphic details, the "flies and the stink" that Bhima must endure, Umrigar makes clear why Bhima prefers to "control her bowels" until she gets to her employer's house (8). Umrigar also makes clear that these conditions are the result of the failure of the state to provide basic civic services, calling attention to the misplaced priorities of a country that spends far more on acquiring nuclear capability and funding the military to crush the independence movement in Kashmir (9).

And yet, as Umrigar also establishes, Bhima is still positioned relatively above the lowest of the low, the Dalit or "Harijan woman who lives at the far end of the slum colony" whom the slum residents individually pay to remove "their piles," and for whose greater abjection and dirtier work Bhima demonstrates an unusual kindness and sympathy (8). Unlike the other residents, Bhima "does not consider herself superior to the poor woman" and "makes it a point to smile at her" (8). In this opening chapter, Umrigar takes care to emphasize the complexity of Bhima, who is cast as poor and downtrodden, but not a mere victim. While the material conditions of Bhima's life seem almost unendurable, her slum-dwelling neighbors also create a varied community: some are petty and competitive, but others show solidarity. In a rich scene, Bibi, a feisty young woman who has adopted Bhima as an aunt, supports and defends her with a caustic wit much appreciated by others, leavening their collective lives with good humor and care (9–10). Though standing in line for the communal toilet, these slum-dwellers display their well-informed currency with national affairs and conviviality. "Who needs nuclear weapons?" jokes someone (also setting the novel's present time as following upon India's nuclear tests of 1998), "they should just unleash Bibi in Kashmir. The snows will melt from the fire in her tongue"; another makes up a song to which they all respond with appreciative laughter (8–9).

By contrast, in a narrative shift that parallels the cinematic technique of cross-cutting, Umrigar opens the second chapter with Sera, Bhima's employer, reveling at the same moment in her only daughter Dinaz's marriage and first pregnancy, and feeling irritated with Bhima for not arriving on time. Umrigar again uses third-person narration to enter into Sera's consciousness, as torn between her desire to reprove Bhima and her understanding of (some of) Bhima's troubles. "Late again. She really needs to talk to Bhima about this daily tardiness," Sera thinks before "feeling a wave of remorse" about her plan to "chastise" Bhima (13). Sera is thus introduced as very much an employer, demanding of Bhima, uncomprehending of the conditions that we have just been asked to understand, and yet still exceptional in her relative kindness. Umrigar asks us to understand Sera as well through her thoughts, relaying her memories of her physically and psychologically abusive late husband Feroz, her consequent relief at Dinaz's better relationship with her husband Viraf, her desire to maintain that relationship at all costs, and her benign curiosity about Bhima's effort to discover the father of Maya's child. Bhima and Sera are thus both introduced as mothers and grandmothers, deeply invested in their families, sharing cultural assumptions about sexuality and marriage, and yet experiencing opposite reactions to a daughter's (or granddaughter's) pregnancy. Like Bhima, Sera betrays a certain misogynistic conventionality as she blames Maya for her pregnancy, and assumes that the girl has been up to "mischief" (13). Unlike Bhima, Sera exists in a world of relatively great privilege, where her greatest discomfort comes from chopping onions, a task she hates and therefore requires of her servant. Indeed, Sera's ability to care for her family, to get credit for making breakfast for her adult daughter and son-in-law, or "children" as she sees them, before they leave for work, literally depends on Bhima's physical labor (13).

Through these alternating perspectives, Umrigar suggests both the convergences and divergences in each woman's understanding of their relationship and relative positions, and how each woman's perspective is inflected by her experience located at the intersection of various social hierarchies. Sera prides herself on being an exceptionally kind employer; over the years she has intervened to help the economically disempowered Bhima in the outside world, getting Bhima's husband a job, ensuring appropriate medical care when he was injured in a factory accident, paying for Maya's education. Sera knows that her neighbors strongly disapprove of her treating Bhima "like a family member," that they criticize her for allowing Bhima to "sit on [Sera's] head" (a repeated phrase which implies that Sera has given too much license to one who should remain low) (44). But she disregards their angry warnings not to treat "servants like queens" who "will take advantage" (170). Sera congratulates herself on what she sees as the understanding between herself and Bhima. "One look at [Bhima's] wan, sallow face tells [Sera] that yesterday's mission was a failure. She raises one eyebrow questioningly, and in answer, Bhima shakes her head slowly from side to side. This is what Sera appreciates most about Bhima—this unspoken language, this intimacy that has developed between them over the years" (17).

Bhima's perspective confirms Sera's kindness and mutual understanding. Bhima's "mission" the day before had been to go to Maya's college to try to locate the father of Maya's child, to persuade him to marry her so that she would not have to have an abortion (17). If Maya was respectably married to a man who could support her, her marriage, even without the college education, would have fulfilled for Bhima an alternative dream of upward mobility. When the college clerk is rude to Bhima, because of her status as a lower-class uneducated woman, Bhima remembers how Sera had accompanied her and Maya when they applied to this college for admission, how Sera had used her upper-class privilege to support and benefit them, not herself: "Sera had pulled herself up to her full height and looked down her long, straight, impervious Parsi nose and told the man, in her best clipped, convent-school accent to kindly watch who he was speaking to, . . . [and] under her haughty, upper-class gaze, the clerk had withered and offered a flurry of apologies" (22–23). In this scene rife with complex intersecting class and gender dynamics, Sera uses her privileges of identity (as an upper-class woman accustomed to deference from lower-class men), and her elite educated English accent, to battle on behalf of Maya and Bhima, both lower-class women treated badly by lower-class men, to demand that they be treated with respect. Umrigar thus emphasizes the subtle micropolitics operative both in these relationships and in the interactions each individual has in her world.

However, Umrigar also shows how Bhima's sense of obligation is mixed with resentment and awareness of contradictions in Sera's condescension. Early in the novel, seeing Bhima in the kitchen scrubbing pots and pans to make them shine, Viraf, Sera's son-in-law, announces that he will buy a dishwasher for the house, but before Bhima can speak, Sera rejects his offer: "My Bhima can put your fancy dishwashers to shame.... Save your money" (19). Sera speaks of Bhima as a possession, a human dishwasher; her priority is not to save Bhima back-breaking labor, but to obtain the cleanest pots. Glowing with a sense of her own exceptionality, Sera exemplifies what sociologist Judith Rollins, in her landmark study *Between Women*, terms maternalism, a form of caring that masks condescension and reassertion of power (173–203). Rollins elaborates on the distinctive micropolitics in female domestic worker-employer relationships (in the United States) as infused by both women's knowledge that they share a "secondary gender position in society" (181). The worker knows that the female employer is not "the ultimate authority in the household" (181); the employer knows that the domestic worker is an extension of herself, a tool to elevate and release her from her devalued domestic responsibilities. This produces both greater comfort between the women (in the privacy and isolation of the home) and two distinctive behavioral patterns, *deference* and *maternalism*, which affirm the employer's superiority, reinforce social hierarchies (198), and "assert dominance" or "mark inequality" (193) in a relation that is not "human to human" but adult to child (186). Deference involves the performance of "ingratiating behaviors" (168) that communicate "appreciation from subordinate to superordinate" such as not initiating conversation or physical contact, using respectful forms of address, maintaining pleasant facial expression (157). Maternalism—derived from paternalism, the obligation to protect and guide in return for work and loyalty, and modified to women's gender roles of "nurturing and attending to affective needs"—involves the giving of gifts, used items, old clothes, advice, or care (178–179). Consequently, Rollins concludes, domestic workers experience *ressentiment*, negative feelings that run deeper because they cannot be expressed against the employers who evoke them (231).

Umrigar highlights these intricate micropolitics as inevitable in such employer and servant interaction in India as well, and renders them from the perspective of Bhima, as experienced by the servant woman. Bhima and Sera are close as women precisely because of the unequal gender dynamics that have long disempowered Sera even as an upper-class woman in her own house in relation to her deeply chauvinist and sexist husband, in a society that continues to devalue woman.[9] At the same time, as a lower-class woman, Bhima has learned over the years to appease her employer, to acknowledge visibly the female employer's relative power over herself, to show requisite deference. But Bhima's feelings are not unmixed with *ressentiment* at Sera's autocratic behavior, such as when she bristles at Sera telling her that Maya must have an abortion (21). Likewise, Bhima's response to the dishwasher comment, unknown to Sera, is silent annoyance, and a struggle to control that annoyance:

> And give [that money] to me instead, Bhima thinks to herself, and then, afraid that one of them will read her mind, she busies herself by concentrating on one

particular food spot. Also she needs a few seconds to fume. Sometimes she can't figure Serabai out. On the one hand it makes her flush with pride when Serabai calls her "my Bhima" and talks about her proprietarily. On the other hand, she always seems to be doing things that undercut Bhima's interests. Like refusing Viraf baba's offer to buy a dishwasher. How nice it would be not to run her arthritic hands in water all day long. (19)

Aware that Sera is thinking about saving her son-in-law's money, and not about Bhima (who is clearly not "family"), Bhima needs time to "fume," to conceal the negative feeling her employer must not see.

Arlie Hochschild has termed such silent self-management "emotional labor," where the employee has to project a requisite demeanor, suppress her own emotions, and artificially induce different emotions to do her physical work and evoke an appropriate emotional response from the customer or employer.[10] Umrigar calls attention to how Bhima has to work on herself to re-manufacture proper feeling: "Oh you ungrateful woman, she chides herself. And who looked after you when you had malaria? . . . Who gave you money just yesterday, so you could take a cab to Maya's college? . . . No, it was this same woman whose salt you eat, who you are thinking ugly thoughts about. Shame on you" (20). Bhima has to project deference and gratitude, and suppress her anger by reminding herself of all she owes Sera, in order to produce Sera's sense of well-being and goodness as an employer. This is an invisible labor and cost borne by the servant that goes unrecognized by others. Through such minutiae, details of everyday life, and use of interiority, Umrigar elucidates the complex emotional texture of this strangely close, yet profoundly unequal, relationship.[11]

Umrigar presents the relationship between Sera and Bhima as neither simple nor one-sided—both are beneficiaries and benefactresses, both have supported each other over the years—and emphasizes both the reciprocity and exceptionality of a relationship that is sustained despite, and indeed depends on, distance. Bhima lives in a filthy slum, Sera in an expensive apartment building in a posh district. Sera drinks tea from a china mug, Bhima from a stainless steel glass set aside for her; "Sera sits on a chair at the table while Bhima squats on her haunches on the floor nearby" (27). Such Indian practices of visible "distinction" are designed to sustain "class domination"; they reflect the "politics of sitting" (Ray and Qayum, 145, 148). Sera knows that, despite her efforts, she cannot overcome her deeply ingrained sense of repulsion for Bhima's servant body, even as she attempts to extend herself to the person. Years earlier, when Bhima got typhoid, and Sera visited her in the slum dwelling, Sera's horror at discovering the gritty realities of slum poverty extended to a horror of Bhima herself. Both ashamed and guilty when faced with "the generosity of the poor" who treat her "like royalty," Sera brought Bhima back to her own apartment and got her own doctor to treat her, but she still made the fevered Bhima sleep outside on "a thin mattress on the balcony" with young Maya "on a bedsheet next to her grandma" because "the thought of [Bhima] sleeping on one of their beds had been too repulsive for Sera" (115). Sera is well aware that "she cannot transcend her middle-class skin," that when Bhima was ill, "she had wanted to protect her daughter from the sheen of dirtiness she now saw each time she looked at her servant" (116). Yet, despite all this, over the years, Sera and Bhima have built an intimate, if asymmetric, understanding of each other's lives, which intersect in the ambiguous space that is at once the employer's home and the servant's place of work. As a daily presence in Sera's home, Bhima knows more about Sera's life than Sera knows about hers, such as the domestic abuse Sera suffered from Feroz, her husband, a secret that Sera keeps hidden even from her own family. And Sera has not forgotten what she owes Bhima, how Bhima had looked after her in a time of extreme need.

Umrigar's language suggests how Bhima has acted as a mother, not only to her own children and grandchild, but also to Sera, her employer. In a powerful scene, Sera remembers how, after her (now deceased) husband Feroz left Sera so violently beaten that her bruises would not heal, Bhima crossed the boundaries of her role as servant and her relegated space in the kitchen and quietly entered Sera's bedroom to provide support, physical healing, and verbal advice. Massaging her homemade balm into Sera's bruises, literally soothing her pain with her "wise hands," Bhima mothered Sera, who felt, in a metaphor that suggests a fetus, like a "small fish floating around in a warm world of darkness and fluids" (109). It was Bhima who instructed Sera to revise her gendered ideology of acquiescence: "Tell your father—he will march in here and break his nose. You are trying to cover up your shame, bai, I know, but it is not your shame. It is Feroz seth's shame, not yours" (111).[12] Bhima has thus mentored the upper-class Sera, joking that she herself would turn her own husband's hands into "pillars of wood" if he should turn on her, offering a proto-feminist solidarity and resistance to cultural and patriarchal hegemony (111).[13]

Sera's response is mixed, revelatory of the disjunction between each woman's understanding of what has passed between them. Despite her Parsi religion, Sera has absorbed a fear of untouchability across class lines, of physical contamination from those who do "dirty work."[14] Though grateful and surprised, she is also horrified by Bhima's physical proximity, the breaking of unspoken taboos: "Sera recoiled. Bhima had never touched her before" (108). Sera's bedroom is a space of only temporary role reversal. Upon return to the kitchen and their conventional roles, Sera is overcome by embarrassment and mortification, "as if Bhima had an eyeglass to her soul, that she had somehow penetrated her body deeper than Feroz ever had" (110). This cross-class homosocial bodily intimacy between women, even in a time of crisis, seems transgressive to Sera, "deeper" than licensed heteronormative marital sex. Sera has no script, except the sexual/erotic, for what has evolved between her and her servant. Class distance and physical decorum are too deeply ingrained in her. She does not want to owe a servant anything—she would rather be the gracious one to whom Bhima owes gratitude. She remembers once catching Dinaz hugging Bhima, and being torn between "pride and awe at the casual ease with which Dinaz had broken an unspoken taboo" and "a feeling of revulsion, so that she had had to suppress the urge to order her daughter to go wash her hands" (29). Obstructed by class and caste prejudice, Sera cannot fully accept the woman-to-woman comfort and support that Bhima provides, or sustain that shift in their power dynamic, or acknowledge what Bhima sees as shared female vulnerability to male violence. By contrast, Bhima takes the event in stride, as a moment of solidarity between women equally vulnerable to male violence. Bhima takes control despite Sera's remonstrance, understanding and accepting Sera's reluctance, and reassuring Sera by maintaining the deferential form of address that indicates recognition of rank: "Shh, shh. Bai, you just let me do what I'm doing" (106). The recipe for her balm, she tells Sera, was acquired from her mother-in-law, who used it when a "village girl was [gang]raped and beaten": it is thus a matrilineal gift, a women's home-remedy that heals where Western medicine is ineffectual (106).

While Bhima goes out of her way to help Sera, Bhima is not the only servant-woman in this novel who has attempted to help an upper-class woman in a situation of distress and oppression. Bhima's muted attempt to intervene against Feroz's abusiveness is anticipated earlier by another older woman servant who witnessed Sera's mother-in-law's abuse of Sera when, as a young bride, Sera lived with her husband's family. When Banu, Feroz's mother, began screaming at Sera for allegedly (and unwittingly) breaking a pollution taboo while menstruating, Gulab, their servant, gently intervened, and tried to separate the women, to stop the situation from escalating (76). Umrigar's repetition of such patterns of intervention suggests that, like Bhima later, as a servant, Gulab had limited power to help, yet felt the call to do something within those limits. When Banu slapped Sera in the kitchen, and then denied it, calling on Gulab as a "witness," Gulab in that moment had no choice but to back her mistress's false claim (81). In Sera's mother-in-law's household, Gulab could speak the truth or offer support openly to Sera. Negotiating her own precarious path through these thickets of abusive power, and across class barriers, Gulab protected herself, claiming not to have seen anything. But like Bhima, as the only silent witness to abuse in the household, Gulab later chose an indirect route to intervene by seeking the help of a patriarchal figure with more power. Gulab went behind Banu's back to tell Freddy, Banu's husband, who enabled Sera to move out of Banu's range of abuse and set up a separate apartment with Feroz: "Banu told me what transpired this morning," Sera remembers him saying (84). Gulab's action resulted in redirecting Sera's life; like Bhima, Gulab also entered Sera's bedroom and offered comfort to the younger woman, "stroking her back" and trying to persuade her to eat (82). But Sera then, as now, was as reluctant to allow a servant woman to comfort her: though she wanted to tell Gulab "of the civil, gentle way she had been raised, . . . her pride rebelled at having to confide in a servant" (82). Bhima goes further than Gulab, in offering the balm and the overt advice to Sera.

Umrigar thus makes it clear that, despite their inequality, Sera owes Bhima, that Sera's beneficence is a form of payback. On many occasions, Bhima has looked after Sera, offering comfort, wisdom, and intervention. When Feroz died suddenly of a heart attack, and Sera wept over him, begging forgiveness in a customary act of wifely self-abasement, it was Bhima who was there with her, in the house, and who provided courage and an inspiring feminist reminder: "nothing for you to seek forgiveness for. Every time the men leave, the women are the ones who ask for forgiveness. You were a good wife, bai. I saw it with my own eyes, day in and day out" (261). And when newly widowed Sera went into a state of depression, it was Bhima who recognized it and told Dinaz, prompting her to move in (292). Yet even such long intimacy, mutual obligation, and bonding cannot produce friendship or uncontaminated trust in the present between employer and servant; despite their individual efforts, both remain ambivalent about the other. Bhima's loyalty remains mixed with resentment; Sera's beneficence with revulsion. Through these dissonances, Umrigar suggests how power asymmetries maintain unbridgeable distances between servant and employer.

Umrigar also establishes a broader picture of servitude, highlighting both how Sera and Bhima's relationship is exceptional and how it compares with the norms between other servants and employers. As important points of comparison, Umrigar includes other more typical employers who, in contrast to Sera, are peremptory, demanding, and self-absorbed. Sera's old friend, Aban, complains about how she has to put up with the "nakhras" (capricious, unreasonable demands) of her maid, and tells Sera she is a "Communist" for defending servants' claims (172–173). Sera's father-in-law tells Sera that his wife is "driving [their servant] Gulab mad with her do-thises and do-thats" (193). Bhima's other employer, also a Parsi lady, is actively mean and nasty, bordering on the insane. She watches over Bhima washing dishes and insists that she must "purify" her house because Bhima, as a Hindu, has polluted it and must pay respects to Lord Zoroaster (294).

Compared to all this, Sera is a boon for Bhima. Nonetheless, Umrigar reminds us, the asymmetry of Bhima's and Sera's positions maintains a level of tension. Individual efforts cannot erase the systemic structural inequalities and consequent relation of domination and subordination between domestic helper and employer. The stunning revelation that Umrigar eventually leads us to is that despite the exceptionality of the relationship built between Bhima and Sera, when faced with the truth that might fracture her own family, the female employer will ultimately fail the woman who has served her so invaluably. Umrigar thus emphasizes the powerful forces that undo even the exceptional efforts of those willing to cross boundaries. The crisis of *Space* turns on the paradox that when pushed to the test, when forced to weigh what she considers her real "family" versus the domestic who helps maintain that family, even the most benign of employers fails disastrously to respond to the call of the domestic worker, to weigh equitably the serving woman's needs, to value adequately her work cementing the employer's family, or to recognize her implicit subordination of her own family's needs. Umrigar's novel puts the onus on readers to think of ways out, individual and systemic, that might honor such unacknowledged ties and ethical claims.

Familial Relations and Intergenerational Consequences of Servitude

Although Umrigar focuses on the relationship between Bhima and Sera in this novel, she also explores how their servant-employer dynamic extends to others in each woman's respective family. Servitude creates a nexus, a web of interdependence, that connects the family members of both servant and employer. The novel is thus also interested in elaborating how the lives of servants' and employers' families are affected by each other. In the past, the relationship between Sera and Bhima has extended to the men in their lives. When Bhima's husband Gopal got hurt in a factory accident, and lay dying of a post-surgery fever and infection in a government hospital after his hand was amputated, Bhima called Sera, whose intervention literally saved his life. Even Bhima's young son Amit knew Sera as a benefactor and beamed "with delight" when she arrived at the hospital (213). Because of Sera, Sera's husband Feroz also became involved. "This fellow is important to our family," Feroz told the neglectful doctor, making clear, "man-to-man," that he did not personally care about a poor man like Gopal, but that he cared about keeping his wife happy with a stable servant situation (215). That Feroz achieved what he wanted by bullying and threatening the lower-class doctor is part of Umrigar's point: in a system where class privilege enables routine mistreatment of those lower on the scale, only exertion and abuse of power are effective, for good or ill. Bhima herself was both indebted to Feroz and wary of Feroz. After Feroz's death, and the entry of Viraf, Sera's son-in-law, into the household, Bhima also serves Viraf, and both trusts and resents him. Feroz and Viraf depend in obvious ways on Bhima's housework for their daily comforts and benefit from the release from housework she provides for their wives.

In the present time of the novel, Umrigar focuses more on the criss-crossing female-to-female bonds that have built up over the years between Bhima and

Dinaz (Sera's daughter) and between Sera and Maya (Bhima's granddaughter). In highlighting the relationship between Bhima and Dinaz, Umrigar presents Dinaz as more exceptional than her mother, less curtailed by the prejudices and beliefs that hamper even Sera, as more exemplary in her progressive ideas and desire to combat social injustice. Dinaz is a figure suggestive perhaps of a new Indian generation (like Umrigar herself) that might take a less accepting approach to the vicissitudes of servitude in their homes.[15] Dinaz's own relationship with Bhima is based on uncomplicated childhood attachment. Sera remembers how, "from the time she was a little girl, Dinaz had never been able to tolerate one unkind word about Bhima," and when her father, Feroz, objected to "that woman... brainwashing" his child, Sera knew it was because "Dinaz saw more of Bhima than she did of Feroz and was treated with more kindness by the servant than by her own father" (68). Extending beyond her purview, Bhima quietly offered love and care to a child in an abusive home. As an adult, though she has given up her dream of being a social worker, Dinaz remembers, and retains her early attachment and solicitude for Bhima, and sense of "fair play" and "thirst for justice" (68). Sera also remembers how Bhima "used to dote on [Dinaz] when Dinaz was a little girl" (112). Bhima remembers that for her, "before there was Maya, there was Dinaz" (288). In the terrible scene at the end of the novel when Sera sacks Bhima and kicks her out of the house, and which I will discuss more below, "dazed" Bhima weeps that she must leave without taking leave of Dinaz, whom she has loved like her own child: " 'Serabai, it was never my desire to hurt you or baby,' she says. 'That girl is like my own' " (304). Umrigar thus highlights the complicated attachments that can form across the deep divides of class in situations of intimacy and care work despite the forces that keep people apart.[16] Bhima sees herself bound by powerful ties of maternal love to "baby," the child in whose home she has worked, in addition to her own flesh and blood.

Sera and Maya also have an unusual, though less tight, connection. Unlike other employers, Sera has taken an interest in her servant's grandchild and provided for her education. Sera remembers Maya as the "orphan girl, painfully thin" who arrived in Bombay with her grandmother after her parents died of AIDS in Delhi, and whom Sera "won over by giving her three pieces of Cadbury's chocolate day after day" (43). When young Maya responded in broken English, Sera decided that "this was an intelligent child and worthy of a life different from what her grandmother could give her" and that "she, Sera, would assume responsibility for Maya's education" (43–44). Again, as with Bhima, Sera exercises both concern and condescension, revealing both unusual compassion and classism. Her intervention is limited to those she sees as deserving; she reads Maya as intelligent because Maya already had some education, in English. (Later, as I discuss briefly below, in her 2016 sequel to this novel, *The Secrets Between Us*, Umrigar presents a better alternative to the matronizing approach of Sera.)

Sera and Maya's relationship is more complicated than Bhima and Dinaz's. When Maya agrees to have an abortion, she insists that Sera, not Bhima, accompany her. "You know they'll take better care of me if someone like her is with me," she says to Bhima (56). Bhima agrees because she knows that "Maya is right. Rich, confident, and well-spoken, Serabai has a way of making doors open like a magician" (56). Much after the abortion, Maya finally reveals to Bhima that it was Viraf who assaulted her. Before the abortion, unable to tell either Bhima or Sera this horrifying truth, Maya counts on Sera to protect her from medical mistreatment in a way that Bhima, as a lower-class woman, cannot. At the same time, to Bhima's horror and surprise, Maya lashes out at Sera in resentment, perhaps partly for what her son-in-law has done, but more clearly, because, unlike Bhima, the young adult college student Maya can see and challenge Sera's habitual condescension to Bhima. When Maya points out bitterly (and rightly) what Bhima does not question, that Sera trusts her apartment key to her neighbor but not to Bhima, Sera is shocked at what she sees as Maya's "hostility," "insolence," and "ingratitude" (118). Importantly, as we will see, it will take Maya's defamiliarizing truth-telling to undo the psychological hegemony of the culture of servitude that Bhima has internalized.

Later, when Bhima discovers that it was Viraf who was the cause of Maya's pregnancy, she realizes that there was another reason for Maya's insistence on Sera accompanying her, that Maya, in her silent resentment, wanted Sera to be involved, to participate unknowingly in the termination of her grandchild's half-sibling, to carry the guilt home to Viraf. Bhima "feels a moment's admiration for the girl. Maya had made sure that the Dubash family was implicated in her child's death, that some of the dark blood stained their hands forever" (282). The scene shows the intricate imbrication of the lives of the families, extending beyond the relationship between Sera and Bhima. As a result of their decades long association, Maya, as the servant's granddaughter and sole dependent, has both benefitted from her grandmother's employer's beneficence and become the victim of sexual assault from a member of Sera's family. Now, she both asks for more help, with the abortion, and makes sure that the family does not remain untouched by the consequences of Viraf's actions. Clearly, Umrigar suggests, servitude has complex and long-reaching consequences for servants' families and familial relationships.

Book One concludes with Maya's abortion and return with Sera from the clinic, with Sera feeling she has fulfilled her debt to Bhima by caring for and chaperoning Maya through this process. In the first half of the novel, Umrigar elucidates the relationship between Sera and Bhima, and shows how it extends to members of both their families. But this novel is also concerned with relationships *within* a servant's family, and how servitude as a system impacts the lives of servants' children and their children. Book Two shifts into the aftermath of the abortion, a pivot point for the novel, as Bhima and Maya begin to repair and rebuild their relationship. Bhima, in an effort to aid Maya's recovery, begins to take her every evening to the seaside and, in response to Maya's questioning, begins to narrate her past, in part to persuade Maya to continue her college education by demonstrating the disastrous consequences that have resulted for Bhima and her family from her illiteracy. Umrigar here emphasizes the cross-generational effects of servitude, the obstructions to the ability of servants to parent and grandparent, and the multiple accumulated disadvantages that are passed down to successive generations by the lack of material resources and the ability to provide guidance to acquire them.

For Bhima, it is now a point of pride, worn literally on the body, that her labor enables Maya's body not to wear the callused mark of menial servitude. The single, determined aspiration of her life is the attempt to build a different life for Maya, an escape from the intergenerational legacy of servitude that Bhima herself inherited. Bhima now knows that for Maya, the only "path" to a "good job . . . the escape from the menial, backbreaking labor that had marred the lives of her mother and her mother before her" is through a college education (21).

> As they walk, Bhima takes Maya's hands in hers. The softness of her granddaughter's hand never fails to thrill her. It is a source of pride to her, this hand, because Bhima has paid for this softness with her own sweat. She remembers her own hands at seventeen—hard and callused from working as a servant from the time she was a child. Ruined from a lifetime of handing the sharp, pointed bristles of the broom, of dipping her hands in ash to scour pots and pans until they sparkled. Maya had escaped that fate. So far. (133)

Umrigar's details call attention to the lasting bodily impact of servitude as arduous menial labor. Bhima is well aware that she has inherited servitude from her mother and passed it on to her own daughter Pooja. As a servant's child, Bhima had no access to education. In a vicious cycle, that lack of education, and her absorption of pernicious gender ideologies from her social environment, led Bhima to devalue education for her own daughter, to push Pooja (Maya's mother) into servitude to pay for Bhima's son Amit's education. Hence Bhima's servitude and lack of education led to her making bad choices that made her daughter also as servant, and actively denied Pooja both material resources and education to earn a better living. In obvious ways, that parental and grandparental lack has both directly and indirectly impacted Maya. Now, able to see the importance of education, and to avert the continuation of that cycle, Bhima is desperate to ensure that Maya should "build a different destiny for herself" (130).

Ironically, as Bhima now tells Maya, when her children were young, her husband Gopal wanted Pooja to be educated, but it was Bhima who opposed it. Now "she felt shame at the memory of how she had argued with Gopal against placing Pooja in school as he had wanted to.... 'She's a girl ... what does she need an education for?'" Bhima had said (204). She wanted Pooja's "extra income" to help pay for Amit's education so that if needed, he could "help his sister later in life" (204). Umrigar thus emphasizes the intersectional, wide-spreading, toxic impact of Bhima's legacy of servitude that led to this preferential treatment of a son, that not only added insult to injury by depriving Pooja of an education and life opportunities, forcing her into poverty at the expense of her brother, but also used her child servant labor to benefit and enrich Amit. Clearly, Bhima understood that in a world structured by gender discrimination, where Amit could succeed with the same education in ways that Pooja could not, this choice would husband the family's resources so that he could then provide for his sister. But, as Bhima subsequently learned, the golden goose could be stolen. To depend on the son providing for the daughter, instead of empowering the daughter to provide for herself, was a mistake, one that many in South Asia more educated than Bhima still continue to make.

Bhima has also learned, at high cost, how her illiteracy made her and her family vulnerable to unscrupulous exploitation and fraud. Because she could not read or write, she was tricked by Gopal's foreman into signing away Gopal's rights to workers' compensation while Gopal lay injured in the hospital (204). Coerced and overpowered by the factory employee who cheated his underclass subordinate to benefit the owners, and who abused his male power and privilege by literally taking Bhima's hand to push her thumbprint onto a contract she could not read, Bhima still blames herself for the inability that led to a chain of disasters: the family's impoverishment from the loss of Gopal's income; Gopal's anger and sense of betrayal; his turn to drinking and gambling; his feeling emasculated at being unable to provide for his family; and eventually, his abandonment of Bhima and Pooja to the city, when he took Amit with him back to his village. Hence the importance of education, Bhima reasserts to Maya with this cautionary tale, as the only way out of servitude and extreme precarity. "Now that Maya knows about her experience with the duplicitous accountant, surely she will understand even more how life treats those without an education," she thinks (246). And though she knows she has made it impossible for Maya to return to her college (by revealing Maya's pregnancy to a classmate), and that it would "awkward to ask Serabai for help to get [Maya] enrolled at a new college, for Maya's sake [she decides] she would ask" (246).

Education as a mode of escape from servitude is the novel's repeated refrain. Sera affirms the necessity of education as even more urgent for Maya than for Dinaz, precisely because Maya, with all the disadvantages of familial servitude, risks falling much further without education than Dinaz does. Sera imagines lecturing Maya on these realities: "Remember, without education, you are nothing. In this city, people with law degrees and Ph.Ds go hungry. . . . It is the same lecture she had given Dinaz years ago. But with Maya, she will add another threat. Without at least a bachelor's degree, you will spend your life sweeping other people's floors and washing their dirty dishes. Is this what you want for yourself—the same life that your mother and grandmother had?" (118). And, as Bhima realizes, someone like Viraf could never understand the immense consequences of his actions, how "his thoughtless pleasure had derailed her Maya's life, has blocked the path that would've taken the girl out of the slum" (283), nor what it means to Bhima:

> How to make him understand that when Maya left for college in the mornings, she used to feel as if everything she had ever gone through in her life—every deprivation, every insult, every betrayal—was worth it if she could provide her grandchild with a life better than what she [Bhima] and her mother and her mother's mother had known. (290)

Umrigar thus also emphasizes that it takes a collective effort, not only an individual one, to enable Maya to complete college and build a career. At the same time, Umrigar builds into this novel a clear recognition that education alone is no silver bullet, that it can at best work as mitigation of extreme indigence and subservience. While even without income, educated status brings some respect and social standing, Bhima also recognizes, on two important occasions, the limitations of education alone, that the world belongs to men with class power: when she sees Feroz bully the hospital doctor, and when Gopal comforts her for having succumbed to the foreman's trickery: "It doesn't matter. One way or the other, they would've tricked us. Because they own the world, you see. They have the machines and the money and the factories and the education. We are just the tools they use to get all these things," he tells her (226).[17] Nonetheless, Gopal's bitter but illuminating truth does not gainsay the greater *gendered* importance for Maya of education as a mode of escape from her inheritance of female servitude: as a woman, Maya cannot even work in a factory as her grandfather could.

Maya is harmed, however, in another way by her grandmother's servitude. As Bhima's granddaughter, Maya herself experiences both first-hand servitude and second-hand servitude. Both make her vulnerable to sexual predation by men in her employer's family. Maya is raped by Viraf because she works part-time for his mother-in-law providing "afternoon tea and dinner" to Sera's bedridden mother-in-law between two nurse shifts (her own servitude) (116). But Maya gets the job working for Sera only because Bhima works for Sera (second-hand servitude). Umrigar makes clear the disjunction between Bhima's and Sera's views of this arrangement. Bhima allows Maya to work for Sera because she sees it as safer for Maya, and can tell herself that Maya is helping Sera: "The thought of Maya working in the homes of strangers made the muscles in Bhima's stomach clench. Working for Serabai, it was easy to pretend that they were simply helping out a family member in need" (130). By contrast, Sera sees it as a way to help Maya, to provide some pocket-money via an "easy job" (116). However, Maya is exposed to Viraf because she is alone in this apartment with him, within the supposed trust and safety of this "family" (130). Umrigar thus highlights the different vicissitudes of domestic servitude for younger women: sexual exploitation when they are isolated and unprotected in the homes of employers without any surveillance. And she further highlights how hollow and dangerous is the rhetoric of family when it gives servants a false sense of security, and induces a (mis) placed trust that will only be betrayed. Umrigar thus builds in the nuances and complexities of South Asian servitude as a system that impacts more than just employer and employee, that produces a culture of extreme entitlement on the one hand, and multiple forms of vulnerability on the other.

Umrigar suggests, however, yet another potent, less obvious, way that Maya is harmed by Bhima's servitude: through Bhima's internalization of inferiority that leads her to overlook the claims of her own family, to show preference for her employers' family, and place undue trust in both Viraf and Sera. Bhima's psychological servitude endangers Maya when it prevents Bhima from suspecting Viraf (or protecting Maya from him), and in fact leads her to castigate Maya for what she assumes is sexual promiscuity. What damages Bhima and Maya's relationship is Bhima's betrayal of her own obligations to her orphaned grandchild, because of her misplaced trust in Sera's family and her consequent inability to trust or prioritize Maya. Hence it is eye-opening for Bhima when Maya reproaches her: "Why are you so fast to blame me for what happened? . . . Is it only your family that you must curse and blame for every act of wickedness and shame? . . . You just assumed that I was the one who did the evil deed. Why, Ma-ma? Why do you love their family even more than you love your own?" (269–270). The process of liberation is gradual, as we will see; it will take the shock of Sera's betrayal to bring home to Bhima the truth of Maya's words. Umrigar thus suggests that education offers a path not just out of material poverty and servitude, but also out of psychological servitude, that Maya's education enables her to educate Bhima, to counter-colonize her mind.

The Crisis, and Ending, of *Space*

Given the significance that *Space* allots to the multiple ramifications of servitude for families, and to the disproportionate impact on servants' families, it is not surprising that the crisis of this novel occurs when the claims of the employer's family directly conflict with those of the servant's family. The final crisis of the novel occurs when Bhima is forced to choose between Dinaz and her own grandchild, between maintaining an untruth that buys Dinaz's fragile happiness at the cost of the truth, and speaking up to defend her own and her grandchild's honor in the face of unjust accusations. When Sera fires Bhima, Umrigar highlights not only the obvious—the employer's asymmetric, unilateral power to terminate employment, and the serving woman's relative lack of agency—but also the consequent identity crisis and emotional disarray for the worker that far exceeds the economic loss of income and financial stability.

Sociologist Handagneu-Sotelo notes that in real domestic worker-vs-employer situations, conflicts often occur over seemingly trivial matters, flaring into "confrontations" where "both women say harsh, regrettable things—things that reveal deep antipathies, . . . as though the previously invisible fissures in their relationship were suddenly magnified and projected into plain view," and result in the worker being fired or walking out (55). Often these conflicts emerge from a discrepancy in the understanding of employer and employee of what the work entails, and hence a failure, on the employer's part, to recognize that "domestic work, especially when it involves childcare, produces relationships that fall somewhere between family and employment yet are often regarded as neither" (Handagneu-Sotelo, 67). The employer fails to respect the worker (or recognize that she is not the "employer's chattel"; 62), or to acknowledge the affective complexity of the work entailed (that "providing daily care for children or the elderly" is "inherently relational," and involves "emotional attachment, affiliation, and intimate knowledge"; 68). And indeed, in Umrigar's novel, this final conflict does surface the fissures in Sera and Bhima's relationship, invisible to them so far, and makes painfully visible the asymmetry of power and precariousness of that relationship. Both Sera and Viraf fail to appreciate fully the attachment and loyalty that Bhima bears to their family and particularly to Dinaz, whom she cared for as a child. As Handagneu-Sotelo also notes, the consequences of the abrupt termination of the relationship are far greater for the worker. What Umrigar adds to this understanding, however, is a powerful portrayal of the enormous emotional and psychological consequences of such a rupture—for Bhima—and the possibility of liberation from mental servitude.

The turning point of *The Space Between Us* occurs when Bhima discovers that Viraf raped Maya, and that Sera's daughter and Bhima's granddaughter are pregnant at the same time by the same man. Umrigar clearly emphasizes the gendered vulnerability to sexual exploitation occasioned by servitude, and excoriates Viraf's hypocrisy and abuse of privilege. But she focuses on the process of Bhima's mental decolonization, her gradual realization of her internalization of inferiority and cooptation by decades of servitude, her implicit trust in the superior goodness of Sera and Sera's family. After Maya challenges her, Bhima begins to see how, all along, she elevated her employer's family above her own, even in her moral judgments. Maya's questions bring an epiphany, revealing to Bhima how she has been hegemonized, how her belief in Sera's family's goodness blinded her into doing injustice to her own. "She remembers Maya's bitter words about how she has treated the Dubash family better than her own. The girl was right—she had slaved and worked for, protected and defended this family as if it were her own" (300–301).

Bhima's initial response, however, is still to protect Sera and Dinaz from this knowledge, rather than seek justice for Maya. She confronts Viraf but decides not to expose him:

> The only way she can hurt Viraf is to share his disgrace with Serabai and Dinaz, to watch the stain of his shame spread over their faces. And this she cannot do. To do this would mean to destroy the only two people who have ever treated her like a human being.... Before there was Maya there was Dinaz, and Dinaz had loved her with an abandon that perhaps only a child can muster.... And Serabai, tall, fair, a sentry who stood at the gates of hell and tried to keep Bhima from being snatched away by the infernal fires.... And now their destiny is in Bhima's hands. (288–289)

Torn between a beloved employer's child and her own, Bhima is able to separate her protectiveness of Sera and Dinaz from her fury at Viraf and desire to exonerate Maya. But Viraf cannot imagine that an illiterate servant woman could exercise such emotional discrimination or self-control. Afraid that Bhima will expose him, Viraf uses old servant stereotypes—dishonesty and unreliability—to manufacture a false accusation. He frames Bhima for stealing money, to get her sacked. Only when Bhima sees "the trap" that Viraf has set for her, does she realize that she had continued to misplace her trust, hegemonized into thinking of every member of the Dubash family as ultimately good, as above her: "she had preferred to believe that he would never strike her family again, that the knowledge that she knew about his guilt was enough to defang him" (300). Goaded beyond control by his threat of the police, and accused by Sera of talking in a "low class way," Bhima, "crazed with outrage and fury," reveals the dark secret that connects their two families: "'Ask him what he did to my Maya if you want the truth,' she says bitterly. Ask him what guilt he is trying to hide. He thinks he can buy my silence for seven hundred rupees?'" (302).

For the first time in their relationship, Bhima and Sera now clash over the families each sees as her own. Sera prioritizes her daughter's happiness over justice to Maya or responsibility to Bhima, while Bhima finally prioritizes her grandchild. Umrigar leaves no ambiguity regarding Sera's moral culpability: after a "stricken moment" when she looks at Viraf, "denial falls on [Sera's] face like a white veil" (303). In this climactic scene, Umrigar draws attention to the ethical failure of the employer, the betrayal of decades of connection and loyalty, and the abjection of the vulnerable older woman-servant. It is important to note here that Sera's lapse is not just a failure to recognize the claims of affective bonds or obligations, but a failure of justice regardless of feeling, a failure to do what is right, to take just action. Refusing to listen, Sera screams at Bhima and calls Maya a "whore," making clear just how hollow the rhetoric of family is: "Just don't involve my family in [Maya's] sickness.... Get out of my sight" (303). Bhima, in a state of shock, and returned to practical reality, abases herself at Sera's feet: "Sobs form like bubbles inside Bhima's throat and rock her frail body. 'Serabai, don't turn me away,' she begs. 'After all these years, where will I go?'" Weeping as she collects her "meager possessions," Bhima realizes she has nowhere to go, no identity apart from being Sera's servant (303). Umrigar's repeated description of Sera's face as "stony as a wall" (303) echoes her earlier description of Viraf's "stony face" (302), suggesting Sera's mirrored loss of humanity, suggesting how Sera has turned out to be a stone idol for Bhima, a member of the upper class that will ultimately cleave only unto their own.

Formally, Umrigar breaks the pattern of Sera and Bhima's alternating perspectives, just as Sera breaks the relationship. The novel ends, not with Sera, whom we never see again, but with Bhima, and her final awakening. The last four chapters are narrated from Bhima's perspective, as if Sera's psyche is no longer worthy of interest, and Bhima has become the only protagonist. Umrigar traces Bhima's changing reactions: Bhima wanders bereft, wondering how Sera will live knowing "her son in law's deceit" (307); is roused to anger, at Sera for accepting Viraf's "obvious lie over [Bhima's] obvious truth," and at herself for caring about another woman replacing her in Sera's house (311); decides to discard her remaining links with Sera—the cardboard box containing her comb, soap, and powder (312); and contemplates suicide. But then, Bhima remembers "a tall gaunt Pathan from Afghanistan," another poor migrant to this metropolis, who sold her children balloons by the seaside, as an exemplar of resilience, courage, and dignity in exile (97). "Empty-handed, he had built a world," she reflects. Recalled from despair by this memory of "loneliness with the recipe for overcoming loneliness," Bhima switches to "taking her orders from a different authority now, following the fluttering sound in her ears ... Freedom. She is almost grateful to Viraf baba now, for his treachery has been the knife that has cut the thread that kept her bound for so long" (314, 315).

This final realization is consolidated by an important symbolic act that bespeaks a certain agency and self-knowledge. The novel holds out no illusion that Bhima's practical problems will be solved. But before she can "confront the terrible reality of unemployment and finding work and all the humiliations that may entail," Bhima feels she "must do this one thing" (316). She spends her last coins buying balloons that she releases over the sea, as if letting go of her dependence on Sera. This seemingly frivolous act that makes her literally penniless can be read as a form of self-cleansing, self-care, and tribute to another destitute urban migrant who exemplified survival and self-reliance. It rehearses the courage that Bhima promises herself she will enact in the future. Bhima can only return to being herself, to mothering Maya, when she realizes how servitude had trapped her in a misplaced dependence on Sera. The novel concludes with Bhima's resolve to continue living, for Maya, and to depend on herself: "A new day. She will face it tomorrow.... along with the rest of Bombay's [poor]" (320).

Umrigar's resolution, while optimistic, has its limitations. First, the relegation of Sera to silence without any further access to her consciousness or perspective seems a narrative cop-out. How are readers to make sense of Sera's failure? Second, the abrupt termination of Sera's family's story and of Sera's perspective renders the narrative mystifyingly incomplete. Umrigar ends that family's story on a cliff-hanger, leaving them on the precipice of Sera's action, as if uninterested in pursuing their story. Readers might question the implausibility of this conclusion. What, we might wonder, will happen when Dinaz returns and finds Bhima gone? Is Dinaz, with her feisty egalitarianism, likely to accept Bhima's dismissal without protest or suspicion? Umrigar also ignores, as do both Sera and Bhima, the important question of whether Dinaz would want to be kept in the dark or stay with such a man were she to know the truth. They overlook the fact that the marital happiness they maternalistically buy Dinaz is founded on a terrible illusion.

Third, Umrigar's ending also leaves in doubt the question of Bhima's (and Maya's) future. Bhima's psychological release from bondage to Sera does not solve the problem of how Bhima will survive, nor does it secure her release from servitude, poverty, and continued degradation. Servitude extends into the outside world, and is not restricted to the boundaries of the home. Bhima does not stop being a servant when she leaves Sera's apartment. She carries her identity of servant with her wherever she goes. Early in the novel, we see how Bhima is treated badly by shopkeepers, who know she is shopping for her mistress, not for herself. When Bhima reproaches the shopkeeper for cheating and giving them rotten potatoes hidden among the good ones, the shopkeeper turns nasty, "It's not your money you're spending, it's your mistress's," he flashes back at Bhima. "You could never afford my wages and my prices, you old woman. Now stop wasting my time" (106). Over and over again, lower-class men treat Bhima with contempt, in stark contrast to their fawning obsequiousness with Sera or other upper-class women. Even at the end, when Bhima is buying balloons with her own money after she has been fired, and is technically no longer a servant, the balloon seller assumes she cannot be buying something so frivolous for herself, and asks conversationally, "Buying for a party for your mistress's house" (317). " 'I have no mistress,'" Bhima replies curtly, realizing how glad she is to be released from that relational identity (317). But servitude is not an identity that is easily shed, not in the eyes of the world, nor even of the servant's own. Bhima is aware that though she has lost this particular mistress, she will have to look for another one, "approach [another family] for another job," that she will remain a servant (316). Even if Bhima can be released from the psychological dependence she has developed with Sera, she cannot end the economic precarity, subordination, and defining identity that come with servitude.

And fourth, while Bhima's determination to persist and her sense of solidarity with Bombay's destitute struggling "millions" (321) can be seen as a tribute to the strength of "the real Bhima and the millions like her" to whom the novel is dedicated, the novel concludes with a solution that is ultimately located in the realm of the private, psychological, and individual, not of the public, collective, or systemic. Bhima's awakening represents an important moment of recovery of strength and independence for her, but includes a troubling tendency for Bhima to blame herself alone, and carries no consciousness of systemic oppression and exploitation, or an expansion of her predicament to other servants or to servitude as a system. Nor is it a solution to the problems that the novel has presented all along: the degradations and exploitations of a cultural system of servitude; the poverty and inequality that are exacerbated by a neoliberal economy; patriarchy coupled with the lack of education that makes illiterate Bhima fall victim to the factory manager who tricks her into signing away her husband's rights to worker's compensation after his crippling injury; the lack of state support, safety nets, or social services such as public healthcare that lead to Bhima's daughter's death from AIDS and the horrific conditions her family suffers; the callous disrespect Bhima suffers from male doctors, educators, clerks, shopkeepers, neighbors, and others who see Bhima as unworthy of humane treatment; and, finally, Sera's betrayal.

These are important shortcomings, though some points can be made in mitigation. The endings of servitude fiction are necessarily difficult to craft because they pose formal (as well as thematic and political) challenges. How is realist fiction to construct a narratively and politically satisfactory resolution that grants agency to the domestic servant while honoring the realities of her disempowerment? *Reef* and *The White Tiger* suggest escape from servitude for the young male servant (respectively through education and business patronage or brutal opportunistic enterprise) only if he can cut off all ties to his past and sacrifice his family. The latter may be more possible for the satiric mode of a novel like *The White Tiger*, less constrained by the bounds of social realism. However, *Space* cannot plausibly present such an option within the limits of its realist framework, nor can it magically transform its world into one where servitude (or the conditions that produce it) does not exist. Though Umrigar deploys the sentimental and melodramatic idiom of mid-nineteenth-century Victorian fiction (not unlike

Charles Dickens or Harriet Beecher Stowe), she cannot resort to conventional forms of closure to resolve the considerable difficulties she presents so well.[18]

It is worth recognizing, therefore, what Umrigar does achieve and what interventions, as servitude fiction, *Space* makes. First, in making a total shift to Bhima and eliminating Sera's narrative and perspective, Umrigar's conclusion seems deigned to thwart, and perhaps restructure, readers' expectations and novelistic conventions. Umrigar chooses deliberately to focus, not on the bourgeois protagonist or her realization, but on Bhima and her gradual change of perspective. In influential nineteenth-century British and American fiction such as George Eliot's *Middlemarch*, or Henry James' *A Portrait of a Lady*, which defined the form, the young upper-class female protagonist experiences betrayal and crisis at the structural center of the novel, going through anguish and turbulence before arriving at strength or resolve, enabling her therefore to move on to make better choices. *Middlemarch* concludes in a happy (second) marriage, while in *Portrait*, Isabel Archer gathers the strength to leave her manipulative husband. In Umrigar's novel, the experience of anguish and epiphany for the elderly servant are situated at the *end* of the novel, after Bhima wanders alone along a beach, wondering whether to kill herself or to struggle on for her granddaughter. Her eventual determination to carry on, finding courage in the example of destitute others, might seem tenuous, but it represents an important change in the conventional plot or form of the Victorian novel. Despite its idiom of sentimentality, at the level of plot and tone, *Space* repudiates sentimental solutions of reunion or reconciliation, holding out no hope that Sera will rethink her actions and come after Bhima, or that Bhima will find another protectress. She leaves open the question of how, despite her fortitude, Bhima will survive, inviting her transnational readers—upper-class Indians and non-Indians alike—to reflect on broader questions of state, institutional, and social responsibility. Leaving us with Bhima as the novel's real protagonist, Umrigar poses Bhima's uncertain future as the prompt for a politicized consciousness of the nation's responsibilities, asking readers to pay attention to the lack of a safety net or social services, gendered and class oppression, and the problems of the system of servitude in a neoliberal economy.

As imaginative work, fiction can both critique existing ills and suggest possible imagined alternatives. Umrigar offers both a powerful critique of the systems it makes visible, and a brief gesture, through a tantalizing glimpse, toward a possible solution. Sera's angry neighbor cites, as a terrible (imagined) outcome of Sera's encouragement of servants' claims, the formation of a domestic workers' "trade union" (28). What the neighbor views as threat is precisely what the novel suggests as a possible solution (28). (Part of the problem of organizing collective bargaining for domestic servants is that they are separated and isolated in employers' homes without a common space to gather, as Ray and Qayum note;

198.) Though *Space* does not, or cannot, present fuller political reform, in the absence of plausible solutions within the reality of the world it creates, the novel does important cultural work in asking its readers to rethink, to understand, to see differently.

Thus, in highlighting the employer's ethical failure, *Space* suggests its different goals. Umrigar gives us no further access to Sera's consciousness, but leaves it to her readers to take the responsibility of finding solutions. A key point about the ending is that Sera fails to recognize what the novel asks its *readers* to recognize: their responsibility to the domestic workers who constitute their societies and their lives. It asks that we reconsider our notions of family and ethical responsibility, precisely by way of the outrage it evokes at Sera's final behavior and the silence to which it relegates her consciousness. Indeed, I would argue that *Space* seeks to inculcate in its readers the very imaginative and empathetic reach into otherness that it exposes as lacking even in such employers as Sera. By formally inviting readers into the interiority and consciousness of someone subject to social subordination, by refusing to subject the servant to narrative subordination, by highlighting conflicting positionalities from within through the use of alternating perspectives, Umrigar's novel attempts to intervene in how readers understand their worlds. *Space* calls attention to the distinctive problems of domestic servitude, the complex gendered micropolitics inevitable between even exceptionally benign employers and employees, the configurations of female servitude in modern urban environments, and the obligations of the educated middle class to the underclass on whom they intimately depend. Umrigar does quietly propose some imagined alternatives: she gestures toward the protections afforded by collective bargaining, and (through Dinaz and Maya, the educated next generation, if not through Sera) a rethinking and restructuring of the systemic culture of servitude that undergirds the South Asian elite, in order to make the promises of postcoloniality available to all.

Second, though Umrigar seems to leave the problem of Dinaz unaddressed, she takes it up, briefly, in a sequel. In 2018, Umrigar published another novel, *The Secrets Between Us*, as a sequel to *Space*. *Secrets* opens three days after *Space* ends, with Dinaz arriving at Bhima's slum lodging with a request to return, and thirty thousand rupees as money owed to Bhima from her month's salary and her savings stored with Sera (to which Dinaz contributes another ten thousand). This money enables Maya to return to college. However, when Bhima determines that Dinaz still does not know the truth, that she has come without Sera or Viraf's knowledge, and that Sera has not admitted to believing Bhima over Viraf, Bhima refuses to return to work for the Dubash family. But Bhima still does not tell Dinaz the truth. Umrigar thus emphasizes both Bhima's pride and moral stance, and Sera's continued moral failure. Later in the novel, Sera does admit privately to Bhima that she believed her, but had to maintain the fiction of Viraf's innocence to maintain her daughter's marriage. (This reconciliation remains incomplete because even when Sera later appears, torn by her choice, and tries to reconcile, she does not rise to the level of exposing Viraf. Hence both Sera and Bhima still collude to maintain the problematic conspiracy of silence that keeps Dinaz in blissful ignorance about her husband.) Umrigar's important point, however, is that Bhima cannot and does not return to serving Sera. Instead, unlike *Space*, *Secrets* imagines another way out of servitude for Bhima herself (and not only for Maya), as Bhima starts to learn how to run a small business as a fruit vendor in partnership with another destitute old woman, Parvati. *Secrets* continues to absent Sera, and instead alternates Bhima's story and perspective with that of Parvati, who was sold into prostitution as a child, and whose life story offers a yet more harrowing saga of gendered descent into exploitation and abuse because of agricultural disaster and abject poverty. Finally, as if to address the third problem I name above, this sequel to *Space* completes the story of Bhima and Maya: Bhima builds an independent economic enterprise; Maya completes her college education and prepares to become a lawyer; and Bhima, in a highly contrived and saccharine ending, reunites with her long-lost son and husband.

To her credit, in this sequel, Umrigar also attempts to offer her readers better imagined alternatives to the kind of employer Sera was even at the best of times. *Secrets* presents as exemplary the figure of Chitra, the Australia-returned lesbian partner of Bhima's new mistress, Sunita. An Indian woman who left India because of its oppressive practices (and who repudiates "stupid customs" like the maintenance of separate utensils for servants; 34), Chitra both prompts Bhima to rethink the status quo she has taken for granted, and provides a better contrast to Sera in her sincere, unrestricted egalitarianism, respect for Bhima, and care for Maya. As Bhima realizes, Chitra "treats Bhima as a respected aunt, rather than as a servant" (131). In retrospect, Bhima sees that unlike Sera, "Chitra treats her as if they are equals" (150), that where Sera gave "charity," Chitra offers Bhima and Maya "friendship" (289). Umrigar suggests that Chitra does so because she has also known cruel social repudiation and marginality, that she is egalitarian because she is queer. After witnessing Chitra targeted by homophobia, Bhima understands that "Chitra's treatment of her was deliberate, a resolve to not inflict on others the kind of pain she herself had known" (154). Unfortunately, worthy though Chitra is as an individual model of an upper-class woman who breaks the mold of South Asian servant-employer relations, as an argument, this connection remains untenable. As we know, and as endless historical examples confirm, one form of social marginality does not automatically produce solidarity or understanding of another. (Men who face racism can be sexist and reinforce patriarchy, women who face sexism still oppress their servants, and so on.)

Finally, to return to *Space*, though the novel does not offer a solution to the systemic problem of servitude, nor does Bhima's final epiphany and psychological break from Sera include an understanding of servitude as systemic, the novel does include throughout an understanding of the system, and of servitude as a cultural, political, and *national* problem.

Umrigar suggests that, while domestic servitude has a long history in India, late twentieth-century structures of neoliberal economic and social inequality, and national/political choices condition Bhima's life, that the conditions that structure Bhima's life are the result of state failures. Like *The White Tiger*, *Space* is set after the 1991 Indian policies of economic "liberalization" that shifted from post-Independence socialism and protectionism to deregulation, increased privatization, foreign investment, IMF debt, consequent SAPs (structural adjustment policies), and cutbacks in social programs, and led to greater poverty and income inequality. Early in the novel, Bhima thinks about the changes in the city, reflected in its name change to Mumbai: "in today's Bombay, it was everybody for himself, and the frail, the weak, the young, and the old entered the overflowing buses at their own peril. Bhima felt as if she barely recognized the city anymore—something snarling and mean and cruel had been unleashed in it" (91). Previously unknown foreign consumer goods—from chocolate, perfume, to air-conditioned cars—flood the markets, and there are constant references to American goods and culture that fascinate the rich, while the poor and vulnerable are more unprotected. An angry shopkeeper "sneers" at Bhima: "'Everything in Mumbai is rotten,' he says loudly. 'The air, . . . the politicians, . . . the public transportation system'" (99). It is, after all, this unscrupulous, union-busting, profit-driven, late capitalist system that lies at the heart of Bhima's troubles, for her family breaks up after her husband's fingers are chopped off in a factory accident even after he warned the manager that the machine was malfunctioning: "Cheaper to pay off a worker like me than to stop for a day to get the machine fixed," he says bitterly (225). Domestic servitude in India is not new, but the specifics of Bhima's conditions of servitude are structured by the new economy and postcolonial (or neocolonial) national decisions that are shaped by larger forces of globalization and dynamics of unequal power between Global North and South. As we will see in the next chapter, Kiran Desai takes on more explicitly these connections between postcolonial servitude within the nation and the effects of globalization, neoliberalism, and neocolonialism.

7
Legacies of Servitude, Global and Local
Kiran Desai's *The Inheritance of Loss*

The Inheritance of Loss opens with a tableau of the judge's chilly household at teatime, introducing its inhabitants, each isolated in his or her own space: Sai, reading on the verandah, glancing up at the towering fog-covered mountain before her; the judge, playing chess by himself; and the cook, working in the "cavernous kitchen, trying to light the damp wood" to make their tea (1). The "cook," as if reduced to his function, is not named, unlike even Mutt, the judge's miniature dog, who cowers under a chair. But from the beginning, Desai calls attention to the outsiderhood and precariousness of the cook, as he works his way around the dark, dank kitchen, literally separate from the main house, and tries to avoid the deadly scorpions that live in the woodpile. Delicately, she invites us into the cook's interiority, his experience of selfhood, and bodily sense of being, as she describes the flame from the fire that overheats him, and the cold that "torture[s] his arthritic knees" (2). By contrast, she presents the self-absorption of the judge, whose awareness of others is limited to the degree that they can provide for his comfort. His first words, addressed to his granddaughter, "Where is the tea," bespeak his expectation both of her and of the cook (2). This opening sets up the Kalimpong household, the main characters and their dynamics, and establishes the servant's interiority as of equal interest to that of his employers'.[1]

Published criticism on this novel, as I elaborate below, tends to overlook Panna Lal the cook, perhaps because Desai chooses to keep him unnamed until the end. Critics usually identify as the main characters Sai, her math tutor Gyan, her grandfather Jemubhai Patel (the judge), and Biju, the cook's son.[2] Those who address minor characters include other regularly named characters: the neighbors Noni and Lola, Uncle Potty and Father Booty, or Bjiu's friend Saeed Saeed. But critics do not include the cook among the major characters, nor do they notice that his perspective and experiences occupy as much narrative space as those of the named major characters.[3] As I will show, this figure of the servant in this novel both occupies significant character space and connects, through the novel's emphasis on domestic servitude and its intergenerational consequences, its explorations of the neoliberal postcolonial state's disarray, ethnic strife, neo-nationalism, intra-state and transnational migrancy, globalization, and the consequent plight of undocumented domestic workers like Biju.

Postcolonial Servitude. Ambreen Hai, Oxford University Press. © Oxford University Press 2024.
DOI: 10.1093/oso/9780197698006.003.0008

From the start, Desai highlights the cook's voice and perspective. Unlike Sai, who thinks about both the "profound" isolation of the giant squid that may (like her) live without ever encountering another of its tribe, and her new romance with Gyan, her young science tutor, the cook thinks about his son, his own loneliness, and his aging body, as he mutters partly to himself and partly to Sai:

> "Terrible," he said. "My bones ache so badly, my joints hurt—I may as well be dead. If not for Biju..." Biju was his son in America. He worked at Don Pollo—or was it The Hot Tomato? Or Ali Baba's Fried Chicken? His father could not remember or understand or pronounce the names, and Biju changed jobs so often, like a fugitive on the run—no papers. (3)

Whereas Umrigar gives us Bhima's perspective through third-person narration, Desai uses three narrative techniques at once, as exemplified in this passage: the cook's own voice, as he complains and expresses self-pity; the narrator's external comment, explaining who Biju is; and free indirect discourse, as the narrator conveys in shorthand, via a barely noticeable shift, the cook's internal sense of confusion, his sorrowful inability to recall where his son works, itself a sign of their separation and disconnection, as well as his constant preoccupation with his beloved and only child.[4]

Thus from the beginning, Desai makes clear how the cook is treated in this house and delineates the microdynamics among the trio that inhabit it. The Anglophile judge irritably demands something to eat with his tea, in the English style to which he is accustomed, without deigning to address the cook; Sai, more sympathetic and understanding of the cook, acts as intermediary and tries to appease her grandfather by explaining that there is no kerosene or gas. "Why the hell can't he make it over wood? All these old cooks can make cakes perfectly fine by building coals around a tin box.... Just too lazy now," he responds (4). These domestic micropolitics are interrupted by (or coupled with) national macropolitics, with the arrival of a group of gun-carrying Gorkha boys, a "ragtag army" of insurgents, Indian Nepalis seeking a separate homeland from India, who demand the judge's rifles. With an undercutting edge of humor, Desai defuses the alarming potential of this scene, commenting on how each acts according to a preexisting gendered and classed script: Sai as frightened heroine in a Bollywood film; the boys as self-imagined romantic heroes-*cum*-rebels; the judge as dignified, calm adult.

But Desai reserves the most attention for the cook, who takes it upon himself to enact the role of the self-abasing abject servant, begging for mercy, almost as a strategy to set the boys at ease, to avert what he recognizes as real danger:

> The cook was hiding under the table and they dragged him out.
>
> "*Ai aaa, ai aaa*," he joined his palms together, begging them, "please, I'm a poor man, please." He held up his arms and cringed as if from an expected blow.

"He hasn't done anything, leave him," said Sai, hating to see him humiliated, hating even more to see that the only path open to him was to humiliate himself further.

"Please living only to see my son please don't kill me please *I'm a poor man spare me.*"

His lines had been honed over centuries, passed down through generations, for poor people needed certain lines; the script was always the same, and they had no option but to beg for mercy. The cook knew instinctively how to cry. (6)

Desai's narrator's unusual commentary makes clear that the cook enacts a role that he has been forced to learn as a mode of survival, a legacy of centuries of self-abasement of the powerless before the powerful. Desai thus calls attention to the strategies of negotiation that the cook's condition of servitude necessitates, elicited by this crisis of postcolonial nationalism. Sai alone cringes as they all witness the cook's self-humiliation, his sacrifice of dignity, as he enacts clownish abjection as a mode of self-preservation. At the same time, his unpunctuated utterance also repeats his single desire, his raison d'etre, "living only to see my son," emphasizing his identity as a father, and not only as a poor man and servant (6). This combination of poignancy with humor, or enhancement of poignancy because of humor, becomes a distinctive aspect of Desai's representation and exploration of servitude in this novel. Soon, as we will see, the cook also becomes the butt of Desai's humor. Unlike Umrigar, Desai uses humor at the expense of the servant, though, as I will suggest, Desai's use of humor is complicated: as he uses humor both to put the cook down and to elicit compassion for him.

Here, the cook's tactic succeeds, as the boys laugh at him, demanding that he make them fried *pakoras*, which he does, "wailing and pleading for his life" (7). By contrast, the boys' treatment of the judge and his response are, unsurprisingly, very different. Motivated by class resentment and ethno-national grievance, and invested in humiliating this representative of Indian political and economic power, the Gorkhas force the judge into his own kitchen, "where he had never been not once," turning "the world upside down" for Sai and the cook (who are "too scared to look"), demanding that the judge lay the tablecloth for them and say "Jai Gorkha" and "I am a fool" (7–8).[5] The judge complies through tight lips, refusing to demean himself, not pleading or begging, until again, the cook's comical response breaks the tension. "Gorkhaland for Gorkhas," echoes Sai, to appease them; "I am a fool," adds the cook, unasked (8). Desai thus highlights the classed and gendered differences among the three, accentuated by the crisis: the judge refusing to kowtow, even as he complies at gunpoint to doing unaccustomed housework that he knows is designed to ridicule him; Sai humbling herself even as she maintains a classed, feminine distance; and the cook, abjecting himself and doing the domestic work expected of him by all. In this tense situation, laced with comedy, Desai keeps the cook in the foreground equally with Sai and the judge, sharing narrative space equally between the employers and the servant.

Indeed, the narrative focus stays with the cook more than with Sai or the judge. When the boys leave, the cook alone breaks down, lamenting in idiomatic Hindi, "*Humara kya hoga, hai hai, humara kya hoga*," which Desai translates as "what will become of us" (9). However, "humara" could also refer in the singular to the cook alone, voicing his sense of himself as the most vulnerable of the three. "Shut up" the judge rebukes him roughly (9). Desai's portrayal of the judge as unsympathetic and contemptuous distances readers from such classed, prejudiced perceptions of the servant. Through this introductory scene, Desai emphasizes, despite the crisis that all three in the house share together, both the differential treatment of the cook by all, and his different behavior, infused with his knowledge of everyone's awareness of his lowly status, and his behavior thereby in accordance, in performance of that servitude. Yet narratively, Desai makes the cook is an equal participant in the household drama, sharing equal character space with his employers. He does not disappear into the background of her story. His subordinate social status, in Woloch's terms, does not relegate him to lesser importance in the narrative itself. Desai's intersectional depiction of the cook highlights differences of class and gender to show how they interlock to constitute his experience, his actions, and his sense of self.

From this emblematic beginning, Desai's narrative further develops the interpersonal dynamics within this household. Desai gives the cook balanced attention, alternating the perspectives of the cook, Sai, and the judge within the same chapter and from chapter to chapter, sometimes so unnoticeably that they seem to bleed into each other. Like Umrigar, Desai alternates characters' perspectives, but unlike Umrigar, Desai does not demarcate separate chapters for servant vs employer. (Desai does use separate chapters for Biju's narrative in the United States, which, as I elaborate below, connect the issue of postcolonial servitude in India to transnational migrancy and the multi-faceted intergenerational consequences of servitude.) Instead, Desai blends the cook's perspectives in more seamlessly with Sai's and the judge's, highlighting the connections, despite the differences. Sometimes a memory or history is triggered by an act or overheard conversation between the other two, sometimes an event or shared experience elucidates their different reactions, or different memories. For instance, the sound of the cook's voice telling fabricated stories about her grandmother to Sai in the kitchen reaches the judge's ears in the drawing room and triggers memories of his past and of his grotesque mistreatment of his wife, which neither the cook nor Sai will ever know (64). This narrative mode and form suggest both the gaps and the interconnections among the three characters, emphasizing their distances and their relationality as they respond to the same thing, shifting from one perspective and story to another. Desai blurs the shift from one to the other and calls for comparison as she highlights their similarities and differences, their knowledge and ignorance about each other.

In the next section, I focus on this interplay of perspectives, memories, thoughts, and feelings among the cook, Sai, and the judge, and in particular on Desai's evocation of the cook's psychology, interiority, and sensibility. Emphasizing Desai's attention to interiority and micropolitics in the relationships among these characters, I focus on the complex cross-generational, cross-gender, and cross-class dynamic between Sai and the cook, though I also attend to the same-gender dynamic between the judge and the cook, and the contrast it implicitly provides with the relationship between Biju and his employers in the United States. Notably, Biju does not have the closeness with his employers' families that the cook has with Sai, nor does he suffer the kind of abuse that the cook does at the hands of the judge. I also address how Desai presents the cook as at once pathetic and comical, endearing, and ridiculous, creating a mode of representation and affect that ranges from the empathetic to the distancing. I then shift in the following section to the intergenerational and secondhand effects of servitude (as with the previous chapter on Umrigar), to examine how Desai presents the relationship between the cook and his son, and the limited options that servant fathers can provide for their children. And finally, I conclude with the crisis at the end, and how Desai, with much greater irony and less sentimentality than Umrigar, addresses the problem of resolution and the future of the servant and his son. I thus argue in this chapter that Desai extends her exploration of postcolonial servitude beyond the borders of the nation to include not only the complexities of cook's narrative, but also of Biju's narrative, to suggest how servitude within the nation extends intergenerationally and internationally in the form of secondhand servitude.

Literary scholars have recognized from the start how *Loss* connects the issues of contemporary globalization, migrancy, and marginalization with (neo) colonialism, imperialism, and postcoloniality. In an important and influential early assessment, Paul Jay argues against the tendency of some scholars to view contemporary globalization as a new phenomenon disjunct from earlier problems created by ethnic rivalries and postcolonial nationalist struggles, and instead argues for the continuity and mirroring of the two, as elaborated in *Loss*.[6] Identifying two main "stories" or "narratives" in the novel by their location— Biju's in New York City, and the other characters in Kalimpong—Jay sets up a comparison between Biju's story as a member of an exploited "underclass of transnational diasporic workers" and the experiences of Sai, Gyan, and the judge, but without giving attention to the cook who in fact connects them (120). Jay also reads the novel as divided between two points of view—Biju's and Sai's (124)—and the problems of Westernization and mobility, hence comparing the journeys of Biju and the judge, and the predicaments of Biju and Gyan. While illuminating, this approach unfortunately sidelines the cook and the issues that his presence in this novel raises.

Others have also focused on globalization and its links to various issues. Angela Poon addresses the costs of globalization highlighted by the novel's use of affect and "hidden private narratives" of the likes of Biju (547). Oana Sabo emphasizes diaspora as a key concept in thinking about *Loss*, as the outcome of both "British colonialism and American neo-imperialism" (381), and argues that "diaspora represents both a socio-political formation and a narrative strategy that underscores socio-economic inequalities in the world and invites readers to think critically about immigration and global capitalism" (375). Elizabeth Jackson explores the usefulness and shortcomings of the concept of cosmopolitanism, which she defines as "an attitude cultivated partly in response to the reality of globalization" (29), and argues, with the examples of Sai's Anglophile neighbors and Biju, that neither elite nor migrant status leads necessarily to cosmopolitanism (38–39). Though she claims, inaccurately, that postcolonial perspectives preclude attention to "class divisions" (37), I find it ironic that she fails to attend to the cook (while focusing on Biju and the judge), and hence to class divisions within the domestic space of the home and the nation. What is needed, to my mind, is more of an intersectional analysis that pays attention to not just abstract, broadly theorized concepts, but to the microdynamics and interplay of specific situational particularities of class, gender, ethnicity, age, and so on.

Still others have focused on related issues, such as violence and terrorism as addressed in the novel. Margaret Scanlon includes *Loss* in her examination of three postcolonial novels written after 9/11 that address terrorism to show how each unsettles the conflation that dominant Western discourses create between "Muslim and terrorist" or immigrant and revolutionary (266). Scanlon argues that the novel uses "disjunctive chronology to prevent the plot of terrorism and counter-terrorism from taking over" and breaks down binaries, so that "in Desai's world the insurgents and terrorists stay home, and the poor go to America to join the underclass, where they are exploited, if not exactly terrorized" (272).

While indebted to the work of these scholars, my focus is somewhat different. Without gainsaying the importance of the connections between globalization and postcolonialism constructed by this novel, I emphasize how the cook and the issue of domestic servitude both crucially connect these issues and how Desai makes servitude in itself a significant issue worthy of attention and exploration. As always, taking an intersectional approach, I explore how Desai elucidates the intricacies of various relationships and psyches as constituted by the interlocking differences of class, gender, age, and so on. As in Adiga's *The White Tiger*, in Desai's *Loss*, the literal servitude of the cook becomes a prism for the failures of the postcolonial state (the disparities of wealth and power, the lack of social services and legal protections, the mistreatment of the poor by state officials like the police). But, through the cook's connection to Biju, Desai also explores the connections among contemporary postcoloniality, global servitude, and migrant labor. It is worth noting that while Biju clearly exemplifies the push-pull effects of transnational service work, Panna Lal his father is also a migrant worker who has journeyed widely within India, from his home village in Eastern Uttar Pradesh to live in Kalimpong, and accompanied the judge "always on tour" around the country for his work under the British (68). Where Biju is an external migrant (from India to the United States), Panna Lal is an internal migrant (from village to city, within India).[7] Moreover, I would contend, domestic servitude in *Loss* is significant not only because it is a mode of connection between its key themes of postcolonialism and globalization, but because it is a vital theme in itself. My goal in what follows is to elucidate how and why that is the case, to unravel Desai's fine delineation of the cook's interiority and his complex relationships, to show how Desai makes the complex of servitude in itself worthy of attention as she focuses on the intricacies, affects, psychological contradictions, and intergenerational consequences of servitude. Paying attention to the cook and to servitude, I suggest, enables us to read this novel afresh.

Interiority and Micropolitics Between the Servant and His Employers

From the beginning, Desai sustains narrative interest in the cook and his perspective, emphasizing the complexity of his reactions, relationships, and understanding of his precarious position in the world. The day after the robbery, the judge sends the cook to fetch the police, even though the cook "protested, knowing from the same accumulated wisdom of the ages that had led him to plead before the intruders that this was not a sensible idea" (11). The judge can dismiss peremptorily, from his position of privilege, the cook's knowledge, learned from generations of poverty and servitude, that the police, as underpaid state officials, would mistreat him and not take him seriously. As does most servitude fiction, Desai suggests that those placed below and targeted by those in power, can see and anticipate the misuse of power against them that those placed above cannot see. (Hence the truism that the view from below is fuller and more accurate than from above, because those privileged cannot see their own privilege.) Desai provides in full the eminent logic of the cook's thought process: "Always bad luck, the police, for if they were being paid off by the robbers, they would do nothing, and if, on the other hand, they were not, then it would be worse, for the boys who came the evening before would take their revenge" (11). We are asked to understand how the cook, at the bottom of every scale, caught between corrupt police and lawless rebels, lives in fear of each form of (masculine) power, knowing that he is unprotected and vulnerable to both. To all this the judge can be oblivious. Hence again the cook longs "for his son, Biju," imagining that at least "a young man on their side" would provide some protection. And again, through free indirect discourse, Desai conveys the cook's voice, his fear, and his consequent enactment of abjection, as he seeks to appease, to avert potential violence through self-diminution and self-abjection:

> In his trembling message, brought forward as if by the motion of his wringing hands, he tried to emphasize how he was just the messenger. He himself had nothing to do with anything and thought it was not worth it to bother the police ... He was a powerless man, barely enough learning to read and write, had worked like a donkey all his life, hoped only to avoid trouble, lived on only to see his son. (12)

Similar to the kind of compassionate narration that Mueenuddin employs, but with an undertone of humor, Desai moves back and forth between the servant's interiority and an external perspective that shows us more than the servant can see. The novel both validates the cook and shows the limitations of his understanding as the police both make clear "their scorn for him" and take seriously the invasion of a judge's home. With nuance, the narrator ensures that readers understand the policemen's view of this complex hierarchy: "As a servant, he was far beneath them, but the robbery of guns from a retired member of the judiciary could not be ignored" (12).

Unlike Umrigar, who oscillates clearly between the perspectives of Bhima and Sera, Desai moves almost imperceptibly among multiple characters' perspectives, interspersed with objective third-person narration. Keeping the cook in the foreground, Desai describes, for example, how the police arrive and deferentially interview the judge, how the cook volunteers that the boys made the judge "set the table and bring the tea," unintentionally making the policemen laugh, and displeasing the judge: "The judge's mouth was a straight grim line. 'Go sit in the kitchen. *Bar bar karta rehta hai*'" (12). It is rare for this usually restrained, Anglophile, self-made man to use Hindi, which Desai does not translate (the judge means that the cook keeps talking nonsense, and butting in unnecessarily), and which is a measure of the judge's annoyance. The judge's humble origins, elaborated later in the novel, may also explain his deeper investment in maintaining a hard distinction between himself and the lower-class cook. Desai also highlights how the police treat the cook, momentarily shifting to their collective perspective to underscore again how quickly and lazily they suspect the servant—"everyone knew it was the servants when it came to robbery"—and yet how, somewhat comically, as lower-class men, they also share in the cook's superstitions about two cobras, "husband and wife," that live nearby (14).

But when the police, removed from the judge's restraining influence, feel at liberty to overturn the cook's meager belongings and rifle through his tiny hut, we get Sai's perspective:

> It pained Sai's heart to see how little he had: a few clothes hung over a string, a single razor blade and a sliver of cheap brown soap, a Kulu blanket that had once been hers, a cardboard case with metal clasps that had belonged to the judge and now contained the cook's papers, the recommendations that had helped him procure his job with the judge, Biju's letters, papers from a court case fought in his village all the way in Uttar Pradesh over the matter of five mango trees that he had lost to his brother.... there was a broken watch that would cost too much to mend, but was still too precious to throw away—he might be able to pawn the parts. They were collected in an envelope and the little wind- up knob skittered out into the grass when the police tore open the seal. (15)

This extraordinary paragraph encompasses, through its minute attention to detail, a synecdochic history of the cook's life, an indicator of its concomitant fragility and resilience. The shift to Sai's perspective reveals what the cook's perspective alone cannot. Sai begins to see and understand, through an extension of empathy, and to invite readers to understand, what the narrator elaborates as the accrued significance of each carefully preserved item: the humble razor and soap that bespeak the effort to maintain daily hygiene; the hand-me-down blanket because he cannot afford to get a new one; the papers that enabled him to get this job and that affirm his identity and claim to land in a faraway village; the letters from his son; the broken watch that represents a hope for the future that is scattered by the policemen's callous officiousness. As Sai witnesses this invasion of the cook's privacy and personhood, she becomes shamefully aware that "the police had exposed the cook's poverty, the fact that he was not looked after, that his dignity had no basis; they ruined the façade and threw it in his face" (20). Sai knows that the cook's poverty and indignity, contingent upon his position as servant to her grandfather, implicates Sai as well. But Desai also gives the cook dignity as he makes the poignant effort to recover his dignity, and as he voices an unexpected understanding for those who have abused him: "Well they have to search everything... Naturally. How are they to know that I am innocent? Most of the time it is the servant that steals" (21).

Desai continues to alternate the cook's perspective with Sai's, throwing light on both, and elucidating their unexpectedly complex relationship:

Sai felt embarrassed. She was rarely in the cook's hut, and when she did come searching for him and enter, he was ill at ease and so was she, something about their closeness being exposed in the end as fake, their friendship composed of shallow things conducted in a broken language, for she was an English-speaker and he was a Hindi-speaker. The brokenness made it easier never to go deep, never to enter into anything that required an intricate vocabulary, yet she always felt tender on seeing his crotchety face, on hearing him haggle in the market, felt pride that she lived with such a difficult man who nonetheless spoke to her with affection, calling her Babyji or Saibaby. (21)

Here Desai renders the complex mix of seventeen-year-old Sai's feelings: her sense of shame and indirect responsibility for the condition of the servant who has effectively parented her for nine years; her awareness, even as she tries to overcome it, of "the gap between them as they stood surveying the mess the police had left in his hut" (with an echo of Umrigar's title); her self-knowledge of disingenuousness in her attempts to pretend that that gap did not exist; and her nonetheless genuine feelings of warmth, belonging, and gratitude for the care that the cook has provided her, an orphan who has received affection from no one else, even as she knows that his terms of address, "Babyji" and "Saibaby," carry the deference of a servant with the claim of belonging to the family in which only she counts as the "baby" (22). They are separated not only by class and gender and age, but also by the language and education that accompany those differences: they literally cannot fully understand each other or each other's world views because of the different languages and discursive systems that constitute them. Sai knows that "she was an English-speaker and he was a Hindi-speaker," and she fears "something about their closeness being exposed in the end as fake" (21). And yet what simultaneously connects them is an interpersonal history of care and connection: they have been thrown together in their isolation, in this house, and in the absence of other familial bonds for either. Despite the gaps between them, Sai is also aware that "she always felt tender on seeing his crotchety face, on hearing him haggle in the market, felt pride that she lived with such a difficult man who nonetheless spoke to her with affection" (21). As we will see, Sai has actually felt jealous of the primary allegiance the cook has to his own child, Biju, as she desires the parental love that the cook reserves for his son. In turn, the cook expects, indeed demands, a reciprocity of filial respect and attachment from Sai. With remarkable nuance, through this alternation, Desai explores this delicate mix of tenderness and distance, across multiple lines of division, in the relationship between Sai and the cook.

In this early scene, Sai helps the cook reassemble his shattered dignity, as she literally helps him regather his scattered possessions. She voices support, recognizing the sense of outrage: "How dare they behave this way to you" (22).

But at the same time, she is aware, as Desai makes us aware, that Sai's understanding of the cook is limited, that she does not understand him. In his hut, the place where Sai tries to connect with the cook and that yet augments the distance between them, she also sees the two photographs that hang on his wall, one of Biju, and one of the cook himself with his (now deceased) wife, and recalls how she had once taken a picture of him unawares, "snuck up on him as he minced an onion, and she had been surprised to see how he felt deeply betrayed," and how he had rushed off to change into his "best clothes" and returned to pose against the more "suitable backdrop" of leather-bound *National Geographics* (15). We understand, as she does not, that he was not averse to having his picture taken, but that he did not want to be recorded unprepared, frozen in his identity as cook, that he wanted to control the terms in which he is remembered. Through this memory, mediated via Sai, Desai intimates poignantly both the servant's unvoiced desire—to be seen, and preserved on film, to project another, imagined, inner sense of self, an alternative, more respectable persona, against the backdrop of American magazines that he cannot read—and Sai's failure to understand that inner life and what constitutes it. Through the intricacies of these thoughts, memories, and inner worlds, Desai evokes the micropolitics and affective complications of this relationship between the older male servant and the young middle-class orphaned girl.

Desai thus also calls attention to the problem of *how* Sai sees him, how Sai is constrained by her own limited framework, the prism (and prison) of her own concerns. Because she is becoming involved with Gyan, Sai wonders about the cook, "if he had loved his wife," imposing her notions of Western romance on a relationship to which she has no access, oblivious to how it may be understood by them in their own socio-economic, cultural contexts (15). Within the same chapter, sometimes the same paragraph, Desai's narrative weaves between these characters, and their knowledge and lack of knowledge of each other. Desai moves, for instance, from what Sai remembers of how she first saw the cook—when he had been the one to receive her at the gate of her grandfather's house when she arrived alone after her parents' death—to a narrative voice that tells us something about him that Sai cannot know:

> ... there had come the cook, bandy-legged up the path, looking as leather-visaged, as weathered and soiled, as he did now [in February 1986], and as he would ten years later. A poverty-stricken man growing into an ancient fast-forward. Compressed childhood, lingering old age. A generation between him and the judge, but you wouldn't know it to look at them. There was age in his temperament, his kettle, his clothes, his kitchen, his voice, his face, in the undisturbed dirt, the undisturbed settled smell of a lifetime of cooking, smoke, and kerosene. (21–22)

This paragraph exemplifies Desai's subtle, almost imperceptible shifts, as it moves from Sai's memory to a third-person narrator's description that extends into a future beyond the novel's ending. The cook is presented here in sentence fragments, as if in broken, fleeting glimpses, from an external vantage point, in a description of his appearance that indicates a lifetime of labor, servitude, and poverty that have literally shaped his body. It is the narrator who notes how the cook has aged before his time, though he is younger than the judge he serves. In the build-up of the detailed, poetic list at the end ("his kettle, his clothes, his kitchen"), Desai renders the him-ness of him, his "temperament" as inextricable from the physical environment that has made the cook who he is.

Whereas the central servant-employer relationship explored in *Space* is between Bhima and Sera, to which relationships between the servant and the employer's family members, such as Dinaz, are narratively subordinated, *Loss* emphasizes the affective connections between the cook and Sai, not between the cook and his male employer, the judge. From the time nine-year-old Sai, a lonely, unwanted orphan raised in an austere convent, arrives at Cho Oyu, the judge's house, it is the cook who welcomes her and makes it a home. He volunteers to become a *de facto* parent: he takes the initiative to make her a motorcar from mashed potatoes for her first dinner (36); he walks her around the neighborhood and introduces her to all the neighbors (47). They share companionable moments, bonding as he tells her (made up) stories about her family, and teaches her how to cook and play:

> Sai liked to keep him company in the kitchen as he told her stories. He gave her bits of dough to roll into *chapatis* and showed her how to make them perfectly round, but hers came out in all kinds of shapes. "Map of India," he would say, dismissing one. "Oofho, now you've made a map of Pakistan," he tossed out the next. Finally he'd let her put one of them on the fire to puff up and if it didn't, "Well, Dog Special Roti," he would say. (63)

With an appealing tenderness, the cook exercises a kind of gentle control, teasing Sai for her childish efforts, and teaching her a certain nationalistic chauvinism as he throws out the roti shaped liked Pakistan. In the kitchen they laugh together, sharing a sense of the ridiculous, as when teenage Sai opens the door and the wind blows flour all over them. Together they make fun of the English, and laugh at themselves, as brown people covered in white flour, appearing white, "*Angrez ke tarah*. Like the English" (115). They are joined momentarily, despite their class differences, in postcolonial harmony against their former colonizers, in their racial sameness (115). Laughter builds community: Sai shares with the cook a sense of warmth and belonging that she does not have with anyone else.

In such moments, they also seem united unconsciously against the Anglophile judge, who does not join in their play.

The emotional connection between the cook and Sai is such that, as a young girl, Sai actually feels jealous of the cook's son, when she realizes that the cook will always love his son more, that his primarily allegiance would always be to his own child:

> ... when [Biju] had visited Kalimpong, ... [Sai] had found her heart shaken by the realization that the cook had his own family and thought of them first. If his son were around, he would pay only the most cursory attention to her. She was just the alternative, the one to whom he gave his affection if he could not have Biju, the real thing. (205)

This jealousy, or Sai's longing to be primary in the cook's affections, is clearly so important that we also hear about it from Biju's perspective, as what Biju did not know when he visited his father at Cho Oyu: "They had stayed up late. They hadn't noticed Sai, then aged thirteen, staring from her bedroom window, jealous of the cook's love for his son" (113). The cook loves his son, to support whom he works as a servant, and from whom he is thereby separated. (Because the cook is a servant, Biju cannot live with his father, and has to live in the village with his grandmother.) Sai cannot know this—all she understands is the diverted attention of the servant. And yet, Desai does not sentimentalize Sai's emotional need, or the cook's kindness to a forlorn child. She makes it clear, from the beginning, how it is a relationship of simultaneous distance and closeness, always marked by their mutual understanding of their inequality. As Sai grows older, the distances grow, even as the attachment remains.

Over the course of the novel, Desai tracks how this relationship changes as Sai's education augments the distance between her and the cook. Though she can laugh *with* him, Sai is not above also laughing *at* him: she laughs at his accent when he speaks a few English words, when his story of how he made "bed tea" for her grandfather (when the judge was doing his administrative rounds in British colonial times) sounds like "Bad tea," phonetically accentuated by Desai as "*Baaad teeee*" (68). Like Rushdie, Desai both contributes to the joke at the servant's expense, making him seem ludicrous, at the same time that she heightens his poignancy, for he neither knows that his pronunciation is wrong, nor that Sai is laughing at him. She presents the cook as at once endearing and ridiculous, moving and absurd. Later, with sensitivity, Desai also shows how the cook gets hurt and annoyed, as Sai becomes more overt in her derision.

When Sai at age sixteen becomes infatuated with Gyan, her math tutor, she turns, not to the judge or to Noni or Lola, people of her own family or class, but to the cook as a source of guidance on matters of love and family history, "pester[ing]" him "about the judge and his wife" (96). The cook obliges by fabricating more stories about what he does not know:

> When I joined the household, all the old servants told me that the death of your grandmother made a cruel man out of your grandfather. She was a great lady, never raised her voice to the servants. How much he loved her! ... But they said he didn't show it. (96)

The cook's words open a window both to a servant's world and to the unevenness of the relationship between the cook and Sai. They indicate how, to servants, the measure of a "great lady" is her treatment of servants; and how the servant (re)constructs the family's past, for Sai's benefit and his own, on frequently false grounds. Earlier, delving into the cook's psyche, Desai explains why the cook feels impelled to make up fake stories that he himself comes to believe in. As a servant, his sense of self and identity are built upon the prestige of his employer. Just as an employer's status depends on his servants, the cook's respect among servants in his community depends on the status of his employer. So he builds it up:

> [The cook] had found that there was nothing so awful as being in the service of a family you couldn't be proud of, that let you down, and showed you up, and made you into a fool. How the other cooks and maids, watchmen and gardeners on the hillside laughed, boasting meanwhile how well *they* were treated by *their* employers....
> So serious was this rivalry that the cook found himself telling lies. Mostly about the past since the present could too easily be picked apart. He fanned a rumor about the judge's past glory, and therefore of his own ...
> The cook had never known the judge's wife, but he claimed that his information had been handed down from the older servants in the household, and eventually, he had grown to believe in his own marvelous story. It gave him a feeling of self-respect ... (63)

As Desai reveals later in the novel, and as Sai and the cook never know, the judge actively hated his wife and, ashamed of her tradition-bound Indianness, treated her with extraordinary brutality. However, in this psychologically astute analysis, Desai suggests, without condemnation, and with sympathy, what cultural ethos and structural conditions of servitude produce the cook's fabrications. These faked stories are produced out of multiple needs—the cook's need to embellish his own position among other servants, and his eagerness to satisfy Sai's need to learn about a family she does not know. His stories enable both to build a sense of place in their world. Desai's narrator moves in and out of the cook's consciousness, locating him in the world he inhabits, showing both how he sees and is seen.

By the time she is sixteen, Sai has started to question the cook, to deploy her critical thinking skills. Sai is less gullible, more skeptical now, as she challenges the cook's recall, or his version. Daringly, she suggests, if her grandfather did not show his love for her grandmother, maybe he did not love her. The cook is so upset by this upending of his picture of the world, this challenge to his veracity, that he loses control, and actually shouts at Sai: "Bite your tongue, you evil girl. Take your words back! ... Of course he loved her" (96). "How did the servants know then?" asks Sai reasonably, to which he responds with unexpected wisdom, as he thinks about his own wife:

"Nobody really knew, but no one said anything in those days, for there are many ways of showing love, not just the way of the movies—which is all you know. You are a very foolish girl. The greatest love is love that's never shown."

"You say anything that suits you."

"Yes, I've found it's the best way," said the cook after thinking some more." (96–97)

As Sai brings the cook to a rare acknowledgment of his fabrications, their conversation produces deeper insights that Sai may not yet understand: that there are indeed "many ways of showing love," and that servants, given their disempowered position, are impelled to say anything that "suits" them.[8]

The dynamic between Sai and the cook changes with the advent of Gyan into their lives. When Gyan first arrives to tutor Sai, the cook acts protectively as self-appointed chaperon: "[he] sat on the stool outside the door, keeping an eye on Sai and the new tutor" (81). But because he is literally kept outside the room, he fails to detect, let alone intervene in, the budding romance. When critics mention this "love affair," they overlook its problematic nature, not least because twenty-year-old Gyan is sexually invasive and betrays the implicit trust placed in a tutor hired to teach alone in her home a sixteen-year-old girl.[9] The cook, "awed" by the "atmosphere" of learning (80), insecure about his own lack of education, and sensing Sai's shift of interest, tries to put down the Nepali Gyan by using ethnic generalizations.

As the cook repeats to Sai a popular South Asian belief that "coastal people" like the Bengalis, who eat more fish, "are more intelligent than inland people" like the Nepalis, Sai at first expresses reproof and skepticism, demonstrating her independent thinking: "Don't be silly," she says, and asks for a reliable source, "Who says?" (81). But when the cook elaborates and insists that he is right, even adding, "Nepalis make good soldiers, coolies, but they are not so bright at their studies. Not their fault, poor things," Sai becomes more contemptuous, like her grandfather. She treats the cook like a lowly unintelligent servant, literally dismissing him: "Go and eat some fish yourself ... One stupid thing after another from your mouth" (82). Desai's depiction here does present the cook as ignorant and prejudiced, as reprehensibly prone to making such ethnic generalizations. Like Rushdie, Desai makes the cook both poignant and ridiculous; and like her mother Anita Desai in *Fire on the Mountain*, Kiran Desai represents the cook as good with children, though as more complex and sympathetic than Ram Lal.[10] Unlike Anita Desai, however, Kiran Desai also makes clear, with greater realism, why he is prone to making such generalizations: he lacks the education that Sai has.

If Sai is positioned in a filial relation to the cook, this scene also reveals an important distinction between Sai and Biju, his actual offspring, and the powerful effects of education. Unlike Biju, who has absorbed his father's beliefs and suspicions of ethnic others, and which, as we will see, ultimately contribute to his failure in the United States, Sai emphatically rejects the prejudices and stereotypes that the cook tries to instill. But Desai also includes the cook's response, for the scene ends with his sense of hurt at Sai's betrayal: "Here I bring you up as my own child with so much love and just see how you are talking to me" (82). Sai may be right, but her manner and tone are disrespectful, and the cook knows it. Yet it is also telling that, with her, he feels he can protest and reproach. He has no such emotional connection or license with the judge, his employer. Later, after Sai has had a falling out with Gyan, she returns to the cook, looking for comfort, yet unable to share her feelings. "You were right about the fish and Nepalis. He isn't very intelligent," she tells him. The cook is gladdened by this affirmation and they return to their old harmony: "'Yes,' said the cook sympathetically, having forecast the boy's stupidity himself" (193). Again, Desai's humor here refuses to sentimentalize or make the cook a victim. He may commiserate with Sai, and rejoice in their reconnection, but he knows nothing about her infatuation with Gyan. What the cook does not get is always part of Desai's comedy. As a narrative gesture, it invites the audience into an ironic, conspiratorial superiority with the narrator above the character who cannot see what we can see.

Unlike Umrigar, who never uses humor at Bhima's expense, and is always careful to maintain Bhima's dignity, Desai's use of humor can at times be self-contradictory, undercutting her otherwise empathetic and sensitive portrayal of the cook. For instance, when he feels particularly distanced and disconnected from Biju in New York, the cook comforts himself with the hope that Biju must be eating well there: "They all grow fat there . . . The cook knew about them all growing fat there. It was one of the things everyone knew" (256). The repetition ironically underscores the cook's over-confidence about his own knowledge, making him seem both comical for his lack of knowledge, and his desire to create a collective "everyone" that supposedly knows what he wants them to know, and yet endearing for his concern for his son. However, when the cook asks Biju if Biju is "fat" and Biju writes back with comic exaggeration that he is himself "times ten," the cook is described as laughing with such delight that "he lay on his back and kicked his legs in the air like a cockroach" (256). Such an uncomfortable moment, reducing the cook to a repulsive scavenging insect, is anomalous, but it does create a distancing effect, as if Desai here pulls back from or disavows the sympathetic close-up she uses elsewhere, and returns to the position of the upper-class gaze.

More continuously, though, Desai uses humor with a complex duality that both slightly diminishes the cook, and heightens the poignancy of his condition. Sometimes, in relation to Sai, she casts the cook as comically effeminate and maternal, like a jealous and reproachful ayah. When, for instance, Sai returns home late after a stolen trip with Gyan, the cook waits anxiously for her at the gate with a lantern, not knowing where she has been. Desai both makes him seem ridiculous and provides an unexpected emotional drama as he tries to guilt Sai:

> His bad-tempered wrinkled face peered from an assortment of mufflers and sweaters. "I've been waiting, waiting . . . In this darkness you have not come home!" he complained, waddling in front of her along the path from gate to house, looking round and womanish. (160)

The cook appears to cross gender lines both in his physical appearance, possibly due to his "assortment" of warm clothing, and his behavior. Both diminish him. The more he behaves like a mother, the more absurd he seems—and the more Sai behaves like a resentful teenager.

> "Why don't you leave me alone?" she said conscious for the first time of the unbearable stickiness of family and friends when she had found freedom and space in love.
> The cook felt hurt to his chutney core. "I'll give you one smack," he shouted. "From childhood I have brought you up! With so much love! Is this any way to talk? Soon I'll die and then who will you turn to? Yes, yes, soon I'll be dead. Maybe then you'll be happy. Here I am, so worried, and there you are, having fun, don't care . . .
> "Ohhoho." As usual she ended by attempting to placate him. He wouldn't be placated and then he was, just a little. (160)

In this oddly moving exchange, Desai maintains a faint strain of the comedic, yet combines it with a delicate, sensitive depiction of the cook's feelings, of the painful wrench caused by this friction, and of Sai's efforts to repair the hurt she has caused, as their adoptive parent-child relationship reveals its fragility. First Desai switches to the cook's perspective, to his feelings, and his voice, as he tells Sai off, claiming the privileges of an old caregiver, and the emotional connection of family. Then, she gives us Sai's perspective, as rebelling against those very demands of care. What we see is the cook's need to parent, to claim parental prerogatives, and Sai's concomitant desire both to separate and to recognize those claims. And we see how they both negotiate around their little rupture, smoothing it over. It is ultimately a gentle quarrel, comfortable in the habit of mutual familiarity, and Sai, who knows she has more power, tries to atone. She soothes the cook, in accordance with her gendered and classed role, showing that she values him, recognizing his need to be valued, as at once servant and adoptive parent, and he allows himself to be mollified, recognizing, in her efforts, the response to his call, and the bond that is thereby restored between them.

Still later, when Sai comes home from Darjeeling, having seen Gyan at a march, and is upset and cannot eat, the cook misunderstands, interpreting it as a rejection of his cooking and care: "At home the cook was waiting, but she went to bed without her dinner, and this greatly offended the cook, who took it to mean that she had eaten fancily in a restaurant and now despised the offerings of home" (240). The cook's investment in Sai's eating and preferring what he has made extends well beyond a pride in his work or in any labor relation—it is a reflection of the imbrication of affect and identity in their relationship. Normally, Sai is "sensitive to his jealousy" and need, and reassures him that his cooking is better, making him "laugh and laugh" with stories of how bad the food was wherever else she ate. But this time, when she fails to maintain this ritual, the cook, almost like a spoiled a child, bangs the dishes and gets told off by the judge. The chapter ends with the cook's emotional upset, his being "beyond caring," his return to servant language with the judge: "Babyji went to sleep. She ate at the hotel" (240). At once heartrending and funny, the scene highlights both the unrepaired rupture of the relationships in the house, and how much Sai and cook, despite their mutual attachment, still do not know about each other. They inhabit the same house, sharing lives and affective ties, yet they know little of the dramas that the other is going through: Sai's romance and its disintegration, the cook's fears about Biju.

That said, even Sai's worst moments are a far cry from the overt contempt for the cook that her grandfather exhibits, whose habitual mode of interaction with the cook, by contrast, is either to ignore him or to use commands or derogatory epithets like "Stupid fool" (115). When the cook abases himself before the Gorkha invaders, the judge is incapable of empathy or any understanding of the cook's behavior as a response to his greater vulnerability. "These damn servants born and brought up to scream," he thinks contemptuously (9). And yet, even for the judge, the habits of a lifetime of being together as master and servant have produced a different kind of tacit affect, of mutual dependence even between these two aging men. When the judge comes home one night and sees the cook hiding in the bushes with the soldiers to whom he sells his homemade liquor, we get a rare moment when the judge reflects on this relationship:

> He knew about this side business of the cook's and ignored it. It was his habit to be master and the cook's to be a servant, but something had changed in their relationship within a system that kept the servant and master both under an illusion of security. (229)

In this odd comment, from the judge's perspective, it becomes clear that the judge chooses to turn a blind eye to the cook's illegal side-business, which the cook would not need to run if the judge paid him more. But it is less clear if, to enact the master, the judge would have to monitor what his servant does, or to let him do it and pretend not to know because it is more dignified not to get involved. In the isolation in which they live, where their mutual interdependence is only stronger, their relationship has changed over the years. By not interfering, the judge allows the cook his false sense of security, and ensures his own. Yet it also makes him complicit and ties them together further. Even for this stiff-necked unaccommodating judge, indulging his servant in this way is the price of cohabitation.

Like Umrigar with Bhima, Desai singles out the cook to provide a detailed, textured account of his interiority and relationships and, as a comparative measure, also surrounds him with other servants to establish the system of servitude in which he is placed, and to offer, by subtle contrast, an understanding of how other dimensions of identity, such as gender or ethnicity, inflect the experience of servitude. Lola, Sai's widowed neighbor and tutor, who lives alone with her sister Noni, responds with instant alarm when she hears about the Gorkha robbery at Cho Oyu. Sai's reassurance that they are protected by a watchman elicits even greater fear, precisely because the watchman is Nepali and likely to be sympathetic to the Gorkha cause: "Who can trust him now? It's always the watchman in a case of robbery.... We had better tell that Budhoo to go" (49–50). Budhoo, a "comforting presence," who has served them for years, is now tainted by suspicion and negative ethnic generalizations: "I tell you, these Neps can't be trusted. And they don't just rob. They think absolutely nothing of murdering as well," Lola asserts (51). Budhoo is the epitome of obliging servility, responding to commands with "*Huzoor*" (a highly deferential term of address translatable as "Lord" or "August Master"), who has given them no reason for such distrust (51). The scene indicates the unreasonable fear and distrust concomitant with the very dependence on the servants employed to guard the rich, heightened when ethnic tensions increase. And indeed, later, when the Gorkha insurgency takes over the area, and Lola and Noni's house is invaded, Budhoo disappears, perhaps precisely because of these suspicions (262).

Desai makes clear how unreasonable Lola and Noni are with their servants. They disapprove of the "way [Sai] had been abandoned to the cook for years," making her prone, they think, to "falling to the level of the servant class" (75). Noni believes in maintaining this distance between the classes, almost on principle, and prides herself for discouraging their maid, Kesang, from "divulging personal information" (75). When Kesang tells them one day of her romance with the milkman, how she had married him despite her parents' opposition, they are shocked to learn that servants have inner lives, emotions, adventures:

> Her love had shocked the sisters. Lola had always professed that servants didn't experience love in the same manner as people like themselves—"their entire structure of relationships is different, it's economic, practical—far more sensible, I'm sure, if only one could manage it oneself." (76)

Desai's humorously satiric portrayal of this exchange makes clear not just how self-deluding Lola's condescension is, but also how problematic her attitude is toward servants whom she regards almost as a different species. The novel shows us how wrong Lola is as it provides by contrast the complex inner world of the cook. Yet he is the only servant in the novel to be given his own perspective and narrative space. Kesang remains a mysterious, unknown figure, whose story remains untold. Perhaps Desai's point is that despite this momentary glimpse of her humanity, her employers refuse to know, and therefore never know, more. Only at the end, Noni realizes, though Lola does not, that "parallel lives" run alongside their own, but rarely intersect (272).

The cook is thus in many ways the linchpin of this novel. He connects all the characters, even filling in for Sai's grandfather and facilitating communication between Sai and the judge. And, as we will see, he creates some of the most intense affects. His emotional connections with Sai and Biju are among the most intricate and powerful in this novel. Via his son Biju, he connects also, as we will see, the novel's explorations of domestic servitude and postcolonial national politics with the problems of globalization, migrancy, and neoliberalism. That he is called just "the cook" throughout is therefore deliberately ironic, because the novel shows him to be much more than a mere functionary. Desai highlights the contrast between how the cook is seen, and who he is, as a full human being. That he is finally named, in the end, at the moment when he is most dehumanized by his employer is doubly ironic and reinforces the violation of that humanity.

Intergenerational Servitude

Like Umrigar, and unlike Gunesekera and Adiga, Kiran Desai explores the intergenerational familial consequences of servitude. The cook, like Bhima, inherits his specific form of domestic servitude as a legacy from a parent of the same gender. Whereas Bhima inherits the cleaning, dishwashing, and all-purpose subsidiary maid's work that is paid less than skilled cooking, Panna Lal inherits the relatively more specialized, higher-paid work of cooking. (In South Asia, male cooks are paid more than female cooks, and more than female servants who are engaged for menial tasks.) Umrigar and Desai both also emphasize how servitude suffuses parent-child relations, how it negatively affects the sense of self of each servant's child, producing a low sense of self-worth or deserving, and how the legacies of servitude produce the lack of material opportunities and knowhow that continue to hamper their efforts to create better lives. Both emphasize how the servant as parent tries to raise his or her child to a higher status than the parent's own, to procure opportunities that would avert servitude for the next generation, but also how the parent's servitude limits, in fact worsens, the possibilities for the next generation. But where Umrigar focuses on female lines of servitude, which are shaped by and reinforce feminine assumptions of gender, Desai focuses on how servitude affects men and their notions of masculinity. As noted in the introduction, most domestic work (particularly cooking, cleaning, and childcare) is feminized labor, traditionally understood as women's work. When men take on these domestic tasks, their sense of masculinity is put in question. In her exploration of male intergenerational servitude, Desai addresses how servitude affects the cook and his son's sense of self and place in the world.

We learn early on that the cook became a servant as a result of his own father's position as a cook. As he tells Sai about how he accompanied her grandfather in the colonial days on his work in the Indian Civil Service, the cook reminisces about this glorious past, "So many servants then," the cook told Sai, "Now, of course, I am the only one" (67). Though the present clearly suggests a decline, as the retired judge can no longer afford the plenitude of servants that he could once, the cook's words also suggest some pride in that he is now the one on whom the family depends for everything. Earlier, the narrator describes the kitchen as now mostly used for storage, with "only a corner being used" by the cook, "the one leftover servant," as if he were himself an unwanted, unconsumed remnant (7). Despite his stories, however, the cook does not tell Sai how he became a servant, a backstory that is supplied instead by the narrator: "He had begun working at ten years old, at a salary half his age, five rupees, as the lowest all-purpose *chokra* boy in the kitchen of a club where his father was pudding cook. At fourteen, he was hired by the judge at twelve rupees a month" (67). The cook's servitude is thus inherited from his father, who worked in colonial times for the "white men" and begged Jemubhai desperately, armed with fake "bought recommendations," to hire his untrained son. The cook, however, having internalized this colonized mentality, saw service with a brown man as a "severe comedown" compared to working for white colonizers (71).[11] Both Jemubhai and the cook thus make do with each other as second best, each recognizing the other as inferior and therefore fitting for himself.

It is therefore deeply ironic that Biju ends up doing, in American restaurant kitchens, exactly what his father and grandfather (respectively) have done in the kitchens of Indian homes and British Indian clubs. Panna Lal's hope (like Bhima's with Maya) is to enable his child to break that legacy of servitude, to the extent that he is willing to send his son halfway around the globe to fulfill this aspiration. These three generations of men in the same servant family reveal a story of decline, not progress, from colonial to postcolonial to globalized economies, where Biju has even less than his father, who had less than *his* father. The inheritance of loss (and servitude) seems compounded and gets worse over the generations, Desai suggests, as Biju becomes a hopelessly exploited and undocumented immigrant kitchen helper, living precariously on the run, while his father at least has risen from untrained helper to cook, even though he is himself, as an all-purpose *generic* cook, as his sole descriptor suggests, of more reduced status than *his* father, the specialized "pudding cook." Unlike Biju, the cook Panna Lal is at least a citizen with a job, though with even less status than his own father had working for the British. All three exhibit degrees of precarity that get worse with each generation.

Like Bhima, the cook tries to break the cycle of servitude in his family. The top priority in his life is to enable Biju *not* to be a servant, to set up his son to be something more. Notably, Desai gives us the judge's condescending perspective as an example of the upper-class failure to understand the cook's desire to avert servitude for his son. When Biju is called for an interview, the judge objects: "Why couldn't Biju plan to work for him when the cook retired?" (197). But the myopically self-centered judge thinks only of who will serve *him*, not of how his servant will survive in retirement. It never occurs to him to offer any provision for that retirement. The cook has literally no economic security or protection for his old age, and like Balram in *The White Tiger*, is incited by the precarity of his future to take action in the present. The cook has to rely only on himself to plan for his old age, by trying to get Biju to do something more remunerative. But the judge does not see this.

Earlier, when the cook's wife died, and he begged temporary leave to return, as his village priests demanded, to protect young Biju from her putatively violent ghost, the judge refused to let him go. Expressing his scorn about the cook's vulnerability to superstition and the extortions of priests, the judge railed at Panna Lal, as if his own efforts uplifting the cook by simply employing him had been wasted:

> "What has your life been for?" said the judge. "You live with me, go to a proper doctor, you have even learned to read and write a little, sometimes you read the newspaper, and all to no purpose! Still the priests make a fool of you, and rob you of your money." (196)

What the judge sees as benefits that raise the cook above others, we see, with the cook, as too minimal to suffice for his son or himself. Because he thinks the poor deserve no better, that what he provides is already a bonus, the judge fails to understand that those securities, though not negligible, fail to protect the cook from the depredations of the cheats and cutthroats around him, that the cook does not have the education, or financial sense, to know how to spend his resources. What the novel provides is this context to understand the cook's consequent desperate attempts to send his son abroad.

Because he knows well what servitude entails, the cook wants more for his son. But ironically, Desai shows, because of his own life of servitude and consequent lack of education and understanding of alternatives, the cook tragically misspends his hard-earned money and savings, not on Biju's education, but on trying to garner a quick fix, or immediate glory, by trying to send Biju abroad, unprepared, unready, with fake papers. Instead of using his precious earnings on an education or training that would provide Biju with the learned skills to get more remunerative work, or a qualify him for a secure form of employment, the cook wastes his money on bribes and the purchase of fake documents. Like Bhima, he is further exploited and defrauded precisely because of his inexperience, his lack of knowhow about how to make it in this world. In his first effort to get Biju a job—doing "drudge" work in the kitchen of an ocean liner with the promise of "legal employment in the USA"—he spends eight thousand rupees plus expenses on what turns out to be a scam (196). Desai makes clear how, in the absence of governmental safeguards, the most vulnerable are further exploited. The cook's and Biju's lack of savvy contributes to their gullibility, to their failure to suspect extortion: "it made sense to them all to pay to get a job" (197). The cook loses all his investment and has no protection, insurance, or recourse, legal or otherwise, no means to recover it. "You've been cheated" laughs a callous observer; "Ah, idiot. Who goes and gives money like that?" comments another (199). What Desai shows instead is how the cook could not know any better, how his circumstances produce such pathetic and desperate measures. And just as Bhima's efforts to make things better for Maya make things worse, it is the cook's tragedy that his efforts to avoid servitude for his offspring leads to further self-sabotage, as his efforts are undermined by his misplaced priorities. He fails to put his money into his son's education, into providing the resources that no one can steal. Effectively, the cook's own servitude and lack of education result in his being exploited and defrauded, until, by an extraordinary chance, Biju gets a tourist visa and becomes, so the cook thinks, "the luckiest boy in the world" (205).

Later, Biju does the same as his father: he spends all his hard-earned savings not on investments that might generate an income, such as setting up a business or acquiring training, but on consumer goods that are stolen from him. At the end, as Biju tries to return to his father in India, he encounters rapacious power-hungry insurgents as well as economic opportunists, and is stripped literally and symbolically of everything he has brought back with him, down to the clothes on his back. Desai's point is that neither the cook nor Biju has the capital to build capital, the knowledge, or the cultural or economic capital to know how to rise out of their situations of precarity. She thus calls attention to the accrued and compounded familial disadvantages of servitude. Her narrative tracks how, though they make their own choices that leads to various disasters, those choices are shaped by their lack of knowledge and resources: their lack of education compounds both father's and son's wrong or misplaced choices.

Like Maya in *Space*, Biju experiences both first-hand and second-hand servitude. The first is more direct, as he becomes effectively a servant in America when he works as an undocumented immigrant for Harish-Harry, his Indian-American employer, at the ironically named Gandhi Café. Literally and figuratively underground, Biju is underpaid, underfed, and exploited by an entrepreneurial fellow-Indian who treats him worse than Biju's erstwhile American employers did because he knows the vulnerability of Biju's situation. Moreover, because they are both Indians of different classes, in their structurally similar relationship in America they import the power dynamics of Indian master-servant relations, almost as a default. Though Biju is technically a restaurant employee, not Harish-Harry's domestic servant, they both replicate the master-servant relation, acceding to and reenacting the same cultural practices and ways of being of Indian servitude with which they are both only too familiar, because their interactions and relations are shaped by their shared memory of those relations.[12] Harish Harry pays Biju less while pretending to do him a kindness as a fellow national; Biju still enacts deference and gratitude, while knowing he is being bilked. Refusing even to get Biju medical attention when Biju slips in the kitchen and breaks his knee, blaming him for his accident, Harish-Harry knows how to mask his inhumanity by bringing him a free gift from the Hindu temple, as if they were indeed tied to each other by other bonds:

> And in that *prasad* Biju knew not to expect anything else. It was a decoy, an old Indian trick of master to servant, the benevolent patriarch garnering the loyalty of the staff; offering slave wages, but now and then a box of sweets, a lavish gift... (207)

Highlighting the language of servitude, Desai calls attention to the situational irony that Biju, whose father's greatest hope in life is to enable his son to escape the life-long servitude he has himself experienced, has in fact ended up a servant, in a far worse situation. Biju's neocolonial servitude is a new mutation, or variant, of the postcolonial servitude that his father knows.

Later, when Biju decides to return to India, too anxious about his father to stay in New York, his travel agent comments on the new transnational servitude of the underclasses fomented by neoliberalism and globalization: "You are making a big mistake. Still a world, my friend, where one side travels to be a servant, and the other side travels to be treated like a king. You want your son to be on this side or that side?" (295). His words emphasize how Biju's first-hand servitude as an undocumented transnational migrant has become both a literal and symbolic condition, and how, if he were to return to India, his familial legacy of servitude would be passed on to *his* son. As Desai repeatedly makes clear, globalization produces both literal and metaphorical servants in the form of poor migrants from the Global South to the North. But the travel agent's warning is important because it also pertains to the generational legacies and consequences of servitude. Returning to India, he insists, is a mistake not only for Biju himself, but also for his (future) son(s). (Again, with notable gender preference, the agent focuses on consequences only for putative male children.) Should he return, Biju would pass on the legacy of servitude to the next generation in his family. The agent sees life in America as offering a chance to break that cycle for Biju's son, if not for himself. What the agent recommends is that Biju remain a servant in America so that his son can escape servitude. The cook's advice replicates this illusive American dream, as he emphasizes the difficulties for the poor in postcolonial India, unknowing of the difficulties Biju faces in America: "Stay there as long as you can. . . . Stay there. Make money. Don't come back here" (209). However, mired in misery and anxiety in America, affected by the selective memory of nostalgia, Biju forgets why he left, as the more knowing narrator reminds us:

> Of course he didn't go over his memories of the village school, of the schoolmaster who failed the children unless paid off by the parents. He didn't think of the roof that flew off each monsoon season . . . He didn't think of all the things that had made him leave in the first place. (296)

As we will see, Desai's bleak ending emphasizes the impossibility of both options; it offers us no hope that Biju will return to a better future. As in *Space*, it is not clear if the next generation will escape being a servant.[13]

I use the term "second-hand servitude," analogous to second-hand smoking, as indicative of the toxic consequences of adjacency to someone else's servitude. Biju experiences the toxic consequences of his father's (and grandfather's) servitude in several different ways. One, as discussed above, as a direct consequence of his father's servitude, the cook's lack of education and resources produces a similar lack of opportunities for Biju, obstructing him through the very ways that Panna Lal tries to build a better future for his son. The cook is cheated, misspends money, and—in the absence of informal guidance or formal support structures such as publicly funded education or vocational training—fails to invest in alternatives that might provide more viable ways out. Two, the cook is limited by both what he knows and does not know. He only seeks work for Biju that is similar to his own. In a system where jobs are only available through connections, where fathers can only wheedle their way to jobs for their sons through the limited networks they have, servants, or cooks, can only find jobs for their sons that also make them into servants, or cooks. (This cycle also replicates gender inequalities—men are hired and paid more than women to cook, and men look for jobs for their sons, not for daughters, because men are singularly burdened by society with the responsibility of providing for their families.) Three, more indirectly, even Biju, in the United States, limits himself by only seeking jobs that involve kitchen work, as if, given his family heritage, he cannot imagine doing anything else to earn a living.

And four, the cook's xenophobia and ethnocentrism further contribute to the bad choices that Biju makes, and that lead him to further disaster, to spurn or fail to avail of the few opportunities that he does get. Biju's downfall in the United States is partly due to his own prejudices, inculcated by the cook. Biju loses the job he has working in a French restaurant because he picks a fight with a Pakistani co-worker. It is his father who has contributed to this nationalist and religious hostility, this adamant refusal to tolerate the diversity Biju encounters in the United States: " 'Beware,' the cook wrote to his son' [upon hearing of Biju's Pakistani co-worker]. 'Beware. Beware. Keep away. Distrust' " (25). Biju does. He brings his unreconstructed ethnocentrisms, his nationalistic chauvinisms with him. He does not have any access to the liberal American college education that attempts to prise people away from such prejudices. Desai notes perspicaciously: "The habit of hate had accompanied Biju, and he found that he possessed an awe of white people, who arguably had done India great harm, and a lack of generosity regarding almost everyone else, who had never done a single harmful thing to India" (86). Though he becomes friends with Saeed Saeed, an Indian Muslim from Zanzibar, he does not learn from Saeed his tolerance and flexibility.[14]

Later, Biju gives up another promising job because he refuses to work in a restaurant where they serve beef. "He'll never make it in America with that kind of attitude," remarks his former employer, and this prediction is proven right by the novel (152). Though "Biju left a new person, a man full to the brim with a wish to live within a narrow purity," feeling a temporary surge of pride and self-worth in asserting his Hinduism, as the narrator's words suggest, that narrowness is precisely what leads him further to curtail his already very limited options (152).[15] After he finds an Indian restaurant that does not serve beef, Biju ends up working for lower pay and greater mistreatment under Harish-Harry. When Biju injures his knee and is unable to access medical help because of fear of deportation, he realizes how Harish abuses the "illegal" workers whom he, deploying the mask-language of servitude, terms a "happy family," precisely because he knows about their vulnerability (162). This illustrative moment then conjoins both first- and second-hand servitude: Biju is treated by his Indian American employer literally as an Indian servant in the terms of Indian servitude; and he lands himself in this fix because of the inadequacies of his father as a provider, model, and teacher, whose reinforcement in his son of ethnic fear and prejudice contributes to this predicament.

However, Desai's portrayal of the cook's and Biju's lives and relationship offers more than a structural understanding. She adds deep psychological complexities of individual desire and feeling, which show how the cook and his son's emotional interactions are intensified and complicated by their conditions of servitude. The cook's love and aspirations for Biju are what drive him first to start an illegal business brewing liquor in his backyard: "He had first started a liquor business on the side for Biju's sake, because his salary had hardly been changed in years" (61). But Desai also complicates the cliché of the self-sacrificing servant-parent, making room in her portrayal for the cook's own desires and aspirations: "This the cook had done for Biju, but also for himself, since the cook's desire was for modernity: toaster ovens, electric shavers, watches, cameras, cartoon colors. He dreamed at night not in Freudian symbols, . . . but in modern codes" (62). The cook's dream of his future with Biju is heartrendingly humble: "He imagined sofa TV bank account. Eventually Biju would make enough and the cook would retire. He would receive a daughter-in-law to serve him food, crick-crack his toes, grandchildren to swat like flies" (19). This unpunctuated list of desired objects suggests their unreality, to him, as if they are necessarily connected, inseparable from one another in his mind.

As a mirror of his own life, the cook's dream is to have someone else serve him. Ironically, the aging servant wants exactly what he has been himself, someone to serve him, to wait on him hand-and-foot, to serve his bodily needs. He wants (unpaid) gendered labor, a woman who will arrive as a daughter-in-law to do the housework that he would be relieved of doing and that is, in his mind, properly woman's work.[16] Then he can rest in manly retirement, where others serve him instead, not as hired servants, but as younger members of his own family, on whom he can legitimately depend both practically and emotionally. Desai's acute evocation of the servant's dream tells us more about his life, his misplaced and misinformed hopes, dreams, and aspirations, and about his assumptions about age, gender, and class.

The cook does not however regard Biju as merely instrumental to his own future. Desai makes clear how much theirs is a relationship of genuine attachment, of an intense emotionality that takes priority over all other relationships, and indeed even above material success. When he receives a letter from Biju telling him about his new job in a bakery, the cook is so filled with joy and pride that he goes around the town proclaiming the news to all and sundry. "My son works in New York," the cook boasted to everyone he met. 'He is the manager of a restaurant business'" (93). Each exaggerates a little, so that the result is a lie: Biju to minimize the ignominy of his precarious position, to prevent his father from worrying and feeling like a failure; and the cook to aggrandize because of his own precarious position, the need to feel pride in himself and his son. To indicate the degree of the heady euphoria that drives the cook to spread this news, Desai repeats the phrase "he told" over and over again, as "he told the doctor, . . . he told those catching their breath . . . resting on the road, he told Mrs. Sen," and Lola, and all he can find (94). In addition, through free indirect discourse, Desai also conveys the cook's need to measure himself against his employer, as what he knows most well: "One day his son would accomplish all that Sai's parents had failed to do, all the judge failed to do" (94). For the servant, the measure of personal success is the achievement of his child, in that the success of the child is the measure of his own. And yet, it is also clear that the cook affirms the value of love, even without money. In a sentence that prefigures the end of the novel, the cook persuades himself to relinquish the desire for money and glory: "Anyway, he said to himself, money wasn't everything. There was the simple happiness of looking after someone and having someone look after you" (95).

In each case, while delineating the intensity of the attachment between father and son, Desai shows how their emotional reactions to each other are complicated by their situations of servitude. When Biju arrives in the United States on a tourist visa and starts working illegally, he is caught in an emotional bind. He minimizes his discomforts, not telling his father about the stringent realities he faces, exaggerating the comforts, trying to reassure, and thus inadvertently contributing to his father's unreal and misplaced expectations.

> "Respected *Pitaji*, no need to worry. Everything is fine. The manager has offered me a full-time waiter position. Uniform and food will be given by them. *Angrezi khana* only, no Indian food, and the owner is not from India. He is from America itself."
>
> "He works for the Americans," the cook reported the contents of the letter to everyone in the market. (16)

In turn, from the other side, Desai also gives us the cook's voice, his pride and hopes for his son, and, in his letters to his son, mixed with self-glory, his anxiety and his insecurity about himself: "He wrote back carefully so his son would not think badly of his less educated father: 'Just make sure you are saving money. Don't lend to anyone and be careful who you talk to. . . . Before you make any decisions talk them over with Nandu'" (20). In this Polonius-like advice (much of which Biju follows to his own detriment, as we have seen), the cook again fosters Biju's xenophobia, his fear and distrust of others of a different ethnicity, race, or religion. He encourages Biju's reliance on, at best, Nandu as the only man from their own village present in New York, as if he alone can be trusted, and thus limits Biju's ability to spread his wings, to develop a broader network. As the cook's misplaced pride leads him to boast of his successful son to others in the town, he is besieged by others pleading for help in getting their own sons to America. The first is another servant, a neighboring watchman: "At first the cook was agitated, upset by the request, felt a war in him between generosity and meanness, but then . . . he began to feel a tingle—the very fact that the watchman had asked! It reestablished Biju in his father's eyes as a fine suited-and-booted-success" (89–90). It is precisely because he has so little that this tiniest boost to his sense of importance puffs the cook up. "A petition improved your status," remarks Desai's narrator (90).

When the cook writes to Biju, however, reality conflicts with fantasy. Desai gives us Biju's mixed reaction of annoyance and helplessness, caught between the need to assure the cook that there is nothing to worry about, and the impossibility of revealing his real position. His father's servitude complicates their relationship. Like his father who makes up stories, Biju lies to his father for his father's sake, precisely because he knows how damaged and fragile is the cook's sense of self. At the same time, he wants his father to do more for him than he can. This duality is captured in Biju's reaction of momentary resentment, as he is caught between a rock and a hard place: "Biju couldn't help but feel a flash of anger at his father for sending him alone to this country, but he knew that wouldn't have forgiven his father for not trying to send him either" (90). The cook's superhuman efforts to send Biju to America become a measure of his love, of his fatherhood, even as, recognizing the contradiction, Biju also experiences filial resentment against that very father for having done what he wanted, for having sent him, lovingly, but unknowingly, to a place where he is so destitute, and so unprotected. Poignantly, what Biju wants from his father, as a servant, is more than he knows his father can possibly provide, precisely because he is a servant. Later, as the requests multiply, Biju gets "violently angry" at his father for these pleas asking him to help various acquaintances' sons (208). What separates father and son are not just physical distances, but also a huge gap in understanding of the conditions Biju faces, and that Biju cannot bring himself to reveal, because he knows how little his father has, how much he has pinned his hopes on his son. And hence the cook imagines a fantasy world, cultivated in part by Biju himself, while Biju cannot on the one hand tell the truth about how bad it is, nor, on the other, tell his father to stop asking. The emotional reactions of each are exacerbated by their respective inherited conditions of servitude.

In Kalimpong, meanwhile, as the weather gets worse, as political tensions increase, and communication with the outside world becomes more difficult, as Biju's letters get wet, or lost, and eventually stop arriving, and the cook starts to lose touch with his son, his anxiety about Biju intensifies: "No way to telephone, no way for letters to get through" (135). Eventually, this nail-biting anxiety, heightened by a pervading sense of insecurity, sends the cook into an almost maddened state, and finally, to a violent crisis with the judge at the end. Building toward that crisis, Desai describes how, as the cook's anxiety intensifies, it materializes in a stark, almost hallucinatory leap of imagination:

> Worried about growing problems in the market and the disruption of supplies due to strikes, the cook was putting some buffalo meat that was growing harder and harder to buy into Mutt's stew. He unwrapped the flank from its newspaper wrapping soaked in blood, and suddenly he had the overwhelming thought that he held two kilos of his son's body there, dead like that. (195)

In this extraordinary moment, possibly a first in South Asian literature, Desai confronts us unexpectedly, powerfully, with the conjunction of servitude and fatherhood (as Umrigar does with servitude and motherhood). What it reveals is the haunting anxiety of a man who lives with the constant fear of loss, of violence to his only child, and the materialization of that anxiety as it erupts into the quotidian task of domestic servitude as the cook prepares meat for his master's pampered dog, meat so expensive that he is not allowed "the luxury" of consuming it himself (316). Through this specter of his son's dismembered body that bursts upon the cook's mind, Desai suggests how he is literally pervaded by an anxiety that takes material shape in the form of the very meat he is holding in his hands, imagined as the flesh of his own precious child. It suggests the sense of constant threat, the unspoken fear that he lives with all the time.

Where should such an idea arise from? In a remarkably probing psychological analysis, Desai shows how the cook's constant anxiety about his son has a history in his own servitude, in the lie he was forced to tell when his wife died and the judge would not allow him to attend the rites demanded by his village priests. Desai gives us this backstory as the cook's memory of his wife's death, as the moment from which this anxiety, intertwined with parental guilt, emanates. The priests insisted that because his wife had died a violent death (by falling from a tree), she was "threatening to take Biju with her," and hence the cook must appease her ghost by sacrificing a chicken (195). When the rationalist (and self-interested) judge dismisses these demands as foolish superstition and Brahmin extortion (or caste oppression), and refuses to let the cook return to his village, the cook produces a "made-up story" to provide a more convincing reason for having to leave (196). But since then, he has been racked by guilt, by the fear that his lie has undermined his efforts to protect his child, that Biju will always be vulnerable to some karma, some evil force that would punish the cook for having tarnished the funeral rites with untruth: "what if the spirit still had a hunger for Biju?" (196). Himself unprotected and beleaguered from all sides—his employer, his priests, the pressures of his fellow villagers and servants—the cook's real social and economic vulnerability becomes heightened into a constant paranoia, a sense of being under threat by amorphous forces beyond his control, imagined in terms of evil forces ready to snatch his child from him. Desai connects this psychic condition emphatically to the cook's condition of servitude. The employer's selfish refusal to accommodate the servant's need and the servant's consequent attempt to circumvent that interdiction heightens the servant's lifelong fear and sense of vulnerability. Unlike the judge, who remains oblivious, it is the cook who carries the lifelong burden of being forced to lie, in the form of guilt and the sense of Biju's vulnerability that constitutes his relationship with this son.

The cook's anxiety, exacerbated by knowledge of precarity, and love for Biju are only matched by Biju's for his father. (By comparison, the upper-class characters, Sai and the judge, manifest no such love or anxiety for each other.) When Biju hears about the unrest in the Darjeeling area, he becomes gradually "convinced his father was dead" (251). Again, through free indirect discourse, Desai relays Biju's implicit knowledge of the disregard and callousness of even those closest to them, which magnifies his fear and sense of insecurity: "The judge wouldn't know how to find him if he would try to find him at all. His unease began to tighten" (251). Yet, when Biju is finally able to make contact via an unprecedented phone call, Desai heightens the poignancy (as well as comedy) of their frantic efforts to connect, as the cook, unexpectedly summoned by the watchman at a neighboring guesthouse to the only available phone, drops his work to rush to receive it, and shouts into it, unaccustomed to talking on the phone, making it even harder for himself to hear his son. Hampered by their own emotional turmoil and by a literally defective transcontinental phone connection, both ask anxious questions, both lie to the other to prevent the other from worrying, and both repeat the phrase "all right" until neither knows what else to say: "Suddenly, after this there was nothing more to say, for while the emotion was there, the conversation was not; one had bloomed, not the other, and they fell abruptly into emptiness" (254). While Biju is tense, having stolen a few moments from work, and paid for a stolen calling card code from an ingenious "bum" (251), the drama on the cook's side is intensified by his new sense of importance, surrounded by the eavesdropping family of his friend the watchman, who wish to "insinuate themselves deeply into the conversation, to *become* it in fact" (252). Servants' families are interested in servants' families—their hopes are invested in each other's successes and failures—and further add to the pressure on each. Desai poignantly compounds the sense of difficulty, deprivation, and stolen opportunity that she makes clear is a pervasive condition of servitude: not only does the cook have no access to a phone in the house where he serves, but he must depend on the generosity of the watchman, another servant, who allows him to use a phone that his absent employers have locked, so that, as the ironic narrator informs us, "the thieving servants might only receive phone calls and not make them" (252).

As the phone call is abruptly disconnected in mid-conversation, the cook is left "trembling," unsure if Biju will call back, while Biju, on the other side, is left feeling bereft, reflecting on how physical distance also disconnects emotional bonds: "If he continued life in New York, he might never see his *pitaji* again.... affection was only a habit after all, and people, they forgot, or they became accustomed to its absence" (255). This is an example of Desai's fabulous writing: insightful, compassionate yet unsentimental, ironic, paradoxical, and profoundly knowing of the brittleness of human relationships under pressure. In this rare moment of wisdom, Biju becomes grievously aware that even love can become attenuated when sustained only on the promise of future reconnection: "They were no longer relevant to each other's lives except for the hope that they would be relevant" (255). As he decides to return to his father, echoing, unknowingly, his father's earlier affirmation that love matters more than money, Biju reflects in an important moment on each mistaken decision:

> Biju had, in his innocence, done just what his father had, in his own innocence, told him to do. What could his father have known? This way of leaving your family for work had condemned them over several generations to have their hearts always in other places, their minds thinking about people elsewhere; they could never be in a single existence at one time. How wonderful it was going to be to have things otherwise. (342)

We know, by the end, how misplaced Biju's hopes are, how things will not be "otherwise." Biju returns to a joyous reunion with his father, but bereft of all that he had earned, with less than he had started with. We do not know what lies in his future, other than perhaps servitude of an even worse kind than that of his father. Desai astutely depicts this condition of familial separation, itself inherited over generations of internal and now external migration, as the condition of cross-generational servitude and, with extraordinary empathy and sensitivity, gives us a measure of its emotional consequences. She shows how parents' servitude makes their children's servitude worse. And she suggests how servitude complicates and intensifies the emotionality of father-son interactions—their desires and feelings for each other are inextricable from their understanding of the precarity of their status as servants and servant's children.

The Crisis, the Ending, and the Future

As we have seen, the final crisis of *Space* centers the servant, and is occasioned by the employer's betrayal of the relationship. In *Loss*, Desai presents the final crisis not through the cook's perspective but through Sai's. In a similarly horrendously painful scene, in which the servant is humiliated and abased before the employer who fails to hear the servant's real calls of distress, or honor the servant's dignity or worth, the cook is violently beaten by the judge and blamed for the loss of the judge's dog. However, unlike *Space*, in *Loss*, the cook is not fired and instead continues in his servant position in the judge's household. Perhaps, Desai suggests through such an ending, there is no end or alternative to servitude for the likes of Panna Lal and his son, or for the impossible choices they have to make.

The final crisis of *Loss* is precipitated by the convergence of two seemingly unrelated chains of events, both of which are connected to the Gorkha insurgency and to the judge's callous disregard of the cook and others in even more precarious positions. As various pressures build at the end of the novel, these two chains of events send the judge and the cook over the edge. One is the loss of the judge's precious dog, Mutt, who is stolen by desperate, impoverished villagers who were spurned by the judge; the second is the cook's experience of a violent riot.

First, after the Gorkha robbery at Cho Oyu (the judge's house), the police wrongly apprehend a poor local man, a "miserable drunk," whom they beat up and torture to the extent that he goes blind (248). When his wife and father show up at the judge's house, "pleading" for help, and begging for food or employment as "servants" while starvation spreads in the besieged valley, the judge forcefully spurns them (288, 310). He refuses to recognize them as having any claim on him, even though his house is the one that was burgled, and for which they have been wrongly punished. He orders the cook, who occupies an in-between, relatively more privileged status compared to these destitute locals, to remove them. Desai highlights how the judge's meanness and hardened refusal are responsible for the loss that ultimately unhinges him: he is punished, with evident poetic justice, when the desperate villagers, to make some money from resale, steal his beloved dog Mutt.

When these villagers first arrive at Cho Oyu, and the judge tells them to take their complaints to the police, the cook remonstrates, because he knows what the police do to the poor and to women: "'You can't send this woman to the police,' said the cook, 'they'll probably assault her'" (289). Indeed, the narrator's added commentary intensifies our sense of the woman's pathetic condition and the significance of the judge's rejection: "The woman looked raped and beaten already. Her clothes were soiled and her teeth ... [were[missing [or] blackened ..., and she was quite bent from carrying stone" (289). But the judge refuses even to learn from the sense or example of humanity offered by his cook: "India was too messy for justice," reflects the judge, "If you let such people get an inch, they'd take everything you had" (289). Fear of the poor, and of loss, seem to compound such elite and prejudiced reactions, in contrast with the cook, who cannot resist handing over a bag of flour. But he is actively prevented, as "the judge barked, 'Don't give them anything,' and continued his chess game" (311). Desai leaves no doubt of the judge's callousness, "adamant" against their pleas, as he dragoons his servant into doing his dirty work for him. She gives us access instead to the cook's thoughts as he follows orders, but is "concerned that they might need a rest before having to walk another five to six hours through the forest to their village" (311). Like Umrigar, Desai highlights the stony hearts of the upper-class employer and contrasts the empathy of the poor for the even poorer. The crises of both novels dramatize, and are caused by, the refusal to recognize the claims of proximate others.

In a second chain of events, as the Gorkha insurgents gain control of the valley, they demand from each family a "man to represent the household in [their] marches" (298). It is part of Desai's humor that the judge insists that the weak, aging cook should represent that requisite masculinity for their household (300). It is also multiply ironic that the judge, by pressing the cook into such service, shunts his own responsibility onto the servant, and effectively designates the servant as a "family" member, while also diminishing the insurgents' cause by sending his servant. However, when the march turns into a violent riot, and the cook flees, after seeing men being beheaded, he goes into a mode of panic and stress from which he cannot recover, and which again triggers his barely dormant anxieties about his son. Desai focuses fully on the cook's bodily and emotional sensations, on his own gradual awareness of them, as his heart beats so fast that the physical and the psychological, the exertion and the fear, become indistinguishable:

> He ran as fast as his lungs and legs would let him, his heart pounding painfully in his chest, ears, throat, each breath poisonous. He managed to get some distance up the steep shortcut to Ringkingpong Road, and there he felt his legs collapse under him, they were trembling so hard.... Clawing at his heart as if it were a door was his panic—a scrabbling rodent creature. (304–305)

The panic is cast as itself a seemingly material thing, a terrified trapped "creature" that hammers at his heart. For the first time, Panna Lal feels that "this place . . . where he had existed in what seemed a sweetness of crabbiness—was showing him now that . . . he wasn't wanted in Kalimpong and he didn't belong. At that moment, a fear overtook him that he might never see his son again" (306). Unable to recover from this experience, badly rattled for days after, he tries to "calm himself," but "he was sure that something even worse stood around the corner. Where was Biju, where was he? He leaped at every shadow" (309). Again, Desai moves between third-person omniscient narration and free indirect discourse, as she gives us the cook's continued agitation, his loss of a sense of security, and his consequent dread about harm coming to his son, the only precious entity he can claim and whose loss he now fears is imminent.

When the judge realizes that Mutt has disappeared, and throws the household into turmoil, these two strains—the judge's loss of his dog, and the cook's fear of loss of his son—converge. As the judge, the cook, and Sai search for Mutt, all three displace onto this tiny dog their intense feelings, their respective grief or guilt about the real or imagined loss of someone else: Sai, for Gyan; the cook for his son; and the judge for the unwanted, mistreated wife he abandoned to be killed by "accident" in a stove fire by her relatives (338). In an almost surreal scene, the judge dreams that Mutt is dead and that the cook confirms it, the dream overtakes reality: " 'Don't touch her! I'll kill you!' screamed the judge aloud, waking himself up, convinced by the logic of his dream" (343). The judge now loses his mind, and turns on the cook in real life, blaming him for the loss of the dog: " 'I'LL KILL YOU! That's it. I've had enough. It's your fault. It was your responsibility to watch her when I went for my bath' " (343–344). Desai leaves no question, via the chain of causation, that it is in fact the judge himself who is to blame and that the servant is scapegoated yet again. What is more significant in this crisis is that the intensity of the judge's unhinged anger in turn unhinges the already fragile cook, who now turns it inward, as he begins to blame himself for all that has gone wrong.

The final crisis is thus triggered by both the judge's actual loss and the cook's fear of loss, as the latter reaches a climactic state of dread, built upon the anxiety and guilt about his son that has been a constant undercurrent since his wife's death. (That guilt is itself a condition, as we have seen, of his servitude.) This key aspect of the novel's ending is overlooked by most critics.[17] As the judge repeats his accusations and threats, the cook "began to weep without looking at anyone or anything and disappeared into the forest. It occurred to him as he stumbled about that he'd done something so awful, he'd be paid by fate and something even more awful would happen" (344). The cook's undercurrent of guilt about having long ago rendered Biju vulnerable resurfaces, exacerbated by his anxiety about being cut off from Biju, and his constant sense of living under the threat of malign forces coming to avenge him for his original failure to protect his son. Where Umrigar presents Bhima as clear about her own innocence in the face of a false accusation, Desai, in a more complex depiction, presents the cook as internalizing the blame, augmenting the guilt he already feels at his inadequacy as a father, superstitiously seeking punishment to forestall misfortune from befalling his son.

In this crisis at the end, both old men seem to lose their minds, as the cook, now drunk on his own home-brewed alcohol, enters the judge's bedroom to beg his employer to beat him, to punish him for his misdeeds. Desai presents a horrifying, seemingly almost implausible scene where the cook utterly abases himself, throwing himself at the judge's feet, while the judge takes up his slipper to hammer the cook's head with blows, and Sai weeps as she tries to stop them. "I'm a bad man," repeats the cook, also weeping, as he confesses to petty thefts that only further accentuate his deprived status, "beat me, sahib, punish me;" "How dare he lose Mutt," rages the judge (351–352). While some critics have found this breakdown incomprehensible, and one even calls it a measure of the cook's "internalized self-hatred,"[18] I would argue that the cook's reaction is in fact neither. A close reading of the novel reveals how Desai sets up this breakdown to be psychologically plausible and understandable. The cook takes upon himself this punishment and degradation in order to save his son. In his internal logic, almost as an unconscious trick, he is trying to avert the harm that he thinks will otherwise fall upon his son from the bad karma that he believes he set in motion when he lied to the judge after his wife's death. In this novel's intricate narrative logic, this crisis is the climax, the culmination of the compound effects of the cook's servitude and his ongoing guilt and love for his son. The cook's begging for punishment is an effort to atone, to reverse the bad karma, and to recover his son. And in fact, so the novel's plot turn suggests, the cook's wager works, because right after, he does in fact recover his son.

As the cook is beaten, the narrator moves from third-person narration to free indirect discourse to evoke the cook's (sub-)consciousness: "The cook didn't mention his son . . . he had none . . . he'd never had one. . . . It was just his hope writing to him . . . Biju was non-existent" (353). Through this reminder, as the cook descends into darkness, the narrator conjures Biju back into existence, as the real underlying cause for this descent into hellish misery, into the blackness of the cook's despair. The fragmentation of Desai's narration at this point, broken into segments separated by dashes, reflects the fragmentation of Panna Lal's mind (353). The cook has given up hope because he believes that he has failed Biju, that he is "useless" to everyone (353). He begs the judge to kill him: "What is my life? It's nothing. Better that it's gone. It's useless to everyone. . . . Kill me!" (353). This seems like an explicit death wish, as if he simply seeks obliteration. But, I would argue, as the narrator reminds us, what underlies it all is in fact Biju, the cook's hope for and guilt about Biju, his only reason for living, as he keeps repeating. This is his way of being of "use" to Biju, by taking upon himself all evil, or, by obliterating himself, the cause, as he sees it, of the harm that threatens Biju. It is after this that the cook is finally named, for the first and last time in the novel. As Sai imagines her grandfather and the cook returning to normal routine, despite this horrible interaction, because both will continue to depend on each other, "Panna Lal bring the tea," she imagines her grandfather saying, in the indefinite future (356). This overt violence is thus only a rare manifestation of the latent violence of their lifelong relations. As the narrator comments drily, "The judge and his cook had lived together for more years than they had with anyone else, practically in the same room, closer to each other than to any other human being and—nothing, zero, no understanding" (344). Though we get the judge's story, and some understanding of his own struggles, there is no excuse for his moral failures.

The novel almost ends with Sai, who flees outside, devastated, resolving to leave: "She felt a glimmer of strength, of resolve. She must leave" (356). And yet she returns, to care for the cook, to make him tea, even as she contemplates the possibilities of starting her own journey away from Kalimpong, a journey different from those of the other characters.[19] The novel ends, however, not with Sai or the judge, but with the ecstatic reunion of the cook and his son, more poignant because Biju returns with nothing, dressed ludicrously in a woman's nightgown. Perhaps the point is that this is what matters, this familial love and joy; it is what Sai and the judge do not have. Desai concludes with a partial moment of hope, or relief, offered very knowingly as brief, a rare lift in the clouds, as the mountain "turned golden with luminous light" as if in a brief and fleeting revelation of truth—the truth of the heart's affections. If the novel begins with Kanchenjunga shrouded in mist and clouds, dimly "visible above the vapor" (1), emblematic of the fog that shrouds their lives, it ends with Kanchenjunga suddenly emerging from the clouds and turning "golden with the kind of luminous light that made you feel briefly, that truth was apparent" (357). Perhaps what Sai sees is that the servant father and son know and have something that she does not: a relationship, however fraught, of love—they have little else but they have each other.

It is perhaps an indicator of the blind spot around servitude in contemporary literary scholarship that despite the critical attention *Loss* has received, few have addressed the significance of the cook or of the sustained emphasis on servitude as a theme in this novel, and its relation to questions of nation and transnationalism. Like Umrigar's *Space*, *Loss* makes narrative choices that reinforce this theme. Through the alternation of perspectives of both employer and servant, and of the family members of each, Umrigar and Desai explore the interiority, the micropolitics, the complex effects of servitude on individuals and relationships, and the deep consequences on generations of lives. Perhaps the most marked difference of Desai's novel consists in its tonality, created by her irony and humor, and her adamant refusal of sentimentality. Desai thus creates a more multi-faceted complexity of tone, a simultaneous closeness and distancing. Desai's conclusion is bleaker than Umrigar's, despite its moment of alleviation. There is no solution for Biju and the cook, as things stand. That is Desai's grim conclusion. We already know that after returning Biju will regret returning, that he will then remember why he left in the first place. Love can (momentarily) alleviate the grimness of the cook and Biju's future, but, as the conclusion suggests, the cook's life will continue unchanged, as will Biju's, unless and until the nation is able to make changes at the macro level, to bring about social justice through political and systemic change.

Conclusion

"She had lived abroad long enough to interpret Sri Lanka with a long-distance gaze"[1]

In a brief but memorable scene in Mira Nair's film adaptation of Jhumpa Lahiri's novel *The Namesake* (2006), as the Bengali American family visits relatives in Calcutta, Gogol, the young protagonist, puts on his sneakers and heads out for an early morning jog. Unaccustomed to this practice, his startled grandmother orders "Chotu," a male servant, to follow the "young master" to make sure he does not get lost. "Keep an eye on him," she instructs Chotu (whose name means "young one"), who has no other name, and who does not appear again in the film (44:55). But even in this one scene (based on a single sentence in Lahiri's novel about the constraints on Gogol in India; Lahiri, 83), Nair provides an unexpectedly empathetic, if somewhat comical, glimpse of servitude in 1990's India (Nair 44:22–46:04). Obeying with alacrity, Chotu instantly drops what he is doing to dash after Gogol. The camera follows the slightly overweight Chotu, in his flapping rubber slippers, huffing and puffing through bustling crowded streets, calling after the oblivious and much more fit Gogol until Chotu literally runs out of breath. Though neither speaks the other's language, Chotu is able to convey to Gogol, through some English words and dramatic gestures, that his heart is beating too fast and that he would die of cardiac arrest if he had to run any more. Concerned and amused, Gogol obligingly gives up his run and agrees to return with Chotu, who sings happily on his unexpected tram ride home.

Gogol's bemusement and unusual response to the servant's importunity bespeaks the second-generation Indian American's lack of familiarity with South Asian cultures of servitude. Gogol smiles cordially at Chotu, treats him with respect and care, and does not brush off Chotu's request. (How unusual it is to see someone of the employer class smiling at a servant. More to the point, we might ask, why is it so unusual?) "Have pity on a fat man," Chotu beseeches, as, in strange moment of intimacy, Chotu takes Gogol's hand and places it upon his heart to prove how fast his heart is beating (45:40). "Don't die," Gogol responds solicitously to Chotu, touching his arm gently, and asks him what he wants: "Wanna go back?" (45:58). Born and raised in the United States, Gogol has no idea why he cannot go jogging in the streets of Calcutta, or why a servant might be sent after him if he tries. It does not occur to him not to accede to the servant, or not to treat him as a fellow human being. By contrast, Gogol's grandmother and even Chotu himself, who have lived all their lives in India, have no doubt that it is the servant's bounden duty to do what the employer demands, even at risk of physical hardship. Where the grandmother expects the servant to keep Gogol safe, Gogol ensures that the servant is safe. This patent disjunction between American guest and Indian hosts is bridged, however, by the South Asian American filmmakers, director Mira Nair and screenwriter Sooni Taraporevala. As diasporic insider/outsiders who both understand the South Asian culture of servitude from the inside and view it from the outside, Nair and Taraporevala implicitly offer a mild critique and suggest an approach toward some amelioration, some mode of recasting a relationship that as yet cannot be wholly transformed or repudiated.

I have argued in this book that in the late twentieth and early twenty-first century, such a new generation of transnational South Asian writers with origins in India, Pakistan, Sri Lanka, and Bangladesh, who have spent significant parts of their lives in the West, has begun to resee, rethink, and defamiliarize accustomed ways of viewing and accepting domestic servitude in their home countries. In their fiction, Daniyal Mueenuddin, Romesh Gunesekera, Aravind Adiga, Thrity Umrigar, and Kiran Desai devise new forms and break from earlier literary conventions in order to make servitude a central question for both literature and for the postcolonial nation. I suggest that it is their insider/outsider status—their knowing from within a specifically South Asian structure of feeling and being, and their ability to see with fresh eyes upon return from elsewhere—that seems conducive to a new critical approach, to new ways of seeing and (re)thinking an otherwise too familiar culture of servitude. They have what, in the epigraph above, Ondaatje calls the "long-distance gaze," or what I call the dual positionality of being situated both within and without a system. As a consequence, they see differently than those situated only within or only without. Using methods of theoretically, politically, and historically informed close reading and intersectional feminism, I show how, unlike earlier Indian English writers who crucially drew upon but decentered servitude, the writers of servitude fiction center both servitude as an issue and the servant as a protagonist with complex subjectivity and interiority, and how they deploy new formal strategies to achieve their goals. I hence identify a new genre of what I call servitude fiction that reformulates literary conventions to center and emphasize marginalized servant perspectives, experiences, and concerns, and that explores in particular the complex affects and paradoxes of intimacy across enormous social divides that constitute relationships in servitude. Ultimately, an effect of this genre is that it raises awareness of a long-overlooked issue and seeks progressively to change normalized ways of seeing, thinking, and acting.

Where Daniyal Mueenuddin uses the form of interlinked short stories in *In Other Rooms, Other Wonders* to examine multiple perspectives and experiences of male and female servants, and to show their interconnections and contrasts, Romesh Gunesekera and Aravind Adiga, in their respective novels *Reef* and *The White Tiger*, invert novelistic convention to center the (male) servant narrator as subject (in every sense) throughout of his own story. Women writers Thrity Umrigar and Kiran Desai, respectively in *A Space Between Us* and *The Inheritance of Loss*, choose instead to share narrative space, to alternate the stories and perspectives of (female and male) servants and employers to track their connections and disconnections, and complexities. Clearly, these are not the first (or last) South Asian writers to write about domestic servitude and how it intersects with gender, class, age, ethnicity, and so on. What I find distinctive about this new wave of servitude fiction is that in each iteration these writers: (i) center the servant's own story, not as subsidiary or appendage to the story of the master; (ii) explore the interiority of the servant; (iii) offer implicit critique of servitude as a system that dehumanizes, degrades, stigmatizes, and enforces abjection; (iv) are interested in the complexities of an individual psyche shaped by servitude and in the peculiar intimacies of relationships shaped and warped by servitude; and (v) suggest possible alternatives or ways out of servitude (primarily education) or invite readers to think about systemic change.[2] Where Daniyal Mueenuddin calls attention both to systemic problems such as feudalism coexisting with late capitalism and to the individual psyches caught within these systems, Gunesekera and Adiga explore the homosocial complexities of relationships between younger male servants and their employers in the context of national unrest or failure, while Umrigar and Desai focus on older male and female servants and employers and explore the intergenerational effects of servitude upon servants and their families.

When I began this project, I did not start out looking for transnational writers. In the course of my research, as I gathered examples of what I saw as a new genre of fiction, I discovered a significant pattern: that the dominant examples were written by transnational South Asian returnees. This is not to say, of course, that all transnational millennial writers focus progressively on servitude. (They do not. Many are focused on other matters and may not notice servitude at all. Others may still replicate unthinkingly some of the conventional modes of representation of servitude and servants.[3]) Nor is this to say that writers who live and write only within South Asia are always unaware of the problems of servitude.[4] To be clear, I am not arguing that *all* contemporary transnational South Asian English literature is more progressive with regard to servitude than domestic fiction; nor am I arguing that *all* novels produced within South Asia are unaware of the problems of domestic servitude. I am arguing, however, for visibly predominant trends. The writers that leaped to my notice as belonging to this emergent wave of servitude fiction happened to be transnational. Many of them live in South Asia after having lived abroad. Travel and displacement, I suggest, enable seeing with fresh eyes, a shift of consciousness. As the filmmaker and scriptwriter Rohena Gera says about the impetus for her 2018 film *Sir* (on which more below), growing up as a middle-class person with live-in cooks, carers, and so on, she was always aware of and questioned the system, but returning from study abroad enabled her to see it anew:

> From a very young age, I struggled with ... this way of living.... That I love this person who has to take care of me as a child, but there is this barrier, and she sits on the floor and eats, and I can go sit on her lap and she'll give you bites, but you know she can't use your chai-mug or whatever ... These are things I carried for a long time. I went away to study in the US and when you come back you see things even more ... it's even more bothersome, and yet you are part of it, you're part of a system.... It's something I carried around for many years like a sort of guilty secret about who I really am.[5]

This shift, I suggest, is also generational. As I show in Part One, early to mid-twentieth-century writers, in particular men, ignored or sidelined servitude. Rushdie, very much a transnational writer, began to pull servants into what I call the middle ground. Many contemporary South Asian writers continue that trend. But some, at the turn of the century, focus on servitude in new ways, and they are predominantly transnational.

Much of this globally published, internationally acclaimed English fiction has begun to influence South Asian writers publishing within South Asia, who are now beginning to pay far more attention to servitude. *Reef*, for example, as discussed in Chapter 4, has generated a number of novels within Sri Lanka that focus on servants, such as Nirmali Hettiarchchi's *Replacements* and Elmo Jayawardena's *Sam's Story* (both first-person male servant narratives that are highly derivative of *Reef*), and Rajiva Wijesinha's *Servants: A Cycle* (an upper-class narrator's recollections of a generation of family servants). *The White Tiger* has also prompted followers, most notably and recently Deepti Kapoor's *Age of Vice* (2023), which replays the narrative of an impoverished young village boy who becomes a servant/driver and is forced to take the fall for a murderous car crash occasioned by the drunken and corrupt scion of a super-rich, super-powerful family. *The White Tiger* has also been adapted into a Hollywood film, directed by Adiga's college friend Ramin Bahrani, released via Netflix in 2021. Very well acted and directed, it was nominated for several awards, including the 2021 Academy Award for Best Adapted Screenplay, and won the Gold List Award for the same category.[6] This film is mostly faithful to the novel, but softens the worst aspects of each character, including that of Balram (played by Adarsh Gourav), who is cast as a much more endearing figure than in the novel.[7] Nonetheless, as a cultural product with greater global reach, the film further works to popularize the important interventions of the novel.

In looking closely at five prominent examples of South Asian English millennial servitude fiction, my goal is to examine some key modes of formal and thematic intervention, not to be exhaustive or encyclopedic. There are undoubtedly many others that I wish I could include, and that were published after I had drafted an already very long book. Servitude fiction is emergent and flourishing with dazzling new iterations. For instance, Neel Mukerhjee's latest book, *A State of Freedom* (2018), consisting of five semi-related sections, has two significant sections on a female servant, albeit one told through the perspective of an upper-class male narrator (a returnee to India from Britain), who becomes fascinated by the life story of his parents' live-out cook Renu, and the other from the perspective of a village girl turned housemaid, Milly, incarcerated in the apartment of the people she serves, who finally makes her escape. And most recently, Tabish Khair's stunning short story, "Namaste Trump" (2023), offers a fabulous satiric account of a middle-class man's guilt about abandoning his disabled servant boy (also called "Chottu") during the COVID-19 pandemic. Narrated by the upper-class male employer, this story carries resonances of Mueenuddin's "About a Burning Girl," as it makes a similar strategic choice to use the point of view of an employer who in the telling unwittingly implicates himself. Gradually revealing himself as a fascistic admirer of Modi and Trump (hence the title), this narrator describes how his family got rid of their house servant when the pandemic hit, and how Chottu was beaten up by the police and sent to a migrant labor center, where he caught and died of COVID. The story ends (spoiler alert) chillingly with the narrator seeing Chottu's ghost in the stairwell after he has been informed that Chottu was cremated; his wife sees Chottu too, but, the narrator realizes, the policemen he summons cannot see what he sees. Only the employers' guilt seems to produce this vision. Khair thus offers a brilliant double turn: first, with Chottu's apparent return to his employers' apartment, we wonder if his death and cremation was a case of mistaken identity, and if Chottu is indeed alive; then, second, it becomes clear that what the narrator and his wife see is indeed a ghost, an emanation of their unconscious, a return of the repressed. Chottu has indeed come home. The servant haunts—and will always haunt—the employer who betrays his dependent's trust, who refused to recognize their implicit bond and abandoned Chottu in a time of dire need. The servant boy, Khair suggests, was clearly not as easily disposable or dispensable as the narrator imagined.[8]

Although I focus in this book on servitude fiction, I want to note briefly that transnational South Asian films have also begun to do similar work. Indian American transnational filmmaker Mira Nair, whose film adaptation of *The Namesake* I discuss above, also made an earlier film, *Monsoon Wedding* (2001) (screenplay by British Indian Sabrina Dhawan), which gives unusually sensitive, sympathetic, and extended attention to a female servant character. *Monsoon Wedding* follows multiple narrative strands as members of an extended family gather in Delhi from all over the Indian diaspora (the United States, Middle East, Australia) to celebrate a wedding. But it also includes, in a minor strain, the growing romance between the Event Manager, P. K. Dubey, and the household's maidservant, Alice. Tillotama Shome plays Alice beautifully as a shy, decorous, somewhat wary, self-abnegating housemaid, responding diligently to everyone's beck and call. Yet Alice has unexpected moments, as the camera stays focused on her, as she cautiously brings water to the wedding planner and his crew and asks shyly if they would like ice, as she casts him a sidelong glance, tilts her head sideways, or joins in the excitement of the women of the household when the groom's family arrives, or eventually dares a heart-wrenching smile. She is smart and knowledgeable, as Dubey discovers when he tentatively hands her his card and email address and tries to explain about "letters you send by computer" (37:20). "Email?" she responds calmly, as he is overcome by embarrassment in case she thought he was talking down to her (37:22).

Dhawan and Nair not only choose to give Alice separate space and her own story within the narrative of the film, but also take time to explore the housemaid's interiority, her secret if innocent desires. In a striking scene, Alice, on her daily round of dusting, ventures into her employers' bedroom, where she is tempted to try on some of the lavish finery and wedding jewelry that has been left lying around (44:44–47:26). As the camera zooms in on her looking at herself in the mirror, the film makes it very clear, with soft romantic music, that this is a girlish game, a form of make-believe, a trying on of a fictive identity, a what-if moment of pure pleasure in a brief hiatus from work. The scene poignantly suggests a hidden, human side to this humble girl playacting for herself, smiling as she imagines herself momentarily in another role, perhaps as a bride. Yet such role-playing is complex, for it in fact prepares her for other future roles and identities. And it offers her a mode of escape, transient but real.

Throughout the scene, there is no question that Alice is honest, that she does not plan to steal a single item, as P. K. Dubey well understands when he accidentally looks in the second-floor window that he has climbed up outside to decorate the house. Smiling indulgently, he gazes upon the unsuspecting girl he himself desires as a bride, recognizing a mirroring of desire in her for a life other than what she currently has. He understands that this is a feminine desire for femininity for a girl denied ordinary everyday pleasure. But unfortunately, his crew, who join him, fall instantly into the clichéd assumption that Alice is a thief, and create an uproar. In a panic, horrified at being seen and misunderstood, Alice shrinks into herself as the camera focuses on her stricken face. The film thus also pushes back against the servant cliché of servant dishonesty: Alice is shown very clearly putting back the jewelry before the men see her. "Chori nahin kar rahi" ("She is not stealing!"), Dubey affirms as he swears at his men (47:22). As Alice becomes withdrawn, sad, and quiet, and Dubey morose and depressed, the film takes another unusual step. Dubey's men recognize that they have made a mistake, and line up to beg Alice's pardon. What is notable here is not just that their apology clears up the misunderstanding and enables the resumption of the burgeoning romance, but that the working-class men patently show respect and consideration for a working-class girl, a domestic servant. The film maintains its interest in Alice to its joyous conclusion, as it uses the technique of cross-cutting between the celebrations of the affluent upper-class and the quieter celebration of the wedding of Dubey and Alice, who is wooed through the continuing motif of marigold flowers, and ends up, smiling shyly, joining in the communal dance at the end. Though Alice is not a protagonist in *Monsoon Wedding*, the film gives unusual attention and subjectivity to this servant figure whose parallel narrative is given an unprecedented importance in South Asian cinema.

It is perhaps no accident, then, that in a recent, more groundbreaking Hindi film set in modern-day Bombay, *Is Love Enough? Sir* (2018), Tillotama Shome plays the role of a housemaid who is the protagonist upon whom the film centers. *Sir* was nominated for fifteen international awards and won eleven, including Best Actress in a Lead Role for Shome, and Best Screenplay for Rohena Gera.[9] Shome is an English-speaking Indian actor, with a degree from New York University; Gera, also the director and co-producer, is likewise a transnational filmmaker (she is Indian, with degrees from Stanford University and Sarah Lawrence College). Described as a "romance" and "drama" in which "a prosperous young Indian man falls in love with his servant, a widow with the dream of becoming a fashion designer,"[10] *Sir* can in fact be seen as both a fantasy (for its ending) and a remarkably well-acted and well-directed exploration of gendered domestic servitude and of possible ways of rethinking it.

Employing the mode of social realism, the film focuses with unprecedented sensitivity and delicacy on Ratna, a young widow who aspires to become a fashion designer and who leaves the village for the city to become a maidservant. With the visual power of the moving image, in detailed, carefully crafted scenes, the film emphasizes both Ratna's fragility and her resilience; it shows her cooking, dusting, cleaning, serving food, eating by herself in the kitchen, sleeping in a tiny servant's room, being insulted by her employer's guests, taking a tailoring course on the side, and, in a rare moment, dancing joyously with her friends at a street festival. Shome's mesmerizing acting—her expressive facial and bodily language—partners well with that of Vivek Gomber, who plays Ashwin, the progressive, America-returned young Indian employer who falls in love with Ratna. The film knowingly takes a huge risk in setting up this relationship, as it presents the two living in close quarters alone in Ashwin's apartment, and gradually developing a mutually respectful emotional bond. As Shome says in an interview with Rajeev Masand, she was "uncomfortable" with the premise and hesitated before accepting this role, in part because the only pairing or love story of a man (or "master") and a maid to be found in India was in pornography, not even in imaginative fiction. As someone from a middle-class background herself who has mostly played people who are "marginalized and poor," she felt a strong sense of responsibility to avoid romanticizing, "misappropriating," or "misrepresenting" Ratna or pandering to voyeurism; she worked hard (and successfully) to emphasize Ratna's "dignity" throughout the film, to maintain Ratna's agency and not cross any lines of decorum and propriety.[11] Before and after every scene, Shome reports, she and Gomber would check in with each other: "Are we safe?" they would ask each other, to maintain a careful balance between Ashwin's power and Ratna's agency, to avoid being read in any moment as Ashwin jeopardizing Ratna having a choice.[12]

Sir thus truly breaks new ground in presenting this relationship, and in centering on a maidservant and her life conditions. As Shome notes, the goal of the film, without being "preachy" or didactic, is to open up questions and introspection even among liberals about their internalized prejudices toward class and servitude. "I know I felt uncomfortable. I know have these prejudices," she confesses disarmingly, but continues:

> It is invisible slavery. . . . We let people service us at such close intimate quarters, and yet can't imagine friendship with them. What is wrong with us? What monsters lurk within us? . . . And we think we are nice people! And yet we have people who are in our homes, in our kitchens, making the food that goes inside our body, and yet we can't imagine falling in love with them, . . . or sharing the same table with them, or using the same bathroom with them.[13]

It is notable that Shome speaks first of friendship, and then of falling in love. She confesses her own initial discomfort with the ending, where Ashish proposes marriage, and Ratna, though she initially disconnects from him, aware of the class barriers, answers his phone call in a moment of reconnection, suggesting that they will reunite. I would say, however, that in moving what is a nuanced, delicate representation of female servitude and the inevitable awkwardness between a young male employer and young female servant the film shows so well into the realm of romance and marriage, the film makes a tricky leap from realism to fantasy. Perhaps the film would work better if it were to restrict itself to exploring that non-romantic discomfort (a complex enterprise in itself) without shifting into a facile romantic resolution. Within the mode of social realism, the ending is implausible. For a modern companionate or "love marriage," those class barriers remain significant: Ratna cannot speak English; she does not have an educational level remotely comparable to Ashwin's; it is hard to imagine how they would negotiate her inability to mix with the class that necessarily constitutes his family and friends. In other words, we might ask, why does the film require a cross-class love story to draw attention to or shift attitudes toward domestic servitude?[14] None of the servitude fiction examined in this study makes such an attempt. The alternatives that this global fiction imagines are more grounded in plausible realities (such as education or entrepreneurship), alternatives that are not cocooned in the fantasy of a heterosexual love story, and that are more concerned with gaining independence, addressing the problems of servitude itself, and contending with social inequality and systemic injustice. Servitude fiction, for all its variety, rarely turns to romance as a solution; it focuses instead on the complexities of a vast variety of other human experiences and interactions shaped by servitude. Its solutions, when implied or proposed, involve the removal of inequality and disrespect and the amelioration of systems that produce the conditions of servitude.

At a crucial moment in the 2018 biopic, *On the Basis of Sex*, feminist lawyer and political activist Dorothy Kenyon tells the young Ruth Bader Ginsburg, "*Change minds first. Then change the law*" (59:13).[15] Servitude fiction and films like *Sir* aim precisely to change minds first, to do the cultural work that is a necessary precursor to changing and implementing laws. I do not claim, in this book, that forms of art and cultural production, like literature or film, can alone change the world. I do suggest, however, that they can prompt awareness of unquestioned norms and shifts in attitudes, and change ways of thinking that might lead to progressive social change. Indeed, they work alongside, perhaps coincident with, other more overt forms of organized activism. Separately, but significantly, in this same time period, international activists and organizers in many countries in South Asia have begun to mobilize to demand more recognition of domestic workers as workers, and to legislate for more protections, benefits, and rights. In 2011, the ILO (International Labor Organization) in Geneva adopted the historic Convention 189 (supplemented by Recommendation 201), which "lays down basic rights and principles, and requires States to take a series of measures with a view to making decent work a reality for domestic workers."[16] But though ratified by some South Asian countries, its provisions have not always led to implementation or changes in law within these countries. As of this writing, some modest changes, however, seem discernible on the horizon.

In Pakistan, although there is as yet no national provision for domestic workers, a bill passed in 2017 is "under discussion by the relevant National Assembly Committee" that aims to bring domestic workers under the same jurisdiction as Pakistan's labor laws.[17] In 2019, a Domestic Workers Act was passed within Pakistan's province of Punjab (later followed by similar ones in Sindh and Islamabad). It specifies a minimum age of fifteen for part-time "light" domestic work, and eighteen for full-time work. Among other provisions, such as forbidding forced labor and discrimination, as well as requiring a contract, wages set at or above minimum wage, consent and compensation for extra work, safety and "dignified working conditions," benefits and medical care, paid leave, and maternity and sick leave, it also "forbids the use of the word 'servant.'"[18] Unfortunately, implementation of this law remains to be desired, since neither workers not employers are aware of its existence. As Shakeeb Asrar notes, "The country's 'informal' workforce has long faced severe exploitation and dehumanization without much intervention from the state" (except when particularly egregious cases of child abuse or sexual abuse hit the news); in addition to legislation, he argues, "changing social norms, employers' expectations, and devoting more resources to implementing existing laws can better protect Pakistan's domestic workers in the future."[19]

In Bangladesh, as the COVID-19 pandemic exacerbated the conditions faced by domestic workers, where many lost their jobs and could not access vaccines, a project funded by Oxfam Canada titled "Securing Rights of Women Domestic Workers in Bangladesh," has worked on distributing provisions and medicine, providing life-skills training (such as learning to negotiate with employers), and raising awareness through such means as social media campaigns and television series.[20] In India, regulation of domestic work remains "de-federalized, with no overarching and binding rules to govern the working conditions of domestic laborers," creating variability by state and little protections for domestic workers who are not covered by labor laws.[21] There are, however, organizations such as the National Domestic Workers Movement that endeavor to fight for domestic workers' rights, and provide educational support, skill training, and legal and medical help.[22] Others include the gender justice movement for domestic workers in India, supported by the Global Fund for Women.[23] Finally, in Sri Lanka, though domestic workers have not been recognized as part of the labor force, in March 2018, the Cabinet approved the Sri Lanka National Action Plan, which would protect human rights, including those of domestic workers, and approved the inclusion of domestic workers under the definition of "workers" under the country's labor laws.[24]

Change is slow. Perhaps one day future readers will look back at servitude fiction as something that called attention to and attempted to change a kind of social injustice that had remained unremarked and unnoticed for too long, and that attempted to craft new forms to sensitize readers and occasion new ways of seeing. For now, I submit, writers like Mueenuddin, Gunesekera, Adiga, Umrigar, and Kiran Desai are important contributors both to a global literature and to a broader global social movement for progressive change.

Notes

Introduction

1. Ama Ata Aidoo, in *No Sweetness Here and Other Stories*.
2. The first wave of postcolonial literature is usually recognized as anticolonial work that struggles to (re)build national(ist) consciousness, to decolonize minds, to challenge by revising colonialist versions of precolonial and colonial histories, to imagine self-determined, egalitarian futures. Prominent examples from South Asia, Africa, and the Caribbean include Raja Rao's *Kanthapura* (1938), Chinua Achebe's *Things Fall Apart* (1958), Ngugi wa Thiong'o's *A Grain of Wheat* (1967), Michelle Cliff's *Abeng* (1984). The second wave addresses the disillusionment that followed after Independence, in the wake of unfulfilled promises, corrupt neocolonial governments, and continued Western neo-imperialism, as in Ayi Kwei Armah's *The Beautyful Ones Are Not Yet Born*, Salman Rushdie's *Midnight's Children* (1981), Arundhati Roy's *The God of Small Things*, and Cliff's *No Telephone to Heaven* (1987). Some identify the third wave of global postcolonial literature as including diasporic, transnational, or postnational literature that addresses concerns both inclusive of and beyond its national context. Amitav Ghosh's *The Glass Palace* (2000), Mohsin Hamid's *The Reluctant Fundamentalist* (2007), or Chimamanda Ngozi Adichie's *Americanah* (2013), would be good examples.
3. The story is also concerned with women and young girls pushed into prostitution under systemic gender inequality.
4. On Aidoo's use of the oral form of the dilemma tale, see Ketu Katrak's Afterword, 135–160.
5. In India the film was violently opposed by Hindu fundamentalists, who called for it to be banned; in the West it was often commended for its courage and sexual progressiveness, though many also challenged its understanding of female same-sex desire as resulting from male abandonment. For a queer postcolonial reading of the film, see Gayatri Gopinath.
6. As we will see, fiction and film produced by employer classes regularly reveal anxiety about this power that servants have. In much British Victorian fiction, a good servant keeps family secrets, while a bad one betrays them. Some twentieth-century British writers cast servants as using their knowledge to take righteous revenge on bad employers. In A. S. Byatt's 1992 novella "Morpho Eugenia," only servants know the dark secret of incest that underlies the seemingly perfect Victorian household, and they finally expose it in an act of protest and resistance when they disrupt the evil son's carryings-on with his sister after he rapes and impregnates a servant child. However, where Byatt's servants push back against a powerful and abusive elite man,

in *Fire*, Mundu aligns himself with the male employer to exert masculine power against vulnerable women who have not acted maliciously.

7. It is almost impossible to think about lesbianism and servitude in South Asia without invoking Ismat Chughtai's famous 1942 Urdu short story "Lihaaf" (often translated as "The Quilt"), which became even more well known when it led to a two-year obscenity trial in Lahore. (The charges were eventually dropped because no explicit reference to sex could be cited, despite the suggestiveness of the story.) *Fire* clearly draws heavily on "Lihaaf" in that the implied cause of lesbianism in both texts is a husband's neglect: in "Lihaaf," the elite husband prefers boys, and therefore his pampered but isolated, childless wife turns to the female household servant who massages her. "Lihaaf" is narrated from the naïve perspective of a child who is herself subjected to the sexual advances of the lady of the house, and who finally understands what is happening when one night, woken by the sounds emanating from her hostess's bed, and terrified by the "elephant" shaped, monstrously shaking quilt, she finally sees what she sees—but refuses to tell—when that eponymous quilt "is lifted" (19). *Fire* substitutes two Hindu women of the same class for the feudal Muslim household in Chughtai's story, and makes a male servant, instead of a female child, the instrument of disclosure. Like *Fire*, "Lihaaf" is not interested in the story or subjectivity of the servant—Chughtai's focus is on the upper-class child's coming to awareness of female sexuality, and on critiquing the system of purdah, or female segregation.

8. Ray and Qayum define "culture" as "the interconnected realms of consciousness and practice, and necessarily encompasses the dimension of power" (3).

9. On the shift from feudal to modern imaginaries, see Ray and Qayum 6–8.

10. Manan Desai notes that for early twentieth-century Leftist and socialist thinkers, the anticolonial struggle was premised on the freedom of the worker from capitalist oppression. As Lenin argued in 1919, "The liberation of the colonies is only thinkable along with the liberation of workers in the metropolis" (quoted by Desai, 85). However, as Sonal Sharma shows, in India, servants were not even recognized as workers within the postcolonial legal frameworks that established protections for factory workers and other forms of labor. While twenty-first-century servitude fiction does not propose communism or the end of capitalism, it does frequently gesture toward more socialist democratic solutions within postcolonial capitalist economies.

11. The National Domestic Workers' Movement in India cites 4.2 million as the official estimate, and 50 million as the unofficial one. They define the domestic worker as follows: "Under the ILO Convention 189, a domestic worker is 'any person engaged in domestic work within an employment relationship.' A domestic worker may work on full-time or part-time basis; may be employed by a single household or by multiple employers; may be residing in the household of the employer (live-in worker) or may be living in his or her own residence (live-out). A domestic worker may be working in a country of which she/he is not a national. Nearly 90% of domestic workers in India are women or children (especially girls), ranging from ages 12 to 75 and it is estimated that 25% among them are below the age of 14. The majority of domestic workers are illiterate. They are engaged in tasks such as cooking, washing, and cleaning, which are traditionally seen as women's work and considered subservient in nature. In India,

the stigma linked to domestic work is heightened by the caste system, since tasks such as cleaning and sweeping are associated with the people belonging to the 'so-called' low castes" (https://ndwm.org/domestic-workers/).
12. https://www.ilo.org/newdelhi/areasofwork/WCMS_141187/lang--en/index.htm.
13. https://paycheck.pk/labour-laws/domestic-workers-in-pakistan.
14. https://www.international.gc.ca/world-monde/stories-histoires/2022/domestic-rights-droits-domestique.aspx?lang=eng. See also https://www.ilo.org/wcmsp5/groups/public/---asia/---ro-bangkok/---ilo-jakarta/documents/presentation/wcms_617648.pdf.
15. International Labor Organization, "Domestic Workers and Decent Work in Sri Lanka," 2020, p.13 (https://www.ilo.org/wcmsp5/groups/public/---asia/---ro-bangkok/---ilo-colombo/documents/publication/wcms_768671.pdf).
16. It is no small irony on Hagedorn's part that this German filmmaker, who is so unused to servants, is discomfited by their presence, claims to value his privacy, and views servitude as a "colonial" problem in the Philippines, himself engages in sex tourism with an impoverished Filipino boy. Hagedorn thus suggests how the global system of postcoloniality places Global South nations and people in such a relation of servitude to the Global North.
17. I draw here upon Arlie Hochschild's important notion of "emotional labor" as the silent invisible work where employees have to project a requisite demeanor, suppress their own emotions, and artificially induce different emotions both to do their own visible work and to evoke the desired emotional response from customers or employers. Hochschild distinguishes *emotional labor* (part of a paid job) from *emotion work* (undertaken in unpaid private or familial situations) by emphasizing three key features: face-to-face interactions; the requirement that workers modulate their own emotions (at emotional cost) to produce requisite emotions in others; the lack of recognition and the invisibility of this part of the job. Hochschild studied airline stewardesses, who were trained to project a welcoming sincerity and suppress annoyance at passengers' unreasonable requests, including sexual advances, but her research has been extended to a variety of non-service professions, including medicine, law, and teaching.
18. As Ray and Qayum note, "In India the hiring of domestic workers is not restricted to the affluent classes but extends to the middle and even lower-middle classes.... The ability to transfer reproductive work to a lower class can be seen as a hallmark of the Indian middle classes" (9). I would only add that this is true across South Asia.
19. To distinguish between class and caste, which may overlap but are not the same, let me note that class is a system of economic and social ranking, within which some mobility is at least theoretically possible, whereas caste is by definition fixed and inherited as a determinant of identity regardless of financial or educational status. In South Asia, the Vedic or Varna caste system is a primary determinant of identity within Hindu cultures, but not among non-Hindus (except converts) even within India, like Muslims or Christians, let alone among Muslim-majority cultures such as in Pakistan or Bangladesh. Hence, I focus on class and other vectors of identity in fiction from contexts in which there is no mention of caste, as in Daniyal Mueenuddin's

stories about farm workers or feudal servants in Pakistan, or Shyam Selvadurai's fiction about class and Sinhalese-Tamil ethnic tensions in Sri Lanka. Of course, class intersects with caste in contexts where caste is relevant, or residual. In a household of Hindu servants, for example, the hierarchy among servants may be shaped by the tasks assigned as well as by caste identity. A person may or may not be employed as a servant depending on caste status. For example, an "untouchable" in Raja Rao's *Kanthapura* or Arundhati's Roy's *The God of Small Things* is not allowed inside the upper-class or upper-caste home and cannot be employed as a domestic servant, and is often distinguished from the domestic servants who work in those homes. There is some debate about whether (residual or retroactively created) caste identities are operative among Muslims in India, since Islam *de jure* does not recognize or sanction caste. Some claim that Indian Muslims *de facto* have a system of social stratification where the "Ashraf" (descendants of Muslims from outside India) distinguish themselves from and look down upon the "Ajlaf" and "Arzal" (descendants of lower-caste converts to Islam). Growing up in Karachi, Pakistan in the 1970s and 1980s, I did not see caste among Muslims. Caste is not integral to Islam. I certainly would not deny that social stratification exists among South Asian Muslims, but I would suggest that it depends primarily on class and ethnicity, not caste, since it is not ordained by religion, nor based on religious categories as the Hindu caste system is. However, the Hindu caste system remains powerful and influential: in the case of converts from Hinduism, some non-Hindu communities remain marked by caste identities, such as the Choohra (formerly sweeper) community, described in Mohammed Hanif's 2011 novel *Our Lady of Alice Bhatti*.

20. As the writer Amitava Kumar remarks sardonically in "Bad News," "In India, even an ordinary middle-class person can employ domestic help. You provide a young man or woman a space to sleep, leftover food, and old clothes, and you are likely to get away with paying as little as fifty dollars a month. A hundred maximum."

21. The protagonist of "A Good Shopkeeper," for instance, an accountant (who loses his job, cannot find another one, and eventually becomes a shopkeeper) has a secret affair with a housemaid, which eases him into his drop in class position (in *Arresting God*). In most of Upadhyay's stories, servants are present as minor characters, but in some they become prominent as witnesses to the misdeeds of their employers (as in "A Servant in the City," about a young village boy seduced by his female employer, in *The Royal Ghosts*), or narrators, as in "A Great Man's House," where an old male servant describes the doings of his master's scheming young wife (in *Arresting God*). However, Upadhyay uses servants to reflect on the employer, not, as in the servitude fiction I discuss in this book, to focus on the inner world of the servant character per se.

22. In a vignette titled "Maid in Iran," for instance, Dumas describes her family's experiences with various couples who worked for them, and how her father paid for one servant's child's education, enabling him to leave servitude behind (*Laughing* 30–41). "In Iran, servants were usually villagers" who worked for "families in the city" and who sometimes "stayed for life," she explains (30). Marjane Satrapi's graphic memoir, *Persepolis*, offers an important example that critiques the system of servitude in Iran.

In an early episode, the young Marjane describes how her maid, who could not read or write, engages in a secret romance with the neighbor's son, enabled by Marjane, the child protagonist, who acts as go-between, and writes letters for her maid. But when the neighbor's son finds out that Mehri is a maid, he abandons her, Marjane's parents admonish their employee, and Marjane learns an important lesson about class inequality in Iran. But Satrapi ends the chapter, "The Letter," by making a broader point about enemies within Iran: at the macro-level, in the public sphere, on "Black Friday," so many Iranian men are killed that "a rumor spread that Israeli soldiers were responsible for the slaughter" (39); simultaneously, at the micro-level, in the private sphere, when Marjane's mother finds out that Mehri took young Marjane to a demonstration, she slaps the maid across the face. Marjane's wry conclusion connects her mother's treatment of the lower-class servant (cross-class violence) in the home with the massacre of Iranian men (political violence) by the Iranian government: "in fact it was really our own who had attacked us" (39). Through ironic juxtaposition, Satrapi thus also calls attention to servitude as a form of political violence.

23. Later, the same rabble rouser uses the language of slavery to make his point even stronger: "In our own country, the country we fight for, we are treated like slaves" (175).

24. Since Robbins' groundbreaking work, recent scholars who study British and American literatures have paid closer attention to a conglomerate of concerns that emerge around questions of literary servitude. Mark Thornton Burnett, for example, examines higher-class cultural anxieties and fears that are expressed via servants in English Renaissance drama, Kristina Straub the constructions of gender and sexuality in intimate domestic affective relations in eighteenth-century British literature, Jean Fernandez the instabilities introduced by servant literacy in nineteenth century British fiction, Mary Wilson the role of domestic servants in modernist women writers' development of experimental forms, and Margaret Jordan the retrospective representations of black servitude in recent African American historical fiction. In the United States, domestic servants from the nineteenth century on were either descendants of, or white immigrants who were compared to, black slaves, so that, as Barbara Ryan argues, the discourse of domestic servitude in the United States has always been tied to the racial history of chattel slavery. Twentieth-century white American literature and film abound in figures of black servants who are descendants of slaves, from Dilsey in Falkner's *The Sound and the Fury* (1929) and Calpurnia in Harper Lee's *To Kill a Mockingbird* (1960) to the black maids or nanny figures in *Gone with the Wind* (1939) and *Imitation of Life* (1934). Black women's writing thematizes this gendered shift from slavery to servitude, as in Maya Angelou's *I Know Why the Caged Bird Sings* (1969), or Toni Morrison's *A Mercy* (2008). Zora Neale Hurston, destitute in later life, ended up herself working as a maid.

25. In his conclusion to *The Servants' Hand*, Bruce Robbins reiterates the "marginal and suggestive" nature of the "literary presence" of servants in canonical British literature (205) as a characteristic of a "long [historical] moment . . . that [had] finally ended" (220–221), and suggests the beginning of a new moment where Third World literature would "bring back the servant" in new ways (223). Decades later, Robbins'

prediction is validated by the work of the writers studied in this book, who bring back the servant as neither marginal nor suggestive but as central: central to our thinking about nation, society, interiority, and literature itself. Yet literary critics have not followed up on the ways that postcolonial literature does in fact return to the servant, for both old and new purposes, or re-presents servitude in entirely new ways.

26. Maryam Mirza's book *Intimate Class Acts* looks at cross-class relationships, from friendships to romances, in Pakistani and Indian women's fiction, and includes servant-employer relationships as well as non-servant ones. Friendship, however, is not a term or concept I find useful in the context of servitude, given the disparities of social location and dynamics of extremely unequal power and obligation between employers and domestic workers (despite undoubtedly affective connections). My book focuses on servitude per se, not on friendship or romance across class differences.

27. Since the end of colonialism in South and Southeast Asia, "industrialization, transnational capitalism, and the global economy have dramatically accelerated the expansion of the domestic worker phenomenon" (Adams and Dickey, 4). This includes both intra-nation (rural to urban) and inter-nation (country to country) worker migration. On female domestic servants in the United States, see Parreñas and Ehrenreich and Hochschild.

28. Servitude is also very different from other care occupations such as nursing, because it is regarded as "unskilled" labor, not as a profession, and is predicated upon the lack of the education that would otherwise qualify the servant for more dignified or higher-paid work.

29. See Ray and Qayum on the maintenance and performance of class distinctions between Bengali servants and employers by emphasis on physical separation in proximate spaces, e.g., places servants are allowed to sit or eat, or use of different utensils (145–166). As Ray and Qayum note, all the servants in their study share the expectation that "they can expect a lifetime of this labor," that "neither marriage nor promotion will likely take them out of this job," and that most likely their children will also be servants (90).

30. As they elaborate, "domestic servitude confuses and complicates the conceptual divide between family and work, custom and contract, affection and duty, the home and the world precisely because the hierarchical arrangements and emotional registers of home and family must coexist with those of workplace and contract in a capitalist world" (Ray and Qayum, 3).

31. As Balram, the servant narrator in Adiga's *The White Tiger*, ironically notes, "A time-honored tradition. Slapping the master when he's asleep. Like jumping on pillows when masters are not around. Or urinating into their plants. Or beating or kicking their pet dogs. Innocent servants' pleasures" (157).

32. See also Sharma on the history of the struggle to gain labor rights for domestic workers in India since Independence in 1947, who are still not legally recognized as workers and therefore not afforded the legal rights or protections available to other workers.

33. See Judith Rollins's classic study of the dynamics between women in employer-servant relations in 1980s Boston, *Between Women: Domestics and their Employers*. Rollins notes how women employers and servants both recognize their relative subordinate position in the gender hierarchy. This recognition and devaluation of women's work informs their interactions, and produces greater comfort working with each other in the isolated space of the home, as well as damaging behavioral patterns such as expected deference and maternalism.
34. I first sketched out this framework in my essay on Daniyal Mueenuddin, published in *Ariel* in 2014.
35. https://www.theguardian.com/world/2013/dec/18/indian-diplomat-strip-search-us-devyani-khobragade. *The Guardian* continues, Khobragade "pleaded not guilty and plans to challenge the arrest on grounds of diplomatic immunity.... If convicted Khobragade faces a maximum sentence of 10 years for visa fraud and five years for making a false declaration." Khobragade was eventually granted diplomatic immunity by the Indian government and enabled to leave the United States, where she was re-indicted under the same charges. See https://thediplomat.com/2014/01/indian-diplomat-leaves-us-after-being-indicted/.
36. CNN, http://www.cnn.com/2013/12/19/world/asia/india-diplomat-politics/index.html.
37. As *The New York Times*, reported, "Ms. Richard's lawyer, Dana Sussman of Safe Horizon, a victim services agency, said: 'My client is frustrated with how the media has portrayed this story and the response from the Indian government. The victim in this case is not the criminal defendant. The victim is the person who worked incredibly long hours and was severely underpaid.'" https://www.nytimes.com/2013/12/20/nyregion/fury-in-india-over-diplomats-arrest-in-new-york.html?_r=0.
38. https://www.hindustantimes.com/india/us-embassy-paid-for-sangeeta-richard-s-family-s-air-tickets/story-26pI4LfLlTAT6u8UAB4FOK.html; https://www.indiatoday.in/india/north/story/devyani-arrest-row-devyani-khobragade-sangeeta-richard-india-us-diplomatic-face-off-222241-2013-12-28.
39. https://www.nytimes.com/2013/12/20/nyregion/fury-in-india-over-diplomats-arrest-in-new-york.html?_r=0.
40. In India, and among Indian Americans, the maid in question, Sangeeta Richards, was blamed for challenging her employer. "Be thankful for what you have," said one Indian American commentator to *The New York Times*; since she got more than what maids get in India (https://www.nytimes.com/2014/01/10/nyregion/claims-of-diplomats-mistreating-household-staff-are-far-from-the-first.html?_r=0).
41. CNN, ibid.
42. https://www.nytimes.com/2017/07/15/world/asia/at-a-luxury-complex-in-india-the-maids-and-the-madams-go-to-war.html.
43. https://www.washingtonpost.com/world/asia_pacific/maids-riot-at-luxury-highrise-exposes-class-divide-in-india/2017/07/12/f126b9e0-4f02-49c5-b8c3-f2ebf8d51ab6_story.html?noredirect=on&utm_term=.01353aefcb33.
44. Ibid.

45. As Walkowitz writes: "Born-translated novels are designed to travel, so they tend to veer away from the modernist emphasis on linguistic experimentation.... Anglophone novels travel especially well because English has become the most-read, most-translated language in the world" (569–571).
46. Koh, Asia Society Interview. As Mueenuddin elaborates, "Half-Pakistani and half-American, I have spent equal amount of time in each country, and so, knowing both cultures well and belonging to both, I equally belong to neither, looking at both with an outsider's eye" (quoted in Murphy).
47. Michele Cliff's novel *No Telephone to Heaven*, for example, opens with a servant's horrific killing of his elite employers and proceeds to illuminate what could lead to such violence; Zadie Smith's short story "The Embassy of Cambodia" is about a girl from the Ivory Coast trapped as a live-in housemaid for a Middle Eastern family in suburban London; Chimamanda Ngozi Adichie's short story "Imitation" suggests the parallels between a wealthy Nigerian man's neglected wife and her Nigerian housemaid in Philadelphia.
48. See also Maryse Jayasuriya's *Terror and Reconciliation: Sri Lankan Anglophone Literature, 1983–2009*, for Sri Lankan writing about the quarter century of ethnic conflict and civil war, and Minoli Salgado's *Writing Sri Lanka: Literature, Resistance, and the Politics of Place*.
49. The term South Asia is used not only in the West but also in South Asia itself as signifying and recognizing a geopolitical entity with shared histories, cultures, and other connections: the region of the Indian subcontinent. Including India, Pakistan, Bangladesh, Sri Lanka, Nepal, Bhutan, Maldives, and sometimes Afghanistan, the term "South Asia" does not assume homogeneity among nations or cultures, but does recognize continuities and resemblances among differences, and the constructedness and provisional nature of national boundaries.
50. Well-known examples of each kind include (from Shakespeare's plays) Stephano and Trinculo in *The Tempest*, who serve as parallels to Antonio and Sebastian, and evidence for Caliban's lower instincts; Malvolio in *Twelfth Night*, who serves as comic relief and contrast with the aristocratic protagonists; the Nurse in *Romeo and Juliet*, who mothers Juliet and enables the romance; Nelly Dean the housekeeper in *Wuthering Heights* and Gabriel Betteredge the butler in *The Moonstone*, who act as minor participants and witnesses to the stories of the families they narrate; the two servants in *Oedipus Rex*, who reveal at the end the horrifying secret of Oedipus's identity; and Thady Quirk the steward in *Castle Rackrent*, who exposes the neglectful practices of Irish landlords in Edgeworth's didactic effort to induce landlords to act more responsibly.
51. Even when a modernist American narrative focuses on a servant, she is described as seen from the outside. The fourth and final section of *The Sound and the Fury* focuses on Dilsey, the black servant, but it is the only section narrated by an unknown third-person narrator. The first three sections are all narrated by white first-person narrators who are main characters and whose subjectivities we are invited to enter. The curious anomaly prompts the question why Faulkner did not attempt to create

Dilsey's voice or tell her part of the story by granting her the position or standpoint of a first-person narrator.

52. Kipling, *Life's Handicap*, 173.
53. Kipling, *Life's Handicap*, 216.
54. Hence Woloch notes a tension in nineteenth-century fiction between democratization and singularity: "the inclusive aesthetics of the nineteenth-century realist tradition—with its dual impulses to bring in a multitude of characters and to bring out the interiority of a singular protagonist—illuminates particularly well the tension between the structural and referential axes of characterization" (30). Structurally, the nineteenth-century novel leans toward affirming the singularity of the protagonist, formally identified through interiority, but referentially, it seeks to include a multitude.
55. Servitude fiction thus faces the problem of relatability: to use the educator Rudine Sims Bishop's terms, for most of its readers, this fiction serves less as a mirror than a window, though it tries to be both. Ultimately, it aspires to be a sliding door.
56. In addition to Gayatri Spivak's most cited "Can the Subaltern Speak," I would direct readers to Linda Alcoff's important essay, "The Problem of Speaking for Others." Spivak has repeatedly clarified her claim that the subaltern cannot speak as meaning that the subaltern cannot be *heard* within the frameworks of dominant discourses. (Interview with Landry and MacLean.)
57. See Ray and Qayum, chapter 4, for the disparity in perspectives of servants and employers when interviewed about their work and lives.
58. Mueenuddin's comment is remarkably similar to Aravind Adiga's response to a similar question (about Adiga's *The White Tiger*): "I don't think a novelist should just write about his own experiences. Yes, I am the son of a doctor, yes, I had a rigorous formal education, but for me the challenge of a novelist is to write about people who aren't anything like me." (Interview with Stuart Jeffries, *The Guardian*, October 16, 2008.)
59. I understand the term "subaltern" to denote colonial or postcolonial non-elite, below the middle class, and not just anyone from a postcolonial country.
60. This line of thinking, if taken to its logical consequence, would spell the end of literary fiction. Should Toni Morrison then not try to represent in *Beloved* the experience of an escaped slave that she has not personally experienced, and so on?
61. Posted May 7, 2010, http://manalkhan.wordpress.com/tag/daniyal-mueenuddin, accessed December 14, 2012.

Chapter 1

1. It is not unusual for writers or characters in Indian fiction to notice the absence of servants when work is not done. In Nayantara Sahgal's *This Time of Morning* (1965), for instance, an upper-class wife notices with annoyance signs of servant incompetence: "With growing frustration she saw that tea was not laid, nor the curtain drawn.

-She called the new bearer—there was a new one every month now that faithful old Haseeb had retired to his village—and told him what to do" (139). This is clearly a gendered responsibility, frequently noted by women writers: the wife is responsible for the supervision of servants, ensuring that domestic work is done, unnoticed by men. After Independence, Sahgal also registers a change in servitude from older, more feudal, to newer, postcolonial forms, where the older, retired servant was more dependable, trained, and life-long, while the new ones fail to fulfil their responsibilities and do not last long.

2. As I elaborate below, Mulk Raj Anand was a notable exception, a pioneer in exposing caste and class oppression and in giving his underclass protagonists some interiority. However, his focus is on didactic protest against extreme forms of social degradation and abuse, not on domestic servitude: Bakha in *Untouchable* (1935) is a sweeper outside the home, while Munoo in *Coolie* (1936), though briefly a servant, is primarily a porter and factory worker. Compared to millennial servitude-fiction writers like Mueenuddin or Adiga, Anand is also less concerned with psychological depth or complexity; his protagonists are more representatives of a generic burdened underclass than individuated nuanced subjectivities.

3. My aim here is not to provide a history of all South Asian writing in English. Recently rediscovered writings, such as Sake Dean Mahomet's *The Travels of Dean Mahomet* (1794), go back to the eighteenth century, but even nineteenth-century fiction, such as for example the first known Anglophone Indian novel, Bankim Chatterjee's *Rajmohan's Wife* (1864), is not as widely known nor as influential in the shaping of the Indian English literary tradition as are the early twentieth-century internationally published writers I discuss in this chapter. My goal is to provide selected examples of modes of addressing servitude in earlier fiction, in order to provide a benchmark for the writers that followed.

4. https://tvtropes.org/pmwiki/pmwiki.php/UsefulNotes/TheBechdelTest. Alison Bechdel herself prefers to call it the Bechdel-Wallace test (https://www.themarysue.com/bechdel-wallace-test-please-alison-bechdel/). Those who critique its minimalism miss the point that it is precisely the minimalism that is revealing of broader cultural norms. Of course more nuanced analytic modes are necessary to assess representations of gender and gender discrimination in any particular text.

5. http://bechdeltest.com/statistics/.

6. Sometimes servants' names in South Asian fiction are themselves literal translations of words that mean "servant" in various Indian languages, e.g., Abdul in *Zohra*, Dasa in R. K. Narayan's short story "A Snake in the Grass," and Ghulam (closer to slave than servant) in Daniyal Mueenuddin's story "About a Burning Girl." The author's choice of such names, however, can itself be read in more than one way, depending on the narrative's bent: it could either deny the character individuality, and indicate that the servant figure is no more than a purely functional signifier in the text of his or her servant function, or, conversely, it can implicitly critique the denial of individuality to the servant by those in his world who treat him as nothing but a servant.

7. For overviews of Indian English literature, see Gopal, *The Indian English Novel*, and Mehrotra, *A History of Indian Literature in English*. Neither of these

include Anglophone literature from other South Asian countries, such as Pakistan or Sri Lanka.
8. For more detail, see Metcalf, Bose and Jalal, and Yasmin Khan.
9. As yet, Narayan is not interested in the figure of the servant per se, so that my reading of the cook here must push against the grain of the text. Narayan's pre-Partition novels remain focused on upper- or middle-class protagonists. This changes in his later short stories, which shift interest to various subaltern figures, though even among those, servants as main characters are rare and few. When Narayan does center on servants as protagonists, the story is told from the point of view of an upper-class narrator who expresses fascination with, incomprehension of, and sometimes condescension toward these ultimately remote figures. (For a fuller discussion, see my essay "No One in the House Knew Her Name.")
10. The first reference to servants in the text makes it clearer that "we" refers to Chaudhuri and his brothers, and does not include their servants: "Often we ran after our cow when the servant took her down for a wash" to the river where the boys "bathed" (5). But, he insists anxiously, they bathed always before, and never with, the cows and elephants (5).
11. The notes explain the term as "the untouchable caste" (187).
12. Arundhati Roy's *The God of Small Things*, for example, describes how the upper caste's fear of pollution dictated that Velutha and his father, because of their untouchable status, had to sweep backward, and Velutha as a child could not touch Ammu's hand even accidentally when he gave her a carved wooden toy. Hence the cook Maria's resentment of the untouchables whom she sees as upstarts for rising above their traditional place.
13. As Ray and Qayum write of a different region in India, "cooks in traditional Bengali Hindu households were almost exclusively Brahmin [highest caste] through the mid-twentieth century" because the main distinction among domestic servants was among those "from whose hand upper-caste Hindu employers could accept water (*jalchal*) and those from whom they could not (*ajalchal*)" (75). Lower-caste servants "performed ritually impure tasks such as cleaning bathrooms" (75). In Hindu households, Muslim servants, if any, performed outdoor tasks, like driving (75).
14. Originally from Urdu/Hindi *qulī*, the word "coolie" means porter, or unskilled low-paid laborer.
15. Anand conflates servitude and slavery here; until he runs away, Munoo is in fact not paid for his labor, for his earnings are taken by his uncle.
16. The novel does present other nameless servant women sexually targeted by Mir Nihal's equally spoiled, immoral son, Asghar. That said, the focus is on his ignominy, not on them.
17. As mentioned in my Introduction, "Lihaaf," Ismat Chughtai's famous story in Urdu, created a scandal because it addressed illicit sexuality, or homosexuality, by portraying a lesbian relationship between an upper-class woman and her maidservant. More common and everyday, but less famously addressed in literature, however, are *homosocial* relations between women employers and women servants. "Lihaaf," while clearly progressive in addressing taboo topics like female sexuality, appears less

progressive if we look critically at its portrayal of the servant woman, Rabbo: "Rabbo! She was black as Begum Jahan was white, like burnt iron ore! Her face was lightly marked with smallpox, her body solidly packed; small, dexterous hands, a tight little paunch and full lips, slightly swollen, which were always moist. A strange and bothersome odour emanated from her body. Those puffy hands were quick as lighting, now at her waist, now her lips, now kneading her things and dashing towards her ankles" (11). Chughtai was a member of the Indian Progressive Writers Association. But her description of Rabbo replays negative servant stereotypes: Rabbo is disfigured, physically unattractive, even repulsive and over-sexed, and by implication seduces the upper-class woman with her "roving hands" (12). Chughtai does not present the servant's interiority or consciousness. We only get the outside perspective of the child narrator and how she views the servant woman.

18. For a fuller discussion of this novel, see my essay, "Adultery Behind Purdah."
19. Attia Hosain's later novel *Sunlight on a Broken Column* (1961) elaborates on these dynamics.
20. Later, in *Storm in Chandigarh* (1969), the upper-class female protagonist is condemned by a female cousin for her putative ineffectuality and slovenliness, as evidenced by her failure to hire and manage servants: "look at the way she lives, everything falling to bits from her chair covers to that impossible servant. She could have found an ayah by this time if she'd made up her mind to" (163).
21. That said, such maltreatment of male servants by upper-class women may also be understood as a form of what Stallybrass and White call "displaced abjection," where women empowered by their class status unconsciously take out on the men under their power the resentment and gendered disempowerment they experience elsewhere in their lives.
22. A good example is the critical moment in Jamaica Kincaid's *Annie John*, when the adolescent eponymous protagonist, living in a colonized Caribbean society, sees her reflection in a shop window and suddenly begins to see herself as black, female, and unattractive, a black sheep like Lucifer, the angel cast out of Paradise.
23. See Ray and Qauym on how the upper classes practice and reinforce class distinction by distancing the servant body (146–156).
24. Anita Desai, (same) Introduction to *Phoenix Fled* and to *Sunlight on a Broken Column* (London: Virago Press, 1988).
25. For an important early reading of Hosain's novel, and for a useful explanation of the pre-Independence feudal *taluqdari* system and its dependence on British patronage, see Needham.
26. Servants as subjects of the narrative also appear in a few of R. K. Narayan's stories in *Lawley Road* (1956) and *Under the Banyan Tree* (1985), which are also all told from an upper-class narrator's perspective. Narayan's early stories offer more static, even condescending portrayals of servants. Though designed to critique the arrogance of the modern bourgeoisie, they are less interested in the subjectivity or complexity of individual servants. See my article, "No One in the House Knew Her Name."
27. This is a nuanced argument I hope to elaborate in another work in progress. Clearly there were trade-offs for Hosain between the form of the short story and the

novel: while the Indian novel form could not yet sustain a servant protagonist, perhaps unacceptable to middle-class readerships and editors, Hosain's novel, with its multiple and complex servant figures, carries more of a biting critique of gendered servitude than even her short stories do, as it presents the intense connection, both affective and analogous, between Laila and Nandi. Nandi is much more than a mere foil for Laila, even though the novel is focused on Laila's changing world and how she perceives and experiences its complexities.

28. Sidhwa's *Cracking India* and Hosseini's *Kite Runner* both use the sexual violation of a servant as an occasion from which the upper-class narrator-protagonist learns. Though expressing guilt and attempted redemption through fictional autobiographical narratives, these novels remain limited to the perspective and consciousness of the upper-class witness-participant, and in my view, precisely because of the guise of sympathy and self-implication, make an ethically troubling, self-aggrandizing, instrumental use of the servant figure, whose interiority or story they are not interested in exploring. For a further discussion of the Ayah in *Cracking India*, see my essay, "Border Work, Border Trouble."

29. Again, in this chapter I offer a broad sweep, to which there are always exceptions (that prove the rule). *The Dark Room*, Narayan's unusual proto-feminist novel of 1938, a strong protest against the treatment of a young wife and mother in middle-class household, uses domestic servants to show how women are treated like servants, or in fact worse, because unlike servants, wives cannot leave, without sacrificing children and status. It also reflects on how servants comment on and are relied upon in the household. This novel suggests, interestingly, that when a male writer focuses on women and domesticity, he too pays more attention to servants

Chapter 2

1. This is not to create a binary between transnational South Asian literature and that produced within South Asia. To be clear, I am not arguing that *all* contemporary transnational South Asian literature is more progressive with regard to servitude than domestic fiction. (Many are not, and some, as I show in this chapter, take a middle ground.) Nor am I arguing that all novels produced within South Asia are unaware of the problems of domestic servitude. However, as I began to research what I saw as an emergent wave of contemporary fiction that made servitude a central concern and that addressed servitude from a new angle—by making formal innovations and ideological shifts, and by proposing new ways of seeing—I found that the ones that leaped to prominence were written by transnational writers. I hypothesize that the reason for this is both generational and the fact that these writers bring a fresh sensibility from their experiences abroad. Travel changes perspectives. That does not mean that writers from within South Asia are not aware of problems of servitude. Moreover, to further complicate such a putative binary, I would point out that many of the writers I discuss live in South Asia. What distinguishes them is that they have all also lived elsewhere.

2. http://www.getty.edu/education/teachers/classroom_resources/curricula/landscapes/ib_calm.html. Accessed January 11, 2021. Objects in the background are the smallest in relative size to those in the middle ground and the foreground, respectively, even if they are located in the center of a composition. As Popular Book media notes, artists distinguish among these three to provide depth to their work: in the foreground, images are "larger, clearer, and brighter," and placed "directly in front of us"; in the middle ground, they are in the "middle of the frame," "perceived as midground"; and in the background, they are "higher in the frame," and "less clear" with "colors less intense."
3. In Pakistani-British Kamila Shamsie's early novels about Westernized Karachi super-elites, for instance, such as *In the City by the Sea* (1998) or *Kartography* (2002), servants are barely mentioned but remain necessary to the maintenance of the lifestyles described. Occasionally we hear of the unnamed ayah who gets fired when a boy expresses ethnic prejudice, or the driver who drops someone off, or the "innumerable servants" of the feudal landlord waiting to carry the visitors' suitcases (*Kartography*, 36).
4. In *The Namesake*, for instance, Lahiri only mentions servants once, when the Ganguli family visits Calcutta, and the Indian American children are thrown off by new experiences, including having their feet measured so that a nameless "servant" can be sent to buy "rubber slippers for them to wear indoors" (82).
5. There are of course exceptions, such as some recent Sri Lankan novels like *Replacements* and *Sam's Story*. These, as I will argue in Chapter 4, have often been influenced by the international success of transnational servitude fiction like *Reef*.
6. It is only in a rare exception, in the short-story form, that Rushdie makes a servant a central character—or so it seems. "The Courter," purportedly about a romance between Mary, the Indian ayah who served the narrator's family for much of her life, and the porter of their apartment building during their 1960s sojourn in England, turns out to be really an autobiographical parable about Rushdie's own better choice (in *East, West*, 173–211.) The story hinges on the (Rushdiean) narrator's realization that unlike Mary, who chose to sacrifice her romance in England to return to India, he himself prefers to refuse the binarism of either/or, and not choose one culture or identity over another. With the luxury of his British passport that allows him to "come and go," he announces, "I buck, I snort, I whiny . . . Ropes, I do not choose between you. Lassoes, lariats, I choose neither of you, and both. . . . I refuse to choose" (211). Finally, the point of this story is to emblazon the narrator's own better (more privileged) choice at the expense of the old woman who raised him, and whose amusingly told story becomes a counter-example to establish the superiority of his own.
7. In Sophocles' *Oedipus Rex*, the man who alone carries a key piece of the puzzle, and reveals at the end that Oedipus was the banished child of Laïos, King of Thebes, and has in fact killed his father and married his mother, is described as a shepherd who "belonged" to Laïos, "born his slave, brought up in his house" (59–60). In the *Odyssey*, upon his return to Ithaca, the disguised Odysseus is recognized by his old nurse, who knows his scar, and who, as his loyal servant, does not betray his secret.

8. Aravind Adiga also constructs the lower-class voice of Balram, the servant narrator-protagonist of *The White Tiger*, and has been severely criticized. But I would distinguish between Rushdie's servant voices, used to make fun of the servant characters (where the humor is at the servants' expense), and, as I elaborate in Chapter 5, Adiga's composite construction, that does not resort to the ungrammatical or stereotypical, and does not make Balram the butt of the humor. Moreover, unlike Rushdie, whose third-person narrator compounds the mockery of the servant, Adiga makes Balram the first-person protagonist, centering the entire novel on the servant, and showing sympathetically how he has become what he has become.
9. Perhaps this inability is meant to be symbolic of Pakistan's independence.
10. As we will see in Chapter 5, in Adiga's *The White Tiger*, the increased proximity in the closed space of the car driven by the chauffeur creates a microcosm of servitude relations that intensifies both employer-servant intimacy and the need to maintain distance.
11. It is no insignificant detail that in this time period, an affluent Tamil family employs Sinhalese servants whom they trust.
12. As Daryl explains to Arjie, "Some Sri Lankan people thought Burgher people were too white to marry their children, and some Burgher people thought Sri Lankan people were too brown to marry theirs" (113).
13. Before he dies, Daryl argues with Amma about the Prevention of Terrorism Act, which has recently been passed (1979), and which he insists is merely a "tool for state terrorism" to put down the Tamil Tigers who were demanding a separate state (Eelam) in the north (107). The chapter also mentions the 1981 burning of the Jaffna library by a Sinhalese mob, locating it clearly at that historical moment.
14. A good example of this is R. K. Narayan's story, "Leela's Friend," where an innocent servant is suspected of stealing a gold necklace, and his attempt to escape the police is interpreted as proof of his guilt. See my essay, "No One in the House Knew Her Name," for a discussion of this and other servant stories by Narayan.
15. I would differentiate Selvadurai's work here from another type of representation and deployment of the servant figure exemplified in Bapsi Sidhwa's *Cracking India* (originally published as *Ice-Candy Man* in 1988) and Khaled Hosseini's *The Kite Runner* (2003). Both novels at first glance appear to locate servant characters in an unusual middle ground. However, in both, a first-person middle-class narrator-protagonist recalls a childhood disrupted by intense national turmoil and political violence, witnessed most immediately when visited upon the bodies of servants to whom she or he is deeply attached. In both, the act of telling seems an effort to atone for a childhood act of betrayal: the Parsi child Lenny, Sidhwa's protagonist, naively gives away the hiding place of her Hindu ayah to Muslim men who then kidnap and rape the servant woman in about-to-be partitioned Pakistan (190–195); the Pashtun child Amir, Hosseini's protagonist, fails to protect Hassan, his servant-playmate, from being raped by a group of rich Pashtun boys who attack Hassan as a member of the minority Hazaras in 1970s Afghanistan (73–79). In both narratives the servant body becomes a displaced site of a sexual violence witnessed and regretted by the protagonist, for whom the event occasions political and ethical awareness, and who tells

the story as a mode of expiation. And in both, the protagonist (or in Lenny's case her female relatives) enacts restitution that highlights their own roles in a rescue mission as saviors of the lower-class victim. Selvadurai resists falling into this trap as he thematizes not the epiphany gained by members of the upper class, nor the melodrama of the servant's victimization, but the problem of instrumentalization itself. Instead of sensationalizing the violence enacted upon the servant, Selvadurai emphasizes the gutsy resistance of the servant boy's mother and the consequent humiliation of Arjie's mother. Nor does Arjie claim to have benefitted or rescued the servant in the end. Arjie's narrative is not motivated by an effort to expiate guilt. The emergent servitude fiction I discuss in following chapters also resists depicting servants as helpless victims, or as an occasion for an upper-class protagonist's moral or political education, or as helpless creatures to be rescued, and focuses instead on servant figures as ethically complex, central subjects in themselves, as having subjectivity and partial agency even in an unforgiving system.

16. Selvadurai's second novel, *Cinnamon Gardens* (1998), arguably gives more narrative space and importance to servants than his first. Though focused on the dual narratives of two upper-class protagonists, an uncle and niece, in early twentieth-century colonial Ceylon, and the parallel pressures of arranged heterosexual marriage on the young girl and the closeted gay man, the plot depends heavily on servants, who have a surprising influence on the lives of the rich. The oldest son in the family has been disowned because he married a servant girl; the gay protagonist has hence not seen his older brother in decades. But he learns at the end that his father, the strict and seemingly upright family patriarch, had repeatedly sexually coerced the girl's mother and attempted to assault the servant girl who then married his brother. This discovery of his father's moral hypocrisy enables liberation for the gay man who then feels able to break out of his autocratic father's grasp. Here the servant does seem instrumental to the protagonist's education. It also turns out that the family bearer (butler) can read and write, and has secretly enabled communication between the protagonist's mother and absent brother, suggesting again the power of the servant in the household. The somewhat melodramatic plot and sentimental rendition of servitude as a subsidiary concern make this novel's approach to servitude less worthy of note.
17. The Prologue and Epilogue are also narrated by an unnamed narrator, presumably Hamid himself, who invites readers implicitly to compare the modern-day characters with their namesakes from Mughal history.
18. Hamid presents a similar male-male dynamic to what Gunesekera's *Reef* and Adiga's *White Tiger* elaborate, but *Moth Smoke* presents only the master's perspective, not the servant's.
19. Stallybrass and White explain displaced abjection as "the process whereby 'low' social groups turn their figurative and actual power, *not* against those in authority, but against those who are even 'lower'" (53).
20. *Brick Lane* was shortlisted for the Booker Prize, the *Guardian* First Book Award, and the National Book Critics Circle Award for Fiction. Ali herself was listed among *Granta*'s "Best of Young British Novelists" in 2003. The novel also occasioned some controversy for its representation of Bangladeshi Muslims from Sylhet.

21. Critics who have discussed Hasina have focused on her experiences as a garment-factory worker but not as a maid, even though this occupies the second half of her narrative.
22. Hasina's unwitting misprision, "falling" for the (Victorian) term "fallen" women, suggests the endless possibility of further decline for women who have had to resort to prostitution.
23. Since all Hasina's letters are in italics, all quotations from them that follow are in italics as in the original text.
24. As I have argued elsewhere ("Motherhood and Domestic Servitude"), though it may seem implausible, disingenuous, or self-interested for an upper-class writer to represent a servant in fiction as experiencing love for her employer's child, many social scientists' work shows that women do in fact develop strong affective ties to the children they are paid to care for, who can either substitute for their own long-separated children, or for the emotional bonding of which they have been deprived. This in no way diminishes their understanding of their own position as subordinate(d) or exploited, and it is in fact one of the paradoxes of servitude that strong positive emotions can co-exist with negative ones.
25. The degree to which Hasina is a reliable narrator remains an open question. There are times, over the decades, when she asks Nazneen not to tell Chanu, Nazneen's husband, about aspects of Hasina's life of which Hasina is ashamed, such as her unwilling descent into prostitution. There is also a five-year gap in Hasina's letters between 1996 and 2001, where we do not know what happens to her. Ali gives readers no access to what Hasina may or may not be concealing or reframing in her letters to her sister.
26. Lovely does finally come through when, at Hasina's urging, Lovely calls the newspapers and pays for the operation of Khurshed, the acid-victim child of Hasina's friend Monju, who herself dies of her wounds (342). But it is the impecunious Hasina who pays for Monju's medical care.
27. This scene is very similar to one in Mira Nair's film *Monsoon Wedding* (2001), where the maidservant (Alice, played by Tillotama Shome) tries on her mistress's jewelry, and is accidentally seen by Dubey (played by Vijay Raaz) the wedding planner, who is falling in love with her. The similarity speaks to the sympathetic attempt in both texts to represent the maids' desire, in scenes of play-acting and self-adornment, a desire to try on, even temporarily, the feminine luxuries and identities they do not have.

Chapter 3

1. See for example Murphy, Rosenberg, and Franks' interview with Mueenuddin.
2. "Daniyal Mueenuddin, "On Writing *In Other Rooms, Other Wonders*," end matter in the paperback edition.
3. In this fifty-two-page story (the longest in the collection), though focused on the luxuries of the super-rich, the word "servant" occurs twenty-one times, separately

from the multiple references to specific types of servants, such as maids, ayahs, gardeners, bearers, cooks, valets, chauffeurs, and drivers.
4. As I discuss in my Introduction, Mueenuddin's fiction, like that of other transnational South Asian writers, is designed to speak to multiple audiences, both local and global, and to perform cultural work on at least two levels, both within and beyond the nation.
5. Adiga in particular has suffered much (ungenerous) critique about his choice to construct the voice of a lower-class character. Umrigar, in *The Space Between Us*, uses third-person narration to alternate between the perspectives of a female servant and her female employer.
6. With more condescension, one critic writes: "India's poor may not bear the burden of a novel but may beautifully fit into the short story" (Gowda, 63).
7. For further elaboration on Narayan's use of the upper-class narrator in his servant stories, see my essay, "No One in the House Knew Her Name."
8. It is worth recalling that "self" and "other" are binary oppositions that we have learned to deconstruct, so that aspects of the "self" remain other to us and aspects of the "other" are like our selves.
9. Herring argues that Bhutto sought to appease industrial capitalists, not to destroy the feudal system through which he was himself a powerful and wealthy landlord. He also quotes Bhutto admitting that "radical land reform [was] . . . politically impossible, explicitly recognizing the power of landed interests" (107, n. 35). See also Saghir Ahmad's important case study.
10. For about half of its seventy-five-year existence to date, Pakistan has been under military rule: under Ayub Khan, 1958–1969; Yahya Khan, 1969–1971; Zia-ul-Haque, 1977–1988; and Pervez Musharraf, 1999–2008. See https://www.britannica.com/place/Pakistan/Government-and-society.
11. In "About a Burning Girl," Mueenuddin presents such a feudal servant as instantly recognizable, as a middle-class judge observes: By his language and manner I knew him to be a serving man of the old type, of the type that believes implicitly in his master's right to be served. They are impossible to get now, unless you own land and bring a man from your own village, and even then you have to choose a simpleton, a real feudal peasant. (106) Mueenuddin thus suggests how servants' identities are both visibly recognizable to others, through their bearing and clothing and deeply internalized servant's self-image. The construction of such identities depends on broader interlocking systems of power.
12. Cara Cilano, "'In a World of Consequences': An Interview with Kamila Shamsie," *Kunapipi: Journal of Postcolonial Writing and Culture* 39.1 (2007): 150–162, p.156.
13. With regard to subaltern issues, for obvious reasons, untouchability is far more common in Indian than in Pakistani writing, since it is a consequence of Hindu, not Muslim, religious tradition. If Pakistani writers address the caste system, it is through its attenuated residuality, as something from the past, lingering as a prejudice, for example, against the sweeper class, some of whom who are perceived as lower-caste Hindus who converted to Christianity. Mohammed Hanif's novel, *Our Lady of Alice Bhatti*, for example, explores the predicament of Christian converts in twenty-first-century Karachi who continue to struggle against caste prejudice.

14. Mueenuddin is by no means unique among South Asian writers who commemorate the formative or lasting power of servants who nurtured them in childhood. Rushdie, for example, in his autobiographical short story, "The Courter," writes fondly of his Indian Christian ayah Mary as "the woman who did as much as my mother to raise my sisters and me" (177). More achingly, Michael Ondaatje, in his poem "Wells," writes of "The tears / I gave to my ayah Rosalin on leaving/ the first home of my life." The ambiguous syntax implies that the home he left was not only Sri Lanka but also the woman who raised him. "More water for her than any other/ that fled my eyes again / this year, remembering her, / a lost almost-mother in those years / of thirsty love" (*Handwriting*, 50). For Ondaatje, this is clearly so searing a memory that he mirrors it in his novel *Anil's Ghost* (2000), when the protagonist Anil, upon return to Sri Lanka after many years, goes first to visit Lalitha, her old nanny: "the old woman was weeping. . . . There was a lost language between them" (22). As women, they express feeling through more physical intimacy: Anil embraces the "tiny aged woman," who runs her hands "over Anil's hair" (22). "She was the one who brought me up," Anil explains to a colleague (24).
15. Meenuddin Interview with Asia Society.
16. In teaching this story, I have found my students disturbed by Nawabdin's callousness at the end, his refusal to help or forgive the dying robber. But Mueenuddin does not present Nawabdin as a hero or exemplar of moral probity. With clear-eyed realism, the story recognizes that in such a dog-eat-dog world, human beings become callous to others whom it is not in their interest to help, and concerned only about those most closely related to them. Such (liberal humanist) expectations of forgiveness or rising above one's circumstances are simply out of place. This is an example, I would argue, of what Stallybrass and White have called "displaced abjection," "the process whereby 'low' social groups turn their figurative and actual power, *not* against those in authority, but against those who are even 'lower'" (53).
17. The asymmetry between servants and employers in this contact zone goes without saying, for no employer depends emotionally on his servants in the way that Rafik depends on his master.
18. Originally titled "The Sparrows of Lahore," the story emphasizes with its new title Saleema's individuality rather than generality.
19. Both these stories are also linked to other stories. "In Other Rooms, Other Wonders" occurs at the same time as "Saleema" and offers a parallel tale of a young woman's determination (and failure) to redress her disadvantages via sex with an older man: Husna, a young opportunistic relative of Harouni's, chooses to forego respectable marriage (114) and to insinuate herself into Harouni's house and bed as a way out of poverty. Harouni dies and Rafik appears in both stories, but neither woman is mentioned in the other's story, as if the two co-exist without intersecting, in the same house. Jaglani does not reappear, but Sohail Harouni's cook does, in "About a Burning Girl" and "A Spoiled Man." Sohail is the young lover in "Our Lady in Paris" and reappears married to a different American woman in "A Spoiled Man."
20. Mueenuddin leaves it ambiguous whether Mustafa in fact seeks merely domestic work for his sister or if he is offering her as sexual bait to curry favor with his master.

21. The title also alludes to Robert Frost's (1934) poem of the same title, suggesting a similar critique of unscrupulous greed for wealth or fame.
22. It is worth noting that none of the stories in Mueenuddin's collection address the conditions faced by older female servants, unlike Attia Hosain's stories "The Loss" or "The Daughter-in-Law." Mueenuddin seems more interested in exploring the consciousnesses of tough young women who break the rules—from the lower-class Saleema and Zainab, to the ambitious middle-class Husna in "In Other Rooms, Other Wonders," to the high society girl Lily in "Lily"—and who, even with wealth and family connections, cannot get what they want, trapped within Pakistan's feudal and sexual system.
23. It seems likely, but remains unconfirmed, that Khadim conspired with his brother to steal their father's savings, and to kill the brother's wife when she seemed about to expose them. In the judge's account, Khadim's brother is designated "the prime mover" (109). Nonetheless, what is extraordinary is that the judge is willing bring back into his home a servant he believes is a thief and a killer.
24. Mueenuddin thus complicates even his portrayal of this corrupt judge, whom he presents here as unexpectedly susceptible to the old man's weeping: "I couldn't bear it, I put my arm around him. He reminded me of the old man who brought me up, whose lap held me, who had callused hands and wore a ring with a cheap red stone, who took me to the zoo and showed me the deer, put me on his shoulders so I could see over the fence" (107). This recognition of a father-son bond across the line of master-servant division, reminiscent of Mueenuddin's description of his own relationship to the old male servant who raised him (quoted above), also induces the judge to find a way to extricate Khadim.
25. It might be tempting to read this story as an allegory of US-Pakistan relations, where American interventions in Pakistan since the 1979 Soviet invasion of Afghanistan have been similarly disastrous. Such a reading could expand the significance of servitude explored in earlier stories into an allegorical representation of Pakistan as a dispossessed, ravaged servant to American interests, a casualty or collateral damage to rivalries between global superpowers. However, such a reading is not one I want to propose. While such a national allegory might seem to increase the scope of Mueenuddin's work, it would overextend into a generality that would flatten the nuance, delicacy, and rich detail, the compassion and empathy for the servant as individual that distinguish his work. I would instead urge a reading that supersedes the national allegory for the particularities, intricacies, and affect of the servant story.

Chapter 4

1. In his 1845 novel *Sybil, or the Two Nations*, Disraeli famously commented on the state of Victorian England: "Two nations; between whom there is no intercourse and no sympathy; who are as ignorant of each other's habits, thoughts, and feelings, as if they were dwellers in different zones, or inhabitants of different planets; who are formed

by a different breeding, are fed by a different food, are ordered by different manners, and are not governed by the same laws: *the rich and the poor*" (Book II, Chapter 2).

2. Other South Asian novels with a servant narrator and protagonist that may come to mind are Elmo Jayawardena's *Sam's Story* (2001) and Nirmali Hettiarachchi's *Replacements* (1998). Both, however, were published locally in Sri Lanka, much after *Reef*, and seem influenced by, if not imitative of, *Reef*, without achieving its level of quality. Both are narrated by a servant boy, who, like Triton, leaves his impoverished village to work for a wealthy "Master" in the city. In *Sam's Story*, the boy is intellectually disabled, and well treated by his master and his family, with whom he finds a happy refuge from the civil war raging in the country, until the master is killed by a terrorist bomb. If the novel critiques servitude, it is only by implication at the end, when Sam is left unprovided for after his master's death. Written in language that reflects awkwardly the simple-mindedness of the servant boy, the novel falls victim to its own mimeticism as it tries to re-create the voice of an illiterate village boy. *Replacements*, though better crafted, literalizes the homoerotic sub-text of *Reef* as lurid melodrama. At once homophobic and improbable, it centers on the sexual assault and exploitation of the servant boy—renamed Charles—by the villainous (closeted homosexual) master, and the revenge of the servant who impregnates the master's wife (who dies). It ends with Charles continuing as servant in the household in which his child is being raised, while the child remains unaware of who is his biological father. Readers might also think of the earlier novel *Giraya* (Wijenaike, 1971), also published in Sri Lanka, which includes some consideration of servants. *Giraya*, however, centers not on a servant, but on the mistreated young woman who becomes the daughter-in-law of a wealthy feudal household. It is told entirely from this unhappy narrator-protagonist's perspective, not a servant's, and in fact reinforces negative servant stereotypes in its representation of an aging female servant as monstrous, lesbian, insane, and violent. For all these reasons, *Giraya* is not what I would consider (anti)servitude fiction. Likewise, yet another Sri Lankan novel, Wijesinha's *Servants: A Cycle* (1995), perhaps also inspired by *Reef*, is told from the perspective of an upper-class man who looks back at multiple servants that served his family, and what he did and did not know about them. This surprising collection of novels concerning servants suggests the influential impact of *Reef*.

3. The British ruled over Sri Lanka (then known as Ceylon) from 1796 to 1948, having taken over from the Dutch, who took over from the Portuguese, who were the first Europeans to conquer the island (in the sixteenth century). After independence in 1948, the United National Party (UNP) enabled relative power-sharing among the elite of Ceylon's various ethnic and religious groups (primarily Sinhalese/Buddhist, Tamil/Hindu, Burgher/Christian). In 1956, the Sinhalese nationalist Sri Lanka Freedom Party (SLFP) came to power, and made Sinhalese the sole official language and promoted Buddhism and Sinhalese culture as a state policy, alienating minority ethnic/religious groups such as Tamils and Christians. By 1965, thanks to an economic crisis, the UNP was re-elected, but their economic policies of privatization led to inflation and rising social inequality. The SLFP joined up with various Marxist parties and returned to power in 1970. The violence that breaks out in 1970–1971

was led by a youth movement that included an armed organization, the JVP, and was violently suppressed by the state. In 1972, a new constitution was written, making Buddhism officially the dominant religion, and the name of the country was changed to Sri Lanka. Rising tensions between the Sinhalese and Tamils, and the Tamil demand for a separate Tamil state, erupted in a horrific civil war in 1983, which lasted until 2009. For a more detailed account, see https://www.britannica.com/place/Sri-Lanka/History.

4. The title also evokes a popular brand of cooking oil, as Anita Mannur notes: *Culinary Fictions: Food in South Asian Diasporic Culture* (Philadelphia: Temple University Press, 2010), 63.

5. Gunesekera unobtrusively provides a few dates or references to historic events to locate Triton's narrative in real time. Triton arrives as an eleven-year-old at Salgado's house in 1962, so he is born in 1951 (15); he is twelve, a year later, when Salgado leaves him alone with Joseph and Joseph attacks him (32); Nili comes for tea for the first time in April 1969 (74); Nili moves in after the Christmas party of 1969 (113); Nili leaves just before the national elections of 1970 (173); Salgado and Triton leave Sri Lanka by the end of 1970 soon after the death of Dias (175); Salgado returns to Sri Lanka in 1983 when the civil war breaks out (188); Triton meets the young refugee at the petrol station over "twenty years" after his own arrival (12). *Reef* was published in 1994.

6. Walter Perera, "Images of Sri Lanka Through Expatriate Eyes: Romesh Gunesekera's Reef," *The Journal of Commonwealth Literature* 30.1 (1995): 63–78.

7. Minoli Salgado, *Writing Sri Lanka: Literature, Resistance and the Politics of Place* (New York: Routledge, 2012).

8. Edward Mallot, "'We Are Only What We Remember, Nothing More': History and Healing in Romesh Gunesekera's *Reef*," *Journal of Commonwealth Literature*, 42.3 (2007): 83–98. Gerd Bayer, "Marine Biology and Scientific Discourse: Gunesekera's Reef as Postcolonial Resistance," in *British Asian Fiction: Framing the Contemporary*, ed. and introd. Neil Murphy et al. (New York: Cambria Press, 2008), 273–287. Melanie Murray, "The Sea and the Erosion of Cultural Identity in Romesh Gunesekera's *Reef*," in *Shared Waters: Sounding in Postcolonial Literatures*, ed. and introd. Stella Borg Barthet (Amsterdam: Brill Academic Publishers, 2009), 217–227.

9. In a somewhat reductive Marxist critique, Lee Erwin argues that in four prize-winning postcolonial novels, including *Reef*, the subaltern figure of the male "laborer" is gradually transformed into an exception who "transcends class" (325). Erwin only cursorily discusses each novel, curiously dismisses education as a mode of escape for the individual concerned, and does not focus on servitude. Erwin, "Domesticating the Subaltern in the Global Novel in English," *Journal of Commonwealth Literature* 47.3 (2012): 325–339. In her article, Lisa Lau very briefly discusses the male servant in four novels (including *Reef* and *White Tiger*) that she approaches sociologically as transparent windows into caste relations. (Lau, "The Male South Asian Domestic Servant: Master Servant Relationships, Class Chasms, and Systematic Emasculation," *The Sri Lanka Journal of the Humanities* 37.1 (2011): 35–54.) By contrast, I focus on servitude as a complex phenomenon that reveals the intersections of class, gender,

sexuality, and ethnicity, among others, and offer a theoretically informed literary analysis of each novelist's strategies in addressing the servant's psychology and interiority, the micropolitics of the relations with the employer, and broader implications for the nation.

10. The similarity is no accident, I suspect, as Adichie picks up with Gunesekera's use of the servant-boy narrator but adapts it to alternate with two other narrative perspectives, to provide contrast and comparison.
11. It is not until the end of Chapter 2, the midpoint of his narrative, that Triton realizes he is only an onlooker, an outsider in this paradise, as he sees Salgado and Nili cuddled up together, lost in their own world, after their Christmas party.
12. The link to Shakespeare's *Tempest* is explicitly signaled by the epigraph of *Reef*, "of his bones are coral made." In the play, these lines are part of Ariel's song, suggestive of the metamorphoses wrought by the sea, designed to frighten Ferdinand into believing that his father is dead. In Gunesekera's novel, the quotation evokes perhaps the paternal-filial relation between Salgado and Triton, who loses Salgado at the end, and the destructive forces, such as interethnic violence, that lead to this loss. The sea symbolizes the forces of destruction, and also of creation, since it produces the coral reef of the title. In a key moment, Salgado describes the polyp coral as "very delicate," "self-renewing," "real flesh," as the protective barrier for the island: having survived for eons, it is easily killed; and then "the sea will rush in," spelling the end of the coastal people, the coast and the land that is their home (58). I cannot discuss in detail here the significance of the novel's constant evocation of the sea, but the epigraph also suggests that the death/loss of Salgado at the end may be productive of a new Triton. Perhaps Triton is "made" of Salgado, who lives on in Triton, always a part of him.
13. In an interview with Rocio Davis, Gunesekera hints that Salgado, with his Western education and maritime interests, gives his servant this new name, suggestive of a new identity and hybridity: "Triton as a child comes without a past, in effect. We know very little about him. We don't even know his name, which he acquires once he enters this other world." "'We Are All Artists of Our Own Lives': A Conversation with Romesh Gunesekera" (Nice, March 21, 1997), *Miscelánea: A Journal of English and American Studies* 55 (2017): 43–54.
14. This dynamic is not limited to male servants and employers. As I discuss in Chapter 2, in Rushdie's *The Satanic Verses*, the ayah likewise mimics her deceased mistress and provokes, in the employer's son, an intense and revealing unease.
15. As we will see in Chapter 5, for Balram, this mimicry unfolds somewhat differently. Balram's master, Ashok, is neither benevolent, nor encouraging of the servant's emulation. And Balram's attempt to become like Ashok is much more ambivalent, where he attempts to look and sound like him, and even takes his name. But by the end, Balram separates in a different way—he refuses to adopt Ashok's *modus operandi*, and insists, when he becomes an employer, that he will conduct himself with a different code of ethics and sense of responsibility.
16. A similar dynamic occurs in *The White Tiger*, when Ashok reconnects with his old girlfriend, who disrupts Ashok's dyadic relationship with Balram. However, this

occurs after Ashok's wife Pinky leaves, and Ashok is living in Delhi, away from his father and brother, leaving him alone with Balram. In *Reef*, Salgado is oddly without family, like Triton, so until Nili arrives, Triton has had no interference or supervision from a mistress, such as a wife or mother might offer. With full control of the household, he also has an unusual hold over his master. Unlike Salgado, who has a wide circle of friends, Triton has no close contact or social relationships with anyone else, which also intensifies his emotional dependence on Salgado.

17. Even if this observation is accurate, a more sympathetic understanding of gender dynamics would suggest that even upper-class women, with less power than men, felt the greater need to assert what power they had on those over whom they could exert it. This is an example of what Stallybrass and White call displaced abjection.

18. In her analysis of food, cooking, and desire in *Reef*, Anita Mannur reads the novel as a queer narrative that shows "how a non-consummated form of same-sex desire can emerge within the heterosexual structure of domestic space" (64). However, Mannur overlooks the simultaneity of same-sex and cross-sex desire that Triton experiences. As I show, Triton desires not only Salgado, but also Nili, in part because he sees her as belonging to Salgado, and because he wants not only Salgado but also to be like Salgado. Triton's desires (and sexuality) are thus not separate from but are deeply structured by his servitude.

19. Such moments do raise the question whether Gunesekera reanimates the problematic stereotype of the oversexed lower-class male servant. There may be an element of that here, but it is to be measured against the force of Gunesekera's attempt to render understandable, with empathy and complexity, the servant's psyche from within, as the reaction of an adolescent boy when placed in such a position. Note also that Triton does nothing inappropriate; he records his inevitable reactions when Nili touches him or comes too close, as if she thinks he is sexless.

20. I am not suggesting that it would be better for Nili to hand her soiled underwear to a woman servant, but that her handing it to Triton carries different meanings. Even without washing machines, when laundry must be hand washed, there are some things one can do for oneself if physically able.

21. This figurative suggestion is literalized and exaggerated in Hettiarachchi's novel *Replacements*, where the boy servant is effectively sold to be subjected to repeat sexual abuse by his secretly gay male master.

22. As Balram says in Adiga's *The White Tiger*, the servant sees only part of the employers' lives: "When you're the driver, you never see the whole picture. Just flashes, glimpses, bit of conversation" (118).

23. Though purportedly drowned, Dias has "never [been] known" to go swimming even in a calm sea, Triton notes (178).

24. Needless to say, such failures of postcoloniality can be attributed both to the failures of postcolonial governments and to the colonial policies that contributed to the creation of religio-ethnic tensions that intensify after independence.

25. *Reef* was written at a time when the end to the civil war was nowhere in sight, from a very different perspective than that of recent Sri Lankan Anglophone fiction, like Nayomi Munaweera's *Island of a Thousand Mirrors* (2012), or Akil Kumarasamy's

Half Gods (2018), which look back to the war from a point secure in the knowledge of that end.
26. Umrigar does imagine an end to servitude for Bhima, but only in her sequel, *The Secrets Between Us*, again in the form of economic enterprise, where Bhima is able to start a small business, with the help of her erstwhile employers. In *The Inheritance of Loss*, Kiran Desai also imagines the possibility of an end to the familial legacy of servitude, not for the cook, but for his son, Biju, via (illegal) immigration to the United States and work in the neoliberal capitalist global system, and suggests why that avenue may prove a failure. Adiga and Gunesekera show little interest in female servants or female servant/employer relations. Adiga presents no women servants at all, while Gunsekera includes two very briefly: the loyal maidservant who helps her angry mistress physically attack the unfaithful master; and the maternal Lucy, who instructs the young Triton and then retires, enabling Triton to take over.

Chapter 5

1. The novel spans the 1990s to the early 2000s, roughly the period of Balram's adolescence and adulthood. As such, it coincides with the period of India's shift from socialist economic policies to economic liberalization and privatization under the aegis of the World Bank and IMF. While this period showed enormous economic growth and increase in GDP and international trade, it also showed hugely increased disparities of income distribution, and massively reduced government spending on social services and public goods, especially health and education. Feminist critics in particular have highlighted the disproportionate effects of SAPs (Structural Adjustment Policies) on women and children in poverty. See for instance Barker and Feiner. Even a policy analyst like Aiyar, who writes for a libertarian think tank like the Cato Institute in Washington DC, and who offers a succinct history of India's economy as (private sector) successes and (government) failures from 1991 onward, states: "What leftist critics have denounced as an era of neoliberalism is better called neo-illiberalism" (1). He cites in particular corruption, criminalization, and extremely poor infrastructure as the problem.
2. Adiga could arguably be criticized for speciesism because of this cluster of animal metaphors that putatively place (and value) the human above the non-human animal. (Speciesism, as Peter Singer originally defined it in *Animal Liberation*, is the assumption that humans are superior to, and therefore justified in, inflicting pain on animals because human interests matter more.) I would respond, however, that while Adiga does assume difference between human and non-human animals, he uses the rhetoric of animality not to suggest that humans are inherently superior to animals or justified in inflicting pain on them, but rather, to render the degradation and dehumanization to which impoverished and oppressed humans are subjected by other humans, to make evident, by comparison, both how humans treat humans worse than how non-human animals treat others of their own species, and far worse than what humans can rightly expect of humans in any society. In so doing, Adiga also

draws attention to the callousness and inhumanity with which animals are treated in India. A counter to charges of speciesism is not to claim equality, or sameness, but, as Peter Singer also argued, to address the lowest common denominator—pain—to base our ethical assessments, not on intelligence or language, but on sentience, to recognize that though humans can build societies, civilization, based on care and community, it is immoral to inflict pain on sentient beings that feel pain.

3. This aspect of this novel has been much misunderstood and consequently heavily criticized. In an early book review, for example, Wendy Singer, a professor of history of South Asia, misses the irony and subtlety altogether, reading it straight as representing "the real depravity of Biharis," and castigating Adiga for "labeling this place [Bihar] 'as Darkness' in contrast to Civilization (Bangalore)," and for following Joseph Conrad and the "stereotypes found in colonial literature." Likewise, Amitava Kumar mistakes "the name Darkness" as referring literally to "the state of Bihar" (his own home-state) (3). In a scholarly article, Ana Mendes accuses Adiga of benefitting from an "alterity industry" by exoticizing India for a Western audience by presenting it via this trope as a place of darkness (277). Such accusations wrongly assume that Adiga speaks only to the West, and indeed they themselves re-center the West. Postcolonial scholars have long recognized that transnational global fiction like Adiga's addresses multiple audiences, including those within the nation, and all around the globe, not just the West. Adiga's satiric work is aimed, I contend, altruistically to urge rectification of wrongs, not to humiliate or pander to Western self-images of superiority.

4. Most critics also miss the allusions to Disraeli and Naipaul and assume that Adiga alludes only to Conrad.

5. Balram introduces himself as living and working literally under the light of a gigantic chandelier, in his tiny "150-square-foot office" as the "chandelier's light spins around the room" (5). Frequently referring back to this chandelier, this monstrous "thing" of light, he tells us, "has a personality of its own," it is a "huge thing, full of small diamond-shaped glass pieces" (as in the 1970s Bollywood films he remembers), from which he has suspended a "midget fan" that produces a "strobe light," which he likens to the "best discos in Bangalore" (5). It is thus literally from the effects of this flamboyant, almost psychedelic kinetic space that Balram's entire narrative is inspired, an alternating mix of darkness and light, as the fan's blades "chop up the chandelier's light and fling it across the room" (5).

6. As I elaborate below, Balram repeatedly likens himself, in a self-dehumanizing move, to a monkey, engaged in mimicry of his master.

7. In paying close attention to such multivalent literary devices and their sustained patterns through the novel (which many critics ignore), I suggest how a more nuanced and accurate reading of the novel may emerge.

8. For *The New York Times*, for instance, Akash Kapur (an Indian) describes Balram as "a roguish criminal with a remarkable capacity for self-justification" (November 7, 2008). Though Kapur recognizes the "landscape of corruption, inequality and poverty" that provides a context for Balram, and the "penetrating social commentary" of the novel, he also faults it for "an absence of human complexity" and seems

unable to see the complexity that Adiga painstakingly delineates. Stuart Jeffries, for *The Guardian*, describes Balram as "an engaging, gobby, megalomaniac, boss-killer of a narrator" (October 16, 2008); Scott Simon, in *NPR*, describes Balram as a "psychopathic" "ambitious, remorseless Indian;" while *Publisher's Weekly* describes him as "a racist, homicidal chauffeur" who "endears himself to readers" even as he "profits from moral ambiguity and outright criminality" (https://www.publishersweekly.com/978-1-4165-6259-7). Literary critic Alexander Adkins calls him a "misanthropic rogue who marks the incursion of neoliberalism into the developing world" (170). Even a scholar like Robbie Goh, who recognizes that "Balram's crimes, horrendous as they are, . . . are mitigated (if not fully exonerated) by the narrative, which presents his actions as largely the effect of the society in which he lives" (335), calls Balram an "unrepentant, vicious thug" (333). Such descriptions name, even pathologize, the actor, not the act, as criminal, as if that criminality is innate, and not a response to the conditions the novel carefully presents.

9. *Kirkus Review*, for examples, states astonishingly, that Adiga "fails to describe the stages by which Balram evolves from solicitous servant into cold-blooded killer" (https://www.kirkusreviews.com/book-reviews/aravind-adiga/the-white-tiger/). My point is precisely that Adiga very much describes with nuance each step in these "stages."

10. Authenticity is also problematic when it becomes a way to dismiss those cast as outsiders when they point out something that insiders do not want to see. Authenticity can be a way of enforcing an in-group's notion of who or what belongs to some self-constructed or invented notion of what is "authentic" and rests on a problematic dichotomy of false or genuine Indianness. Postcolonial and related fields have long established that outsiders and those on the margins can see and expose what insiders often cannot see. Adiga's novel is too easily dismissed by those who claim he is an outsider (because of his Western education) and therefore should not expose the "sordid" social ills that he rightly sees and critiques. It is a way to silence critique. *Accuracy* might be a better concept than authenticity—but in any case, literature cannot be measured merely in terms of its ability to mirror a putative reality. Certainly, a working-class man like Balram would not speak English, but the novel sets up Balram's narrative as a literary fiction or imagined translation for larger purposes than mere verisimilitude.

11. Interview with Lee Thomas, April 15, 2009.

12. See for instance Adkins and Nandi.

13. See Peters, Walther, Lochner, Ratti, Khor.

14. Schotland, for example, examines violence in Richard Wright's *Native Son* (which Adiga has cited as an influence), though she omits, even as she cites Fanon, to address (as Fanon did) the systemic and literal violence committed by the oppressors that prompts the violence committed by the oppressed.

15. For instance, in his essay on the extent to which a disprivileged subject can deliver justice, Manav Ratti sees Balram as embodying "subalternism," but not servitude (230).

16. Critics often mistakenly read the novel as Balram *writing* this letter to Jiabao, but Balram states very clearly that in fact he is "dictating" this "letter" (3), and that he

cannot "speak English," let alone write it (1). Alone in his office at midnight, he says, it is "a good time for [him] to *talk*" (5, my emphasis). Even the otherwise excellent film adaptation of the novel (2021), directed by Adiga's college friend Ramin Bahrani, misses this crucial point. In the film Balram not only speaks English, but is also presented as writing emails to Jiabao.

17. As I note above, Adiga has been criticized, unfairly, both for the alleged inauthenticity of his narrator's voice (how dare an educated man make an uneducated man sound like an educated man), and, contrarily, for its unlikeliness (how can an uneducated man produce such prose). My point is precisely that Adiga does not attempt verisimilitude. He emphasizes from the beginning that Balram does not speak English, that this narrative presents a mediated voice. Indeed this dictated narrative suggests at best an aspiration that may remain unfulfilled, for it may never reach its intended audience, the Chinese premier, for whom it may or may not be translated.

18. This sense of the importance of telling the truth is clearly shared by Adiga as well, as a literary and ethical imperative. In an interview with Stephen Moss, Adiga describes his research traveling around India, listening to ordinary people talking on the street, because he was "determined to be truthful." Adiga quotes Naipaul: "The truth about India is not what you think, but what they are living."

19. As I discuss in my introduction, many postcolonial male writers (Gunesekera, Adiga, Rushdie, Ghosh) use the language of "servant" and "servitude" to connect domestic servitude with colonialism, where the former becomes a ready analogy for the latter.

20. Critics who see Balram as having achieved success fail to see Adiga's irony, and the extent to which Balram's gains at the end are extremely limited. Socially, he is not part of the upper class, and he has certainly not changed caste (which is not changeable), as one critic avers.

21. While Muslim South Asians might include descendants of Arabs or Central Asians who came with various waves of invaders and settled and mixed with South Asians (unlike British imperialists who maintained separation and returned "home" to Britain), the majority of South Asian Muslims are descendants of Hindus who converted to Islam. Nor does such an Islamophobic ideology and revisionist history acknowledge that even at the peak of the power of the Mughal Empire, many Hindu dynasties maintained their independence and ruled in India longer than Muslim ones did.

22. That said, I would agree with Robbie Goh's point that Balram is primarily a reliable narrator (Goh, 340), not an unreliable one, in the sense that Balram does not deliberately lie or mislead. The narrative and contexts he presents are not open to doubt, but his understanding of what he describes is clearly limited.

23. This is not to condescend to Balram, who can see astutely much of what upper-classes cannot. But it is to recognize that ignorance and misprision are the consequence of larger systemic failures, not just of the individual. Indeed, the novel underscores the toxic acculturating environment from which Balram absorbs some of his horrific ideas. His grandmother Kusum, for example, inculcates horrific sexism when she urges Balram to marry: "We'll fix up the wedding for later this year, ok? We've already found someone for you—a nice plump duck. The moment she has her menstrual

cycle, she can come here" (73). Where would Balram learn alternative notions or respect for women if his own grandmother presents him with a child-bride in such animalistic and rapacious terms?

24. Toward the end of his narrative, for instance, Balram states again: "Iqbal, that great poet, was so right. The moment you recognize what is beautiful in this world, you stop being a slave. To hell with the Naxals and their guns shipped from China. If you taught every poor boy how to paint, that would be end of the rich in India" (236). In other words, the import of weapons and communist ideologies is less effective, Balram suggests, than the radical potential of art, which can inspire greater rebellion and struggle against oppression, perhaps through its capacity to create a new vision by inculcating an aesthetic sensibility.

25. Though I cannot elaborate on this here, there are many ways in which Adiga's novel draws upon Ishiguro's as an important precursor and intertext, not least with the structural element of a servant narrator who reveals unconsciously in and through his narration how servitude has shaped and damaged his consciousness.

26. Balram's lack of a formal education is important enough for him to repeat this point many times. Again, at the end of the chapter, he asserts, "I gave myself a better education at the tea shop than I could have got at any school" (33).

27. Another powerful example occurs in one of Balram's many trenchant remarks, when he comments directly on democracy: "If *I* were making a country, I'd get the sewage pipes first, then the democracy" (81). Citizens cannot participate effectively, he means, when they are not provided with basic necessities. Balram elaborates, with bitter sarcasm, "I've got no problem with democracy, Mr. Jibao. Far from it, I owe democracy a lot—even my birthday" (81). He does not know his real age, or his birthday, which were arbitrarily assigned to him when his employer, a teashop owner, sold his employees' votes. "There was an election coming up, and the tea shop owner had already sold us. He had sold our fingerprints—the inky fingerprints which the illiterate person makes on the ballot paper to indicate his vote" (82). The irony is that Balram is not illiterate, but he is nonetheless forced to relinquish his identity and his right to vote. (Adiga's language of selling here evokes slavery.) Such interlocking systems of oppression—denial of education, denial of opportunity, corruption—produce a vicious cycle: not only can Balram not vote, but he cannot vote to produce betterment or change from the conditions that prevent him from voting.

28. In a key moment, Balram describes himself as akin to Iqbal's Devil, the Lucifer figure, the Blakeian Romantic hero who dared to challenge God: "When I remember Iqbal's Devil, as I do often, lying here under my chandelier, I think of the little black figure [Balram himself] in a wet khaki uniform who is climbing up the entranceway to a black fort . . . surrounded by a group of amazed monkeys" (75). Here Balram sees himself in his mind's eye as both literally and figuratively climbing to get away from his village, both one of (akin to) and apart from the monkeys who watch and gibber around him.

29. It is no small detail that, to celebrate the conclusion of his training, Balram's driving instructor takes him to have his first experience with a prostitute. "I've taught you to be a driver and a man," he declares subsequently (49). Manhood or masculinity is

defined and understood here as coterminous with sexual prowess: becoming a "good driver," he instructs Balram, entails being aggressive, foul-mouthed, and cutthroat competitive, to survive in the "jungle" of the road (48).

30. Soon after, Balram confirms this sense of Ashok's weakness: "I realized that this tall, broad-shouldered, handsome, foreign-educated man . . . was weak, helpless, absent-minded, and completely unprotected by the usual instincts that run in the blood of a landlord" (120). This is why later he picks Ashok as the one to kill, not Ashok's brother, the Mongoose.

31. On emotional labor (versus emotional work) as invisible work of suppression or self-redirection of emotion for a job, see my earlier endnote.

32. It is important to note that Balram's horror of the extended family and its exploitative demands is distinct from his feeling for his immediate family (his parents and brother), for whom he evinces deep attachment. Adiga shows how this joint family, headed by Balram's ruthless and self-serving grandmother Kusum, merely deploys the discourse of family to make deeply destructive demands. In a telling moment, upon return to his village, Balram realizes that his brother Kishan now looks like their deceased father and is similarly trapped within this system that consumes him. Balram looks at the chicken curry served him by the "grinning" Kusum and experiences a powerful revulsion and revelation: "There was red, curried bone and flesh in front of me—and it seemed to me that they had served me flesh from Kishan's own body on that plate" (73). It is when Balram understands this guise of the familial as ultimately cannibalistic, that he refuses to participate in this system or become victim to it.

33. See Laura Kipnis, on bourgeois disgust. Pinky's disgust here is learned, an intersectional effect of her gendered and classed identity.

34. Fanon speaks of third person consciousness in terms of racialized colonialism, where the black man internalizes the view of himself that he sees via the white gaze—he sees himself as he is seen, another form of subjection in that he cannot see him on his own terms, but only through the terms imposed on him by the other.

35. Soon after this event, Balram copies his master, using the same phrase to lash out at someone even more disempowered than himself, a poor street vendor: "How *stupid* can you people get" (174). But unlike Ashok, in this telling moment, Balram enacts a form of displaced abjection, taking out on someone weaker what has been done to him.

36. This is not to imply that someone like Balram has no choice. However, someone in conditions like Balram's has much more *restricted* choice to act ethically, and judgments of ethical action have to be context specific.

37. This is not to claim too much for Balram, especially on his attitude to women. Earlier, Balram undoubtedly behaves very badly, for example, with another prostitute. As he tries to imitate Ashok, and attempts higher status by paying for a blonde prostitute, and he discovers he has been cheated, that she is just an Indian woman with dyed hair, he slaps her and demands his money back (200). However, this episode is more complex than it seems. It begins with empathy. Balram recognizes, upon first meeting, her attempts to ingratiate as subordinate to power: "She gave me a big smile—I knew it well: it was the smile a servant gives a master" (199). Next, it includes a sense of

connection that Balram knowingly repudiates because he is attempting, in this rare moment, to exert power, precisely when he has very little. When he learns that her family gave her no name but "girl," he contemplates rescuing her like a film hero, but then, makes a self-ironic joke that that could only happen "in the Hindi film they'll make of my life" (199). In the gritty reality he inhabits, he suggests with full self-knowledge of his own failings, he cannot act like such a hero. But he is able to see and expose the absurdity of such unrealistic, sentimental forms of popular cultural representations.

38. Adiga's notion of Darkness as the result of inequity and unjust division of resources thus also alludes to Rushdie's *Haroun*. As Haroun learns to his amazement, "Thanks to the genius of the Eggheads . . . , the rotation of Kahani has been brought under control. As a result the Land of Gup is bathed in Endless Sunshine, while over in Chup it's always the middle of the night" (80). In a wonderful fantasy of restorative justice, the problems of the Moon Kahani are resolved when Haroun disrupts this unjust arrangement and makes the moon rotate again, so that sunlight is shared, and its world no longer split between "Perpetual Darkness" and "Eternal Daylight" (172).

39. In a notable exploration of the problem of justice in the novel, Manav Ratti concludes that Adiga's sense of justice is "individualistic, not concerned with the social or collective good, or caste or class upliftment. Balram's is an individual journey; the novel does not show the group or collective realization of caste and class justice. Distributive justice would give all members of a subordinated group equality and opportunity. . . . Balram's justice would appear more rectificatory than distributive or social" (Ratti, 234–235). While I agree with what Ratti says here about Balram, I would disagree that Adiga is guilty of the same limitation. Adiga's novel ironizes Balram and does not idealize him. It points to the problems that remain unfixed and that are not within the purview of someone like Balram to fix. The novel is designed not to provide an ideal solution, but to show precisely how Balram's ending is a failure of the ideal, how, despite his struggles, Balram cannot imagine or achieve distributive social justice. That, Adiga suggests, remains precisely a (trans)national and collective responsibility. In my view, *The White Tiger* does not condone or promote the hyper-individualism of neoliberal ideology, as some critics have argued. Rather, it both critiques that ideology and shows how it thrives in conjunction with feudalist exploitation in India. Balram finally escapes the horrors of servitude and dire poverty by killing his employer, but he is hardly upheld as an epitome of success or achievement: though he gains financial independence at the end, he remains isolated, ignorant, and paranoid, hoping at best that through education, he can provide his nephew with the upward social mobility Balram himself cannot have.

Chapter 6

1. A search on the MLA bibliography for scholarship on this novel yields about ninety-eight hits (July 2023). An entire anthology of critical essays by Indian scholars has been devoted to this one novel alone.

2. By contrast, an MLA bibliographic search on *Space* yields only about three hits. My essay, "Motherhood and Domestic Servitude in Transnational Women's Fiction: Thrity Umrigar's *The Space Between Us* and Mona Simpson's *My Hollywood*," *Contemporary Literature* 57.4 (Winter 2016): 500–540, offers the first published scholarly analysis of Umrigar's work and places it in relation to global women's fiction on female servants. This chapter reworks my earlier argument about Umrigar's novel, places it in relation to other South Asian servitude fiction, and sets up a comparison with Kiran Desai's novel.
3. Though there are other characters whose perspectives and memories are occasionally given space, such as Gyan and Noni, these four are the main characters whose perspectives are given prominence, and that are regularly explored and sustained through the novel.
4. In one of the few critical essays published to date about Umrigar's novel, Geetanjali Chanda discusses the creation of a "horizontal community formation" within the home (119), or "female friendships" across class divides that enable a "womenspace . . . within a dominant, patriarchal space," and that empower women even though they do not dismantle existing power structures (121). However, in a remarkable instance of a blind spot that prevents the scholar from seeing the servant as a protagonist even when the novel clearly casts Bhima as one, Chanda discusses *Space* as if it had only one protagonist, the upper-class woman, Sera. To see Bhima as not a protagonist of this novel ignores its formal and structural features, such as the alternation of perspective between Sera and Bhima, the more than equal space given to Bhima's narrative, and the conclusion.
5. Other novels, such as Imbolo Mbue's *Behold the Dreamers* (2016) and Kazuo Ishiguro's *The Remains of the Day* (1989), explore in more depth the ethical conundrums faced by servants under conditions of extreme exigency.
6. In *Cultures of Servitude*, Ray and Qayum begin with "an iconic scene" from Satyajit Ray's *Apu Trilogy*, where Apu's newly widowed mother, who has become a cook in a rich feudal household in order to provide for her son, realizes she cannot bear to see him become a servant, and leaves, taking him with her (1).
7. In my experience teaching this novel, I have found that young women students, especially from the Global North, initially see Bhima as unkind and unsympathetic for her attitude toward Maya, until they learn more about this background.
8. It is hard to believe that someone like Bhima, who knows well about the pervasiveness of rape culture and the extreme sexual vulnerability of poor women, would not even consider that Maya may not have chosen to have sex, and would so unthinkingly blame the victim. It is one of the weaknesses of this novel that Umrigar often deploys for dramatic effect what is psychologically implausible. Bhima's discovery later that Maya was assaulted by Viraf triggers the final crisis of the novel, but unfortunately this plot twist comes at the expense of making Bhima seem remarkably obtuse and misogynistic.
9. Even in the present, after Feroz's death, both Sera and her daughter Dinaz replay and reaffirm these gender dynamics, as they pamper Viraf, now the man of the house, even though he has moved in to live in Sera's home. In cringeworthy scenes, both

women appease him when he is unreasonable, confirming the continuity of these gender inequalities in the home (67).
10. Hochschild initially studied flight attendants, who were trained to project a welcoming sincerity and to suppress annoyance at passengers' unreasonable requests, including sexual advances. Her research has been extended to a variety of non-service professions, including medicine, law, and teaching. Hochschild distinguishes *emotional labor* (part of a paid job) from *emotion work* (undertaken in unpaid private situations) by emphasizing its three features: face-to-face interactions, the requirement that workers modulate their own emotions (at emotional cost) to produce requisite emotions in others, and the lack of recognition or invisibility of this part of the job.
11. At another key moment, Bhima reenacts this form of emotional labor when she is with Viraf, and he talks about arranging an abortion for Maya: "Instead of the gratitude she knows she ought to feel, Bhima is shocked to feel a deep resentment at Viraf's words.... To punish herself for her uncharitable thoughts, Bhima digs her right thumb into the palm of heft hand until the pain makes her wince" (94). Not only does Bhima stifle that feeling and stop herself from expressing her sense of intrusion from this unfeeling man—since she needs his and Sera's help—but she actually physically inflicts pain on herself to suppress the feeling that she is surprised to have, the resentment at her employers' privilege, at their unconsciousness of their privilege, and their presumption in thinking that they know better and can tell her what to do with her family.
12. Later, as if she has internalized what Bhima tells her, Sera's language echoes Bhima's, as she blames herself for putting up with Feroz's abuse: "the first time he hit you, you should have left. And you should never have covered up for him, never allowed his shame to become your shame," Sera tells herself (168).
13. In teaching this novel, I have found that my students sometimes object that Bhima's solution is not feminist, since she advises turning to a man for help, Sera's father, a form of patriarchal power that would counter that of her husband. I point out that Umrigar is careful to maintain social realism here, that Bhima knows that as a servant she can only intervene indirectly and covertly, that she is too vulnerable to do anything more directly herself. If she did, Feroz would simply throw her out. She is strategic: knows she cannot overthrow the patriarchy, but Bhima's feminism consists in her solidarity with and courageous support of Sera, and her refusal to acquiesce in an exploitative system.
14. I take this phrase from the title of sociologist Bridget Anderson's important book.
15. It is perhaps incompatible with this portrayal that Dinaz is so lacking in discernment as to be married to a man who is the most heinously villainous in his treatment of servants and women.
16. Such representations cannot simply be dismissed as disingenuousness on the part of upper-class writers, and can instead be understood as recognition of complex social and psychological realities. Contemporary social science research confirms that in fact real emotional bonds do form among caregivers and the children they care for. In her interviews with women of color from the Global South who work in the United

States as child caregivers, Arlie Hochschild cites numerous attestations to such attachments, developed in part as the result of isolation and "redirected" longing for their own children: "Rowena calls Noa, the American child she tends, 'my baby.' ... As Rowena explained, 'I give Noa what I can't give to my children. ... She makes me feel like a mother'" ("Love & Gold," 16, 23, in *Global Woman*, ed. Barbara Ehrenreich and Arlie Hochschild, 2002). This is to say not that the exploited do not recognize their exploitation, but that the formation of cross-class or cross-race emotional bonds can occur despite that knowledge.

17. As a character, Gopal voices other illuminating insights, such as his explicit statement that the accident was not his fault, as the foreman falsely claims, but that it was the result of the factory-owners' deliberate negligence and willingness to risk workers' safety instead of the loss of a day's work. Gopal had warned them of the likelihood of such accidents days before it occurred, but was ignored. Umrigar's Marxist understanding comes through in this critique of a brutal capitalist system enabled by a state that does not penalize such negligence, and in fact enables it by not making such corporations accountable for the cost of lawsuits or workers' compensation.

18. It has to be said that Umrigar's depiction of various scenes and exchanges can be saccharine and overdone, not unlike a Bollywood film.

Chapter 7

1. Though published in 2006, the novel is set in 1986, in the Himalayan town of Kalimpong in West Bengal, near Darjeeling. The events in the present take place between February to December 1986 and include the Gorkha uprising, the demand for a separate state by ethnic Nepalis, which led to a siege and struggle with the Indian army.

2. For example, in her excellent reading of *Loss* as a postcolonial critique of globalization, Angela Poon highlights the novel's use of "the invisible script or hidden private narrative to foreground the problems of injustice and inequality" (547), and reads *Loss* as an "interlocking" (554) or "multiply braided narrative" (550) of three journeys—the judge's, Biju's, and Sai's. But Poon omits to note the hidden narrative of Bjiu's father, the cook, even though the novel concludes with Sai thinking "of the judge's journey, of the cook's journey, [and] of Biju's," as she contemplates beginning her own (356). Or, in her account of master-servant relations as an analogy for colonizer-colonized and First World–Third World "servicing" nations in *Loss* (19), Elif Oztabak-Avci views the servant figure as a literary tool to critique social "'domestic' inequalities" (9) but, after briefly mentioning the cook, focuses on Biju as an example of undocumented immigrant workers in the United States, global inequality, and relations between developing and developed nations. By contrast, I explore the servitude evoked by the cook as an affective and material complex that is not merely a metaphor for something else. As an important exception, Paul Jay does include the cook as one of the four main characters in the Kalimpong part of the narrative, but

he still sees the novel as focused only on Sai and Biju: "Throughout the novel the reader moves back and forth between Sai's point of view and Biju's in a way that sets up a complex dialogue between the two characters' experiences" (124). As I show, the novel in fact gives unusual and equal space to the cook's point of view and emphasizes his interiority.
3. Elizabeth Jackson, for instance, lists the major and minor characters of this novel and altogether omits to mention the cook (26).
4. Babli Sinha is unusual in her attention to form, though her focus is on how the novel critiques neoliberalism in India. Sinha argues that Desai uses "the technique of free indirect discourse to convey the inner emotions of the characters who undergo the social upheavals of neoliberal India" and engage readers' empathy for their suffering (293), but accuses Desai of nihilism because Desai's characters "do not seem able to experience [empathy] for each other," and claims that Desai's technique thereby sets her readers above and "outside the processes of exploitation highlighted in the novel" (302). I see Desai using multiple techniques, such as dialogue and narrator commentary, as well as free indirect discourse, to convey characters' emotions as well as the nuances of their interrelations and social situations. Moreover, as I show below, even if not all of Desai's characters show empathy, many do, including Sai for the cook, and the cook for those less fortunate then himself. I read Desai as manifesting not nihilism, but a grittier realism or ironic pessimism combined with compassion.
5. See Ostabak-Avci's excellent reading of this inversion of hierarchies as designed by the Nepali insurgents to undermine the judge's status as both a gentleman and a representative of the state that oppresses them (12).
6. As he writes, "On its surface, the novel seems to be telling two very different stories, one rooted in contemporary economic and cultural politics of globalization, the other in an older, fading history of ancient territorial disputes, ethnic rivalries and nationalist aspirations. Read more carefully, however, it becomes clear that the two narratives are linked in a way that underscores the continuity between the stories they tell, emphasizing the extent to which the relationship between migration, identity, and belonging under the forces of globalization mirror longstanding problems created by territorial, cultural, and personal disputes about identity among national groups" (Jay, 119). See also Oztabak-Avci, who rightly emphasizes how the novel delineates India's "double positioning" as at once subject to past colonialism and present neocolonialism, and as itself a colonizing/imperial force or "regional hegemon" in relation to neighboring poorer countries like Nepal and Bangladesh (without) and to Indian Nepalese citizens (within) (15).
7. Indeed, nearly all the servants we see in servitude fiction (from Saleema to Khadim, to Triton, Balram, and Bhima) are such internal migrants, from village to city, within the nation.
8. In the narrative logic of this novel, the cook's (false) stories also carry unexpected power, and indirect responsibility for the home invasion and theft of the judge's guns. Later, it turns out, Sai naively repeats to Gyan what the cook has boastfully told her—that her grandfather was a great hunter and his rifles are still powerful—which leads to the theft, for Gyan foolishly passes on this information to his insurgent friends

(256). The cook's unchecked desire for glory thus boomerangs on the household. "The cook couldn't help but enjoy himself, and the more he repeated his stories, the more they became truer than the truth" (257).

9. Paul Jay, 128. Describing Gyan as Sai's "boyfriend," Jay imposes terminology and concepts not used by either the author or the characters (128). It is perhaps telling that Sai's romance with Gyan takes off at a moment when the cook fails to chaperone Sai (125). When Gyan has to stay overnight because of bad weather, the cook leaves Sai alone for the first time with Gyan to go read his son's letters. His prioritization of Biju leads him to neglect Sai, who then is left vulnerable to Gyan's overtures. Later, Desai gives us the cook's perspective, as, attuned to Sai like a vigilant mother, he senses something in the air: "Was there a strange atmosphere in the room? But Sai and Gyan seemed immersed in the newspapers again, and he confused their sense of ripening anticipation with his own, because that morning, two letters from Biju had arrived in the post . . . and all evening he had been savoring the thought of them" (135).

10. It is worth noting, though I cannot discuss it more fully here, that Kiran Desai's *Loss* in many ways rewrites her mother's *Fire on a Mountain*. Both are set in a remote hill-station in the Himalayas, both are concerned with an old and affluent retiree, visited by a grandchild, and cared for by an old male cook on whom they depend entirely. Both cooks are good with children, both tell stories and welcome the unwanted child. The cooks even bear similar names: Panna Lal and Ram Lal. However, Kiran Desai revises the cook into a figure much more poignant, complex, and humanized.

11. Though the contexts are very different (imperial Britain vs postcolonial India), the father-son intergenerational servitude of Panna Lal is reminiscent of the father-son dynamic in Ishiguro's *The Remains of the Day*, where the father likewise ingrains in the son his sense of self and identity as a servant. But where Mr. Stevens teaches his son to be the perfect butler to a British aristocrat, Panna Lal's father teaches his son to internalize racialized and colonialized as well as classed inferiority.

12. Notably, in a telling moment, Harish-Harry's Americanized daughter resists the gendered role of subservience within the family by using the language of servitude: "I didn't ask to be born. You had me for your own selfish reasons, wanted a servant, didn't you? But in this country, Dad, nobody's going to wipe your ass for free" (165). Through this startling comment, Desai indicates both how servitude is understood as menial (and manual) intimate labor, with no recompense, and how diasporic Indians transport the culture of servitude with them. But only in America can a daughter have the gumption to talk back to her father in this way, suggesting also how the privileged upper class can use the lens of servitude metaphorically to repudiate exploitation, whereas for domestic servants that condition is only too real and literal.

13. As we have seen in the Chapter 6, Umrigar's sequel does imagine an escape for Maya and Bhima, though only because of the beneficence of an employer, not because of systemic change.

14. This is not to suggest that Desai holds up Saeed Saeed as an admirable figure. As Jackson suggests, Desai's satiric depiction of Saeed Saeed as an opportunist willing to "cheat and hustle" shows what kind of immigrant succeeds in America (38).

15. Scholars who see Biju's failure in America as solely the result of geopolitical inequalities overlook the extent to which the novel also highlights Biju's own unfortunate choices in contributing to that failure.
16. This desire is very similar to that of the old woman servant in Attia Hosain's short story, "The Daughter-in-Law," who also desires a daughter-in-law over whom she can finally exert some power, and who can serve her as she has served others.
17. Of the few critics who attend to this ending, even fewer note that the cook is beaten, but none read the beating as a result of the judge's mistreatment of the locals who were wrongly punished for the theft of the judge's guns, or connect the cook's self-abasement to his anxiety and guilt about his son. See for instance Scanlan, who describes but does not attempt to explain these events as other than revealing the "resilience of the poorest people": "a destitute couple kidnaps Mutt and the judge berates [Panna Lal] for failing to find her. As if craving abasement, he urges the judge to beat him" (273).
18. Sinha, 299.
19. As an English-speaking, educated, young, middle-class Indian woman in the late twentieth century, Sai's journey would necessarily be different, by virtue of her gender and class, than those of any of the male characters. Paul Jay views Sai's hopes of escape as already doomed by the conditions highlighted by Biju's return, spelling a "dead-end" for all the characters (136). But this pessimistic reading ignores the difference of status that Sai enjoys (even under the conditions of globalization and inequality). Despite her nationality and gender, Sai belongs among the haves, not the have-nots; she can get a visa, go legitimately to college, and land among the elite, like the Indian women students in New York to whom the undocumented Biju delivers Chinese food (56). I do not, however, read too much hope in the novel's ending, as some critics do. Poon, for example, sees promise for the future for all the characters, despite the losses of the past and present: "For only when the characters have experienced nothingness can they hope to gain something. . . . Loss is not necessarily forever—not extinction, but the possible prelude to something else. . . . Thus the novel seems to say, in its expansive humanistic vision, that the loss we inherit is ours to make good" (555). Such general optimism rests at best upon individual recovery or redemption. The novel certainly presents individual moments of relief in interpersonal interactions, but suggests, in its bleak presentation of global and local systemic inequalities and injustices, that the answer lies in collective and systemic change, not in individual resilience or transformation.

Conclusion

1. Ondaatje, *Anil's Ghost*, 11.
2. Some early readers of this manuscript suggested other examples of South Asian fiction that precede the works I focus on, as if I had missed an important counter-example. They pointed to Sri Lankan writer Punyekante Wijenaike's 1971 novella *Giraya*. But *Giraya* is not servitude fiction. Composed "mainly of diary entries . . . written by

Kamini, the young daughter-in-law of an elite, English-speaking Sinhalese family, living in a feudal manor" (Mohan, 29), this Gothic novella is told from this upper-class woman's perspective, who is occasionally sympathetic to the mistreatment of feudal servants in her in-laws' home. In fact, the novella engages in the demonization of homosexuality and negative stereotyping of an old woman servant who is cast as grotesquely lesbian, insane, evil, and violent, and who eventually murders her lover-mistress, Kamini's oppressive mother-in-law. This aspect of *Giraya* seems like a warped expansion of the influential Urdu short story "Lihaaf."

3. For example, in *A Golden Age*, her 2007 novel about the 1971 civil war between East and West Pakistan, transnational Bangladeshi writer Tahmima Anam often mentions servants but keeps them as background presences. Rehana, the middle-class widowed protagonist, dismisses her servants after she loses her children (147), but her affluent neighbor, Mrs. Chowdhury, continues to enjoy the benefits of a cook, driver, and bearer even during the struggle for Bangladeshi independence, as does Rehana's Pakistani brother-in-law when he arrives in what was then East Pakistan to supervise the Pakistani army. Focused on narrating the effects of the war on middle-class Bengali women and families, Anam seems at best peripherally aware of domestic servitude even in a novel concerned with (middle-class) female domesticity amid war. By contrast, Pakistani British writer Kamila Shamsie, in her early novels set in relatively peaceful 1980s Pakistan, seems more oblivious to the many cooks, maids, drivers, and so on that necessarily surround and serve the spoilt ultra-rich elite whose shenanigans occupy her attention. In *Kartography* (2002), for example, the US-college-returned protagonist and her friends cheerfully use powerplay with the watchman at a friend's house to gain access (136). *Salt and Saffron* (2000) overtly protests an aristocratic family's ostracism of an aunt who eloped with a cook, but itself reinforces the class separatism on which the upper-class protagonist and her family depend.

4. The novels produced within South Asia that I discuss in this book are primarily from the 1930s to 1970s, and I discuss them as mixed in their approaches to servitude. As I show in Chapter 1, women writers from mid-century onward were more attentive and empathetic than their male contemporaries to the complexities and power dynamics of servitude. A late twentieth-century writer like Shashi Deshpande likewise focuses on women of the middle classes, but her protagonists, like Jaya in *That Long Silence* (1989), are often empathetically aware of the connections and disconnections between themselves and the women servants upon whom they depend. The difference is that such writers rarely choose to center upon servants as protagonists, or sustain an investigation into a servant character's interiority.

5. https://www.youtube.com/watch?v=age3eodOoyk (5:04–5:40).
6. https://www.imdb.com/title/tt6571548/awards/?ref_=tt_awd.
7. The film leaves out, for instance, Balram's degrading references to sex and women and his experiences with prostitution, as well as the novel's depiction of rape as a form of feudal terrorism. Somewhat contradictorily, it also makes Ashok and Pinky nicer

and more ethical than they are in the novel: when the critical car accident occurs, it is Balram who urges Ashok to leave the scene, whereas in the novel, Ashok and Balram act in concert, silently.

8. This story is based on the very real crisis occasioned by the COVID-19 lockdown when middle-class employers, especially the elderly, who relied upon regular cooks, housecleaners, and so on had to make do without any domestic help, and domestic workers who needed money were sent away and not paid. See for instance "Coronavirus: How India's Lockdown Sparked a Debate Over Maids," BBC News, May 6, 2020, https://www.bbc.com/news/world-asia-india-52529922.
9. https://www.imdb.com/title/tt7142506/awards/?ref_=tt_awd. *Sir* is available via streaming on Netflix.
10. https://www.imdb.com/title/tt7142506/. Tellingly, this description centers the male employer, not the servant girl at the heart of the film. In fact, his is more of a supporting role.
11. https://www.youtube.com/watch?v=l1-3owCWphs (3:15–4:40).
12. Ibid. (8:55–9:37).
13. Ibid. (12:17–13:12).
14. It may be possible to argue that the film's ending gestures toward a utopian possibility, a politics of suggesting not what is but what may be. However, to my mind, in the context of servitude, utopianism would mean elimination of servitude and its attendant associations of degradation and inequality, not a marriage that retains enormous differentials of power.
15. Directed by Mimi Leder and written by Daniel Stiepleman.
16. https://www.ilo.org/wcmsp5/groups/public/@ed_protect/@protrav/@travail/documents/publication/wcms_161104.pdf.
17. https://paycheck.pk/labour-laws/domestic-workers-in-pakistan.
18. Ibid.
19. https://pulitzercenter.org/stories/commentary-safeguarding-pakistans-domestic-workers-will-take-more-just-laws.
20. https://www.international.gc.ca/world-monde/stories-histoires/2022/domestic-rights-droits-domestique.aspx?lang=eng.
21. https://thewire.in/labour/indian-domestic-workers-chri-labour-code. Again, extreme cases of abuse occasionally hit the news, and offenders are tried under child-trafficking or sexual-harassment laws. See for example https://www.bbc.com/news/world-asia-india-64594779.
22. https://ndwm.org/domestic-workers/.
23. https://www.globalfundforwomen.org/movements/domestic-workers-rights-movement/.
24. https://www.ilo.org/wcmsp5/groups/public/---asia/---ro-bangkok/---ilo-colombo/documents/publication/wcms_768671.pdf (p. 13). Many South Asian domestic workers (mostly women) who migrate to work in the Middle East and send remittances home also face abusive and exploitative conditions in these countries. Changing laws and practices in Middle Eastern countries likewise remain part of the

global effort to bring about progressive change. See for example https://www.nytimes.com/2020/07/06/world/middleeast/coronavirus-saudi-domestic-workers-maids-arab.html and https://blogs.lse.ac.uk/internationaldevelopment/2019/07/04/migrant-domestic-workers-in-the-middle-east-between-state-ignorance-and-obsolete-laws/. "According to the ILO, while Latin American countries have made the greatest legal advances, the Middle East and Asia remain the worst places to be a domestic worker." https://www.buzzfeednews.com/article/miriamberger/the-middle-east-is-the-worst-place-to-be-a-domestic-worker-n.

Works Cited

Adams, Kathleen, and Sara Dickey, eds. "Introduction." *Home and Hegemony: Domestic Service and Identity Politics in South and Southeast Asia*. Ann Arbor: University of Michigan Press, 2000, 1–30.
Adichie, Chimamanda Ngozi. "Imitation." *The Thing Around Your Neck*. New York: Knopf, 2009, 22–42.
Adiga, Aravind. *White Tiger*. New York: Free Press, 2008.
Adkins, Alexander. "Neoliberal Disgust in Aravind Adiga's *The White Tiger*." *Journal of Modern Literature* 42.3 (2019): 169–188.
Ahmad, Saghir. *Class and Power in a Punjabi Village*. Introd. Kathleen Gough. New York: Monthly Review, 1977.
Alcoff, Linda. "The Problem of Speaking for Others." *Cultural Critique* 20 (1991–1992): 5–32.
Ali, Ahmed. *Twilight in Delhi*. 1940. Karachi: Oxford University Press, 1984.
Ali, Monica. *Brick Lane*. New York: Scribner, 2003.
Aidoo, Ama Ata. "For Whom Things Did Not Change." *No Sweetness Here and Other Stories*. 1970. New York: Feminist Press, 1995, 8–29.
Aiyar, Swaminathan S. "Twenty- Five Years of Indian Economic Reform." Cato Institute, Policy Analysis No. 803, October 26, 2016. https://www.cato.org/policy-analysis/twenty-five-years-indian-economic-reform.
Anand, Mulk Raj. *Coolie*. 1936. New Delhi: Penguin, 1993.
Anand, Mulk Raj. *Untouchable*. 1935. London: Penguin, 1986.
Anderson, Bridget. *Doing the Dirty Work? The Global Politics of Domestic Labor*. New York: Zed Books, 2000.
Angelou, Maya. *I Know Why the Caged Bird Sings*. New York: Random House, 1969.
Asrar, Shakeeb. "'Are We Not Humans?': Pakistan's Domestic Workers Confront Abuse." https://www.csmonitor.com/World/Asia-South-Central/2021/0830/Are-we-not-humans-Pakistan-s-domestic-workers-confront-abuse. *Christian Science Monitor*, August 30, 2021.
Attridge, Derek. *The Singularity of Literature*. London: Routledge, 2004.
Bal, Mieke. *Narratology: Introduction to the Theory of Narrative*. Toronto: University of Toronto Press, 1985.
Barker, Drucilla K., and Susan F. Feiner. "Globalization Is a Feminist Issue." *Liberating Economics: Feminist Perspectives on Families, Work, and Globalization*. Ann Arbor: University of Michigan Press, 2004, 95–117.
Basu, Moni. "Indian Reaction to Diplomat's Arrest." *CNN.com*. Cable News Network, December 19, 2013. Web. January 25, 2014. https://www.cnn.com/2013/12/19/world/asia/india-diplomat-politics/index.html
Bishop, Rudine Sims. 1990. "Mirrors, Windows, and Sliding Glass Doors: Multicultural Literacy." https://scenicregional.org/wp-content/uploads/2017/08/Mirrors-Windows-and-Sliding-Glass-Doors.pdf.

Black, Shameem. *Fiction Across Borders: Imagining the Lives of Others in Late Twentieth-Century Novels*. New York: Columbia University Press, 2009.
Bose, Sugata, and Ayesha Jalal. *Modern South Asia*. New York: Routledge, 1998.
Brontë, Charlotte. *Jane Eyre*. 1847. Norton Critical Edition. Ed. Richard Dunn. New York: Norton, 2001.
Burnett, Mark Thornton. *Masters and Servants in English Renaissance Drama and Culture*. New York: St. Martin's, 1997.
Butler, Judith. *Gender Trouble: Feminism and the Subversion of Identity*. New York: Routledge, 1990.
Byatt, A. S. "Morpho Eugenia." *Angels and Insects*. New York: Vintage, 1992, 1–183.
Chanda, Geetanjali Singh. "'Womenspace': Negotiating Class and Gender in Indian English Novels." *Emerging South Asian Women Writers: Essays and Interviews*. Ed. Feroza Jussawalla and Deborah Weagel. New York: Peter Lang, 2016, 117–134.
Chaudhuri, Nirad. *The Autobiography of an Unknown Indian*. 1951. New York: Addison, 1989.
Cheesman, David. *Landlord Power and Rural Indebtedness in Colonial Sind: 1865–1901*. Surrey: Curzon, 1997.
Chughtai, Ismat. *The Quilt and Other Stories*. Transl. Tahira Naqvi and Syeda Hameed. Karachi: Oxford University Press, 1996.
Cliff, Michele. *No Telephone to Heaven*. New York: Vintage, 1987.
Crenshaw, Kimberlé. "Demarginalizing the Intersection of Race and Sex: A Black Feminist Critique of Antidiscrimination Doctrine, Feminist Theory and Antiracist Politics." *The University of Chicago Legal Forum* 140.1 (1989): 139–167.
Crenshaw, Kimberlé. "Mapping the Margins: Intersectionality, Identity Politics, and Violence Against Women of Color." *Stanford Law Review* 43.6 (1991): 1241–1299.
Damrosch, David. *What Is World Literature?* Princeton, NJ: Princeton University Press, 2003.
Desai, Anita. *Cry, The Peacock*. 1963. New Delhi: Orient Paperbacks, 1980.
Desai, Anita. *Fire on the Mountain*. New York: King Penguin, 1977.
Desai, Kiran. *The Inheritance of Loss*. New York: Grove Press, 2006.
Desai, Manan. *The United States of India: Anticolonial Literature and Transnational Refraction*. Philadelphia: Temple University Press, 2020.
Deshpande, Shashi. *That Long Silence*. New Delhi: Penguin, 1988.
Dumas, Firoozeh. *Laughing Without an Accent: Adventures of a Global Citizen*. New York: Random House, 2008.
Eagleton, Terry. *How to Read Literature*. New Haven, CT: Yale University Press, 2013.
Ehrenreich, Barbara, and Arlie Russell Hochschild, eds. Introduction. *Global Woman: Nannies, Maids, and Sex Workers in the New Economy*. New York: Holt, 2004. 1–14.
Faulkner, William. *The Sound and the Fury*. 1929. New York: Vintage Books, 1984.
Fernandez, Jean. *Victorian Servants, Class, and the Politics of Literacy*. New York: Routledge, 2010.
Franks, Alan. "Alan Franks Interviews Daniyal Mueenuddin." *Times*, July 11, 2009. Web. June 15, 2010. https://www.thetimes.co.uk/article/alan-franks-interviews-daniyal-mueenuddin-xr2nqxmcxvm
Frost, Robert. "Provide, Provide." 1936.
Futehally, Zeenuth. *Zohra*. 1951. Ed. Rummana Futehally Denby. New Delhi: Oxford University Press, 2004.

George, Rosemary Marangoly. "Domestic." *Keywords for American and Cultural Studies*. Ed. Bruce Burgett and Glenn Hendler. New York: New York University Press, 2007, 88.
Gera, Rohena (dir). *Sir*. Platoon One Films: Netflix, 2018.
Ghosh, Amitav. *The Hungry Tide*. New York: Houghton Mifflin, 2004.
Girard, René. *Deceit, Desire, and the Novel: Self and Other in Literary Structure*. 1961. Transl. Yvonne Freccero. Baltimore: Johns Hopkins University Press, 1965.
Goh, Robbie. "Narrating 'Dark' India in *Londonstani* and *The White Tiger*: Sustaining Identity in the Diaspora." *Journal of Commonwealth Literature* 46.2 (2011): 327–344.
Goonetilleke, D. C. R. A. *Sri Lankan English Literature and the Sri Lankan People, 1917–2003*. Colombo: Vijitha Yapa Publications, 2005.
Gopal, Priyamvada. *The Indian English Novel: Nation, History, Narration*. New York: Oxford University Press, 2009.
Gopinath, Gayatri. *Impossible Desires: Queer Diasporas and South Asian Public Cultures*. Durham, NC: Duke University Press, 2005.
Gray, Thomas. "Elegy Written in a Country Churchyard." 1751.
Gunesekera, Romesh. *Monkfish Moon*. New York: Riverhead Books, 1992.
Gunesekera, Romesh. *Reef*. New York: Riverhead Books, 1994.
Habib, Shahnaz. Interview with Daniyal Mueenuddin. *New Yorker*, March 3, 2009. https://www.newyorker.com/books/page-turner/the-exchange-daniyal-mueenuddin
Hagedorn, Jessica. *Dogeaters*. New York: Penguin, 1990.
Haggard, H. Rider. *King Solomon's Mines*. 1885. Ed. Dennis Butts. Oxford: Oxford University Press, 1989.
Hai, Ambreen. "Border Work, Border Trouble: Postcolonial Feminism and the Ayah in Bapsi Sidhwa's *Cracking India*." *Modern Fiction Studies* 46.2 (June 2000): 379–426.
Hai, Ambreen. "Motherhood and Domestic Servitude in Transnational Women's Fiction: Thrity Umrigar's *The Space Between Us* and Mona Simpson's *My Hollywood*." *Contemporary Literature* 57.4 (Winter 2016): 500–540.
Hai, Ambreen. "'No One in the House Knew Her Name': Servant Problems in R. K. Narayan's Short Stories." *South Asian Review* 39.3-4 (2019): 335–353. (Reprinted in *Vulnerable South Asias: Precarities, Resistance, and Care Communities*. Ed. Pallavi Rastogi. Routledge, 2021, 70–88.)
Hai, Ambreen. "Postcolonial Servitude: Interiority and System in Daniyal Mueenuddin's *In Other Rooms, Other Wonders*." *Ariel: A Review of International English Literature* 45.3 (July 2014): 33–73.
Hamid, Mohsin. *Moth Smoke*. London: Granta, 2000.
Hamid, Mohsin. *The Reluctant Fundamentalist*. New York: Harcourt, 2007.
Hanif, Mohammad. *Our Lady of Alice Bhatti*. London: Random House, 2011.
Herring, Ronald J. *Land to the Tiller: The Political Economy of Agrarian Reform in South Asia*. New Haven, CT: Yale University Press, 1983.
Hettiarachchi, Nirmali. *Replacements*. Sri Lanka: Hettiarachichi, 1998 (self-published).
Hochschild, Arlie Russell. 1983. *The Managed Heart: Commercialization of Human Feeling*. Berkeley: University of California Press, 2003.
Hondagneu-Sotelo, Pierrette. "Blowups and Other Unhappy Endings." *Global Woman*. Ed. Barbara Ehrenreich and Arlie Hochschild, New York: Holt, 2002, 55–69.
Hosain, Attia. *Phoenix Fled*. 1953. London: Virago, 1988.
Hosain, Attia. *Sunlight on a Broken Column*. 1961. London: Penguin, 1988.
Hosseini, Khaled. *The Kite Runner*. New York: Riverhead, 2003.

Ishiguro, Kazuo. *The Remains of the Day*. New York: Vintage, 1989.

Jackson, Elizabeth. "Globalization, Diaspora, and Cosmopolitanism in Kiran Desai's *The Inheritance of Loss*." *Ariel: A Review of International English Literature* 47.4 (2016): 25–43.

Jani, Pranav. *Decentering Rushdie: Cosmopolitanism and the Indian Novel in English*. Columbus: Ohio State University Press, 2010.

Jay, Paul. *Global Matters: The Transnational Turn in Literary Studies*. Ithaca, NY: Cornell University Press, 2010.

Jayasuriya, Maryse. *Terror and Reconciliation: Sri Lankan Anglophone Literature, 1983–2009*. New York: Lexington, 2012.

Jayawardena, Elmo. *Sam's Story*. Sri Lanka: Vijitha Yapa Publications, 2001.

Jeffries, Stuart. "Booker Prize: Roars of Anger." *The Guardian*. October 16, 2008. https://www.theguardian.com/books/2008/oct/16/booker-prize

Jordan, Margaret I. *African-American Servitude and Historical Imaginings*. New York: Palgrave, 2004.

Joyce, James. *Ulysses: The Corrected Text*. 1920. New York: Random House, 1986.

Katrak, Ketu. Afterword to *No Sweetness Here and Other Stories*. 1970. New York: Feminist Press, 1995, 135–160.

Kanwal, Aroosa, and Saiyma Aslam, eds. *The Routledge Companion to Pakistani Anglophone Writing: Origins, Contestations, New Horizons*. London: Routledge, 2018.

Kapur, Akash. "The Secret of His Success: *The White Tiger*." *The New York Times*. November 7, 2008.

Keen, Suzanne. *Empathy and the Novel*. New York: Oxford University Press, 2007.

Khair, Tabish. "Namaste Trump." *The Massachusetts Review* 64.1 (Spring 2023): 37–48.

Khan, Manal Ahmad. "Daniyal Mueenuddin: In Other Rooms, Other Wonders, and Other Pakistans." *Windswept Words*. Wordpress, May 7, 2010. Web. December 14, 2012. https://windsweptwords.com/2010/05/

Khan, Yasmin. *The Great Partition: The Making of India and Pakistan*. New Haven, CT: Yale University Press, 2007.

Khor, Lena. "Can the Subaltern Right Wrongs?: Human Rights and Development in Aravind Adiga's *The White Tiger*." *South Central Review* 29.1 (2012): 41–67.

Kincaid, Jamaica. *Annie John*. New York: Penguin, 1983.

Kipling, Rudyard. *Life's Handicap: Being Stories of Mine Own People*. 1891. Ed P. N. Furbank. New York: Penguin, 1987.

Kipling, Rudyard. *Something of Myself*. 1937. Cambridge: Cambridge University Press, 1990.

Kipnis, Laura. "(Male) Desire and (Female) Disgust: Reading *Hustler*." *Ecstasy Unlimited: On Sex, Capital, Gender, and Aesthetics*. Minneapolis: University of Minnesota Press, 1993, 219–242.

Koh, Helen. "Daniyal Mueenuddin and Mohsin Hamid: Two 'Internally Displaced' Writers." *Asia Society*, February 23, 2009. https://asiasociety.org/daniyal-mueenuddin-and-mohsin-hamid-two-internally-displaced-writers

Kristeva, Julia. *Powers of Horror: An Essay on Abjection*. Transl. Leon S. Roudiez. New York: Columbia University Press, 1982.

Kumar, Amitava. "'Bad News': Authenticity and the South Asian Political Novel," *Boston Review*, November 1, 2008. https://www.bostonreview.net/articles/kumar-bad-news/

Kumar, Priya. *Limiting Secularism: The Ethics of Coexistence in Indian Literature and Film*. Minneapolis: University of Minnesota Press, 2008.

Kirkus Reviews. White Tiger. February 15, 2008. https://www.kirkusreviews.com/book-reviews/aravind-adiga/the-white-tiger/.
Kumarasamy, Akil. *Half Gods*. New York: Picador, 2018.
LaCapra, Dominic. *History, Politics and the Novel*. New York: Cornell University Press, 1987.
Lahiri, Jhumpa. *The Namesake*. New York: Houghton Mifflin, 2003.
Lahiri, Tripti. *Maid in India: Stories of Inequality and Opportunity Inside Our Homes*. New Delhi: Aleph Book Company, 2017.
Lazarus, Neil. "Introducing Postcolonial Studies." *The Cambridge Companion to Postcolonial Literary Studies*. Ed. Neil Lazarus. Cambridge: Cambridge University Press, 2004, 1–16.
Lee, Harper. *To Kill a Mockingbird*. 1960. New York: Harper Perennial, 2002.
Lim, Shirley Geok-lin, et al., eds. *Transnational Asian American Literature: Sites and Transits*. Philadelphia: Temple University Press, 2006.
Lochner, Liani. "The Politics of Precarity: Contesting Neoliberalism's Subjects in Aravind Adiga's *The White Tiger*." *English Academy Review* 31.2 (2014): 35–48.
Markandaya, Kamala. *Nectar in a Sieve*. New York: Penguin Signet, 1956.
Markandaya, Kamala. *A Silence of Desire*. New York: John Day, 1960.
Markandaya, Kamala. *Some Inner Fury*. 1955. Gurgaon, India: Penguin, 2009.
Mehrotra, Arvind. *A History of Indian Literature in English*. New York: Columbia University Press, 2003.
Mehta, Aban. *The Domestic Servant Class*. Bombay, 1960.
Mehta, Deepa (dir.). *Fire* (film). Trial By Fire Films, 1996.
Mendes, Ana. "Exciting Tales of Exotic Dark India: Aravind Adiga's *The White Tiger*." *The Journal of Commonwealth Literature* 45.2 (2010): 275–293.
Metcalf, Barbara and Thomas. *A Concise History of Modern India*, New York: Cambridge University Press, 2006.
Mirza, Maryam. *Intimate Class Acts: Friendship and Desire in Indian and Pakistani Women's Fiction*. New Delhi: Oxford University Press, 2016.
Mistry, Rohinton. *Family Matters*. New York: Vintage, 2002.
Mohan, Anupama. "*Giraya* and the Gothic Space: Nationalism and the Novel in Sri Lanka." *University of Toronto Quarterly* 84.4 (2015): 29–53.
Mohsin, Moni. *The End of Innocence*. London: Penguin, 2006.
Morrison, Toni. *Beloved*. New York: Vintage, 1987.
Morrison, Toni. *A Mercy*. New York: Vintage, 2008.
Moss, Stephen. "Aravind Adiga: 'I was Afraid *The White Tiger* Would Eat Me Up Too.'" *The Guardian*, August 25, 2017. https://www.theguardian.com/books/2017/aug/25/aravind-adiga-books-interview-selection-day-the-white-tiger
Mueenuddin, Daniyal. *In Other Rooms, Other Wonders*. New York: Norton, 2009.
Mueenuddin, Daniyal. "An Interview with Daniyal Mueenuddin." *BookBrowse*. Web. February 9, 2010. https://www.bookbrowse.com/author_interviews/full/index.cfm/author_number/1659/daniyal-mueenuddin
Mueenuddin, Daniyal. "On Writing *In Other Rooms, Other Wonders*," end-matter in the paperback edition, 2010.
Mueenuddin, Daniyal. "Sameer and the Samosas." *New Yorker*, December 3, 2012, 62–71.
Mukherjee, Neel. *A State of Freedom*. New York: Norton, 2017.
Munaweera, Nayomi. *Island of a Thousand Mirrors*. New York: St. Martin's, 2012.
Murphy, Richard McGill. "Pakistan's New Literary Star." *Daily Beast*, February 23, 2009. https://www.thedailybeast.com/pakistans-new-literary-star

Naipaul, V. S. *A Bend in the River*. New York: Vintage, 1979.
Nair, Mira (dir.). *Monsoon Wedding*. New York: Mirabai Films, 2001.
Nair, Mira (dir.). *The Namesake*. New York: Mirabai Films, 2007.
Nandi, Swaralipi. "Narrative Ambiguity and the Neoliberal Bildungsroman in Aravind Adiga's *The White Tiger*." *Journal of Narrative Theory* 47.2 (2017): 276–301.
Naqvi, Syed Nawab Haider, Mahmood Hasan Khan, and M. Ghaffar Chaudhry, eds. *Land Reforms in Pakistan: A Historical Perspective*. Islamabad: Pakistan Institute of Development Economics, 1987.
Narayan, R. K. *The Bachelor of Arts*. Chicago: University of Chicago Press, 1980.
Narayan, R. K. *The Dark Room*. 1938. Chicago: University of Chicago Press, 1981.
Narayan, R. K. *Swami and Friends*. 1935. Chicago: University of Chicago Press, 1980.
Needham, Anuradha Dingwaney. "Multiple Forms of (National) Belonging: Attia Hosain's *Sunlight on a Broken Column*." *Modern Fiction Studies* 39.1 (1993): 93–111.
Nixon, Rob. *Slow Violence and the Environmentalism of the Poor*. Cambridge: Harvard University Press, 2011.
North, Joseph. *Literary Criticism: A Concise Political History*. Cambridge: Harvard University Press, 2017.
Ondaatje, Michael. *Anil's Ghost*. New York: Vintage, 2000.
Ondaatje, Michael. *Handwriting*. New York: Knopf, 1999.
Ong, Aihwa. *Flexible Citizenship: The Cultural Logics of Transnationality*. Durham, NC: Duke University Press, 1999.
Oztabak-Avci, Elif. "Entanglement of the Domestic and the Global: A View of Globalization from Below in Desai's *The Inheritance of Loss*." *Mapping Cultural Identities and Intersections: Imagological Readings*. Ed. Onorina Botezat and Mustafa Kirca, Newcastle upon Tyne, UK: Cambridge Scholars Publishing, 2019, 8–28.
Parreñas, Rhacel Salazar. *Servants of Globalization: Women, Migration and Domestic Work*. Stanford: Stanford University Press, 2001.
Peters, Susanne. "The Pragmatics of Contained Excessiveness: Humour in Aravind Adiga's *The White Tiger*." *Pragmatic Perspectives on Postcolonial Discourse: Linguistics and Literature*. Ed. and introd. Christoph Schubert. Newcastle upon Tyne, UK: Cambridge Scholars Publishing, 2016, 114–134.
Poon, Angela. "(In)visible Scripts, Hidden Costs: Narrating the Postcolonial Globe in Kiran Desai's *The Inheritance of Loss*." *Journal of Postcolonial Writing* 50.5 (2014): 547–558.
Pratt, Mary Louise. *Imperial Eyes: Travel Writing and Transculturation*. New York: Routledge, 1992.
Publisher's Weekly. "The White Tiger." 2008.
Rahman, Mushtaqur. "Pakistan." *Agrarian Egalitarianism: Land Tenures and Land Reforms in South Asia*. Ed. Mushtaqur Rahman. Iowa City: Kendall, 1981, 133–192.
Raj, K. N. "Land Reforms in India and Pakistan: A Comparative Review." *The Post-Colonial State and Social Transformation in India and Pakistan*. Ed. S. M. Naseem and Khalid Nadvi. Karachi: Oxford University Press, 2002, 131–141.
Rao, Raja. *Kanthapura*. 1938. New York: New Directions, 1967.
Ratti, Manav. "Justice, Subalternism, and Literary Justice: Aravind Adiga's *The White Tiger*." *The Journal of Commonwealth Literature* 55.2 (2020): 228–245.
Ray, Raka, and Seemin Qayum. *Cultures of Servitude: Modernity, Domesticity, and Class in India*. Stanford, CA: Stanford University Press, 2009.
Richardson, Samuel. *Pamela*. 1740. New York: Oxford University Press, 2001.

Robbins, Bruce. *The Servant's Hand: English Fiction from Below*. 1986. Durham, NC: Duke University Press, 1993.

Rollins, Judith. *Between Women: Domestics and their Employers*. Philadelphia: Temple University Press, 1985.

Rosenberg, Amy. Review, "In Other Rooms, Other Wonders." *BookForum*, February/March 2009. https://www.bookforum.com/print/1505/in-other-rooms-other-wonders-by-daniyal-mueenuddin-3261

Roy, Arundhati. *The God of Small Things*. New York: Random House, 1997.

Rushdie, Salman. "The Courter." *East, West*. New York: Pantheon, 1994. 173–211.

Rushdie, Salman. *Haroun and the Sea of Stories*. New York: Penguin, 1990.

Rushdie, Salman. *Midnight's Children*. New York: Penguin, 1981.

Rushdie, Salman. *The Moor's Last Sigh*. New York: Pantheon Books, 1995.

Rushdie, Salman. "Outside the Whale." *Imaginary Homelands*. New York: Viking Penguin, 1991, 87–101.

Rushdie, Salman. *The Satanic Verses*. New York: Viking Penguin, 1989.

Rushdie, Salman. *Shalimar the Clown*. New York: Random House, 2005.

Rushdie, Salman. *Shame*. New York: Vintage Aventura, 1983.

Ryan, Barbara. *Love, Wages, Slavery: The Literature of Servitude in the United States*. Urbana: University of Illinois Press, 2006.

Sabo, Oana. "Disjunctures and Diaspora in Kiran Desai's *The Inheritance of Loss*." *The Journal of Commonwealth Literature* 47.3 (2012): 375–392.

Sahgal, Nayantara. *The Day in Shadow*. New York: Norton, 1971.

Sahgal, Nayantara. *Storm in Chandigarh*. 1969. India: Penguin, 1988.

Sahgal, Nayantara. *This Time of Morning*. 1965. New York: Harper Collins, 2008.

Sahgal, Nayantara. *A Time to Be Happy*. London: Victor Gollancz, 1958.

Salgado, Minoli. *Writing Sri Lanka: Literature, Resistance and the Politics of Place*. New York: Routledge, 2007.

Satrapi, Marjane. *Persepolis*. New York: Pantheon, 2003.

Scanlon, Margaret. "Migrating from Terror: The Postcolonial Novel after September 11." *Journal of Postcolonial Writing* 46.4 (2010): 266–278.

Schotland, Sara. "Breaking Out of the Rooster Coop: Violent Crime in Aravind Adiga's *White Tiger* and Richard Wright's *Native Son*." *Comparative Literature Studies* 48.1 (2011): 1–19.

Selvadurai, Shyam. *Cinnamon Gardens*. Gurgaon, India: Penguin, 1998.

Selvadurai, Shyam. *Funny Boy*. New York: Harvest, 1994.

Selznick, David O. (dir). *Gone With the Wind* (film). Selznick International Pictures. 1939.

Shamsie, Kamila. *Kartography*. New York: Harcourt, 2002.

Sharma, Sonal. "Domestic Workers, Class-Hegemony, and the Indian State: A Sociological Perspective on Ideology." *South Asian History and Culture* 13.4 (2022): 528–545.

Sidhwa, Bapsi. *Cracking India*. Minneapolis: Milkweed, 1999.

Silverman, Jacob. Review of *In Other Rooms, Other Wonders*, by Daniyal Mueenuddin. *Bookslut*. March 2009. Web. December 14, 2012. https://www.powells.com/post/reviewaday/a-review-of-in-other-rooms-other-wonders

Simon, Scott. "In *White Tiger*, Killer Exploits India's Caste System." *NPR*. May 17, 2008. https://www.npr.org/transcripts/90452769

Singer, Peter. *Animal Liberation: A New Ethics for Our Treatment of Animals*. New York: Harper Collins, 1975.

Singer, Wendy. "Review of Adiga's *The White Tiger*." *The Kenyon Review*, Winter 2009. https://kenyonreview.org/kr-online-issue/2009-winter/selections/review-of-arav ind-adigas-the-white-tiger/?_gl=1%2Alxvkxi%2A_ga%2AMTIxNDk3NzU5MC4xN zAxMDE0Nzc2%2A_ga_HKRGCMX9KD%2AMTcwMTAyNDQ5OC4yLjAuMTc wMTAyNDQ5OC4wLjAuMA..&_ga=2.146273852.949230911.1701014776-1214977 590.1701014776

Sinha, Babli. "Collective Suffering and the Possibility of Empathy in Karan Mahajan's *The Association of Small Bombs* and Kiran Desai's *The Inheritance of Loss*." *The Journal of Commonwealth Literature* 54.2 (2019): 292–302.

Smith, Zadie. *The Embassy of Cambodia*. London: Hamish Hamilton, Penguin, 2013.

Sophocles. *The Oedipus Cycle*. Transl. Dudley Fitts and Robert Fitzgerald. New York: Houghton Mifflin, 1967.

Spivak, Gayatri. "Can the Subaltern Speak?" *Colonial Discourse and Post-Colonial Theory: A Reader*. Ed. Patrick Williams and Laura Chrisman. New York: Columbia University Press, 1994, 66–111.

Spivak, Gayatri. "Subaltern Talk: Interview with the Editors." *The Spivak Reader*. Ed. Donna Landry and Gerald MacLean. New York: Routledge, 1996, 287–308.

Stahl, John M. (dir). *Imitation of Life* (film). Universal Pictures, 1934.

Stallybrass, Peter, and Allon White. *The Politics and Poetics of Transgression*. Ithaca, NY: Cornell Universiyt Press, 1986.

Straub, Kristina. *Domestic Affairs: Intimacy, Eroticism and Violence between Servants and Masters in Eighteenth Century Britain*. Baltimore: Johns Hopkins University Press, 2009.

Thomas, Lee. Interview with Adiga. April 15, 2009. https://fictionwritersreview.com/ interview/interiew-with-aravind-adiga-the-white-tiger/.

Thiong'o, Ngũgĩ wa. *A Grain of Wheat*. 1967. New York: Penguin, 1986.

Umrigar, Thrity. "Looking Back: Interview with Thrity Umrigar." Conducted by Arthur J. Pais. *India Abroad: The Magazine*, M9. December 23, 2011.

Umrigar, Thrity. *The Secrets Between Us*. New York: Harper, 2018.

Umrigar, Thrity. *The Space Between Us*. New York: Harper, 2005.

Upadhyay, Samrat. *Arresting God in Kathmandu*. New York: Houghton Mifflin, 2001.

Upadhyay, Samrat. *The Royal Ghosts*. New York: Houghton Mifflin, 2006.

Walkowitz, Rebecca L. "Comparison Literature." *New Literary History* 40.3 (2009): 567–582.

Walther, Sundhya. "Fables of the Tiger Economy: Subalternity in Aravind Adiga's *The White Tiger*." *Modern Fiction Studies* 60.3 (2014): 580–598.

Wijenaike, Punyakante. *Giraya*. Colombo, Ceylon: Lake House, 1971.

Wijesinha, Rajiva. *Servants: A Cycle*. Colombo, Sri Lanka: McCallum Books, 1995.

Wilson, Mary. *The Labors of Modernism: Domesticity, Servants, and Authorship in Modernist Fiction*. Burlington, VT: Ashgate, 2013.

Woloch, Alex. *The One Vs. The Many: Minor Characters and the Space of the Protagonist in the Novel*. Princeton, NJ: Princeton University Press, 2003.

Index

For the benefit of digital users, indexed terms that span two pages (e.g., 52–53) may, on occasion, appear on only one of those pages.

abasement, 3–4, 6–7, 14, 16–17, 18–19, 121, 129–30, 231, 257, 267, 276–77, 285–86, 301–2, 316, 319
abjection, 4, 7, 8, 61–62, 68–69, 77, 104–5, 126–27, 129–30, 142–43, 144–45, 154–55, 171–72, 198–99, 212, 226, 238–39, 251, 255, 276–77, 281–82, 285–86, 290–91, 324
abortion, 112–13, 262–64, 270–72
abuse:
    colonialism and, 59
    domestic, 256, 264–65
    home and, 6, 28–29, 102, 208–9
    by police, 120, 121–22
    of power, 9–10, 28–29, 108, 112–13, 125–27, 164, 165–66, 249–50, 255, 268, 272, 275–76
    resisting, 26–27
    servitude and, 19–20, 26–27, 28–29, 35–36, 55, 60–62, 75, 77–78, 79, 96, 102, 105–6, 108–10, 111–13, 116–17, 121–22, 125–27, 132–33, 165–66, 169–70, 208–9, 266–67, 275–76, 288, 292
    sexual, 157
    systemic, 60, 130–31, 142–43
    vulnerability and, 18, 121, 309–10
acquiescence, 17–18, 26–27, 79–80, 96–97, 101, 131–32, 136, 163, 222, 236–37, 265. *See also* resistance
activism, 330–31
Adams, Kathleen, 20–21
Adichie, Chimamanda Ngozi, 30
    Half of a Yellow Sun, 181
Adiga, Aravind, 5–6, 23, 50, 52–53, 145, 252–53, 323
    White Tiger, The, 11, 21–22, 174–77, 207–51, 279–80, 324, 325–26
aesthetics, 4–5, 14–15, 24, 31. *See also* form, formalism
affect, 8, 216, 289
    attachment and, 253–54, 255
    interpersonal, 7
    labor and, 11, 255, 264
    narrative fiction and, 14–15
    nation and, 28
    of servitude, 21, 101, 125–27, 130–31, 135, 145, 146–47, 152–53, 171, 174–75, 180, 181–83, 184–86, 191–97, 202–3, 206, 207–8, 226–28, 232, 235–37, 240–41, 262–64, 268–69, 275, 276–77, 292–94, 295–96, 299–302, 303, 313, 323
    See also individual emotions by name
age, aging, 4–5, 7, 8, 42, 69–70, 104–5, 156–57, 253, 255, 258–59, 292–95, 305, 310
agency, 8, 30
    characterization and, 52, 155
    education and, 182–83
    gender and, 131, 136–37, 157, 159, 161, 164, 210, 274–75
    limited, 20–21, 277–78
    postcolonialism and, 14–15
    servitude and, 8, 20–21, 30, 52, 79–80, 81, 91–92, 93–94, 110, 122–23, 130, 131–33, 136–37, 145–46, 155, 157–58, 159, 161, 173, 174–75, 178–79, 181, 182–83, 188, 189–90, 205–6, 210, 218–19, 226, 251, 274–75, 277–78, 279–80, 328–29
    See also resistance
agricultural workers, 71–72, 149–50
Aidoo, Ama Ata, "For Whom Things Do Not Change," 1–2, 4
Alcoff, Linda, 41, 43
Ali, Ahmed, 50–51
    Twilight in Delhi, 64–66
Ali, Monica, 7, 23
    Brick Lane, 97–98, 131–37
alienation, 90–91, 238–39, 246
All-India Progressive Writers Association, 53–54
altruism, 7, 11, 134–35, 215, 249
ambition, xvi, 189
Anand, Mulk Raj, 7, 12–13, 28–29, 50–51
    Coolie, 60–63
    Untouchable, 59–60
animal, animalization, 86–87, 96, 112, 210–11, 216, 219–20, 222, 246, 248–49

anticolonialism, 8, 59, 78
anxiety, 10, 82, 94–95, 110, 154, 201–2, 308, 311–12, 313–15, 316–18
Asrar, Shakeeb, 330–31
attachment:
  ambivalence and, 207, 253–54, 255, 292–93
  conflict and, 275
  desire and, 174–75, 179–80, 184–85, 202–4, 214, 226, 227–28
  gender and, 22, 68–69, 90–91, 214, 268–69
  resentment and, 6, 11
  servitude and, xii, 132–33, 152–53, 310–12
  See also relationality
Attridge, Derek, 23–24
Austen, Jane, 25, 31–32
authenticity, 39–41, 215–16
ayah (nanny), viii, 21–22, 34, 71, 84, 85–86, 91–92, 98–99, 100, 103–4, 108, 109, 110–14, 117, 300–1

Bahrani, Ramin, 325–26
Baker, Jo, 30
Bal, Mieke, 155–56
Baldwin, James, 42–43
Bangladesh, 131
  civil war, 53, 149
  genocide in, 107–8
  "Securing Rights of Women Domestic Workers in Bangladesh" project with Oxfam Canada, 331
  servitude in, 9
  See also Ali, Monica
Battle of Plassey, 53
Bayer, Gerd, 180
bearer (butler), 18, 21–22, 34, 71, 72–74, 79–81, 84, 101, 113
Bechdel test, 51–53
belonging:
  family and, 3–4, 67, 68–69, 71, 292–93
  nation and, x, 28, 215
  servitude and, 127, 183–84, 191–92, 205, 295–96
  unbelonging, 96–97
beneficence, beneficiary, 81, 122–23, 130, 135–36, 169–70, 264–65, 267, 270
  class and, 198–99, 203–4
  colonialism and, 151
benevolence, 124–25, 175, 177–79, 181–82, 206
betrayal, xvii, 1–4, 64–65, 85–86, 128, 172, 240–41, 242–44, 251, 255, 272, 274, 276–77, 279, 280, 299, 316, 326
Bhabha, Homi, 188
Bhutto, Zulfikar Ali, 149–50

Bildungsroman, 7–8, 179
Black, Shameem, 40, 43, 154
body, 3, 171–72, 173, 194–96, 198, 260, 284, 294–95
  class and, 114
  identity and, 17–18
  servitude and, 56, 61–62, 142–43, 218–19, 231, 238–39, 264–66, 271
  social location and, 114
Booker Prize, 11, 12–13, 174, 215, 252
British East India Company, 53
Brontë, Anne, *Agnes Grey*, 31–32
Brontë, Charlotte, *Jane Eyre*, 31–33
Brontë, Emily, *Wuthering Heights*, 31
butler, 31–32, 73–75, 171, 193, 224
Butler, Judith, 153

capitalism, 6–7, 18–20, 28–29, 71–72, 94, 147–48, 217, 228, 232–33, 250–51, 282–83
car, 175, 176, 208–9, 212, 222. *See also* home
care, care work, 14–15, 27–28, 33, 240–41, 255, 262–63, 268–69, 292–93
caste, 8, 11–13, 25–26, 28–29, 58–60, 68–69, 74, 94, 116–17, 221–22, 224–25, 228, 265–66. *See also* class
character, characterization, 37–39, 99–100, 194–95
  attention and, 38
  character space, 94, 97, 99–100, 110–11, 256–57, 284, 286–88
  complexity, 91–92
  focalization, 155–57, 158, 159–61, 163
  foregrounding, 142, 143–44, 145, 146–47
  identification, 157
  minor, 2, 37–38, 64–65, 77, 129–30, 284
  modernity and, 78
  naming and, 51–53, 71, 73–74, 108–9, 113, 116–17, 120, 169, 187, 227–28, 284, 303
  narrative and, 37–39, 64–65
  protagonist, 142, 174–75, 178–79, 207–8, 220, 227–28, 277, 278, 326–28
Chaudhuri, Nirad, 50–51
  Autobiography of an Unknown Indian, 56–57, 224–25
chauffeur, 18, 21–22, 71, 73–74, 75, 114, 161–62, 208–9. *See also* driver
Chughtai, Ismat, 53–54
citizenship, 13–14, 16–17, 28, 68–69, 216, 223–25
  vulnerability and, 1, 8, 43–44, 176, 208
civil disobedience, 53
civility, 181–82, 188
civilization, 50–51, 56, 66–67, 87–88

INDEX

class, xvii, 5–6, 11–12, 30, 42, 90–91, 252
  body and, 114
  caste and, 59–60
  citizenship and, 224–25
  colonialism and, 62–63
  decorum and, xv
  descent, 123–24, 125–27, 128–30
  domesticity and, ix
  education and, 100–1
  elite, 50, 51, 55–56, 57–58, 77–78, 114–15, 150–51, 183–84
  entitlement and, 128
  exploitation, 116, 198–99
  fiction and, 236–37
  gender and, 8, 21–23, 26, 32, 53–55, 59, 60–62, 63, 66–71, 81–82, 88, 89, 93–94, 96, 114–15, 119–20, 123, 191, 197, 200, 214, 239, 252, 253, 256, 262, 263–64, 265–67, 272–73, 278–79, 285, 286–87
  home and, 96–97
  ideology and, 42, 242
  in India, vii–viii
  inequality, 116, 121–22, 175–76, 181, 256
  intimacy and, 18, 98–99
  landowners, 147–50
  mobility, 62–63, 115, 123–27, 183–84
  narrative and, 216–17, 253–54, 256, 258
  in Pakistan, viii
  postcolonialism and, vii–viii, 41–42, 289
  power and, 7, 89
  race and, 33
  relations across, 101
  resentment and, 286–87
  servitude and, vii–ix, 1–2, 4–7, 10–13, 15–20, 21–23, 26, 27, 31–33, 39–40, 41–42, 50–51, 52–53, 54–58, 59–63, 65, 66–69, 71, 75–78, 81–82, 83–84, 88, 90, 91–93, 94–95, 96–97, 98–102, 103, 106, 113, 114–15, 116, 117, 119–27, 128–31, 135–37, 142–43, 167–68, 176, 177–79, 181, 197, 198–99, 200, 203–4, 214, 215, 237–40, 242, 252–54, 260–67, 268–69, 272, 276–77, 278–79, 281, 287–89, 292–93, 295–96, 300–1, 302–3, 308, 316–17, 328–30
  sexuality and, 119, 120
  socialization and, 115
  in South Asia, ix
  subjectivity and, 52–53, 54–55, 56–58
  as systemic structure, 60–62
  transgressing, xv, 66–67, 74, 89, 254
  in United States, vii–viii
  violence and, 204–5
  vulnerability and, 121–22

cleaner, viii, 12–13, 18, 21–22, 60, 124
close reading, 23–24, 323
coercion, 9, 59, 132–33, 240–41, 272
collective bargaining, 280–81
Collins, Wilkie, 31
colonialism, 252, 288–89
  capitalism and, 28–29, 71–72, 94–95
  class and, 12–14, 16, 18, 50–51, 54–55, 56, 58, 61–65, 94–95
  literature and, 33–37, 150, 211
  nation and, 43–44, 147–49, 151, 198–99, 205, 217–18, 220, 224–25, 256–57
  race and, 33, 36–37, 256–57, 295–96
  servitude and, 1, 8–9, 11–14, 18, 21, 73–74, 101, 149–51, 304–5
  subjectivity and, 188
colorism, 92, 118–19. *See also* racism *under* race
comedy, 7–8, 33, 55–56, 62–63, 76, 79, 100–1, 106, 108, 111–12, 116–17, 137, 153, 166–68, 216, 220, 233, 251, 252, 260–61, 285, 286–87, 299–301, 302–3, 317–18, 320–21. *See also* irony; satire
community, 50–51, 71, 72–73, 134–35, 152–53, 232–33, 236, 251, 260–61, 295–97. *See also* solidarity
companionship, companionability, xvi, 103–4, 295–96, 329–30
comparative framework, 29–30
conflict, 165, 209–10, 253–54, 255, 274–75, 281
Conrad, Joseph, 211
contact zone, 6, 7, 21, 152–53, 160, 176
cook, x–xii, 21–22, 54–56, 60, 74–75, 77, 84–85, 92, 100–1, 134–35, 175, 187–88, 190–92, 196–97, 208–9, 252, 256–57, 258, 284–321. *See also* Desai, Kiran: *The Inheritance of Loss*; Gunesekera, Romesh: *Reef*
corruption, 1–2, 21–22, 102, 108, 120, 123–24, 129, 150–51, 152–53, 155, 166–67, 168, 175, 207–8, 213, 216, 221–22, 224–25, 245–46, 251, 290–91
cosmopolitanism, 289
COVID-19 pandemic, 326, 331
crime, criminality, 117–277, 326–28. *See also* robbery; theft
critical race theory, 28–29

Dalit caste, ix, 59–60, 71–72
Damrosch, David, 44
dark, darkness, 211–12, 233–34, 249–50, 251. *See also* light, lightness
decorum, xv, 3–4, 163, 169–70, 188, 191, 238, 265–66, 328–29

deference, 16–17, 27, 129–30, 162–63, 196, 262–64, 265–66
degradation, 14, 17–18, 19–20, 116, 137, 169, 183–84, 207–8, 210–11, 218–19, 226, 229–30, 232–33, 236, 243–44, 278–79, 319, 324
dehumanization, 79, 84–87, 106, 127, 160–61, 183, 207–8, 210–11, 214, 218–19, 232–33, 242–43
Deleuze, Gilles, 40–41
democracy, vii, 8, 16–17, 18
  failure of, 208, 216, 223–25, 239–40, 251
dependence, vii–viii, 10–11, 21, 32, 84, 89, 90–91, 96, 136, 192, 201–2, 277–78, 301–2
  interdependence, 7, 128, 130–31, 178–79, 183, 187–88
  mutual, 6, 26–27, 301–2
  See also independence
Desai, Anita, 7, 50–51, 82–83, 88–89
  Cry, The Peacock, 83–84
  Fire on the Mountain, 84–88, 298–99
Desai, Kiran, 5–6, 13–14, 23, 52–53, 323
  Inheritance of Loss, The, 13–14, 252–59, 284–321, 324
desire, xvi–xvii, 2, 118–19, 132–33, 142–43, 159, 171, 189, 190–91, 192–93, 194, 197, 216, 226–29, 293–94, 310, 326–28
  erotics of inequality, 214
  homoerotic, 174–75, 183, 187–88, 191–93, 226–27, 235–36
  triangulated, 174–75, 187–88, 193–94, 197, 214, 235, 238–39
destitution, 9, 28–29, 72–73, 113, 132, 141, 151–52, 279, 280, 312, 316
detachment, 6–7, 210. *See also* distance
devotion, 34, 111, 124, 169–71, 175, 179–80, 183, 191, 203, 227–28, 235–36, 237, 240–41
diaspora, 89, 96, 97–98, 113, 115, 175, 177–78, 180–81, 252–53, 288–89, 322–23, 326–27
Dickey, Sara, 20–21
dignity, 6–7, 19–20, 26, 91–92, 112–13, 115, 134–35, 219, 229–30, 277, 285–86, 292, 316, 328–29
dirt, dirtiness, 85–86, 94–95, 110, 126–27, 264–66
disenfranchisement, 1, 11–12, 18, 50–51, 81–82, 128–29, 131, 175, 215, 223–24
disgust, 57, 84–86, 229–30, 238–39
disillusionment, 1–2, 8, 93, 118–19, 166–67, 179, 197, 202–3, 209–10, 225–26
displacement, 4, 13–14, 94, 103–5, 126–27, 149–50, 155–56, 217, 324–25
dispossession, 11–12, 155–56, 169–70
disrupt, disruption, xvi, 38, 41–42, 190–91, 246

distance:
  class and, 18, 56, 121, 126–27, 265–66, 286–87, 302–3
  gender and, 88, 126–27, 176–77, 286–87
  narrative, 93, 146–47, 166–67, 175, 178–79, 180, 220, 258, 287–88, 299–300, 320–21
  proximity and, 173
  servitude and, xi, 6–7, 17, 21, 32–33, 57, 65–68, 77, 90, 123, 152–53, 162–63, 173, 177–78, 196–97, 253–54, 258, 267, 293–94, 296
  See also proximity
docility, 35–36
domesticity. *See* home
domination, 17, 20–21, 96–97, 267–68. *See also* subordination
Downton Abbey, 162–63
driver, viii, 21–22, 175, 208–10, 212–13, 227–28, 233, 235–36, 237, 325–26. *See also* Adiga, Aravind: *The White Tiger*; chauffeur
drugs, drug use, 92–93, 123–24, 125–27, 160–61
Dumas, Firoozeh, 12–13
duty, 100, 159, 322–23

Eagleton, Terry, 23–24
economy:
  global, 250–51, 257
  informal, 8–9
  injustice, 175–76, 279
  nation and, 149–50, 198–99, 283, 305
  precarity and, 6, 278–79, 305, 313–14
  representational, 4
  servitude and, 9, 30, 72–73, 103, 179, 239, 274–75, 280
  stages of, 147–48
  See also capitalism; neoliberalism
education, xi–xii, 6–7, 16–17, 31–32, 34, 53–55, 67–68, 70, 100–1, 115, 174–75, 182–83, 190, 205–6, 219, 221, 223–25, 249, 255–56, 259, 262, 270–73, 279, 296, 298–99
egalitarianism, 1–2, 4–5, 18, 58–59, 68–69, 96, 100–1, 253, 282
Eliot, George, 280
elitism, ix, 9, 27, 43–44, 50, 51, 55–56, 57–58, 77–78, 114, 115, 183–84, 281, 316–17. *See also* class
emotion. *See* affect
empathy, 14–15, 82–89, 91–95, 101, 103, 141, 142, 143–45, 147, 154–55, 157, 161, 165–66, 232, 248–49, 257–58
ethics, 5, 154–55, 276–77
  absence of, 214–15
  concern for other, 7
  intervention, 14–15

obligations, 8
responsibility and, 281–82
servitude and, 96, 123, 248, 249–50, 251, 255–56
of speaking for, 215, 217
subaltern, 248
ethnicity, 4–5, 7, 8, 16–17, 25–26, 42, 118–19, 120, 121–22, 180–81, 256–57, 286–87
ethnocentrism, 309
ethnic minority criticism, 40
exception, exceptionality, 31, 183–84, 206, 211, 251, 261, 262–63, 264–65, 267–68
exploitation, 9, 11, 27, 60, 92, 113, 116, 157, 161, 173, 198–99, 208, 221–22, 239–40, 257, 272, 279, 281–82, 306–7

family, 18–19, 49
joint system, 208, 218
obligation, 274
servitude and, 3–4, 54–55, 231, 234–35, 238, 239–40, 242–44, 249, 255, 261–62, 265, 267–68, 270–72, 273–77, 281
fantasy, 178–79, 206, 328–30
fascism, 223–24
fate, fatalism, 131–32, 136–37
fear, xvi, 10–11, 117, 119
feeling. *See* affect
feminism, 15–16, 23–24, 28–29, 40, 93–94, 144–45
intersectionality and, 22–23, 323
feudalism, 28–29, 71–72, 94, 142, 143–45, 147–52, 155, 207–8, 216, 221–22, 228–30, 234–35, 251
fiction:
border-crossing, 40, 42–43, 154
global Anglophone South Asian, 4–6, 16, 18, 27–28, 29–30, 44, 50–51, 71–72, 142, 324–26
millennial, 97–98, 118, 142, 324–26
politics of, 236–37, 280–81
representation and, 14–15, 24, 37–39, 40–42, 43, 61–62, 66–67, 80, 137, 144–45, 215–16, 279–80
servitude, 5–7, 9–11, 14–16, 20, 25–26, 27–28, 29–44, 50–53, 71–72, 89, 94–95, 96–98, 118, 123, 137, 142, 144–45, 178–79, 188, 279–80, 323–26, 329–30, 331
See also realism
film, 2–5, 51–52, 162–63, 322–23, 324–30
focalization, 155–57, 158, 159–61, 163, 260, 261
footman, 31–32, 193
form, formalism, 7–8, 14–15, 23–25, 142–43, 144–47, 168–69, 254, 257–58, 280, 323.
See also narrative, narration

Forster, E. M., *A Passage to India*, 73–74
Foucault, Michel, 20–21, 40–41
free indirect discourse, 14–15, 133–34, 154, 157, 254, 285, 290–91, 310–11, 314–15, 317–18, 319–20
freedom:
ethics and, 214–15
postcolonialism and, 1, 8
servitude and, 1, 144, 175, 178–79, 217–18, 219–20, 243, 247–48, 255
See also independence
friendship, 131, 267, 282, 329–30
Futehally, Zeenuth, 23, 50–51, 66–67, 70–71
Zohra, 67–70

Gandhi, Mahatma, 53, 58
Gandhi, Leela, 188
Ganguly, Sumit, 26
gardener, viii, 1, 12–13, 21–22, 73–74, 83, 116–17, 187–88
gaze, 56, 194–95, 213, 238–39, 299–300, 323
gender, xvii, 11–12, 25–26, 30, 42–43, 90–91
abjection and, 77
agency and, 136–37
bonds between women, 94–95, 268–72
class and, 8, 21–23, 26, 32, 53–55, 59, 60–62, 63, 66–71, 81–82, 88, 89, 93–94, 96, 114–15, 119–20, 123, 191, 197, 200, 214, 239, 252, 253, 256, 262–64, 265–67, 272–73, 278–79, 285, 286–87
colonialism and, 63
decorum and, xv
desexualized surrogate mother or nanny, 98–99, 111, 112
education and, 53–55, 67–68, 70, 256, 272–73
effeminacy and, 1–2, 198, 240–41, 300–1, 303–4
entitlement and, 128
equality, 4–5, 8–9, 60–62, 64–65, 70, 79–80, 115, 218, 219–21, 256, 257
home and, vii–viii, 22, 66–67, 75–76, 77, 78–79, 101, 108–9
identity and, 21–22, 66–67
independence and, 131
intersectionality and, 22–23
justice and, xi, 331
labor, vii–viii, 15–16, 77
masculinity and manhood, xi–xii, 1–2, 3–4, 36–37, 110–11, 114–15, 176–77, 214, 219–20, 238, 303–4
norms of, 3–4
patriarchy and, x, 3–4, 54–55, 64–65, 67–68, 79–80, 93–94, 109, 131–32, 165, 166–67, 169–70, 238, 265

gender (*cont.*)
  performance, 233
  politics and, 53–54, 66–67
  power and, 89, 99–100, 161–62, 163–67, 175, 226–27, 272–73
  race and, 33
  relationality and, 22, 94–95
  representation and, 51–52
  resistance and, 219–20
  servitude and, 1–2, 4, 6–9, 21–23, 26, 32, 33, 36–37, 50–51, 57–59, 60–61, 64–68, 69–73, 74–77, 78–84, 88, 93, 94–95, 96, 98–100, 102, 103–4, 106–7, 108–9, 110, 111–13, 114–15, 119–20, 123, 128, 131–33, 134–35, 142–45, 146–47, 156–58, 159, 161–67, 169–70, 175, 176–77, 192–93, 198, 200, 203, 206, 207–8, 214, 218, 219–20, 221, 233, 238–39, 240–41, 247–48, 251, 252, 253, 255–57, 262–64, 265–67, 268–72, 275–76, 278–79, 281, 288, 292–93, 300–1, 303–4, 310, 328–30
  sexism, 40, 51–52
  sexual exploitation and, 22, 64–65, 75, 93–94, 98–99
  sexuality and, 72–73
  solidarity and, xi, 131
  subjectivity and, 103–4, 159, 207–8, 214, 247–48
  subordination, 80–81, 102
  transgressing, xv, 66–67
  vulnerability and, 255–56, 260, 265–66, 273–74, 275–76, 281–82
George, Rosemary Marangoly, 5–6
Gera, Rohena, Sir - *Is Love Enough?* 324–25, 328–30
Ghana, 1
Ghosh, Amitav, *The Hungry Tide*, 96
Girard, René, 193, 197
global, globalization, 5–6, 15–16, 18, 27–30, 44, 142, 175, 250–51, 252, 256–57, 282–83, 284, 288–90, 308
Global Fund for Women, 331
Godwin, William, 31
Goonetilleke, D. C. R. A., 29–30
Gopal, Priyamvada, 29–30
Gosford Park, 162–63
governess, 31–33
gratitude, xii, 183, 228–29, 242–43, 244–45, 264, 265–66, 292–93, 307
Gray, Thomas, 173
guard, guardian, 21–22, 70, 72, 73–74, 84, 100, 144, 169–71, 205, 302
guilt, 72–73, 75, 90–91, 102–3, 104–5, 106–7, 168, 177, 182–83, 232, 244–45, 264–65, 270, 276, 300–1, 313–14, 318–20, 326

Gunesekera, Romesh, 5–6, 23, 52–53, 145, 252–53, 323
  Monkfish Moon, 177–78
  Reef, 174–206, 207–11, 216–17, 279–80, 324, 325–26

Hagedorn, Jessica, *Dogeaters*, 10
Haggard, H. Rider, 33–34
Hai, Ambreen, 375
Hamid, Mohsin, 7, 13–14, 23, 141
  Moth Smoke, 97–98, 123–31
  Reluctant Fundamentalist, The, 13–14
Handagneu-Sotelo, Pierrette, 275
Hettiarchchi, Nirmali, *Replacements*, 325–26
hierarchy, 151–52, 156–57, 161–62, 167–68, 171–72, 262–64, 265–66
  of servants, 232–33
Hinduism
  fundamentalism, 117
  gender and, 80–81
  nationalism, 220
  in Pakistan, xv
  servitude and, 73–75, 221–22
  See also caste
HIV/AIDS, 259, 269, 279
Hochschild, Arlie, 264
home, ix, 3–4, 5–6, 14–15, 89, 94–95, 98, 101, 191, 216
  access to, 59–60
  car as extension of, 208–9
  class and, 96–97
  gender and, 22, 75–76, 77, 78–79, 206, 207–8, 257, 281, 293–94
  intimacy and, 18–19, 22, 36
  labor and, vii–viii, 18–20, 54–55
  micropolitics of, 8, 20–21, 51, 66–67, 86, 98, 103–4, 142–43, 206, 207–8, 255, 257, 258–59, 262–64, 281, 285, 288, 293–94, 320–21
  nation and, 5–6, 8, 109–10, 128–29, 135, 175, 203–5, 242, 285, 289, 320–21
  order and, 76–77, 100, 108–9
  power and, 11–12, 183–84
  servitude and, 6, 10–11, 18–19, 28–29, 76–77, 231, 236–37
  social differences and, 64–65, 66–67, 72–73, 83, 102
  space of, 119, 175, 197, 208–9
  as unregulated and unobserved, 6, 7, 11–12
  as workplace, 11–12, 18–20, 264–65
homelessness, 9, 237–38
homoeroticism, 22–23, 174–75, 176, 183–84, 193, 226–28. *See also* desire
homosexuality, 108–9, 118–19. *See also* queer, queerness

homosociality, 124, 174–75, 176, 214, 226, 265–66, 324
honor, x, 3–4, 36–37, 91–92, 159, 214–15, 249–50, 274–75, 316
Hosain, Attia, 23, 50–51, 53–54, 66–67, 82–83, 145, 151–52
　Phoenix Fled, 88–93
　Sunlight on a Broken Column, 88–89, 93–94
Hosseini, Khaled, *The Kite Runner*, 12–13
human rights, 38, 216, 331
humiliation, xi–xii, 1–2, 6–7, 60, 105–6, 142–43, 157, 224–25, 285–86, 316
humility, 1, 16–17, 52, 153, 171–72, 286–87
humor. *See* comedy

identity, identification, xii, 14–15
　character and, 157
　disidentification, 258
　gender and, 1–2, 21–22, 66–67
　intersectionality and, 22–23, 42–43, 144–45
　performing, 153
　relational, 278–79
　representation and, 40–42
　servitude and, 7, 8, 9, 17–19, 20, 30, 32, 50, 62, 66–67, 68, 80–82, 101, 114, 115, 128, 153, 160, 172, 174–75, 185, 186–87, 199, 217–18, 227–28, 232, 235, 238–39, 255, 256, 278–79, 285–86, 292, 293–94, 296–97, 301, 302
ideology, 11, 32–34, 35, 41–42, 96–97, 155–56, 178–79, 183–84, 185, 216, 220, 228, 232–33, 236–37, 240–41, 242, 271
imitation, 175, 188, 194–95, 208–9, 212–13, 227, 232, 238–39, 243–44. *See also* mimicry
immigration, x, 16–17, 42–43, 131, 256–57, 289, 305, 307. *See also* migrant, migrancy
imperialism, 13–14, 33, 256–57, 288–89. *See also* colonialism
indenture, 6, 18
independence, xii, 32, 62, 131, 174–75, 178–79, 185–86, 187, 190, 191–92, 216–17, 220, 255, 279, 329–30
　national, 1–2, 8, 13–14, 28–29, 53–54, 66–67, 71–72, 73–74, 77–78, 82, 88, 98–99, 101, 108–9, 148–50, 151–52, 283
India, 98–99, 175
　All-India Muslim League, 53
　failures of, 282–83
　First War of Independence (Indian "Mutiny"), 53, 64–65, 148–49
　Indian Emergency, 107–8
　National Congress, 53
　National Domestic Workers Movement, 331
　neoliberalism and, 176, 216, 217
　Quit India resolution, 53
　regulation of domestic work, 331
　as two countries, 211–12
individual, individualism, 94, 110–11, 116–17, 228, 279
industrialization, 18
inequality, 17–18, 26–27, 28–29, 60–62, 103, 104–5, 122–23, 141, 175–76, 256
　systemic structural, 154, 267–68, 279, 282–83
insider-outsider, 3–4, 28, 43–44, 96–97, 143–44, 201, 215, 237, 323
interdependence. *See under* dependence
interiority, 2–3, 5–6, 9–10, 14–16, 17–18, 30, 38–39, 52–53, 57–58, 60–62, 68, 80–81, 90, 91–94, 99–100, 106, 134, 142–43, 144–45, 146–47, 151–53, 154–57, 159, 160–61, 163–66, 167–68, 169–73, 176–77, 178–79, 180, 185, 255, 258–59, 281, 284–85, 288, 290–91, 293–94, 302–3, 310, 313–15, 317–21, 323–24, 326–28
　access to, 126–28, 155–56, 158, 177–78, 190
interior monologue, 52–53, 174–75, 220
International Labor Organization (ILO), 8–9
　Convention 189, 330
intersectionality, 22–23, 42–94, 144–45, 256, 271–72, 289–90, 323
intertextuality, 29–30, 175–76, 233–34
intimacy, 6, 7, 8, 9, 14–15, 18–19, 21, 22, 66–67, 68–69, 71, 74, 89, 113, 117–18, 120, 132–33, 174–75, 176, 183, 188, 194, 198, 208–9, 212–13, 216, 229–30, 231, 235–36, 253–54, 264–66, 267, 268–69, 323
　between classes. 98–99
　exploitation and, 173
　home and, 18–19, 22, 36
invisible, 7–8, 11–12, 15–16, 18, 27, 30, 43–44, 49, 83–84, 87–88, 94–95, 102, 191–92, 264. *See also* visible, visibility
irony, 23–24, 39, 104–5, 120–21, 128, 167–68, 169–70, 176, 211–12, 222–23, 229–30, 236–37, 251, 254, 258, 317–18, 320–21. *See also* comedy; satire
Ishiguro, Kazuo, 30
　Remains of the Day, The, 224–25
Islamicism, 131, 149–50
Islamophobia, 131

Jackson, Elizabeth, 289
Jahan, Rashid, 53–54
Jallianwalla Bagh massacre, 53
James, Henry, 280
Jani, Pranav, 29–30
Jay, Paul, 27–28, 288–89

Jayawardena, Elmo, *Sam's Story*, 325–26
jemadarni (sweepress), viii
Joyce, James, 13–14
justice, 122–23, 160–61, 169, 216, 251, 276–77
  economic, 175–76
  injustice, xi, 6, 60, 93–94, 137, 204–5
  social, 25–26, 28–29, 141, 268–69

Kapoor, Deepti, *Age of Vice*, 325–26
Kapur, Akash, 215
Keen, Suzanne, 157
Khair, Tabish, "Namaste Trump," 326
Khan, Ayub, 149
Khobragade, Devyani, 25–26
Khurshid, Salman, 26
Kipling, Rudyard, 33
  "At the End of the Passage," 35–36
  "Return of Imray, The," 36–37
  Something of Myself, 34
  "Strange Ride of Morrowbie Jukes, The," 35
Kristeva, Julia, 4
Kumar, Amitava, 215–16
Kumar, Priya, 29–30

labor, 271, 275
  as abject, 101
  capitalism and, 18–19
  care work, 255, 262–63, 268–69
  child, 135–36
  dehumanizing, 210–11
  divisions of, 64–65, 83
  domestic, 18, 31–32, 36, 49, 98–99
  emotional, 11, 232, 264
  factory, 19–20
  feminization of, 1–2, 15–16, 77, 198, 203, 240–41, 303–4, 310
  home and, vii–viii, 18–20, 54–55
  intellectual, 31–32
  invisible, 11, 83–84, 87–88, 264
  laws, 330–31
  menial, 6
  sexual, 1–2, 72–73
  "unskilled," 16–17
  withholding, 10
LaCapra, Dominic, 43–44
Lahiri, Jhumpa, 98
  Namesake, The, 322–23
Lahiri, Tripti, *Maid in India*, 11–12, 27
land ownership, 147–50
language, of servitude, 52–53, 107–8, 109–10, 111–12, 115, 129–30, 133–34, 307
Lazarus, Neil, 42
leisure, xvi, 18–19, 54–55, 87–88, 113
life writing, 226

light, lightness, 211–12, 233–34, 249–50, 251.
  See also dark, darkness
literacy, x, 6–7, 8–9, 16–17, 182–83, 205–6, 219, 259. *See also* education
literature, ix, 12–16, 18
  attentiveness to, 23–24
  British, 31–38
  colonial, 33–37
  experimentation, 5–6
  interiority and, 9–10
  invisibility and, 7
  as making an argument, 5–6, 7–8, 9–11
  margins of, xvi
  nation and, 29–30, 44
  politics of, 23–25, 43–44
  reality and, 24–25
  representation and, 39–44
  servitude in, ix, 2, 7, 9–11, 12–16, 18, 23–25, 27–30, 31–39, 42–44
  South Asian Anglophone, 29–31
  transnational and global, 27–30, 44
  See also fiction; narrative, narration
loyalty, 3–4, 18–19, 33–34, 35–36, 102, 110, 125, 228–29, 267, 275, 276–77
luxury, 79, 86–87, 101, 114, 136, 236, 313

maid, 21–22, 25–27, 31–32, 64–65, 68–70, 71, 75–76, 79, 131–33, 134–36, 157, 252, 303–4, 326–30
Mallot, Edward, 180
Mannur, Anita, 180
margin, marginality, xvi, 2–4, 5–6, 9, 25, 31, 96–97, 108, 137, 170–71, 282, 288–89, 323
  short story and, 146–47
Markandaya, Kamala, 23, 28–29, 50–51, 66–67
  Nectar in a Sieve, 71–73
  Silence of Desire, A, 75–77
  Some Inner Fury, 73–75
mask, xvi, 10–11
maternalism, 262–63
Mbue, Imbolo, 30
McLeod, John, 188
mediation, 57, 81–82, 157, 193, 216–17, 293–94
Mehrotra, Arvind, 29–30
Mehta, Deepa, *Fire*, 2–4
memory, 175, 180–81, 284, 288–90
migrant, migrancy, 11–12, 18, 27–28, 71–72, 113, 115, 149–50, 180–81, 252, 256–57, 259
militancy, xvi
mimesis, 24–25, 180, 193, 215–16
mimicry, 189, 208–9, 227, 232, 238–39, 243–44
  colonial, 188
  See also imitation

mirror, mirroring, xvii, 80–81, 108–9, 119, 123–24, 125–28, 131–32, 180–81, 208–9, 212–13, 227, 238–39, 243–46, 247, 326–28
Mistry, Rohinton, *Family Matters*, 49
mobility, social, 6–7, 75–76, 262, 288–89
modernism, 90
modernity, 2, 6–7, 9, 18, 78
Moore, George, 31
morality, 194–95, 211
   authority and, 127
   class and, 183–84
   decline and, 130–31
   See also ethics
Mueenuddin, Daniyal, ix, 5–6, 17–18, 23, 40–41, 44, 50, 52–53, 323
   In Other Rooms, Other Wonders, 12–13, 28, 141–73, 324, 326
Mukherjee, Neel, 52–53
   State of Freedom, A, 16–17, 20, 96, 326
multivocality, 254
Murphy, Richard, 141, 147–48
Murray, Melanie, 180
mutuality, 6, 26–27, 86, 114–15, 128, 151–52, 159, 178–79, 187–88, 213, 253–54, 255, 267, 300–2, 328–29. *See also* relationality

Naipaul, V. S.:
   Area of Darkness, An, 211
   Bend in the River, A, 10
Nair, Mira:
   Monsoon Wedding, 326–28
   Namesake, The, 322–23
name, naming, 51–53, 71, 73–74, 108–9, 113, 116–17, 120, 129–30, 169, 187, 227–28, 284, 303
nanny, 21–22, 25–26, 98–99, *See also* ayah
Narayan, R. K., 12–13, 23, 50–51
   Bachelor of Arts, The, 54–55
   Swami and Friends, 55–56
   Under the Banyan Tree, 146–47
narrative, narration:
   affect and, 288, 289
   background and, 49–51, 55–56, 57–59, 64–65, 74–75, 87–88, 98
   character and, 37–39, 64–65
   class and, 216–17, 253–54, 256, 258
   closure and, 279–80
   distance and, 288
   elite, 50, 51, 55–56, 57–58
   first-person, 14–15, 52–53, 66–67, 90–92, 118–19, 134, 147, 169–70, 174–75, 177
   focalization and, 147, 151–52, 155–57, 158, 159–61, 163, 260, 261
   form and, 254, 258
   multiple narrators, 7–8
   perspective and, 154–55, 158, 159–61, 165, 166–67, 169–70, 173, 174–75, 177–79, 277, 278, 280–82, 284–85, 287–88, 290–95, 296–97, 300–1, 302–3, 326–28
   power and, 258
   proximity and, 97–98
   retrospective, 216–17, 225–27, 233–34
   self-effacement in, 154
   servitude and, 31, 84, 90, 128–29, 132–34, 145, 174–75, 216–18
   situation, 157
   social and, 37–39, 123–24, 287
   space of, 110–11, 132–33, 252–54, 256–58, 284, 286–88, 302–3, 326–28
   subordination, 37–39, 52–53, 281
   theory, 157
   third-person, 7–8, 52–53, 83, 90, 92–93, 133, 145, 147, 154, 157, 169–70, 177–78, 258, 260, 261, 285, 291–95, 317–18, 319–20
   unreliable, 7–8
   See also perspective
nation, nationalism, x, 4–5, 30, 42–43, 59, 71, 98–99, 217, 256–57, 284, 309
   affective connection to, 28
   citizenship and, 216
   cross-national comparisons, 29–30
   democracy and, 16–17
   disorder and, 109–10
   ethnicity and, 286–87
   feudalism and, 147–49, 151–52, 155
   home and, 5–6, 8, 109–10, 135, 175, 203–5, 242, 285, 289, 320–21
   injustice and, 123
   literature and, 27–28, 29–30, 43–44
   modernity and, 6–7
   postcolonial, 28, 43–44, 150–52, 155, 175–77, 198–99, 211, 214, 215, 217, 223–24, 251, 252, 282–83, 284, 285–86, 288–89, 323
   responsibility and, 280
   servitude and, 9, 13–14, 26, 176, 198–99, 224–25
   vulnerable citizens, 176
   See also democracy; state
naukar (Hindi/Urdu for servant), 20
neocolonialism, 1–2, 115–16, 211, 216, 282–83, 288–89. *See also* colonialism
neoliberalism, 124–25, 128–29, 175, 176, 207–8, 216, 217, 228, 232–33, 250–51, 252, 256–57, 279, 282–83, 284, 308
New Criticism, The 23–24
Nixon, Rob, 42–43
Non-Cooperation Movement, 53
non-violence, 53, 59

North, Joseph, 23–24
novel, 146–47
    ending, 279–80
    form of, 257, 258, 280
    marriage plot, 7–8
    See also literature; narrative, narration

O'Connor, Frank, *The Lonely Voice*, 146–47
obligation, 6, 18, 77, 90–91, 239, 262–63
    of employer to servant, xi, 8, 18–19, 151–52, 255, 276–77, 281
    to family, 84, 274
    mutual, 253–54, 255–56, 267
Ondaatje, Michael, 323
Ong, Aihwa, 28
oppression, xi, 1–2, 20–21, 60, 71–72, 93–94, 216, 221–23, 279
orality, 216–17
orientalism, 40
Orwell, George, 14
other, otherness, xvi, 5, 7, 9, 12–13, 18, 28–29, 33, 36, 39, 56, 80–81, 83–84, 96, 99–100, 121, 122–23, 188, 242–43, 281, 316–17
    speaking for, 40–41, 43
outsider. *See* insider-outsider
Oxfam Canada, 331

painting, xv, 97
Pakistan, ix, 53
    Domestic Workers Act (Punjab), 330–31
    feudalism and, 147–50, 151–52
    history of, 148–50
    inequality and, 141, 149–50
    labor laws, 330–31
    neoliberalism and, 124–25, 128–29
Partition, ix, 53, 67, 68–69, 71, 88–89, 150, 155–56
passivity, 83, 87, 131, 136, 163, 242–43
patriarchy. *See under* gender
Perera, Walter, 180
performance, 55, 153
    of deference, 27
    gender, 233
    of servitude, 127, 162, 228–29
perspective, 154–55, 158, 159–61, 165, 166–67, 169–70, 173
    alternating, 257–58, 261–62, 281–82, 287–88, 291–93, 320–21
    class and, 253–54
    distance and, 175
    from below, 5–6
    narrative, 252–54, 256–58, 281–82, 294–95, 296–97, 300–1, 302–3, 320–21, 326–28

of servant, 132–34, 174–79, 194–95, 207–8, 216–18, 263–64, 277, 278, 280, 284–85, 290–91, 296–97, 300–1, 302–3, 323–24, 326–28
    See also narrative, narration
photography, 97
plot. *See* narrative, narration
poetry, 223
police violence, x–xi, 26–27, 59, 121–23, 171–72
politics:
    citizenship and, 223–25
    corruption and, 207–8, 251
    fiction and, 236–37
    gender and, 53–54, 66–67
    home and, 98, 103–4, 128–29, 198–99
    intervention, 14–15
    of literature, 23–25, 43–44
    of postcolonial nation, 175–76, 220
    of servitude, 20–21, 135–36, 214, 218–19, 221–22, 223–25
    social location and, 42, 43
    systems and, 135–36, 214, 221–25
    violence and, 119, 120, 121–23, 175–76
Poon, Angela, 289
positionality, 13–14, 33, 41–42, 43, 219–20, 281, 323
postcolonial criticism, 6–7, 23–24, 28–29, 30, 40, 42–43
postcolonialism, ix, 1–2, 5, 6–8, 11–14, 16, 18, 21, 28, 34, 41–42, 149–50, 151–52, 173, 175–77, 198–99, 207–8, 211, 214, 215, 217, 220, 223–24, 251, 252, 256–57, 282–83, 284, 285–86, 288–90, 323. *See also under* nation, nationalism
poverty, 8–9, 11–12, 31–32, 55–57, 173, 175–76, 259, 264–65, 278–79, 281–82, 292
power, xvi, 3–4, 5–6, 10, 14–15, 20, 43–44, 90–91
    abuse of, 28–29, 59, 60–62, 125–26
    asymmetry of, 275
    boundaries of, 69–70
    disempowerment, 7, 26–27, 157, 160–61
    feudalism and, 151
    gendered, 226–27, 272–73
    hierarchy and, 50, 142–43
    home and, 11–12, 183–84
    inequality, 89, 112–13, 116, 183, 188, 206
    narrative and, 258
    negotiating, 20–21
    powerlessness, 4, 18
    relations of, 7, 8, 185
    representation and, 15–16
    servitude and, 18, 21, 106, 110, 144–45, 147, 156–57, 162–66, 170–71, 172, 176, 183,

185, 188, 208–9, 255, 257, 262–64, 265–68, 274–75, 290–91, 298
  social location and, 100, 121, 123, 128–29
  speaking to, 121–23
  status and, 55, 57–58
  subordination and, 155
  systems of, 142–43, 144–45, 154–55, 159, 160–62, 163–67, 168, 169, 170–71, 172–73, 175–76
Pratt, Mary Louise, 21
precarity, precariousness, 10–11, 71–72, 108–9, 122–23, 124–25, 151–52, 184–85, 190, 201–2, 216, 244–45, 272, 275, 278–79, 284, 305–7, 310–11, 314–15
privacy, private, 65, 70, 144–45, 183, 201, 203, 236–37, 279
privilege, vii–viii, x, 1–2, 6, 8, 11–12, 21–22, 59–60, 101, 116, 122–23, 262
  representation and, 40–41, 42–43
progressivism, 96–98
projection, xvii
protagonist. *See under* character
protest, ix–x, 25–27, 32, 53, 116, 160–61.
  See also resistance
proximity, 6, 8, 14–15, 21, 57, 65, 84, 117–18, 183, 194, 195–96, 197, 230, 235, 258, 265–66, 296, 316–17
  distance and, 173
  in narrative, 97–98, 101
psyche, psychology. *See* interiority; subjectivity
psychoanalysis, 188
purdah (female segregation), 67–68, 69–71, 93–94

Qayum, Seemin, 6–7, 9, 17, 18–19, 22–23, 29, 58, 66–67, 90–91
queer, queerness, 2–3, 118–19, 282. *See also* desire; sexuality

race, 11–12, 30, 42–43, 295–96
  class and, 33
  gender and, 33
  racism, 40, 92, 118–19, 131, 256–57
  servitude and, 1–2, 13–14, 16–17, 33–37, 56, 74, 79–80, 114–15, 169–70
  social hierarchy and, 36–37
  transgressing, 74
  whiteness, 36–37, 63
Rao, Raja, 7, 23, 50–51
  Kanthapura, 58–59
rationality, 10, 35–37, 190
Ray, Raka, 6–7, 9, 17, 18–19, 22–23, 29, 58, 66–67, 90–91

realism, 24–25, 100, 101, 146–47, 229–30, 279–80, 298–99
  magical, 103, 110, 112–13
  social, 7–8, 103, 176, 185, 215–16, 328–30
reciprocity, 68, 158, 183, 196, 264–65, 292–93
reform, 20, 58, 149, 280–81
refuge, 9, 98–99, 124–25, 130–33, 137, 176, 179, 181–82, 197, 205–6
refusal, ix–x, 26–27, 154–55, 316–17
relationality, 14–15, 20–21, 218–19
  across class, 101
  affective, 101
  complexity of, 9–10
  between servants, 144, 145, 158–60, 184–85, 232–33
  between servants and employers, 86, 90–92, 110–11, 120, 124–28, 130–31, 142–45, 151–53, 161–66, 169–72, 174–75, 176–80, 181–83, 184–86, 187–88, 190–97, 202–3, 206, 207–10, 212–14, 226–28, 231–32, 235–36, 238, 240–41, 252, 253–54, 257–59, 261–65, 267–72, 275–77, 278–79, 292–98, 299–302, 324
  between women, 94–95
religion, 4–5, 7, 8, 16–17, 25–26, 36–37, 58–59, 64–66, 68–69, 106, 116, 221–22, 233–34, 251
representation, 24–25
  dehumanization and, 84–86
  distancing effect, 180, 220, 288, 299–300
  gender and, 51–52
  right to, 39–40, 42–43
  of servitude, 52–53
  across social difference, 28–29, 39–42, 43–44
  violence of, 40, 41–42
  See also narrative, narration
reputation, 75, 91–92
resentment, x–xii, xvi, 6, 26–27, 105–6, 267, 286–87, 312
resistance, 8, 10, 11, 14–15, 19–21, 26–27, 32, 50, 99–100, 101, 108, 113, 123, 135, 145–46, 178–79, 200–1, 210, 218–20, 223, 233–34, 236–37, 243, 251, 265. *See also* agency
respect, respectability, 19–20, 26, 36–37, 64, 65–66, 113, 115, 127, 129–30, 147, 163–64, 202–3, 218–19, 232–33, 262, 292–94, 296–97
  disrespect, 81–82, 157–58, 185, 279, 299, 329–30
responsibility, vii–viii, 8, 36–37, 41–43, 54–55, 66–67, 74–77, 78, 119, 123, 154–55, 183, 240–41, 249–50, 253, 255–56, 262–63, 280–81, 292–93, 317–18, 328–29. *See also* obligation

ressentiment, 262–64. *See also* resentment
retaliation, 11, 59
Richards, I. A., 23–24
Richards, Sangeeta, 25–26
Richardson, Samuel, 31
robbery, x–xi, 134–35, 154–55, 290–92. *See also* crime, criminality; theft
Robbins, Bruce, 3–4, 15–16, 25, 31
Rodriguez, Richard, 42–43
Rollins, Judith, 262–63
romance, 118–19, 179, 188, 190–93, 294–95, 327–28, 329–30
Rosenberg, Amy, 141
Roy, Arundhati; *The God of Small Things*, 12–13
Rushdie, Salman, 7, 12–13, 23, 97–98, 298–99
 "The Courter," *East, West*, 379
 Fury, 117–18
 Golden House, The, 117–18
 Ground Beneath Her Feet, The, 117–18
 Haroun and the Sea of Stories, 250–51
 Midnight's Children, 19–20, 49–50, 98–108, 216–17
 Moor's Last Sigh, The, 116–17, 137
 "Outside the Whale," 14
 Satanic Verses, The, 113–16
 Shalimar the Clown, 117–18
 Shame, 108–13

Sabo, Oana, 289
Sahgal, Nayantara, 23, 50–51, 66–67, 77–78
 Day in Shadow, The, 79–82
 This Time of Morning, 82
 Time to Be Happy, A, 78–79
Salgado, Minoli, 180
Salt March, 53
Saro-Wiwa, Ken, 42–43
satire, 7–8, 100–1, 103, 106, 107–9, 111–14, 116–17, 137, 176, 211, 215–17, 220. *See also* comedy; irony
Satrapi, Marjane, 12–13
Scanlon, Margaret, 289
secret, secrecy, 3–4, 10, 66–67, 102–3, 104–5, 106–7, 110, 208–9, 233, 239, 264–65, 276
self, selfhood, 32, 123, 186–87, 192, 217–19, 238–39, 240–41, 243, 245–46, 247, 255, 284, 287, 296–97, 303–4, 312
 abjection and, 4
 concern for other, 7
 interiority and, 80–81
 other and, 56
 self-making, 189
 self-sufficiency, vii
 servitude and, 9–11, 207–8
 See also identity; subjectivity

Selvadurai, Shyam, 7, 23
 Funny Boy, 97–98, 118–23
sentimentality, 255–56, 279–80
servant, servitude, xi–xii, 6–7, 14–15, 82, 110
 absence of, vii–viii
 in art, xvi–xvii, 4–8
 as background, xvi, 2–3, 5, 37–38, 49–51, 55–56, 57–59, 64–67, 71, 74–75, 79–80, 82, 87–88, 97, 98, 100, 102–3, 113
 centering, 323–24
 critique of, 72–73, 79–80, 96–98, 114, 185, 215, 233–34, 250–51, 279, 280–83, 322–24, 330–31
 cross-generational effects of, 8, 18–19, 255, 256, 257, 258–59, 270–75, 288, 303–15, 320–21
 culture of, 16–17, 18–19, 20, 29, 126–27, 155, 177–78, 229–30, 232–33, 236, 240–43, 251, 270, 279, 281, 307, 322–23
 distance and, 32–33, 35–36, 152–53, 162–63, 173, 178–79, 196–97, 258, 288, 293–94, 296, 299–300, 302–3
 education and, 16–17, 31–32, 100–1, 115, 174–75, 182–83, 190, 205–6, 219, 221, 223–25, 249, 255–56, 259, 262, 270–73, 279, 296, 298–99
 empathy for, 82–90, 91–95, 101, 103, 141–45, 147, 154–55, 157, 161, 165–66, 232, 248–49, 258
 escape from, 130–31, 136–37, 205–6, 207, 210, 247–49, 251, 252, 255–56, 279–80, 281–82, 324
 fear of, xvi, 117, 119
 foregrounding, 5–6, 37–39, 49, 52–53, 89, 96–97, 142, 143–47, 174–75, 176, 286–87
 function in representational economy, 4–5, 7–8, 9–10, 14–16, 24–25, 30–40, 49–53, 54–58, 62–68, 74–75, 81, 82, 84, 85–86, 87–88, 89–90, 94, 99–100, 101–3, 107–8, 112–13, 123, 128–29, 130–31, 132–33, 160–61, 176, 252–54, 256–58, 287, 289–90, 320–21
 inner lives of, 9–11, 14–16, 17–18, 30, 38–39, 52–53, 57–58, 60–62, 68, 90, 91–94, 99–100, 106, 126–28, 134, 142–43, 144–45, 147, 151–53, 154–57, 158–59, 160–61, 163–66, 167–68, 169–73, 176–80, 185, 190, 255, 258–59, 260, 281, 284–85, 288, 290–91, 293–94, 302–3, 310, 313–15, 317–21, 323–24, 326–28
 invisibility of, 12–16, 25–29, 30, 44, 49–50, 83–84, 87–88, 94–95, 102
 language of, 107–8, 109–10, 111–12, 115, 129–30, 133–34, 307

legal or social protections for, 27
in literature, ix, 2, 9–11, 12–16, 18, 23–25, 27–30, 31–39, 42–44
as marginal, xvi, 2–4, 5–6, 7, 9, 25, 31, 96–97, 108, 137, 146–47, 170–71, 323
mask of, xvi, 10–13
middle ground, 97–98, 99–100, 113, 123, 124, 130–31, 137
as mirror, 24, 80–81, 108–9, 119, 123–24, 125–28, 131–32
naming, 51–53, 71, 73–74, 108–9, 113, 116–17, 120, 169, 187, 227–28, 284, 303
plot and, 2
postcolonial, 1–2, 5, 8, 11–16, 21, 149–50, 173, 175–77, 207–8, 214, 252, 257, 282–83, 285–86, 288, 289–90
as protagonist, 142, 207–28, 252–54, 256–57, 277, 278, 326–28
as social and economic system, 1–2, 6–7, 8–10, 16–18, 21–22, 30–31, 39–40, 41–42, 43–44, 54–56, 57–58, 59, 70–73, 92, 103, 104–5, 109, 113, 114, 116, 128–30, 137, 142–43, 147, 149–50, 152–54, 157–58, 159, 161–62, 164, 168, 169–71, 172–73, 175–76, 198–99, 203–4, 207–8, 214, 218–19, 221–25, 234–35, 245–46, 250–51, 257, 267–68, 273–74, 278–79, 281, 282–83, 289–90, 302–3, 324, 329–30
in South Asia, 6–7, 8–9, 11–14, 16–17, 18–20, 25–30, 38–42, 43–44, 58–59, 64–65, 115, 149–50, 322–23, 330–31
space of, 236–37
speaking for, 2
stereotypes of, 3, 35–36, 60–62, 65–68, 83–87, 92–93, 94–95, 98–100, 105, 106–9, 110, 111–13, 116, 117–18, 145, 168, 178–79, 183–84, 214–15, 236–37, 276, 326–28
as threat, xvi–xvii, 3
tradition and, 67–68, 74–77, 144, 177–78, 190
transnational contexts, 5–6, 27–30, 41–42, 44, 96–97, 308, 324–25, 328
as unknowable, 36–37
sexual exploitation, 75, 93–95, 98–99, 112–14, 120, 121, 145, 157–58, 161, 162–66, 184–85, 255–56, 270, 273–74, 275–76
sexuality, 1–2, 6–8, 11–12, 30, 42–43, 57, 65, 66–67, 88, 108–9, 114–15, 118–19, 142–43, 145, 176–77, 194–98, 201–2, 238–39
alternative, 4–5, 118–19, 121
class and, 119, 120
illicit, 3, 4, 69–70
prostitution and, 72–73, 93
transgressing, 120
See also desire; queer, queerness

shame, 4–5, 7, 26, 72–73, 93–94, 235, 264–65, 292–93, 296–97
Shamsie, Kamila, 12–13, 141, 150
Sharma, Sonal, 8–9
short story, 7–8, 89–90
form of, 142–47, 168–69
perspective and, 145–46, 147, 151–52
social marginality and, 146–47
Sidhwa, Bapsi, *Cracking India*, ix
Silverman, Jacob, 141
Simpson, Mona, 30
slavery, 6, 18
Smith, Zadie, 30
social, 115
corruption and, 175
hierarchy and, 36–37, 58–59, 68–69
inequality, 60–62, 92, 104–5, 122–23, 175, 245–46
location, 42, 100, 114, 116–17, 128–31, 137
narrative and, 37–39, 123–24, 287
power and, 100, 121, 128–29, 160–61
servitude and, 9, 129–31, 137
See also positionality
solidarity, xi, 19–20, 36, 131, 134–35, 232–33, 236, 260–61, 265–66, 279, 282
space:
exterior, 144
of home, 119, 175, 197, 208–9, 231
interior, 144
light and dark, 211–12
liminal, 119
narrative, 252–54, 256–58, 284, 286–88, 302–3, 326–28
of servitude, 236–37
speaking for, 39–42, 43, 215, 216–17
Spivak, Gayatri, 40–41
Sri Lanka, 53, 118–19, 175
civil war, 177, 180–81
National Action Plan, 331
starvation, 9, 11–12
state:
failures of, 130–31, 207–8, 215, 216, 217, 260, 280, 282–83, 284
neoliberal, 207–8, 215, 216, 217
responsibility of, 8
safety nets, 279
status and, xvi, 6–7, 31, 38–39, 55, 57–59, 65–66, 67, 73–74, 75–76, 80–81, 94, 124–27, 130–31, 264–65, 296–97
See also nation, nationalism
Steel, Flora Annie, 33
Stevenson, Robert Louis, 33
stigma, stigmatization, 4–5, 7, 8, 18–19, 20, 26–27, 59–60, 65–66

Stockett, Kathryn, 30
subaltern, subalternity, 4–5, 7, 11–12, 16, 18, 20–21, 39–42, 62, 71–72, 133, 147, 150, 176, 215, 216, 248
subjection, 14–15, 26, 61–62, 103–4, 217–18
subjectivity, 5–6, 15–16, 21–22, 134, 142–43, 159, 168, 169, 175–76, 185, 214–15, 216, 226, 232, 242–43, 247–48, 254, 258–59, 275–76, 323–24, 326–28
    class and, 52–53, 54–55, 56–58
    contact zones and, 21
    distance from, 147
    gender and, 103–4, 159, 207–8, 214, 247–48
    servitude and, 50, 52–53, 57–58, 60–62, 89–94, 103–5
    See also identity; self, selfhood
subordination, 6–7, 8, 13–14, 20–21, 27, 32, 33, 37–39, 56, 80–81, 96–97, 102, 106, 136, 155, 161–62, 172, 267–68, 278–79, 281
subservience, 116, 142–43, 187, 188, 200, 203
surveillance, 3–4, 76–77, 120, 212–13
syncretism, xv

Taraporevala, Sooni, 322–23
terrorism, 289
theft, 105–6, 116–17, 120–21, 124–25, 209–10, 245–46, 276, 326–28. *See also* crime, criminality; robbery
Thiong'o, Ngũgĩ wa, 13–14
tradition, 18, 74–77, 144, 177–78, 190
translation, 27–28, 143–44, 216–17
Truong, Monique, 30
trust, trustworthiness, xi, 3, 6, 91–92, 276

Umrigar, Thrity, 5–6, 23, 28, 50, 52–53, 145, 323
    Secrets Between Us, The, 281–82
    Space Between Us, The, 21–22, 252–83, 316, 320–21, 324
untouchability, 7, 11–12, 58, 59–60, 116–17, 265–66. *See also* caste

Upadhyay, Samrat
    Arresting God in Kathmandu, 12–13
    Royal Ghosts, The, 12–13
Upstairs,Downstairs, 162–63

violence, 11, 125–27, 201–2, 216, 289, 319–20
    class, 204–5
    colonial, 59
    feudal, 221–22, 228–29, 230
    police, 26–27, 59, 121–23, 171–72
    political, 119, 120, 121–23, 175–76
    representational, 40, 41–42
    of servant, 117–18
    sexual, 75, 93–95, 98–99, 112–14, 120, 121, 145, 157–58, 161, 162–66, 184–85, 255–56, 270, 273–74, 275–76
visible, visibility, 7–8, 137, 142–43, 168, 169, 194–96, 236. *See also* invisible
visual arts, 97
vulnerability, x, 8, 18, 22, 30, 36–37, 43–44, 71–72, 100, 117, 120–23, 124–25, 130–31, 152–53, 155, 157–58, 161, 166–67, 177–78, 234–35, 237–38, 249–50, 251, 255–56, 260, 265–66, 273–74, 276–77, 281–82, 290–91, 306–7, 313–14

Walkowitz, Rebecca, 27–28
watchman, 21–22. *See also* guard
wet-nurse, 67
Wijesinha, Rajiva, *Servants: A Cycle*, 325–26
Williams, Raymond, 16
Woloch, Alex, 37–38, 287
world literature, 44

xenophobia, 131, 309. *See also* racism *under* race

Zainab Market (Karachi), xv
zenana (women's quarters), 65, 67, 68–70
Zia-ul-Haque, Muhammad, 149–50